HOLT McDOUGAL

# Western World

**Christopher L. Salter**

HISTORY

## HOLT McDOUGAL

HOUGHTON MIFFLIN HARCOURT

# Author

## Dr. Christopher L. Salter

Dr. Christopher L. "Kit" Salter is Professor Emeritus of geography and former Chair of the Department of Geography at the University of Missouri. He did his undergraduate work at Oberlin College and received both his M.A. and Ph.D. degrees in geography from the University of California at Berkeley.

Dr. Salter is one of the country's leading figures in geography education. In the 1980s he helped found the national Geographic Alliance network to promote geography education in all 50 states. In the 1990s Dr. Salter was Co-Chair of the National Geography Standards Project, a group of distinguished geographers who created *Geography for Life* in 1994, the document outlining national standards in geography. In 1990 Dr. Salter received the National Geographic Society's first-ever Distinguished Geography Educator Award. In 1992 he received the George Miller Award for distinguished service in geography education from the National Council for Geographic Education. In 2006 Dr. Salter was awarded Lifetime Achievement Honors by the Association of American Geographers for his transformation of geography education.

Over the years, Dr. Salter has written or edited more than 150 articles and books on cultural geography, China, field work, and geography education. His primary interests lie in the study of the human and physical forces that create the cultural landscape, both nationally and globally.

ISBN-13 978-0-547-48495-2

1 2 3 4 5 6 7 8 9 10  0914  19 18 17 16 15 14 13 12 11 10

4500263433            ^ B C D E F G

# Reviewers

## Academic Reviewers

**Elizabeth Chako, Ph.D.**
Department of Geography
The George Washington University

**Altha J. Cravey, Ph.D.**
Department of Geography
University of North Carolina

**Eugene Cruz-Uribe, Ph.D.**
Department of History
Northern Arizona University

**Toyin Falola, Ph.D.**
Department of History
University of Texas

**Sandy Freitag, Ph.D.**
Director, Monterey Bay History and
    Cultures Project
Division of Social Sciences
University of California,
    Santa Cruz

**Oliver Froehling, Ph.D.**
Department of Geography
University of Kentucky

**Reuel Hanks, Ph.D.**
Department of Geography
Oklahoma State University

**Phil Klein, Ph.D.**
Department of Geography
University of Northern Colorado

**B. Ikubolajeh Logan, Ph.D.**
Department of Geography
Pennsylvania State University

**Marc Van De Mieroop, Ph.D.**
Department of History
Columbia University
New York, New York

**Christopher Merrett, Ph.D.**
Department of History
Western Illinois University

**Thomas R. Paradise, Ph.D.**
Department of Geosciences
University of Arkansas

**Jesse P.H. Poon, Ph.D.**
Department of Geography
University at Buffalo–SUNY

**Robert Schoch, Ph.D.**
CGS Division of Natural Science
Boston University

**Derek Shanahan, Ph.D.**
Department of Geography
Millersville University
Millersville, Pennsylvania

**David Shoenbrun, Ph.D.**
Department of History
Northwestern University
Evanston, Illinois

**Sean Terry, Ph.D.**
Department of Interdisciplinary
    Studies, Geography and
    Environmental Studies
Drury University
Springfield, Missouri

## Educational Reviewers

**Dennis Neel Durbin**
Dyersburg High School
Dyersburg, Tennessee

**Carla Freel**
Hoover Middle School
Merced, California

**Tina Nelson**
Deer Park Middle School
Randallstown, Maryland

**Don Polston**
Lebanon Middle School
Lebanon, Indiana

**Robert Valdez**
Pioneer Middle School
Tustin, California

## Teacher Review Panel

**Heather Green**
LaVergne Middle School
LaVergne, Tennessee

**John Griffin**
Wilbur Middle School
Wichita, Kansas

**Rosemary Hall**
Derby Middle School
Birmingham, Michigan

**Rose King**
Yeatman-Liddell School
St. Louis, Missouri

**Mary Liebl**
Wichita Public Schools USD 259
Wichita, Kansas

**Jennifer Smith**
Lake Wood Middle School
Overland Park, Kansas

**Melinda Stephani**
Wake County Schools
Raleigh, North Carolina

# Contents

## UNIT 1 Introduction to Geography

**CHAPTER 3** Climate, Environment, and Resources....................48

CHAPTER 18  **Northern Europe** . . . . . . . . . . . . . . . . .446

![HISTORY] **VIDEO**
**Winston Churchill**

# References

Available @

**⬈ hmhsocialstudies.com**

• Facts About the World
• Regions of the World Handbook
• Standardized Test-Taking Strategies
• Economics Handbook

**HISTORY**
MADE EVERY DAY.

**HISTORY**™ is the leading destination for revealing, award-winning, original non-fiction series and event-driven specials that connect history with viewers in an informative, immersive and entertaining manner across multiple platforms. HISTORY is part of A&E Television Networks (AETN), a joint venture of Hearst Corporation, Disney/ABC Television Group and NBC Universal, an award-winning, international media company that also includes, among others, A&E Network™, BIO™, and History International™.

**HISTORY** programming greatly appeals to educators and young people who are drawn into the visual stories our documentaries tell. Our Education Department has a long-standing record in providing teachers and students with curriculum resources that bring the past to life in the classroom. Our content covers a diverse variety of subjects, including American and world history, government, economics, the natural and applied sciences, arts, literature and the humanities, health and guidance, and even pop culture.

The HISTORY website, located at **www.history.com**, is the definitive historical online source that delivers entertaining and informative content featuring broadband video, interactive timelines, maps, games, podcasts and more.

**"We strive to engage, inspire and encourage the love of learning..."**

Since its founding in 1995, HISTORY has demonstrated a commitment to providing the highest quality resources for educators. We develop multimedia resources for K–12 schools, two- and four-year colleges, government agencies, and other organizations by drawing on the award-winning documentary programming of A&E Television Networks. We strive to engage, inspire and encourage the love of learning by connecting with students in an informative and compelling manner. To help achieve this goal, we have formed a partnership with Houghton Mifflin Harcourt.

The Idea Book for Educators

Classroom resources that bring the past to life

Live webcasts

HISTORY Take a Veteran to School Day

In addition to premium video-based resources, **HISTORY** has extensive offerings for teachers, parents, and students to use in the classroom and in their in-home educational activities, including:

▶ *The Idea Book for Educators* is a biannual teacher's magazine, featuring guides and info on the latest happenings in history education to help keep teachers on the cutting edge.

▶ **HISTORY Classroom (www.history.com/classroom)** is an interactive website that serves as a portal for history educators nationwide. Streaming videos on topics ranging from the Roman aqueducts to the civil rights movement connect with classroom curricula.

▶ **HISTORY email newsletters** feature updates and supplements to our award-winning programming relevant to the classroom with links to teaching guides and video clips on a variety of topics, special offers, and more.

▶ **Live webcasts** are featured each year as schools tune in via streaming video.

▶ **HISTORY Take a Veteran to School Day** connects veterans with young people in our schools and communities nationwide.

In addition to **HOUGHTON MIFFLIN HARCOURT**, our partners include the *Library of Congress*, the *Smithsonian Institution*, *National History Day*, *The Gilder Lehrman Institute of American History*, the *Organization of American Historians*, and many more. HISTORY video is also featured in museums throughout America and in over 70 other historic sites worldwide.

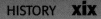

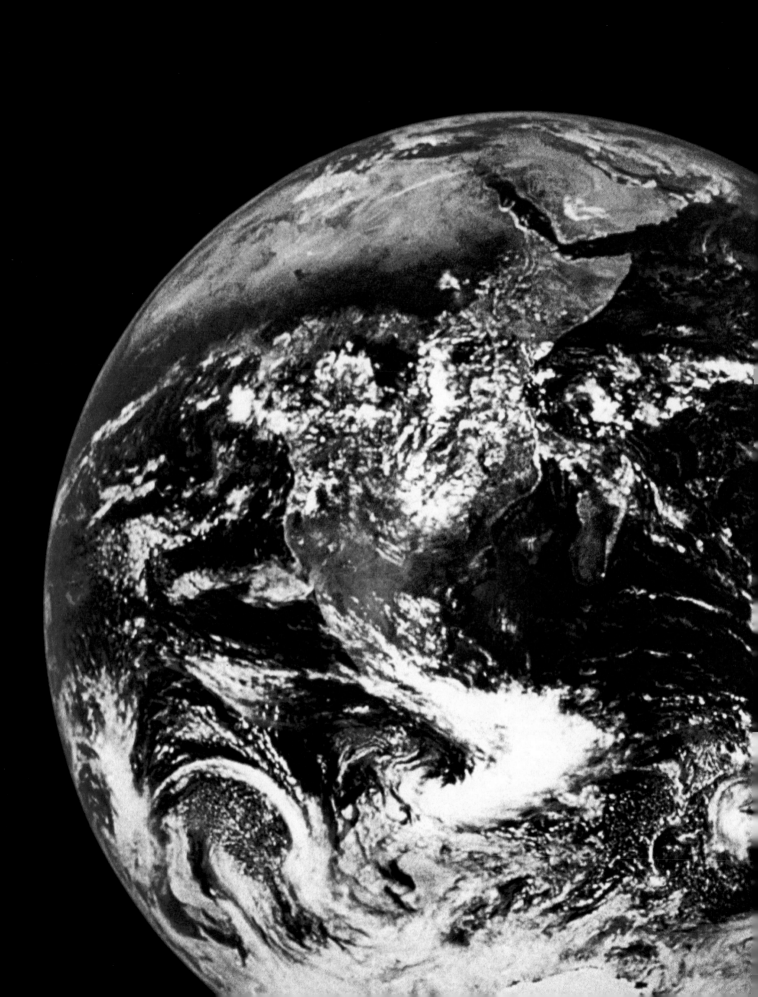

# Geography and Map Skills Handbook

## Contents

Throughout this textbook, you will be studying the world's people, places, and landscapes. One of the main tools you will use is the map—the primary tool of geographers. To help you begin your studies, this Geography and Map Skills Handbook explains some of the basic features of maps. For example, it explains how maps are made, how to read them, and how they can show the round surface of Earth on a flat piece of paper. This handbook will also introduce you to some of the types of maps you will study later in this book. In addition, you will learn about the different kinds of features on Earth and about how geographers use themes and elements to study the world.

📐 hmhsocialstudies.com  **INTERACTIVE MAPS**

**Geography Skills** With map zone geography skills, you can go online to find interactive versions of the key maps in this book. Explore these interactive maps to learn and practice important map skills and bring geography to life.

You can access all of the interactive maps in this book through the Interactive Student Edition at

📐 hmhsocialstudies.com

# Mapping the Earth
## Using Latitude and Longitude

A **globe** is a scale model of the Earth. It is useful for showing the entire Earth or studying large areas of Earth's surface.

To study the world, geographers use a pattern of imaginary lines that circles the globe in east-west and north-south directions. It is called a **grid**. The intersection of these imaginary lines helps us find places on Earth.

The east-west lines in the grid are lines of **latitude**, which you can see on the diagram. Lines of latitude are called **parallels** because they are always parallel to each other. These imaginary lines measure distance north and south of the **equator**. The equator is an imaginary line that circles the globe halfway between the North and South Poles. Parallels measure distance from the equator in **degrees**. The symbol for degrees is °. Degrees are further divided into **minutes**. The symbol for minutes is ´. There are 60 minutes in a degree. Parallels north of the equator are labeled with an N. Those south of the equator are labeled with an S.

The north-south imaginary lines are lines of **longitude**. Lines of longitude are called **meridians**. These imaginary lines pass through the poles. They measure distance east and west of the **prime meridian**. The prime meridian is an imaginary line that runs through Greenwich, England. It represents 0° longitude.

Lines of latitude range from 0°, for locations on the equator, to 90°N or 90°S, for locations at the poles. Lines of longitude range from 0° on the prime meridian to 180° on a meridian in the mid-Pacific Ocean. Meridians west of the prime meridian to 180° are labeled with a W. Those east of the prime meridian to 180° are labeled with an E. Using latitude and longitude, geographers can identify the exact location of any place on Earth.

## Lines of Latitude

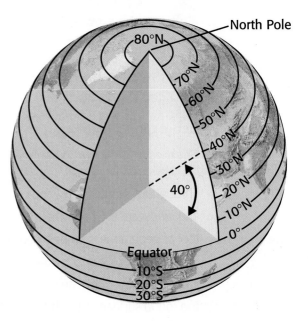

## Lines of Longitude

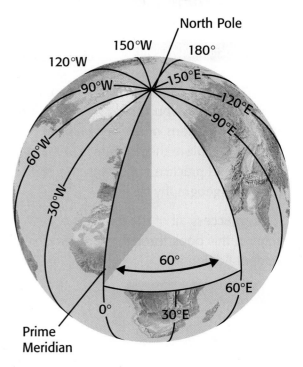

## Northern Hemisphere

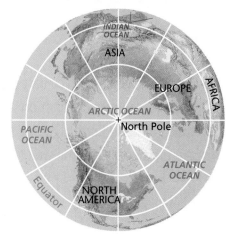

The equator divides the globe into two halves, called **hemispheres**. The half north of the equator is the Northern Hemisphere. The southern half is the Southern Hemisphere. The prime meridian and the 180° meridian divide the world into the Eastern Hemisphere and the Western Hemisphere. Look at the diagrams on this page. They show each of these four hemispheres.

Earth's land surface is divided into seven large landmasses, called **continents**. These continents are also shown on the diagrams on this page. Landmasses smaller than continents and completely surrounded by water are called **islands**.

Geographers organize Earth's water surface into major regions too. The largest is the world ocean. Geographers divide the world ocean into the Pacific Ocean, the Atlantic Ocean, the Indian Ocean, and the Arctic Ocean. Lakes and seas are smaller bodies of water.

## Southern Hemisphere

## Western Hemisphere

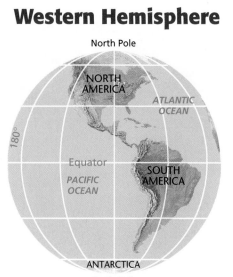

## Eastern Hemisphere

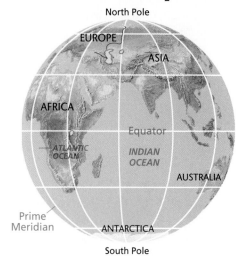

# Mapmaking
## Understanding Map Projections

A **map** is a flat diagram of all or part of Earth's surface. Mapmakers have created different ways of showing our round planet on flat maps. These different ways are called **map projections**. Because Earth is round, there is no way to show it accurately on a flat map. All flat maps are distorted in some way. Mapmakers must choose the type of map projection that is best for their purposes. Many map projections are one of three kinds: cylindrical, conic, or flat-plane.

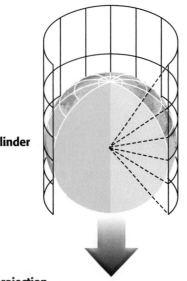

Paper cylinder

## Cylindrical Projections

Cylindrical projections are based on a cylinder wrapped around the globe. The cylinder touches the globe only at the equator. The meridians are pulled apart and are parallel to each other instead of meeting at the poles. This causes landmasses near the poles to appear larger than they really are. The map below is a Mercator projection, one type of cylindrical projection. The Mercator projection is useful for navigators because it shows true direction and shape. However, it distorts the size of land areas near the poles.

Mercator projection

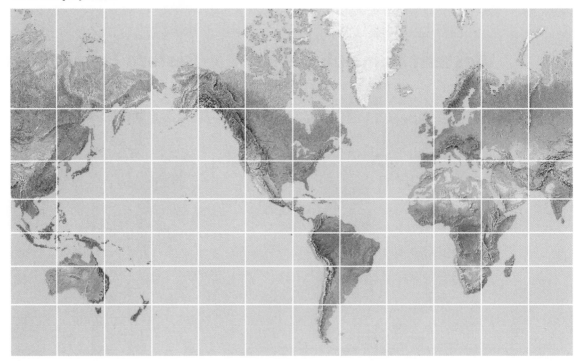

## Conic Projections

Conic projections are based on a cone placed over the globe. A conic projection is most accurate along the lines of latitude where it touches the globe. It retains almost true shape and size. Conic projections are most useful for showing areas that have long east-west dimensions, such as the United States.

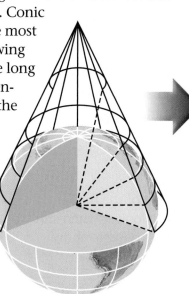

**Paper cone**

**Conic projection**

## Flat-plane Projections

Flat-plane projections are based on a plane touching the globe at one point, such as at the North Pole or South Pole. A flat-plane projection is useful for showing true direction for airplane pilots and ship navigators. It also shows true area. However, it distorts the true shapes of landmasses.

**Flat-plane projection**

**Flat plane**

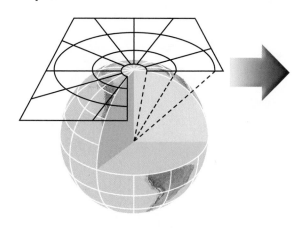

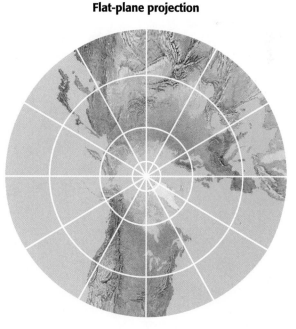

# Map Essentials
## How to Read a Map

Maps are like messages sent out in code. To help us translate the code, mapmakers provide certain features. These features help us understand the message they are presenting about a particular part of the world. Of these features, almost all maps have a title, a compass rose, a scale, and a legend. The map below has these four features, plus a fifth—a locator map.

### ❶ Title

A map's **title** shows what the subject of the map is. The map title is usually the first thing you should look at when studying a map, because it tells you what the map is trying to show.

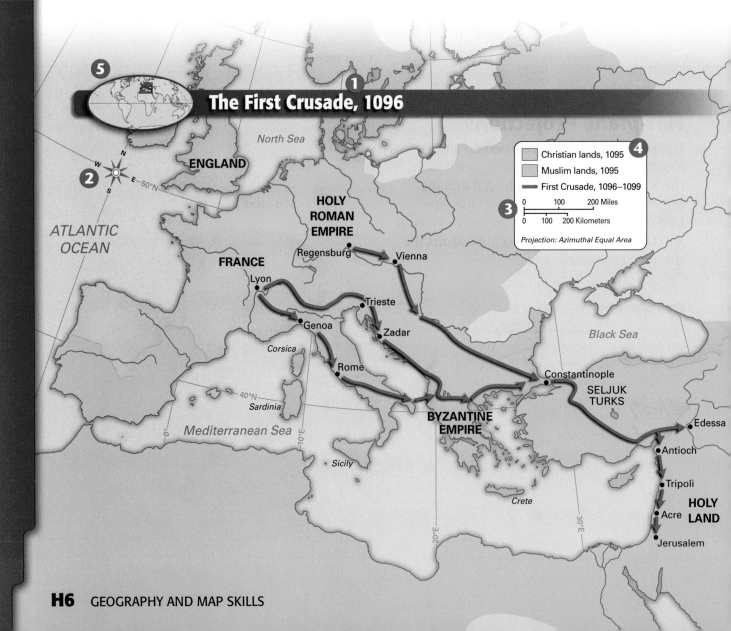

The First Crusade, 1096

North Sea

ENGLAND

ATLANTIC OCEAN

HOLY ROMAN EMPIRE

Regensburg · Vienna

FRANCE

Lyon

Genoa · Trieste · Zadar

Corsica

Rome

Sardinia · 40°N

Mediterranean Sea · 10°E

Sicily

Crete

BYZANTINE EMPIRE

Black Sea

Constantinople

SELJUK TURKS

Edessa

Antioch

Tripoli

HOLY LAND

Acre

Jerusalem

Christian lands, 1095
Muslim lands, 1095
First Crusade, 1096–1099

0    100    200 Miles
0   100   200 Kilometers

Projection: Azimuthal Equal Area

50°N

## ❷ Compass Rose

A directional indicator shows which way north, south, east, and west lie on the map. Some mapmakers use a "north arrow," which points toward the North Pole. Remember, "north" is not always at the top of a map. The way a map is drawn and the location of directions on that map depend on the perspective of the mapmaker. Most maps in this textbook indicate direction by using a compass rose. A **compass rose** has arrows that point to all four principal directions.

## ❸ Scale

Mapmakers use scales to represent the distances between points on a map. Scales may appear on maps in several different forms. The maps in this textbook provide a **bar scale**. Scales give distances in miles and kilometers.

To find the distance between two points on the map, place a piece of paper so that the edge connects the two points. Mark the location of each point on the paper with a line or dot. Then, compare the distance between the two dots with the map's bar scale. The number on the top of the scale gives the distance in miles. The number on the bottom gives the distance in kilometers. Because the distances are given in large intervals, you may have to approximate the actual distance on the scale.

## ❹ Legend

The **legend**, or key, explains what the symbols on the map represent. Point symbols are used to specify the location of things, such as cities, that do not take up much space on the map. Some legends show colors that represent certain features like empires or other regions. Other maps might have legends with symbols or colors that represent features such as roads. Legends can also show economic resources, land use, population density, and climate.

## ❺ Locator Map

A **locator map** shows where in the world the area on the map is located. The area shown on the main map is shown in red on the locator map. The locator map also shows surrounding areas so the map reader can see how the information on the map relates to neighboring lands.

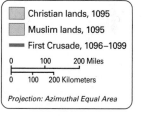

# Working with Maps
## Using Different Kinds of Maps

As you study the world's regions and countries, you will use a variety of maps. Political maps and physical maps are two of the most common types of maps you will study. In addition, you will use special-purpose maps. These maps might show climate, population, resources, ancient empires, or other topics.

## Political Maps

Political maps show the major political features of a region. These features include country borders, capital cities, and other places. Political maps use different colors to represent countries, and capital cities are often shown with a special star symbol.

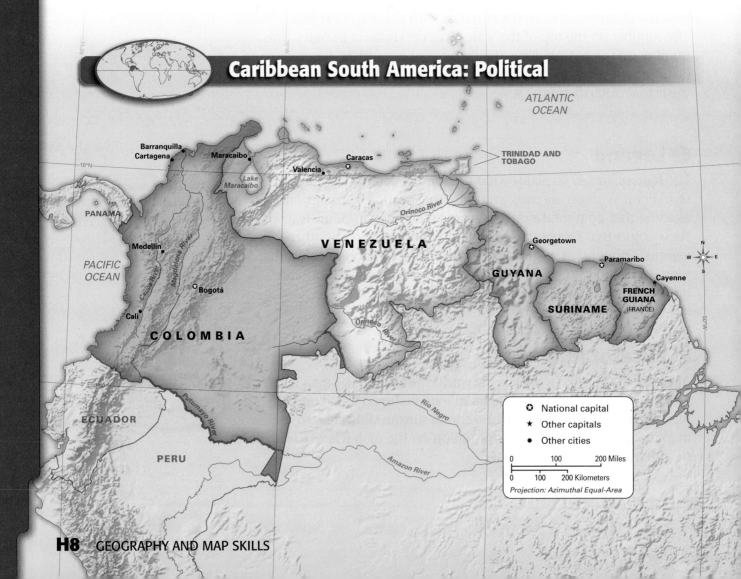

**Caribbean South America: Political**

ATLANTIC OCEAN

Barranquilla
Cartagena
Maracaibo
Caracas
Valencia
Lake Maracaibo
TRINIDAD AND TOBAGO
PANAMA
Orinoco River
VENEZUELA
Georgetown
Medellín
Paramaribo
Cayenne
PACIFIC OCEAN
GUYANA
Bogotá
Cali
SURINAME
FRENCH GUIANA (FRANCE)
Orinoco River
COLOMBIA
0° Equator
ECUADOR
Rio Negro
PERU
Amazon River

✪ National capital
★ Other capitals
● Other cities

0       100      200 Miles
0   100   200 Kilometers
Projection: Azimuthal Equal-Area

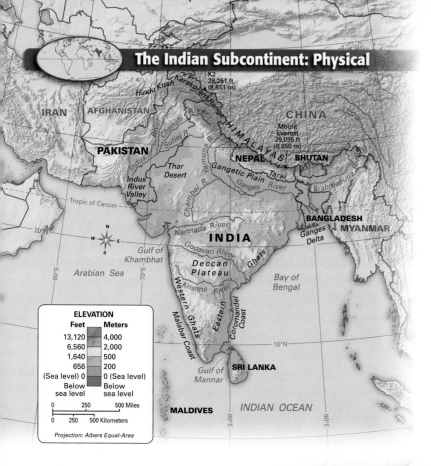

## The Indian Subcontinent: Physical

IRAN

AFGHANISTAN

CHINA

Hindu Kush

Karakoram Range

K2
28,261 ft
(8,611 m)

Indus River

Chenab R.

Sutlej R.

HIMALAYAS

Mount Everest
29,035 ft
(8,850 m)

PAKISTAN

NEPAL

BHUTAN

Thar Desert

Gangetic Plain

Tarai

Yamuna R.

Ganges River

Brahmaputra River

Indus River Valley

Chambal R.

Tropic of Cancer

BANGLADESH

MYANMAR

Narmada River

Ganges Delta

INDIA

Godavari River

Ghats

Gulf of Khambhat

Deccan Plateau

Krishna River

Eastern Ghats

Western Ghats

Arabian Sea

Bay of Bengal

Malabar Coast

Coromandel Coast

10°N

**ELEVATION**

| Feet | | Meters |
|---|---|---|
| 13,120 | | 4,000 |
| 6,560 | | 2,000 |
| 1,640 | | 500 |
| 656 | | 200 |
| (Sea level) 0 | | 0 (Sea level) |
| Below sea level | | Below sea level |

0    250    500 Miles

0    250    500 Kilometers

*Projection: Albers Equal-Area*

Gulf of Mannar

SRI LANKA

MALDIVES

INDIAN OCEAN

## Physical Maps

Physical maps show the major physical features of a region. These features may include mountain ranges, rivers, oceans, islands, deserts, and plains. Often, these maps use different colors to represent different elevations of land. As a result, the map reader can easily see which areas are high elevations, like mountains, and which areas are lower.

## Special-Purpose Maps

Special-purpose maps focus on one special topic, such as climate, resources, or population. These maps present information on the topic that is particularly important in the region. Depending on the type of special-purpose map, the information may be shown with different colors, arrows, dots, or other symbols.

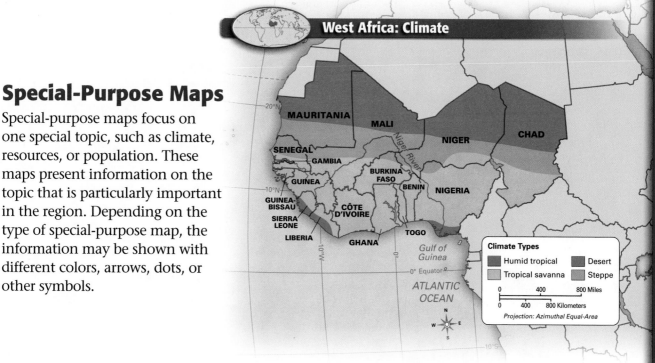

## West Africa: Climate

MAURITANIA

MALI

NIGER

CHAD

SENEGAL

GAMBIA

Niger River

GUINEA

BURKINA FASO

BENIN

NIGERIA

GUINEA-BISSAU

CÔTE D'IVOIRE

SIERRA LEONE

LIBERIA

GHANA

TOGO

Gulf of Guinea

0° Equator

ATLANTIC OCEAN

10°S

**Climate Types**

■ Humid tropical   ■ Desert

■ Tropical savanna   ■ Steppe

0    400    800 Miles

0    400    800 Kilometers

*Projection: Azimuthal Equal-Area*

**Using Maps in Geography** The different kinds of maps in this textbook will help you study and understand geography. By working with these maps, you will see what the physical geography of places is like, where people live, and how the world has changed over time.

# Geographic Dictionary

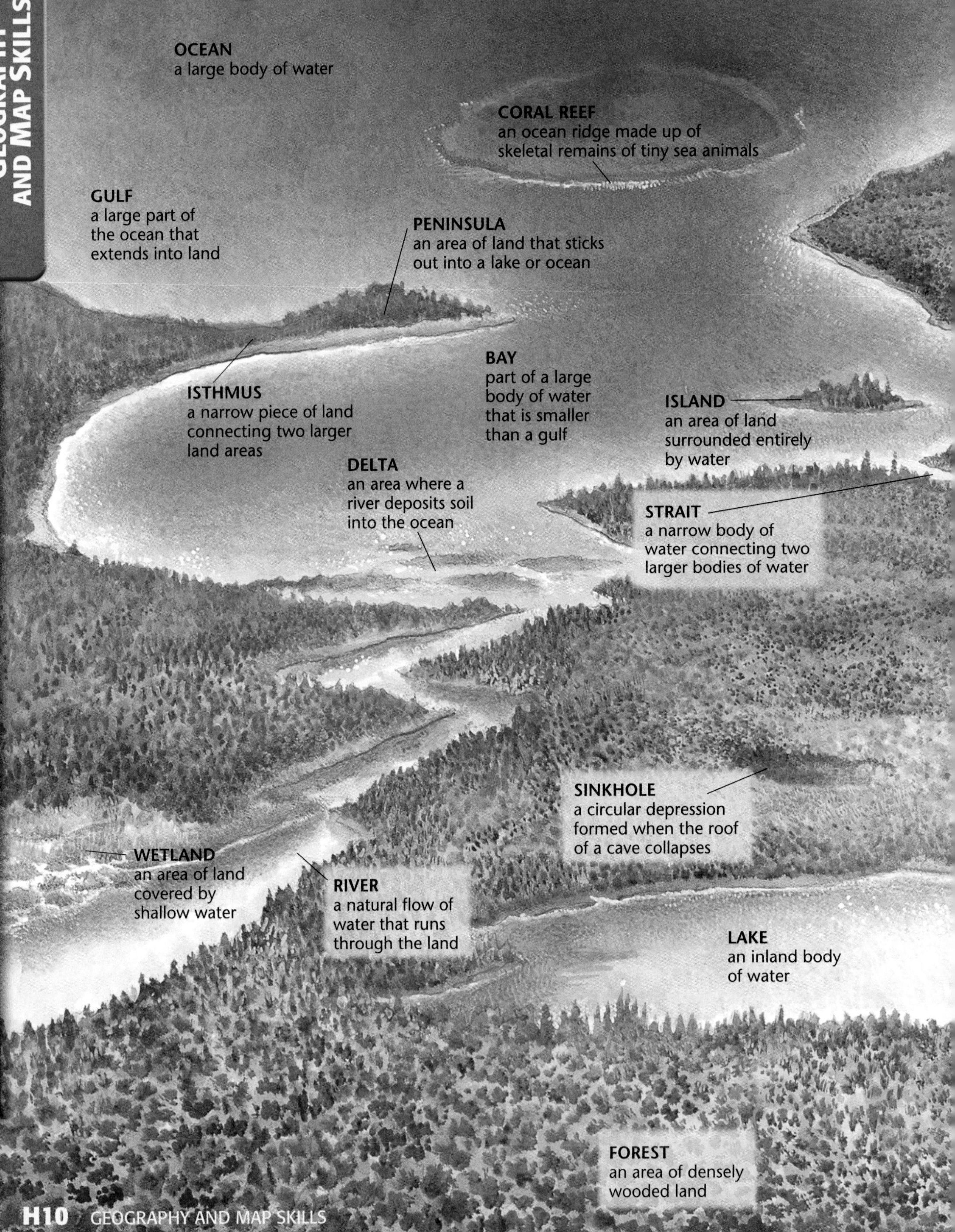

**OCEAN**
a large body of water

**CORAL REEF**
an ocean ridge made up of
skeletal remains of tiny sea animals

**GULF**
a large part of
the ocean that
extends into land

**PENINSULA**
an area of land that sticks
out into a lake or ocean

**ISTHMUS**
a narrow piece of land
connecting two larger
land areas

**BAY**
part of a large
body of water
that is smaller
than a gulf

**ISLAND**
an area of land
surrounded entirely
by water

**DELTA**
an area where a
river deposits soil
into the ocean

**STRAIT**
a narrow body of
water connecting two
larger bodies of water

**SINKHOLE**
a circular depression
formed when the roof
of a cave collapses

**WETLAND**
an area of land
covered by
shallow water

**RIVER**
a natural flow of
water that runs
through the land

**LAKE**
an inland body
of water

**FOREST**
an area of densely
wooded land

**COAST**
an area of land near the ocean

**MOUNTAIN**
an area of rugged land that generally rises higher than 2,000 feet

**VALLEY**
an area of low land between hills or mountains

**GLACIER**
a large area of slow-moving ice

**VOLCANO**
an opening in Earth's crust where lava, ash, and gases erupt

**CANYON**
a deep, narrow valley with steep walls

**HILL**
a rounded, elevated area of land smaller than a mountain

**PLAIN**
a nearly flat area

**DUNE**
a hill of sand shaped by wind

**OASIS**
an area in the desert with a water source

**DESERT**
an extremely dry area with little water and few plants

**PLATEAU**
a large, flat, elevated area of land

GEOGRAPHY AND MAP SKILLS

# Themes and Essential Elements of Geography

*by Dr. Christopher L. Salter*

To study the world, geographers have identified 5 key themes, 6 essential elements, and 18 geography standards.

"How should we teach and learn about geography?" Professional geographers have worked hard over the years to answer this important question.

In 1984 a group of geographers identified the 5 Themes of Geography. These themes did a wonderful job of laying the groundwork for good classroom geography. Teachers used the 5 Themes in class, and geographers taught workshops on how to apply them in the world.

By the early 1990s, however, some geographers felt the 5 Themes were too broad. They created the 18 Geography Standards and the 6 Essential Elements. The 18 Geography Standards include more detailed information about what geography is, and the 6 Essential Elements are like a bridge between the 5 Themes and 18 Standards.

Look at the chart to the right. It shows how each of the 5 Themes connects to the Essential Elements and Standards. For example, the theme of Location is related to The World in Spatial Terms and the first three Standards. Study the chart carefully to see how the other themes, elements, and Standards are related.

The last Essential Element and the last two Standards cover The Uses of Geography. These key parts of geography were not covered by the 5 Themes. They will help you see how geography has influenced the past, present, and future.

## 5 Themes of Geography

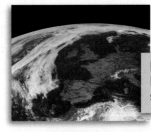

**Location** The theme of location describes where something is.

**Place** Place describes the features that make a site unique.

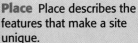

**Regions** Regions are areas that share common characteristics.

**Movement** This theme looks at how and why people and things move.

**Human-Environment Interaction** People interact with their environment in many ways.

# 6 Essential Elements

 **Geography Standards**

1. How to use maps and other tools
2. How to use mental maps to organize information
3. How to analyze the spatial organization of people, places, and environments

**I. The World in Spatial Terms**

4. The physical and human characteristics of places
5. How people create regions to interpret Earth
6. How culture and experience influence people's perceptions of places and regions

**II. Places and Regions**

7. The physical processes that shape Earth's surface
8. The distribution of ecosystems on Earth

9. The characteristics, distribution, and migration of human populations
10. The complexity of Earth's cultural mosaics
11. The patterns and networks of economic interdependence on Earth
12. The patterns of human settlement
13. The forces of cooperation and conflict

**III. Physical Systems**

**IV. Human Systems**

14. How human actions modify the physical environment
15. How physical systems affect human systems
16. The distribution and meaning of resources

**V. Environment and Society**

17. How to apply geography to interpret the past
18. How to apply geography to interpret the present and plan for the future

**VI. The Uses of Geography**

# Become an Active Reader

Did you ever think you would begin reading your social studies book by reading about *reading*? Actually, it makes better sense than you might think. You would probably make sure you knew some soccer skills and strategies before playing in a game. Similarly, you need to know something about reading skills and strategies before reading your social studies book. In other words, you need to make sure you know whatever you need to know in order to read this book successfully.

## Tip #1

## Read Everything on the Page!

*You can't follow the directions on the cake-mix box if you don't know where the directions are!* Cake-mix boxes always have directions on them telling you how many eggs to add or how long to bake the cake. But, if you can't find that information, it doesn't matter that it is there.

Likewise, this book is filled with information that will help you understand what you are reading. If you don't study that information, however, it might as well not be there. Let's take a look at some of the places where you'll find important information in this book.

### The Chapter Opener
The chapter opener gives you a brief overview of what you will learn in the chapter. You can use this information to prepare to read the chapter.

### The Section Openers
Before you begin to read each section, preview the information under What You Will Learn. There you'll find the main ideas of the section and key terms that are important in it. Knowing what you are looking for before you start reading can improve your understanding.

### Boldfaced Words
Those words are important and are defined somewhere on the page where they appear—either right there in the sentence or over in the side margin.

### Maps, Charts, and Artwork
These things are not there just to take up space or look good! Study them and read the information beside them. It will help you understand the information in the chapter.

### Questions at the End of Sections
At the end of each section, you will find questions that will help you decide whether you need to go back and re-read any parts before moving on. If you can't answer a question, that is your cue to go back and re-read.

### Questions at the End of the Chapter
Answer the questions at the end of each chapter, even if your teacher doesn't ask you to. These questions are there to help you figure out what you need to review.

Tip #2

# Use the Reading Skills and Strategies in Your Textbook

Good readers use a number of skills and strategies to make sure they understand what they are reading. In this textbook you will find help with important reading skills and strategies such as "Using Prior Knowledge," and "Understanding Main Ideas."

We teach the reading skills and strategies in several ways. Use these activities and lessons and you will become a better reader.

- First, on the opening page of every chapter we identify and explain the reading skill or strategy you will focus on as you work through the chapter. In fact, these activities are called "Focus on Reading."

- Second, as you can see in the example at right, we tell you where to go for more help. The back of the book has a reading handbook with a full-page practice lesson to match the reading skill or strategy in every chapter.

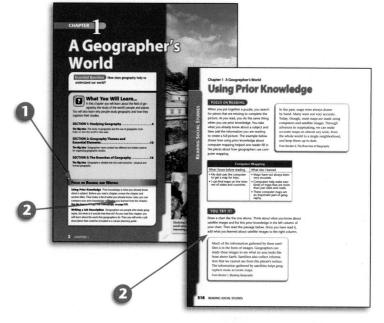

- Third, we give you short practice activities and examples as you read the chapter. These activities and examples show up in the margin of your book. Again, look for the words, "Focus on Reading."

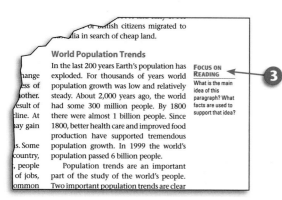

**World Population Trends**

In the last 200 years Earth's population has exploded. For thousands of years world population growth was low and relatively steady. About 2,000 years ago, the world had some 300 million people. By 1800 there were almost 1 billion people. Since 1800, better health care and improved food production have supported tremendous population growth. In 1999 the world's population passed 6 billion people.

Population trends are an important part of the study of the world's people. Two important population trends are clear

**FOCUS ON READING**
What is the main idea of this paragraph? What facts are used to support that idea?

- Finally, we provide another practice activity in the Chapter Review at the end of every chapter. That activity gives you one more chance to make sure you know how to use the reading skill or strategy.

**FOCUS ON READING AND WRITING**

**Understanding Main Ideas** *Read the paragraph in question 15 below. Then, write out the main idea of the paragraph.*

15. The ancient Greeks were the first to practice democracy. Since then many countries have adopted democratic government. The United Kingdom, South Korea, and Ghana all practice democracy. Democracy is the most widely used government in the world today.

16. **Creating a Poster** Review your notes about the world's cultures, populations, governments, and economies. Then, select a topic for your poster. On large sheet of paper, write a title that identifies your topic. Illustrate your poster with images that support your topic. Write a short caption explaining each image.

## Tip #3

# Pay Attention to Vocabulary

It is no fun to read something when you don't know what the words mean, but you can't learn new words if you only use or read the words you already know. In this book, we know we have probably used some words you don't know. But, we have followed a pattern as we have used more difficult words.

- First, at the beginning of each section you will find a list of key terms that you will need to know. Be on the lookout for those words as you read through the section. You will find that we have defined those words right there in the paragraph where they are used. Look for a word that is in boldface with its definition highlighted in yellow.

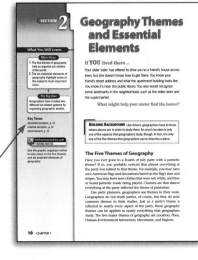

- Second, when we use a word that is important in all classes, not just social studies, we define it in the margin under the heading Academic Vocabulary. You will run into these academic words in other textbooks, so you should learn what they mean while reading this book.

## Tip #4

# Read Like a Skilled Reader

***You won't be able to climb to the top of Mount Everest if you do not train!*** If you want to make it to the top of Mount Everest then you must start training to climb that huge mountain.

Training is also necessary to become a good reader. You will never get better at reading your social studies book—or any book for that matter—unless you spend some time thinking about how to be a better reader.

## Skilled readers do the following:

1. They preview what they are supposed to read before they actually begin reading. When previewing, they look for vocabulary words, titles of sections, information in the margin, or maps or charts they should study.

2. They get ready to take some notes while reading by dividing their notebook paper into two parts. They title one side "Notes from the Chapter" and the other side "Questions or Comments I Have."

3. As they read, they complete their notes.

4. They read like **active readers**. The Active Reading list below shows you what that means.

5. Finally, they use clues in the text to help them figure out where the text is going. The best clues are called signal words. These are words that help you identify chronological order, causes and effects, or comparisons and contrasts.

**Chronological Order Signal Words:** *first, second, third, before, after, later, next, following that, earlier, subsequently, finally*

**Cause and Effect Signal Words:** *because of, due to, as a result of, the reason for, therefore, consequently, so, basis for*

**Comparison/Contrast Signal Words:** *likewise, also, as well as, similarly, on the other hand*

## Active Reading

There are three ways to read a book: You can be a turn-the-pages-no-matter-what type of reader. These readers just keep on turning pages whether or not they understand what they are reading. Or, you can be a stop-watch-and-listen kind of reader. These readers know that if they wait long enough, someone will tell them what they need to know. Or, you can be an active reader. These readers know that it is up to them to figure out what the text means. Active readers do the following as they read:

**Predict** what will happen next based on what has already happened. When your predictions don't match what happens in the text, re-read the confusing parts.

**Question** what is happening as you read. Constantly ask yourself why things have happened, what things mean, and what caused certain events. Jot down notes about the questions you can't answer.

**Summarize** what you are reading frequently. Do not try to summarize the entire chapter! Read a bit and then summarize it. Then read on.

**Connect** what is happening in the section you're reading to what you have already read.

**Clarify** your understanding. Be sure that you understand what you are reading by stopping occasionally to ask yourself whether you are confused by anything. Sometimes you might need to re-read to clarify. Other times you might need to read further and collect more information before you can understand. Still other times you might need to ask the teacher to help you with what is confusing you.

**Visualize** what is happening in the text. In other words, try to see the events or places in your mind. It might help you to draw maps, make charts, or jot down notes about what you are reading as you try to visualize the action in the text.

# Social Studies Words

As you read this textbook, you will be more successful if you learn the meanings of the words on this page. You will come across these words many times in your social studies classes, like geography and history. Read through these words now to become familiar with them before you begin your studies.

## Social Studies Words

### WORDS ABOUT TIME

| | |
|---|---|
| **AD** | refers to dates after the birth of Jesus |
| **BC** | refers to dates before Jesus's birth |
| **BCE** | refers to dates before Jesus's birth, stands for "before the common era" |
| **CE** | refers to dates after Jesus's birth, stands for "common era" |
| **century** | a period of 100 years |
| **decade** | a period of 10 years |
| **era** | a period of time |
| **millennium** | a period of 1,000 years |

### WORDS ABOUT THE WORLD

| | |
|---|---|
| **climate** | the weather conditions in a certain area over a long period of time |
| **geography** | the study of the world's people, places, and landscapes |
| **physical features** | features on Earth's surface, such as mountains and rivers |
| **region** | an area with one or more features that make it different from surrounding areas |
| **resources** | materials found on Earth that people need and value |

### WORDS ABOUT PEOPLE

| | |
|---|---|
| **anthropology** | the study of people and cultures |
| **archaeology** | the study of the past based on what people left behind |
| **citizen** | a person who lives under the control of a government |
| **civilization** | the way of life of people in a particular place or time |
| **culture** | the knowledge, beliefs, customs, and values of a group of people |
| **custom** | a repeated practice or tradition |
| **economics** | the study of the production and use of goods and services |
| **economy** | any system in which people make and exchange goods and services |
| **government** | the body of officials and groups that run an area |
| **history** | the study of the past |
| **politics** | the process of running a government |
| **religion** | a system of beliefs in one or more gods or spirits |
| **society** | a group of people who share common traditions |
| **trade** | the exchange of goods or services |

# Academic Words

What are academic words? They are important words used in all of your classes, not just social studies. You will see these words in other textbooks, so you should learn what they mean while reading this book. Review this list now. You will use these words again in the chapters of this book.

## Academic Words

| | | | | |
|---|---|---|---|---|
| **advocate** | to plead in favor of | | **incentive** | something that leads people to follow a certain course of action |
| **affect** | to change or influence | | **influence** | change or have an effect on |
| **agreement** | a decision reached by two or more people or groups | | **innovation** | a new idea or way of doing something |
| **aspects** | parts | | **logical** | reasoned, well thought out |
| **cause** | to make something happen | | **neutral** | unbiased, not favoring either side in a conflict |
| **consequences** | the effects of a particular event or events | | **policy** | rule, course of action |
| **contemporary** | modern | | **primary** | main, most important |
| **contract** | a binding legal agreement | | **process** | a series of steps by which a task is accomplished |
| **development** | the process of growing or improving | | **purpose** | the reason something is done |
| **distinct** | clearly different and separate | | **reaction** | a response to something |
| **element** | part | | **rebel** | to fight against authority |
| **establish** | to set up or create | | **strategy** | a plan for fighting a battle or war |
| **facilitate** | to make easier | | **structure** | the way something is set up or organized |
| **factor** | cause | | **traditional** | customary, time-honored |
| **features** | characteristics | | **vary** | to be different |
| **function** | use or purpose | | | |
| **implications** | consequences | | | |

# Making This Book Work for You

Studying geography will be easy for you with this textbook. Take a few minutes now to become familiar with the easy-to-use structure and special features of your book. See how it will make geography come alive for you!

## Unit

Each unit begins with a satellite image, a regional atlas, and a table with facts about each country. Use these pages to get an overview of the region you will study.

## Regional Atlas

The maps in the regional atlas show some of the key physical and human features of the region.

**Facts about Countries** See which countries are included in each region and learn some important facts about them with these helpful tables.

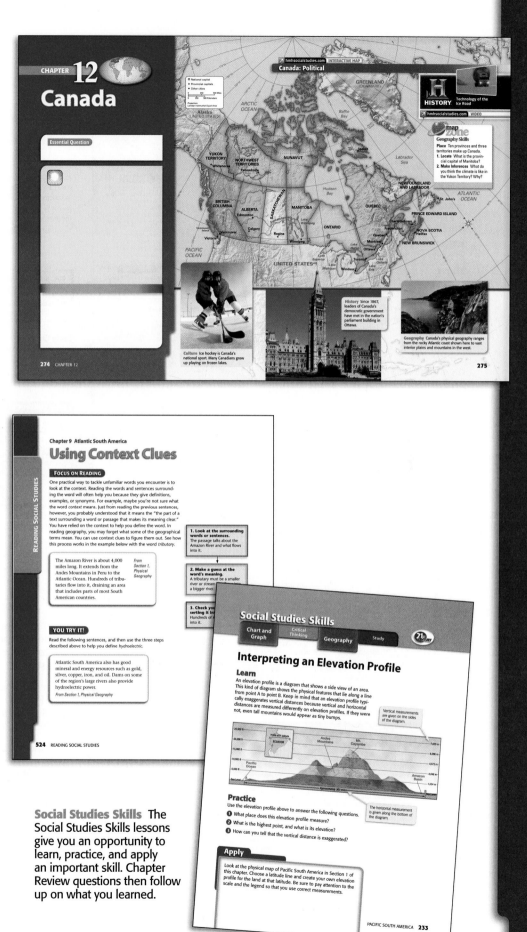

## Chapter

Each regional chapter begins with a preview of what you will learn and a map of the region. Special instruction is also given in reading and skills.

## Reading Social Studies

Chapter reading lessons give you skills and practice to help you read the textbook. More help with each lesson can be found in the back of the book. Margin notes and questions in the chapter make sure you understand the reading skill.

## Social Studies Skills

The Social Studies Skills lessons give you an opportunity to learn, practice, and apply an important skill. Chapter Review questions then follow up on what you learned.

# Section

The section opener pages include Main Ideas, an overarching Big Idea, and Key Terms and Places. In addition, each section includes these special features:

**If YOU Lived There . . .** Each section begins with a situation for you to respond to, placing you in a place that relates to the content you will be studying in the section.

**Building Background** Building Background connects what will be covered in each section with what you already know.

**Short Sections of Content** The information in each section is organized into small chunks of text that you can easily understand.

**Taking Notes** Suggested online graphic organizers help you read and take notes on the important ideas in the section.

---

**SECTION 2**

# History and Culture

## What You Will Learn...

### Main Ideas

1. Early cultures of Mexico included the Olmec, the Maya, and the Aztec.
2. Mexico's period as a Spanish colony and its struggles since independence have shaped its culture.
3. Spanish and native cultures have influenced Mexico's customs and traditions today.

### The Big Idea

Native American cultures and Spanish colonization shaped Mexican history and culture.

### Key Terms

empire, p. 147
mestizos, p. 148
missions, p. 148
haciendas, p. 148

hmhsocialstudies.com
**TAKING NOTES**

Use the graphic organizer online to organize your notes on Mexico's history and culture.

### If YOU lived there...

You belong to one of the native Indian peoples in southern Mexico in the early 1500s. Years ago, the Aztec rulers went to war against your people. They took many captives. They have always treated you cruelly. Now some strangers have come from across the sea. They want your people to help them conquer the Aztecs.

**Will you help the strangers fight the Aztecs? Why or why not?**

**BUILDING BACKGROUND** Mexico was home to several of the earliest advanced cultures in the Americas. Early farmers there developed crops that became staples in much of North America. Mexico also has valuable minerals, which drew Spanish conquerors and colonists. Spanish culture blended with native Mexican cultures.

### Early Cultures

People first came to Mexico many thousands of years ago. As early as 5,000 years ago, they were growing beans, peppers, and squash. They also domesticated an early form of corn. Farming allowed these people to build the first permanent settlements in the Americas.

**Early Cultures of Mexico**

hmhsocialstudies.com
**ANIMATED GEOGRAPHY**

**Olmec**

- The Olmec made sculptures of giant stone heads.
- The heads may have represented rulers or gods.

---

**ACADEMIC VOCABULARY**
affect to change or influence

Northern Mexico's closeness to the border has **affected** the region's culture as well as its economy. American television, music, and other forms of entertainment are popular there. Many Mexicans cross the border to shop, work, or live in the United States. While many people cross the border legally, the U.S. government tries to prevent Mexicans and others from crossing the border illegally.

### Southern Mexico

Southern Mexico is the least populated and industrialized region of the country. Many people in this region speak Indian languages and practice traditional ways of life. Subsistence farming and slash-and-burn agriculture are common.

**FOCUS ON READING**
What do you think makes southern Mexico vital to the country's economy?

However, southern Mexico is vital to the country's economy. Sugarcane and coffee, two major export crops, grow well in the region's warm, humid climate. Also, oil production along the Gulf coast has increased in recent years. The oil business has brought more industry and population growth to this coastal area of southern Mexico.

Another place in southern Mexico that has grown in recent years is the Yucatán Peninsula. Maya ruins, beautiful sunny beaches, and clear blue water have made tourism a major industry in this area. Many cities that were just tiny fishing villages only 20 years ago are now booming with new construction for the tourist industry.

Mexico will continue to change in the future. Changes are likely to bring more development. However, maintaining the country's unique regional cultures may be a challenge as those changes take place.

**READING CHECK** Comparing and Contrasting
What similarities and differences exist between greater Mexico City and southern Mexico?

**SUMMARY AND PREVIEW** Mexico has a democratic government and a growing economy. It also has distinct regions with different cultures, economies, and environments. In the next chapter you will learn about the countries to the south of Mexico.

### Section 3 Assessment

hmhsocialstudies.com
**ONLINE QUIZ**

**Reviewing Ideas, Terms, and Places**

1. **a. Define** What is the term for the practice of burning forest in order to clear land for planting?
   **b. Compare and Contrast** How is Mexico's government similar to and different from the government of the United States?
2. **a. Identify** What is an environmental problem found in **Mexico City**?
   **b. Make Inferences** What conditions in Mexico lead some Mexicans to cross the border into the United States?
   **c. Develop** If you were to start a business in Mexico, what type of business would you start and where would you start it? Explain your decisions.

**Critical Thinking**

3. **Finding Main Ideas** Review your notes on Mexico's economy. Then use a chart like this one to show what parts of the economy are important in each region.

| Greater Mexico City | Central Mexico | Northern Mexico | Southern Mexico |
|---|---|---|---|
| | | | |

**FOCUS ON WRITING**

4. **Describing Mexico Today** Write some details about the four culture regions of Mexico. Which details will you include in your poem?

---

**Reading Check** Questions end each section of content so you can check to make sure you understand what you just studied.

**Summary and Preview** The Summary and Preview connects what you studied in the section to what you will study in the next section.

**Section Assessment** Finally, the section assessment boxes make sure that you understand the main ideas of the section. We also provide assessment practice online!

# Features

Your book includes many features that will help you learn about geography, such as Close-up and Satellite View.

**Satellite View**
See and explore the world through satellite images.

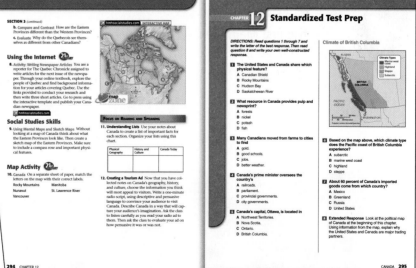

## Venice

Venice, in northeastern Italy, is one of the country's most visited tourist attractions. Look at the image of Venice above, taken by an orbiting satellite. Does it look like other cities you have seen? What may not be obvious is that the paths that wind their way through the city are not roads, but canals. In fact, Venice has very few roads. This is because the city was built on islands—118 of them! People move about the city on boats that navigate along the canals. Every year, millions of tourists travel to Venice to see the sights as they are rowed along the scenic waterways.

**Contrasting** How is Venice unlike other cities you have studied?

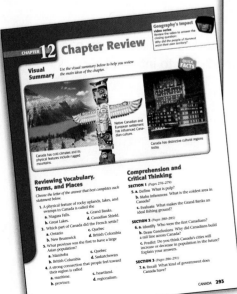

**Close-up** These features help you see how people live and what places look like around the world.

# Chapter Review

At the end of each chapter, the Chapter Review will help you review key concepts, analyze information critically, complete activities, and show what you have learned.

**Standardized Test Practice** Practice for standardized tests with the last page of each chapter before moving on to another region of the world!

# Scavenger Hunt

Are you ready to explore the world of geography? *Holt McDougal Social Studies: Western World* is your ticket to this exciting world. Before you begin your journey, complete this scavenger hunt to get to know your book and discover what's inside.

**On a separate sheet of paper**, fill in the blanks to complete each sentence below. In each answer, one letter will be in a yellow box. When you have answered every question, copy these letters in order to reveal the answer to the question at the bottom of the page.

**1** According to the Table of Contents, Section 2 of Chapter 18 is called The ☐☐☐☐☐☐ Isles. What else does the Table of Contents show?

**2** The first term listed in the English and Spanish Glossary is ☐☐☐☐☐☐☐☐ location. What does this term mean?

**3** The first word of the first Main Idea on page 248 is ☐☐☐☐☐.

**4** The first entry listed under "B" in the Index is ☐☐☐☐☐☐☐.

**5** Page 29 includes a Focus on Culture feature called The Midnight ☐☐☐. What other features can you find in this book?

**6** Page 549 of the Atlas shows a map of ☐☐☐☐☐.

**7** The Social Studies Skill lesson on page 180 will teach you to interpret a ☐☐☐☐☐☐ ☐☐☐☐.

## Fact!

One of the most popular foods in the United States was named after a German city. What city was it?

☐☐☐☐☐☐☐

# Introduction to Geography

## Deserts

Huge deserts, such as the Sahara in North Africa, are visible from space and appear yellow and brown.

## Oceans

About 71 percent of Earth's surface is covered by vast amounts of salt water, which form the world's oceans.

>665.00'

# UNIT 1

# Introduction to Geography

**Explore the Satellite Image**
Human-made machines that orbit Earth, called satellites, send back images of our planet like this one. What can you learn about Earth from studying this satellite image?

## Frozen Lands

Earth's icy poles are frozen year-round and appear a brilliant white from space. These frozen lands contain much of Earth's freshwater.

>>>>>>665·00'

# CHAPTER 1

# A Geographer's World

**Essential Question** How does geography help us understand our world?

## What You Will Learn...

In this chapter you will learn about the field of geography, the study of the world's people and places. You will also learn why people study geography and how they organize their studies.

## FOCUS ON READING AND WRITING

**Using Prior Knowledge** Prior knowledge is what you already know about a subject. Before you read a chapter, review the chapter and section titles. Then make a list of what you already know. Later, you can compare your prior knowledge with what you learned from the chapter. See the lesson, Using Prior Knowledge, on page 516.

**Writing a Job Description** Geographers are people who study geography, but what is it exactly that they do? As you read this chapter, you will learn about the work that geographers do. Then you will write a job description that could be included in a career-planning guide.

**Studying the World** Exploring the world takes people to exciting and interesting places.

HISTORY  Satellites

↗ hmhsocialstudies.com  VIDEO

**ANALYSIS SKILL**  **ANALYZING VISUALS**

This village is in the country of Nepal. It rests high in the Himalayas, the highest mountains in the world.

**What is the land around the village like? How can you tell that people live in this area?**

**Human Geography** Geography is also the study of people. It asks where people live, what they eat, what they wear, and even what kinds of animals they keep.

**Physical Geography** Geography is the study of the world's land features, such as this wind-swept rock formation in Arizona.

3

# Studying Geography

## If YOU lived there...

You have just moved to Miami, Florida, from your old home in Pennsylvania. Everything seems very different—from the weather and the trees to the way people dress and talk. Even the streets and buildings look different. One day you get an e-mail from a friend at your old school. "What's it like living there?" he asks.

**How will you describe your new home?**

**BUILDING BACKGROUND** Often, when you are telling someone about a place they have never been, what you are describing is the place's geography. What the place looks like, what kind of weather it has, and how people live there are all parts of its geography.

## What Is Geography?

Think about the place where you live. What does the land look like? Are there tall mountains nearby, or is the land so flat that you can see for miles? Is the ground covered with bright green grass and trees, or is the area part of a sandy desert?

Now think about the weather in your area. What is it like? Does it get really hot in the summer? Do you see snow every winter? How much does it rain? Do tornadoes ever strike?

Finally, think about the people who live in your town or city. Do they live mostly in apartments or houses? Do most people own cars, or do they get around town on buses or trains? What kinds of jobs do adults in your town have? Were most of the people you know born in your town, or did they move there?

The things that you have been thinking about are part of your area's geography. **Geography** is the study of the world, its people, and the landscapes they create. To a geographer, a place's **landscape** is all the human and physical features that make it unique. When they study the world's landscapes, geographers ask questions much like the ones you just asked yourself.

## Geography as a Science

Many of the questions that geographers ask deal with how the world works. They want to know what causes mountains to form and what creates tornadoes. To answer questions like these, geographers have to think and act like scientists.

As scientists, geographers look at data, or information, that they gather about places. Gathering data can sometimes lead geographers to fascinating places. They might have to crawl deep into caves or climb tall mountains to make observations and take measurements. At other times, geographers study sets of images collected by satellites orbiting high above Earth.

However geographers gather their data, they have to study it carefully. Like other scientists, geographers must examine their findings in great detail before they can learn what all the information means.

## Geography as a Social Science

Not everything that geographers study can be measured in numbers, however. Some geographers study people and their lives. For example, they may ask why countries change their governments or why people in a place speak a certain language. This kind of information cannot be measured.

Because it deals with people and how they live, geography is sometimes called a social science. A **social science** is a field that studies people and the relationships among them.

The geographers who study people do not dig in caves or climb mountains. Instead, they visit places and talk to the people who live there. They want to learn about people's lives and communities.

**READING CHECK** **Analyzing** In what ways is geography both a science and a social science?

## What Is Geography?

Geography is the study of the world, its people, and the landscapes they create. To study a place's geography, we look at its physical and human features.

The physical features of Algeria include huge deserts full of tall sand dunes.

Many Algerians live in small villages like this one. The village is one of Algeria's human features.

Together, Algeria's physical and human features create the country's landscape.

**ANALYSIS SKILL ANALYZING VISUALS**

What is the landscape of this part of Algeria like?

## Looking at the World

Whether they study volcanoes and storms or people and cities, geographers have to look carefully at the world around them. To fully understand how the world works, geographers often look at places at three different levels.

### Local Level

Some geographers study issues at a local level. They ask the same types of questions we asked at the beginning of this chapter: How do people in a town or community live? What is the local government like? How do the people who live there get around? What do they eat?

By asking these questions, geographers can figure out why people live and work the way they do. They can also help people improve their lives. For example, they can help town leaders figure out the best place to build new schools, shopping centers, or sports complexes. They can also help the people who live in the city or town plan for future changes.

### Regional Level

Sometimes, though, geographers want to study a bigger chunk of the world. To do this, they divide the world into regions. A **region** is a part of the world that has one or more common features that distinguish it from surrounding areas.

Some regions are defined by physical characteristics such as mountain ranges, climates, or plants native to the area. As a result, these types of regions are often easy to identify. The Rocky Mountains of the western United States, for example, make up a physical region. Another example of this kind of region is the Sahara, a huge desert in northern Africa.

Other regions may not be so easy to define, however. These regions are based on the human characteristics of a place, such as language, religion, or history. A place in which most people share these kinds of characteristics can also be seen as a region. For example, most people in Scandinavia, a region in northern Europe, speak similar languages and practice the same religion.

## Looking at the World

Geographers look at the world at many levels. At each level, they ask different questions and discover different types of information. By putting information gathered at different levels together, geographers can better understand a place and its role in the world.

**ANALYZING VISUALS** Based on these photos, what are some questions a geographer might ask about London?

**Local Level** This busy neighborhood in London, England, is a local area. A geographer here might study local foods, housing, or clothing.

Regions come in all shapes and sizes. Some are small, like the neighborhood called Chinatown in San Francisco. Other regions are huge, like the Americas. This huge region includes two continents, North America and South America. The size of the area does not matter, as long as the area shares some characteristics. These shared characteristics define the region.

Geographers divide the world into regions for many reasons. The world is a huge place and home to billions of people. Studying so large an area can be extremely difficult. Dividing the world into regions makes it easier to study. A small area is much easier to examine than a large area.

Other geographers study regions to see how people interact with one another. For example, they may study a city such as London, England, to learn how the city's people govern themselves. Then they can compare what they learn about one region to what they learn about another region. In this way, they can learn more about life and landscapes in both places.

## Global Level

Sometimes geographers do not want to study the world just at a regional level. Instead they want to learn how people interact globally, or around the world. To do so, geographers ask how events and ideas from one region of the world affect people in other regions. In other words, they study the world on a global level.

Geographers who study the world on a global level try to find relationships among people who live far apart. They may, for example, examine the products that a country exports to see how those products are used in other countries.

In recent decades, worldwide trade and communication have increased. As a result, we need to understand how our actions affect people around the world. Through their studies, geographers provide us with information that helps us figure out how to live in a rapidly changing world.

**READING CHECK** **Finding Main Ideas** At what levels do geographers study the world?

**Regional Level** As a major city, London is also a region. At this level, a geographer might study the city's population or transportation systems.

**Global Level** London is one of the world's main financial centers. Here a geographer might study how London's economy affects the world.

# The Geographer's Tools

Geographers use many tools to study the world. Each tool provides part of the information a geographer needs to learn what a place is like.

**ANALYZING VISUALS** What information could you learn from each of these tools?

A geographer can use a globe to see where a place, such as the United States, is located.

### High School Soccer Participation

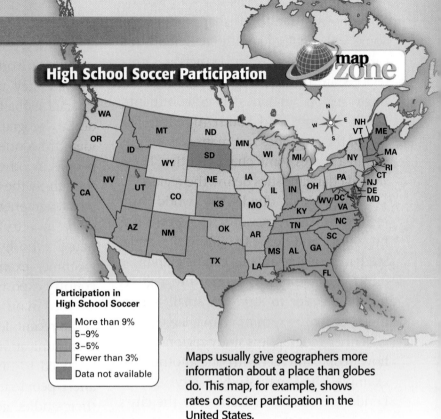

**Participation in High School Soccer**

- More than 9%
- 5–9%
- 3–5%
- Fewer than 3%
- Data not available

Maps usually give geographers more information about a place than globes do. This map, for example, shows rates of soccer participation in the United States.

## The Geographer's Tools

Have you ever seen a carpenter building or repairing a house? If so, you know that builders need many tools to do their jobs correctly. In the same way, geographers need many tools to study the world.

### Maps and Globes

**FOCUS ON READING**

What do you already know about maps and globes?

The tools that geographers use most often in their work are maps and globes. A **map** is a flat drawing that shows all or part of Earth's surface. A **globe** is a spherical, or ball-shaped, model of the entire planet.

Both maps and globes show what the world looks like. They can show where mountains, deserts, and oceans are. They can also identify and describe the world's countries and major cities.

There are, however, major differences between maps and globes. Because a globe is spherical like Earth, it can show the world as it really is.

A map, though, is flat. It is not possible to show a spherical area perfectly on a flat surface. To understand what this means, think about an orange. If you took the peel off of an orange, could you make it lie completely flat? No, you could not, unless you stretched or tore the peel first.

The same principle is true with maps. To draw Earth on a flat surface, people have to distort, or alter, some details. For example, places on a map might look to be farther apart than they really are, or their shapes or sizes might be changed slightly.

Still, maps have many advantages over globes. Flat maps are easier to work with than globes. Also, it is easier to show small areas like cities on maps than on globes.

In addition, maps usually show more information than globes. Because globes are more expensive to make, they do not usually show anything more than where places are and what features they have.

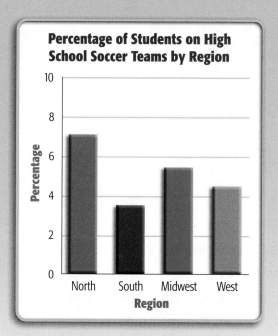

**Percentage of Students on High School Soccer Teams by Region**

Charts and graphs are also tools geographers can use to study information. They are often used when geographers want to compare numbers, such as the number of students who play soccer in each region of the country.

Maps, on the other hand, can show all sorts of information. Besides showing land use and cities, maps can include a great deal of information about a place. A map might show what languages people speak or where their ancestors came from. Maps like the one on the opposite page can even show how many students in an area play soccer.

## Satellite Images

Maps and globes are not the only tools that geographers use in their work. As you have already read, many geographers study information gathered by satellites.

Much of the information gathered by these satellites is in the form of images. Geographers can study these images to see what an area looks like from above Earth. Satellites also collect information that we cannot see from the planet's surface. The information gathered by satellites helps geographers make accurate maps.

## Other Tools

Geographers also use many other tools. For example, they use computer programs to create, update, and compare maps. They also use measuring devices to record data. In some cases, the best tools a geographer can use are a notebook and tape recorder to take notes while talking to people. Armed with the proper tools, geographers learn about the world's people and places.

**READING CHECK** **Summarizing** What are some of the geographer's basic tools?

**SUMMARY AND PREVIEW** Geography is the study of the world, its people, and its landscapes. In the next section, you will learn about two systems geographers use to organize their studies.

## Section 1 Assessment

hmhsocialstudies.com
ONLINE QUIZ

### Reviewing Ideas, Terms, and Places

1. **a. Define** What is **geography**?
   **b. Explain** Why is geography considered a science?
2. **a. Identify** What is a **region**? Give two examples.
   **b. Elaborate** What global issues do geographers study?
3. **a. Describe** How do geographers use satellite images?
   **b. Compare and Contrast** How are maps and globes similar? How are they different?

### Critical Thinking

4. **Summarizing** Draw three ovals like the ones shown here. Use your notes to fill the ovals with information about geography, geographers, and their tools.

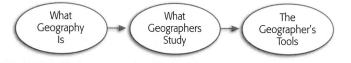

What Geography Is → What Geographers Study → The Geographer's Tools

### FOCUS ON WRITING

5. **Describing a Field** Based on what you have learned, what might attract people to work in geography? In your notebook, list some details about geography that might make people interested in working in the field.

# Geography Themes and Essential Elements

## What You Will Learn...

### Main Ideas

1. The five themes of geography help us organize our studies of the world.
2. The six essential elements of geography highlight some of the subject's most important ideas.

### The Big Idea

Geographers have created two different but related systems for organizing geographic studies.

### Key Terms

absolute location, *p. 12*
relative location, *p. 12*
environment, *p. 12*

hmhsocialstudies.com
**TAKING NOTES**

Use the graphic organizer online to take notes on the five themes and six essential elements of geography.

## If **YOU** lived there...

Your older sister has offered to drive you to a friend's house across town, but she doesn't know how to get there. You know your friend's street address and what the apartment building looks like. You know it's near the public library. You also would recognize some landmarks in the neighborhood, such as the video store and the supermarket.

**What might help your sister find the house?**

**BUILDING BACKGROUND** Like drivers, geographers have to know where places are in order to study them. An area's location is only one of the aspects that geographers study, though. In fact, it is only one of the five themes that geographers use to describe a place.

## The Five Themes of Geography

Have you ever gone to a Fourth of July party with a patriotic theme? If so, you probably noticed that almost everything at the party was related to that theme. For example, you may have seen American flags and decorations based on the flag's stars and stripes. You may have seen clothes that were red, white, and blue or heard patriotic music being played. Chances are that almost everything at the party reflected the theme of patriotism.

Like party planners, geographers use themes in their work. Geographers do not study parties, of course, but they do note common themes in their studies. Just as a party's theme is reflected in nearly every aspect of the party, these geography themes can be applied to nearly everything that geographers study. The five major themes of geography are Location, Place, Human-Environment Interaction, Movement, and Regions.

# The Five Themes of Geography

Geographers use five major themes, or ideas, to organize and guide their studies.

**Location** The theme of location describes where something is. The mountain shown above, Mount Rainier, is in west-central Washington.

**Place** Place describes the features that make a site unique. For example, Washington, D.C., is our nation's capital and has many great monuments.

**UNITED STATES**

**Regions** Regions are areas that share common characteristics. The Mojave Desert, shown here, is defined by its distinctive climate and plant life.

**Movement** This theme looks at how and why people and things move. Airports like this one in Dallas, Texas, help people move around the world.

**Human-Environment Interaction** People interact with their environments in many ways. Some, like this man in Florida, use the land to grow crops.

**ANALYSIS SKILL** | **ANALYZING VISUALS**

Which of the five themes deals with the relationships between people and their surroundings?

## Location

Every point on Earth has a location, a description of where it is. This location can be expressed in many ways. Sometimes a site's location is expressed in specific, or absolute, terms, such as an address. For example, the White House is located at 1600 Pennsylvania Avenue in the city of Washington, D.C. A specific description like this one is called an **absolute location**. Other times, the site's location is expressed in general terms. For example, Canada is north of the United States. This general description of where a place lies is called its **relative location**.

## Place

Another theme, Place, is closely related to Location. However, Place does not refer simply to where an area is. It refers to the area's landscape, the features that define the area and make it different from other places. Such features could include land, climate, and people. Together, they give a place its own character.

## Human-Environment Interaction

FOCUS ON READING
What do you know about environments?

In addition to looking at the features of places, geographers examine how those features interact. In particular, they want to understand how people interact with their environment—how people and their physical environment affect each other. An area's **environment** includes its land, water, climate, plants, and animals.

People interact with their environment every day in all sorts of ways. They clear forests to plant crops, level fields to build cities, and dam rivers to prevent floods. At the same time, physical environments affect how people live. People in cold areas, for example, build houses with thick walls and wear heavy clothing to keep warm. People who live near oceans look for ways to protect themselves from storms.

## Movement

People are constantly moving. They move within cities, between cities, and between countries. Geographers want to know why and how people move. For example, they ask if people are moving to find work or to live in a more pleasant area. Geographers also study the roads and routes that make movement so common.

## Regions

You have already learned how geographers divide the world into many regions to help the study of geography. Creating regions also makes it easier to compare places. Comparisons help geographers learn why each place has developed the way it has.

**READING CHECK** **Finding Main Ideas** What are the five themes of geography?

The six essential elements are used by geographers to organize their studies and are closely related to the geography standards. Each element includes several of the standards, as listed in the chart.

**ANALYZING VISUALS** How many of the six essential elements can you see illustrated in this photo?

# The Six Essential Elements

The five themes of geography are not the only system geographers use to study the world. They also use a system of standards and essential **elements**. Together, these standards and essential elements identify the most important ideas in the study of geography. These ideas are expressed in two lists.

The first list is the national geography standards. This is a list of 18 basic ideas that are central to the study of geography. These standards are listed in black type on the chart below.

The essential elements are based on the geography standards. Each element is a big idea that links several standards together. The six essential elements are The World in Spatial Terms, Places and Regions, Physical Systems, Human Systems, Environment and Society, and The Uses of Geography. On the chart, they are shown in purple.

Read through that list again. Do you see any similarities between geography's six essential elements and its five themes? You probably do. The two systems are very similar because the six essential elements build on the five themes.

ACADEMIC VOCABULARY
**element** part

## The Essential Elements and Geography Standards

### The World in Spatial Terms

- How to use maps and other geographic representations, tools, and technologies to acquire, process, and report information from a spatial perspective
- How to use mental maps to organize information about people, places, and environments in a spatial context
- How to analyze the spatial organization of people, places, and environments on Earth's surface

### Places and Regions

- The physical and human characteristics of places
- How people create regions to interpret Earth's complexity
- How culture and experience influence people's perceptions of places and regions

### Physical Systems

- The physical processes that shape the patterns of Earth's surface
- The characteristics and spatial distribution of ecosystems on Earth's surface

### Human Systems

- The characteristics, distributions, and migration of human populations on Earth's surface
- The characteristics, distribution, and complexity of Earth's cultural mosaics
- The patterns and networks of economic interdependence on Earth's surface
- The processes, patterns, and functions of human settlement
- How the forces of cooperation and conflict among people influence the division and control of Earth's surface

### Environment and Society

- How human actions modify the physical environment
- How physical systems affect human systems
- Changes that occur in the meaning, use, distribution, and importance of resources

### The Uses of Geography

- How to apply geography to interpret the past
- How to apply geography to interpret the present and plan for the future

## BOOK
# Geography for Life

*The six essential elements were first outlined in a book called* Geography for Life. *In that book, the authors—a diverse group of geographers and teachers from around the United States—explained why the study of geography is important.*

"Geography *is* for life in every sense of that expression: lifelong, life-sustaining, and life-enhancing. Geography is a field of study that enables us to find answers to questions about the world around us—about where things are and how and why they got there."

"Geography focuses attention on exciting and interesting things, on fascinating people and places, on things worth knowing because they are absorbing and because knowing about them lets humans make better-informed and, therefore, wiser decisions."

"With a strong grasp of geography, people are better equipped to solve issues at not only the local level but also the global level."

–from *Geography for Life,*
by the Geography Education Standards Project

**ANALYSIS SKILL** **ANALYZING PRIMARY SOURCES**

**Why do the authors of these passages think that people should study geography?**

For example, the element Places and Regions combines two of the five themes of geography—Place and Regions. Also, the element called Environment and Society deals with many of the same issues as the theme Human-Environment Interaction.

There are also some basic differences between the essential elements and the themes. For example, the last element, The Uses of Geography, deals with issues not covered in the five themes. This element examines how people can use geography to plan the landscapes in which they live.

Throughout this book, you will notice references to both the themes and the essential elements. As you read, use these themes and elements to help you organize your own study of geography.

**READING CHECK** **Summarizing** What are the six essential elements of geography?

**SUMMARY AND PREVIEW** You have just learned about the themes and elements of geography. Next, you will explore the branches into which the field is divided.

## Section 2 Assessment

hmhsocialstudies.com
ONLINE QUIZ

### Reviewing Ideas, Terms, and Places

1. **a. Define** What is the difference between a place's **absolute location** and its **relative location**? Give one example of each type of location.
   **b. Contrast** How are the themes of Location and Place different?
   **c. Elaborate** How does using the five themes help geographers understand the places they study?
2. **a. Identify** Which of the five themes of geography is associated with airports, highways, and the migration of people from one place to another?
   **b. Explain** How are the geography standards and the six essential elements related?
   **c. Compare** How are the six essential elements similar to the five themes of geography?

### Critical Thinking

3. **Categorizing** Draw a chart like the one below. Use your notes to list the five themes of geography, explain each of the themes, and list one feature of your city or town that relates to each.

| Theme | | | | | |
|---|---|---|---|---|---|
| Explanation | | | | | |
| Feature | | | | | |

### FOCUS ON WRITING

4. **Including Themes and Essential Elements** The five themes and six essential elements are central to a geographer's job. How will you mention them in your job description? Write down some ideas.

# Social Studies Skills

Chart and Graph

Critical Thinking

Geography

Study

# Analyzing Satellite Images

## Learn

In addition to maps and globes, satellite images are among the geographer's most valuable tools. Geographers use two basic types of these images. The first type is called true color. These images are like photographs taken from high above Earth's surface. The colors in these images are similar to what you would see from the ground. Vegetation, for example, appears green.

The other type of satellite image is called an infrared image. Infrared images are taken using a special type of light. These images are based on heat patterns, and so the colors on them are not what we might expect. Bodies of water appear black, for example, since they give off little heat.

## Practice

Use the satellite images on this page to answer the following questions.

**1** On which image is vegetation red?

**2** Which image do you think probably looks more like Italy does from the ground?

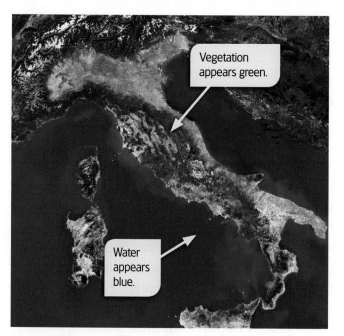

**True color satellite image of Italy**

**Infrared satellite image of Italy**

## Apply

Search the Internet to find a satellite image of your state or region. Determine whether the image is true color or infrared. Then write three statements that describe what you see on the image.

# The Branches of Geography

## What You Will Learn...

### Main Ideas

1. Physical geography is the study of landforms, water bodies, and other physical features.
2. Human geography focuses on people, their cultures, and the landscapes they create.
3. Other branches of geography examine specific aspects of the physical or human world.

### The Big Idea

Geography is divided into two main branches—physical and human geography.

## Key Terms

physical geography, *p. 16*
human geography, *p. 18*
cartography, *p. 19*
meteorology, *p. 20*

hmhsocialstudies.com
**TAKING NOTES**

Use the graphic organizer online to take notes on the branches of geography.

## If YOU lived there...

You are talking to two friends about the vacations their families will take this summer. One friend says that his family is going to the Grand Canyon. He is very excited about seeing the spectacular landscapes in and around the canyon. Your other friend's family is going to visit Nashville, Tennessee. She is looking forward to trying new foods at the city's restaurants and touring its museums.

**Which vacation sounds more interesting? Why?**

**BUILDING BACKGROUND** Geography is the study of the world and its features. Some features are physical, like the Grand Canyon. Others are human, like restaurants and museums. The main branches of geography focus on these types of features.

## Physical Geography

Think about a jigsaw puzzle. Seen as a whole, the puzzle shows a pretty or interesting picture. To see that picture, though, you have to put all the puzzle pieces together. Before you assemble them, the pieces do not give you a clear idea of what the puzzle will look like when it is assembled. After all, each piece contains only a tiny portion of the overall image.

In many ways, geography is like a huge puzzle. It is made up of many branches, or divisions. Each of these branches focuses on a single part of the world. Viewed separately, none of these branches shows us the whole world. Together, however, the many branches of geography improve our understanding of our planet and its people.

Geography's two main branches are physical geography and human geography. The first branch, **physical geography**, is the study of the world's physical features—its landforms, bodies of water, climates, soils, and plants. Every place in the world has its own unique combination of these features.

**Physical Geography**

The study of Earth's physical features, including rivers, mountains, oceans, weather, and other features, such as Victoria Falls in southern Africa

**Human Geography**

The study of Earth's people, including their ways of life, homes, cities, beliefs, and customs, like those of these children in Malawi, a country in central Africa

**Geography**

The study of Earth's physical and cultural features

## The Physical World

What does it mean to say that physical geography is the study of physical features? Physical geographers want to know all about the different features found on our planet. They want to know where plains and mountain ranges are, how rivers flow across the landscape, and why different amounts of rain fall from place to place.

More importantly, however, physical geographers want to know what causes the different shapes on Earth. They want to know why mountain ranges rise up where they do and what causes rivers to flow in certain directions. They also want to know why various parts of the world have very different weather and climate patterns.

To answer these questions, physical geographers take detailed measurements. They study the heights of mountains and the temperatures of places. To track any changes that occur over time, physical geographers keep careful records of all the information they collect.

## Uses of Physical Geography

Earth is made up of hundreds of types of physical features. Without a complete understanding of what these features are and the effect they have on the world's people and landscapes, we cannot fully understand our world. This is the major reason that geographers study the physical world—to learn how it works.

There are also other, more specific reasons for studying physical geography, though. Studying the changes that take place on our planet can help us prepare to live with those changes. For example, knowing what causes volcanoes to erupt can help us predict eruptions. Knowing what causes terrible storms can help us prepare for them. In this way, the work of physical geographers helps us adjust to the dangers and changes of our world.

**READING CHECK** **Analyzing** What are some features in your area that a physical geographer might study?

## Eratosthenes
(c. 276–c. 194 BC)

Did you know that geography is over 2,000 years old? Actually, the study of the world is even older than that, but the first person ever to use the word *geography* lived then. His name was Eratosthenes (er-uh-TAHS-thuh-neez), and he was a Greek scientist and librarian. With no modern instruments of any kind, Eratosthenes figured out how large Earth is. He also drew a map that showed all of the lands that the Greeks knew about. Because of his many contributions to the field, Eratosthenes has been called the Father of Geography.

**Generalizing** Why is Eratosthenes called the Father of Geography?

# Human Geography

The physical world is only one part of the puzzle of geography. People are also part of the world. **Human geography** is the study of the world's people, communities, and landscapes. It is the second major branch of geography.

## The Human World

Put simply, human geographers study the world's people, past and present. They look at where people live and why. They ask why some parts of the world have more people than others, and why some places have almost no people at all.

Human geographers also study what people do. What jobs do people have? What crops do they grow? What makes them move from place to place? These are the types of questions that geographers ask about people around the world.

Because people's lives are so different around the world, no one can study every aspect of human geography. As a result, human geographers often specialize in a smaller area of study. Some may choose to study only the people and landscapes in a certain region. For example, a geographer may study only the lives of people who live in West Africa.

Other geographers choose not to limit their studies to one place. Instead, they may choose to examine only one aspect of people's lives. For example, a geographer could study only economics, politics, or city life. However, that geographer may compare economic patterns in various parts of the world to see how they differ.

## Uses of Human Geography

Although every culture is different, people around the world have some common needs. All people need food and water. All people need shelter. All people need to deal with other people in order to survive.

Human geographers study how people in various places address their needs. They look at the foods people eat and the types of governments they form. The knowledge they gather can help us better understand people in other cultures. Sometimes this type of understanding can help people improve their landscapes and situations.

On a smaller scale, human geographers can help people design their cities and towns. By understanding where people go and what they need, geographers can help city planners place roads, shopping malls, and schools. Geographers also study the effect people have on the world. As a result, they often work with private groups and government agencies who want to protect the environment.

**READING CHECK** **Summarizing** What do human geographers study?

## Other Fields of Geography

Physical geography and human geography are the two largest branches of the subject, but they are not the only ones. Many other fields of geography exist, each one devoted to studying one aspect of the world.

Most of these fields are smaller, more specialized areas of either physical or human geography. For example, economic geography—the study of how people make and spend money—is a branch of human geography. Another specialized branch of human geography is urban geography, the study of cities and how people live in them. Physical geography also includes many fields, such as the study of climates. Other fields of physical geography are the studies of soils and plants.

## Cartography

One key field of geography is **cartography**, the science of making maps. You have already seen how important maps are to the study of geography. Without maps, geographers would not be able to study where things are in the world.

In the past, maps were always drawn by hand. Many were not very accurate. Today, though, most maps are made using computers and satellite images. Through advances in mapmaking, we can make accurate maps on almost any scale, from the whole world to a single neighborhood, and keep them up to date. These maps are not only used by geographers. For example, road maps are used by people who are planning long trips.

## CONNECTING TO Technology

### Computer Mapping

In the past, maps were drawn by hand. Making a map was a slow process. Even the simplest map took a long time to make. Today, however, cartographers have access to tools people in the past—even people who lived just 50 years ago—never imagined. The most important of these tools are computers.

Computers allow us to make maps quickly and easily. In addition, they let us make new types of maps that people could not make in the past.

The map shown here, for example, was drawn on a computer. It shows the number of computer users in the United States who were connected to the Internet on a particular day. Each of the lines that rises off of the map represents a city in which people were using the Internet. The color of the line indicates the number of computer users in that city. As you can see, this data resulted in a very complex map.

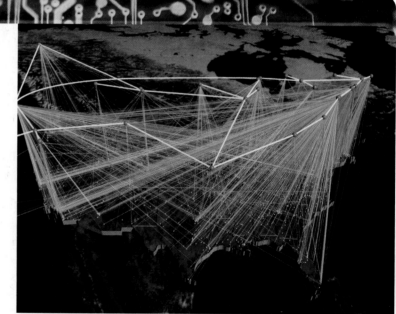

Making such a map required cartographers to sort through huge amounts of complex data. Such sorting would not have been possible without computers.

**Contrasting** How are today's maps different from those created in the past?

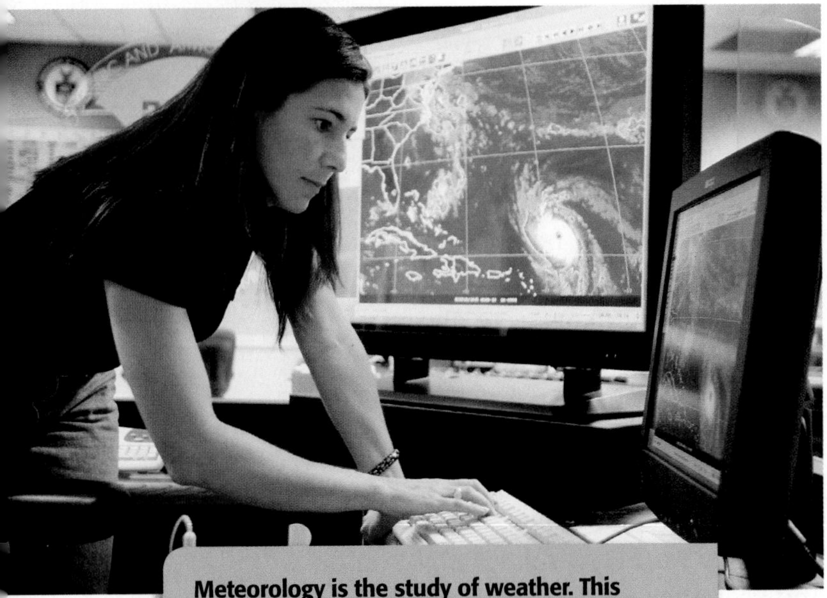

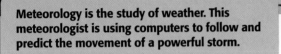

Meteorology is the study of weather. This meteorologist is using computers to follow and predict the movement of a powerful storm.

## Hydrology

Another important branch of geography is hydrology, the study of water on Earth. Geographers in this field study the world's river systems and rainfall patterns. They study what causes droughts and floods and how people in cities can get safe drinking water. They also work to measure and protect the world's supply of water.

## Meteorology

Have you ever seen the weather report on television? If so, you have seen the results of another branch of geography. This branch is called **meteorology**, the study of weather and what causes it.

Meteorologists study weather patterns in a particular area. Then they use the information to predict what the weather will be like in the coming days. Their work helps people plan what to wear and what to do on any given day. At the same time, their work can save lives by predicting the arrival of terrible storms. These predictions are among the most visible ways in which the work of geographers affects our lives every day.

**READING CHECK** Finding Main Ideas What are some major branches of geography?

**SUMMARY AND PREVIEW** In this section, you learned about two main branches of geography, physical and human. In the next chapter, you will learn more about the physical features that surround us and the processes that create them.

## Section 3 Assessment

### Reviewing Ideas, Terms, and Places

1. a. **Define** What is **physical geography**?
   b. **Explain** Why do we study physical geography?
2. a. **Identify** What are some things that people study as part of **human geography**?
   b. **Summarize** What are some ways in which the study of human geography can influence our lives?
   c. **Evaluate** Which do you think would be more interesting to study, physical geography or human geography? Why?
3. a. **Identify** What are two specialized fields of geography?
   b. **Analyze** How do cartographers contribute to the work of other geographers?

### Critical Thinking

4. **Comparing and Contrasting** Draw a diagram like the one shown here. In the left circle, list three features of physical geography from your notes. In the right circle, list three features of human geography. Where the circles overlap, list one feature they share.

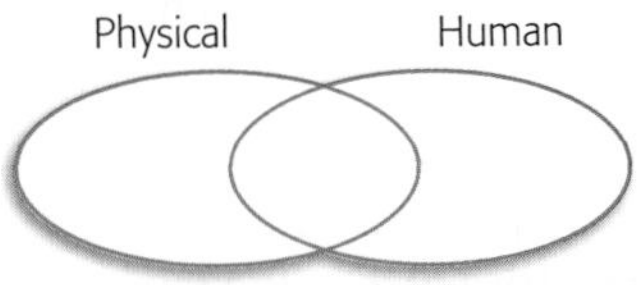

Physical     Human

### FOCUS ON WRITING

5. **Choosing a Branch** Your job description should point out to people that there are many branches of geography. How will you note that?

# Chapter Review

**Geography's Impact**
**video series**
Review the video to answer the closing question:
*Why do you think it might be valuable to know the absolute location of a place?*

## Visual Summary

*Use the visual summary below to help you review the main ideas of the chapter.*

**QUICK FACTS**

Physical geography—the study of the world's physical features—is one main branch of geography.

Human geography—the study of the world's people and how they live—is the second main branch.

Geographers use many tools to study the world. The most valuable of these tools are maps.

## Reviewing Vocabulary, Terms, and Places

*Match the words in the columns with the correct definitions listed below.*

1. geography
2. physical geography
3. human geography
4. element
5. meteorology
6. region
7. cartography
8. map
9. landscape
10. globe

**a.** a part of the world that has one or more common features that make it different from surrounding areas

**b.** a flat drawing of part of Earth's surface

**c.** a part

**d.** a spherical model of the planet

**e.** the study of the world's physical features

**f.** the study of weather and what causes it

**g.** the study of the world, its people, and the landscapes they create

**h.** the science of making maps

**i.** the physical and human features that define an area and make it different from other places

**j.** the study of people and communities

## Comprehension and Critical Thinking

**SECTION 1** *(Pages 4–9)*

**11. a. Identify** What are three levels at which a geographer might study the world? Which of these levels covers the largest area?

**b. Compare and Contrast** How are maps and globes similar? How are they different?

**c. Elaborate** How might satellite images and computers help geographers improve their knowledge of the world?

## SECTION 2 (Pages 10–14)

**12. a. Define** What do geographers mean when they discuss an area's landscape?

**b. Explain** Why did geographers create the five themes and the six essential elements?

**c. Predict** How might the five themes and six essential elements help you in your study of geography?

## SECTION 3 (Pages 16–20)

**13. a. Identify** What are the two main branches of geography? What does each include?

**b. Summarize** How can physical geography help people adjust to the dangers of the world?

**c. Elaborate** Why do geographers study both physical and human characteristics of places?

# Using the Internet

**14. Activity: Using Maps** Through your online textbook, explore how maps can help you understand your community and learn about its features. Then search the Internet to find a map of your community. Use the map to find the locations of at least five important features. For example, you might locate your school, the library, a park, or major highways. Be creative and find other places you think your classmates should be aware of.

↗ hmhsocialstudies.com

# Social Studies Skills

**Analyzing Satellite Images** *Use the satellite images of Italy from the Social Studies Skills lesson in this chapter to answer the following questions.*

**15.** On which image do forests appear more clearly, the true-color or the infrared image?

**16.** What color do you think represents mountains on the infrared satellite image?

**17.** Why might geographers use satellite images like these while making maps of Italy?

# Map Activity

**18. Sketch Map** Draw a map of your school and the surrounding neighborhood. Your map should include major features like streets and buildings. Use the map shown here as an example.

## FOCUS ON READING AND WRITING

**19. Using Prior Knowledge** Create a chart with three columns. In the first column, list what you knew about geography before you read the chapter. In the second column, list what you learned in the chapter. In the third column, list questions that you now have about geography.

**20. Writing Your Job Description** Review your notes on the different jobs geographers do. Then write your job description. You should begin your description by explaining why the job is important. Then identify the job's tasks and responsibilities. Finally, tell what kind of person might do well as a geographer.

# Standardized Test Prep

*DIRECTIONS: Read questions 1 through 7 and write the letter of the best response. Then read question 8 and write your own well-constructed response.*

**1** Which of the following subjects would a human geographer study the most?

   A mountains

   B populations

   C rivers

   D volcanoes

**2** The study of weather is called

   A meteorology.

   B hydrology.

   C social science.

   D cartography.

**3** A region is an area that has

   A one or more common features.

   B no people living in it.

   C few physical features.

   D set physical boundaries.

**4** How many essential elements of geography have geographers identified?

   A two

   B four

   C six

   D eight

**5** The physical and human characteristics that define an area are its

   A landscape.

   B location.

   C region.

   D science.

## The United States

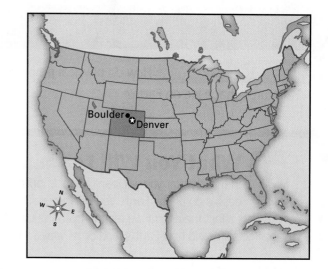

**6** Which of the five themes of geography would a geographer most likely study using this map?

   A movement

   B location

   C human-environment interaction

   D landscape

**7** The smallest level at which a geographer might study a place is

   A microscopic.

   B local.

   C regional.

   D global.

**8** **Extended Response** Look at the map of the United States above. Do you think this map is more likely to be used by a physical geographer or by a human geographer? Give two reasons for your answer. Then write two statements about what a geographer could find on this map.

# CHAPTER 2

# Planet Earth

**Essential Question** How do physical processes and features shape life on Earth?

## What You Will Learn...

In this chapter you will learn about important processes on planet Earth. You will discover how Earth's movements affect the energy we receive from the sun, how water affects life, and how Earth's landforms were made.

### FOCUS ON READING AND WRITING

**Using Word Parts** Sometimes you can figure out the meaning of a word by looking at its parts. A root is the base of the word. A prefix attaches to the beginning, and a suffix attaches to the ending. When you come across a word you don't know, check to see whether you recognize its parts. **See the lesson, Using Word Parts, on page 517.**

**Writing a Haiku** Join the poets who have celebrated our planet for centuries. Write a haiku, a short poem, about planet Earth. As you read the chapter, gather information about changes in the sun's energy, Earth's water supply, and shapes on the land. Then choose the most intriguing information to include in your haiku.

**Energy from the Sun** The planet's movement creates differences in the amount of energy Earth receives from the sun.

**HISTORY**

How the Earth Was Made

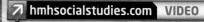

↗ hmhsocialstudies.com  VIDEO

**ANALYSIS SKILL**  **ANALYZING VISUALS**

Many of Earth's features are visible from space. This photo, taken from a satellite orbiting the planet, shows part of the North American continent.

**Which of Earth's features are visible in this photo?**

**Land** Forces on and under Earth's surface have shaped the different landforms on our planet. Geographers study how mountains and other landforms were made.

**Water on Earth** Water is essential for life on Earth. Much of the planet's water supply is stored in Earth's oceans and ice caps.

**25**

# Earth and the Sun's Energy

## What You Will Learn...

### Main Ideas

1. Earth's movement affects the amount of energy we receive from the sun.
2. Earth's seasons are caused by the planet's tilt.

### The Big Idea

Earth's movement and the sun's energy interact to create day and night, temperature changes, and the seasons.

## Key Terms

solar energy, *p. 26*
rotation, *p. 26*
revolution, *p. 27*
latitude, *p. 27*
tropics, *p. 29*

hmhsocialstudies.com
### TAKING NOTES

Use the graphic organizer online to take notes on Earth's movement and the seasons.

## If YOU lived there...

You live in Chicago and have just won an exciting prize—a trip to Australia during winter vacation in January. As you prepare for the trip, your mother reminds you to pack shorts and a swimsuit. You are confused. In January you usually wear winter sweaters and a heavy jacket.

**Why is the weather so different in Australia?**

**BUILDING BACKGROUND** Seasonal differences in weather are an important result of Earth's constant movement. As the planet moves, we experience changes in the amount of energy we receive from the sun. Geographers study and explain why different places on Earth receive differing amounts of energy from the sun.

## Earth's Movement

Energy from the sun helps crops grow, provides light, and warms Earth. It even influences the clothes we wear, the foods we eat, and the sports we play. All life on Earth requires **solar energy**, or energy from the sun, to survive. The amount of solar energy places on Earth receive changes constantly. Earth's rotation, revolution, and tilt, as well as latitude, all affect the amount of solar energy parts of the planet receive from the sun.

### Rotation

Imagine that Earth has a rod running through it from the North Pole to the South Pole. This rod represents Earth's axis—an imaginary line around which a planet turns. As Earth spins on its axis, different parts of the planet face the sun. It takes Earth 24 hours, or one day, to complete this rotation. A **rotation** is one complete spin of Earth on its axis. As Earth rotates during this 24-hour period, it appears to us that the sun moves across the sky. The sun seems to rise in the east and set in the west. The

## Solar Energy

Earth's tilt and rotation cause changes in the amount of energy we receive from the sun. As Earth rotates on its axis, energy from the sun creates periods of day and night. Earth's tilt causes some locations, especially those close to the equator, to receive more direct solar energy than others.

**HISTORY** VIDEO
Secrets of the Sun

↗ hmhsocialstudies.com

←23.5°

North Pole

Equator

Sun's Rays

South Pole

**ANALYSIS SKILL** **ANALYZING VISUALS**

Is the region north or south of the equator receiving more solar energy? How can you tell?

sun, however, does not move. It is actually Earth's rotation that creates the sense of the sun's movement.

Earth's rotation also explains why day changes to night. As you can see in the illustration, solar energy strikes only the half of Earth facing the sun. Warmth and light from the sun create daytime. At the same time, the half of the planet facing away from the sun experiences the cooler temperatures and darkness of night. Earth's rotation causes regular shifts from day to night. As a result, levels of solar energy on Earth constantly change.

### Revolution

As Earth spins on its axis, it also follows a path, or orbit, around the sun. Earth's orbit around the sun is not a perfect circle. Sometimes the orbit takes Earth closer to the sun, and at other times the orbit takes it farther away. It takes 365¼ days for Earth to complete one **revolution**, or trip around the sun. We base our calendar year on the time it takes Earth to complete its orbit around the sun. To allow for the fraction of a day, we add an extra day—February 29—to our calendar every four years.

### Tilt and Latitude

Another **factor** affecting the amount of solar energy we receive is the planet's tilt. As the illustration shows, Earth's axis is not straight up and down. It is actually tilted at an angle of 23½ degrees from vertical. At any given time of year, some locations on Earth are tilting away from the sun, and others are tilting toward it. Places tilting toward the sun receive more solar energy and experience warmer temperatures. Those tilting away from the sun receive less solar energy and experience cooler temperatures.

A location's **latitude**, the distance north or south of Earth's equator, also affects the amount of solar energy it receives. Low-latitude areas, those near the equator like Hawaii, receive direct rays from the sun all year. These direct rays are more intense and produce warmer temperatures. Regions with high latitudes, like Antarctica, are farther from the equator. As a result, they receive indirect rays from the sun and have colder temperatures.

**ACADEMIC VOCABULARY**

factor cause

**READING CHECK** Finding Main Ideas What factors affect the solar energy Earth receives?

## The Seasons

**FOCUS ON READING**

The prefix *hemi-* means half. What does the word *hemisphere* mean?

Does the thought of snow in July or 100-degree temperatures in January seem odd to you? It might if you live in the Northern Hemisphere, where cold temperatures are common in January, not July. The planet's changing seasons explain why we often connect certain weather with specific times of the year, like snow in January. Seasons are periods during the year that are known for a particular type of weather. Many places on Earth experience four seasons—winter, spring, summer, and fall. These seasons are based on temperature and length of day. In some parts of the world, however, seasons are based on the amount of rainfall.

## Winter and Summer

The change in seasons is created by Earth's tilt. As you can see in the illustration below, while one of Earth's poles tilts away from the sun, the other tilts toward it. During winter part of Earth is tilted away from the sun, causing less direct solar energy, cool temperatures, and less daylight. Summer occurs when part of Earth is tilted toward the sun. This creates more direct solar energy, warmer temperatures, and longer periods of daylight.

Because of Earth's tilt, the Northern and Southern hemispheres experience opposite seasons. As the North Pole tilts toward the sun in summer, the South Pole tilts away

## The Seasons: Northern Hemisphere

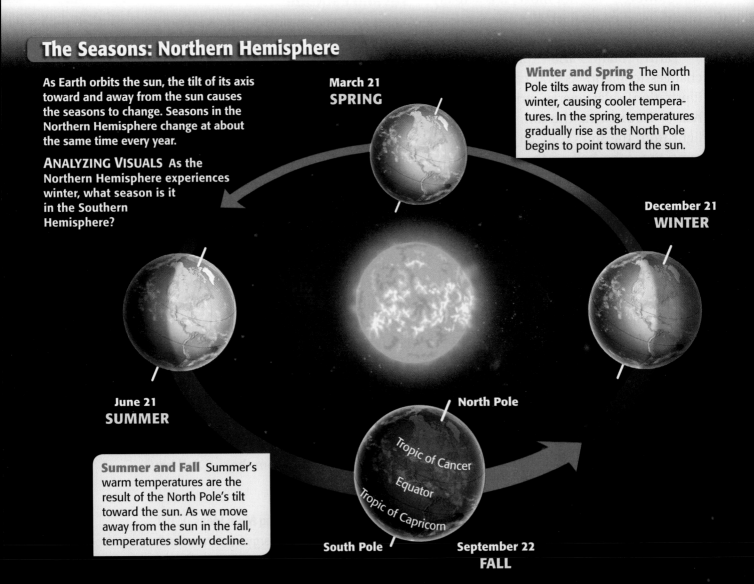

As Earth orbits the sun, the tilt of its axis toward and away from the sun causes the seasons to change. Seasons in the Northern Hemisphere change at about the same time every year.

**ANALYZING VISUALS** As the Northern Hemisphere experiences winter, what season is it in the Southern Hemisphere?

**Winter and Spring** The North Pole tilts away from the sun in winter, causing cooler temperatures. In the spring, temperatures gradually rise as the North Pole begins to point toward the sun.

March 21
**SPRING**

December 21
**WINTER**

June 21
**SUMMER**

**Summer and Fall** Summer's warm temperatures are the result of the North Pole's tilt toward the sun. As we move away from the sun in the fall, temperatures slowly decline.

North Pole

Tropic of Cancer

Equator

Tropic of Capricorn

South Pole

September 22
**FALL**

from it. As a result, the Southern Hemisphere experiences winter. Likewise, when it is spring in the Northern Hemisphere, it is fall in the Southern Hemisphere.

## Spring and Fall

As Earth orbits the sun, there are periods when the poles tilt neither toward nor away from the sun. These periods mark spring and fall. During the spring, as part of Earth begins to tilt toward the sun, solar energy increases. Temperatures slowly start to rise, and days grow longer. In the fall the opposite occurs as winter approaches. Solar energy begins to decrease, causing cooler temperatures and shorter days.

## Rainfall and Seasons

Some regions on Earth have seasons marked by rainfall rather than temperature. This is true in the **tropics**, regions close to the equator. At certain times of year, winds bring either dry or moist air to the tropics, creating wet and dry seasons. In India, for example, seasonal winds called monsoons bring heavy rains from June to October and dry air from November to January.

**READING CHECK** **Identifying Cause and Effect** What causes the seasons to change?

## The Midnight Sun

Can you imagine going to sleep late at night with the sun shining in the sky? People who live near the Arctic and Antarctic circles experience this every summer, when they can receive up to 24 hours of sunlight a day. The time-lapse photo below shows a typical sunset during this period—except the sun never really sets! This phenomenon is known as the midnight sun. For locations like Tromso, Norway, this means up to two months of constant daylight each summer. People living near Earth's poles often use the long daylight hours to work on outdoor projects in preparation for winter, when they can receive 24 hours of darkness a day.

**Predicting** How might people's daily lives be affected by the midnight sun?

**SUMMARY AND PREVIEW** Solar energy is crucial for all life on the planet. Earth's position and movements affect the amount of energy we receive from the sun and determine our seasons. Next, you will learn about Earth's water supply and its importance to us.

## Section 1 Assessment

hmhsocialstudies.com
ONLINE QUIZ

### Reviewing Ideas, Terms, and Places

1. **a. Identify** What is **solar energy**, and how does it affect Earth?
   **b. Analyze** How do **rotation** and tilt each affect the amount of solar energy that different parts of Earth receive?
   **c. Predict** What might happen if Earth received less solar energy than it currently does?
2. **a. Describe** Name and describe Earth's seasons.
   **b. Contrast** How are seasons different in the Northern and Southern hemispheres?
   **c. Elaborate** How might the seasons affect human activities?

### Critical Thinking

3. **Identifying Cause and Effect** Use your notes and the diagram to identify the causes of seasons.

### FOCUS ON WRITING

4. **Describing the Seasons** What are the seasons like where you live? In your notebook, jot down a few notes that describe the changing seasons.

# Water on Earth

## If **YOU** lived there...

You live in the desert Southwest, where heavy water use and a lack of rainfall have led to water shortages. Your city plans to begin a water conservation program that asks people to limit how much water they use. Many of your neighbors have complained that the program is unnecessary. Others support the plan to save water.

**How do you feel about the city's water plan?**

> **BUILDING BACKGROUND** Although water covers much of Earth's surface, water shortages, like those in the American Southwest, are common all over the planet. Because water is vital to the survival of all living things, geographers study Earth's water supply.

## Earth's Water Supply

Think of the different uses for water. We use water to cook and clean, we drink it, and we grow crops with it. Water is used for recreation, to generate electricity, and even to travel from place to place. Water is perhaps the most important and abundant resource on Earth. In fact, water covers some two-thirds of the planet. Understanding Earth's water supply and how it affects our lives is an important part of geography.

### What You Will Learn...

**Main Ideas**

1. Salt water and freshwater make up Earth's water supply.
2. In the water cycle, water circulates from Earth's surface to the atmosphere and back again.
3. Water plays an important role in people's lives.

**The Big Idea**

Water is a dominant feature on Earth's surface and is essential for life.

**Key Terms**

freshwater, *p. 31*
glaciers, *p. 31*
surface water, *p. 31*
precipitation, *p. 31*
groundwater, *p. 32*
water vapor, *p. 32*
water cycle, *p. 33*

hmhsocialstudies.com
TAKING NOTES

Use the graphic organizer online to take notes on Earth's water.

### Earth's Distribution of Water

Earth's water supply is divided into two main types—salt water and freshwater. Humans, plants, and animals rely on Earth's freshwater supply for survival.

## Salt Water

Although water covers much of the planet, we cannot use most of it. About 97 percent of the Earth's water is salt water. Because salt water contains high levels of salt and other minerals, it is unsafe to drink.

In general, salt water is found in Earth's oceans. Oceans are vast bodies of water covering some 71 percent of the planet's surface. Earth's oceans are made up of smaller bodies of water such as seas, gulfs, bays, and straits. Altogether, Earth's oceans cover some 139 million square miles (360 million square km) of the planet's surface.

Some of Earth's lakes contain salt water. The Great Salt Lake in Utah, for example, is a saltwater lake. As salt and other minerals have collected in the lake, which has no outlet, the water has become salty.

## Freshwater

Since the water in Earth's oceans is too salty to use, we must rely on other sources for freshwater. **Freshwater**, or water without salt, makes up only about 3 percent of our total water supply. Much of that freshwater is locked in Earth's **glaciers**, large areas of slow-moving ice, and in the ice of the Antarctic and Arctic regions. Most of the freshwater we use everyday is found in lakes, in rivers, and under Earth's surface.

One form of freshwater is surface water. **Surface water** is water that is found in Earth's streams, rivers, and lakes. It may seem that there is a great deal of water in our lakes and rivers, but only a tiny amount of Earth's water supply—less than 1 percent—comes from surface water.

Streams and rivers are a common source of surface water. Streams form when precipitation collects in a narrow channel and flows toward the ocean. **Precipitation** is water that falls to Earth's surface as rain, snow, sleet, or hail. In turn, streams join together to form rivers. Any smaller stream or river that flows into a larger stream or river is called a tributary. For example, the Missouri River is the largest tributary of the Mississippi River.

Lakes are another important source of surface water. Some lakes were formed as rivers filled low-lying areas with water. Other lakes, like the Great Lakes along the U.S.–Canada border, were formed when glaciers carved deep holes in Earth's surface and deposited water as they melted.

Most of Earth's available freshwater is stored underground. As precipitation falls to Earth, much of it is absorbed into the ground, filling spaces in the soil and rock.

**Salt Water** Earth's oceans contain some 97 percent of the planet's water supply. Unfortunately, this water is too salty to drink.

**Freshwater** Freshwater from lakes, rivers, and streams makes up only a fraction of Earth's water supply.

Water found below Earth's surface is called **groundwater**. In some places on Earth, groundwater naturally bubbles from the ground as a spring. More often, however, people obtain groundwater by digging wells, or deep holes dug into the ground to reach the water.

**READING CHECK** Contrasting How is salt water different from freshwater?

⌐ hmhsocialstudies.com **INTERACTIVE ART**
**Close-up**

# The Water Cycle

Energy from the sun drives the water cycle. Surface water evaporates into Earth's atmosphere, where it condenses, then falls back to Earth as precipitation. This cycle repeats continuously, providing us with a fairly constant water supply.

## The Water Cycle

When you think of water, you probably visualize a liquid—a flowing stream, a glass of ice-cold water, or a wave hitting the beach. But did you know that water is the only substance on Earth that occurs naturally as a solid, a liquid, and a gas? We see water as a solid in snow and ice and as a liquid in oceans and rivers. Water also occurs in the air as an invisible gas called **water vapor**.

Water is always moving. As water heats up and cools down, it moves from the planet's surface to the atmosphere, or the mass of air that surrounds Earth. One of the most important processes in nature

Condensation occurs when water vapor cools and forms clouds.

When the droplets in clouds become too heavy, they fall to Earth as precipitation.

Runoff is excess precipitation that flows over land into rivers, streams, and oceans.

**ANALYSIS SKILL** **ANALYZING VISUALS**
How does evaporation differ from precipitation?

is the water cycle. The **water cycle** is the movement of water from Earth's surface to the atmosphere and back.

The sun's energy drives the water cycle. As the sun heats water on Earth's surface, some of that water evaporates, or turns from liquid to gas, or water vapor. Water vapor then rises into the air. As the vapor rises, it cools. The cooling causes the water vapor to condense, or change from a vapor into tiny liquid droplets. These droplets join together to form clouds. If the droplets become heavy enough, precipitation occurs—that is, the water falls back to Earth as rain, snow, sleet, or hail.

When that precipitation falls back to Earth's surface, some of the water is absorbed into the soil as groundwater. Excess water, called runoff, flows over land and collects in streams, rivers, and oceans. Because the water cycle is constantly repeating, it allows us to maintain a fairly constant supply of water on Earth.

**READING CHECK** **Finding Main Ideas** What is the water cycle?

As energy from the sun heats water on Earth's surface, the water evaporates, or turns to water vapor, and rises to the atmosphere.

# Water and People

How many times a day do you think about water? Many of us rarely give it a second thought, yet water is crucial for survival. Water problems such as the lack of water, polluted water, and flooding are concerns for people all around the world. Water also provides us with <u>countless</u> benefits, such as energy and recreation.

## Water Problems

One of the greatest water problems people face is a lack of available freshwater. Many places face water shortages as a result of droughts, or long periods of lower-than-normal precipitation. Another cause of water shortages is overuse. In places like the southwestern United States, where the population has grown rapidly, the heavy demand for water has led to shortages.

Even where water is plentiful, it may not be clean enough to use. If chemicals and household wastes make their way into streams and rivers, they can contaminate the water supply. Polluted water can carry diseases. These diseases may harm humans, plants, and animals.

Flooding is another water problem that affects people around the world. Heavy rains often lead to flooding, which can damage property and threaten lives. One example of dangerous flooding occurred in Bangladesh in 2004. Severe floods there destroyed roads and schools, affecting about 25 million people.

## Water's Benefits

Water does more than just quench our thirst. It provides us with many benefits, such as food, power, and even recreation.

Water's most important benefit is that it provides us with food to eat. Everything we eat depends on water. For example, fruits and vegetables need water to grow.

**FOCUS ON READING**
Look at the word *countless* in this paragraph. The suffix *-less* means unable to. What does *countless* mean?

## The Benefits of Water

Many people take advantage of the recreational and agricultural benefits that water provides.

Animals also need water to live and grow. As a result, we use water to farm and raise animals so that we will have food to eat.

Water is also an important source of energy. Using dams, we harness the power of moving water to produce electricity. Electricity provides power to air-condition or heat our homes, to run our washers and dryers, and to keep our food cold.

Water also provides us with recreation. Rivers, lakes, and oceans make it possible for us to swim, to fish, to surf, or to sail a boat. Although recreation is not critical for our survival, it does make our lives richer and more enjoyable.

**READING CHECK** **Summarizing** How does water affect people's lives?

**SUMMARY AND PREVIEW** In this section you learned that water is essential for life on Earth. Next, you will learn about the shapes on Earth's surface.

## Section 2 Assessment

hmhsocialstudies.com
ONLINE QUIZ

### Reviewing Ideas, Terms, and Places

1. **a. Describe** Name and describe the different types of water that make up Earth's water supply.
   **b. Analyze** Why is only a small percentage of Earth's **freshwater** available to us?
   **c. Elaborate** In your opinion, which is more important—**surface water** or **groundwater**? Why?
2. **a. Recall** What drives the **water cycle**?
   **b. Make Inferences** From what bodies of water do you think most evaporation occurs? Why?
3. **a. Define** What is a drought?
   **b. Analyze** How does water support life on Earth?
   **c. Evaluate** What water problem do you think is most critical in your community? Why?

### Critical Thinking

4. **Sequencing** Draw the graphic organizer at right. Then use your notes and the graphic organizer to identify the stages in Earth's water cycle.

### FOCUS ON WRITING

5. **Learning about Water** Consider what you have learned about water in this section. How might you describe water in your haiku? What words might you use to describe Earth's water supply?

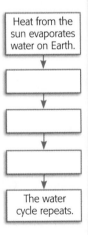

Heat from the sun evaporates water on Earth.

↓

↓

↓

The water cycle repeats.

# The Land

## If YOU lived there...

You live in the state of Washington. All your life, you have looked out at the beautiful, cone-shaped peaks of nearby mountains. One of them is Mount Saint Helens, an active volcano. You know that in 1980 it erupted violently, blowing a hole in the mountain and throwing ash and rock into the sky. Since then, scientists have watched the mountain carefully.

**How do you feel about living near a volcano?**

**BUILDING BACKGROUND** Over billions of years, many different forces have changed Earth's surface. Processes deep underground have built up landforms and even shifted the position of continents. Wind, water, and ice have also shaped the planet's landforms. Changes in Earth's surface continue to take place.

## Landforms

Do you know the difference between a valley and a volcano? Can you tell a peninsula from a plateau? If you answered yes, then you are familiar with some of Earth's many landforms. **Landforms** are shapes on the planet's surface, such as hills or mountains. Landforms make up the landscapes that surround us, whether it's the rugged mountains of central Colorado or the flat plains of Oklahoma.

Earth's surface is covered with landforms of many different shapes and sizes. Some important landforms include:

- mountains, land that rises higher than 2,000 feet (610 m)
- valleys, areas of low land located between mountains or hills
- plains, stretches of mostly flat land
- islands, areas of land completely surrounded by water
- peninsulas, land surrounded by water on three sides

Because landforms play an important role in geography, many scientists study how landforms are made and how they affect human activity.

**READING CHECK** **Summarizing** What are some common landforms?

## What You Will Learn...

### Main Ideas
1. Earth's surface is covered by many different landforms.
2. Forces below Earth's surface build up our landforms.
3. Forces on the planet's surface shape Earth's landforms.
4. Landforms influence people's lives and culture.

### The Big Idea
Processes below and on Earth's surface shape the planet's physical features.

### Key Terms
landforms, *p. 35*
continents, *p. 36*
plate tectonics, *p. 36*
lava, *p. 37*
earthquakes, *p. 38*
weathering, *p. 39*
erosion, *p. 39*

**hmhsocialstudies.com**
**TAKING NOTES**

Use the graphic organizer online to take notes on Earth's landforms.

# Forces below Earth's Surface

Geographers often study how landforms are made. One explanation for how landforms have been shaped involves forces below Earth's surface.

## Earth's Plates

ACADEMIC VOCABULARY

**structure** the way something is set up or organized

To understand how these forces work, we must examine Earth's **structure**. The planet is made up of three layers. A solid inner core is surrounded by a liquid layer, or mantle. The solid outer layer of Earth is called the crust. The planet's **continents**, or large landmasses, are part of Earth's crust.

Geographers use the theory of plate tectonics to explain how forces below Earth's surface have shaped our landforms. The theory of **plate tectonics** suggests that Earth's surface is divided into a dozen or so slow-moving plates, or pieces of Earth's crust. As you can see in the image below, some plates, like the Pacific plate, are quite large. Others, like the Nazca plate, are much smaller. These plates cover Earth's entire surface. Some plates are under the ocean. These are known as ocean plates. Other plates, known as continental plates, are under Earth's continents.

Why do these plates move? Energy deep inside the planet puts pressure on Earth's crust. As this pressure builds up, it forces the plates to shift. Earth's tectonic plates all move. However, they move in different directions and at different speeds.

## The Movement of Continents

Earth's tectonic plates move slowly—up to several inches per year. The continents, which are part of Earth's plates, shift as the plates move. If we could look back some 200 million years, we would see that the continents have traveled great distances. This idea is known as continental drift.

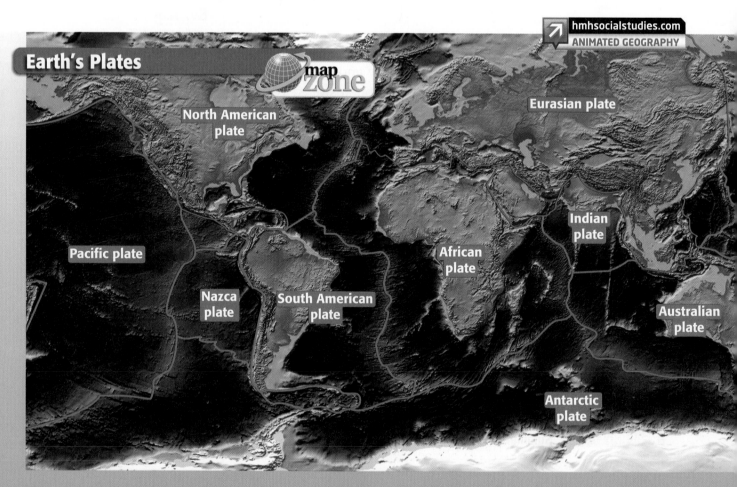

**Earth's Plates**

map zone

hmhsocialstudies.com
ANIMATED GEOGRAPHY

North American plate

Eurasian plate

Pacific plate

Indian plate

African plate

Nazca plate

South American plate

Australian plate

Antarctic plate

The theory of continental drift, first developed by Alfred Wegener, states that the continents were once united in a single supercontinent. According to this theory, Earth's plates shifted over millions of years. As a result, the continents slowly separated and moved to their present positions.

Earth's continents are still moving. Some plates move toward each other and collide. Other plates separate and move apart. Still others slide past one another. Over time, colliding, separating, and sliding plates have shaped Earth's landforms.

## Plates Collide

As plates collide, the energy created from their collision produces distinct landforms. The collision of different types of plates creates different shapes on Earth's surface. Ocean trenches and mountain ranges are two examples of landforms produced by the collision of tectonic plates.

### BIOGRAPHY

### Alfred Wegener
(1880–1930)

German scientist Alfred Wegener's fascination with the similarities between the western coast of Africa and the eastern coast of South America led to his theory of continental drift. Wegener argued that the two continents had once been joined together. Years of plate movement broke the continents apart and moved them to their current locations. It was only after Wegener's death that his ideas became a central part of the theory of plate tectonics.

The theory of plate tectonics suggests that the plates that make up Earth's crust are moving, usually only a few inches per year. As Earth's plates collide, separate, and slide past each other, they create forces great enough to shape many of Earth's landforms.

ANALYZING VISUALS Looking at the map, what evidence indicates that plates have collided or separated?

When two ocean plates collide, one plate pushes under the other. This process creates ocean trenches. Ocean trenches are deep valleys in the ocean floor. Near Japan, for example, the Pacific plate is slowly moving under other plates. This collision has created several deep ocean trenches, including the world's deepest trench, the Mariana Trench.

Ocean plates and continental plates can also collide. When this occurs, the ocean plate drops beneath the continental plate. This action forces the land above to crumple and form a mountain range. The Andes in South America, for example, were formed when the South American and Nazca plates collided.

The collision of two continental plates also results in mountain-building. When continental plates collide, the land pushes up, sometimes to great heights. The world's highest mountain range, the Himalayas, formed when the Indian plate crashed into the Eurasian plate. In fact, the Himalayas are still growing as the two plates continue to crash into each other.

## Plates Separate

A second type of plate movement causes plates to separate. As plates move apart, gaps between the plates allow magma, a liquid rock from the planet's interior, to rise to Earth's crust. **Lava**, or magma that reaches Earth's surface, emerges from the gap that has formed. As the lava cools, it builds a mid-ocean ridge, or underwater mountain. For example, the separation of the North American and Eurasian plates formed the largest underwater mountain, the Mid-Atlantic Ridge. If these mid-ocean ridges grow high enough, they can rise above the surface of the ocean, forming volcanic islands. Iceland, on the boundary of the Eurasian and North American plates, is an example of such an island.

**FOCUS ON READING**
The suffix –sion means the act of. What does the word collision mean?

## Plates Slide

Tectonic plates also slide past each other. As plates pass by one another, they sometimes grind together. This grinding produces **earthquakes**—sudden, violent movements of Earth's crust. Earthquakes often take place along faults, or breaks in Earth's crust where movement occurs. In California, for example, the Pacific plate is sliding by the edge of the North American plate. This has created the San Andreas Fault zone, an area where earthquakes are quite common.

The San Andreas Fault zone is one of many areas that lie along the boundaries of the Pacific plate. The frequent movement of this plate produces many earthquakes and volcanic eruptions along its edges. In fact, the region around the Pacific plate, called the Ring of Fire, is home to most of the world's earthquakes and volcanoes.

**READING CHECK** **Finding Main Ideas** What forces below Earth's surface shape landforms?

## Plate Movement

The movement of tectonic plates has produced many of Earth's landforms. Volcanoes, islands, and mountains often result from the separation or collision of Earth's plates.

**ANALYZING VISUALS** What type of landform is created by the collision of two continental plates?

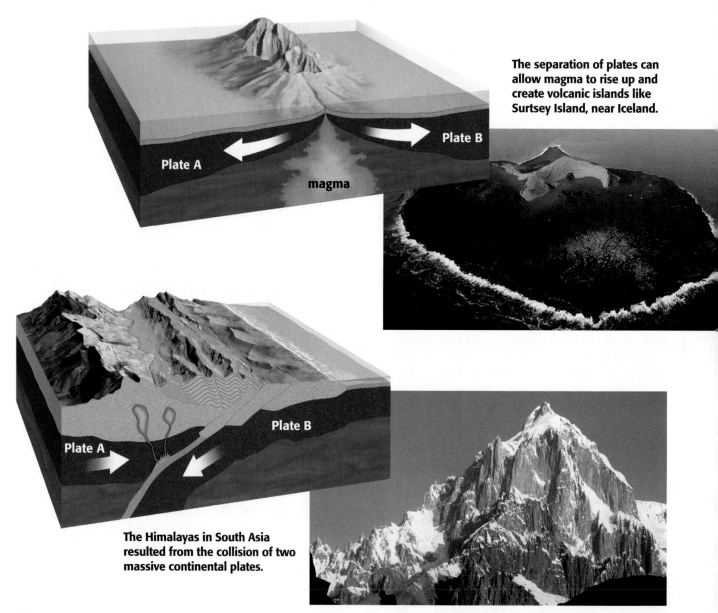

Plate A    Plate B
magma

The separation of plates can allow magma to rise up and create volcanic islands like Surtsey Island, near Iceland.

Plate A    Plate B

The Himalayas in South Asia resulted from the collision of two massive continental plates.

# Forces on Earth's Surface

For millions of years, the movement of Earth's tectonic plates has been building up landforms on Earth's surface. At the same time, other forces are working to change those very same landforms.

Imagine a small pile of dirt and rock on a table. If you poured water on the pile, it would move the dirt and rock from one place to another. Likewise, if you were to blow at the pile, the rock and dirt would also move. The same process happens in nature. Weather, water, and other forces change Earth's landforms by wearing them away or reshaping them.

## Weathering

One force that wears away landforms is weathering. **Weathering** is the process by which rock is broken down into smaller pieces. Several factors cause rock to break down. In desert areas, daytime heating and nighttime cooling can cause rocks to crack. Water may get into cracks in rocks and freeze. The ice then expands with a force great enough to break the rock. Even the roots of trees can pry rocks apart.

Regardless of which weathering process is at work, rocks eventually break down. These small pieces of rock are known as sediment. Once weathering has taken place, wind, ice, and water often move sediment from one place to another.

## Erosion

Another force that changes landforms is the process of erosion. **Erosion** is the movement of sediment from one location to another. Erosion can wear away or build up landforms. Wind, ice, and water all cause erosion.

Powerful winds often cause erosion. Winds lift sediment into the air and carry it across great distances. On beaches and in deserts, wind can deposit large amounts of sand to form dunes. Blowing sand can also wear down rock. The sand acts like sandpaper to polish and wear away at rocks. As you can see in the photo below, wind can have a dramatic effect on landforms.

Earth's glaciers also have the power to cause massive erosion. Glaciers, or large, slow-moving sheets of ice, build up when winter snows do not melt the following summer. Glaciers can be huge. Glaciers in Greenland and Antarctica, for example, are great sheets of ice up to two miles (3 km) thick. Some glaciers flow slowly downhill like rivers of ice. As they do so, they erode the land by carving large U-shaped valleys and sharp mountain peaks. As the ice flows downhill, it crushes rock into sediment and can move huge rocks long distances.

## Wind Erosion

Landforms in Utah's Canyonlands National Park have been worn away mostly by thousands of years of powerful winds.

39

Water is the most common cause of erosion. Waves in oceans and lakes can wear away the shore, creating jagged coastlines, like those on the coast of Oregon. Rivers also cause erosion. Over many years, the flowing water can cut through rock, forming canyons, or narrow areas with steep walls. Arizona's Horseshoe Bend and Grand Canyon are examples of canyons created in this way.

Flowing water shapes other landforms as well. When water deposits sediment in new locations, it creates new landforms. For example, rivers create floodplains when they flood their banks and deposit sediment along the banks. Sediment that is carried by a river all the way out to sea creates a delta. The sediment settles to the bottom, where the river meets the sea. The Nile and Mississippi rivers have created two of the world's largest river deltas.

**READING CHECK** **Comparing** How are weathering and erosion similar?

## Water Erosion

For millions of years, the Colorado River has worn away the rock at Horseshoe Bend in Arizona.

# Landforms Influence Life

Why do you live where you do? Perhaps your family moved to the desert to avoid harsh winter weather. Or possibly one of your ancestors settled near a river delta because its fertile soil was ideal for growing crops. Maybe your family wanted to live near the ocean to start a fishing business. As these examples show, landforms exert a strong influence on people's lives. Earth's landforms affect our settlements and our culture. At the same time, we affect the landforms around us.

Earth's landforms can influence where people settle. People sometimes settle near certain landforms and avoid others. For example, many settlements are built near fertile river valleys or deltas. The earliest urban civilization, for example, was built in the valley between the Tigris and Euphrates rivers. Other times, landforms discourage people from settling in a certain place. Tall, rugged mountains, like the Himalayas, and harsh desert climates, like the Sahara, do not usually attract large settlements.

Landforms affect our culture in ways that we may not have noticed. Landforms often influence what jobs are available in a region. For example, rich mineral deposits in the mountains of Colorado led to the development of a mining industry there. Landforms even affect language. On the island of New Guinea in Southeast Asia, rugged mountains have kept the people so isolated that more than 700 languages are spoken on the island today.

People sometimes change landforms to suit their needs. People may choose to modify landforms in order to improve their lives. For example, engineers built the Panama Canal to make travel from the Atlantic Ocean to the Pacific Ocean easier. In Southeast Asia, people who farm on steep hillsides cut terraces into the slope to

## Living with Landforms

The people of Rio de Janeiro, Brazil, have learned to adapt to the mountains and bays that dominate their landscape.

**ANALYZING VISUALS** How have people in Rio de Janiero adapted to their landscape?

create more level space to grow their crops. People have even built huge dams along rivers to divert water for use in nearby towns or farms.

**READING CHECK** **Analyzing** What are some examples of humans adjusting to and changing landforms?

**SUMMARY AND PREVIEW** Landforms are created by actions deep within the planet's surface, and they are changed by forces on Earth's surface, like weathering and erosion. In the next chapter you will learn how other forces, like weather and climate, affect Earth's people.

## Section 3 Assessment

### Reviewing Ideas, Terms, and Places

1. **a. Describe** What are some common **landforms**?
   **b. Analyze** Why do geographers study landforms?
2. **a. Identify** What is the theory of **plate tectonics**?
   **b. Compare and Contrast** How are the effects of colliding plates and separating plates similar and different?
   **c. Predict** How might Earth's surface change as tectonic plates continue to move?
3. **a. Recall** What is the process of **weathering**?
   **b. Elaborate** How does water affect sediment?
4. **a. Recall** How do landforms affect life on Earth?
   **b. Predict** How might people adapt to life in an area with steep mountains?

### Critical Thinking

5. **Analyzing** Use your notes and the chart below to identify the different factors that alter Earth's landforms and the changes that they produce.

| Factor | Change in Landform |
|---|---|
|  |  |
|  |  |
|  |  |

### FOCUS ON WRITING

6. **Writing about Earth's Land** Think of some vivid words you could use to describe Earth's landforms. As you think of them, add them to your notebook.

# The Ring of Fire

**Essential Elements**

The World in Spatial Terms
Places and Regions
**Physical Systems**
Human Systems
Environment and Society
The Uses of Geography

**Background** Does "the Ring of Fire" sound like the title of a fantasy novel? It's actually the name of a region that circles the Pacific Ocean known for its fiery volcanoes and powerful earthquakes. The Ring of Fire stretches from the tip of South America all the way up to Alaska, and from Japan down to the islands east of Australia. Along this belt, the Pacific plate moves against several other tectonic plates. As a result, thousands of earthquakes occur there every year, and dozens of volcanoes erupt.

## The Eruption of Mount Saint Helens

One of the best-known volcanoes in the Ring of Fire is Mount Saint Helens in Washington State. Mount Saint Helens had been dormant, or quiet, since 1857. Then in March 1980, it began spitting out puffs of steam and ash. Officials warned people to leave the area. Scientists brought in equipment to measure the growing bulge in the mountainside. Everyone feared the volcano might erupt at any moment.

On May 18, after a sudden earthquake, Mount Saint Helens let loose a massive explosion of rock and lava. Heat from the blast melted snow on the mountain, which

### Ring of Fire

map zone

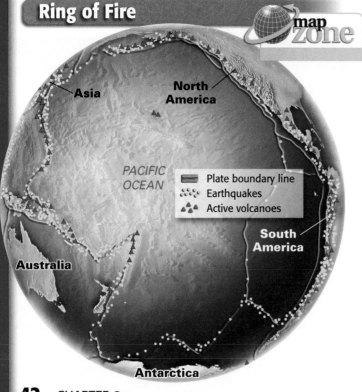

PACIFIC OCEAN

Asia
North America
South America
Australia
Antarctica

Plate boundary line
Earthquakes
Active volcanoes

### THE WORLD ALMANAC
Facts about the World

## Major Eruptions in the Ring of Fire

| Volcano | Year |
|---|---|
| Tambora, Indonesia | 1815 |
| Krakatau, Indonesia | 1883 |
| **Mount Saint Helens, United States** | **1980** |
| Nevado del Ruiz, Colombia | 1985 |
| Mount Pinatubo, Philippines | 1991 |

⇗ hmhsocialstudies.com

**Mount Saint Helens, 1980**
The 1980 eruption of Mount Saint Helens blew ash and hot gases miles into the air. Today, scientists study the volcano to learn more about predicting eruptions.

mixed with ash to create deadly mudflows. As the mud quickly poured downhill, it flattened forests, swept away cars, and destroyed buildings. Clouds of ash covered the land, killing crops, clogging waterways, and blanketing towns as far as 200 miles (330 km) away. When the volcano finally quieted down, 57 people had died. Damage totaled nearly $1 billion. If it were not for the early evacuation of the area, the destruction could have been much worse.

**What It Means** By studying Mount Saint Helens, scientists learned a great deal about stratovolcanoes. These are tall, steep, cone-shaped volcanoes that have violent eruptions. Stratovolcanoes often form in areas where tectonic plates collide.

Because stratovolcanoes often produce deadly eruptions, scientists try to predict when they might erupt. The lessons learned from Mount Saint Helens helped scientists warn people about another stratovolcano, Mount Pinatubo in the Philippines. That eruption in 1991 was the second-largest of the 1900s. It was far from the deadliest, however. Careful observation and timely warnings saved thousands of lives.

The Ring of Fire will always remain a threat. However, the better we understand its volcanoes, the better prepared we'll be when they erupt.

## Geography for Life Activity

1. How did the eruption of Mount Saint Helens affect the surrounding area?

2. Why do scientists monitor volcanic activity?

3. **Investigating the Effects of Volcanoes** Some volcanic eruptions affect environmental conditions around the world. Research the eruption of either Mount Saint Helens or the Philippines' Mount Pinatubo to find out how its eruption affected the global environment.

# Social Studies Skills

# Using a Physical Map

## Learn

Physical maps show important physical features, like oceans and mountains, in a particular area. They also indicate an area's elevation, or the height of the land in relation to sea level.

When you use a physical map, there are important pieces of information you should always examine.

- Identify physical features. Natural features, such as mountains, rivers, and lakes, are labeled on physical maps. Read the labels carefully to identify what physical features are present.

- Read the legend. On physical maps, the legend indicates scale as well as elevation. The different colors in the elevation key indicate how far above or below sea level a place is.

## Practice

Use the physical map of India at right to answer the questions below.

**1** What landforms and bodies of water are indicated on the map?

**2** What is the highest elevation in India? Where is it located?

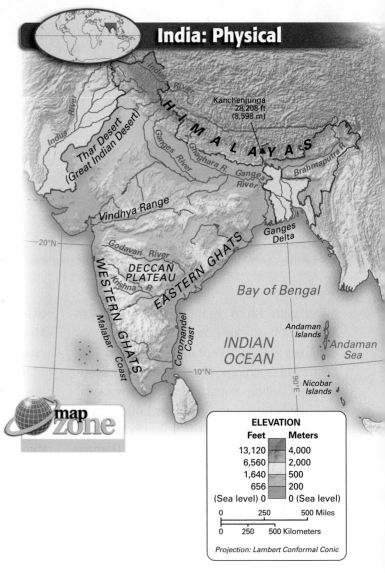

India: Physical

**ELEVATION**

| Feet | Meters |
|---|---|
| 13,120 | 4,000 |
| 6,560 | 2,000 |
| 1,640 | 500 |
| 656 | 200 |
| (Sea level) 0 | 0 (Sea level) |

0        250        500 Miles

0     250     500 Kilometers

*Projection: Lambert Conformal Conic*

## Apply

Locate the physical map of Africa in the atlas in the back of the book. Use the map to answer the questions below.

1. Which region has the highest elevation?

2. What bodies of water surround Africa?

3. What large island is located off the east coast of Africa?

# Chapter Review

**Geography's Impact**
video series
Review the video to answer the closing question:
*What are some reasons for water shortages, and what can be done to solve this problem?*

## Visual Summary

*Use the visual summary below to help you review the main ideas of the chapter.*

QUICK FACTS

The amount of solar energy Earth receives changes based on Earth's movement and position.

Water is crucial to life on Earth. Our abundant water supply is stored in oceans, in lakes, and underground.

Earth's various landforms are shaped by complex processes both under and on the planet's surface.

## Reviewing Vocabulary, Terms, and Places

*For each statement below, write T if it is true and F if it is false. If the statement is false, write the correct term that would make the sentence a true statement.*

1. **Weathering** is the movement of sediment from one location to another.

2. Because high **latitude** areas receive indirect rays from the sun, they have cooler temperatures.

3. Most of our **groundwater** is stored in Earth's streams, rivers, and lakes.

4. It takes 365¼ days for Earth to complete one **rotation** around the sun.

5. Streams are formed when **precipitation** collects in narrow channels.

6. **Earthquakes** cause erosion as they flow down-hill, carving valleys and mountain peaks.

7. The planet's tilt affects the amount of **erosion** Earth receives from the sun.

## Comprehension and Critical Thinking

**SECTION 1** *(Pages 26–29)*

8. **a. Identify** What factors influence the amount of energy that different places on Earth receive from the sun?

**b. Analyze** Why do the Northern and Southern hemispheres experience opposite seasons?

**c. Predict** What might happen to the amount of solar energy we receive if Earth's axis were straight up and down?

**SECTION 2** *(Pages 30–34)*

9. **a. Describe** What different sources of water are available on Earth?

**b. Draw Conclusions** How does the water cycle keep Earth's water supply relatively constant?

**c. Elaborate** What water problems affect people around the world? What solutions can you think of for one of those problems?

10. **a. Define** What is a landform? What are some common types of landforms?

   **b. Analyze** Why are Earth's landforms still changing?

   **c. Elaborate** What physical features dominate the landscape in your community? How do they affect life there?

# Using the Internet 21ST CENTURY

11. **Activity: Researching Earth's Seasons** Earth's seasons not only affect temperatures, they also affect how much daylight is available during specific times of the year. Through your online textbook, research Earth's seasons and view animations to see how seasons change. Then use the interactive worksheet to answer some questions about what you learned.

hmhsocialstudies.com

# Social Studies Skills

**Using a Physical Map** *Examine the physical map of the United States in the back of this book. Use it to answer the questions below.*

12. What physical feature extends along the Gulf of Mexico?

13. What mountain range in the West lies above 6,560 feet?

14. Where does the elevation drop below sea level?

# Map Activity 21ST CENTURY

**Physical Map** *Use the map on the right to answer the questions that follow.*

15. Which letter indicates a river?

16. Which letter on the map indicates the highest elevation?

17. The lowest elevation on the map is indicated by which letter?

18. An island is indicated by which letter?

19. Which letter indicates a large body of water?

20. Which letter indicates an area of land between 1,640 feet and 6,560 feet above sea level?

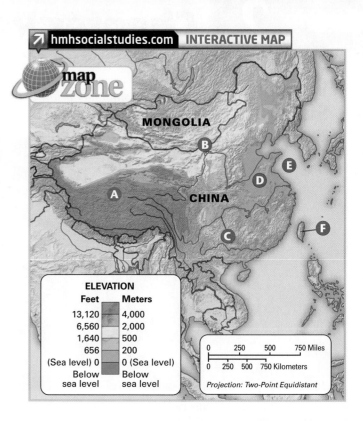

hmhsocialstudies.com **INTERACTIVE MAP**

map zone

MONGOLIA

CHINA

**ELEVATION**

| Feet | | Meters |
|---|---|---|
| 13,120 | | 4,000 |
| 6,560 | | 2,000 |
| 1,640 | | 500 |
| 656 | | 200 |
| (Sea level) 0 | | 0 (Sea level) |
| Below sea level | | Below sea level |

0   250   500   750 Miles
0   250   500   750 Kilometers

*Projection: Two-Point Equidistant*

## FOCUS ON READING AND WRITING

**Using Word Parts** *Use what you learned about prefixes, suffixes, and word roots to answer the questions below.*

21. The prefix *in-* means not. What do the words *invisible* and *inactive* mean?

22. The suffix *-ment* means action or process. What does the word *movement* mean?"

23. **Writing a Haiku** Look back through your notes about Earth. Choose one aspect of Earth to describe in a haiku. A haiku is a three-line poem that consists of 17 syllables—five in the first line, seven in the second line, and five in the third line. Be sure to use descriptive words to paint a picture of planet Earth.

# Standardized Test Prep

*DIRECTIONS: Read questions 1 through 7 and write the letter of the best response. Then read question 8 and write your own well-constructed response.*

**1** **Which regions on Earth have seasons tied to the amount of rainfall?**

A  polar regions

B  the tropics

C  the Northern Hemisphere

D  high latitudes

**2** **Most of Earth's water supply is made up of**

A  groundwater.

B  water vapor.

C  freshwater.

D  salt water.

**3** **The theory of continental drift explains how**

A  Earth's continents have moved thousands of miles.

B  Earth's axis has moved to its current position.

C  mountains and valleys are formed.

D  sediment moves from one place to another.

**4** **Which of the following is a cause of erosion?**

A  evaporation

B  ice

C  plate collisions

D  Earth's tilt

**5** **Changes in solar energy that create day and night are a result of**

A  the movement of tectonic plates.

B  Earth's rotation.

C  the revolution of Earth around the sun.

D  Earth's tilt.

## The Water Cycle

**6** **In the illustration above, which letter *best* reflects the process of evaporation?**

A  W

B  X

C  Y

D  Z

**7** **Which of the following is *most likely* a cause of water pollution?**

A  River water is used to produce electricity.

B  Heavy rainfall causes a river to overflow its banks.

C  Chemicals from a factory seep into the local water supply.

D  Groundwater is used faster than it can be replaced.

**8** **Extended Response Question** Use the water cycle diagram above to explain how Earth's water cycle affects our water supply.

# Climate, Environment, and Resources

**Essential Question** What factors shape Earth's different environments?

 ## What You Will Learn...

In this chapter you will learn about weather and climate. You will also learn about how living things and the environment are connected and about natural resources.

**FOCUS ON READING AND VIEWING**

**Understanding Cause and Effect** A cause makes something happen. An effect is the result of a cause. Words such as *because*, *result*, *since*, and *therefore* can signal causes or effects. As you read, look for causes and effects to understand how things relate. **See the lesson, Understanding Cause and Effect, on page 518.**

**Writing a Weather Report** You have likely seen a TV weather report, which tells the current weather conditions and predicts future conditions. After reading this chapter, prepare a weather report for a reason and place of your choosing. Present your report to the class and then view your classmates' reports.

**Climate** Earth has many climates, such as the dry climate of the region shown here.

ANALYSIS
SKILL  ANALYZING VISUALS

This photo shows a severe thunderstorm. These storms produce violent weather, such as heavy rainfall and strong winds, which affects people's lives.

**How do you think this storm might have affected the people who lived in this area?**

**Environments** Living things, such as this koala, depend on their surroundings.

**Natural Resources** Earth provides many valuable and useful natural resources, such as oil.

# Weather and Climate

## What You Will Learn...

### Main Ideas

1. While weather is short term, climate is a region's average weather over a long period.
2. The amount of sun at a given location is affected by Earth's tilt, movement, and shape.
3. Wind and water move heat around Earth, affecting how warm or wet a place is.
4. Mountains influence temperature and precipitation.

### The Big Idea

The sun, location, wind, water, and mountains affect weather and climate.

### Key Terms

weather, *p. 50*
climate, *p. 50*
prevailing winds, *p. 51*
ocean currents, *p. 52*
front, *p. 53*

hmhsocialstudies.com
TAKING NOTES

Use the graphic organizer online to take notes on the factors that affect weather and climate.

## If YOU lived there...

You live in Buffalo, New York, at the eastern end of Lake Erie. One evening in January, you are watching the local TV news. The weather forecaster says, "A huge storm is brewing in the Midwest and moving east. As usual, winds from this storm will drop several feet of snow on Buffalo as they blow off Lake Erie."

**Why will winds off the lake drop snow on Buffalo?**

**BUILDING BACKGROUND** All life on Earth depends on the sun's energy and on the cycle of water from the land to the air and back again. In addition, sun and water work with other forces, such as wind, to create global patterns of weather and climate.

## Understanding Weather and Climate

"Climate is what you expect; weather is what you get."
—Robert Heinlein, from *Time Enough for Love*

What is it like outside right now where you live? Is it hot, sunny, wet, cold? Is this what it is usually like outside for this time of year? The first two questions are about **weather**, the short-term changes in the air for a given place and time. The last question is about **climate**, a region's average weather conditions over a long period.

Weather is the temperature and precipitation from hour to hour or day to day. "Today is sunny, but tomorrow it might rain" is a statement about weather. Climate is the expected weather for a place based on data and experience. "Summer here is usually hot and muggy" is a statement about climate. The factors that shape weather and climate include the sun, location on Earth, wind, water, and mountains.

**READING CHECK** **Finding Main Ideas** How are weather and climate different from each other?

## Sun and Location

Energy from the sun heats the planet. Different locations receive different amounts of sunlight, though. Thus, some locations are warmer than others. The differences are due to Earth's tilt, movement, and shape.

You have learned that Earth is tilted on its axis. The part of Earth tilted toward the sun receives more solar energy than the part tilted away from the sun. As the Earth revolves around the sun, the part of Earth that is tilted toward the sun changes during the year. This process creates the seasons. In general, temperatures in summer are warmer than in winter.

Earth's shape also affects the amount of sunlight different locations receive. Because Earth is a sphere, its surface is rounded. Therefore, solar rays are more direct and concentrated near the equator. Nearer the poles, the sun's rays are less direct and more spread out.

As a result, areas near the equator, called the lower latitudes, are mainly hot year-round. Areas near the poles, called the higher latitudes, are cold year-round. Areas about halfway between the equator and poles have more seasonal change. In general, the farther from the equator, or the higher the latitude, the colder the climate.

**READING CHECK** **Summarizing** How does Earth's tilt on its axis affect climate?

## Wind and Water

Heat from the sun moves across Earth's surface. The reason is that air and water warmed by the sun are constantly on the move. You might have seen a gust of wind or a stream of water carrying dust or dirt. In a similar way, wind and water carry heat from place to place. As a result, they make different areas of Earth warmer or cooler.

## Global Wind Systems

**Prevailing winds blow in circular belts across Earth. These belts occur at about every 30° of latitude.**

**ANALYZING VISUALS** Which direction do the prevailing winds blow across the United States?

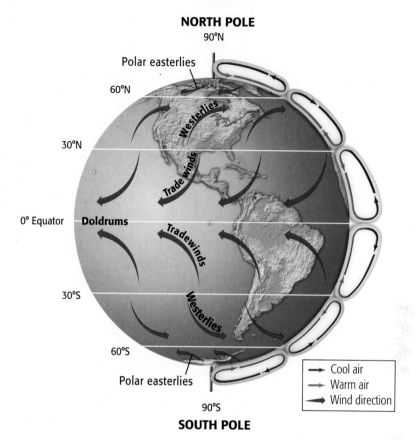

### Global Winds

Wind, or the sideways movement of air, blows in great streams around the planet. **Prevailing winds** are winds that blow in the same direction over large areas of Earth. The diagram above shows the patterns of Earth's prevailing winds.

To understand Earth's wind patterns, you need to think about the weight of air. Although you cannot feel it, air has weight. This weight changes with the temperature. Cold air is heavier than warm air. For this reason, when air cools, it gets heavier and sinks. When air warms, it gets lighter and rises. As warm air rises, cooler air moves in to take its place, creating wind.

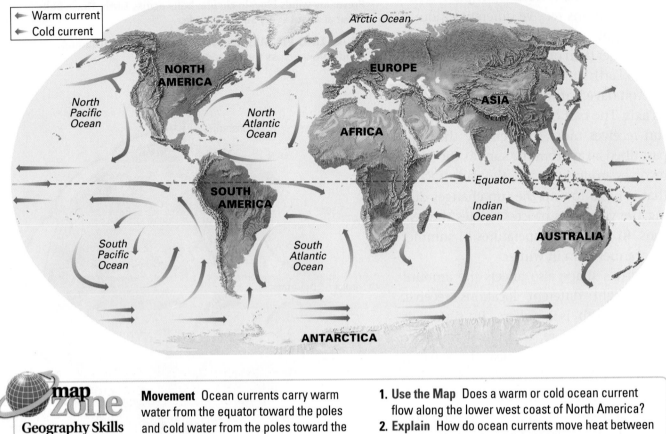

Warm current
Cold current

Arctic Ocean
NORTH AMERICA
EUROPE
ASIA
North Pacific Ocean
North Atlantic Ocean
AFRICA
Equator
SOUTH AMERICA
Indian Ocean
South Pacific Ocean
South Atlantic Ocean
AUSTRALIA
ANTARCTICA

**map zone**
**Geography Skills**

**Movement** Ocean currents carry warm water from the equator toward the poles and cold water from the poles toward the equator. The currents affect temperature.

1. **Use the Map** Does a warm or cold ocean current flow along the lower west coast of North America?
2. **Explain** How do ocean currents move heat between warmer and colder areas of Earth?

**FOCUS ON READING**
What is the effect of Earth's rotation on prevailing winds?

On a global scale, this rising, sinking, and flowing of air creates Earth's prevailing wind patterns. At the equator, hot air rises and flows toward the poles. At the poles, cold air sinks and flows toward the equator. Meanwhile, Earth is rotating. Earth's rotation causes prevailing winds to curve east or west rather than flowing directly north or south.

Depending on their source, prevailing winds make a region warmer or colder. In addition, the source of the winds can make a region drier or wetter. Winds that form from warm air or pass over lots of water often carry moisture. In contrast, winds that form from cold air or pass over lots of land often are dry.

## Ocean Currents

Like wind, **ocean currents**—large streams of surface seawater—move heat around Earth. Winds drive these currents. The map above shows how Earth's ocean currents carry warm or cool water to different areas. The water's temperature affects air temperature near it. Warm currents raise temperatures; cold currents lower them.

The Gulf Stream is a warm current that flows north along the U.S. East Coast. It then flows east across the Atlantic to become the North Atlantic Drift. As the warm current flows along northwestern Europe, it heats the air. Westerlies blow the warmed air across Europe. This process makes Europe warmer than it otherwise would be.

## Large Bodies of Water

Large bodies of water, such as an ocean or sea, also affect climate. Water heats and cools more slowly than land does. For this reason, large bodies of water make the temperature of the land nearby milder. Thus, coastal areas, such as the California coast, usually do not have as wide temperature ranges as inland areas.

As an example, the state of Michigan is largely surrounded by the Great Lakes. The lakes make temperatures in the state milder than other places as far north.

## Wind, Water, and Storms

If you watch weather reports, you will hear about storms moving across the United States. Tracking storms is important to us because the United States has so many of them. As you will see, some areas of the world have more storms than others do.

Most storms occur when two air masses collide. An air mass is a large body of air. The place where two air masses of different temperatures or moisture content meet is a **front**. Air masses frequently collide in regions like the United States, where the westerlies meet the polar easterlies.

Fronts can produce rain or snow as well as severe weather such as thunderstorms and icy blizzards. Thunderstorms produce rain, lightning, and thunder. In the United States, they are most common in spring and summer. Blizzards produce strong winds and large amounts of snow and are most common during winter.

Thunderstorms and blizzards can also produce tornadoes, another type of severe storm. A tornado is a small, rapidly twisting funnel of air that touches the ground. Tornadoes usually affect a limited area and last only a few minutes. However, they can be highly destructive, uprooting trees and tossing large vehicles through the air. Tornadoes can be extremely deadly as well.

In 1925 a tornado that crossed Missouri, Illinois, and Indiana left 695 people dead. It is the deadliest U.S. tornado on record.

The largest and most destructive storms, however, are hurricanes. These large, rotating storms form over tropical waters in the Atlantic Ocean, usually from late summer to fall. Did you know that hurricanes and typhoons are the same? Typhoons are just hurricanes that form in the Pacific Ocean.

## Extreme Weather

Severe weather is often dangerous and destructive. In the top photo, rescuers search for people during a flood in Yardley, Pennsylvania. Below, a tornado races across a wheat field.

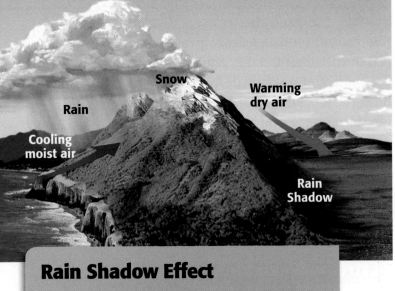

## Rain Shadow Effect

Most of the moisture in the ocean air falls on the mountainside facing the wind. Little moisture remains to fall on the other side, creating a rain shadow.

Labels: Snow, Warming dry air, Rain, Cooling moist air, Rain Shadow

## Mountains

Mountains can influence an area's climate by affecting both temperature and precipitation. Many high mountains are located in warm areas yet have snow at the top all year. How can this be? The reason is that temperature decreases with elevation—the height on Earth's surface above sea level.

Mountains also create wet and dry areas. Look at the diagram at left. A mountain forces air blowing against it to rise. As it rises, the air cools and precipitation falls as rain or snow. Thus, the side of the mountain facing the wind is often green and lush. However, little moisture remains for the other side. This effect creates a rain shadow, a dry area on the mountainside facing away from the direction of the wind.

**READING CHECK**  Finding Main Ideas  How does temperature change with elevation?

**SUMMARY AND PREVIEW** As you can see, the sun, location on Earth, wind, water, and mountains affect weather and climate. In the next section you will learn what the world's different climate regions are like.

Hurricanes produce drenching rain and strong winds that can reach speeds of 155 miles per hour (250 kph) or more. This is more than twice as fast as most people drive on highways. In addition, hurricanes form tall walls of water called storm surges. When a storm surge smashes into land, it can wipe out an entire coastal area.

**READING CHECK**  Analyzing  Why do coastal areas have milder climates than inland areas?

## Section 1 Assessment

### Reviewing Ideas, Terms, and Places

1. a. **Recall**  What shapes **weather** and **climate**?
   b. **Contrast**  How do weather and climate differ?
2. a. **Identify**  What parts of Earth receive the most heat from the sun?
   b. **Explain**  Why do the poles receive less solar energy than the equator does?
3. a. **Describe**  What creates wind?
   b. **Summarize**  How do **ocean currents** and large bodies of water affect climate?
4. a. **Define**  What is a rain shadow?
   b. **Explain**  Why might a mountaintop and a nearby valley have widely different temperatures?

### Critical Thinking

5. **Identifying Cause and Effect**  Draw a chart like this one. Use your notes to explain how each factor affects climate.

| | Effect on Climate |
|---|---|
| Sun and Location | |
| Wind | |
| Water | |
| Mountains | |

### FOCUS ON VIEWING

6. **Writing about Weather and Climate**  Jot down information to include in your weather report. For example, you might want to include a term such as fronts or describe certain types of storms such as hurricanes or tornadoes.

# World Climates

## If YOU lived there...

You live in Colorado and are on your first serious hike in the Rocky Mountains. Since it is July, it is hot in the campground in the valley. But your guide insists that you bring a heavy fleece jacket. By noon, you have climbed to 11,000 feet. You are surprised to see patches of snow in shady spots. Suddenly, you are very happy that you brought your jacket!

**Why does it get colder as you climb higher?**

**BUILDING BACKGROUND** While weather is the day-to-day changes in a certain area, climate is the average weather conditions over a long period. Earth's different climates depend partly on the amount of sunlight a region receives. Differences in climate also depend on factors such as wind, water, and elevation.

## Major Climate Zones

In January, how will you dress for the weekend? In some places, you might get dressed to go skiing. In other places, you might head out in a swimsuit to go to the beach. What the seasons are like where you live depends on climate.

Earth is a patchwork of climates. Geographers identify these climates by looking at temperature, precipitation, and native plant life. Using these items, we can divide Earth into five general climate zones—tropical, temperate, polar, dry, and highland.

The first three climate zones relate to latitude. Tropical climates occur near the equator, in the low latitudes. Temperate climates occur about halfway between the equator and the poles, in the middle latitudes. Polar climates occur near the poles, in the high latitudes. The last two climate zones occur at many different latitudes. In addition, geographers divide some climate zones into more specific climate regions. The chart and map on the next two pages describe the world's climate regions.

**READING CHECK** Drawing Inferences Why do you think geographers consider native plant life when categorizing climates?

---

### What You Will Learn...

#### Main Ideas

1. Geographers use temperature, precipitation, and plant life to identify climate zones.
2. Tropical climates are wet and warm, while dry climates receive little or no rain.
3. Temperate climates have the most seasonal change.
4. Polar climates are cold and dry, while highland climates change with elevation.

#### The Big Idea

Earth's five major climate zones are identified by temperature, precipitation, and plant life.

#### Key Terms

monsoons, *p. 58*
savannas, *p. 58*
steppes, *p. 59*
permafrost, *p. 61*

hmhsocialstudies.com
TAKING NOTES

Use the graphic organizer online to take notes on Earth's major climate zones.

# World Climate Regions

To explore the world's climate regions, start with the chart below. After reading about each climate region, locate the places on the map that have that climate. As you locate climates, look for patterns. For example, places near the equator tend to have warmer climates than places near the poles. See if you can identify some other climate patterns.

Tropical climate

| Climate | | Where is it? | What is it like? | Plants |
|---|---|---|---|---|
| **Tropical** | HUMID TROPICAL | On and near the equator | Warm with high amounts of rain year-round; in a few places, monsoons create extreme wet seasons | Tropical rain forest |
| | TROPICAL SAVANNA | Higher latitudes in the tropics | Warm all year; distinct rainy and dry seasons; at least 20 inches (50 cm) of rain during the summer | Tall grasses and scattered trees |
| **Dry** | DESERT | Mainly center on 30° latitude; also in middle of continents, on west coasts, or in rain shadows | Sunny and dry; less than 10 inches (25 cm) of rain a year; hot in the tropics; cooler with wide daytime temperature ranges in middle latitudes | A few hardy plants, such as cacti |
| | STEPPE | Mainly bordering deserts and interiors of large continents | About 10–20 inches (25–50 cm) of precipitation a year; hot summers and cooler winters with wide temperature ranges during the day | Shorter grasses; some trees and shrubs by water |
| **Temperate** | MEDITERRANEAN | West coasts in middle latitudes | Dry, sunny, warm summers; mild, wetter winters; rain averages 15–20 inches (30–50 cm) a year | Scrub woodland and grassland |
| | HUMID SUBTROPICAL | East coasts in middle latitudes | Humid with hot summers and mild winters; rain year-round; in paths of hurricanes and typhoons | Mixed forest |
| | MARINE WEST COAST | West coasts in the upper-middle latitudes | Cloudy, mild summers and cool, rainy winters; strong ocean influence | Evergreen forests |
| | HUMID CONTINENTAL | East coasts and interiors of upper-middle latitudes | Four distinct seasons; long, cold winters and short, warm summers; average precipitation varies | Mixed forest |

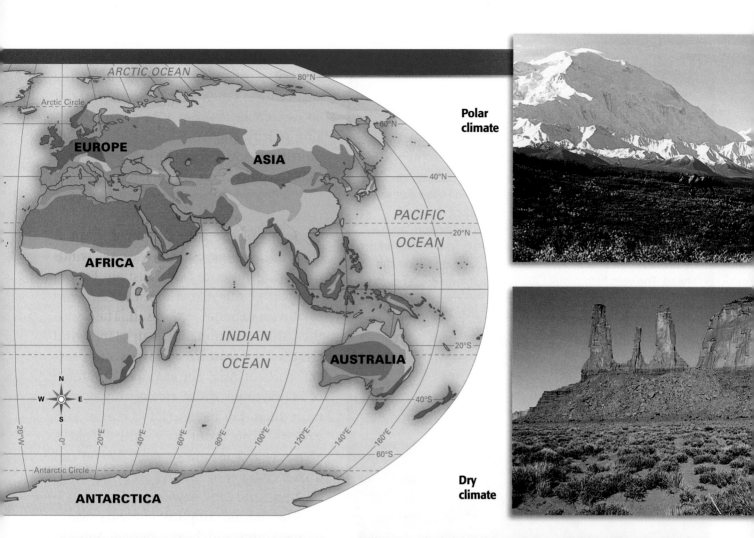

Polar climate

Dry climate

| Climate | | Where is it? | What is it like? | Plants |
|---------|---|--------------|------------------|--------|
| Polar | SUBARCTIC | Higher latitudes of the interior and east coasts of continents | Extremes of temperature; long, cold winters and short, warm summers; little precipitation | Northern ever-green forests |
| Polar | TUNDRA | Coasts in high latitudes | Cold all year; very long, cold winters and very short, cool summers; little precipitation; permafrost | Moss, lichens, low shrubs |
| Polar | ICE CAP | Polar regions | Freezing cold; snow and ice; little precipitation | No vegetation |
| Highland | HIGHLAND | High mountain regions | Wide range of temperatures and precipitation amounts, depending on elevation and location | Ranges from forest to tundra |

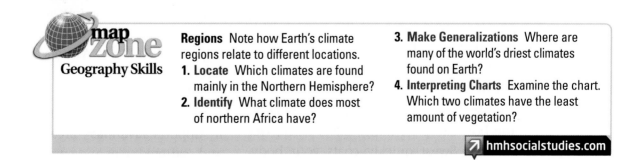

**map zone**
**Geography Skills**

**Regions** Note how Earth's climate regions relate to different locations.
1. **Locate** Which climates are found mainly in the Northern Hemisphere?
2. **Identify** What climate does most of northern Africa have?
3. **Make Generalizations** Where are many of the world's driest climates found on Earth?
4. **Interpreting Charts** Examine the chart. Which two climates have the least amount of vegetation?

hmhsocialstudies.com

## The Tuareg of the Sahara.

In the Sahara, the world's largest desert, temperatures can top 130°F (54°C). Yet the Tuareg (TWAH-reg) of North and West Africa call the Sahara home—and prefer it. The Tuareg have raised camels and other animals in the Sahara for more than 1,000 years. The animals graze on sparse desert plants. When the plants are gone, the Tuareg move on.

In camp, Tuareg families live in tents made from animal skins. Some wealthier Tuareg live in adobe homes. The men traditionally wear blue veils wrapped around their face and head. The veils help protect against windblown desert dust.

**Summarizing** How have the Tuareg adapted to life in a desert?

## Tropical and Dry Climates

Are you the type of person who likes to go to extremes? Then tropical and dry climates might be for you. These climates include the wettest, driest, and hottest places on Earth.

### Tropical Climates

Our tour of Earth's climates starts at the equator, in the heart of the tropics. This region extends from the Tropic of Cancer to the Tropic of Capricorn. Look back at the map to locate this region.

**Humid Tropical Climate** At the equator, the hot, damp air hangs like a thick, wet blanket. Sweat quickly coats your body.

Welcome to the humid tropical climate. This climate is warm, muggy, and rainy year-round. Temperatures average about 80°F (26°C). Showers or storms occur almost daily, and rainfall ranges from 70 to more than 450 inches (180 to 1,140 cm) a year. In comparison, only a few parts of the United States average more than 70 inches (180 cm) of rain a year.

Some places with a humid tropical climate have **monsoons**, seasonal winds that bring either dry or moist air. During one part of the year, a moist ocean wind creates an extreme wet season. The winds then shift direction, and a dry land wind creates a dry season. Monsoons affect several parts of Asia. For example, the town of Mawsynram, India, receives on average more than 450 inches (1,140 cm) of rain a year—all in about six months! That is about 37 feet (11 m) of rain. As you can imagine, flooding during wet seasons is common and can be severe.

The humid tropical climate's warm temperatures and heavy rainfall support tropical rain forests. These lush forests contain more types of plants and animals than anywhere else on Earth. The world's largest rain forest is in the Amazon River basin in South America. There you can find more than 50,000 species, including giant lily pads, poisonous tree frogs, and toucans.

**Tropical Savanna Climate** Moving north and south away from the equator, we find the tropical savanna climate. This climate has a long, hot, dry season followed by short periods of rain. Rainfall is much lower than at the equator but still high. Temperatures are hot in the summer, often as high as 90°F (32°C). Winters are cooler but rarely get cold.

This climate does not receive enough rainfall to support dense forests. Instead, it supports **savannas**—areas of tall grasses and scattered trees and shrubs.

## Dry Climates

Leaving Earth's wettest places, we head to its driest. These climates are found in a number of locations on the planet.

**Desert Climate** Picture the sun baking down on a barren wasteland. This is the desert, Earth's hottest and driest climate. Deserts receive less than 10 inches (25 cm) of rain a year. Dry air and clear skies produce high daytime temperatures and rapid cooling at night. In some deserts, highs can top 130°F (54°C)! Under such conditions, only very hardy plants and animals can live. Many plants grow far apart so as not to compete for water. Others, such as cacti, store water in fleshy stems and leaves.

**Steppe Climate** Semidry grasslands or prairies—called **steppes** (STEPS)—often border deserts. Steppes receive slightly more rain than deserts do. Short grasses are the most common plants, but shrubs and trees grow along streams and rivers.

**READING CHECK** **Contrasting** What are some ways in which tropical and dry climates differ?

## Temperate Climates

If you enjoy hot, sunny days as much as chilly, rainy ones, then temperate climates are for you. *Temperate* means "moderate" or "mild." These mild climates tend to have four seasons, with warm or hot summers and cool or cold winters.

Temperate climates occur in the middle latitudes, the regions halfway between the equator and the poles. Air masses from the tropics and the poles often meet in these regions, which creates a number of different temperate climates. You very likely live in one, because most Americans do.

**Mediterranean Climate** Named for the region of the Mediterranean Sea, this sunny, pleasant climate is found in many popular vacation areas. In a Mediterranean climate, summers are hot, dry, and sunny. Winters are mild and somewhat wet. Plant life includes shrubs and short trees with scattered larger trees. The Mediterranean climate occurs mainly in coastal areas. In the United States, much of California has this climate.

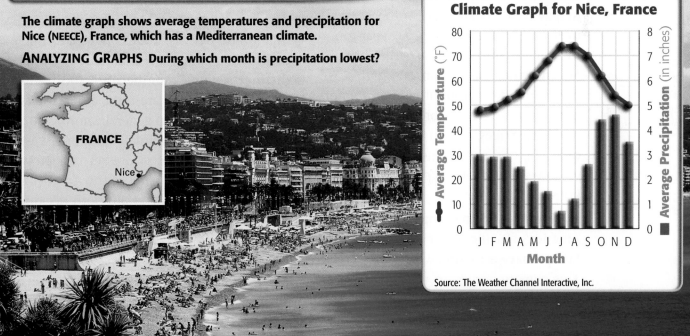

## Mediterranean Climate

The climate graph shows average temperatures and precipitation for Nice (NEECE), France, which has a Mediterranean climate.

**ANALYZING GRAPHS** During which month is precipitation lowest?

FRANCE
Nice

**Climate Graph for Nice, France**

Source: The Weather Channel Interactive, Inc.

# Highland Climates

Mount Kilimanjaro is the tallest mountain in Africa. Although Kilimanjaro is only about 200 miles (320 km) south of the equator, snow blankets its highest peak.

Kilimanjaro rises to 19,341 ft (5,895 m). The snow-covered summit has an ice cap climate.

Climate and plant life ranges from rain forest, to steppe, to desert, to tundra.

A tropical savanna climate is found around the base of Mount Kilimanjaro.

**ANALYSIS SKILL** **ANALYZING VISUALS**
Which type of tropical climate is found on Mount Kilimanjaro?

**Humid Subtropical Climate** The southeastern United States is an example of the humid subtropical climate. This climate occurs along east coasts near the tropics. In these areas, warm, moist air blows in from the ocean. Summers are hot and muggy. Winters are mild, with occasional frost and snow. Storms occur year-round. In addition, hurricanes can strike, bringing violent winds, heavy rain, and high seas.

A humid subtropical climate supports mixed forests. These forests include both deciduous trees, which lose their leaves each fall, and coniferous trees, which are green year-round. Coniferous trees are also known as evergreens.

**Marine West Coast Climate** Parts of North America's Pacific coast and of western Europe have a marine west coast climate. This climate occurs on west coasts where winds carry moisture in from the seas.

The moist air keeps temperatures mild year-round. Winters are foggy, cloudy, and rainy, while summers can be warm and sunny. Dense evergreen forests thrive in this climate.

**Humid Continental Climate** Closer to the poles, in the upper–middle latitudes, many inland and east coast areas have a humid continental climate. This climate has four **distinct** seasons. Summers are short and hot. Spring and fall are mild, and winters are long, cold, and in general, snowy.

This climate's rainfall supports vast grasslands and forests. Grasses can grow very tall, such as in parts of the American Great Plains. Forests contain both deciduous and coniferous trees, with coniferous forests occurring in the colder areas.

**READING CHECK** **Categorizing** Which of the temperate climates is too dry to support forests?

**ACADEMIC VOCABULARY**

distinct
clearly different and separate

# Polar and Highland Climates

Get ready to feel the chill as we end our tour in the polar and highland climates. The three polar climates are found in the high latitudes near the poles. The varied highland climate is found on mountains.

**Subarctic Climate** The subarctic climate and the tundra climate described below occur mainly in the Northern Hemisphere south of the Arctic Ocean. In the subarctic climate, winters are long and bitterly cold. Summers are short and cool. Temperatures stay below freezing for about half the year. The climate's moderate rainfall supports vast evergreen forests called taiga (TY-guh).

**Tundra Climate** The tundra climate occurs in coastal areas along the Arctic Ocean. As in the subarctic climate, winters are long and bitterly cold. Temperatures rise above freezing only during the short summer. Rainfall is light, and only plants such as mosses, lichens, and small shrubs grow.

In parts of the tundra, soil layers stay frozen all year. Permanently frozen layers of soil are called **permafrost**. Frozen earth absorbs water poorly, which creates ponds and marshes in summer. This moisture causes plants to burst forth in bloom.

**Ice Cap Climate** The harshest places on Earth may be the North and South poles. These regions have an ice cap climate. Temperatures are bone-numbingly cold, and lows of more than –120°F (–84°C) have been recorded. Snow and ice remain year-round, but precipitation is light. Not surprisingly, no vegetation grows. However, mammals such as penguins and polar bears thrive.

**Highland Climates** The highland climate includes polar climates plus others. In fact, this mountain climate is actually several climates in one. As you go up a mountain, the climate changes. Temperatures drop, and plant life grows sparser. Going up a mountain can be like going from the tropics to the poles. On very tall mountains, ice coats the summit year-round.

**FOCUS ON READING**
What is the effect of elevation on climate?

**READING CHECK** **Comparing** How are polar and highland climates similar?

**SUMMARY AND PREVIEW** As you can see, Earth has many climates, which we identify based on temperature, precipitation, and native plant life. In the next section you will read about how nature and all living things are connected.

---

## Section 2 Assessment

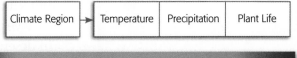

hmhsocialstudies.com
ONLINE QUIZ

### Reviewing Ideas, Terms, and Places

1. **a. Recall** Which three major climate zones occur at certain latitudes?
   **b. Summarize** How do geographers categorize Earth's different climates?
2. **a. Define** What are **monsoons**?
   **b. Make Inferences** In which type of dry climate do you think the fewest people live, and why?
3. **a. Identify** What are the four temperate climates?
   **b. Draw Conclusions** Why are places with a Mediterranean climate popular vacation spots?
4. **a. Describe** What are some effects of **permafrost**?
   **b. Explain** How are highland climates unique?

### Critical Thinking

5. **Categorizing** Create a chart like the one below for each climate region. Then use your notes to describe each climate region's average temperatures, precipitation, and native plant life.

| Climate Region → | Temperature | Precipitation | Plant Life |
|---|---|---|---|

### FOCUS ON VIEWING

6. **Discussing World Climates** Add information about the climate of the place you have selected, such as average temperature and precipitation.

# Natural Environments

## What You Will Learn...

### Main Ideas

1. The environment and life are interconnected and exist in a fragile balance.
2. Soils play an important role in the environment.

### The Big Idea

Plants, animals, and the environment, including soil, interact and affect one another.

### Key Terms

environment, *p. 62*
ecosystem, *p. 63*
habitat, *p. 64*
extinct, *p. 64*
humus, *p. 65*
desertification, *p. 65*

hmhsocialstudies.com
**TAKING NOTES**

Use the graphic organizer online to take notes on Earth's natural environments.

## If **YOU** lived there...

When your family moved to the city, you were sure you would miss the woods and pond near your old house. Then one of your new friends at school told you there's a large park only a few blocks away. You wondered how interesting a city park could be. But you were surprised at the many plants and animals that live there.

**What environments might you see in the park?**

**BUILDING BACKGROUND** No matter where you live, you are part of a natural environment. From a desert to a rain forest to a city park, every environment is home to a unique community of plant and animal life. These plants and animals live in balance with nature.

## The Environment and Life

If you saw a wild polar bear outside your school, you would likely be shocked. In most parts of the United States, polar bears live only in zoos. This is because plants and animals must live where they are suited to the **environment**, or surroundings. Polar bears are suited to very cold places with lots of ice, water, and fish. As you will see, living things and their environments are connected and affect each other in many ways.

### Limits on Life

The environment limits life. As our tour of the world's climates showed, factors such as temperature, rainfall, and soil conditions limit where plants and animals can live. Palm trees cannot survive at the frigid North Pole. Ferns will quickly wilt and die in deserts, but they thrive in tropical rain forests.

At the same time, all plants and animals are adapted to specific environments. For example, kangaroo rats are adapted to dry desert environments. These small rodents can get all the water they need from food, so they seldom have to drink water.

## Connections in Nature

The interconnections between living things and the environment form ecosystems. An **ecosystem** is a group of plants and animals that depend on each other for survival and the environment in which they live. Ecosystems can be any size and can occur wherever air, water, and soil support life. A garden pond, a city park, a prairie, and a rain forest are all examples of ecosystems.

The diagram below shows a forest ecosystem. Each part of this ecosystem fills a certain role. The sun provides energy to the plants, which use the energy to make their own food. The plants then serve as food, either directly or indirectly, for all other life in the forest. When the plants and animals die, their remains break down and provide nutrients for the soil and new plant growth. Thus, the cycle continues.

**Close-up**

# A Forest Ecosystem

A forest is one type of ecosystem. The plants and animals in the forest depend on one another and the forest environment for survival.

1 Sunlight is the source of energy for most living things.

2 Plants use the energy in sunlight to make food. They serve as the basis for other life in the ecosystem.

5 Larger predators, such as mountain lions, compete for the prey that is available.

4 Predators, such as wolves and hawks, eat rabbits and other prey for energy.

3 Animals such as rabbits eat plants and gain some of their energy.

**ANALYSIS SKILL** **ANALYZING VISUALS**

**What might happen in the forest ecosystem above if the number of rabbits fell significantly?**

## Changes to Environments

The interconnected parts of an ecosystem exist in a fragile balance. For this reason, a small change to one part can affect the whole system. A lack of rain in the forest ecosystem could kill off many of the plants that feed the rabbits. If the rabbits die, there will be less food for the wolves and mountain lions. Then they too may die.

Many actions can affect ecosystems. For example, people need places to live and food to eat, so they clear land for homes and farms. Clearing land has **consequences**, however. It can cause the soil to erode. In addition, the plants and animals that live in the area might be left without food and shelter.

Actions such as clearing land and polluting can destroy habitats. A **habitat** is the place where a plant or animal lives. The most diverse habitats on Earth are tropical rain forests. People are clearing Earth's rain forests for farmland, lumber, and other reasons, though. As a result, these diverse habitats are being lost.

**ACADEMIC VOCABULARY**

consequences
the effects of a particular event or events

**FOCUS ON READING**

What are some causes of habitat destruction?

Extreme changes in ecosystems can cause species to die out, or become **extinct**. As an example, flightless birds called dodos once lived on Mauritius (maw-RI-shuhs), an island in the Indian Ocean. When people began settling on the island, their actions harmed the dodos' habitat. First seen in 1507, dodos were extinct by 1681.

Recognizing these problems, many countries are working to balance people's needs with the needs of the environment. The United States, for example, has passed many laws to limit pollution, manage forests, and protect valuable ecosystems.

**READING CHECK** Drawing Inferences How might one change affect an entire ecosystem?

## Soil and the Environment

As you know, plants are the basis for all food that animals eat. Soils help determine what plants will grow and how well. Because soils support plant life, they play an important role in the environment.

## CONNECTING TO Science

### Soil Factory

The next time you see a fallen tree in the forest, do not think of it as a dead log. Think of it as a soil factory. A fallen tree is buzzing with the activity of countless insects, bacteria, and other organisms. These organisms invade the fallen log and start to break the wood down.

As the tree decays and crumbles, it turns into humus. Humus is a rich blend of organic material. The humus mixes with the soil and broken rock material. These added nutrients then enrich the soil, making it possible for new trees and plants to grow. Fallen trees provide as much as one-third of the organic material in forest soil.

**Summarizing** What causes a fallen tree to change into soil?

Fertile soils are rich in minerals and **humus** (HYOO-muhs), decayed plant or animal matter. These soils can support abundant plant life. Like air and water, fertile soil is essential for life. Without it, we could not grow much of the food we eat.

Soils can lose fertility in several ways. Erosion from wind or water can sweep topsoil away. Planting the same crops over and over can also rob soil of its fertility. When soil becomes worn out, it cannot support as many plants. In fragile dry environments this can lead to the spread of desertlike conditions, or **desertification**. The spread of desertlike conditions is a serious problem in many parts of the world.

**READING CHECK** **Analyzing** What do fertile soils contain, and why are these soils important?

**SUMMARY AND PREVIEW** Living things and the environment are connected, but changes can easily upset the balance in an ecosystem. Because they support plant life, soils are important parts of ecosystems. In the next section you will learn about Earth's many resources.

## Soil Layers

The three layers of soil are the topsoil, subsoil, and broken rock. The thickness of each layer depends on the conditions in a specific location.

**ANALYZING VISUALS** In which layer of soil are most plant roots and insects found?

Topsoil

Subsoil

Broken Rock

Solid Rock

## Section 3 Assessment

hmhsocialstudies.com
ONLINE QUIZ

### Reviewing Ideas, Terms, and Places

1. **a. Define** What is an **ecosystem**, and what are two examples of ecosystems?
   **b. Summarize** How do nature and people change ecosystems?
   **c. Elaborate** Why can plants and animals not live everywhere?

2. **a. Recall** What is **humus**, and why is it important to soil?
   **b. Identify Cause and Effect** What actions can cause **desertification**, and what might be some possible effects?
   **c. Elaborate** Why it is important for geographers and scientists to study soils?

### Critical Thinking

3. **Identifying Cause and Effect** Review your notes. Then use a chart like this one to identify some of the causes and effects of changes to ecosystems.

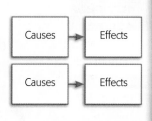

| Causes | → | Effects |
| Causes | → | Effects |

### FOCUS ON VIEWING

4. **Writing about Natural Environments** Jot down ideas about how different types of weather might affect the environment of the place you chose. For example, how might lack of rain affect the area?

# Earth's Changing Environments

**PANGAEA**

**Pangaea** About 250 million years ago, all of Earth's continents were connected, forming one giant landmass called Pangaea.

hmhsocialstudies.com
ANIMATED GEOGRAPHY

What was North America like 74 million years ago, when dinosaurs roamed Earth? You might be surprised to learn that it was a very different place. Earth's environments are always changing. The map at right shows North America in the age of dinosaurs. Back then, the climate was warm and humid, and large inland seas covered much of the land. The region's plants and animals were completely different. Slowly, however, things changed. Some major event, possibly an asteroid impact, wiped out the dinosaurs. Over time, North America's environments changed into the ones that exist today.

**HISTORY**

VIDEO
Future Chill

hmhsocialstudies.com

**What Survived** Dinosaurs, such as the plant-eating ceratopsian at left, are long gone. But insects, such as cockroaches and dragonflies, are still around.

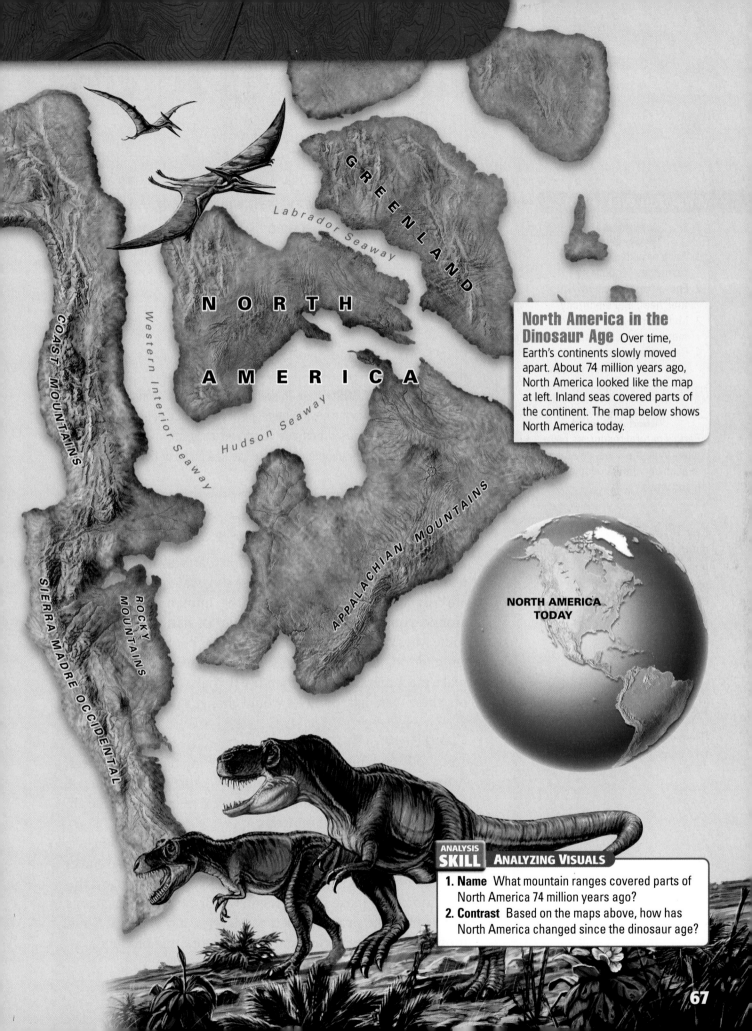

G R E E N L A N D

Labrador Seaway

N O R T H

A M E R I C A

Western Interior Seaway

Hudson Seaway

COAST MOUNTAINS

SIERRA MADRE OCCIDENTAL

ROCKY MOUNTAINS

APPALACHIAN MOUNTAINS

**North America in the Dinosaur Age** Over time, Earth's continents slowly moved apart. About 74 million years ago, North America looked like the map at left. Inland seas covered parts of the continent. The map below shows North America today.

**NORTH AMERICA TODAY**

ANALYSIS
**SKILL** **ANALYZING VISUALS**

1. **Name** What mountain ranges covered parts of North America 74 million years ago?
2. **Contrast** Based on the maps above, how has North America changed since the dinosaur age?

**ANALYSIS SKILL** **ANALYZING VISUALS**

1. **Name** What mountain ranges covered parts of North America 74 million years ago?
2. **Contrast** Based on the maps above, how has North America changed since the dinosaur age?

# Natural Resources

## If YOU lived there...

You live in Southern California, where the climate is warm and dry. Every week, you water the grass around your house to keep it green. Now the city has declared a "drought emergency" because of a lack of rain. City officials have put limits on watering lawns and on other uses of water.

**How can you help conserve scarce water?**

**BUILDING BACKGROUND** In addition to plant and animal life, other resources in the environment greatly influence people. In fact, certain vital resources, such as water, soils, and minerals, may determine whether people choose to live in a place or how wealthy people are.

## Earth's Valuable Resources

Think about the materials in nature that you use. You have learned about the many ways we use sun, water, and land. They are just a start, though. Look at the human-made products around you. They all required the use of natural materials in some way. We use trees to make paper for books. We use petroleum, or oil, to make plastics for cell phones. We use metals to make machines, which we then use to make many items. Without these materials, our lives would change drastically.

### Using Natural Resources

Trees, oil, and metals are all examples of natural resources. A **natural resource** is any material in nature that people use and value. Earth's most important natural resources include air, water, soils, forests, and minerals.

Understanding how and why people use natural resources is an important part of geography. We use some natural resources just as they are, such as wind. Usually, though, we change natural resources to make something new. For example, we change metals to make products such as bicycles and watches. Thus, most natural resources are raw materials for other products.

## What You Will Learn...

### Main Ideas

1. Earth provides valuable resources for our use.
2. Energy resources provide fuel, heat, and electricity.
3. Mineral resources include metals, rocks, and salt.
4. Resources shape people's lives and countries' wealth.

### The Big Idea

Earth's natural resources have many valuable uses, and their availability affects people in many ways.

### Key Terms

natural resource, *p. 68*
renewable resources, *p. 69*
nonrenewable resources, *p. 69*
deforestation, *p. 69*
reforestation, *p. 69*
fossil fuels, *p. 69*
hydroelectric power, *p. 70*

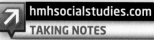

hmhsocialstudies.com
**TAKING NOTES**

Use the graphic organizer online to take notes on Earth's resources.

## Reforestation

Members of the Green Belt Movement plant trees in Kenya. Although trees are a renewable resource, some forests are being cut down faster than new trees can replace them. Reforestation helps protect Earth's valuable forestlands.

**ANALYZING VISUALS** How does reforestation help the environment?

### Types of Natural Resources

We group natural resources into two types, those we can replace and those we cannot. **Renewable resources** are resources Earth replaces naturally. For example, when we cut down a tree, another tree can grow in its place. Renewable resources include water, soil, trees, plants, and animals. These resources can last forever if used wisely.

Other natural resources will run out one day. These **nonrenewable resources** are resources that cannot be replaced. For example, coal formed over millions of years. Once we use the coal up, it is gone.

### Managing Natural Resources

People need to manage natural resources to protect them for the future. Consider how your life might change if we ran out of forests, for example. Although forests are renewable, we can cut down trees far faster than they can grow. The result is the clearing of trees, or **deforestation**.

By managing resources, however, we can repair and prevent resource loss. For example, some groups are engaged in **reforestation**, planting trees to replace lost forestland.

**READING CHECK** Contrasting How do renewable and nonrenewable resources differ?

**BIOGRAPHY**

### Wangari Maathai
(1940– )

Can planting a tree improve people's lives? Wangari Maathai thinks so. Born in Kenya in East Africa, Maathai wanted to help people in her country, many of whom were poor. She asked herself what Kenyans could do to improve their lives. "Planting a tree was the best idea that I had," she says. In 1977 Maathai founded the Green Belt Movement to plant trees and protect forestland. The group has now planted more than 30 million trees across Kenya! These trees provide wood and prevent soil erosion. In 2004 Maathai was awarded the Nobel Peace Prize. She is the first African woman to receive this famous award.

## Energy Resources

Every day you use plants and animals from the dinosaur age—in the form of energy resources. These resources power vehicles, produce heat, and generate electricity. They are some of our most important and valuable natural resources.

### Nonrenewable Energy Resources

Most of the energy we use comes from **fossil fuels**, nonrenewable resources that formed from the remains of ancient plants and animals. The most important fossil fuels are coal, petroleum, and natural gas.

Coal has long been a reliable energy source for heat. However, burning coal causes some problems. It pollutes the air and can harm the land. For these reasons, people have used coal less as other fuel options became available.

FOCUS ON
READING
In the second
sentence on this
page, what cause
does the word
*because* signal?
What is the effect
of this cause?

Today we use coal mainly to create electricity at power plants, not to heat single buildings. Because coal is plentiful, people are looking for cleaner ways to burn it.

Petroleum, or oil, is a dark liquid used to make fuels and other products. When first removed from the ground, petroleum is called crude oil. This oil is shipped or piped to refineries, factories that process the crude oil to make products. Fuels made from oil include gasoline, diesel fuel, and jet fuel. Oil is also used to make petrochemicals, which are processed to make products such as plastics and cosmetics.

As with coal, burning oil-based fuels can pollute the air and land. In addition, oil spills can harm wildlife. Because we are so dependent on oil for energy, however, it is an extremely valuable resource.

The cleanest-burning fossil fuel is natural gas. We use it mainly for heating and cooking. For example, your kitchen stove may use natural gas. Some vehicles run on natural gas as well. These vehicles cause less pollution than those that run on gasoline.

## Renewable Energy Resources

Unlike fossil fuels, renewable energy resources will not run out. They also are generally better for the environment. On the other hand, they are not available everywhere and can be costly.

The main alternative to fossil fuels is **hydroelectric power**—the production of electricity from waterpower. We obtain energy from moving water by damming rivers. The dams harness the power of moving water to generate electricity.

Hydroelectric power has both pros and cons. On the positive side, it produces power without polluting and lessens our use of fossil fuels. On the negative side, dams create lakes that replace existing resources, such as farmland, and disrupt wildlife habitats.

Another renewable energy source is wind. People have long used wind to power windmills. Today we use wind to power wind turbines, a type of modern windmill. At wind farms, hundreds of turbines create electricity in windy places.

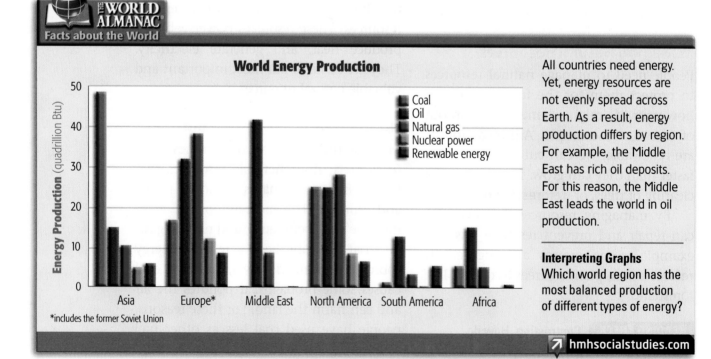

**THE WORLD ALMANAC**
**Facts about the World**

**World Energy Production**

Energy Production (quadrillion Btu)

- Coal
- Oil
- Natural gas
- Nuclear power
- Renewable energy

Asia   Europe*   Middle East   North America   South America   Africa

*includes the former Soviet Union

All countries need energy. Yet, energy resources are not evenly spread across Earth. As a result, energy production differs by region. For example, the Middle East has rich oil deposits. For this reason, the Middle East leads the world in oil production.

**Interpreting Graphs**
Which world region has the most balanced production of different types of energy?

hmhsocialstudies.com

A third source of renewable energy is heat from the sun and Earth. We can use solar power, or power from the sun, to heat water or homes. Using special solar panels, we turn solar energy into electricity. We can also use geothermal energy, or heat from within Earth. Geothermal power plants use steam and hot water located within Earth to create electricity.

### Nuclear Energy

A final energy source is nuclear energy. We obtain this energy by splitting atoms, small particles of matter. This process uses the metal uranium, so some people consider nuclear energy a nonrenewable resource. Nuclear power does not pollute the air, but it does produce dangerous wastes. These wastes must be stored for thousands of years before they are safe. In addition, an accident at a nuclear power plant can have terrible effects.

**READING CHECK** Drawing Inferences Why might people look for alternatives to fossil fuels?

## Mineral Resources

Like energy resources, mineral resources can be quite valuable. These resources include metals, salt, rocks, and gemstones.

Minerals fulfill countless needs. Look around you to see a few. Your school building likely includes steel, made from iron. The outer walls might be granite or limestone. The window glass is made from quartz, a mineral in sand. From staples to jewelry to coins, metals are everywhere.

Minerals are nonrenewable, so we need to conserve them. Recycling items such as aluminum cans will make the supply of these valuable resources last longer.

**READING CHECK** Categorizing What are the major types of mineral resources?

### From the Ground to the Air

The photo shows a bauxite mine. Bauxite is used to make aluminum. This metal is used in many products, such as jet planes. See how many other products made from aluminum you can name.

## Resources and People

Natural resources vary from place to place. The resources available in a region can shape life and wealth for the people there.

### Resources and Daily Life

The natural resources available to people affect their lifestyles and needs. In the United States we have many different kinds of natural resources. We can choose among many different ways to dress, eat, live, travel, and entertain ourselves. People in places with fewer natural resources will likely have fewer choices and different needs than Americans.

For example, people who live in remote rain forests depend on forest resources for most of their needs. These people may craft containers by weaving plant fibers together. They may make canoes by hollowing out tree trunks. Instead of being concerned about money, they might be more concerned about food.

## Resources and Wealth

The availability of natural resources affects countries' economies as well. For example, the many natural resources available in the United States have helped it become one of the world's wealthiest countries. In contrast, countries with few natural resources often have weak economies.

Some countries have one or two valuable resources but few others. For example, Saudi Arabia is rich in oil but lacks water for growing food. As a result, Saudi Arabia must use its oil profits to import food.

**READING CHECK** **Identifying Cause and Effect** How can having few natural resources affect life and wealth in a region or country?

**SUMMARY AND PREVIEW** You can see that Earth's natural resources have many uses. Important natural resources include air, water, soils, forests, fuels, and minerals. In the next chapter you will read about the world's people and cultures.

## Products from Petroleum

This Ohio family shows some common products made from petroleum, or oil.

**ANALYZING VISUALS** What petroleum-based products can you identify in this photo?

## Section 4 Assessment

### Reviewing Ideas, Terms, and Places

1. **a. Define** What are **renewable resources** and **nonrenewable resources**?
   **b. Explain** Why is it important for people to manage Earth's natural resources?
   **c. Develop** What are some things you can do to help manage and conserve natural resources?
2. **a. Define** What are **fossil fuels**, and why are they significant?
   **b. Summarize** What are three examples of renewable energy resources?
   **c. Predict** How do you think life might change as we begin to run out of petroleum?
3. **a. Recall** What are the main types of mineral resources?
   **b. Analyze** What are some products that we get from mineral resources?

4. **a. Describe** How do resources affect people?
   **b. Make Inferences** How might a country with only one valuable resource develop its economy?

### Critical Thinking

5. **Categorizing** Draw a chart like this one. Use your notes to identify and evaluate each energy resource.

| | Fossil Fuels | Renewable Energy | Nuclear Energy |
|---|---|---|---|
| Pros | Pros | Pros | Pros |
| Cons | Cons | Cons | Cons |

### FOCUS ON VIEWING

6. **Noting Details about Natural Resources** What natural resources does the place you chose have? Note ways to refer to some of these resources (or the lack of them) in your weather report.

# from
# The River

## by Gary Paulsen

**About the Reading** *In the novel* The River, *a teenager named Brian has already proven his ability to survive in the wilderness. On this trip into the wilderness, he is accompanied by a man who wants to learn survival skills from him. With only a pocket knife and a transistor radio as tools, the two men meet challenges that at first appear too difficult to overcome. In the following passage from the novel, the men have just arrived in the wilderness.*

**AS YOU READ** Notice how Brian uses his senses to predict how some natural resources can help him survive.

He didn't just hear birds singing, not just a background sound of birds, but each bird. He listened to each bird. Located it, knew where it was by the sound, listened for the sound of alarm. He didn't just see clouds, but light clouds, scout clouds that came before the heavier clouds that could mean rain and maybe wind. ❶ The clouds were coming out of the northwest, and that meant that weather would come with them. Not could, but would. There would be rain. Tonight, late, there would be rain.

His eyes swept the clearing. . . There was a stump there that probably held grubs; hardwood there for a bow, and willows there for arrows; a game trail, . . . porcupines, raccoons, bear, wolves, moose, skunk would be moving on the trail and into the clearing. ❷ He flared his nostrils, smelled the air, pulled the air along the sides of his tongue in a hissing sound and tasted it, but there was nothing. Just summer smells. The tang of pines, soft air, some mustiness from rotting vegetation. No animals. ❸

**GUIDED READING**

**WORD HELP**

**grubs** soft, thick wormlike forms of insects
**flared** widened
**tang** sharp, biting smell
**mustiness** damp, stale smell

❶ Scout clouds are clouds that appear to be searching for other clouds to come.

❷ Brian notes that the stump likely holds grubs. He can eat the grubs for food.

❸ Brian does not smell any animals nearby.

*Why might Brian want to know if animals are around?*

## Connecting Literature to Geography

1. **Predicting** Brian observes the clouds and can tell from their appearance and movement that rain is coming. What might be some ways that he can use his environment to prepare for the rain?

2. **Finding Main Ideas** The environment provides many resources that we can use, from wood to plants to animals. What resources does Brian identify around him that he can use to survive?

# Analyzing a Bar Graph

## Learn

Bar graphs are drawings that use bars to show data in a clear, visual format. Use these guidelines to analyze bar graphs.

- Read the title to identify the graph's subject and purpose.

- Read the graph's other labels. Note what the graph is measuring and the units of measurement being used. For example, this bar graph is measuring precipitation by climate. The unit of measurement is inches. If the graph uses colors, note their purpose.

- Analyze and compare the data. As you do, note any increases or decreases and look for trends or changes over time.

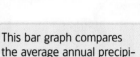

This bar graph compares the average annual precipitation of six climate regions.

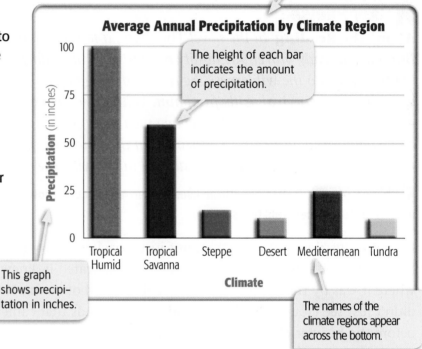

**Average Annual Precipitation by Climate Region**

The height of each bar indicates the amount of precipitation.

This graph shows precipitation in inches.

The names of the climate regions appear across the bottom.

## Practice

❶ On the bar graph above, which climate region has the highest average annual precipitation?

❷ Which two climate regions have about the same amount?

❸ Which climate region receives an average of between 50 and 75 inches of precipitation each year?

## Apply

Examine the World Energy Production Today bar graph in Section 4. Then use the graph to answer the following questions.

**1.** Which region produces the most oil?

**2.** Which three regions produce little or no nuclear power?

**3.** Based on the graph, what type of energy resource do most Asian countries likely use?

# Chapter Review

**Geography's Impact**
video series
Review the video to answer the closing question:
*How are climate and weather different, and how does the influence they have differ?*

## Visual Summary

*Use the visual summary below to help you review the main ideas of the chapter.*

QUICK FACTS

Earth has a wide range of climates, which we identify by precipitation, temperature, and native plant life.

Plants, animals, and the environment are interconnected and affect one another in many ways.

Earth's valuable natural resources, such as air, water, forests, and minerals, have many uses and affect people's lives.

## Reviewing Vocabulary, Terms, and Places

*Unscramble each group of letters below to spell a term that matches the given definition.*

1. **usumh**—decayed plant or animal matter
2. **tahrewe**—changes or conditions in the air at a certain time and place
3. **netorietfaosr**—planting trees where forests were
4. **neticxt**—completely died out
5. **estpep**—semidry grassland or prairie
6. **sifeticatorined**—spread of desertlike conditions
7. **laitemc**—an area's weather patterns over a long period of time
8. **arsmofrtpe**—permanently frozen layers of soil
9. **snonomo**—winds that change direction with the seasons and create wet and dry periods
10. **vansanas**—areas of tall grasses and scattered shrubs and trees

## Comprehension and Critical Thinking

**SECTION 1** (Pages 50–54)

11. **a. Identify** What five factors affect climate?

    **b. Analyze** Is average annual precipitation an example of weather or climate?

    **c. Evaluate** Of the five factors that affect climate, which one do you think is the most important? Why?

**SECTION 2** (Pages 55–61)

12. **a. Recall** What are the five major climate zones?

    **b. Explain** How does latitude relate to climate?

    **c. Elaborate** Why do you think the study of climate is important in geography?

**SECTION 3** (Pages 62–65)

13. **a. Define** What is an ecosystem, and why does it exist in a fragile balance?

## SECTION 3 (continued)

**b. Explain** Why are plants an important part of the environment?

**c. Predict** What might be some results of desertification?

## SECTION 4 (Pages 68–72)

**14. a. Define** What are minerals?

**b. Contrast** How do nonrenewable resources and renewable resources differ?

**c. Elaborate** How might a scarcity of natural resources affect life in a region?

## Using the Internet 21ST CENTURY

**15. Activity: Experiencing Extremes** Could you live in a place where for part of the year it is always dark and temperatures plummet to –104°F? What if you had to live in a place where it is always wet and stormy? Through your online textbook, learn more about some of the world's extreme climates. Then create a poster that describes some of those climates and the people, animals, and plants that live in them.

 hmhsocialstudies.com

## Social Studies Skills

**Analyzing a Bar Graph** *Examine the bar graph titled Average Annual Precipitation by Climate Region in the Social Studies Skills for this chapter. Then use the bar graph to answer the following questions.*

**16.** Which climate region receives an average of 100 inches of precipitation a year?

**17.** Which climate region receives an average of 25 inches of precipitation a year?

**18.** What is the difference in average annual precipitation between tropical humid climates and Mediterranean climates?

## Map Activity 21ST CENTURY

**19. Prevailing Winds** On a separate sheet of paper, match the letters on the map with their correct labels.

| equator | South Pole | westerly |
| North Pole | trade wind | |

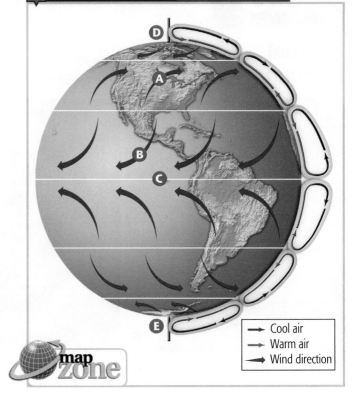

hmhsocialstudies.com **INTERACTIVE MAP**

map zone

→ Cool air
→ Warm air
→ Wind direction

**Understanding Cause and Effect** *Answer the following questions about causes and effects.*

**20.** What causes desertification?

**21.** What are the effects of abundant natural resources on a country's economy?

**22. Presenting and Viewing a Weather Report** Select a place and a season to write a weather report about. Describe the weather and predict upcoming weather. Present your report to your class. Use a professional, friendly tone of voice and make frequent eye contact with your audience. Then view your classmates' weather reports. Be prepared to give feedback on the content and their presentation techniques.

# Standardized Test Prep

*DIRECTIONS: Read questions 1 through 7 and write the letter of the best response. Then read question 8 and write your own well-constructed response.*

**1** The cold winds that flow away from the North and South poles are the

A doldrums.

B polar easterlies.

C trade winds.

D westerlies.

**2** Which climate zone occurs only in the upper latitudes?

A highland

B temperate

C tropical

D polar

**3** Where are the most diverse habitats on Earth found?

A steppe

B tropical rain forest

C tropical savanna

D tundra

**4** What is the cleanest burning fossil fuel?

A coal

B natural gas

C oil

D petroleum

**5** Which renewable energy source uses the heat of Earth's interior to generate power?

A geothermal energy

B hydroelectric energy

C nuclear energy

D solar energy

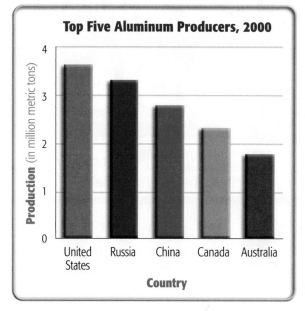

Top Five Aluminum Producers, 2000

**6** Based on the graph above, which country produced about 2.8 million tons of aluminum in 2000?

A Australia

B China

C Russia

D United States

**7** Which of the following form over tropical waters and are Earth's largest and most destructive storms?

A blizzards

B hurricanes

C thunderstorms

D tornadoes

**8** **Extended Response** Forces such as the sun, latitude, wind, and water shape climate. Examine the World Climate Regions map in Section 2. Describe two climate patterns that you see on the map and explain how various forces combine to create the two patterns.

# The World's People

**Essential Question** What concepts help geographers understand the world's people?

## What You Will Learn...

In this chapter you will learn what culture is and how it changes over time. You will also learn about population, different types of governments and economic systems, and globalization.

### FOCUS ON READING AND WRITING

**Understanding Main Ideas** A main idea is the central idea around which a paragraph or passage is organized. As you read, ask yourself what each paragraph is about. Look for a sentence or two that summarizes the main point of the entire paragraph. **See the lesson, Understanding Main Ideas, on page 519.**

**Creating a Poster** Think of some great posters you have seen at the movies, in bus stations, or in the halls of your school. They likely all had a colorful image that captured your attention and a few words that explained the main idea. Read this chapter about the world's people. Then create a poster that includes words and images that summarize the chapter's main ideas.

**Culture** Thousands of different cultures make up our world. Clothing, language, and music are just some parts of culture.

ANALYSIS
**SKILL** **ANALYZING VISUALS**

Many of the world's people come together every four years to compete in the Olympics.

**What indicates that some of the people in this photo are from different parts of the world?**

**Population** Geographers study human populations like this one in India to learn where and why people live in certain places.

**Global Connections** Technology allows people in remote places around the world to communicate.

# Culture

## If YOU lived there...

You live in New York City, and your young cousin from out of state has come to visit. As you take her on a tour of the city, you point out the different cultural neighborhoods, like Chinatown, Little Italy, Spanish Harlem, and Koreatown. Your cousin isn't quite sure what culture means or why these neighborhoods are so different.

**How can you explain what culture is?**

## What You Will Learn...

### Main Ideas

1. Culture is the set of beliefs, goals, and practices that a group of people share.
2. The world includes many different culture groups.
3. New ideas and events lead to changes in culture.

### The Big Idea

Culture, a group's shared practices and beliefs, differs from group to group and changes over time.

### Key Terms

culture, *p. 80*
culture trait, *p. 81*
culture region, *p. 82*
ethnic group, *p. 83*
cultural diversity, *p. 83*
cultural diffusion, *p. 85*

hmhsocialstudies.com
TAKING NOTES

Use the graphic organizer online to take notes on culture.

**BUILDING BACKGROUND** For hundreds of years, immigrants from around the world have moved to the United States to make a new home here. They have brought with them all the things that make up culture—language, religion, beliefs, traditions, and more. As a result, the United States has one of the most diverse cultures in the world.

## What Is Culture?

If you traveled around the world, you would experience many different sights and sounds. You would probably hear unique music, eat a variety of foods, listen to different languages, see distinctive landscapes, and learn new customs. You would see and take part in the variety of cultures that exist in our world.

### A Way of Life

What exactly is culture? **Culture** is the set of beliefs, values, and practices that a group of people has in common. Culture includes many aspects of life, such as language and religion, that we may share with people around us. Everything in your day-to-day life is part of your culture, from the clothes you wear to the music you hear to the foods you eat.

On your world travels, you might notice that all societies share certain cultural features. All people have some kind of government, educate their children in some way, and create some type of art or music. However, not all societies practice their culture in the same way. For example, in Japan the school year begins in the spring, and students wear school uniforms. In the United States, however, the school year begins in the late

## Culture Traits

These students in Japan and Kenya have some culture traits in common, like eating lunch at school. Other culture traits are different.

**ANALYZING VISUALS** What culture traits do these students share? Which are different?

summer, and most schools do not require uniforms. Differences like these are what make each culture unique.

### Culture Traits

Cultural features like starting the school year in the spring or wearing uniforms are types of culture traits. A **culture trait** is an activity or behavior in which people often take part. The language you speak and the sports you play are some of your culture traits. Sometimes a culture trait is shared by people around the world. For example, all around the globe people participate in the game of soccer. In places as different as Germany, Nigeria, and Saudi Arabia, many people enjoy playing and watching soccer.

While some culture traits are shared around the world, others change from place to place. One example of this is how people around the world eat. In China most people use chopsticks to eat their food. In Europe, however, people use forks and spoons. In Ethiopia, many people use bread or their fingers to scoop their food.

### Development of Culture

How do cultures develop? Culture traits are often learned or passed down from one generation to the next. Most culture traits develop within families as traditions, foods, or holiday customs are handed down over the years. Laws and moral codes are also passed down within societies. Many laws in the United States, for example, can be traced back to England in the 1600s and were brought by colonists to America.

Cultures also develop as people learn new culture traits. Immigrants who move to a new country, for example, might learn to speak the language or eat the foods of their adopted country.

Other factors, such as history and the environment, also affect how cultures develop. For example, historical events changed the language and religion of much of Central and South America. In the 1500s, when the Spanish conquered the region, they introduced their language and Roman Catholic faith. The environment in which we live can also shape culture.

**FOCUS ON READING**
What is the main idea of this paragraph?

For example, the desert environment of Africa's Sahara influences the way people who live there earn a living. Rather than grow crops, they herd animals that have adapted to the harsh environment. As you can see, history and the environment affect how cultures develop.

**READING CHECK** Finding Main Ideas What practices and customs make up culture?

## Culture Groups

Earth is home to thousands of different cultures. People who share similar culture traits are members of the same culture group. Culture groups can be based on a variety of factors, such as age, language, or religion. American teenagers, for example, can be said to form a culture group based on location and age. They share similar tastes in music, clothing, and sports.

### Culture Regions

When we refer to culture groups, we are speaking of people who share a common culture. At other times, however, we need to refer to the area, or region, where the culture group is found. A **culture region** is an area in which people have many shared culture traits.

In a specific culture region, people share certain culture traits, such as religious beliefs, language, or lifestyle. One well-known culture region is the Arab world. As you can see at right, an Arab culture region spreads across Southwest Asia and North Africa. In this region, most people write and speak Arabic and are Muslim. They also share other traits, such as foods, music, styles of clothing, and architecture.

Occasionally, a single culture region dominates an entire country. In Japan, for example, one primary culture dominates the country. Nearly everyone in Japan speaks the same language and follows the same practices. Many Japanese bow to their elders as a sign of respect and remove their shoes when they enter a home.

A single country may also include more than one culture region within its borders. Mexico is one of many countries that is made up of different culture regions. People in northern Mexico and southern Mexico, for example, have different culture traits. The culture of northern Mexico tends to be more modern, while traditional culture remains strong in southern Mexico.

A culture region may also stretch across country borders. As you have already learned, an Arab culture region dominates much of Southwest Asia and North Africa. Another example is the Kurdish culture region, home to the Kurds, a people that live throughout Turkey, Iran, and Iraq.

## Arab Culture Region

Culture regions are based on shared culture traits. Southwest Asia and North Africa make up an Arab culture region based on ethnic heritage, a common language, and religion. Most people in this region are Arab, speak and write Arabic, and practice Islam.

## Cultural Diversity

As you just learned, countries may contain several culture regions within their borders. Often, these culture regions are based on ethnic groups. An **ethnic group** is a group of people who share a common culture and ancestry. Members of ethnic groups often share certain culture traits such as religion, language, and even special foods.

Some countries are home to a variety of ethnic groups. For example, more than 100 different ethnic groups live in the East African country of Tanzania. Countries with many ethnic groups are culturally diverse. **Cultural diversity** is the state of having a variety of cultures in the same area. While cultural diversity creates an interesting mix of ideas, behaviors, and practices, it can also lead to conflict.

In some countries, ethnic groups have been in conflict. In Canada, for example, some French Canadians want to separate from the rest of Canada to preserve their language and culture. In the 1990s ethnic conflict in the African country of Rwanda led to extreme violence and bloodshed.

Although ethnic groups have clashed in some culturally diverse countries, they have cooperated in others. In the United States, for example, many different ethnic groups live side by side. Cities and towns often celebrate their ethnic heritage with festivals and parades, like the Saint Patrick's Day Parade in Boston or Philadelphia's Puerto Rican Festival.

**READING CHECK** **Making Inferences** Why might cultural diversity cause conflict?

Many people share Arab culture traits. An Omani boy, above, and Palestinian girls, at left, share the same language and religion.

**ANALYZING VISUALS** What culture traits do you see in the photos?

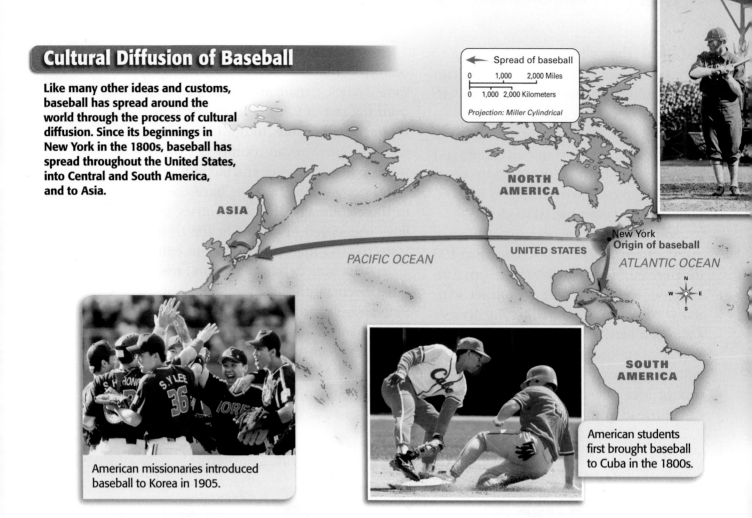

## Cultural Diffusion of Baseball

Like many other ideas and customs, baseball has spread around the world through the process of cultural diffusion. Since its beginnings in New York in the 1800s, baseball has spread throughout the United States, into Central and South America, and to Asia.

Spread of baseball

0    1,000    2,000 Miles

0   1,000  2,000 Kilometers

Projection: Miller Cylindrical

NORTH AMERICA

ASIA

PACIFIC OCEAN

UNITED STATES

New York
Origin of baseball

ATLANTIC OCEAN

SOUTH AMERICA

American missionaries introduced baseball to Korea in 1905.

American students first brought baseball to Cuba in the 1800s.

## Changes in Culture

You've read books or seen movies set in the time of the Civil War or in the Wild West of the late 1800s. Think about how our culture has changed since then. Clothing, food, music—all have changed drastically. When we study cultural change, we try to find out what caused the changes and how those changes spread from place to place.

### How Cultures Change

Cultures change constantly. Some changes happen rapidly, while others take many years. What causes cultures to change? **Innovation** and contact with other people are two key causes of cultural change.

New ideas often bring about cultural changes. For example, when Alexander Graham Bell invented the telephone, it changed how people communicate with each other. Other innovations, such as motion pictures, changed how people spend their free time. More recently, the creation of the Internet dramatically altered the way people find information, communicate, and shop.

Cultures also change as societies come into contact with each other. For example, when the Spanish arrived in the Americas, they introduced firearms and horses to the region, changing the lifestyle of some Native American groups. At the same time, the Spaniards learned about new foods like potatoes and chocolate. These foods then became an important part of Europeans' diet. The Chinese had a similar influence on Korea and Japan, where they introduced Buddhism and written language.

ACADEMIC VOCABULARY

**innovation**
a new idea or way of doing something

Organized baseball began in New York around 1845 and quickly spread around the world.

**ANALYSIS SKILL** **ANALYZING VISUALS**

Where did baseball begin, and to what parts of the world did it eventually spread?

## How Ideas Spread

You have probably noticed that a new slang word might spread from teenager to teenager and state to state. In the same way, clothing styles from New York or Paris might become popular all over the world. More serious cultural traits spread as well. Religious beliefs or ideas about government may spread from place to place. The spread of culture traits from one region to another is called **cultural diffusion**.

Cultural diffusion often occurs when people move from one place to another. For example, when Europeans settled in the Americas, they brought their culture along with them. As a result, English, French, Spanish, and Portuguese are all spoken in the Americas. American culture also spread as pioneers moved west, taking with them their form of government, religious beliefs, and customs.

Cultural diffusion also takes place as new ideas spread from place to place. As you can see on the map above, the game of baseball first began in New York, then spread throughout the United States. As more and more people learned the game, it spread even faster and farther. Baseball eventually spread around the world. Wearing blue jeans became part of our culture in a similar way. Blue jeans originated in the American West in the mid-1800s. They gradually became popular all over the country and the world.

**READING CHECK** **Finding Main Ideas** How do cultures change over time?

**SUMMARY AND PREVIEW** In this section you learned about the role that culture plays in our lives and how our cultures change. Next, you will learn about human populations and how we keep track of Earth's changing population.

## Section 1 Assessment

hmhsocialstudies.com
ONLINE QUIZ

### Reviewing Ideas, Terms, and Places

1. **a. Define** What is **culture**?
   **b. Analyze** What influences the development of culture?
   **c. Elaborate** How might the world be different if we all shared the same culture?
2. **a. Identify** What are the different types of **culture regions**?
   **b. Analyze** How does **cultural diversity** affect societies?
3. **a. Describe** How does **cultural diffusion** take place?
   **b. Make Inferences** How can the spread of new ideas lead to cultural change?
   **c. Evaluate** Do you think that cultural diffusion has a positive or a negative effect? Explain your answer.

### Critical Thinking

4. **Finding Main Ideas** Using your notes and a chart like the one here, explain the main idea of each aspect of culture in your own words.

| Culture Traits | Culture Groups | Cultural Change |
|---|---|---|
|  |  |  |

### FOCUS ON WRITING

5. **Writing about Culture** What key words about culture can you include on your poster? What images might you include? Jot down your ideas in your notebook.

# Population

## If YOU lived there...

You live in Mexico City, one of the largest and most crowded cities in the world. You realize just how crowded it is whenever you ride the subway at rush hour! You love the excitement of living in a big city. There is always something interesting to do. At the same time, the city has a lot of crime. Heavy traffic pollutes the air.

**What do you like and dislike about living in a large city?**

## Population Patterns

How many people live in your community? Do you live in a small town, a huge city, or somewhere in between? Your community's **population**, or the total number of people in a given area, determines a great deal about the place in which you live. Population influences the variety of businesses, the types of transportation, and the number of schools in your community.

Because population has a huge impact on our lives, it is an important part of geography. Geographers who study human populations are particularly interested in patterns that emerge over time. They study such information as how many people live in an area, why people live where they do, and how populations change. Population patterns like these can tell us much about our world.

### Population Density

Some places on Earth are crowded with people. Others are almost empty. One statistic geographers use to examine populations is **population density**, a measure of the number of people living in an area. Population density is expressed as persons per square mile or square kilometer.

---

# World Population Density

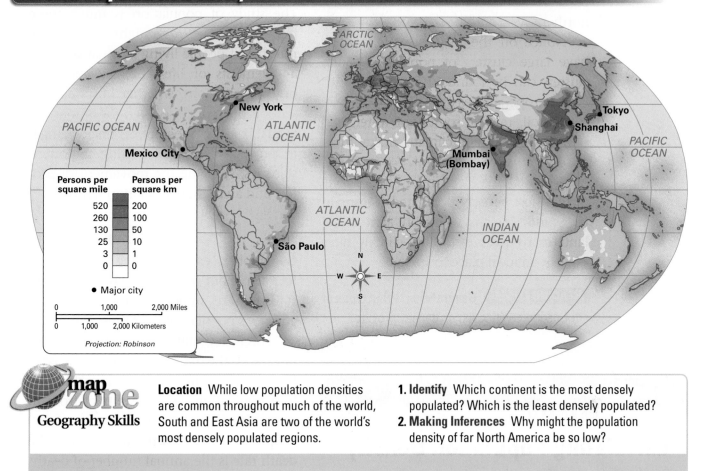

**map zone** **Geography Skills**

**Location** While low population densities are common throughout much of the world, South and East Asia are two of the world's most densely populated regions.

1. **Identify** Which continent is the most densely populated? Which is the least densely populated?
2. **Making Inferences** Why might the population density of far North America be so low?

---

Population density provides us with important information about a place. The more people per square mile in a region, the more crowded, or dense, it is. Japan, for example, has a population density of 880 people per square mile (340 per square km). That is a high population density. In many parts of Japan, people are crowded together in large cities, and space is very limited. In contrast, Australia has a very low population density. Only 6 people per square mile (2 per square km) live there. Australia has many wide-open spaces with very few people.

How do you think population density affects life in a particular place? In places with high population densities, the land is often expensive, roads are crowded, and buildings tend to be taller. On the other hand, places with low population densities tend to have more open spaces, less traffic, and more available land.

## Where People Live

Can you tell where most of the world's people live by examining the population density map above? The reds and purples on the map indicate areas of very high population density, while the light yellow areas indicate sparse populations. When an area is thinly populated, it is often because the land does not provide a very good life. These areas may have rugged mountains or harsh deserts where people cannot grow crops. Some areas may be frozen all year long, making survival there very difficult.

↗ hmhsocialstudies.com
**ANIMATED GEOGRAPHY**
Earth at Night

For these reasons, very few people live in parts of far North America, Greenland, northern Asia, and Australia.

Notice on the map that some areas have large clusters of population. Such clusters can be found in East and South Asia, Europe, and eastern North America. Fertile soil, reliable sources of water, and a good agricultural climate make these good regions for settlement. For example, the North China Plain in East Asia is one of the most densely populated regions in the world. The area's plentiful agricultural land, many rivers, and mild climate have made it an ideal place to settle.

**READING CHECK** **Generalizing** What types of information can population density provide?

## CONNECTING TO Math

$-2x(x^2-2x+$

# Calculating Population Density

Population density measures the number of people living in an area. To calculate population density, divide a place's total population by its area in square miles (or square kilometers). For example, if your city has a population of 100,000 people and an area of 100 square miles, you would divide 100,000 by 100. This would give you a population density of 1,000 people per square mile ( 100,000 ÷ 100 = 1,000 ).

**Analyzing** If a city had a population of 615,000 and a total land area of 250 square miles, what would its population density be?

| City | Population | Total Area (square miles) | Population Density (people per square mile) |
|---|---|---|---|
| Adelaide, Australia | 1,145,000 | 336 | 3,408 |
| Lima, Peru | 8,012,000 | 1,029 | 7,786 |
| Nairobi, Kenya | 3,010,000 | 266 | 11,316 |

$6+x-54÷102=9y$ $8+x^2-33×157+x^2-ab÷102=8$

# Population Change

The study of population is much more important than you might realize. The number of people living in an area affects all elements of life—the availability of housing and jobs, whether hospitals and schools open or close, even the amount of available food. Geographers track changes in populations by examining important statistics, studying the movement of people, and analyzing population trends.

### Tracking Population Changes

Geographers examine three key statistics to learn about population changes. These statistics are important for studying a country's population over time.

Three key statistics—birthrate, death rate, and the rate of natural increase—track changes in population. Births add to a population. Deaths subtract from it. The annual number of births per 1,000 people is called the **birthrate**. Similarly, the death rate is the annual number of deaths per 1,000 people. The birthrate minus the death rate equals the percentage of natural increase, or the rate at which a population is changing. For example, Denmark has a rate of natural increase of 0.05%. This means it has slightly more births than deaths and a very slight population increase.

Population growth rates differ from one place to another. In some countries, populations are growing very slowly or even shrinking. Many countries in Europe and North America have very low rates of natural increase. In Russia, for example, the birthrate is about 10.8 and the death rate is 16.1. The result is a negative rate of natural increase and a shrinking population.

In most countries around the world, however, populations are growing. Mali, for example, has a rate of natural increase of about 3.3 percent. While that may sound

## Irish Migration

**Irish Migration to the United States, 1845–1855**

Source: *Historical Statistics of the United States*

The failure of Ireland's most important food crop, the potato, caused widespread starvation. Disease and high food prices forced many Irish to flee to America in search of a better life.

**ANALYZING GRAPHS** In what year did Irish migration to the United States peak?

small, it means that Mali's population is expected to double in only 21 years! High population growth rates can pose some challenges, as governments try to provide enough jobs, education, and medical care for their rapidly growing populations.

## Migration

A common cause of population change is migration. **Migration** is the process of moving from one place to live in another. As one country loses citizens as a result of migration, its population can decline. At the same time, another country may gain population as people settle there.

People migrate for many reasons. Some factors push people to leave their country, while other factors pull, or attract, people to new countries. Warfare, a lack of jobs, or a lack of good farmland are common push factors. For example, during the Irish potato famine of the mid-1800s, poverty and disease forced some 1.5 million people to leave Ireland. Opportunities for a better life often pull people to new countries. For example, in the 1800s and early 1900s thousands of British citizens migrated to Australia in search of cheap land.

## World Population Trends

In the last 200 years Earth's population has exploded. For thousands of years world population growth was low and relatively steady. About 2,000 years ago, the world had some 300 million people. By 1800 there were almost 1 billion people. Since 1800, better health care and improved food production have supported tremendous population growth. In 1999 the world's population passed 6 billion people.

Population trends are an important part of the study of the world's people. Two important population trends are clear today. The first trend indicates that the population growth in some of the more industrialized nations has begun to slow.

**FOCUS ON READING**
What is the main idea of this paragraph? What facts are used to support that idea?

# World Population Growth

Advances in food production and health care have dramatically lowered death rates. As a result, the global population has seen incredible growth over the last 200 years.

**ANALYZING GRAPHS** By how much did the world's population increase between 1800 and 2000?

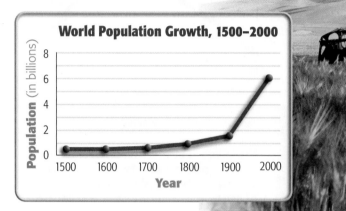

**World Population Growth, 1500–2000**

Source: *Atlas of World Population History*

For example, Germany and France have low rates of natural increase. A second trend indicates that less industrialized countries, like Nigeria and Bangladesh, often have high growth rates. These trends affect a country's workforce and government aid.

**READING CHECK** **Summarizing** What population statistics do geographers study? Why?

**SUMMARY AND PREVIEW** In this section you have learned where people live, how crowded places are, and how population affects our world. Geographers study past and present population patterns in order to plan for the future. In the next section, you will learn how governments and economies affect people on Earth.

## Section 2 Assessment

### Reviewing Ideas, Terms, and Places

1. **a. Identify** What regions of the world have the highest levels of **population density**?
   **b. Draw Conclusions** What information can be learned by studying population density?
   **c. Evaluate** Would you prefer to live in a region with a dense or a sparse population? Why?
2. **a. Describe** What is natural increase? What can it tell us about a country?
   **b. Analyze** What effect does **migration** have on human populations?
   **c. Predict** What patterns do you think world population might have in the future?

### Critical Thinking

3. **Summarizing** Draw a graphic organizer like the one here. Use your notes to write a sentence that summarizes each aspect of the study of population.

   Population Patterns

   Population Change

### FOCUS ON WRITING

4. **Discussing Population** What effect does population have on our world? Write down some words and phrases that you might use on your poster to explain the importance of population.

# Government and Economy

## If YOU were there...

You live in Raleigh, North Carolina. Your class at school is planning a presentation about life in the United States for a group of visitors from Japan. Your teacher wants you to discuss government and economics in the United States. As you prepare for your speech, you wonder what you should say.

**How do government and economics affect your life?**

> **BUILDING BACKGROUND** Although you probably don't think about them every day, your country's government and economy have a big influence on your life. That is true in every country in every part of the world. Governments and economic systems affect everything from a person's rights to the type of job he or she has.

## Governments of the World

Can you imagine what life would be like if there were no rules? Without ways to establish order and ensure justice, life would be chaotic. That explains why societies have governments. Our governments make and enforce laws, regulate business and trade, and provide aid to people. Governments help shape the culture and economy of a country as well as the daily lives of the people who live there.

### Democratic Governments

Many countries—including the United States, Canada, and Mexico—have democratic governments. A **democracy** is a form of government in which the people elect leaders and rule by majority. In most democratic countries, citizens are free to choose representatives to make and enforce the laws. Voters in the United States, for example, elect members of Congress, who make the laws, and the president, who enforces those laws.

# Governments of the World

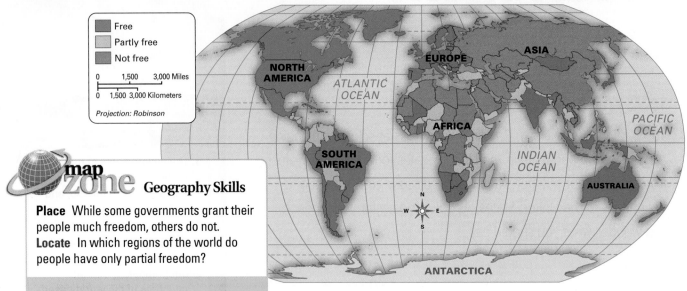

Free

Partly free

Not free

0    1,500    3,000 Miles

0   1,500   3,000 Kilometers

Projection: Robinson

NORTH AMERICA

ATLANTIC OCEAN

SOUTH AMERICA

EUROPE

ASIA

AFRICA

PACIFIC OCEAN

INDIAN OCEAN

AUSTRALIA

ANTARCTICA

**map zone Geography Skills**

**Place** While some governments grant their people much freedom, others do not.
**Locate** In which regions of the world do people have only partial freedom?

Source: *Freedom House*

**FOCUS ON READING**

Main ideas are not always stated in the first sentence. Which sentence in this paragraph states the main idea?

Most democratic governments in the world work to protect the freedoms and rights of their people, such as the freedom of speech and the freedom of religion. Other democracies, however, restrict the rights and freedoms of their people. Not all democratic governments in the world are completely free.

## Other Types of Government

Not all of the world's countries, however, are democracies. Several other types of government are found in the world today, including monarchies, dictatorships, and Communist states.

Monarchy is one of the oldest types of government in the world. A monarchy is ruled directly by a king or queen, the head of a royal family. Saudi Arabia is an example of a monarchy. The Saudi king has executive, legislative, and judicial powers. In some monarchies, power is in the hands of just one person. As a result, the people have little say in their government. Other monarchies, however, like Norway and Spain, use many democratic practices.

Dictatorship is a type of government in which a single, powerful ruler has total control. This leader, called a dictator, often rules by force. Iraq under Saddam Hussein was an example of a dictatorship. People who live under a dictatorship are not free. They have few rights and no say in their own government.

Yet another form of government is communism. **Communism** is a political system in which the government owns all property and dominates all aspects of life in a country. Leaders of most Communist governments are not elected by citizens. Rather, they are chosen by the Communist Party or by Communist leaders. In most Communist states, like Cuba and North Korea, the government strictly controls the country's economy and the daily life of its people. As a result, people in Communist states often have restricted rights and very little freedom.

**READING CHECK** **Supporting a Point of View** Why might people prefer to live in a democracy as opposed to a dictatorship?

# Economies of the World

One important function of government is to monitor a country's economy. The economy is a system that includes all of the activities that people and businesses do to earn a living. Countries today use a mix of different economic activities and systems.

## Economic Activity

Every country has some level of economic activity. Economic activities are ways in which people make a living. Some people farm, others manufacture goods, while still others provide services, such as driving a taxi or designing skyscrapers. Geographers divide these economic activities into four different levels.

The first level of economic activity, the primary industry, uses natural resources or raw materials. People in these industries earn a living by providing raw materials to others. Farming, fishing, and mining are all examples of primary industries. These activities provide raw materials such as grain, seafood, and coal for others to use.

Secondary industries perform the next step. They use natural resources or raw materials to manufacture other products. Manufacturing is the process in which raw materials are changed into finished goods. For example, people who make furniture might take wood and make products such as tables, chairs, or desks. Automobile manufacturers use steel, plastic, glass, and rubber to put together trucks and cars.

In the third level of activity, or tertiary industry, goods and services are exchanged. People in tertiary industries sell the furniture, automobiles, or other products made in secondary industries. Other people, like health care workers or mechanics, provide services rather than goods. Teachers, store clerks, doctors, and TV personalities are all engaged in this level of economic activity.

## Economic Activity

### Primary Industry

Primary industries use natural resources to make money. Here a farmer sells milk from dairy cows to earn a living.

### Secondary Industry

Secondary economic activities use raw materials to produce or manufacture something new. In this case, the milk from dairy cows is used to make cheese.

### Tertiary Industry

Tertiary economic activities provide services to people and businesses. This grocer selling cheese in a market is involved in a tertiary activity.

### Quaternary Industry

Quaternary industries process and distribute information. Skilled workers research and gather information. Here, inspectors examine and test the quality of cheese.

The highest level of economic activity, quaternary industry, involves the research and distribution of information. People making a living at this level work with information rather than goods, and often have specialized knowledge and skills. Architects, lawyers, and scientists all work in quaternary industries.

## Economic Systems

Just as economic activities are organized into different types, so are our economic systems. Economic systems can be divided into three types: traditional, market, and command. Most countries today use a mix of these economic systems.

One economic system is a **traditional** economy, a system in which people grow their own food and make their own goods. Trade may take place through barter, or the exchange of goods without the use of money. Rural and remote communities often have a mostly traditional economy.

ACADEMIC
VOCABULARY
**traditional**
customary,
time-honored

The most common economic system used around the world today is a market economy. A **market economy** is a system based on private ownership, free trade, and competition. Individuals and businesses are free to buy and sell what they wish. Prices are determined by the supply and demand for goods. This is sometimes called capitalism. The United States is one of many countries that use this system.

A third system is a **command economy**, a system in which the central government makes all economic decisions. The government decides what goods to produce, how much to produce, and what prices will be. While no country has a purely command economy, the economies of North Korea and Cuba are close to it. The Communist governments of these nations own and control most businesses.

**READING CHECK** **Summarizing** What economic systems are used in the world today?

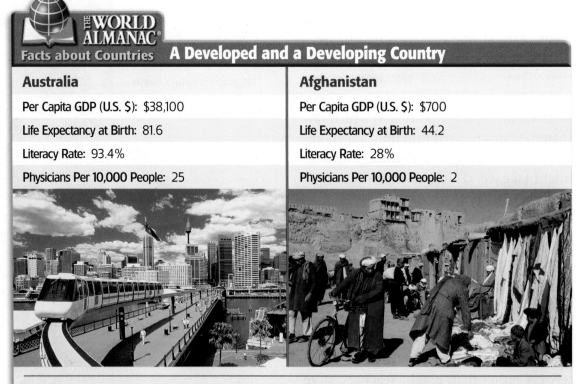

### THE WORLD ALMANAC
### Facts about Countries
### A Developed and a Developing Country

| Australia | Afghanistan |
|---|---|
| Per Capita GDP (U.S. $): $38,100 | Per Capita GDP (U.S. $): $700 |
| Life Expectancy at Birth: 81.6 | Life Expectancy at Birth: 44.2 |
| Literacy Rate: 93.4% | Literacy Rate: 28% |
| Physicians Per 10,000 People: 25 | Physicians Per 10,000 People: 2 |

**Contrasting** How does the quality of life in Afghanistan differ from that in Australia?

hmhsocialstudies.com

# Economic Development

Economic systems and activities affect a country's economic development, or the level of economic growth and quality of life. Geographers often group countries into two basic categories—developed and developing countries—based on their level of economic development.

## Economic Indicators

Geographers use economic indicators, or measures of a country's wealth, to decide if a country is developed or developing. One such measure is gross domestic product. **Gross domestic product (GDP)** is the value of all goods and services produced within a country in a single year. Another indicator is a country's per capita GDP, or the total GDP divided by the number of people in a country. As you can see in the chart, per capita GDP allows us to compare incomes among countries. Other indicators include the level of industrialization and overall quality of life. In other words, we look at the types of industries and technology a country has, in addition to its level of health care and education.

## Developed and Developing Countries

Many of the world's wealthiest and most powerful nations are **developed countries**, countries with strong economies and a high quality of life. Developed countries like Germany and the United States have a high per capita GDP and high levels of industrialization. Their health care and education systems are among the best in the world. Many people in developed countries have access to technology.

The world's poorer nations are known as **developing countries**, countries with less productive economies and a lower quality of life. Almost two-thirds of the people in the world live in developing countries. These developing countries have a lower per capita GDP than developed countries. Most of their citizens work in farming or other primary industries. Although these countries typically have large cities, much of their population still lives in rural areas. People in developing countries usually have less access to health care or technology. Guatemala, Nigeria, and Afghanistan are all developing countries.

**READING CHECK** **Analyzing** What factors separate developed and developing countries?

**SUMMARY AND PREVIEW** The world's countries have different governments, economies, and levels of development. Next, you will learn how people are linked in a global community.

## Section 3 Assessment

hmhsocialstudies.com
ONLINE QUIZ

### Reviewing Ideas, Terms, and Places

1. **a. Identify** What are some different types of government?
   **b. Elaborate** Under which type of government would you most want to live? Why?
2. **a. Describe** What are the levels of economic activity?
   **b. Evaluate** Which economic system do you think is best? Explain your answer.
3. **a. Define** What is **gross domestic product**?
   **b. Contrast** In what ways do **developed countries** differ from **developing countries**?

### Critical Thinking

4. **Categorizing** Draw a chart like the one here. Use the chart and your notes to

| Types of Government | Economic Systems | Economic Development |
|---|---|---|
|  |  |  |

identify the different governments, economies, and levels of economic development in the world today.

### FOCUS ON WRITING

5. **Thinking about Government and Economy** What kinds of images and words could you use to present the main ideas behind the world's governments and economies?

# Organizing Information

## Learn

Remembering new information is easier if you organize it clearly. As you read and study, try to organize what you are learning. One way to do this is to create a graphic organizer. Follow these steps to create a graphic organizer as you read.

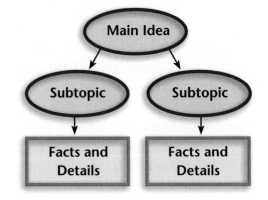

- Identify the main idea of the passage. Write the main idea in a circle at the top of your page.

- As you read, look for subtopics under the main idea. On your paper, draw a row of circles below the main idea, one for each subtopic. Write the subtopics in the circles.

- Below each subtopic, draw a big box. Look for facts and supporting details for each subtopic. List them in the box below the subtopic.

## Practice

Read the passage below carefully. Then use the graphic organizer above to organize the information from the passage.

> Cultures change slowly over time. New ideas and new people can often lead to cultural change.
>
> Cultures often change as new ideas are introduced to a society. New ways of doing things, new inventions, and even new beliefs can all change a culture. One example of this is the spread of computer technology. As people adopted computers, they learned a new language and new work habits.
>
> Cultures also change when new people introduce their culture traits to a society. For example, as immigrants settle in the United States, they add new culture traits, like food, music, and clothing, to American culture.

## Apply

Turn to Section 1 and read the passage titled Culture Regions. Draw a graphic organizer like the one above. Then follow the steps to organize the information you have read. The passage will have two or more subtopics. Add additional circles and rectangles for each additional subtopic you find.

# Global Connections

## If YOU lived there...

You live in Louisville, Kentucky, and you have never traveled out of the United States. However, when you got ready for school this morning, you put on a T-shirt made in Guatemala and jeans made in Malaysia. Your shoes came from China. You rode to school on a bus with parts manufactured in Mexico. At school, your class even took part in a discussion with students in Canada.

**What makes your global connections possible?**

> **BUILDING BACKGROUND** Trade and technology have turned the world into a "global village." People around the world wear clothes, eat foods, and use goods made in other countries. Global connections are bringing people around the world closer than ever before.

## Globalization

In just seconds an e-mail message sent by a teenager in India beams all the way to a friend in London. A band in Seattle releases a song that becomes popular in China. People from New York to Singapore respond to a crisis in Brazil. These are all examples of **globalization**, the process in which countries are increasingly linked to each other through culture and trade.

What caused globalization? Improvements in transportation and communication over the past 100 years have brought the world closer together. Airplanes, telecommunications, and the Internet allow us to communicate and travel the world with ease. As a result, global culture and trade have increased.

### Popular Culture

What might you have in common with a teenager in Japan? You probably have more in common than you think. You may use similar technology, wear similar clothes, and watch many of the same movies. You share the same global popular culture.

**What You Will Learn...**

**Main Ideas**

1. Globalization links the world's countries together through culture and trade.
2. The world community works together to solve global conflicts and crises.

**The Big Idea**

Fast, easy global connections have made cultural exchange, trade, and a cooperative world community possible.

**Key Terms**

globalization, *p. 97*
popular culture, *p. 98*
interdependence, *p. 99*
United Nations (UN), *p. 99*
humanitarian aid, *p. 100*

hmhsocialstudies.com
**TAKING NOTES**

Use the graphic organizer online to take notes on globalization and the world community.

More and more, people around the world are linked through popular culture. **Popular culture** refers to culture traits that are well known and widely accepted. Food, sports, music, and movies are all examples of our popular culture.

The United States has great influence on global popular culture. For example, American soft drinks are sold in almost every country in the world. Many popular American television shows are broadcast internationally. English has become the major global language. One-quarter of the world's people speak English. It has become the main language for international music, business, science, and education.

At the same time, the United States is influenced by global culture. Martial arts movies from Asia attract large audiences in the United States. Radio stations in the United States play music by African, Latin American, and European musicians. We even adopt many foreign words, like *sushi* and *plaza*, into English.

Close-up

# A Global Economy

The growth of the global economy has affected many businesses, especially the automobile industry. Automakers can now buy parts from countries all around the world, depending on where they can get the best price.

Many engines are man-ufactured in the United States and Canada.

Bumpers are often designed and produced in France, Germany, and the United States.

Tires come from a number of countries, including Mexico, South Korea, or Chile.

## Global Trade

Globalization not only links the world's people, but it also connects businesses and affects trade. For centuries, societies have traded with each other. Improvements in transportation and communication have made global trade quicker and easier. For example, a shoe retailer in Chicago can order the sneakers she needs on a Web site from a company in China. The order can be flown to Chicago the next day and sold to customers that afternoon.

Many cars feature windows manufactured in Venezuela or the United States.

Seats are sometimes assembled in Japan from covers sewn in Mexico.

**ANALYSIS SKILL** **ANALYZING VISUALS**

From what different countries do automotive parts often originate?

The expansion of global trade has increased interdependence among the world's countries. **Interdependence** is a relationship between countries in which they rely on one another for resources, goods, or services. Many companies in one country often rely on goods and services produced in another country. For example, automakers in Europe might purchase auto parts made in the United States or Japan. Consumers also rely on goods produced elsewhere. For example, American shoppers buy bananas from Ecuador and tomatoes from Mexico. Global trade gives us access to goods from around the world.

**READING CHECK** **Finding Main Ideas** How has globalization affected the world?

## A World Community

Some people call our world a global village. What do you think this means? Because of globalization, the world seems smaller. Places are more connected. What happens in one part of the world can affect the entire planet. Because of this, the world community works together to promote cooperation among countries in times of conflict and crisis.

The world community encourages cooperation by working to resolve global conflicts. From time to time, conflicts erupt among the countries of the world. Wars, trade disputes, and political disagreements can threaten the peace. Countries often join together to settle such conflicts. In 1945, for example, 51 nations created the United Nations. The **United Nations (UN)** is an organization of the world's countries that promotes peace and security around the globe.

The world community also promotes cooperation in times of crisis. A disaster may leave thousands of people in need.

**FOCUS ON READING**

What is the main idea of this paragraph? What facts are used to support that idea?

## HISTORIC DOCUMENT
# The Charter of the United Nations

*Created in 1945, the United Nations is an organization of the world's countries that works to solve global problems. The Charter of the United Nations outlines the goals of the UN, some of which are included here.*

> We the Peoples of the United Nations Determined ...
>
> to save succeeding generations from the scourge [terror] of war ...
>
> to practice tolerance and live together in peace with one another as good neighbors, and
>
> to unite our strength to maintain international peace and security, and
>
> to ensure ... that armed forces shall not be used, save [except] in the common interest, and
>
> to employ international machinery [systems] for the promotion of the economic and social advancement of all peoples,
>
> Have Resolved to Combine our Efforts to Accomplish these Aims.
>
> —*from the Charter of the United Nations*

**ANALYSIS SKILL** **ANALYZING PRIMARY SOURCES**

**What are some of the goals of the United Nations?**

Earthquakes, floods, and drought can cause crises around the world. Groups from many nations often come together to provide **humanitarian aid**, or assistance to people in distress.

Organizations representing countries around the globe work to help in times of crisis. For example, in 2004 a tsunami, or huge tidal wave, devastated parts of Southeast Asia. Many organizations, like the United Nations Children's Fund (UNICEF) and the International Red Cross, stepped in to provide humanitarian aid to the victims of the tsunami. Some groups lend aid to refugees, or people who have been forced to flee their homes. Groups like Doctors Without Borders give medical aid to those in need around the world.

**READING CHECK** **Analyzing** How has globalization promoted cooperation?

**SUMMARY** In this section you learned how globalization links the countries of the world through shared culture and trade. Globalization allows organizations around the world to work together. They often solve conflicts and provide humanitarian aid.

## Section 4 Assessment

hmhsocialstudies.com
ONLINE QUIZ

### Reviewing Ideas, Terms, and Places
1. **a. Describe** What is **globalization**?
   **b. Make Inferences** How has **popular culture** influenced countries around the world?
   **c. Evaluate** In your opinion, has globalization hurt or helped the people of the world?
2. **a. Define** What is **humanitarian aid**?
   **b. Draw Conclusions** How has globalization promoted cooperation among countries?
   **c. Predict** What types of problems might lead to international cooperation?

### Critical Thinking
3. **Identifying Cause and Effect** Use your notes and the graphic organizer at right to identify the effects that globalization has on our world.

Globalization → Effects / Effects / Effects

### FOCUS ON WRITING
4. **Writing about Global Connections** What aspects of globalization could you include in your poster? Jot down your ideas in your notebook.

# Chapter Review

**Geography's Impact**
**video series**
Review the video to answer the closing question:
*Why do you think some peoples must work to preserve their cultures in the modern world?*

## Visual Summary

*Use the visual summary below to help you review the main ideas of the chapter.*

QUICK FACTS

The world has many different cultures, or shared beliefs and practices.

The world's people practice different economic activities and systems.

Globalization brings people around the world closer than ever before.

## Reviewing Vocabulary, Terms, and Places

*Choose one word from each word pair to correctly complete each sentence below.*

1. Members of a/an _____ often share the same religion, traditions, and language. **(ethnic group/population)**

2. People in a _____ are free to buy and sell goods as they please. **(command economy/ market economy)**

3. Organizations like the International Red Cross provide _____ to people in need around the world. **(humanitarian aid/cultural diffusion)**

4. _____, the process of moving from one place to live in another, is a cause of population change. **(Population density/Migration)**

5. A country with a strong economy and a high standard of living is considered a _____. **(developed country/developing country)**

## Comprehension and Critical Thinking

**SECTION 1** *(Pages 80–85)*

6. **a. Describe** What is cultural diversity?

   **b. Analyze** What causes cultures to change over time?

   **c. Elaborate** Describe some of the culture traits practiced by people in your community.

**SECTION 2** *(Pages 86–90)*

7. **a. Describe** What does population density tell us about a place?

   **b. Draw Conclusions** Why do certain areas attract large populations?

   **c. Elaborate** Why do you think it is important for geographers to study population trends?

**SECTION 3** *(Pages 91–95)*

8. **a. Recall** What is a command economy?

**SECTION 3** (continued)

**b. Make Inferences** Why might developing countries have only primary and secondary economic activities?

**c. Evaluate** Do you think government is important in our everyday lives? Why or why not?

**SECTION 4** (Pages 97–100)

**9. a. Describe** How have connections among the world's countries improved?

**b. Analyze** What impact has globalization had on world trade and culture?

**c. Evaluate** What do you think has been the most important result of globalization? Why?

## Social Studies Skills

**10. Organizing Information** Practice organizing information by creating a graphic organizer for Section 3. Use the main ideas on the first page of the section for your large circles. Then write the subtopics under each main idea. Finally, identify supporting details for each subtopic.

## Using the Internet

**11. Activity: Writing a Report** Population changes have a huge impact on the world around us. Countries around the world must deal with shrinking populations, growing populations, and other population issues. Through your online textbook, explore the issues surrounding global population. Then imagine you have been asked to report on global population trends to the United Nations. Write a report in which you identify world population trends and their impact on the world today.

↗ hmhsocialstudies.com

## Map Activity

**Population Density** *Use the map to the right to answer the questions that follow.*

**12.** What letter on the map indicates the least crowded area?

**13.** What letter on the map indicates the most densely crowded area?

**14.** Which letter indicates a region with 260–520 people per square mile (100–200 people per square km)?

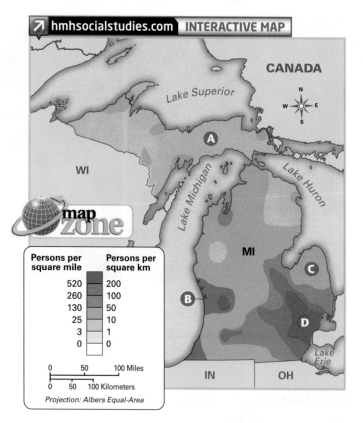

↗ hmhsocialstudies.com   **INTERACTIVE MAP**

| Persons per square mile | Persons per square km |
|---|---|
| 520 | 200 |
| 260 | 100 |
| 130 | 50 |
| 25 | 10 |
| 3 | 1 |
| 0 | 0 |

0    50    100 Miles
0    50   100 Kilometers
*Projection: Albers Equal-Area*

**FOCUS ON READING AND WRITING**

**Understanding Main Ideas** *Read the paragraph in question 15 below. Then, write out the main idea of the paragraph.*

**15.** The ancient Greeks were the first to practice democracy. Since then many countries have adopted democratic government. The United Kingdom, South Korea, and Ghana all practice democracy. Democracy is the most widely used government in the world today.

**16. Creating a Poster** Review your notes about the world's cultures, populations, governments, and economies. Then, select a topic for your poster. On large sheet of paper, write a title that identifies your topic. Illustrate your poster with images that support your topic. Write a short caption explaining each image.

# Standardized Test Prep

DIRECTIONS: Read questions 1 through 7 and write the letter of the best response. Then read question 8 and write your own well-constructed response.

**1** **Which of the following is *most likely* a culture trait?**

A religion

B population density

C interdependence

D cultural diffusion

**2** **What developments led to the rapid increase in world population in the last 200 years?**

A a decline in migration

B improvements in technology and communication

C a decrease in standard of living

D improvements in health care and agriculture

**3** **Which economic system is used in the United States?**

A market economy

B command economy

C traditional economy

D domestic economy

**4** **A government in which a single, powerful ruler exerts complete control is a**

A Communist state.

B democracy.

C dictatorship.

D republic.

**5** **Global connections have improved as a result of**

A population growth.

B cultural diversity.

C the spread of democratic government.

D improvements in technology.

## Developed and Developing Countries

| Country | Per Capita GDP (U.S. $) | Life Expectancy at Birth | TVs per 1,000 People |
|---|---|---|---|
| Cameroon | $2,400 | 53.0 | 34 |
| Singapore | $30,900 | 81.8 | 341 |
| Ukraine | $7,600 | 67.9 | 433 |
| Uruguay | $10,700 | 76.5 | 531 |

**6** **Which of the countries in the chart above is *most likely* a developed country?**

A Cameroon

B Singapore

C Ukraine

D Uruguay

**7** **Which of the following is an example of economic interdependence?**

A Cattle ranchers in Oklahoma sell beef to grocery stores in Maryland.

B Students in Germany use the Internet to communicate with scientists in Brazil.

C Construction companies in Canada build skyscrapers with steel imported from the United States.

D Immigrants from Russia settle in London.

**8** **Extended Response** Using the data in the chart above, write a paragraph in which you compare and contrast the standard of living in Ukraine and Singapore.

# Explaining a Process

**Assignment**
Write a paper explaining one of these topics:
- how water recycles on Earth
- how agriculture developed

**H**ow does soil renewal work? How do cultures change? Often the first question we ask about something is how it works or what process it follows. One way we can answer these questions is by writing an explanation.

## 1. Prewrite

### Choose a Process
- Choose one of the topics above to write about.
- Turn your topic into a big idea, or thesis. For example, your big idea might be "Water continually circulates from Earth's surface to the atmosphere and back."

> **TIP** **Organizing Information** Explanations should be in a logical order. You should arrange the steps in the process in chronological order, the order in which the steps take place.

### Gather and Organize Information
- Look for information about your topic in your textbook, in the library, or on the Internet.
- Start a plan to organize support for your big idea. For example, look for the individual steps of the water cycle.

## 2. Write

### Use a Writer's Framework

> **A Writer's Framework**
>
> **Introduction**
> - Start with an interesting fact or question.
> - Identify your big idea.
>
> **Body**
> - Create at least one paragraph for each point supporting the big idea. Add facts and details to explain each point.
> - Use chronological order or order of importance.
>
> **Conclusion**
> - Summarize your main points in your final paragraph.

## 3. Evaluate and Revise

### Review and Improve Your Paper
- Re-read your paper and make sure you have followed the framework.
- Make the changes needed to improve your paper.

### Evaluation Questions for an Explanation of a Process
1. Do you begin with an interesting fact or question?
2. Does your introduction identify your big idea? Does it provide any background information your readers might need?
3. Do you have at least one paragraph for each point you are using to support the big idea?
4. Do you include facts and details to explain and illustrate each point?
5. Do you use chronological order or order of importance to organize your main points?

## 4. Proofread and Publish

### Give Your Explanation the Finishing Touch
- Make sure you have capitalized the first word in every sentence.
- Check for punctuation at the end of every sentence.
- Think of a way to share your explanation.

## 5. Practice and Apply

Use the steps and strategies outlined in this workshop to write your explanation. Share your paper with others and find out whether the explanation makes sense to them.

# The Americas

## The Great Lakes

Five huge lakes in North America known as the Great Lakes make up the largest group of fresh water lakes on Earth.

## The Andes

Stretching along South America's western coast, the Andes are the longest mountain range in the world.

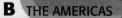

# The Americas

## The Amazon

In the heart of South America, the Amazon rain forest is home to millions of plant and animal species.

**Explore the Satellite Image**
Forests, mountains, and plains stretch from north to south across the Americas. How do you think the features you can see on this satellite image influence life in the Americas?

## The Satellite's Path

>44'56.08<

>>>>>>>>>665.00'87<

567.476.348

+799

+803

+966

+355

456.094.

## The Americas: Physical

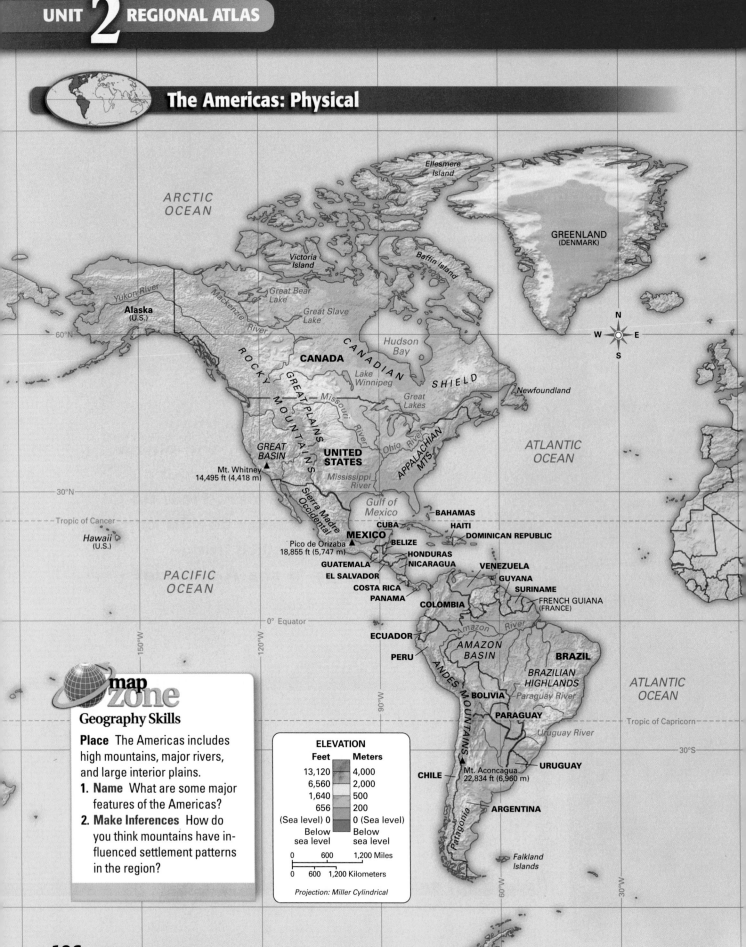

ARCTIC OCEAN

Ellesmere Island

GREENLAND (DENMARK)

Victoria Island

Baffin Island

Yukon River

Great Bear Lake

Mackenzie River

Great Slave Lake

Alaska (U.S.)

60°N

ROCKY MOUNTAINS

CANADA

CANADIAN SHIELD

Hudson Bay

Lake Winnipeg

Great Lakes

Newfoundland

GREAT PLAINS

Missouri River

GREAT BASIN

UNITED STATES

Ohio River

APPALACHIAN MTS.

ATLANTIC OCEAN

Mt. Whitney 14,495 ft (4,418 m)

Mississippi River

30°N

Tropic of Cancer

Sierra Madre Occidental

Gulf of Mexico

BAHAMAS

Hawaii (U.S.)

CUBA

HAITI

DOMINICAN REPUBLIC

MEXICO

Pico de Orizaba 18,855 ft (5,747 m)

BELIZE

HONDURAS

GUATEMALA

NICARAGUA

EL SALVADOR

VENEZUELA

GUYANA

SURINAME

PACIFIC OCEAN

COSTA RICA

PANAMA

COLOMBIA

FRENCH GUIANA (FRANCE)

0° Equator

ECUADOR

Amazon River

150°W

120°W

PERU

AMAZON BASIN

BRAZIL

BRAZILIAN HIGHLANDS

ATLANTIC OCEAN

ANDES MOUNTAINS

BOLIVIA

Paraguay River

PARAGUAY

Uruguay River

Tropic of Capricorn

30°S

CHILE

Mt. Aconcagua 22,834 ft (6,960 m)

URUGUAY

ARGENTINA

Patagonia

Falkland Islands

90°W

60°W

30°W

N
W E
S

### map zone

### Geography Skills

**Place** The Americas includes high mountains, major rivers, and large interior plains.

1. **Name** What are some major features of the Americas?

2. **Make Inferences** How do you think mountains have influenced settlement patterns in the region?

**ELEVATION**

| Feet | Meters |
|---|---|
| 13,120 | 4,000 |
| 6,560 | 2,000 |
| 1,640 | 500 |
| 656 | 200 |
| (Sea level) 0 | 0 (Sea level) |
| Below sea level | Below sea level |

0      600      1,200 Miles

0   600   1,200 Kilometers

*Projection: Miller Cylindrical*

**Facts about the World**

## Geographical Extremes: The Americas

| | |
|---|---|
| **Longest River** | Amazon River, Brazil/Peru: 4,000 miles (6,435 km) |
| **Highest Point** | Mt. Aconcagua, Argentina: 22,834 feet (6,960 m) |
| **Lowest Point** | Death Valley, United States: 282 feet (86 m) below sea level |
| **Highest Recorded Temperature** | Death Valley, United States: 134°F (56.6°C) |
| **Lowest Recorded Temperature** | Snag, Canada: −81.4°F (−63°C) |
| **Wettest Place** | Lloro, Colombia: 523.6 inches (1,329.9 cm) average precipitation per year |
| **Driest Place** | Arica, Chile: .03 inches (.08 cm) average precipitation per year |
| **Highest Waterfall** | Angel Falls, Venezuela: 3,212 feet (979 m) |
| **Most Tornadoes** | United States: More than 1,000 per year |

**Death Valley, United States**

hmhsocialstudies.com

## Size Comparison: The United States and the Americas

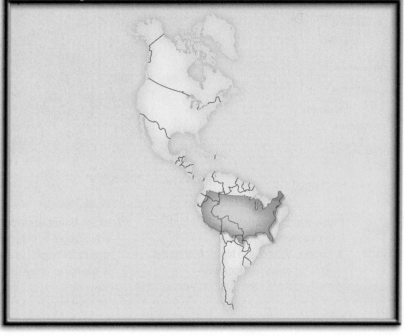

## North America: Political

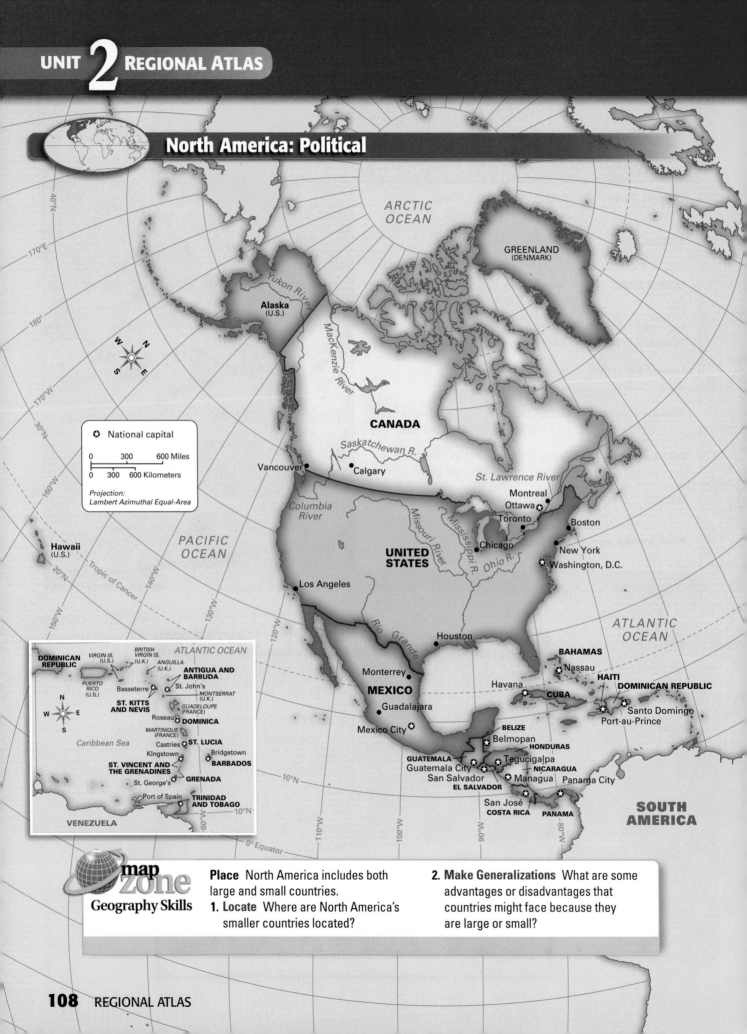

ARCTIC OCEAN

GREENLAND (DENMARK)

Yukon River

Alaska (U.S.)

MacKenzie River

CANADA

Saskatchewan R.

Vancouver • Calgary

St. Lawrence River

Montreal
Ottawa ✪
Toronto
Boston •

Columbia River

Missouri River

Mississippi R.

Chicago •

Ohio R.

New York •
✪ Washington, D.C.

PACIFIC OCEAN

Hawaii (U.S.)

UNITED STATES

Los Angeles •

Tropic of Cancer

ATLANTIC OCEAN

Rio Grande

Houston •

BAHAMAS
✪ Nassau

Monterrey •

Havana ✪

HAITI
DOMINICAN REPUBLIC

MEXICO

CUBA

• Guadalajara

Santo Domingo ✪
Port-au-Prince ✪

Mexico City ✪

BELIZE
Belmopan ✪
HONDURAS
GUATEMALA ✪ Tegucigalpa
Guatemala City ✪ NICARAGUA
San Salvador ✪ Managua   Panama City
EL SALVADOR

San José ✪
COSTA RICA   PANAMA

SOUTH AMERICA

0° Equator

**Legend**

✪ National capital

0    300    600 Miles
0  300  600 Kilometers

Projection:
Lambert Azimuthal Equal-Area

### Caribbean inset

DOMINICAN REPUBLIC
VIRGIN IS. (U.S.)
BRITISH VIRGIN IS. (U.K.)
ANGUILLA (U.K.)
ANTIGUA AND BARBUDA
PUERTO RICO (U.S.)
Basseterre
St. John's
MONTSERRAT (U.K.)
ST. KITTS AND NEVIS
GUADELOUPE (FRANCE)
Roseau ✪ DOMINICA
MARTINIQUE (FRANCE)
Castries ✪ ST. LUCIA
Caribbean Sea
Kingstown   Bridgetown
ST. VINCENT AND THE GRENADINES   BARBADOS
St. George's   GRENADA
Port of Spain ✪ TRINIDAD AND TOBAGO
VENEZUELA
ATLANTIC OCEAN

**map zone**
**Geography Skills**

**Place** North America includes both large and small countries.

**1. Locate** Where are North America's smaller countries located?

**2. Make Generalizations** What are some advantages or disadvantages that countries might face because they are large or small?

# The Americas

Cartagena
Caracas
VENEZUELA
Georgetown
Paramaribo
GUYANA
French Guiana
(FRANCE)
SURINAME
Bogotá
COLOMBIA
0° Equator
Quito
ECUADOR
Galápagos
Islands
Guayaquil
Manaus
Amazon River
PACIFIC
OCEAN
PERU
BRAZIL
Lima
Salvador
La Paz
BOLIVIA
Brasília
Sucre
ATLANTIC
OCEAN
Tropic of Capricorn
Parana River
PARAGUAY
Rio de
Janeiro
CHILE
São Paulo
Asunción
Córdoba
URUGUAY
Santiago
Buenos Aires
Montevideo
ARGENTINA
Falkland
Islands
South Georgia
Island

National capital

| 0 | 300 | 600 Miles |
| 0 | 300 | 600 Kilometers |

Projection:
Lambert Azimuthal Equal-Area

## map zone

### Geography Skills

**Place** South America includes 12 countries and one overseas department of France.

**1. Name** Which country is by far the largest in South America?

**2. Compare** Compare this map to the physical map of the Americas. What physical feature separates Chile and Argentina?

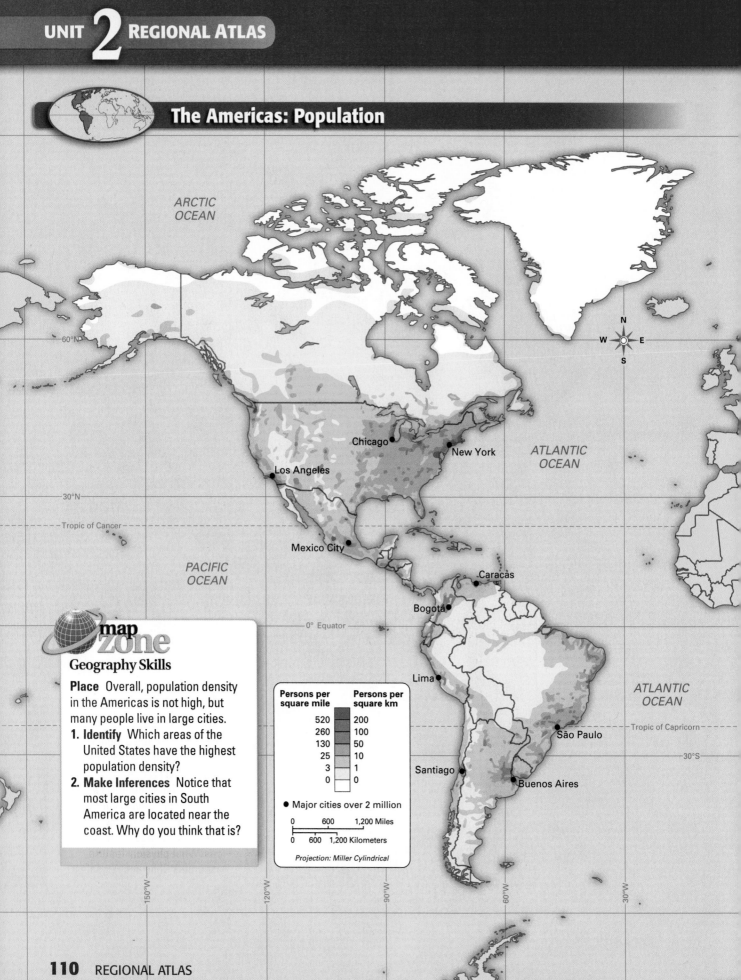

The Americas: Population

ARCTIC OCEAN

60°N

Chicago

New York

ATLANTIC OCEAN

Los Angeles

30°N

Tropic of Cancer

Mexico City

PACIFIC OCEAN

Caracas

Bogotá

0° Equator

Lima

ATLANTIC OCEAN

Tropic of Capricorn

São Paulo

30°S

Santiago

Buenos Aires

**Geography Skills**

**Place** Overall, population density in the Americas is not high, but many people live in large cities.

1. **Identify** Which areas of the United States have the highest population density?

2. **Make Inferences** Notice that most large cities in South America are located near the coast. Why do you think that is?

| Persons per square mile | Persons per square km |
|---|---|
| 520 | 200 |
| 260 | 100 |
| 130 | 50 |
| 25 | 10 |
| 3 | 1 |
| 0 | 0 |

● Major cities over 2 million

0      600      1,200 Miles

0    600   1,200 Kilometers

*Projection: Miller Cylindrical*

150°W    120°W    90°W    60°W    30°W

## The Americas: Climate

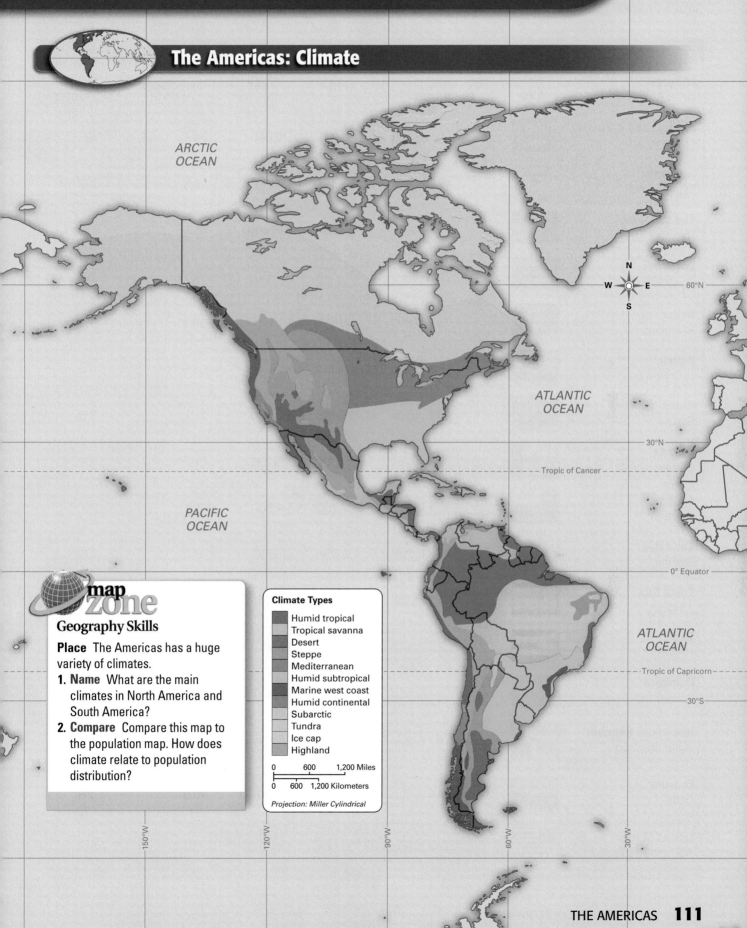

ARCTIC
OCEAN

ATLANTIC
OCEAN

PACIFIC
OCEAN

ATLANTIC
OCEAN

N
W · E
S

60°N

30°N

Tropic of Cancer

0° Equator

Tropic of Capricorn

30°S

150°W   120°W   90°W   60°W   30°W

**map zone**

**Geography Skills**

**Place** The Americas has a huge variety of climates.

1. **Name** What are the main climates in North America and South America?

2. **Compare** Compare this map to the population map. How does climate relate to population distribution?

**Climate Types**

- Humid tropical
- Tropical savanna
- Desert
- Steppe
- Mediterranean
- Humid subtropical
- Marine west coast
- Humid continental
- Subarctic
- Tundra
- Ice cap
- Highland

0    600    1,200 Miles

0   600  1,200 Kilometers

*Projection: Miller Cylindrical*

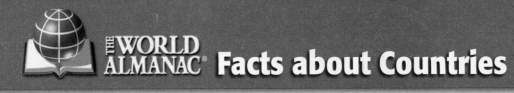
## The Americas

| COUNTRY<br>CAPITAL | FLAG | POPULATION | AREA<br>(sq mi) | PER CAPITA<br>GDP<br>(U.S. $) | LIFE<br>EXPECTANCY<br>AT BIRTH | TVS PER<br>1,000 PEOPLE |
|---|---|---|---|---|---|---|
| **Antigua and Barbuda**<br>St. John's | | 85,632 | 171 | $19,600 | 74.3 | 493 |
| **Argentina**<br>Buenos Aires | | 40.9 million | 1,068,302 | $14,200 | 76.5 | 293 |
| **The Bahamas**<br>Nassau | | 309,156 | 5,382 | $29,600 | 65.8 | 243 |
| **Barbados**<br>Bridgetown | | 284,589 | 166 | $19,100 | 73.2 | 290 |
| **Belize**<br>Belmopan | | 307,899 | 8,867 | $8,400 | 68.3 | 183 |
| **Bolivia**<br>La Paz, Sucre | | 9.8 million | 424,164 | $4,500 | 66.6 | 118 |
| **Brazil**<br>Brasília | | 198.7 million | 3,286,488 | $10,200 | 71.9 | 333 |
| **Canada**<br>Ottawa | | 33.5 million | 3,855,101 | $39,100 | 81.3 | 709 |
| **Chile**<br>Santiago | | 16.6 million | 292,260 | $14,900 | 77.3 | 240 |
| **Colombia**<br>Bogotá | | 45.6 million | 439,736 | $8,800 | 72.6 | 279 |
| **Costa Rica**<br>San José | | 4.3 million | 19,730 | $11,500 | 77.5 | 229 |
| **Cuba**<br>Havana | | 11.5 million | 42,803 | $9,500 | 77.3 | 248 |
| **Dominica**<br>Roseau | | 72,660 | 291 | $9,900 | 75.4 | 232 |
| **Dominican Republic**<br>Santo Domingo | | 9.7 million | 18,815 | $8,200 | 73.4 | 96 |
| **Ecuador**<br>Quito | | 14.6 million | 109,483 | $7,500 | 76.9 | 213 |
| **United States**<br>Washington, D.C. | | 307.2 million | 3,794,083 | $46,900 | 78.2 | 844 |

| COUNTRY<br>Capital | FLAG | POPULATION | AREA<br>(sq mi) | PER CAPITA GDP<br>(U.S. $) | LIFE<br>EXPECTANCY<br>AT BIRTH | TVS PER 1,000<br>PEOPLE |
|---|---|---|---|---|---|---|
| **El Salvador**<br>San Salvador | | 7.2 million | 8,124 | $6,200 | 72.2 | 191 |
| **Grenada**<br>Saint George's | | 90,739 | 133 | $12,900 | 65.6 | 376 |
| **Guatemala**<br>Guatemala City | | 13.3 million | 42,043 | $5,300 | 70.1 | 61 |
| **Guyana**<br>Georgetown | | 772,298 | 83,000 | $3,800 | 66.5 | 70 |
| **Haiti**<br>Port-au-Prince | | 9 million | 10,714 | $1,300 | 57.6 | 5 |
| **Honduras**<br>Tegucigalpa | | 7.8 million | 43,278 | $4,100 | 69.4 | 95 |
| **Jamaica**<br>Kingston | | 2.8 million | 4,244 | $7,500 | 73.7 | 191 |
| **Mexico**<br>Mexico City | | 111.2 million | 761,606 | $14,200 | 75.9 | 272 |
| **Nicaragua**<br>Managua | | 5.9 million | 49,998 | $2,900 | 71.3 | 69 |
| **Panama**<br>Panama City | | 3.4 million | 30,193 | $11,700 | 77 | 192 |
| **Paraguay**<br>Asunción | | 7 million | 157,047 | $4,200 | 75.7 | 205 |
| **Peru**<br>Lima | | 29.5 million | 496,226 | $8,500 | 70.5 | 147 |
| **Saint Kitts and Nevis**<br>Basseterre | | 40,131 | 101 | $19,500 | 73.1 | 256 |
| **Saint Lucia**<br>Castries | | 160,267 | 238 | $11,100 | 76.3 | 368 |
| **Saint Vincent and the<br>Grenadines;** Kingstown | | 104,574 | 150 | $10,200 | 74.4 | 230 |
| **United States**<br>Washington, D.C. | | 307.2 million | 3,794,083 | $46,900 | 78.2 | 844 |

| COUNTRY<br>Capital | FLAG | POPULATION | AREA<br>(sq mi) | PER CAPITA GDP<br>(U.S. $) | LIFE<br>EXPECTANCY<br>AT BIRTH | TVS PER 1,000<br>PEOPLE |
|---|---|---|---|---|---|---|
| **Suriname**<br>Paramaribo | | 481,267 | 63,039 | $8,900 | 73.6 | 241 |
| **Trinidad and Tobago**<br>Port-of-Spain | | 1.2 million | 1,980 | $23,600 | 67.1 | 337 |
| **Uruguay**<br>Montevideo | | 3.5 million | 68,039 | $12,400 | 76.2 | 531 |
| **Venezuela**<br>Caracas | | 26.8 million | 352,144 | $13,500 | 73.6 | 185 |
| **United States**<br>Washington, D.C. | | 307.2 million | 3,794,083 | $46,900 | 78.2 | 844 |

**ANALYSIS SKILL  ANALYZING TABLES**

1. Compare the information for the United States, Canada, Brazil, and Mexico. How do these four countries compare?
2. Which country has the lowest per capita GDP?

## Largest Cities and Urban Populations

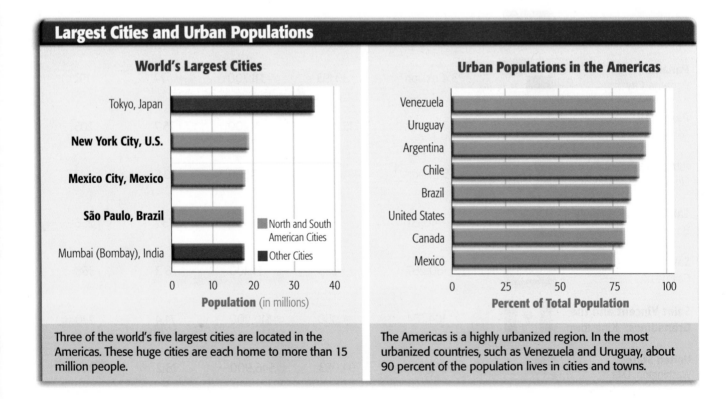

### World's Largest Cities

Tokyo, Japan
New York City, U.S.
Mexico City, Mexico
São Paulo, Brazil
Mumbai (Bombay), India

North and South American Cities
Other Cities

0   10   20   30   40
**Population** (in millions)

### Urban Populations in the Americas

Venezuela
Uruguay
Argentina
Chile
Brazil
United States
Canada
Mexico

0   25   50   75   100
**Percent of Total Population**

Three of the world's five largest cities are located in the Americas. These huge cities are each home to more than 15 million people.

The Americas is a highly urbanized region. In the most urbanized countries, such as Venezuela and Uruguay, about 90 percent of the population lives in cities and towns.

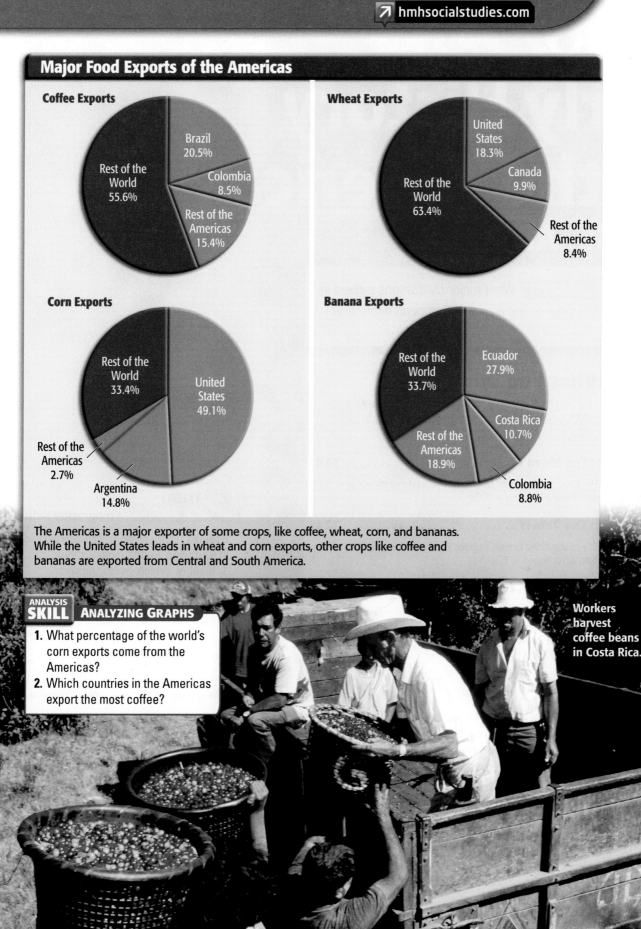

# Major Food Exports of the Americas

**Coffee Exports**

- Brazil 20.5%
- Colombia 8.5%
- Rest of the Americas 15.4%
- Rest of the World 55.6%

**Wheat Exports**

- United States 18.3%
- Canada 9.9%
- Rest of the Americas 8.4%
- Rest of the World 63.4%

**Corn Exports**

- United States 49.1%
- Argentina 14.8%
- Rest of the Americas 2.7%
- Rest of the World 33.4%

**Banana Exports**

- Ecuador 27.9%
- Costa Rica 10.7%
- Colombia 8.8%
- Rest of the Americas 18.9%
- Rest of the World 33.7%

The Americas is a major exporter of some crops, like coffee, wheat, corn, and bananas. While the United States leads in wheat and corn exports, other crops like coffee and bananas are exported from Central and South America.

**ANALYSIS SKILL ANALYZING GRAPHS**

1. What percentage of the world's corn exports come from the Americas?
2. Which countries in the Americas export the most coffee?

Workers harvest coffee beans in Costa Rica.

# Early History of the Americas

## 500 BC–AD 1537

**Essential Question** What major civilizations thrived in the Americas prior to the arrival of European explorers?

## What You Will Learn...

In this chapter you will learn about the location, growth, and decline of the Maya, Aztec, and Inca civilizations in the Americas.

### FOCUS ON READING AND WRITING

**Setting a Purpose** Setting a purpose for your reading can help give you a focus. Before you read, look at pictures and headings to find out what the text is about. Then decide what your purpose in reading the text is. Keep your purpose in mind as you read. **See the lesson, Setting a Purpose, on page 520.**

**Writing a Newspaper Article** You are a writer for a European newspaper who is traveling with some explorers to the Americas. As you read this chapter, you will decide what you want to share with readers in a newspaper article—the land, the people, or the events that occurred after the explorers arrived.

PACIFIC OCEAN

140°W · 130°W · 120°W · 110°W

**map zone** **Geography Skills**

**Regions** Three great civilizations existed in North and South America before 1537.
1. **Identify** Which civilization was located in South America?
2. **Make Inferences** What do you think happened when the Spanish arrived in the Americas?

**The Maya** The Maya traded jade between their cities in Mesoamerica.

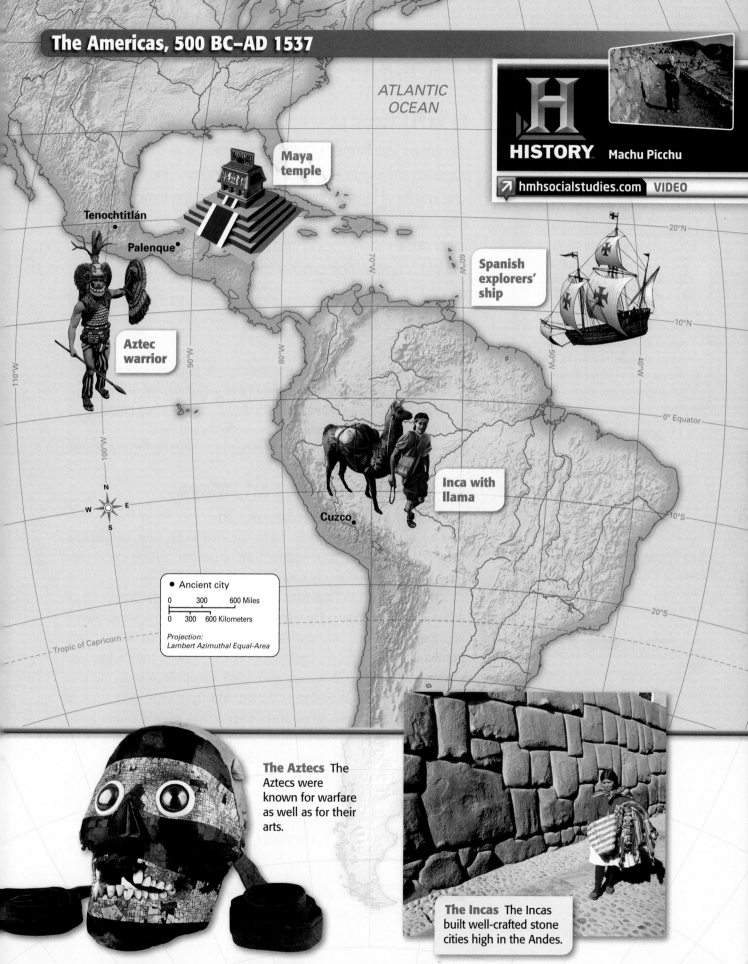

# The Americas, 500 BC–AD 1537

ATLANTIC OCEAN

**HISTORY** Machu Picchu

↗ hmhsocialstudies.com VIDEO

Maya temple

Tenochtitlán

Palenque

Aztec warrior

Spanish explorers' ship

20°N

10°N

0° Equator

10°S

20°S

Inca with llama

Cuzco

• Ancient city

0   300   600 Miles
0   300   600 Kilometers

*Projection: Lambert Azimuthal Equal-Area*

Tropic of Capricorn

**The Aztecs** The Aztecs were known for warfare as well as for their arts.

**The Incas** The Incas built well-crafted stone cities high in the Andes.

# The Maya

## If YOU lived there...

You are a Maya farmer, growing corn in fields outside a city. Often you enter the city to join in religious ceremonies. You watch the king and his priests standing at the top of a tall pyramid. They wear capes of brightly colored feathers and gold ornaments that glitter in the sun. Far below them, thousands of worshippers crowd into the plaza with you to honor the gods.

**How do these ceremonies make you feel?**

**BUILDING BACKGROUND** Religion was very important to the Maya, one of the early peoples in the Americas. The Maya believed the gods controlled everything in the world around them.

## Geography and the Early Maya

The region known as Mesoamerica stretches from the central part of Mexico south to include the northern part of Central America. It was in this region that a people called the Maya (MY-uh) developed a remarkable civilization.

Around 1000 BC the Maya began settling in the lowlands of what is now northern Guatemala. Thick tropical forests covered most of the land, but the people cleared areas to farm. They grew a variety of crops, including beans, squash, avocados, and **maize**, or corn. The forests provided valuable resources, too. Forest animals such as deer, rabbits, and monkeys were sources of food. In addition, trees and other forest plants made good building materials. For example, some Maya used wooden poles and vines, along with mud, to build their houses.

The early Maya lived in small, isolated villages. Eventually, though, these villages started trading with one another and with other groups in Mesoamerica. As trade increased, the villages grew. By about AD 200, the Maya had begun to build large cities in Mesoamerica.

**READING CHECK** Finding Main Ideas How did the early Maya make use of their physical environment?

---

## What You Will Learn...

### Main Ideas

1. Geography helped shape the lives of the early Maya.
2. During the Classic Age, the Maya built great cities linked by trade.
3. Maya culture included a strict social structure, a religion with many gods, and achievements in science and the arts.
4. The decline of Maya civilization began in the 900s.

### The Big Idea

The Maya developed an advanced civilization that thrived in Mesoamerica from about 250 until the 900s.

### Key Terms and Places

maize, *p. 118*
Palenque, *p. 119*
observatories, *p. 122*

hmhsocialstudies.com
TAKING NOTES

Use the graphic organizer online to organize your notes on the Maya.

# The Classic Age

The Maya civilization reached its height between about AD 250 and 900. This time in Maya history is known as the Classic Age. During this time, Maya territory grew to include more than 40 large cities. Each had its own government and its own king. No single ruler united the many cities into one empire.

Instead, the Maya cities were linked through trade. People exchanged goods for products that were not available locally. Look at the trade routes on the map to see the goods that were available in different areas of Maya civilization. For example, the warm lowlands were good for growing cotton and cacao (kuh-KOW), the source of chocolate. But lowland crops did not grow well in the cool highlands. Instead, the highlands had valuable stones, such as jade and obsidian. People carried these and other products along trade routes.

Through trade, the Maya got supplies for construction. Maya cities had grand buildings, such as palaces decorated with carvings and paintings. The Maya also built stone pyramids topped with temples. Some temples honored local kings. For example, in the city of **Palenque** (pah-LENG-kay), the king Pacal (puh-KAHL) had a temple built to record his achievements.

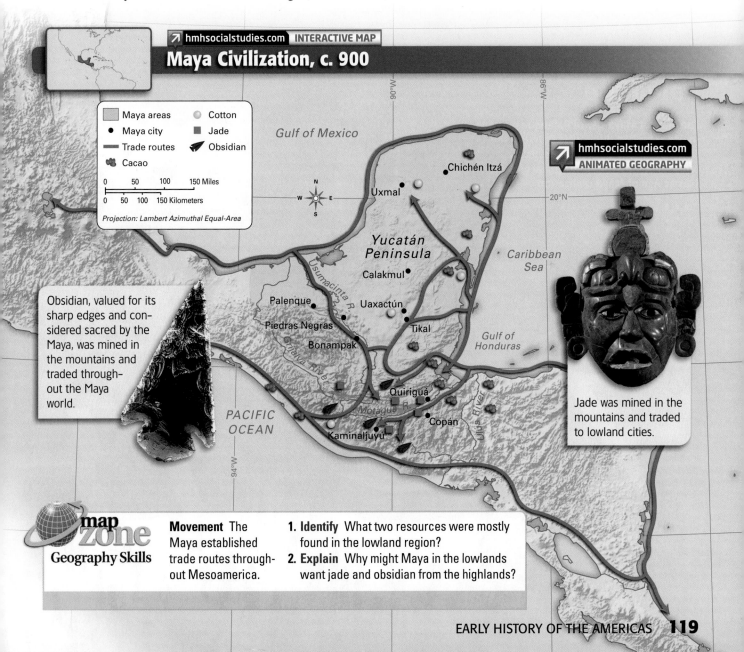

↗ hmhsocialstudies.com **INTERACTIVE MAP**

## Maya Civilization, c. 900

↗ hmhsocialstudies.com **ANIMATED GEOGRAPHY**

**Legend:**
- Maya areas
- Maya city
- Trade routes
- Cacao
- Cotton
- Jade
- Obsidian

0  50  100  150 Miles
0  50  100  150 Kilometers
Projection: Lambert Azimuthal Equal-Area

Gulf of Mexico

Chichén Itzá

Uxmal

Yucatán Peninsula

Calakmul

Caribbean Sea

Palenque

Uaxactún

Piedras Negras

Tikal

Bonampak

Gulf of Honduras

Usumacinta R.

Chixoy River

Quiriguá

Motagua R.

Copán

Ulúa River

PACIFIC OCEAN

Kaminaljuyú

20°N

90°W · 98°W · 94°W

Obsidian, valued for its sharp edges and considered sacred by the Maya, was mined in the mountains and traded throughout the Maya world.

Jade was mined in the mountains and traded to lowland cities.

**map zone**
**Geography Skills**

**Movement** The Maya established trade routes throughout Mesoamerica.

1. **Identify** What two resources were mostly found in the lowland region?
2. **Explain** Why might Maya in the lowlands want jade and obsidian from the highlands?

In addition to palaces and temples, the Maya built canals and paved large plazas, or open squares, for public gatherings. Farmers used stone walls to shape hillsides into flat terraces so they could grow crops on them. Almost every Maya city also had a stone court for playing a special ball game. Using only their heads, shoulders, or hips, players tried to bounce a heavy rubber ball through stone rings attached high on the court walls. The winners of these games received jewels and clothing. The losers were often killed.

**READING CHECK** **Analyzing** Why is Maya civilization not considered an empire?

## Maya Culture

In Maya society, people's daily lives were heavily influenced by two main forces. One was the social structure, and the other was religion.

### Social Structure

The king held the highest position in Maya society. The Maya believed their kings were related to the gods, so Maya kings had religious as well as political authority. Priests, rich merchants, and noble warriors were also part of the upper class. Together with the king, these people held all the power in Maya society.

Close-up

# Palenque

The ancient Maya city of Palenque was a major power on the border between the Maya highlands and lowlands. Its great temples and plazas were typical of the Classic Age of Maya civilization.

Flat terraces made more land usable for farming.

Priests led religious ceremonies from the tops of temples.

Most Maya, though, belonged to the lower class. This group was made up of farming families who lived outside the cities. The women cared for the children, cooked, made yarn, and wove cloth. The men farmed, hunted, and crafted tools.

Lower-class Maya had to "pay" their rulers by giving the rulers part of their crops and goods such as cloth and salt. They also had to help construct temples and other public buildings. If their city went to war, Maya men had to serve in the army, and if captured in battle, they often became slaves. Slaves carried goods along trade routes or worked for upper-class Maya as servants or farmers.

## Religion

The Maya worshipped many gods, such as a creator, a sun god, a moon goddess, and a maize god. Each god was believed to control a different aspect of daily life.

According to Maya beliefs, the gods could be helpful or harmful, so people tried to please the gods to get their help. The Maya believed their gods needed blood to prevent disasters or the end of the world. Every person offered blood to the gods by piercing their tongue or skin. On special occasions, the Maya made human sacrifices. They usually used prisoners captured in battle, offering their hearts to stone carvings of the gods.

Maya temples were shaped like mountains, which the Maya considered sacred because they allowed people to approach the gods.

### BIOGRAPHY

## Pacal
(603–683)

Pacal became king of the Maya city of Palenque when he was just 12 years old. As king, Pacal led many important community events, such as religious dances and public meetings. When he died, he was buried at the bottom of the Temple of the Inscriptions shown to the near left.

Maya buildings were covered with stucco and painted in bright colors.

ANALYSIS
**SKILL** **ANALYZING VISUALS**

In what ways might Palenque's setting have helped the city? In what ways might it have hurt the city?

# Maya Astronomy and Writing

October 28, AD 709

She is letting blood.

Lady Xoc

The Maya studied the stars from their observatory (left) at Chichén Itzá. The stone carving (above) shows a religious ceremony.

**ANALYZING VISUALS** What is happening in this religious ceremony?

## Achievements

**FOCUS ON READING**
What will be your purpose in reading about Maya achievements?

The Maya's religious beliefs led them to make impressive advances in science. They built large **observatories**, or buildings from which people could study the sky, so their priests could watch the stars and plan the best times for religious festivals. With the knowledge they gained about astronomy, the Maya developed two calendars. One, with 365 days, guided farming activities, such as planting and harvesting. This calendar was more accurate than the one used in Europe at that time. The Maya also had a separate 260-day calendar that they used for keeping track of religious events.

The Maya were able to measure time accurately partly because they were skilled mathematicians. They created a number system that helped them make complex calculations, and they were among the first people with a symbol for zero. The Maya used their number system to record key dates in their history.

The Maya also developed a writing system. Anthropologists, or scholars who study people and cultures, have figured out that symbols used in Maya writing represented both objects and sounds. The Maya carved these symbols into large stone tablets to record their history. They also wrote in bark-paper books and passed down stories and poems orally.

The Maya created amazing art and architecture as well. Their jade and gold jewelry was exceptional. Also, their huge temple-pyramids were masterfully built. The Maya had neither metal tools for cutting nor wheeled vehicles for carrying heavy supplies. Instead, workers used obsidian tools to cut limestone into blocks. Then workers rolled the giant blocks over logs and lifted them with ropes. The Maya decorated their buildings with paintings.

**READING CHECK** **Categorizing** What groups made up the different classes in Maya society?

# Decline of Maya Civilization

Maya civilization began to collapse in the AD 900s. People stopped building temples and other structures. They left the cities and moved back to the countryside. What caused this collapse? Historians are not sure, but they think that a combination of factors was probably responsible.

One factor could have been the burden on the common people. Maya kings forced their subjects to farm for them or work on building projects. Perhaps people didn't want to work for the kings. They might have decided to **rebel** against their rulers' demands and abandon their cities.

Increased warfare between cities could also have caused the decline. Maya cities had always fought for power. But if battles became more widespread or destructive, they would have disrupted trade and cost many lives. People might have fled from the cities for their safety.

A related theory is that perhaps the Maya could not produce enough food to feed everyone. Growing the same crops year after year would have weakened the soil. In addition, as the population grew, the demand for food would have increased. To meet this demand, cities might have begun competing fiercely for new land. But the resulting battles would have hurt more crops, damaged more farmland, and caused even greater food shortages.

Climate change could have played a role, too. Scientists know that Mesoamerica suffered from droughts during the period when the Maya were leaving their cities. Droughts would have made it hard to grow enough food to feed people in the cities.

Whatever the reasons, the collapse of Maya civilization happened gradually. The Maya scattered after 900, but they did not disappear entirely. In fact, the Maya civilization later revived in the Yucatán Peninsula. By the time Spanish conquerors reached the Americas in the 1500s, though, Maya power had faded.

**READING CHECK** **Summarizing** What factors may have caused the end of Maya civilization?

> **SUMMARY AND PREVIEW** The Maya built a civilization that peaked between about 250 and 900 but later collapsed for reasons still unknown. In Section 2 you will learn about another people who lived in Mesoamerica, the Aztecs.

**HISTORY**

**VIDEO**
The
Disappearance

⬈ hmhsocialstudies.com

**ACADEMIC VOCABULARY**
**rebel** to fight against authority

---

## Section 1 Assessment

⬈ hmhsocialstudies.com
ONLINE QUIZ

### Reviewing Ideas, Terms, and Places

1. **a. Recall** What resources did the Maya get from the forest?
   **b. Elaborate** How do you think Maya villages grew into large cities?
2. **a. Describe** What features did Maya cities include?
   **b. Make Inferences** How did trade strengthen the Maya civilization?
3. **a. Identify** Who belonged to the upper class in Maya society?
   **b. Explain** Why did the Maya build **observatories**?
   **c. Rank** What do you think was the most impressive cultural achievement of the Maya? Why?
4. **a. Describe** What happened to the Maya after 900?
   **b. Evaluate** What would you consider to be the key factor in the collapse of Maya civilization? Explain.

### Critical Thinking

5. **Evaluating** Draw a diagram like the one to the right. Use your notes to rank Maya achievements, with the most important at the top.

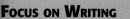

**FOCUS ON WRITING**

6. **Gathering Information about the Maya** Part of your article will probably be devoted to the Maya. Use the map and pictures in this section to help you decide what to write about. How would you describe the land and the Maya cities? What could you add about the history and culture of the Maya? Take notes on your ideas.

# The Aztecs

## What You Will Learn...

### Main Ideas

1. The Aztecs built a rich and powerful empire in central Mexico.
2. Social structure, religion, and warfare shaped life in the empire.
3. Hernán Cortés conquered the Aztec Empire in 1521.

### The Big Idea

The strong Aztec Empire, founded in central Mexico in 1325, lasted until the Spanish conquest in 1521.

### Key Terms and Places

Tenochtitlán, *p. 124*
causeways, *p. 124*
conquistadors, *p. 128*

hmhsocialstudies.com
TAKING NOTES

Use the graphic organizer online to organize your notes on the Aztecs.

## If YOU lived there...

You live in a village in southeastern Mexico that is ruled by the powerful Aztec Empire. Each year your village must send the emperor many baskets of corn. You have to dig gold for him, too. One day some pale, bearded strangers arrive by sea. They want to overthrow the emperor, and they ask for your help.

**Should you help the strangers? Why or why not?**

**BUILDING BACKGROUND** The Aztecs ruled a large empire in Mesoamerica. Each village they conquered had to contribute heavily to the Aztec economy. This system helped create a mighty state, but one that did not inspire loyalty.

## The Aztecs Build an Empire

The first Aztecs were farmers who migrated from the north to central Mexico. Finding the good farmland already occupied, they settled on a swampy island in the middle of Lake Texcoco (tays-KOH-koh). There, in 1325, they began building their capital and conquering nearby towns.

War was a key factor in the Aztecs' rise to power. The Aztecs fought fiercely and demanded tribute payments from the people they conquered. The cotton, gold, and food that poured in as a result became vital to their economy. The Aztecs also controlled a huge trade network. Merchants carried goods to and from all parts of the empire. Many merchants doubled as spies, keeping the rulers informed about what was happening in their lands.

War, tribute, and trade made the Aztec Empire strong and rich. By the early 1400s the Aztecs ruled the most powerful state in Mesoamerica. Nowhere was the empire's greatness more visible than in its capital, **Tenochtitlán** (tay-nawch-teet-LAHN).

To build this amazing island city, the Aztecs first had to overcome many geographic challenges. One problem was the difficulty getting to and from the city. The Aztecs addressed this challenge by building three wide **causeways**—raised roads across water or wet ground—to connect the island to the lakeshore.

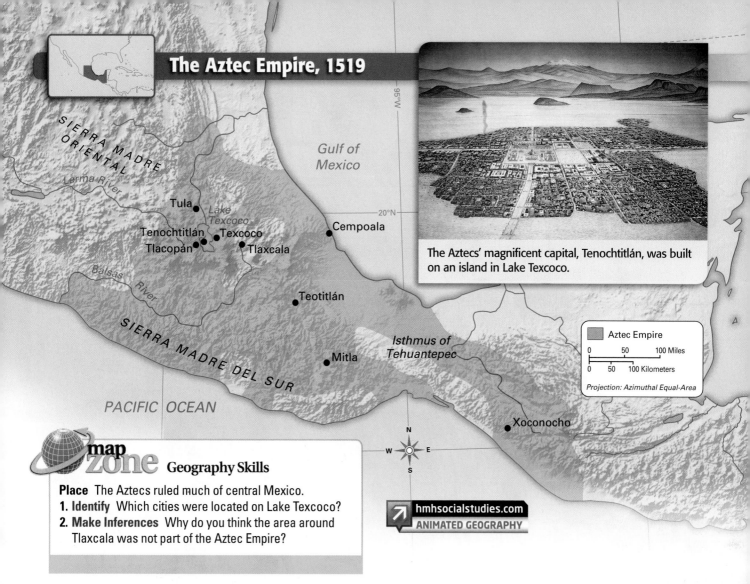

## The Aztec Empire, 1519

SIERRA MADRE ORIENTAL

Lerma River

Tula

Lake Texcoco

Tenochtitlán  Texcoco

Tlacopán  Tlaxcala

Balsas River

SIERRA MADRE DEL SUR

PACIFIC OCEAN

Gulf of Mexico

20°N

Cempoala

Teotitlán

Mitla

Isthmus of Tehuantepec

Xoconocho

95°W

N W E S

The Aztecs' magnificent capital, Tenochtitlán, was built on an island in Lake Texcoco.

Aztec Empire

0  50  100 Miles
0  50  100 Kilometers

Projection: Azimuthal Equal-Area

### map zone Geography Skills

**Place** The Aztecs ruled much of central Mexico.
1. **Identify** Which cities were located on Lake Texcoco?
2. **Make Inferences** Why do you think the area around Tlaxcala was not part of the Aztec Empire?

hmhsocialstudies.com
ANIMATED GEOGRAPHY

They also built canals that crisscrossed the city. The causeways and canals made travel and trade much easier.

Tenochtitlán's island location also limited the amount of land available for farming. To solve this problem, the Aztecs created floating gardens called *chinampas* (chee-NAHM-pahs). They piled soil on top of large rafts, which they anchored to trees that stood in the water.

The Aztecs made Tenochtitlán a truly magnificent city. Home to some 200,000 people at its height, it had huge temples, a busy market, and a grand palace.

**READING CHECK** Finding Main Ideas How did the Aztecs rise to power?

## Life in the Empire

The Aztecs' way of life was as distinctive as their capital city. They had a complex social structure, a demanding religion, and a rich culture.

### Aztec Society

The Aztec emperor, like the Maya king, was the most important person in society. From his great palace, he attended to law, trade, tribute, and warfare. Trusted nobles helped him as tax collectors, judges, and other government officials. These noble positions were passed down from fathers to sons, and young nobles went to school to learn their responsibilities.

**THE IMPACT TODAY**

Mexico's capital, Mexico City, is located where Tenochtitlán once stood.

# Close-up
# Tenochtitlán

The Aztecs turned a swampy, uninhabited island into one of the largest and grandest cities in the world. The first Europeans to visit Tenochtitlán were amazed. At the time, the Aztec capital was about five times bigger than London.

The Great Temple stood at the heart of the city. On top of the temple were two shrines—a blue shrine for the rain god and a red shrine for the sun god.

Gold, silver, cloaks, and precious stones were among the many items sold at the market.

A network of canals linked different parts of the city.

Aztec farmers grew crops on floating gardens called *chinampas*.

**ANALYSIS SKILL** **ANALYZING VISUALS**

What is the most important building in this picture? How can you tell?

## Aztec Ceremonial Jewelry

Aztec artists were very skilled. They created detailed and brightly colored items. This double-headed serpent was probably worn during religious ceremonies. The man on the right is wearing it on his chest.

**ANALYZING VISUALS**
What are some features of Aztec art that you can see in these pictures?

Just below the emperor and his nobles was a class of warriors and priests. Aztec warriors were highly respected and had many privileges, but priests were more influential. They led religious ceremonies and, as keepers of the calendars, decided when to plant and harvest.

The next level of Aztec society included merchants and artisans. Below them, in the lower class, were farmers and laborers, who made up the majority of the population. Many didn't own their land, and they paid so much in tribute that they often found it tough to survive. Only slaves, at the very bottom of society, struggled more.

### Religion and Warfare

Like the Maya, the Aztecs worshipped many gods whom they believed controlled both nature and human activities. To please the gods, Aztec priests regularly made human sacrifices. Most victims were battle captives or slaves. In bloody ritual ceremonies, priests would slash open their victims' chests to "feed" human hearts and blood to the gods. The Aztecs sacrificed as many as 10,000 people a year. To supply enough victims, Aztec warriors often fought battles with neighboring peoples.

### Cultural Achievements

As warlike as the Aztecs were, they also appreciated art and beauty. Architects and sculptors created fine stone pyramids and statues. Artisans used gold, gems, and bright feathers to make jewelry and masks. Women embroidered colorful designs on the cloth they wove.

The Aztecs valued learning as well. They studied astronomy and devised a calendar much like the Maya one. They kept detailed written records of historical and cultural events. They also had a strong oral tradition. Stories about ancestors and the gods were passed from one generation to the next. The Aztecs also enjoyed fine speeches and riddles such as these:

"What is a little blue-green jar filled with popcorn? Someone is sure to guess our riddle: it is the sky.
What is a mountainside that has a spring of water in it? Our nose."
–Bernardino de Sahagún, from Florentine Codex

Knowing the answers to riddles showed that one had paid attention in school.

**READING CHECK** **Identifying Cause and Effect** How did Aztec religious practices influence warfare?

# Cortés Conquers the Aztecs

**FOCUS ON READING**
If your purpose is to learn about the end of the Aztecs, how will reading about the Spanish help you?

In the late 1400s the Spanish arrived in the Americas, seeking adventure, riches, and converts to Catholicism. One group of **conquistadors** (kahn-KEES-tuh-dohrz), or Spanish conquerors, reached Mexico in 1519. Led by Hernán Cortés (er-NAHN kawr-TEZ), their motives were to find gold, claim land, and convert the native peoples to Christianity.

The Aztec emperor, Moctezuma II (MAWK-tay-SOO-mah), cautiously welcomed the strangers. He believed Cortés to be the god Quetzalcoatl (ket-suhl-kuh-WAH-tuhl), whom the Aztecs believed had left Mexico long ago. According to legend, the god had promised to return in 1519.

Moctezuma gave the Spanish gold and other gifts, but Cortés wanted more. He took the emperor prisoner, enraging the Aztecs, who attacked the Spanish. They managed to drive out the conquistadors, but Moctezuma was killed in the fighting.

Within a year, Cortés and his men came back. This time they had help from other peoples in the region who resented the Aztecs' harsh rule. In addition, the Spanish had better weapons, including armor, cannons, and swords. Furthermore, the Aztecs were terrified of the enemy's big horses—animals they had never seen before. The Spanish had also unknowingly brought diseases such as smallpox to the Americas. Diseases weakened or killed thousands of Aztecs. In 1521 the Aztec Empire came to an end.

**READING CHECK** **Summarizing** What factors helped the Spanish defeat the Aztecs?

**SUMMARY AND PREVIEW** The Aztec Empire, made strong by warfare and tribute, fell to the Spanish in 1521. In the next section you will learn about another empire in the Americas, that of the Incas.

---

## Section 2 Assessment

hmhsocialstudies.com
ONLINE QUIZ

### Reviewing Ideas, Terms, and Places

1. **a. Recall** Where and when did Aztec civilization develop?
   **b. Explain** How did the Aztecs in **Tenochtitlán** adapt to their island location?
   **c. Elaborate** How might Tenochtitlán's location have been both a benefit and a hindrance to the Aztecs?

2. **a. Recall** What did the Aztecs feed their gods?
   **b. Rate** Consider the roles of the emperor, warriors, priests, and others in Aztec society. Who do you think had the hardest role? Explain.

3. **a. Identify** Who was Moctezuma II?
   **b. Make Generalizations** Why did allies help Cortés defeat the Aztecs?
   **c. Predict** The Aztecs vastly outnumbered the **conquistadors**. If the Aztecs had first viewed Cortés as a threat rather than a god, how might history have changed?

### Critical Thinking

4. **Evaluating** Draw a diagram like the one shown. Use your notes to identify three factors that contributed to the Aztecs' power. Put the factor you consider most important first and put the least important last. Explain your choices.

   | 1. | 2. | 3. |
   |----|----|----|

### FOCUS ON WRITING

5. **Describing the Aztec Empire** Tenochtitlán would certainly be described in your article. Make notes about how you would describe it. Be sure to explain the causeways, chinampas, and other features. What activities went on in the city? Your article should also describe the events that occurred when the Spanish discovered the Aztec capital. Make notes on the fall of the Aztec Empire.

# The Incas

## If **YOU** lived there...

You live in the Andes Mountains, where you raise llamas. You weave their wool into warm cloth. Last year, soldiers from the powerful Inca Empire took over your village. They brought in new leaders, who say you must all learn a new language and send much of your woven cloth to the Inca ruler. They also promise that the government will provide for you in times of trouble.

**How do you feel about living in the Inca Empire?**

> **BUILDING BACKGROUND** The Incas built their huge empire by taking over village after village in South America. They brought many changes to the people they conquered before they were themselves conquered by the Spanish.

## The Incas Create an Empire

While the Aztecs were ruling Mexico, the Inca Empire arose in South America. The Incas began as a small tribe in the Andes. Their capital was **Cuzco** (KOO-skoh) in what is now Peru.

In the mid-1400s a ruler named Pachacuti (pah-chah-KOO-tee) began to expand Inca territory. Later leaders followed his example, and by the early 1500s the Inca Empire was huge. It stretched from what is now Ecuador south to central Chile. It included coastal deserts, snowy mountains, fertile valleys, and thick forests. About 12 million people lived in the empire. To rule effectively, the Incas formed a strong central government.

## What You Will Learn...

### Main Ideas

1. The Incas created an empire with a strong central government in South America.
2. Life in the Inca Empire was influenced by social structure, religion, and the Incas' cultural achievements.
3. Francisco Pizarro conquered the Incas and took control of the region in 1537.

### The Big Idea

The Incas controlled a huge empire in South America, but it was conquered by the Spanish.

### Key Terms and Places

Cuzco, *p. 129*
Quechua, *p. 130*
masonry, *p. 131*

**hmhsocialstudies.com**
TAKING NOTES

Use the graphic organizer online to organize your notes on the Inca Empire.

The Incas lived in a region of high plains and mountains.

### Pachacuti

(Died 1471 )

Pachacuti became the Inca ruler in about 1438. Under his rule the Inca Empire began a period of great expansion. Pachacuti, whose name means "he who remakes the world," had the Inca capital at Cuzco rebuilt. He also established an official Inca religion.

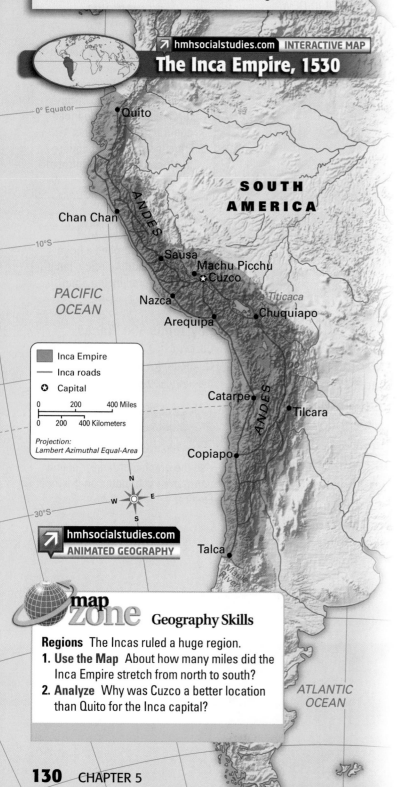

↗ hmhsocialstudies.com **INTERACTIVE MAP**

## The Inca Empire, 1530

0° Equator

Quito

SOUTH AMERICA

Chan Chan

10°S

ANDES

Sausa

Machu Picchu
☆ Cuzco

PACIFIC OCEAN

Nazca

Lake Titicaca

Arequipa

Chuquiapo

| | Inca Empire |
|---|---|
| — | Inca roads |
| ☆ | Capital |

0    200    400 Miles

0    200    400 Kilometers

Projection:
Lambert Azimuthal Equal-Area

Catarpe

Tilcara

ANDES

Copiapo

N
W E
S

30°S

↗ hmhsocialstudies.com
**ANIMATED GEOGRAPHY**

Talca

Maule River

ATLANTIC OCEAN

### map zone   Geography Skills

**Regions** The Incas ruled a huge region.
1. **Use the Map** About how many miles did the Inca Empire stretch from north to south?
2. **Analyze** Why was Cuzco a better location than Quito for the Inca capital?

## Central Rule

Pachacuti did not want the people he conquered to have too much power. He began a policy of removing local leaders and replacing them with new officials whom he trusted. He also made the children of conquered leaders travel to Cuzco to learn about Inca government and religion. When the children were grown, they were sent back to govern their villages, where they taught their people about the Incas' history, traditions, and way of life.

As another way of unifying the empire, the Incas used an official Inca language, **Quechua** (KE-chuh-wuh). Although people spoke many other languages, all official business had to be done in Quechua. Even today, many people in Peru and the other former Inca lands still speak Quechua.

## A Well-Organized Economy

The Inca government strictly controlled the economy and told each household what work to do. Most Incas had to spend time working for the government as well as themselves. Farmers tended government land in addition to their own. Villagers made cloth and other goods for the army. Some Incas served as soldiers, worked in mines, or built roads and bridges. In this way the people paid taxes in the form of labor rather than money. This labor tax system was called the *mita* (MEE-tah).

Another feature of the Inca economy was that there were no merchants or markets. Instead, government officials would distribute goods collected through the *mita*. Leftover goods were stored in the capital for emergencies. If a natural disaster struck, or if people simply could not care for themselves, the government provided supplies to help them.

**READING CHECK** Summarizing How did the Incas control their empire?

# Life in the Inca Empire

Because the rulers controlled Inca society so closely, the common people had little personal freedom. At the same time, the government protected the general welfare of all in the empire. But that did not mean everyone was treated equally.

## Social Divisions

Inca society had two main social classes. The emperor, government officials, and priests made up the upper class. Members of this class lived in stone houses in Cuzco and wore the best clothes. They did not have to pay the labor tax, and they enjoyed many other privileges. The Inca rulers, for example, could relax in luxury at Machu Picchu (MAH-choo PEEK-choo). This royal retreat lay nestled high in the Andes.

The people of the lower class in Inca society included farmers, artisans, and servants. There were no slaves, however, because the Incas did not practice slavery. Most Incas were farmers. In the warmer valleys they grew crops such as maize and peanuts. In the cooler mountains they carved terraces into the hillsides and grew potatoes. High in the Andes, people raised llamas—South American animals related to camels—for wool and meat.

Lower-class Incas dressed in plain clothes and lived simply. By law, they could not own more goods than just what they needed to survive. Most of what they made went to the *mita* and the upper class.

## Religion

The Inca social structure was partly related to religion. For example, the Incas thought that their rulers were related to the sun god and never really died. As a result, priests brought mummies of former kings to many ceremonies. People gave these royal mummies food and gifts.

Most Incas were farmers. The Incas in this drawing from the mid-1500s are harvesting potatoes.

THE GRANGER COLLECTION, NEW YORK

Inca ceremonies included sacrifices. But unlike the Maya and the Aztecs, the Incas rarely sacrificed humans. They sacrificed llamas, cloth, or food instead.

In addition to practicing the official religion, people outside Cuzco worshipped other gods at local sacred places. The Incas believed certain mountaintops, rocks, and springs had magical powers. Many Incas performed sacrifices at these places as well as at the temple in Cuzco.

## Achievements

Inca temples were grand buildings. The Incas were master builders, known for their expert **masonry**, or stonework. They cut stone blocks so precisely that they did not need cement to hold them together. The Incas also built a major network of roads.

The Incas produced works of art as well. Artisans made pottery as well as gold and silver jewelry. They even created a life-sized cornfield of gold and silver, crafting each cob, leaf, and stalk individually. Inca weavers also made some of the finest textiles in the Americas.

**FOCUS ON READING**
What will be your purpose in reading about Inca achievements?

## Inca Arts

Inca arts included beautiful textiles and gold and silver objects.

Inca artisans made many silver offerings to the gods.

The Incas are famous for their textiles. Inca weavers made cloth from cotton and from the wool of llamas.

**ANALYSIS SKILL** **ANALYZING VISUALS**

What are some features of Inca art that you can see in these pictures?

Inca artisans also made many gold objects, such as this mask.

While such artifacts tell us much about the Incas, nothing was written about their empire until the Spanish arrived. Indeed, the Incas had no writing system. Instead, they kept records with knotted cords called *quipus* (KEE-pooz). Knots in the cords stood for numbers. Different colors represented information about crops, land, and other important topics.

The Incas also passed down their stories and history orally. People sang songs and told stories about daily life and military victories. Official "memorizers" learned long poems about Inca legends and history. When the conquistadors arrived, the Inca records were written in Spanish and Quechua. We know about the Incas from these records and from the stories that survive in the songs and religious practices of the people in the region today.

**READING CHECK** **Contrasting** How did daily life differ for upper- and lower-class Incas?

## Pizarro Conquers the Incas

The arrival of conquistadors changed more than how the Incas recorded history. In the late 1520s a civil war began in the Inca Empire after the death of the ruler. Two of the ruler's sons, Atahualpa (ah-tah-WAHL-pah) and Huáscar (WAHS-kahr), fought to claim the throne. Atahualpa won the war in 1532, but fierce fighting had weakened the Inca army.

On his way to be crowned as king, Atahualpa got news that a band of about 180 Spanish soldiers had arrived in the Inca Empire. They were conquistadors led by Francisco Pizarro. When Atahualpa came to meet the group, the Spanish attacked. They were greatly outnumbered, but they caught the unarmed Incas by surprise. They quickly captured Atahualpa and killed thousands of Inca soldiers.

To win his freedom, Atahualpa asked his people to fill a room with gold and silver for Pizarro. Incas brought jewelry, statues, and other valuable items from all parts of the empire. Melted down, the gold and silver may have totaled 24 tons. The precious metals would have been worth millions of dollars today. Despite this huge payment, the Spanish killed Atahualpa. They knew that if they let the Inca ruler live, he might rally his people and defeat the smaller Spanish forces.

Some Incas did fight back after the emperor's death. In 1537, though, Pizarro defeated the last of the Incas. Spain took control over the entire Inca Empire and ruled the region for the next 300 years.

**READING CHECK** Identifying Cause and **Effect** What events ended the Inca Empire?

**SUMMARY AND PREVIEW** The Incas built a huge empire in South America. But even with a strong central government, they could not withstand the Spanish conquest in 1537. In the next chapters you will learn about how the Americas have changed since the great civilizations of the Maya, Aztecs, and Incas and what these places are like today.

## BIOGRAPHY

# Atahualpa
(1502–1533)

Atahualpa was the last Inca emperor. He was a popular ruler, but he didn't rule for long. At his first meeting with Pizarro, he was offered a religious book to convince him to accept Christianity. Atahualpa held the book to his ear and listened. When the book didn't speak, Atahualpa threw it on the ground. The Spanish considered this an insult and a reason to attack.

**Identifying Bias** How do you think the Spanish viewed non-Christians?

## BIOGRAPHY

# Francisco Pizarro
(1475–1541)

Francisco Pizarro organized expeditions to explore the west coast of South America. His first two trips were mostly uneventful. But on his third trip, Pizarro met the Incas. With only about 180 men, he conquered the Inca Empire, which had been weakened by disease and civil war. In 1535 Pizarro founded Lima, the capital of modern Peru.

**Predicting** If Pizarro had not found the Inca Empire, what do you think might have happened?

---

## Section 3 Assessment

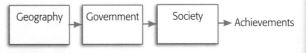
hmhsocialstudies.com
ONLINE QUIZ

### Reviewing Ideas, Terms, and Places

1. **a. Identify** Where was the Inca Empire located? What kinds of terrain did it include?
   **b. Evaluate** Do you think the *mita* system was a good government policy? Why or why not?
2. **a. Describe** What was a unique feature of Inca **masonry**?
   **b. Make Inferences** How might the Inca road system have helped strengthen the empire?
3. **a. Recall** When did the Spanish defeat the last of the Incas?
   **b. Analyze** Why do you think Pizarro was able to defeat the much larger forces of the Incas? Name at least two possible reasons.

### Critical Thinking

4. **Analyzing** Draw a diagram like the one below. Using your notes, write a sentence in each box about how that topic influenced the next topic.

   Geography → Government → Society → Achievements

### FOCUS ON WRITING

5. **Adding Information about the Inca Empire** Your article would also describe the Inca Empire. Include some comments about how the Incas' building activities related to their environment. Also, note what happened when the Spanish arrived.

# Geography and History

# North America's Native Cultures

Native Americans once lived all over North America. Their lifestyles varied depending on their local landscapes. Many Native Americans still carry on the traditions of their ancestors.

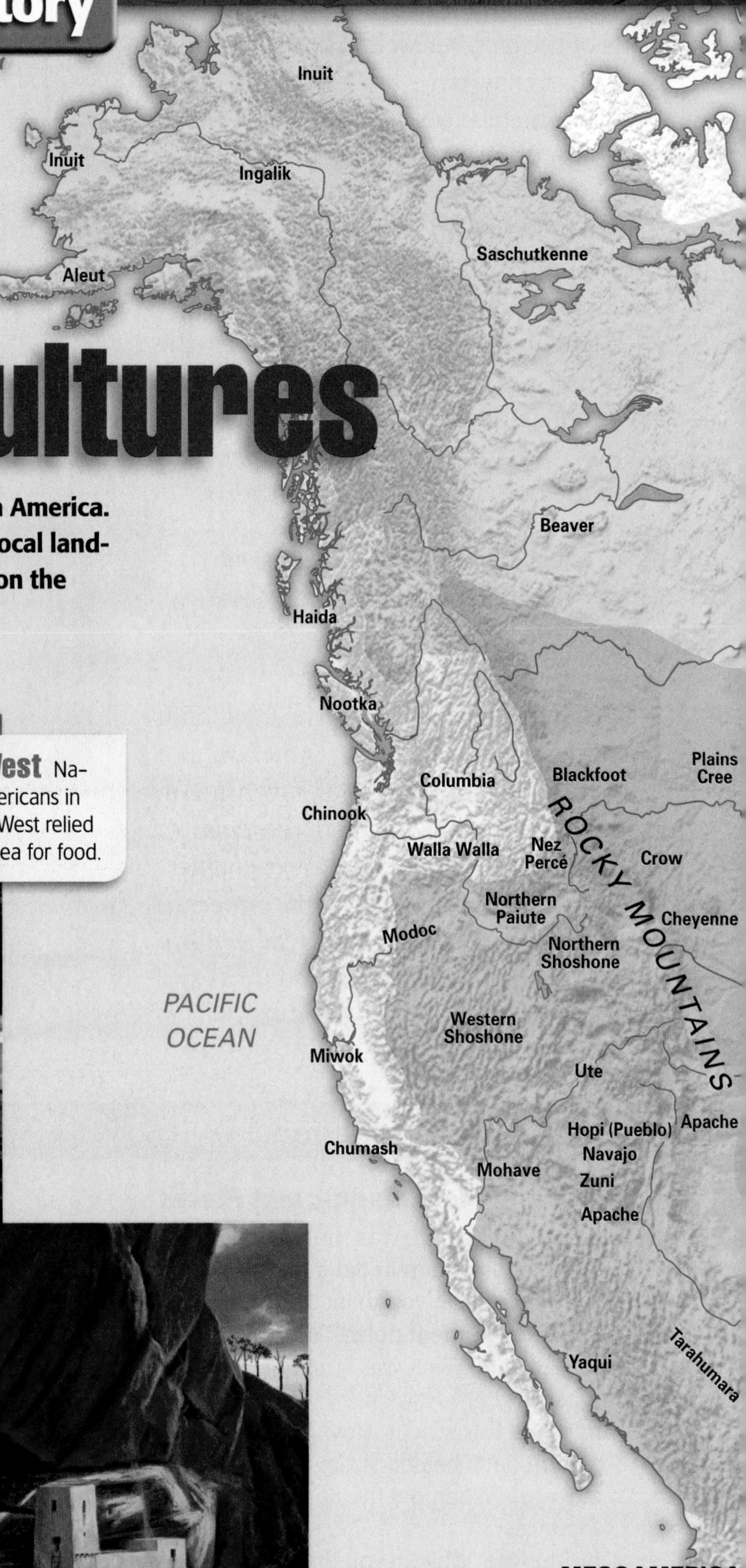

**Far West** Native Americans in the Far West relied on the sea for food.

**Desert West** In the Desert West, Native Americans dealt with their dry, rocky environment by building their homes into the sides of cliffs.

Bering Sea

Inuit
Inuit
Ingalik
Saschutkenne
Aleut
Beaver
Haida
Nootka
Columbia
Plains Cree
Blackfoot
Chinook
Walla Walla
Nez Percé
Crow
Northern Paiute
Cheyenne
Modoc
Northern Shoshone
ROCKY MOUNTAINS
Western Shoshone
Ute
Miwok
Hopi (Pueblo)
Apache
Chumash
Mohave
Navajo
Zuni
Apache
Yaqui
Tarahumara

PACIFIC OCEAN

**MESOAMERICA**

Arctic and Subarctic
Eastern Woodlands
Great Plains
Desert West
Far West

0    150    300 Miles
0    150    300 Kilometers

Projection: Azimuthal Equal-Area

**Arctic and Subarctic** In the cold north, Native Americans adapted to life in permanent snow and ice.

Inuit

Hudson Bay

Inuit

Naskapi

Beothuk

Swampy Cree

Montagnais

**NORTH AMERICA**

Micmac

Algonquian

Pequot
Mohegan

Iroquois
Mohawk
Narraganset

Great Lakes

Teton Sioux

Omaha

Powhatan

Shawnee

Cherokee

Osage

Chickasaw

ATLANTIC OCEAN

**Eastern Woodlands** The forests of the east provided Native Americans there with good building material.

Kiowa

Comanche
Wichita

Choctaw

Caddo

Seminole

Gulf of Mexico

**Great Plains** Native Americans moved around the Great Plains in search of good hunting grounds.

N
W    E
S

Caribbean Sea

**ANALYSIS SKILL** | **ANALYZING VISUALS**

1. **Regions** In what region did the Osage live?
2. **Human-Environment Interaction** What resources did Native Americans in the Far West use?

# Social Studies Skills

# Analyzing Information

## Learn

An important skill to learn is analyzing information presented in the text you read. One way to do this is to identify main ideas and supporting details. Everything in the paragraph should support the main idea.

After you identify the main idea, watch out for anything that is not related to it or necessary for its understanding. Don't let that extra information distract you from the most important material.

## Practice

Look at the paragraph on this page about communication in the Maya civilization. Some unrelated and unnecessary information has been added so that you can learn to identify it. Use the paragraph to answer the questions here.

❶ Which sentence expresses the main idea? What details support it?

❷ What information is unnecessary or unrelated to the main idea?

---

### The Maya

**Communication** The Maya developed an advanced form of writing that used many symbols. Our writing system uses 26 letters. They recorded information on large stone monuments. Some early civilizations drew pictures on cave walls. The Maya also made books of paper made from the bark of fig trees. Fig trees need a lot of light.

**Religion** The Maya believed in many gods and goddesses. More than 160 gods and goddesses are named in a single Maya manuscript. Among the gods they worshipped were a corn god, a rain god, a sun god, and a moon goddess. The early Greeks also worshipped many gods and goddesses.

---

## Apply

Use the passage on this page about Maya religion to answer the following questions.

1. What is the main idea of the paragraph?

2. What details support the main idea?

3. What information is unnecessary or unrelated?

# Chapter Review

**Geography's Impact**
video series
Review the video to answer the closing question:
*How do archaeologists know the Maya built their pyramids without the aid of metal tools?*

## Visual Summary

*Use the visual summary below to help you review the main ideas of the chapter.*

QUICK FACTS

**The Maya**
The Maya traded valuable goods like jade along trade routes that linked their great cities.

**The Aztecs**
The Aztec capital, Tenochtitlán, was a huge, bustling city. People came to its marketplace from all over the empire.

**The Incas**
The Incas are known for their organized empire, impressive stone-work, and crafts in gold and silver.

## Reviewing Vocabulary, Terms, and Places

*For each statement below, write T if it is true and F if it is false. If the statement is false, replace the underlined term with one that would make the sentence a true statement.*

1. The main crops of the Maya included <u>maize</u> and beans.

2. The <u>Quechua</u> came to the Americas to find land, gold, and converts to Catholicism.

3. <u>Palenque</u>, located on a swampy island, was the capital of the Aztec Empire.

4. Maya priests studied the sun, moon, and stars from stone <u>observatories</u>.

5. The official language of the Inca Empire was <u>Cuzco</u>.

6. The Aztecs built raised roads called <u>masonry</u> to cross from Tenochtitlán to the mainland.

7. <u>Tenochtitlán</u> was the Inca capital.

8. Many people in Mesoamerica died at the hands of the <u>conquistadors</u>.

## Comprehension and Critical Thinking

**SECTION 1** *(Pages 118–123)*

9. **a. Recall** Where did the Maya live, and when was their Classic Age?

   **b. Analyze** What was the connection between Maya religion and astronomy? How do you think this connection influenced Maya achievements?

   **c. Elaborate** Why did Maya cities trade with each other? Why did they fight?

**SECTION 2** *(Pages 124–128)*

10. **a. Describe** What was Tenochtitlán like? Where was it located?

    **b. Make Inferences** Why do you think warriors had many privileges and were such respected members of Aztec society?

**SECTION 2** (continued)

**c. Evaluate** What factor do you think played the biggest role in the Aztecs' defeat? Defend your answer.

**SECTION 3** (Pages 129–133)

**11. a. Identify** Name two Inca leaders and explain their roles in Inca history.

**b. Draw Conclusions** What geographic and cultural problems did the Incas overcome to rule their empire?

**c. Elaborate** Do you think most people in the Inca Empire appreciated or resented the *mita* system? Explain your answer.

## Using the Internet

**12. Activity: Making Diagrams** In this chapter you learned about the rise and fall of the Maya, Aztecs, and Incas. Through your online textbook, track the rise and fall of empires in the Americas. Then create a diagram that shows the factors that cause empires to form and the factors that cause empires to fall apart.

hmhsocialstudies.com

## Social Studies Skills

**Analyzing Information** *In the passage below, the first sentence expresses the main idea. One of the following sentences is nonessential to the main idea. Identify the nonessential sentence.*

**13.** Cacao beans had great value to the Maya. Cacao trees are evergreens. They were the source of chocolate, known as a favorite food of rulers and the gods. The Maya also used cacao beans as money.

## Map Activity

**14. Early History of the Americas** On a separate sheet of paper, match the letters on the map with their correct labels.

Palenque      Tenochtitlán

Cuzco

**FOCUS ON READING AND WRITING**

**15. Setting a Purpose** Look back over the information about the Maya in Section 1. For each blue heading, write down the purpose of reading that text. Then describe how reading the text below each heading achieves your purpose.

**16. Writing Your Article** Now that you have collected information about the Americas, you are ready to write a newspaper article. Your purpose is to inform readers in Europe about these fascinating civilizations. Write a headline or title and a two- or three-sentence introduction to the civilizations. Then write a short paragraph about one aspect of each civilization. Choose the most interesting topic to discuss. For example, you might discuss their religion, their social structure, or their scientific achievements.

# Standardized Test Prep

DIRECTIONS: Read questions 1 through 6 and write the letter of the best response. Then read question 7 and write your own well-constructed response.

**1** Maya, Aztec, and Inca societies were similar in many ways. Which of the following practices was common to all three civilizations?

A developing calendars

B keeping written historical records

C building stone temples

D practicing slavery

**2** Farming was important to the Maya, the Aztecs, and the Incas. Which of the following statements about farming is false?

A The Maya grew crops on *chinampas*.

B Farmers in all three civilizations grew maize, but only the Incas raised llamas.

C Maya farmers might not have been able to produce enough food to feed the entire population.

D Maya and Aztec priests decided the best times to plant and harvest.

**3** Which of the following factors helped the Spanish to conquer the Aztecs and the Incas?

A a greater number of soldiers

B superior weapons

C surprise attacks

D good knowledge of the land

**4** Which of the following was a possible reason for the decline of Maya civilization?

A increased warfare and lack of good farmland

B the arrival of Spanish conquistadors and spread of disease

C the development and misuse of guns

D floods that destroyed crops and cities

## Early Civilizations of the Americas

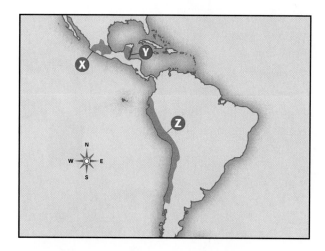

**5** The Aztec and Inca empires are indicated on the map above by

A X for the Inca and Y for the Aztec.

B Y for the Aztec and Z for the Inca.

C Y for the Inca and Z for the Aztec.

D X for the Aztec and Z for the Inca.

**6** Which statement *best* describes the social structure in Maya, Aztec, and Inca civilizations?

A The ruler held the highest position in society, and merchants held the lowest.

B The Aztecs had a simpler class structure than the Maya or the Incas.

C Social divisions were very important to the Maya and the Aztecs, but power and wealth were equally distributed in the Inca Empire.

D Social class helped shape daily life, with the upper class enjoying special privileges made possible by the labor of the common people.

**7** **Extended Response** Use the map above and your knowledge of the Maya and Aztecs to write a brief essay comparing and contrasting the two civilizations. Be sure to discuss the physical geography, achievements, and decline of both civilizations.

# THE Maya

**The Maya developed one of the most advanced civilizations in the Americas, but their story is shrouded in mystery.** Around A.D. 250, the Maya began to build great cities in southern Mexico and Central America. They developed a writing system, practiced astronomy, and built magnificent palaces and pyramids with little more than stone tools. Around A.D. 900, however, the Maya abandoned their cities, leaving their monuments to be reclaimed by the jungle and, for a time, forgotten.

Explore some of the incredible monuments and cultural achievements of the ancient Maya online. You can find a wealth of information, video clips, primary sources, and more at ↗ **hmhsocialstudies.com** .

"Thus let it be done! Let the emptiness be filled! Let the water recede and make a void, let the earth appear and become solid; let it be done . . . "Earth!" they said, and instantly it was made."

### The Popol Vuh

Read the document to learn how the Maya believed the world was created.

### Destroying the Maya's Past

Watch the video to learn how the actions of one Spanish missionary nearly destroyed the written record of the Maya world.

### Finding the City of Palenque

Watch the video to learn about the great Maya city of Palenque and the European discovery of the site in the eighteenth century.

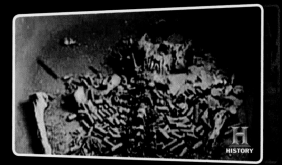

### Pakal's Tomb

Watch the video to explore how the discovery of the tomb of a great king helped archaeologists piece together the Maya past.

# Mexico

**Essential Question** What are the major physical, cultural, and economic features of Mexico?

## What You Will Learn...

In this chapter you will learn about Mexico's physical geography. You will also study the influence of early cultures and Spanish colonial history on Mexico's culture. Today, Mexico is experiencing many changes in its government and economy.

### FOCUS ON READING AND WRITING

**Predicting** Predicting is trying to guess what will happen next. As you read a chapter, stop along the way and consider what you have read. Does the text provide any clues about what will happen next? If it does, see if you can make a prediction about the text. **See the lesson, Predicting, on page 521.**

**Writing an "I Am" Poem** Countries have stories to tell, just like people do. As you read this chapter, gather details about Mexico—how it looks, what its history was like, and what it is like today. Then write an "I Am" poem from the point of view of Mexico telling what you have learned.

Tijuana

30°N

*Gulf of California*

25°N

Tropic of Cancer

*PACIFIC OCEAN*

### Geography Skills

**Location** Mexico is located just south of the United States.
1. **Locate** What is the absolute location of Mexico's capital?
2. **Make Inferences** Do you think Tijuana or Mérida is more influenced by the United States? Why?

**Culture** Brightly costumed dancers perform a traditional dance in Cancún.

# Mexico: Political

UNITED STATES

Ciudad Juárez

Chihuahua

Rio Grande
Rio Bravo

Monterrey

MEXICO

Gulf of Mexico

N
W   E
S

○ National capital
• Other cities

0        100           300 Miles
0   100   200 Kilometers
Projection: Lambert Conformal Conic

25°N

Tropic of Cancer

Yucatán Channel

Cancún
Mérida
Cozumel Island

20°N

Bay of Campeche

Guadalajara

Rio Lerma

Mexico City
Puebla

Balsas River

Veracruz

Usumacinta R.

Caribbean Sea

Oaxaca

Acapulco

Grijalva River

85°W

CENTRAL AMERICA

Gulf of Tehuantepec

105°W

100°W

95°W

90°W

**Geography** Much of Mexico's landscape is dry, with high plateaus and mountains.

**History** The Spanish brought Christianity to Mexico and built churches like this one.

**141**

# Physical Geography

## What You Will Learn...

### Main Ideas

1. Mexico's physical features include plateaus, mountains, and coastal lowlands.
2. Mexico's climate and vegetation include deserts, tropical forests, and cool highlands.
3. Key natural resources in Mexico include oil, silver, gold, and scenic landscapes.

### The Big Idea

Mexico is a large country with different natural environments in its northern, central, and southern regions.

### Key Terms and Places

Río Bravo (Rio Grande), *p. 142*
peninsula, *p. 142*
Baja California, *p. 142*
Gulf of Mexico, *p. 142*
Yucatán Peninsula, *p. 142*
Sierra Madre, *p. 143*

**hmhsocialstudies.com**
TAKING NOTES

Use the graphic organizer online to organize your notes on Mexico's physical geography.

## If YOU lived there...

You live on Mexico's Pacific coast. Sunny weather and good beaches bring tourists year-round. Now you are on your way to visit a cousin in Puebla, in the highlands. To get there, you will have to take a bus along the winding roads of the steep Sierra Madre Occidental. This rugged mountain range runs along the coast. You have never been to the interior of Mexico before.

**What landscapes will you see on your trip?**

**BUILDING BACKGROUND** Mexico is part of Latin America, a region in the Western Hemisphere where Spanish and Portuguese culture shaped life. Mexico is also part of North America, along with the United States and Canada. Unlike its northern neighbors, Mexico's landscape consists mainly of highlands and coastal plains.

## Physical Features

Mexico, our neighbor to the south, shares a long border with the United States. Forming part of this border is one of Mexico's few major rivers, the **Río Bravo**. In the United States this river is called the Rio Grande. At other places along the U.S.–Mexico border it is impossible to tell where one country ends and the other country begins.

### Bodies of Water

As you can see on the map, except for its border with the United States, Mexico is mostly surrounded by water. Mexico's border in the west is the Pacific Ocean. Stretching south into the Pacific Ocean from northern Mexico is a narrow **peninsula**, or piece of land surrounded on three sides by water, called **Baja California**. To the east, Mexico's border is the **Gulf of Mexico**. The Gulf of Mexico is separated from the Caribbean Sea by a part of Mexico called the **Yucatán** (yoo-kah-TAHN) **Peninsula**.

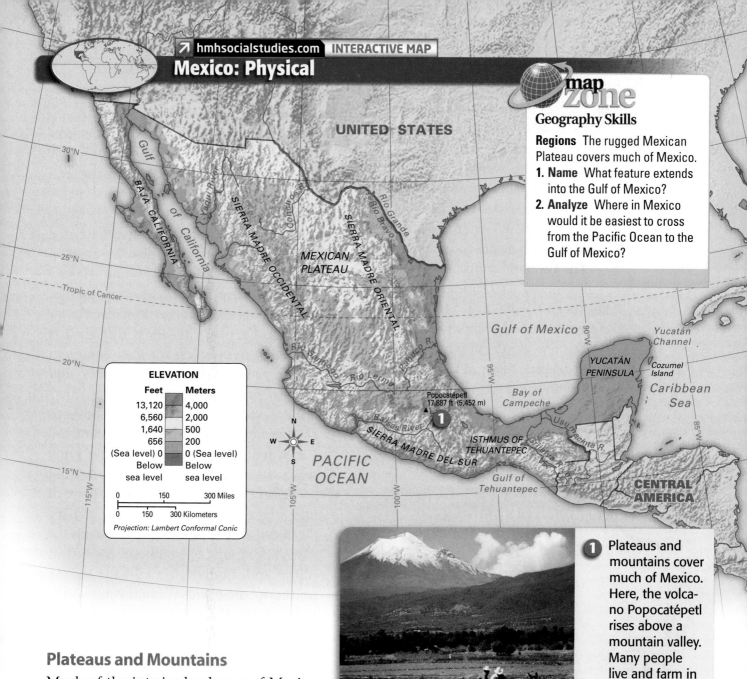

**UNITED STATES**

Gulf of California

BAJA CALIFORNIA

SIERRA MADRE OCCIDENTAL

Rio Colorado

Conchos R.

Rio Grande

Rio Bravo

**MEXICAN PLATEAU**

SIERRA MADRE ORIENTAL

Rio Santiago

Rio Lerma

Panuco R.

**Gulf of Mexico**

Yucatán Channel

**YUCATÁN PENINSULA**

Cozumel Island

**Caribbean Sea**

Popocatépetl 17,887 ft (5,452 m)

Balsas River

SIERRA MADRE DEL SUR

Bay of Campeche

Usumacinta R.

Grijalva River

ISTHMUS OF TEHUANTEPEC

Gulf of Tehuantepec

**CENTRAL AMERICA**

**PACIFIC OCEAN**

30°N
25°N
Tropic of Cancer
20°N
15°N
115°W
110°W
105°W
100°W
95°W
90°W
85°W

**map zone**
**Geography Skills**

**Regions** The rugged Mexican Plateau covers much of Mexico.
1. **Name** What feature extends into the Gulf of Mexico?
2. **Analyze** Where in Mexico would it be easiest to cross from the Pacific Ocean to the Gulf of Mexico?

**ELEVATION**

| Feet | Meters |
|---|---|
| 13,120 | 4,000 |
| 6,560 | 2,000 |
| 1,640 | 500 |
| 656 | 200 |
| (Sea level) 0 | 0 (Sea level) |
| Below sea level | Below sea level |

0      150      300 Miles
0   150   300 Kilometers

*Projection: Lambert Conformal Conic*

**1** Plateaus and mountains cover much of Mexico. Here, the volcano Popocatépetl rises above a mountain valley. Many people live and farm in the mountain valleys.

## Plateaus and Mountains

Much of the interior landscape of Mexico consists of a high, mostly rugged region called the Mexican Plateau. The plateau's lowest point is more than a half mile above sea level. Its highest point is close to two miles above sea level. The entire plateau spreads between two mountain ranges that rise still higher. One range, the Sierra Madre Oriental, lies in the east. The other, the Sierra Madre Occidental, lies in the west. Together, these two mountain ranges and another shorter one in southern Mexico make up the **Sierra Madre** (SYER-rah MAH-dray), or "mother range."

Between the two ranges in the south lies the Valley of Mexico. Mexico City, the country's capital, is located there. The mountains south of Mexico City include towering, snowcapped volcanoes. Volcanic eruptions, as well as earthquakes, are a threat there. The volcano Popocatépetl (poh-puh-cah-TE-pet-uhl) near Mexico City has been active as recently as 2010.

**FOCUS ON READING**

What do you think the text will discuss next?

## Coastal Lowlands

From the highlands in central Mexico, the land slopes down to the coasts. Beautiful, sunny beaches stretch all along Mexico's eastern and western coasts. The plain that runs along the west coast is fairly wide in the north. It becomes narrower in the south. On the east side of the country, the Gulf coastal plain is wide and flat. The soils and climate there are good for farming.

ACADEMIC
VOCABULARY
**vary** to be
different

The Yucatán Peninsula in the southeast is also mostly flat. Limestone rock underlies much of the area. Erosion there has created caves and sinkholes, steep-sided depressions that form when the roof of a cave collapses. Many of these sinkholes are filled with water.

**READING CHECK** **Summarizing** What are Mexico's major physical features?

# Climate and Vegetation

From snowcapped mountain peaks to warm, sunny beaches, Mexico has many different climates. You can see Mexico's climate regions on the map below. This great variety of climates results in several different types of vegetation.

In some areas, changes in elevation cause climates to **vary** widely within a short distance. For example, the areas of high elevation on the Mexican Plateau can have surprisingly cool temperatures. At times, freezing temperatures reach as far south as Mexico City—even though it is located in the tropics. Mexico's mountain valleys generally have mild climates, and many people have settled there.

The valleys along Mexico's southern coastal areas also have pleasant climates. Warm temperatures and a summer rainy season support the forests that cover about 25 percent of Mexico's land area. Tropical rain forests provide a home for jaguars, monkeys, anteaters, and other animals.

While most of southern Mexico is warm and humid, the climate in the northern part of the Yucatán Peninsula is hot and dry. The main vegetation there is scrub forest.

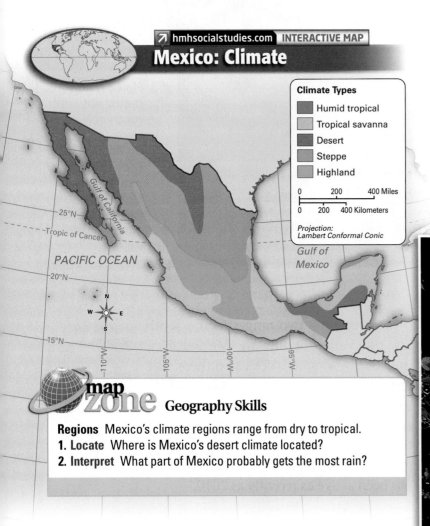

↗ hmhsocialstudies.com **INTERACTIVE MAP**

## Mexico: Climate

**Climate Types**
- Humid tropical
- Tropical savanna
- Desert
- Steppe
- Highland

0   200   400 Miles
0   200   400 Kilometers

Projection:
Lambert Conformal Conic

Gulf of California

25°N

Tropic of Cancer

PACIFIC OCEAN

20°N

N
W    E
S

15°N

110°W    105°W    100°W    95°W

Gulf of Mexico

**map zone** **Geography Skills**

**Regions** Mexico's climate regions range from dry to tropical.
1. **Locate** Where is Mexico's desert climate located?
2. **Interpret** What part of Mexico probably gets the most rain?

**A Tropical Climate**
A tropical savanna climate supports lush vegetation along Mexico's southern beaches.

Like the Yucatán Peninsula in the south, most of northern Mexico is dry. The deserts in Baja California and the northern part of the plateau get little rainfall. Desert plants and dry grasslands are common in the north. Cougars, coyotes, and deer live in some areas of the desert.

**READING CHECK** Analyzing Why does Mexico City sometimes experience freezing temperatures even though it is in the tropics?

## Natural Resources

Mexico is rich in natural resources. One of its most important resources is petroleum, or oil. Oil reserves are found mainly under the southern and Gulf coastal plains as well as offshore in the Gulf of Mexico. Mexico sells much of its oil to the United States.

Before oil was discovered in Mexico, minerals were the country's most valuable resource. Some gold and silver mines that were begun many centuries ago are still in operation. In addition, new mines have been developed in Mexico's mountains. Today Mexico's mines produce more silver than any other country in the world. Mexican mines also yield large amounts of copper, gold, lead, and zinc.

Another important resource is water. The refreshing water surrounding Mexico draws many tourists to the country's scenic beaches. Unfortunately, water is limited in many parts of Mexico. Water scarcity is a serious issue.

**READING CHECK** Finding Main Ideas What is one of Mexico's most important resources?

**SUMMARY AND PREVIEW** The natural environments of Mexico range from arid plateaus in the north to humid, forested mountains in the south. Next, you will study the history and culture of Mexico.

## Section 1 Assessment

hmhsocialstudies.com
ONLINE QUIZ

### Reviewing Ideas, Terms, and Places

1. **a. Describe** What is the interior of Mexico like?
   **b. Analyze** Do you think the **Yucatán Peninsula** is a good place for farming? Explain your answer.
2. **a. Recall** What is the climate like in the northern part of the Yucatán Peninsula?
   **b. Explain** Why can climates sometimes vary widely within a short distance?
   **c. Elaborate** How do you think climate and vegetation affect where people live in Mexico?
3. **a. Identify** Where are Mexico's oil reserves located?
   **b. Make Inferences** What problems might water scarcity cause for Mexican citizens?
   **c. Elaborate** How are Mexico's location, climate, and physical features also natural resources?

### Critical Thinking

4. **Categorizing** Draw a chart like the one here. Using your notes, list the geographical features found in northern Mexico and southern Mexico.

|  | Geography |
|---|---|
| Northern Mexico |  |
| Southern Mexico |  |

### FOCUS ON WRITING

5. **Telling What Mexico Looks Like** What features of Mexico's physical geography will you include in your "I Am" poem? Write notes about the physical features, climate and vegetation, and natural resources of Mexico.

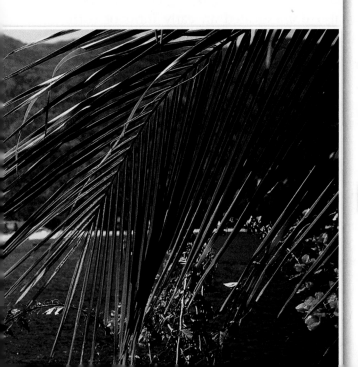

# History and Culture

## What You Will Learn...

### Main Ideas

1. Early cultures of Mexico included the Olmec, the Maya, and the Aztec.
2. Mexico's period as a Spanish colony and its struggles since independence have shaped its culture.
3. Spanish and native cultures have influenced Mexico's customs and traditions today.

### The Big Idea

Native American cultures and Spanish colonization shaped Mexican history and culture.

### Key Terms

empire, *p. 147*
mestizos, *p. 148*
missions, *p. 148*
haciendas, *p. 148*

hmhsocialstudies.com
**TAKING NOTES**

Use the graphic organizer online to organize your notes on Mexico's history and culture.

## If **YOU** lived there...

You belong to one of the native Indian peoples in southern Mexico in the early 1500s. Years ago, the Aztec rulers went to war against your people. They took many captives. They have always treated you cruelly. Now some strangers have come from across the sea. They want your people to help them conquer the Aztecs.

**Will you help the strangers fight the Aztecs? Why or why not?**

**BUILDING BACKGROUND** Mexico was home to several of the earliest advanced cultures in the Americas. Early farmers there developed crops that became staples in much of North America. Mexico also has valuable minerals, which drew Spanish conquerors and colonists. Spanish culture blended with native Mexican cultures.

## Early Cultures

People first came to Mexico many thousands of years ago. As early as 5,000 years ago, they were growing beans, peppers, and squash. They also domesticated an early form of corn. Farming allowed these people to build the first permanent settlements in the Americas.

### Early Cultures of Mexico

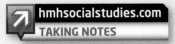
hmhsocialstudies.com
**ANIMATED GEOGRAPHY**

**Olmec**

- The Olmec made sculptures of giant stone heads.
- The heads may have represented rulers or gods.

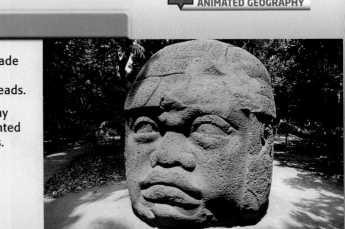

## Olmec

By about 1500 BC the Olmec people in Mexico were living in small villages. The Olmec lived on the humid southern coast of the Gulf of Mexico, where they built temples and giant statues. They also traded carved stones like jade and obsidian with other cultures in eastern Mexico.

## Maya

A few hundred years later, the Maya built on the achievements of the Olmec. Between about AD 250 and 900, the Maya built large cities in Mexico and Central America. In these cities they built stone temples to worship their gods. They studied the stars and developed a detailed calendar. They also kept written records that scholars still study today to learn about Maya history. However, scholars do not fully understand why Maya civilization suddenly collapsed sometime after 900.

## Aztec

After the decline of the Maya civilization, people called the Aztecs moved to central Mexico from the north. In 1325 they built their capital on an island in a lake. Known as Tenochtitlán (tay-nawch-teet-LAHN), this capital grew into one of the largest and most impressive cities of its time.

The Aztecs also built a large, powerful empire. An **empire** is a land with different territories and peoples under a single ruler.

### CONNECTING TO Technology

hmhsocialstudies.com
ANIMATED GEOGRAPHY

## Chinampas

The Aztecs practiced a form of raised-field farming in the swampy lake areas of central Mexico. They called these raised fields *chinampas*. To make them, Aztec farmers piled earth on rafts anchored to trees in the lake. There they grew the corn, beans, and squash that most people ate.

**Analyzing** Why do you think the Aztecs decided to build raised fields for their crops?

The Aztecs planted trees in the lake to anchor the rafts.

The Aztecs built their empire through conquest. They defeated their neighboring tribes in war. Then they forced the other people to pay taxes and to provide war captives for sacrifice to the Aztec gods.

**READING CHECK** **Summarizing** What were some achievements of Mexico's early cultures?

### Maya

- The Maya had a trade network between cities.
- This Maya pyramid stands in Uxmal.

### Aztec

- The Aztecs built the first empire in the Americas.
- Aztec artisans made art like this turquoise mask.

## Colonial Mexico and Independence

**FOCUS ON READING**
What do you think will happen to the Aztec Empire?

In spite of its great size and power, the Aztec Empire did not last long after the first Europeans landed in Mexico. In 1519 Hernán Cortés, a Spanish soldier, arrived in Mexico with about 600 men. These conquistadors (kahn-KEES-tuh-dawrz), or conquerors, gained allies from other tribes in the region. They also had guns and horses, which the Aztecs had never seen before. The new weapons terrified the Aztecs and gave the Spanish an advantage.

The Spanish also unknowingly brought European diseases such as smallpox. The Aztecs had no resistance to these diseases, so many of them died. Greatly weakened by disease, the Aztecs were defeated. In 1521 Cortés claimed the land for Spain.

### Colonial Times

After the conquest, Spanish and American Indian peoples and cultures mixed. This mixing formed a new Mexican identity. Spaniards called people of mixed European and Indian ancestry **mestizos** (me-STEE-zohs). When Africans were brought to America as slaves, they added to this mix of peoples. The Spaniards called people of mixed European and African ancestry mulattoes (muh-LAH-tohs). Africans and American Indians also intermarried.

Life in colonial Mexico was greatly influenced by the Roman Catholic Church. Large areas of northern Mexico were left to the church to explore and to rule. Church outposts known as **missions** were scattered throughout the area. Priests at the missions learned native languages and taught the Indians Spanish. They also worked to convert the American Indians to Catholicism.

In addition to spreading Christianity, the Spaniards wanted to find gold and silver in Mexico. American Indians and enslaved Africans did most of the hard physical labor in the mines. As a result, many died from disease and overwork.

Like mining, agriculture became an important part of the colonial economy. After the conquest, the Spanish monarch granted **haciendas** (hah-see-EN-duhs), or huge expanses of farm or ranch land, to some favored people of Spanish ancestry. Peasants, usually Indians, lived and worked on these haciendas. The haciendas made their owners very wealthy.

### Hidalgo Calls for Independence

Miguel Hidalgo (center, in black) calls for independence from Spain in 1810. The famous Mexican painter Juan O'Gorman painted this image.

**ANALYZING VISUALS** What kinds of people joined Hidalgo in his revolt?

## Independence

Spain ruled Mexico for almost 300 years before the people of Mexico demanded independence. The revolt against Spanish rule was led by a Catholic priest named Miguel Hidalgo. In 1810, he gave a famous speech calling for the common people to rise up against the Spanish. Hidalgo was killed in 1811, but fighting continued until Mexico won its independence in 1821.

## Later Struggles

Fifteen years after Mexico gained its independence, a large area, Texas, broke away. Eventually, Texas joined the United States. As a result, Mexico and the United States fought over Texas and the location of their shared border. This conflict led to the Mexican-American War, in which Mexico lost nearly half its territory to the United States.

In the mid-1800s, Mexico faced other challenges. During this time, the popular president Benito Juárez helped Mexico survive a French invasion. He also made reforms that reduced the privileges of the church and the army.

In spite of these reforms, in the early 1900s the president helped the hacienda owners take land from peasants. Also, foreign companies owned huge amounts of land in Mexico and, in turn, influenced Mexican politics. Many Mexicans thought the president gave these large landowners too many privileges.

As a result, the Mexican Revolution broke out in 1910. The fighting lasted 10 years. One major result of the Mexican Revolution was land reform. The newly formed government took land from the large landowners and gave it back to the peasant villages.

**READING CHECK** **Sequencing** What events occurred after Mexico gained independence?

---

### BIOGRAPHY

## Benito Juárez
(1806–1872)

Benito Juárez was Mexico's first president of Indian heritage. A wise and passionate leader, Juárez stood up for the rights of all Mexicans. As the minister of justice, he got rid of special courts for members of the church and the military. As president, he passed reforms that laid the foundation for a democratic government. Today he is considered a national hero in Mexico.

**Drawing Conclusions** How may Juárez's heritage have affected his efforts for Mexico's citizens?

---

## Culture

Mexico's history has **influenced** its culture. For example, one major influence from history is language. Most Mexicans speak Spanish because of the Spanish influence in colonial times. Another influence from Spain is religion. About 90 percent of all Mexicans are Roman Catholic.

However, Mexico's culture also reflects its American Indian heritage. For example, many people still speak American Indian languages. In Mexico, a person's language is tied to his or her ethnic group. Speaking an American Indian language identifies a person as Indian.

Mexicans also have some unique cultural practices that combine elements of Spanish influence with the influence of Mexican Indians. An example of this combining can be seen in a holiday called Day of the Dead. This holiday is a day to remember and honor dead ancestors.

**ACADEMIC VOCABULARY**
influence change or have an effect on

**VIDEO**
The Peasant Revolution
hmhsocialstudies.com

## Day of the Dead

Everyone is sad when a loved one dies. But during Day of the Dead, Mexicans celebrate death as part of life. This attitude comes from the Mexican Indian belief that the souls of the dead return every year to visit their living relatives. To prepare for this visit, Mexican families gather in graveyards. They clean up around their loved one's grave and decorate it with flowers and candles. They also set out food and drink for the celebration. Favorite foods often include sugar candy skulls, chocolate coffins, and sweet breads shaped like bones.

**Summarizing** Why do Mexicans celebrate Day of the Dead?

Mexicans celebrate Day of the Dead on November 1 and 2. These dates are similar to the dates that the Catholic Church honors the dead with All Souls' Day. The holiday also reflects native customs and beliefs about hopes of life after death.

**READING CHECK** **Categorizing** What aspects of Mexican culture show the influence of Spanish rule?

**SUMMARY AND PREVIEW** Mexico's early cultures formed great civilizations, but after the conquest of the Aztec Empire, power in Mexico shifted to Spain. Spain ruled Mexico for nearly 300 years before Mexico gained independence. Mexico's history and its mix of Indian and Spanish backgrounds have influenced the country's culture. In the next section you will learn about life in Mexico today.

## Section 2 Assessment

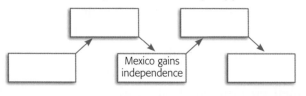
hmhsocialstudies.com
ONLINE QUIZ

### Reviewing Ideas, Terms, and Places

**1. a. Recall** Where in Mexico did the Olmec live?
**b. Explain** How did the Aztecs build and rule their **empire**?
**c. Elaborate** Why do you think scholars are not sure what caused the end of Maya civilization?

**2. a. Identify** Who began the revolt that led to Mexico's independence?
**b. Explain** What was Mexico like in colonial times?
**c. Predict** How may history have been different if the Aztecs had defeated the Spanish?

**3. a. Identify** What Mexican holiday honors dead ancestors?
**b. Summarize** How did Mexico's colonial past shape its culture?

### Critical Thinking

**4. Sequencing** Draw a diagram like the one below. Then, using your notes, list the major events in Mexico's history in the order they happened.

Mexico gains independence

### FOCUS ON WRITING

**5. Learning about History and Culture** Mexico's history is full of fascinating stories. In your notebook, jot down ideas about people and stories from Mexico's history.

# Taking Notes

## Learn

Taking notes can help you remember what you have learned from your textbook or in class. To be effective, your notes must be clear and organized. One good way to organize your notes is in a chart like the one here. Use the following steps to help you take useful notes:

• Before you read: Divide a page in your notebook into two columns as shown.

• While you read: Write down your notes in phrases or sentences in the large column on the right.

• After you read: Review your notes. Then in the small column on the left, jot down ideas, key terms, or questions in your own words based on the notes you took.

| Recall | Notes |
|---|---|
| New Mexican identity | - Spanish and American Indian cultures mixed.<br>  - mestizos<br>- Africans came as slaves. |
| Influence on Catholic Church | - Life in colonial Mexico was influenced by the Roman Catholic Church.<br>  - missions<br>  - Priests taught Spanish. |
| Economy: mining and agriculture | - Spaniards were interested in gold and silver.<br>  - American Indians and enslaved Africans worked in mines.<br>- Agriculture was important.<br>  - haciendas |

## Practice

Answer the following questions about taking notes.

❶ Where should you write your notes while you read or listen in class?

❷ How can jotting down key ideas, terms, and questions help you clarify your notes after you take them?

## Apply

Look back at Section 1 of this chapter. Divide your paper into two columns and take notes on the section using the suggestions above. Then answer the following questions.

**1.** What ideas or questions did you write in the Recall column on the left?

**2.** What are some advantages of taking notes?

# Mexico Today

## What You Will Learn...

### Main Ideas

1. Government has traditionally played a large role in Mexico's economy.
2. Mexico has four distinct culture regions.

### The Big Idea

Mexico has four culture regions that all play a part in the country's government and economy.

### Key Terms and Places

inflation, *p. 152*
slash-and-burn agriculture, *p. 153*
cash crop, *p. 153*
Mexico City, *p. 154*
smog, *p. 154*
maquiladoras, *p. 155*

hmhsocialstudies.com
**TAKING NOTES**

Use the graphic organizer online to take notes on Mexico's government and economy.

## If YOU lived there...

For many years, your family has lived in a small village in southern Mexico. Jobs are scarce there. Your older brother and sisters talk about moving to a larger city. Big cities may provide some more opportunities, but they can be crowded and noisy. Many people from your village have already gone to the city.

**How do you feel about moving to the city?**

**BUILDING BACKGROUND** After Mexico gained independence, many government leaders did not rule democratically. For years the Mexican people had little say in their government. But changes in the 1990s and 2000s led toward more democracy and prosperity.

## Government and Economy

Today people in Mexico can vote in certain elections for the first time. People can find jobs in cities and buy their families a home. More children are able to attend school. In recent years, changes in Mexico's government and economy have made improvements like these possible.

### Government

Mexico has a democratic government. However, Mexico is not like the United States where different political parties have always competed for power. In Mexico the same political party controlled the government for 71 years. But this control ended in 2000 when Mexicans elected Vicente Fox their president. Fox represented a different political party.

For many years, Mexico's government controlled most of the country's economic activity. Today the government has less control of the economy.

### Economy

Mexico is a developing country. It has struggled with debts to foreign banks, unemployment, and inflation. **Inflation** is a rise in prices that occurs when currency loses its buying power.

Although living standards in Mexico are lower than in many other countries, Mexico's economy is growing. The North American Free Trade Agreement (NAFTA), which took effect in 1994, has made trade among Mexico, the United States, and Canada easier. Mexico's agricultural and industrial exports have increased since NAFTA went into effect.

**Agriculture** Agriculture has long been a key part of the Mexican economy. This is true even though just 13 percent of the land is good for farming. Many farmers in southern Mexico practice **slash-and-burn agriculture**, which is the practice of burning forest in order to clear land for planting.

The high market demand for food in the United States has encouraged many farmers in Mexico to grow cash crops. A **cash crop** is a crop that farmers grow mainly to sell for a profit. Trucks bring cash crops like fruits and vegetables from Mexico to the United States.

**Industry** Oil is also an important export for Mexico. Many Mexicans work in the oil, mining, and manufacturing industries. These industries are growing.

The fastest-growing industrial centers in Mexico lie along the U.S. border. Because wages are relatively low in Mexico, many U.S. and foreign companies have built factories in Mexico. Mexican workers in these factories assemble goods for export to the United States and other countries. Some Mexican workers also come to the United States to look for jobs that pay more than they can make at home.

**Tourism** Tourism is another important part of Mexico's economy. Many tourists visit old colonial cities and Maya and Aztec monuments. Coastal cities and resorts such as Cancún and Acapulco are also popular with tourists.

**READING CHECK** **Summarizing** How is the government's role in the economy changing?

**HISTORY**

VIDEO
Mexico in the Modern Era

↗ hmhsocialstudies.com

↗ hmhsocialstudies.com
ANIMATED GEOGRAPHY
Resources and Products of Mexico

## Satellite View

Smoke

Fire

Many people in Mexico are subsistence farmers. They do not own much land and grow only enough food to feed their families. To gain more land, farmers in southern Mexico burn patches of forest. The fires clear the trees and kill weeds, and ash from the fires fertilizes the soil. However, growing the same crops year after year drains valuable nutrients from the soil. The farmers then have to burn new forest land.

In the satellite image here, agricultural fires appear as red dots. As you can see, the fires create a lot of smoke. Wind then blows the smoke great distances. Every few years, when the conditions are right, smoke from agricultural fires in Mexico reaches as far as the southern United States. The smoke can cause health problems for some people.

**Analyzing** What direction was the wind blowing in this image?

**Northern Mexico** Northern Mexico's land is generally too dry to be much good for farming, but ranching is an important part of the region's economy.

**ANALYSIS SKILL** **ANALYZING INFORMATION**
How do you think life in greater Mexico City differs from life in northern Mexico?

**Central Mexico** The architecture and cobble-stone streets of many towns in central Mexico reflect the region's Spanish colonial heritage.

## Mexico's Culture Regions

Although all Mexicans share some cultural characteristics, we can divide Mexico into four regions based on regional differences. These four culture regions differ from each other in their population, resources, climate, and other features.

### Greater Mexico City

Greater Mexico City includes the capital and about 50 smaller cities near it. With a population of more than 19 million, **Mexico City** is the world's second-largest city and one of the most densely populated urban areas. Thousands of people move there every year looking for work.

While this region does provide job and educational opportunities not so easily found in the rest of the country, its huge population causes problems. For example, Mexico City is very polluted. Factories and cars release exhaust and other pollutants into the air. The surrounding mountains trap the resulting **smog**—a mixture of smoke, chemicals, and fog. Smog can cause health problems like eye irritation and breathing difficulties.

Another problem that comes from crowding is poverty. Wealth and poverty exist side by side in Mexico City. The city has large urban slums. The slums often exist right next to modern office buildings, apartments, museums, or universities.

**Greater Mexico City** Traffic clogs Mexico City's busy streets. Taxis, buses, and private cars zoom past modern office buildings and old colonial government buildings.

**Southern Mexico** While poverty is a problem in much of southern Mexico, some people make money selling traditional handicrafts to tourists.

## Central Mexico

North of greater Mexico City lies Mexico's central region. Many cities in this region were established as mining or ranching centers during the colonial period. Mexico's colonial heritage can still be seen today in these cities and towns. For example, small towns often have a colonial-style church near a main central square. The central square, or plaza, has served for hundreds of years as a community meeting spot and market area.

In addition to small colonial towns, central Mexico has many fertile valleys and small family farms. Farmers in this region grow vegetables, corn, and wheat for sale, mostly to cities in Mexico.

While central Mexico has always been a mining center, in recent years the region has also attracted new industries from overcrowded Mexico City. As a result, some cities in the region, such as Guadalajara, are growing rapidly.

## Northern Mexico

Northern Mexico has become one of the country's richest and most modern areas. Trade with the United States has helped the region's economy grow. Monterrey and Tijuana are now major cities there. Many U.S.- and foreign-owned factories called **maquiladoras** (mah-kee-lah-DORH-ahs) have been built along Mexico's long border with the United States.

ACADEMIC VOCABULARY
**affect** to change or influence

Northern Mexico's closeness to the border has **affected** the region's culture as well as its economy. American television, music, and other forms of entertainment are popular there. Many Mexicans cross the border to shop, work, or live in the United States. While many people cross the border legally, the U.S. government tries to prevent Mexicans and others from crossing the border illegally.

## Southern Mexico

Southern Mexico is the least populated and industrialized region of the country. Many people in this region speak Indian languages and practice traditional ways of life. Subsistence farming and slash-and-burn agriculture are common.

FOCUS ON READING
What do you think makes southern Mexico vital to the country's economy?

However, southern Mexico is vital to the country's economy. Sugarcane and coffee, two major export crops, grow well in the region's warm, humid climate. Also, oil production along the Gulf coast has increased in recent years. The oil business has brought more industry and population growth to this coastal area of southern Mexico.

Another place in southern Mexico that has grown in recent years is the Yucatán Peninsula. Maya ruins, beautiful sunny beaches, and clear blue water have made tourism a major industry in this area. Many cities that were just tiny fishing villages only 20 years ago are now booming with new construction for the tourist industry.

Mexico will continue to change in the future. Changes are likely to bring more development. However, maintaining the country's unique regional cultures may be a challenge as those changes take place.

**READING CHECK** Comparing and Contrasting What similarities and differences exist between greater Mexico City and southern Mexico?

**SUMMARY AND PREVIEW** Mexico has a democratic government and a growing economy. It also has distinct regions with different cultures, economies, and environments. In the next chapter you will learn about the countries to the south of Mexico.

## Section 3 Assessment

hmhsocialstudies.com
ONLINE QUIZ

### Reviewing Ideas, Terms, and Places

1. a. **Define** What is the term for the practice of burning forest in order to clear land for planting?
b. **Compare and Contrast** How is Mexico's government similar to and different from the government of the United States?
2. a. **Identify** What is an environmental problem found in **Mexico City**?
b. **Make Inferences** What conditions in Mexico lead some Mexicans to cross the border into the United States?
c. **Develop** If you were to start a business in Mexico, what type of business would you start and where would you start it? Explain your decisions.

### Critical Thinking

3. **Finding Main Ideas** Review your notes on Mexico's economy. Then use a chart like this one to show what parts of the economy are important in each region.

| Greater Mexico City | Central Mexico | Northern Mexico | Southern Mexico |
|---|---|---|---|
| | | | |

### FOCUS ON WRITING

4. **Describing Mexico Today** Write some details about the four culture regions of Mexico. Which details will you include in your poem?

**156** CHAPTER 6

# Chapter Review

**Geography's Impact**
video series
Review the video to answer the closing question:
*Do you think emigration from Mexico to the United States hurts or helps Mexico? Why?*

## Visual Summary

*Use the visual summary below to help you review the main ideas of the chapter.*

QUICK FACTS

The physical geography of Mexico includes a high region of plateaus and mountains.

The Spanish conquered the Aztecs and ruled Mexico for about 300 years until the Mexicans gained independence.

Greater Mexico City, one of Mexico's four culture regions, is the center of Mexico's government and economy.

## Reviewing Vocabulary, Terms, and Places

*Unscramble each group of letters below to spell a term that matches the given definition.*

1. **pmreie**—a land with different territories and peoples under a single ruler

2. **tflinnaoi**—a rise in prices that occurs when currency loses its buying power

3. **mogs**—a mixture of smoke, chemicals, and fog

4. **snipluane**—a piece of land surrounded on three sides by water

5. **ztosemsi**—people of mixed European and Indian ancestry

6. **hacs rpoc**—a crop that farmers grow mainly to sell for a profit

7. **ssnmiosi**—church outposts

8. **dqamiuarsloa**—U.S.- and foreign-owned factories in Mexico

9. **ndhceiasa**—expanses of farm or ranch land

## Comprehension and Critical Thinking

**SECTION 1** *(Pages 143–145)*

10. **a. Define** What is the Mexican Plateau? What forms its edges?

   **b. Contrast** How does the climate of Mexico City differ from the climate in the south?

   **c. Evaluate** What do you think would be Mexico's most important resource if it did not have oil? Explain your answer.

**SECTION 2** *(Pages 146–150)*

11. **a. Recall** What early civilization did the Spanish conquer when they came to Mexico?

   **b. Analyze** How did Spanish rule influence Mexico's culture?

   **c. Evaluate** Which war—the war for independence, the Mexican War, or the Mexican Revolution—do you think changed Mexico the most? Explain your answer.

**12. a. Describe** What are Mexico's four culture regions? Describe a feature of each.

**b. Analyze** What regions do you think are the most popular with tourists? Explain your answer.

**c. Evaluate** What are two major drawbacks of slash-and-burn agriculture?

# Using the Internet 21ST CENTURY

**13. Activity: Writing a Description** Colorful textiles, paintings, and pottery are just some of the many crafts made throughout Mexico. Each region in Mexico has its own style of crafts and folk art. Through your online textbook, visit some of the different regions of Mexico and explore their arts and crafts. Pick a favorite object from each region. Learn about its use, its design, how it was made, and the people who made it. Then write a brief paragraph that describes each object and its unique characteristics.

↗ hmhsocialstudies.com

# Social Studies Skills

**14. Taking Notes** Look back at the information in Section 3 about Mexico's government and economy. Then use a chart like this one to take notes on the information in your book.

| Recall | Notes |
|--------|-------|
|        |       |
|        |       |
|        |       |

# Map Activity 21ST CENTURY

**15. Mexico** On a separate sheet of paper, match the letters on the map with their correct labels.

Gulf of Mexico          Baja California

Río Bravo (Rio Grande)  Tijuana

Yucatán Peninsula        Mexico City

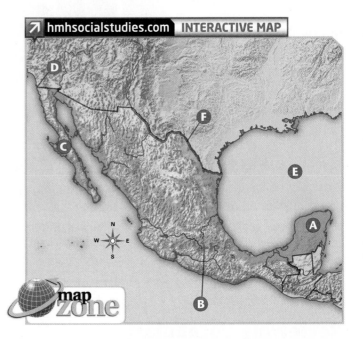

↗ hmhsocialstudies.com   INTERACTIVE MAP

map zone

**FOCUS ON READING AND WRITING**

**16. Predicting** Now you can use your skills in predicting to think about events that might happen in the future. Reread the text in your book about Mexico's economy. Write three to four sentences about how you think the economy might change in the future.

**17. Writing an "I Am" Poem** Now it is time to write your poem. Title your poem "I am Mexico" and make it six lines long. Use each line to give details about Mexico, such as "I have towering, snowcapped volcanoes." Make sure at least one line deals with physical geography, one line with history and culture, and one line with Mexico today. Your poem does not need to rhyme, but you should try to use vivid language.

DIRECTIONS: *Read questions 1 through 6 and write the letter of the best response. Then read question 7 and write your own well-constructed response.*

**1** **What physical features make up much of central Mexico?**

A plateaus and mountains

B peninsulas

C beaches and lowlands

D sinkholes

**2** **What early culture in Mexico did the Spanish conquer?**

A Olmec

B Maya

C Aztec

D conquistador

**3** **Which of the following was a way in which the Spanish affected Mexico during colonial times?**

A granted land to the native people

B set up missions and taught about Christianity

C started the Mexican Revolution

D gave away half of Mexico to the United States

**4** **Where are Mexico's fastest-growing industrial centers?**

A on the Gulf coast

B in Mexico City

C on the Yucatán Peninsula

D along the U.S. border

**5** **What factor helps classify Mexico as a developing country?**

A high unemployment

B few political parties

C an economy based on oil and tourism

D relatively high living standards

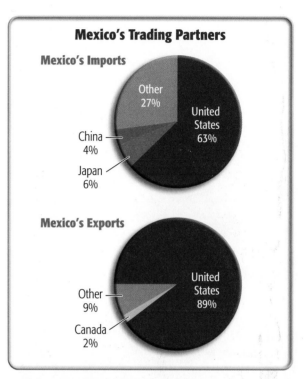

Source: *World Almanac and Book of Facts,* 2005

**6** **Based on the graphs above, which of the following statements is false?**

A The United States is Mexico's biggest trading partner.

B The United States imports 63% of its goods from Mexico.

C 89% of Mexico's exports go to the United States.

D Imports from Japan make up 6% of Mexico's total imports.

**7** **Extended Response** Look at the graphs above and the information in Section 3. Then write a brief essay explaining how NAFTA has influenced Mexico.

# Mexico

**Teotihuacán, established around 200 B.C., was the first great civilization of ancient Mexico.** At its height around the middle of the first millennium A.D., the "City of the Gods" was one of the largest cities in the world. It covered 12 square miles and was home to some 200,000 people. The Pyramid of the Sun, above, was the largest building in Teotihuacán.

For centuries after the fall of Teotihuacán, present-day Mexico was home to a number of great empires, including the highly sophisticated Aztec civilization. The arrival of the Spanish in the early 1500s forever changed life for Mexico's ancient peoples, and Mexican culture today is dominated by a blend of indigenous and Spanish cultures.

Explore the history of Mexico from ancient to modern times online. You can find a wealth of information, video clips, primary sources, activities, and more at ⬇ hmhsocialstudies.com.

### The Arrival of the Spanish

Watch the video to learn how the arrival of the conquistadors led to the fall of the Aztec Empire.

### Miguel Hidalgo's Call to Arms

Watch the video to learn about Miguel Hidalgo's path from priest to revolutionary leader.

### Mexico in the Modern Era

Watch the video to learn about the role of oil in the industrialization of Mexico's economy.

### Mexico's Ancient Civilizations

Watch the video to learn about the great civilizations that arose in ancient Mexico.

# Central America and the Caribbean

**Essential Question** How have Central America and the Caribbean been shaped by geography and history?

## What You Will Learn...

In this chapter you will learn about the beautiful physical landscapes of Central America and the Caribbean. You will also study the history of the region along with the people who live there and the way they live today.

### FOCUS ON READING & WRITING

**Understanding Comparison-Contrast** When you compare, you look for ways in which things are alike. When you contrast, you look for ways in which things are different. As you read the chapter, look for ways you can compare and contrast information. **See the lesson, Understanding Comparison-Contrast, on page 522.**

**Creating a Travel Guide** People use travel guides to learn more about places they want to visit. As you read about Central America and the Caribbean in this chapter, you will collect information about places tourists might visit. Then you will create your own travel guide for visitors to one of these vacation spots.

**History** The Spanish built forts like this one in Puerto Rico to defend their islands and protect the harbors from pirates.

Gulf of Mexico

MEXICO

Belmopan
BELIZE

GUATEMALA
Guatemala City

HONDURAS
Tegucigalpa

San Salvador
EL SALVADOR

PACIFIC OCEAN

NICARAGUA
Managua
San Juan River

COSTA RICA
San José

○ National capital

| 0 | 100 | 200 Miles |
| 0 | 100 | 200 Kilometers |

*Projection: Azimuthal Equal-Area*

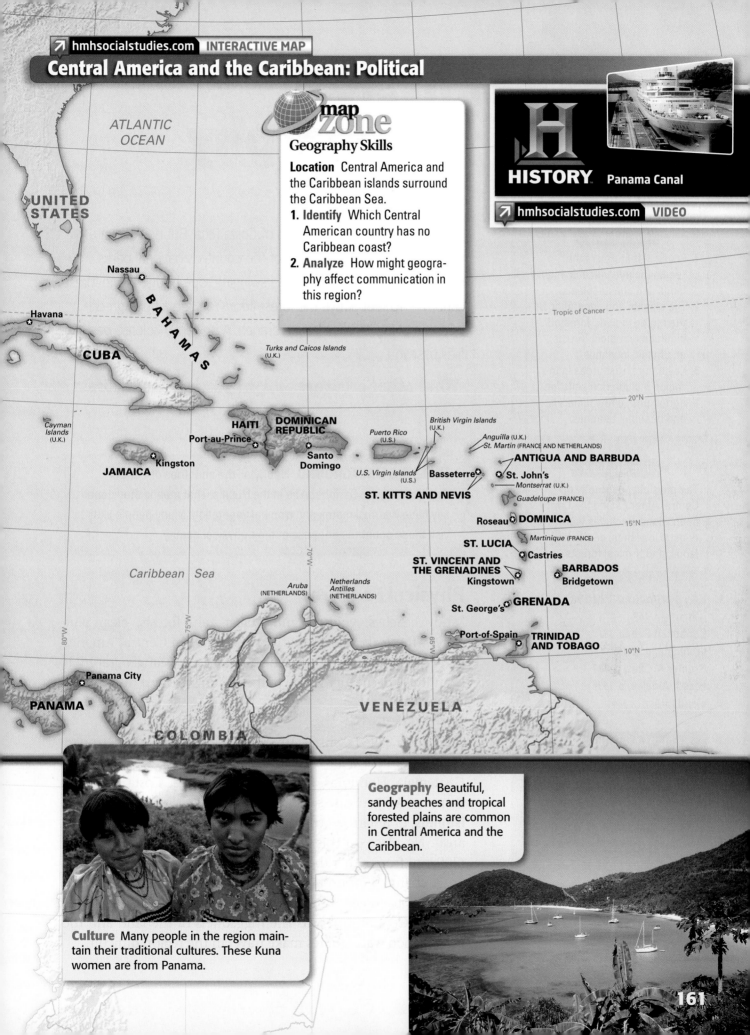

ATLANTIC OCEAN

### map zone
**Geography Skills**

**Location** Central America and the Caribbean islands surround the Caribbean Sea.
1. **Identify** Which Central American country has no Caribbean coast?
2. **Analyze** How might geography affect communication in this region?

**H HISTORY** Panama Canal

hmhsocialstudies.com  VIDEO

UNITED STATES

Nassau ✪

Havana ✪

B A H A M A S

CUBA

Turks and Caicos Islands (U.K.)

Tropic of Cancer

20°N

Cayman Islands (U.K.)

HAITI
Port-au-Prince ✪

DOMINICAN REPUBLIC
Santo Domingo ✪

Puerto Rico (U.S.)

British Virgin Islands (U.K.)

Anguilla (U.K.)
St. Martin (FRANCE AND NETHERLANDS)

ANTIGUA AND BARBUDA
✪ St. John's

JAMAICA
✪ Kingston

U.S. Virgin Islands (U.S.)

Basseterre ✪

Montserrat (U.K.)

Guadeloupe (FRANCE)

ST. KITTS AND NEVIS

Roseau ✪ DOMINICA

15°N

ST. LUCIA
✪ Castries

Martinique (FRANCE)

Caribbean Sea

70°W

75°W

80°W

Aruba (NETHERLANDS)

Netherlands Antilles (NETHERLANDS)

ST. VINCENT AND THE GRENADINES
Kingstown

BARBADOS
Bridgetown

St. George's ✪ GRENADA

65°W

Port-of-Spain ✪ TRINIDAD AND TOBAGO

10°N

Panama City ✪

PANAMA

VENEZUELA

COLOMBIA

**Geography** Beautiful, sandy beaches and tropical forested plains are common in Central America and the Caribbean.

**Culture** Many people in the region maintain their traditional cultures. These Kuna women are from Panama.

# Physical Geography

## What You Will Learn...

### Main Ideas

1. Physical features of the region include volcanic highlands and coastal plains.
2. The climate and vegetation of the region include forested highlands, tropical forests, and humid lowlands.
3. Key natural resources in the region include rich soils for agriculture, a few minerals, and beautiful beaches.

### The Big Idea

The physical geography of Central America and the Caribbean islands includes warm coastal lowlands, cooler highlands, and tropical forests.

### Key Terms and Places

isthmus, *p. 162*
Caribbean Sea, *p. 162*
archipelago, *p. 163*
Greater Antilles, *p. 163*
Lesser Antilles, *p. 163*
cloud forest, *p. 164*

hmhsocialstudies.com
TAKING NOTES

Use the graphic organizer online to take notes on Mexico's physical geography.

## If YOU lived there...

You live in San José, the capital of Costa Rica. But now you are visiting a tropical forest in one of the country's national parks. You make your way carefully along a swinging rope bridge in the forest canopy—40 feet above the forest floor! You see a huge green iguana making its way along a branch. A brilliantly colored parrot flies past you.

**What other creatures might you see in the forest?**

**BUILDING BACKGROUND** Nearly all the countries of Central America and the Caribbean lie in the tropics. That means they generally have warm climates and tropical vegetation. Many people like to visit these countries because of their physical beauty.

## Physical Features

Sandy beaches, volcanic mountains, rain forests, clear blue water—these are images many people have of Central America and the Caribbean islands. This region's physical geography is beautiful. This beauty is one of the region's greatest resources.

### Central America

The region called Central America is actually the southern part of North America. Seven countries make up this region: Belize, Guatemala, Honduras, El Salvador, Nicaragua, Costa Rica, and Panama. As you can see on the map, Central America is an **isthmus**, or a narrow strip of land that connects two larger land areas. No place on this isthmus is more than about 125 miles (200 km) from either the Pacific Ocean or the **Caribbean Sea**.

A chain of mountains and volcanoes separates the Pacific and Caribbean coastal plains, and only a few short rivers flow through Central America. The ruggedness of the land and the lack of good water routes make travel in the region difficult.

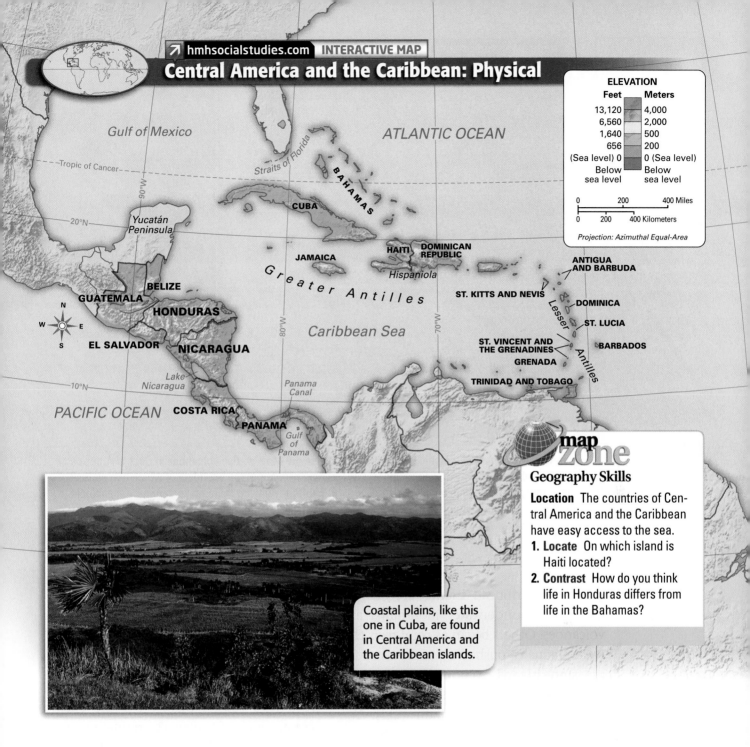

## Central America and the Caribbean: Physical

Gulf of Mexico

ATLANTIC OCEAN

Tropic of Cancer

Straits of Florida

BAHAMAS

CUBA

20°N

Yucatán
Peninsula

JAMAICA

Greater Antilles

HAITI   DOMINICAN
REPUBLIC

Hispaniola

ANTIGUA
AND BARBUDA

BELIZE

ST. KITTS AND NEVIS

GUATEMALA

DOMINICA

HONDURAS

Caribbean Sea

Lesser   ST. LUCIA

N
W   E
S

EL SALVADOR   NICARAGUA

ST. VINCENT AND
THE GRENADINES   BARBADOS

Antilles

10°N

Lake
Nicaragua

Panama
Canal

GRENADA

TRINIDAD AND TOBAGO

PACIFIC OCEAN   COSTA RICA

PANAMA   Gulf
of
Panama

**ELEVATION**

| Feet | | Meters |
|------|--|--------|
| 13,120 | | 4,000 |
| 6,560 | | 2,000 |
| 1,640 | | 500 |
| 656 | | 200 |
| (Sea level) 0 | | 0 (Sea level) |
| Below sea level | | Below sea level |

0   200   400 Miles
0   200   400 Kilometers

Projection: Azimuthal Equal-Area

**map zone**

**Geography Skills**

**Location** The countries of Central America and the Caribbean have easy access to the sea.
1. **Locate** On which island is Haiti located?
2. **Contrast** How do you think life in Honduras differs from life in the Bahamas?

Coastal plains, like this one in Cuba, are found in Central America and the Caribbean islands.

## The Caribbean Islands

Across the Caribbean Sea from Central America lie hundreds of islands known as the Caribbean islands. They make up an **archipelago** (ahr-kuh-PE-luh-goh), or large group of islands. Arranged in a long curve, the Caribbean islands stretch from the southern tip of Florida to northern South America. They divide the Caribbean Sea from the Atlantic Ocean.

There are two main island groups in the Caribbean. The four large islands of Cuba, Jamaica, Hispaniola, and Puerto Rico make up the **Greater Antilles** (an-TI-leez). Many smaller islands form the **Lesser Antilles**. They stretch from the Virgin Islands to Trinidad and Tobago. A third island group, the Bahamas, lies in the Atlantic Ocean southeast of Florida. It includes nearly 700 islands and thousands of reefs.

**FOCUS ON READING**
How are the Greater and Lesser Antilles different?

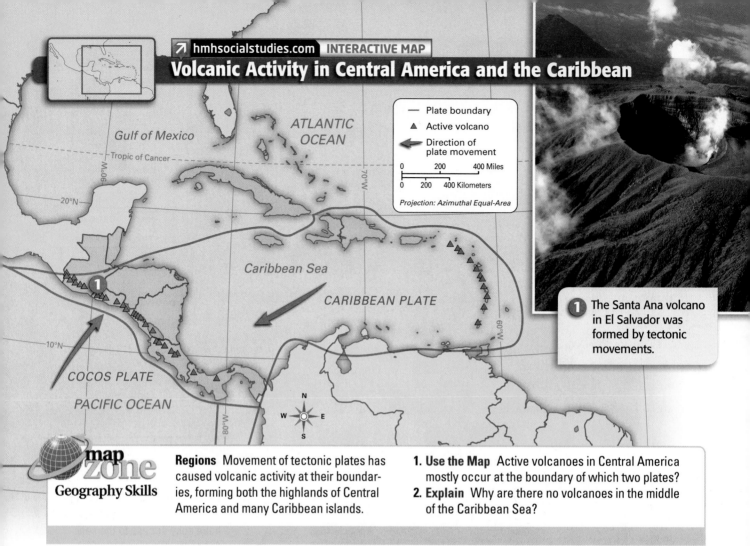

ATLANTIC OCEAN

Gulf of Mexico

Tropic of Cancer

20°N

90°W

70°W

Caribbean Sea

CARIBBEAN PLATE

10°N

COCOS PLATE

PACIFIC OCEAN

80°W

60°W

N W E S

— Plate boundary
▲ Active volcano
← Direction of plate movement

0    200    400 Miles
0   200   400 Kilometers
*Projection: Azimuthal Equal-Area*

**1** The Santa Ana volcano in El Salvador was formed by tectonic movements.

**map zone**
**Geography Skills**

**Regions** Movement of tectonic plates has caused volcanic activity at their boundaries, forming both the highlands of Central America and many Caribbean islands.

1. **Use the Map** Active volcanoes in Central America mostly occur at the boundary of which two plates?
2. **Explain** Why are there no volcanoes in the middle of the Caribbean Sea?

Many Caribbean islands are actually the tops of underwater mountains and volcanoes. Others began as coral reefs that were gradually pushed up to become flat limestone islands. Colliding tectonic plates have pushed this region's land up out of the sea over several million years. You can see these tectonic plates on the map above. Notice how the land follows the boundaries of the plates. Earthquakes and volcanic eruptions occur frequently as these plates shift. When such events do occur, they can cause great damage to the region and its people.

**READING CHECK** **Comparing** What physical features do Central America and the Caribbean islands have in common?

## Climate and Vegetation

Central America and the Caribbean islands are generally sunny and warm. Humid tropical and tropical savanna climates are common in the islands and on Central America's coastal plains. On the Pacific coast, much of the area's original savanna vegetation has been cleared. It has been replaced by plantations and ranches. The opposite coast, along the Caribbean, has areas of tropical rain forest.

Inland mountain areas contain cool, humid climates. Some mountainous parts of Central America are covered with dense cloud forest. A **cloud forest** is a moist, high-elevation tropical forest where low clouds are common. These forests are home to numerous plant and animal species.

Temperatures in most of Central America and the Caribbean do not change much from day to night or from summer to winter. Instead, the change in seasons is marked by a change in rainfall. Winters in the region are generally dry, while it rains nearly every day during the summers.

From summer to fall, hurricanes are a threat in the region. These tropical storms bring violent winds, heavy rain, and high seas. Most hurricanes occur between June and November. Their winds and flooding can cause destruction and loss of life.

**READING CHECK** **Generalizing** Where would one find the coolest temperatures in the region?

## Resources

The region's best resources are its land and climate. These factors make tourism an important industry. They also influence agriculture. Agriculture in the region can be profitable where volcanic ash has enriched the soil. Coffee, bananas, sugarcane, and cotton grow well and are major crops. Timber is exported from the rain forests.

Although its land and climate make good agricultural resources, the region has few mineral resources. Energy resources are also limited. Central America and the Caribbean islands must rely on energy imports, which limits their development.

**READING CHECK** **Analyzing** Why would having few energy resources limit economic development?

**SUMMARY AND PREVIEW** Central America and the Caribbean islands share volcanic physical features and a warm, tropical climate good for agriculture. In the next section you will learn about the history and culture of Central America.

### Satellite View

Strong hurricane winds spin around a calm center point called the eye.

### Hurricane Isabel

Hurricanes are rotating storms that bring heavy rain and winds that can reach speeds higher than 155 miles per hour (249 kph). This image shows Hurricane Isabel sweeping through the Caribbean Sea in 2003. Strong hurricanes like this one can shatter houses and hurl cars through the air.

**Analyzing** How can you tell the storm is rotating?

## Section 1 Assessment

hmhsocialstudies.com
ONLINE QUIZ

### Reviewing Ideas, Terms, and Places

1. **a. Define** What is an **isthmus**?
   **b. Explain** How has tectonic activity affected Central America and the Caribbean islands?
2. **a. Describe** What is a **cloud forest**?
   **b. Make Inferences** Why do temperatures in the region change little from summer to winter?
3. **a. Recall** What crops grow well in the region?
   **b. Evaluate** Do you think tourists who want to go to the beach are more likely to visit Guatemala or the Bahamas? Explain your answer.

### Critical Thinking

4. **Categorizing** Draw a diagram like the one here. Using your notes, write descriptive phrases about the physical features, climate, and resources of both places.

| Central America | Caribbean Islands |
|---|---|
| | |

### FOCUS ON WRITING

5. **Writing about Geography** What information about the physical geography of the region might interest readers of your travel guide? Jot down some ideas.

# Central America

## If YOU lived there...

You live in El Salvador, in a town that is still living with the effects of a civil war 20 years ago. Your parents and your older neighbors still speak about those years with fear. One effect of the war was damage to the economy. Many people have gone to Mexico to try to make a better life. Now your parents are talking about going there to look for work. But you are not sure.

**How do you feel about leaving your home?**

## What You Will Learn...

### Main Ideas

1. The history of Central America was mostly influenced by Spain.
2. The culture of Central America is a mixture of Native American and European traditions.
3. The countries of Central America today have challenges and opportunities.

### The Big Idea

Central America's native traditions and colonial history have created a mixed culture, unstable governments, and uncertain economies.

### Key Terms and Places

ecotourism, *p. 170*
civil war, *p. 170*
Panama Canal, *p. 171*

hmhsocialstudies.com
**TAKING NOTES**

Use the graphic organizer online to organize your notes on Central America.

**BUILDING BACKGROUND** All the countries of Central America were once colonies of European nations. Years of colonial rule made it hard for most of these countries to establish strong economies or democratic governments. Today things are slowly improving.

## History

Many countries of Central America have a shared history. This shared history has been influenced by the Maya, the Spanish, and the United States.

### Early History

In several Central American countries, the Maya were building large cities with pyramids and temples by about AD 250. The Maya abandoned most of their cities around 900, but the ruins of many ancient cities still stand in the region today. People of Maya descent still live in Guatemala and Belize. In fact, many ancient Maya customs still influence modern life there.

Hundreds of years later, in the early 1500s, most of Central America came under European control. Spain claimed most of the region. Britain claimed what is now Belize and also occupied part of Nicaragua's coast. The Spanish established large plantations in their colonies to grow crops like tobacco and sugarcane. They made Central American Indians work on the plantations or in gold mines elsewhere in the Americas. In addition, Europeans brought many enslaved Africans to the region to work on plantations and in mines.

## One-Crop Economies

The economies of many Central American countries relied on only one crop—bananas. The U.S.-based United Fruit Company was the biggest banana exporter and the largest employer in the region for many years. The old photo below shows the company's hiring hall in Guatemala.

**ANALYZING VISUALS** Why do workers place cushions between bananas?

### Central America Since Independence

The Spanish colonies of Central America declared independence from Spain in 1821, but much of the region remained joined together as the United Provinces of Central America. The countries of Costa Rica, Nicaragua, Honduras, El Salvador, and Guatemala separated from each other in 1838 to 1839. Panama remained part of Colombia until 1903. Belize did not gain independence from Britain until 1981.

For most countries in Central America, independence brought little change. The Spanish officials left, but wealthy landowners continued to run the countries and their economies. The plantation crops of bananas and coffee supported Central American economies.

In the early to mid-1900s, one landowner in particular, the U.S.-based United Fruit Company, controlled most of the banana production in Central America. To help its business, the company developed railroads and port facilities. This kind of development helped transportation and communications in the region.

Many people resented the role of foreign companies, however. They thought it was wrong that only a few people should own so much land while many people struggled to make a living. In the mid- to late 1900s, demands for reforms led to armed struggles in Guatemala, El Salvador, and Nicaragua. Only in recent years have these countries achieved peace.

**READING CHECK** **Evaluating** How did Spain influence the region's history?

## Culture

Central America's colonial history has influenced its culture. The region's people, languages, religion, and festivals reflect both Spanish and native practices.

### People and Languages

Most of the people in Central America are mestizos, or people of mixed European and Indian ancestry. Various Indian peoples descended from the ancient Maya live in places such as the Guatemalan Highlands.

People of African ancestry also make up a significant minority in this region. They live mostly along the Caribbean coast.

In some countries in Central America, many people still speak the native Indian languages. In places that were colonized by England, English is spoken. For example, it is the official language of Belize. In most countries, however, Spanish is the official language. The Spanish colonization of Central America left this lasting mark on the region.

**Close-up**

# A Market in Guatemala

Villages in Guatemala and all over Central America hold weekly markets. On market day, people come from all around to buy and sell food and other items. The market is also an important gathering spot for the community. Scenes like this one are typical in the region.

The Catholic church is a major influence in most towns.

Patterns on women's clothing are unique to the village where the woman lives.

## Religion, Festivals, and Food

Many Central Americans practice a religion brought to the region by Europeans. Most people are Roman Catholic because Spanish missionaries taught the Indians about Catholicism. However, Indian traditions have influenced Catholicism in return. Also, Protestant Christians are becoming a large minority in places such as Belize.

Religion has influenced celebrations in towns throughout the region. For example, to celebrate special saints' feast days, some people carry images of the saint in parades through the streets. Easter is a particularly important holiday. Some towns decorate whole streets with designs made of flowers and colorful sawdust.

During festivals, people eat **traditional** foods. Central America shares some of its traditional foods, like corn, with Mexico. The region is also known for tomatoes, hot peppers, and cacao (kuh-KOW), which is the source of chocolate.

**READING CHECK** **Contrasting** How is Belize culturally different from the rest of the region?

**ACADEMIC VOCABULARY**

**traditional**
customary, time-honored

Tourists contribute to the local economy when they buy crafts.

People often spend all day at the market and need to eat lunch there.

**ANALYSIS SKILL** **ANALYZING VISUALS**

How do the contributions of tourists and Guatemalans affect the local economy differently?

## Central America Today

The countries of Central America share similar histories and cultures. However, they all face their own economic and political challenges today. In 2005 Costa Rica, the Dominican Republic, El Salvador, Guatemala, Honduras, and Nicaragua signed the Central American Free Trade Agreement (CAFTA) with the United States to help increase trade among the countries.

### Guatemala

Guatemala is the most populous country in Central America. More than 13 million people live there. About 60 percent of Guatemalans are mestizo and European. About 40 percent are Central American Indians. Many speak Maya languages.

Most people in Guatemala live in small villages in the highlands. Fighting between rebels and government forces there killed some 200,000 people between 1960 and 1996. Guatemalans are still recovering from this conflict.

Coffee, which grows well in the cool highlands, is Guatemala's most important crop. The country also is a major producer of cardamom, a spice used in Asian foods.

### Belize

Belize has the smallest population in Central America. The country does not have much land for agriculture, either. But **ecotourism**—the practice of using an area's natural environment to attract tourists—has become popular lately. Tourists come to see the country's coral reefs, Maya ruins, and coastal resorts.

### Honduras

Honduras is a mountainous country. Most people live in mountain valleys and along the northern coast. The rugged land makes transportation difficult and provides little land where crops can grow. However, citrus fruits and bananas are important exports.

### El Salvador

In El Salvador, a few rich families own much of the best land while most people live in poverty. These conditions were a reason behind a long civil war in the 1980s. A **civil war** is a conflict between two or more groups within a country. The war killed many people and hurt the economy.

El Salvador's people have been working to rebuild their country since the end of the war in 1992. One advantage they have in this rebuilding effort is the country's fertile soil. People are able to grow and export crops such as coffee and sugarcane.

### Nicaragua

Nicaragua has also been rebuilding since the end of a civil war. In 1979, a group called the Sandinistas overthrew a dictator.

Many Nicaraguans supported the Sandinistas, but rebel forces aided by the United States fought the Sandinistas for power. The civil war ended in 1990 when elections ended the rule of the Sandinistas. Nicaragua is now a democracy.

## Costa Rica

Unlike most other Central American countries, Costa Rica has a history of peace. It also has a stable, democratic government. The country does not even have an army. Peace has helped Costa Rica make progress in reducing poverty.

Agricultural products like coffee and bananas are important to Costa Rica's economy. Also, many tourists visit Costa Rica's rich tropical rain forests.

## Panama

Panama is the narrowest, southernmost country of Central America. Most people live in areas near the **Panama Canal**. Canal fees and local industries make the canal area the country's most prosperous region.

The Panama Canal provides a link between the Pacific Ocean, the Caribbean Sea, and the Atlantic Ocean. The United States finished building the canal in 1914. For years the Panama canal played an important role in the economy and politics of the region. The United States controlled the canal until 1999. Then, as agreed to in a treaty, Panama finally gained full control of the canal.

**READING CHECK** **Drawing Inferences** Why do you think Panama might want control of the canal?

**FOCUS ON READING**
What word in the paragraphs on Costa Rica signals contrast?

**SUMMARY AND PREVIEW** Native peoples, European colonizers, and the United States have influenced Central America's history and culture. Today most countries are developing stable governments. Their economies rely on tourism and agriculture. In the next section you will learn about the main influences on the Caribbean islands and life there today.

## Section 2 Assessment

### Reviewing Ideas, Terms, and Places

1. **a. Recall** What parts of Central America did the British claim?
   **b. Analyze** How did independence affect most Central American countries?
   **c. Elaborate** What benefits and drawbacks might there be to the United Fruit Company's owning so much land?
2. **a. Identify** What language do most people in Central America speak?
   **b. Explain** How have native cultures influenced cultural practices in the region today?
3. **a. Define** What is a **civil war,** and where in Central America has a civil war been fought?
   **b. Explain** Why might some people practice **ecotourism**?
   **c. Elaborate** Why is the **Panama Canal** important to Panama? Why is it important to other countries?

### Critical Thinking

4. **Summarizing** Copy the graphic organizer below. Using your notes, write at least one important fact about each Central American country today.

| Guatemala | |
|-----------|---|
| Belize | |
| Honduras | |
| El Salvador | |
| Nicaragua | |
| Costa Rica | |
| Panama | |

### FOCUS ON WRITING

5. **Describing Central America** Note details about the history, culture, and life today of people in Central America. Which details will appeal to people who are thinking of visiting the region?

# The Panama Canal

The Panama Canal links the Atlantic and Pacific oceans. Built in the early 1900s, workers on the canal faced tropical diseases and the dangers of blasting through solid rock. The result of their efforts was an amazing feat of engineering. Today some 13,000 to 14,000 ships pass through the canal each year.

## Routes Before and After the Panama Canal

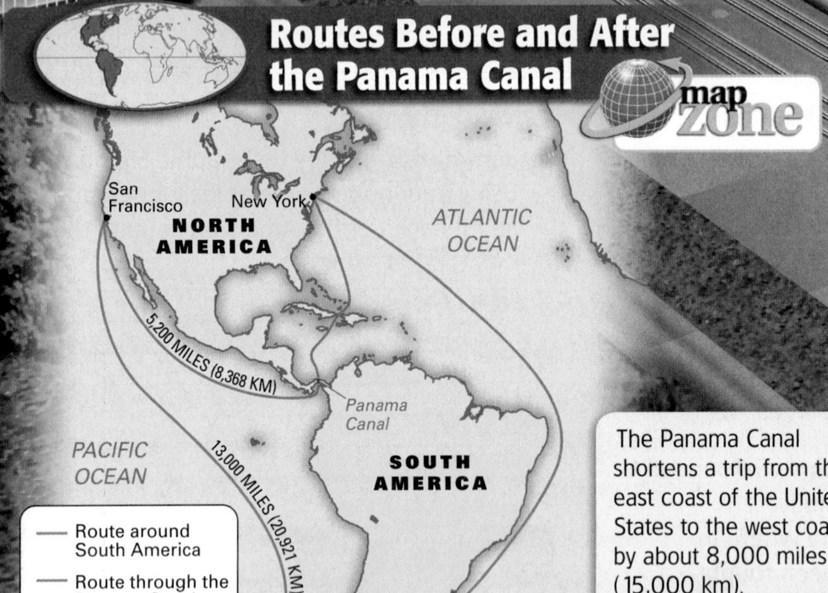

**map zone**

San Francisco
New York

**NORTH AMERICA**

*ATLANTIC OCEAN*

5,200 MILES (8,368 KM)

*Panama Canal*

**SOUTH AMERICA**

*PACIFIC OCEAN*

13,000 MILES (20,921 KM)

— Route around South America

— Route through the Panama Canal

0    750    1,500 Miles
0    750    1,500 Kilometers

*Projection: Azimuthal Equal-Area*

The Panama Canal shortens a trip from the east coast of the United States to the west coast by about 8,000 miles (15,000 km).

**Crossing a Continent**
The Panama Canal takes ships from sea level, across a mountain range, and back to sea level.

Caribbean Sea

Gatún Locks

Gatún Lake

Pedro Miguel Locks

Miraflores Locks

Pacific Ocean

Trains help guide large ships through the canal.

These locks act as doors to different compartments of the canal. Underground pumps raise and lower the water in each compartment like an elevator.

**HISTORY**  VIDEO  Panama Canal
↗ hmhsocialstudies.com

**ANALYSIS SKILL  ANALYZING VISUALS**

1. Why was Panama a good location for a canal?
2. Why must ships be raised and lowered in order to get through the canal?

# The Caribbean Islands

## What You Will Learn...

### Main Ideas

1. The history of the Caribbean islands includes European colonization followed by independence.
2. The culture of the Caribbean islands shows signs of past colonialism and slavery.
3. Today the Caribbean islands have distinctive governments with economies that depend on agriculture and tourism.

### The Big Idea

The Caribbean islands have a rich history and culture influenced by European colonization.

### Key Terms and Places

dialect, *p. 176*
commonwealth, *p. 177*
refugee, *p. 177*
Havana, *p. 178*
cooperative, *p. 178*

hmhsocialstudies.com
**TAKING NOTES**

Use the graphic organizer online to organize your notes on the Caribbean islands.

## If YOU lived there...

You are a young sailor on Christopher Columbus's second voyage to the New World. The year is 1493. Now that your ship is in the Caribbean Sea, you are sailing from island to island. You have seen volcanoes and waterfalls and fierce natives. Columbus has decided to establish a trading post on one of the islands. You are part of the crew who will stay there.

### What do you expect in your new home?

**BUILDING BACKGROUND** In the late 1400s and early 1500s, European nations began to compete for colonies. Sailing for Spain, Christopher Columbus made four voyages to the Americas. He and his men discovered and explored many islands.

## History

When Christopher Columbus discovered America in 1492, he actually discovered the Caribbean islands. These islands now include 13 independent countries. The countries themselves show the influence of those first European explorers.

### Early History

Christopher Columbus first sailed into the Caribbean Sea from Spain in 1492. He thought he had reached the Indies, or the islands near India. Therefore, he called the Caribbean islands the West Indies and the people who lived there Indians.

Spain had little interest in the smaller Caribbean islands, but the English, French, Dutch, and Danish did. In the 1600s and 1700s, these countries established colonies on the islands. They built huge sugarcane plantations that required many workers. Most Caribbean Indians had died from disease, so Europeans brought Africans to work as slaves. Soon Africans and people of African descent outnumbered Europeans on many islands.

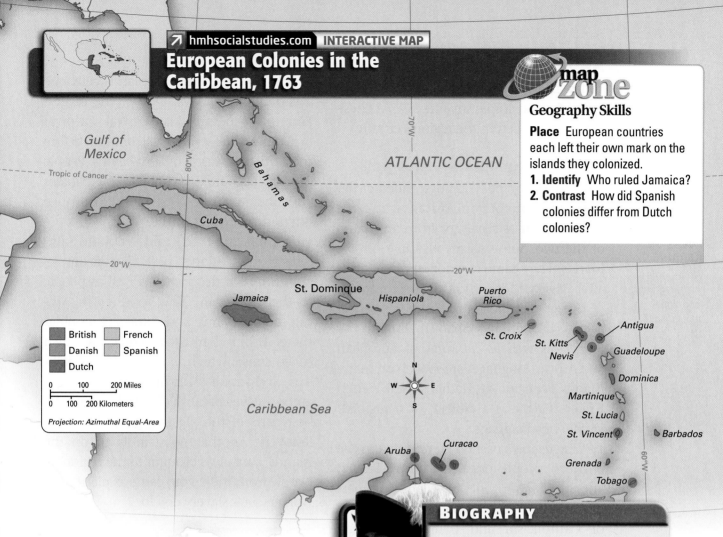

## European Colonies in the Caribbean, 1763

Gulf of Mexico

Tropic of Cancer

ATLANTIC OCEAN

Bahamas

Cuba

Jamaica

St. Dominque

Hispaniola

Puerto Rico

St. Croix

St. Kitts
Nevis

Antigua

Guadeloupe

Dominica

Martinique

St. Lucia

St. Vincent

Barbados

Grenada

Tobago

Caribbean Sea

Aruba

Curacao

| | |
|---|---|
| British | French |
| Danish | Spanish |
| Dutch | |

0    100    200 Miles
0    100    200 Kilometers

*Projection: Azimuthal Equal-Area*

**map Zone**

**Geography Skills**

**Place** European countries each left their own mark on the islands they colonized.
1. **Identify** Who ruled Jamaica?
2. **Contrast** How did Spanish colonies differ from Dutch colonies?

## Independence

A slave revolt led by Toussaint-L'Ouverture (too-sahn loo-ver-toor) eventually helped Haiti win independence from France in 1804. Along with independence came freedom for the slaves in Haiti. Ideas of independence then spread throughout the Americas.

By the mid-1800s, the Dominican Republic had gained independence. The United States won Cuba from Spain, but Cuba gained independence in 1902. The other Caribbean countries did not gain independence until more than 40 years later, after World War II. At that time, the Europeans transferred political power peacefully to most of the islands.

Many Caribbean islands still are not independent countries. For example, the islands of Martinique and Guadeloupe are

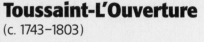

## BIOGRAPHY

### Toussaint-L'Ouverture
(c. 1743–1803)

Toussaint-L'Ouverture was born a slave. A few years after he gained his freedom, a slave revolt broke out in Haiti. Toussaint soon realized the rebels did not have very good leaders, so he went on to form an army of his own. He proved to be an excellent army general. He later became a popular governor of Haiti, gaining the respect of both black and white people on the island.

still French possessions. Each has its own elected government and is also represented in the French government. Most people on these islands seem not to wish for independence from their ruling countries.

**READING CHECK** **Identifying Points of View**
Why might an island's people not be interested in gaining independence?

## Culture

Today nearly all Caribbean islands show signs of past colonialism and slavery. These signs can be seen in the region's culture.

### People, Languages, and Religion

Most islanders today are descended either from Europeans or from Africans who came to the region as slaves, or from a mixture of the two. Some Asians also live on the islands. They came to work on plantations after slavery ended in the region.

Languages spoken in the region reflect a colonial heritage. Spanish, English, or French as well as mixtures of European and African languages are spoken on many islands. For example, Haitians speak French Creole. Creole is a **dialect**, or a regional variety of a language.

The region's past is also reflected in the religions people practice. Former French and Spanish territories have large numbers of Catholics. People also practice a blend of Catholicism and traditional African religions. One blended religion is Santería.

**FOCUS ON READING**

What words in the paragraph on food signal comparison?

### Festivals and Food

People on the Caribbean islands celebrate a variety of holidays. One of the biggest and most widespread is Carnival. Carnival is a time of feasts and celebration before the Christian season of Lent begins. People usually celebrate Carnival with big parades and fancy costumes. Festivals like Carnival often include great music.

Caribbean food and cooking also reflect the region's past. For example, slave ships carried foods as well as people to the Caribbean. Now foods from Africa, such as yams and okra, are popular there. Also, in Barbados, people eat a dish called souse, which is made of pigs' tails, ears, and snouts. This dish was developed among slaves because slaveholders ate the best parts of the pig and gave slaves the leftovers. Another popular flavor on the islands, curry, was brought to the region by people from India who came as plantation workers after slavery ended.

**READING CHECK** **Generalizing** How does Caribbean culture reflect African influences?

---

### THE WORLD ALMANAC
**Facts about Countries** — Languages of the Caribbean

| Language | Countries |
|---|---|
| English | Antigua and Barbuda, Barbados, Trinidad and Tobago |
| Creole English | Saint Kitts and Nevis, Grenada, Jamaica, Bahamas |
| Creole French | Haiti, Dominica, Saint Lucia |
| Spanish | Cuba, Puerto Rico, Dominican Republic |

**Interpreting Charts** What language do people speak in Barbados?

BIBLIOTHEQUE UNIVERSITAIRE

hmhsocialstudies.com

# Caribbean Music

The Caribbean islands have produced many unique styles of music. For example, Jamaica is famous as the birthplace of reggae. Merengue is the national music and dance of the Dominican Republic. Trinidad and Tobago is the home of steel-drum and calypso music.

Here, a band in the Grenadines performs on steel drums. Steel-drum bands can include as few as 4 or as many as 100 musicians. The instruments are actually metal barrels like the kind used for shipping oil. The end of each drum is hammered into a curved shape with multiple grooves and bumps. Hitting different-sized bumps results in different notes.

**Drawing Inferences** What role might trade have played in the development of steel-drum music?

# The Caribbean Islands Today

Many Caribbean islands share a similar history. Still, each island has its own economy, government, and culture.

## Puerto Rico

Once a Spanish colony, Puerto Rico today is a U.S. commonwealth. A **commonwealth** is a self-governing territory associated with another country. Puerto Ricans are U.S. citizens, but they do not have voting representation in Congress.

Overall, Puerto Rico's economy has benefitted from U.S. aid and investment. Still, wages are lower and unemployment is higher on the island than in the United States. Many Puerto Ricans have moved to the United States for better paying jobs. Today, Puerto Ricans debate whether their island should remain a U.S. commonwealth, become an American state, or become an independent nation.

## Haiti

Haiti occupies the western part of the island of Hispaniola. Haiti's capital, Port-au-Prince, is the center of the nation's limited industry. Most Haitians farm small plots. Coffee and sugarcane are among Haiti's main exports.

Haiti is the poorest country in the Americas. Its people have suffered under a string of corrupt governments during the last two centuries. Violence, political unrest, and poverty have created many political refugees. A **refugee** is someone who flees to another country, usually for political or economic reasons. Many Haitian refugees have come to the United States.

On January, 12, 2010, a catastrophic earthquake struck close to Port-au-Prince. The quake devastated Haiti, leaving about 230,000 Haitians dead, 300,000 injured, and over a million homeless. Today, many Haitians continue working to rebuild their lives and nation.

### Dominican Republic

The Dominican Republic occupies the eastern part of Hispaniola. The capital is Santo Domingo. Santo Domingo was the first permanent European settlement in the Western Hemisphere.

The Dominican Republic is not a rich country. However, its economy, health care, education, and housing are more developed than Haiti's. Agriculture is the basis of the economy in the Dominican Republic. The country's tourism industry has also grown in recent years. Beach resorts along the coast are popular with many tourists from Central and South America as well as from the United States.

### Cuba

Cuba is the largest and most populous country in the Caribbean. It is located just 92 miles (148 km) south of Florida. **Havana**, the capital, is the country's largest and most important city.

Cuba has been run by a Communist government since Fidel Castro came to power in 1959. At that time, the government took over banks, large sugarcane plantations, and other businesses. Many of these businesses were owned by U.S. companies. Because of the takeovers, the U.S. government banned trade with Cuba and restricted travel there by U.S. citizens.

Today the government still controls the economy. Most of Cuba's farms are organized as cooperatives or government-owned plantations. A **cooperative** is an organization owned by its members and operated for their mutual benefit.

Besides controlling the economy, Cuba's government also controls all the newspapers, television, and radio stations. While many Cubans support these policies, others oppose them. Some people who oppose the government have become refugees in the United States. Many Cuban refugees have become U.S. citizens.

**Cubans Divided**

Government-sponsored rallies are a part of Cuban life. Meanwhile, some Cubans try to flee their country on tiny rafts.

**ANALYZING VISUALS** How can you tell that the people in the raft are trying to flee Cuba?

## Other Islands

The rest of the Caribbean islands are small countries. Jamaica is the largest of the remaining Caribbean countries. The smallest country is Saint Kitts and Nevis. It is not even one-tenth the size of Rhode Island, the smallest U.S. state!

A number of Caribbean islands are not independent countries but territories of other countries. These territories include the U.S. and British Virgin Islands. The Netherlands and France also still have some Caribbean territories.

Some of these islands have enough land to grow some coffee, sugarcane, or spices. However, most islands' economies are based on tourism. Hundreds of people on the islands work in restaurants and hotels visited by tourists. While tourism has provided jobs and helped economies, not all of its effects have been positive. For example, new construction sometimes harms the same natural environment tourists come to the islands to enjoy.

**READING CHECK** **Contrasting** How are the governments of Puerto Rico and Cuba different?

## Caribbean Tourism
Tourism has helped Caribbean economies. New developments, like this hotel in Saint Martin, have also changed many islands' landscapes.

**SUMMARY AND PREVIEW** The Caribbean islands were colonized by European countries, which influenced the culture of the islands. Today the islands have different types of governments but similar economies. Next, you will read about countries in South America that are also located near the Caribbean Sea.

---

## Section 3 Assessment

hmhsocialstudies.com
ONLINE QUIZ

### Reviewing Ideas, Terms, and Places

1. **a. Describe** What crop was the basis of the colonial economy on the Caribbean islands?
   **b. Make Inferences** Why do you think most smaller Caribbean countries were able to gain independence peacefully?
2. **a. Define** What is a **dialect**?
   **b. Explain** In what ways have African influences shaped Caribbean culture?
3. **a. Recall** What is a **refugee**, and from what Caribbean countries have refugees come?
   **b. Make Inferences** Why do you think many Cubans support their government's policies?
   **c. Evaluate** What would be the benefits and drawbacks for Puerto Rico if it became a U.S. state?

### Critical Thinking

4. **Summarizing** Look over your notes. Then use a diagram like this one to note specific influences on the region and where they came from in each circle. You may add more circles if you need to.

Caribbean Islands

### FOCUS ON WRITING

5. **Telling about the Caribbean Islands** These islands have a fascinating history and a rich culture. Take notes about them for your travel guide.

# Interpreting a Climate Graph

## Learn

A climate graph is a visual representation of the climate in a certain region. The graph shows the average precipitation and average temperature for each month of the year.

Use the following tips to help you interpret a climate graph:

- The months of the year are labeled across the bottom of the graph.
- The measurements for monthly average temperatures are found on the left side of the graph.
- The measurements for monthly average precipitation are found on the right side of the graph.

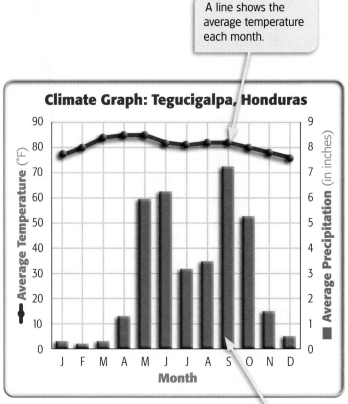

A line shows the average temperature each month.

**Climate Graph: Tegucigalpa, Honduras**

Source: The Weather Channel Interactive, Inc.

Bars show the average precipitation each month.

## Practice

Use the climate graph here to answer the following questions.

❶ What four months get the highest amount of precipitation?

❷ What months get fewer than two inches of precipitation?

❸ What is the average temperature in February?

## Apply

Using the Internet, an almanac, or a newspaper, look up the monthly average temperatures and precipitation for your home town. Then make your own climate graph using that information.

# Chapter Review

**Geography's Impact**
video series
Review the video to answer the closing question:
*Why do so many visitors to the Caribbean come from the United States and Canada?*

## Visual Summary

*Use the visual summary below to help you review the main ideas of the chapter.*

QUICK FACTS

The region's landscapes include warm coastal lowlands and cool highland regions with tropical forests.

Native cultures still influence Central America. Today governments and economies there are changing.

The Caribbean islands have a history of colonial rule. Today many countries' economies there depend on tourism.

## Reviewing Vocabulary, Terms, and Places

*Choose one word from each word pair to correctly complete each sentence below.*

1. A(n) _____ is a narrow strip of land that connects two larger land areas. **(archipelago/ isthmus)**

2. A _____ is a self-governing territory associated with another country. **(commonwealth/ cooperative)**

3. A _____ is someone who flees to another country, usually for political or economic reasons. **(traditional/refugee)**

4. The United States controlled the _____ until 1999. **(Caribbean Sea/Panama Canal)**

5. The large islands of Cuba, Jamaica, Hispaniola, and Puerto Rico make up the _____. **(Greater Antilles/Lesser Antilles)**

6. _____ is found in the mountainous part of Central America. **(Cloud forest/Havana)**

## Comprehension and Critical Thinking

**SECTION 1** *(Pages 162–165)*

7. **a. Describe** What process has formed many of the Caribbean islands? Describe the effect this process has on the region today.

   **b. Compare and Contrast** How are summer and winter similar in Central America and the Caribbean? How are the seasons different?

   **c. Elaborate** What kinds of damage might hurricanes cause? What damage might earthquakes and volcanic eruptions cause?

**SECTION 2** *(Pages 166–171)*

8. **a. Identify** In what Central American country is English the official language?

   **b. Make Inferences** Why do you think people of African ancestry live mainly along the coast?

   **c. Elaborate** How might recent political conflict have affected development in some countries?

## SECTION 3 *(Pages 174–179)*

**9. a. Recall** What country was the first to gain independence? Who led the revolt that led to independence?

**b. Analyze** How does tourism impact the smaller islands of the Caribbean?

**c. Evaluate** What might be some benefits and drawbacks of working for a cooperative?

## Social Studies Skills

**Interpreting a Climate Graph** *Use the climate graph below to answer the questions that follow.*

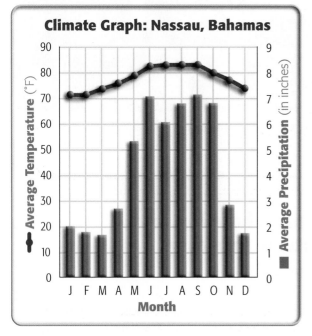

Source: The Weather Channel Interactive, Inc.

**10.** What two months get the most rainfall?

**11.** What is the average temperature in December?

## Using the Internet

**12. Activity: Taking an Ecotour** Ecotourism is all about visiting places to appreciate the environment. Through your online textbook, take your own Internet ecotour of Central America and the Caribbean islands. Visit the Web sites to learn more about some of the people and places you have read about in this chapter. Then create a postcard from a place you visited on your trip.

↗ hmhsocialstudies.com

## Map Activity

**13. Central America and the Caribbean** On a separate sheet of paper, match the letters on the map with their correct labels.

Guatemala            Caribbean Sea

Panama               Puerto Rico

Havana, Cuba         Lesser Antilles

### FOCUS ON READING AND WRITING

**14. Understanding Comparison-Contrast** Look back over the section on physical geography. Then write a paragraph comparing and contrasting Central America with the Caribbean islands. Consider their physical features, climates, landscapes, and resources.

**15. Creating a Travel Guide** Choose one place in this region to be the subject of your travel guide. Then look over your notes for facts about that place to interest your reader. Your guide should begin with a paragraph describing the outstanding physical features of the place. Your second paragraph should identify interesting details about its history and culture. End with a sentence that might encourage your readers to visit. Include two images in your guide to show off the features of the place you have chosen.

# Standardized Test Prep

DIRECTIONS: *Read questions 1 through 7 and write the letter of the best response. Then read question 8 and write your own well-constructed response.*

**1** Which country is an example of an isthmus?

A Guatemala

B Bahamas

C Panama

D Cuba

**2** Which European country established the most colonies in the Greater Antilles?

A France

B Spain

C England

D Netherlands

**3** Which country has a Communist government?

A Cuba

B Puerto Rico

C Dominican Republic

D Haiti

**4** Which of the following countries has remained at peace since independence?

A Guatemala

B El Salvador

C Nicaragua

D Costa Rica

**5** Which of the following sentences about the region's economy is false?

A Coffee and bananas are major export crops.

B The region has good energy resources.

C The region's climate, land, and history attract many tourists.

D Most countries have limited economic development.

## Languages of Central America

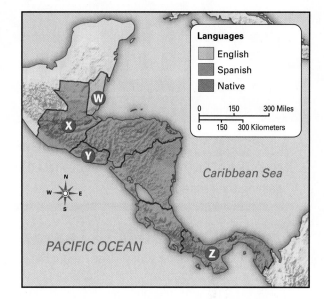

**6** On the map above, which letter represents the country where English is spoken?

A W

B X

C Y

D Z

**7** On the map above, which letters represent countries whose people speak either Spanish or a native language?

A W and X

B X and Y

C Y and Z

D X and Z

**8** **Extended Response** Using the map above and your knowledge of Central America, write a description of influences on culture in Central America today.

**CHAPTER 8**

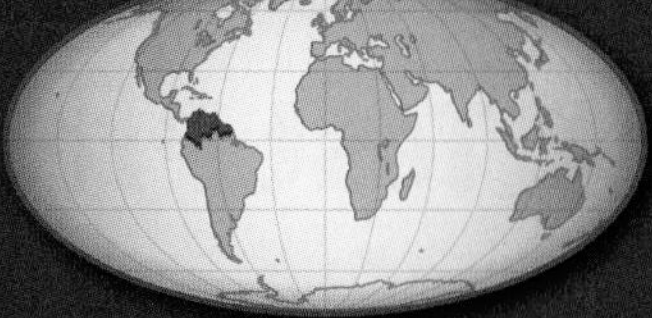

# Caribbean South America

Caribbean Sea

Barranquilla
Cartagena
Maracaibo
Lake Maracaibo
PANAMA
Medellín
Magdalena River
PACIFIC OCEAN
Cauca River
Bogotá
Cali
COLOMBIA
0° Equator
Putumayo River
ECUADOR
PERU

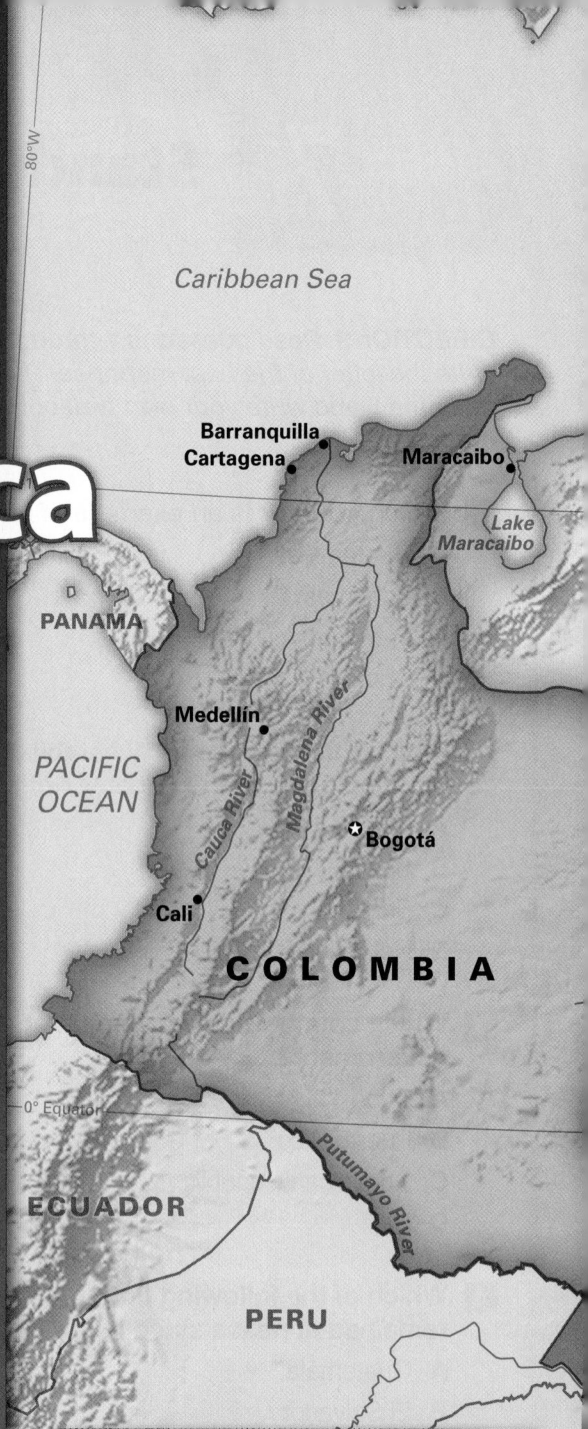

**Essential Question** What challenges have the countries of Caribbean South America faced since gaining their independence?

## ? What You Will Learn...

In this chapter you will learn about the physical geography, history, and cultures of Colombia, Venezuela, Guyana, Suriname, and French Guiana. These countries make up the region of Caribbean South America.

### FOCUS ON READING AND WRITING

**Identifying Supporting Details** Supporting details are the facts and examples that provide information to support the main ideas of a chapter, section, or paragraph. At the beginning of each section in this book, there is a list of main ideas. As you read this chapter, look for the details that support each section's main ideas. **See the lesson, Identifying Supporting Details, on page 523.**

**Writing a Letter** You live in a country in Caribbean South America. Your pen pal in the United States has asked you to write a letter telling her about life in your region. As you read this chapter, collect details to include in your letter. Your friend will want to know about your country as well as the whole region.

**History** The architecture of Cartagena, Colombia, reflects the city's Spanish colonial past.

# Caribbean South America: Political

**Legend**

- ✪ National capital
- ★ Other capitals
- ● Other cities

0    100    200 Miles
0    100    200 Kilometers
*Projection: Azimuthal Equal-Area*

ATLANTIC OCEAN

60°W

TRINIDAD AND TOBAGO

Caracas ✪
Valencia ●

*Orinoco River*

**VENEZUELA**

Georgetown ★
**GUYANA**

Paramaribo ★
Cayenne ★

**SURINAME**

**FRENCH GUIANA**
(FRANCE)

50°W

*Orinoco River*

*Rio Negro*

**BRAZIL**

*Amazon River*

N
W · E
S

**map zone**

### Geography Skills

**Place** Most of Caribbean South America is located on the Caribbean Sea.

1. **Identify** What is the capital of Venezuela?
2. **Contrast** How is Colombia's location different from Venezuela's location?

**Culture** Cowboys called llaneros work on the plains of Venezuela.

**Geography** Dense rain forest covers much of Suriname.

**185**

# Physical Geography

## What You Will Learn...

### Main Ideas

1. Caribbean South America has a wide variety of physical features and wildlife.
2. The region's location and elevation both affect its climate and vegetation.
3. Caribbean South America is rich in resources, such as farmland, oil, timber, and rivers for hydroelectric power.

### The Big Idea

Caribbean South America is a region with diverse physical features, wildlife, climates, and resources.

### Key Terms and Places

Andes, *p. 186*
cordillera, *p. 186*
Guiana Highlands, *p. 187*
Llanos, *p. 187*
Orinoco River, *p. 188*

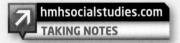
hmhsocialstudies.com
TAKING NOTES

Use the graphic organizer online to take notes on the physical geography of Caribbean South America.

## If YOU lived there...

You live in Caracas, Venezuela, but this is your first visit to the great Orinoco River. You've heard about the fierce creatures that live in the river, so you think your guide is kidding when he says he's going to catch a piranha. You're expecting a monster and are surprised when he pulls up a small orange fish. It has many sharp teeth, but it's only seven inches long!

**What other animals might you see in the region?**

**BUILDING BACKGROUND** The narrow Isthmus of Panama joins the continent of South America at its northwestern corner, the country of Colombia. Like the countries of Central America, the five countries in Caribbean South America border the Caribbean Sea. They all vary in landscape, climate, and culture and have large rivers and rugged mountains.

## Physical Features and Wildlife

If you were traveling through the region of Caribbean South America, you might see the world's highest waterfall, South America's largest lake, and even the world's largest rodent! As you can see on the map, the geography of this region includes rugged mountains, highlands, and plains drained by huge river systems.

### Mountains and Highlands

The highest point in the region is in Colombia, a country larger than California and Texas combined. On the western side of Colombia the **Andes** (AN-deez) reach 18,000 feet (5,490 m). The Andes form a **cordillera** (kawr-duhl-YER-uh), a mountain system made up of roughly parallel ranges. Some of the Andes' snowcapped peaks are active volcanoes. Eruptions and earthquakes shake these mountains frequently.

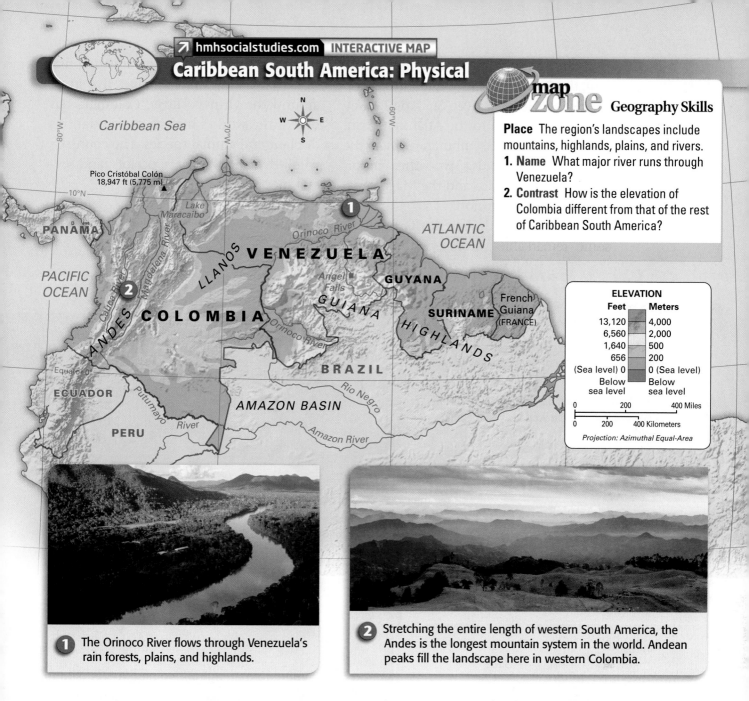

## Caribbean South America: Physical

**map zone** Geography Skills

**Place** The region's landscapes include mountains, highlands, plains, and rivers.
1. **Name** What major river runs through Venezuela?
2. **Contrast** How is the elevation of Colombia different from that of the rest of Caribbean South America?

Caribbean Sea

Pico Cristóbal Colón
18,947 ft (5,775 m)

PANAMA

Lake Maracaibo

LLANOS

VENEZUELA

Orinoco River

ATLANTIC OCEAN

PACIFIC OCEAN

Magdalena River

Cauca River

ANDES

COLOMBIA

Angel Falls

GUIANA

GUYANA

SURINAME

French Guiana (FRANCE)

HIGHLANDS

Orinoco River

BRAZIL

Rio Negro

ECUADOR

Putumayo River

AMAZON BASIN

Amazon River

PERU

**ELEVATION**

| Feet | | Meters |
|---|---|---|
| 13,120 | | 4,000 |
| 6,560 | | 2,000 |
| 1,640 | | 500 |
| 656 | | 200 |
| (Sea level) 0 | | 0 (Sea level) |
| Below sea level | | Below sea level |

0   200   400 Miles
0   200   400 Kilometers
Projection: Azimuthal Equal-Area

(1) The Orinoco River flows through Venezuela's rain forests, plains, and highlands.

(2) Stretching the entire length of western South America, the Andes is the longest mountain system in the world. Andean peaks fill the landscape here in western Colombia.

Lying on the Caribbean coast, Venezuela is located in the middle of the other countries in the region. Venezuela's highest elevation is in the **Guiana Highlands**, which stretch into Guyana and Suriname. For millions of years, wind and rain have eroded these highlands' plateaus. However, some of the steep-sided plateaus are capped by sandstone layers that have resisted erosion. These unusual flat-topped formations are sometimes called *tepuís* (tay-PWEEZ). The *tepuís* create a dramatic landscape as they rise about 3,000 to 6,000 feet (900 to 1,800 m) above the surrounding plains.

## Plains, Rivers, and Wildlife

As you look at the map above, notice how much the elevation drops between the highlands and the Andes. This region of plains is known as the **Llanos** (YAH-nohs). The Llanos is mostly grassland with few trees. At a low elevation and not much vegetation, these plains flood easily.

FOCUS ON
READING
What details in
this paragraph
support this
section's first
main idea?

Flowing for about 1,600 miles (2,575 km), the **Orinoco** (OHR-ee-NOH-koh) **River** is the region's longest river. Snaking its way through Venezuela to the Atlantic Ocean, the Orinoco and its tributaries drain the plains and highlands. Two other important rivers, the Cauca and the Magdalena, drain the Andean region.

Caribbean South America is home to some remarkable wildlife. For example, hundreds of bird species, meat-eating fish called piranhas, and crocodiles live in or around the Orinoco River. Colombia has one of the world's highest concentrations of plant and animal species. The country's wildlife includes jaguars, ocelots, and several species of monkeys.

**READING CHECK** **Summarizing** What are the region's major physical features?

## Venezuela's Canaima National Park

Covering almost 3 million acres of eastern Venezuela, Canaima National Park is one of the largest national parks in the world.

**ANALYZING VISUALS** What do you think attracts millions of people from around the world to visit Canaima National Park?

Dropping more than 3,200 feet (975 m), Angel Falls is the world's highest waterfall.

A rocky *tepuí* rises from the park's flat plains. Hundreds of these flat-topped mountains are scattered throughout the park.

The red-billed toucan is among the almost 500 species of birds that live in the park.

## Climate and Vegetation

Caribbean South America's location near the equator means that most of the region has warm temperatures year-round. However, temperatures do vary with elevation. For example, in the Andes, as you go up in elevation, the temperature can drop rapidly—about four degrees Fahrenheit every 1,000 feet (305 m).

In contrast, the vast, flat landscape of the Llanos region has a tropical savanna climate. Here, both the wet and dry seasons provide favorable conditions for grasslands to grow.

Rain forests, another type of landscape, thrive in the humid tropical climate of southern Colombia. This area is a part of the Amazon Basin. Here, rain falls throughout the year, watering the forest's huge trees. These trees form a canopy where the vegetation is so dense that sunlight barely shines through to the jungle floor.

**READING CHECK** Analyzing What causes the region's temperatures to vary?

## Resources

Good soil and moderate climates help make most of Caribbean South America a rich agricultural region. Major crops include rice, coffee, bananas, and sugarcane.

In addition, the region has other valuable resources, such as oil, iron ore, and coal. Both Venezuela and Colombia have large oil-rich areas. Forests throughout the region provide timber. While the seas provide plentiful fish and shrimp, the region's major rivers are used to generate hydroelectric power.

**READING CHECK** Summarizing How do geographic factors affect economic activities in Caribbean South America?

**SUMMARY AND PREVIEW** In this section you learned that the physical geography of Caribbean South America includes mountains, highlands, plains, and rivers. The region's location near the equator and its elevation affect the region's climate. In the next section you will learn about Colombia's history, people, and economy. You will also learn about the challenges Colombia is facing today, which include a civil war.

---

### Section 1 Assessment

hmhsocialstudies.com
ONLINE QUIZ

**Reviewing Ideas, Terms, and Places**

1. **a. Recall** Where are the **Andes** located?
   **b. Explain** How are the rock formations called *tepuís* unusual?
   **c. Elaborate** Why do the **Llanos** in Colombia and Venezuela flood easily?
2. **a. Describe** In the Andes, how does the temperature change with elevation?
   **b. Make Inferences** How does the region's location near the equator affect its climate?
3. **a. Identify** What is a major resource in both Venezuela and Colombia?
   **b. Explain** Which resource provides hydroelectric power?

**Critical Thinking**

4. **Categorizing** Use your notes to identify four types of physical features in the region. Write each type in one of the small circles of the diagram.

Physical Features

**FOCUS ON WRITING**

5. **Describing Physical Geography** Take notes about the physical features, wildlife, climate, vegetation, and resources of the region. After you decide which country you are living in, collect more details about it.

# Colombia

## If YOU lived there...

You live in the beautiful colonial city of Cartagena, on the coast of the Caribbean. Your family runs a small restaurant there. You're used to the city's wide beaches and old colonial buildings with wooden balconies that overhang the street. Now you are on your way to visit your cousins. They live on a cattle ranch on the inland plains region called the Llanos.

**How do you think life on the ranch is different from yours?**

**BUILDING BACKGROUND** Like most of the countries of Central and South America, Colombia was once a colony of Spain. Colombians gained their independence from Spain in 1819. The new country was then named after the explorer Christopher Columbus.

## Colombia's History

Giant mounds of earth, mysterious statues, and tombs—these are the marks of the people who lived in Colombia more than 1,500 years ago. Colombia's history begins with these people. It also includes conquest by Spain and, later, independence.

### The Chibcha

Have you heard of the legend of El Dorado (el duh-RAH-doh), or the Golden One? That legend about

**This gold Chibcha artifact represents the ceremonial raft used by their king.**

---

## What You Will Learn...

### Main Ideas

1. Native cultures, Spanish conquest, and independence shaped Colombia's history.
2. In Colombia today, the benefits of a rich culture and many natural resources contrast with the effects of a long period of civil war.

### The Big Idea

Spanish conquest, valuable resources, and civil war have shaped the history, culture, and economy of Colombia.

### Key Terms and Places

Cartagena, *p. 191*
Bogotá, *p. 192*
guerrillas, *p. 193*

hmhsocialstudies.com
TAKING NOTES

Use the graphic organizer online to organize your notes on Colombia.

a land rich in gold was inspired by the Chibcha culture in Colombia. The Chibcha covered their new rulers in gold dust. Then they took each ruler to a lake to wash the gold off. As the new ruler washed, the Chibcha threw gold and emerald objects into the water. A well-developed civilization, they practiced pottery making, weaving, and metalworking. Their gold objects were among the finest in ancient America.

## Spanish Conquest

In about 1500 Spanish explorers arrived on the Caribbean coast of South America. The Spaniards wanted to expand Spain's new empire. In doing so, the Spanish conquered the Chibcha and seized much of their treasure. Soon after claiming land for themselves, the Spaniards founded a colony and cities along the Caribbean coast.

One colonial city, **Cartagena**, was a major naval base and commercial port in the Spanish empire. By the 1600s Spaniards and their descendants had set up large estates in Colombia. Spanish estate owners forced South American Indians and enslaved Africans to work the land.

## Independence

In the late 1700s people in Central and South America began struggling for independence from Spain. After independence was achieved, the republic of Gran Colombia was created. It included Colombia, Ecuador, Panama, and Venezuela. In 1830 the republic dissolved, and New Granada, which included Colombia and Panama, was created.

After independence, two different groups of Colombians debated over how Colombia should be run. One group wanted the Roman Catholic Church to participate in government and education. On the other hand, another group did not want the church involved in their lives.

## Cartagena's Spanish Fort

Imagine you are a Spanish colonist living in Cartagena, Colombia, in the 1600s. Your city lies on the Caribbean coast and has been attacked by English pirates several times. They have stolen tons of silver and gold that were waiting shipment to Spain. How do you protect your city from these pirates? Build an enormous fort, of course! You make sure to design the fort's walls to deflect the cannonballs that the pirates shoot from their ships. Today this fort still stands on a peninsula outside Cartagena. A statue commemorates one of the heroes that defended the city from attack.

**Drawing Conclusions** Why did the Spanish want to defend Cartagena from the pirates?

Outbreaks of violence throughout the 1800s and 1900s killed thousands. Part of the problem had to do with the country's rugged geography, which isolated people in one region from those in another region. As a result, they developed separate economies and identities. Uniting these different groups into one country was hard.

**READING CHECK** **Drawing Conclusions** How did Spanish conquest shape Colombia's history and culture?

## Daily Life in Colombia

Different regions of Colombia are home to diverse ethnic groups.

**ANALYZING VISUALS** What are some of the goods sold in this market?

Colombians of African descent unload their goods at a local market near the Pacific coast.

## Colombia Today

Colombia is Caribbean South America's most populous country. The national capital is **Bogotá**, a city located high in the eastern Andes. Although Colombia is rich in culture and resources, more than 40 years of civil war have been destructive to the country's economy.

### People and Culture

Most Colombians live in the fertile valleys and river basins among the mountain ranges, where the climate is moderate and good for farming. Rivers, such as the Cauca and the Magdalena, flow down from the Andes to the Caribbean Sea. These rivers provide water and help connect settlements located between the mountains and the coast. Other Colombians live on cattle ranches scattered throughout the Llanos. Few people live in the tropical rainforest regions in the south.

Because the physical geography of Colombia isolates some regions of the country, the people of Colombia are often known by the region where they live. For example, those who live along the Caribbean coast are known for songs and dances influenced by African traditions.

**FOCUS ON READING**
In the first paragraph under Economy, find at least three details to support the idea stated in the first sentence.

Colombian culture is an interesting mix of influences:

- Music: traditional African songs and dances on the Caribbean coast and South American Indian music in remote areas of the Andes
- Sports: soccer, as well as a traditional Chibcha ring-toss game called *tejo*
- Religion: primarily Roman Catholicism
- Official language: Spanish
- Ethnic groups: 58 percent mestizo; also Spanish, African, and Indian descent

### Economy

Colombia's economy relies on several valuable resources. Rich soil, steep slopes, and tall shade trees produce world-famous Colombian coffee. Other major export crops include bananas, sugarcane, and cotton. Many farms in Colombia produce flowers that are exported around the world. In fact, 80 percent of the country's flowers are shipped to the United States.

Colombia's economy depends on the country's valuable natural resources. Recently oil has become Colombia's major export. Other natural resources include iron ore, gold, and coal. Most of the world's emeralds also come from Colombia.

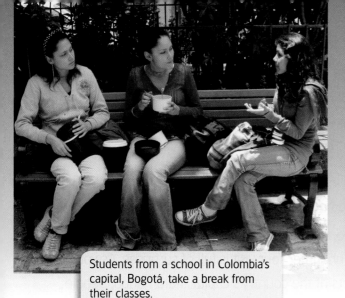

Students from a school in Colombia's capital, Bogotá, take a break from their classes.

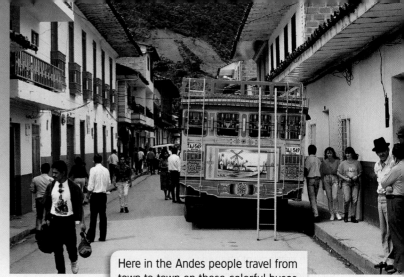

Here in the Andes people travel from town to town on these colorful buses, called *chivas*.

## Civil War

Civil war is a major problem in Colombia today. Many different groups have waged war with each other and with Colombia's government. For more than 40 years, these heavily armed militant groups have controlled large areas of the country.

One of these groups is an army of **guerrillas**, or members of an irregular military force. These guerrillas want to overthrow the government. The guerrillas, as well as other militant groups, have forced farmers off their land and caused thousands of Colombians to flee the country. All of these groups are also involved in growing crops of the illegal coca plant. This plant is used to make cocaine, a dangerous drug.

Because of the instability caused by civil war, the future of Colombia is uncertain. However, the Colombian government has passed new laws that make it harder for the guerrillas and other militant groups to operate freely. In addition, the United States provides assistance to Colombia's government. Colombia is one of the top recipients of U.S. foreign aid.

**READING CHECK** **Drawing Conclusions** How do you think civil war affects daily life in Colombia?

**SUMMARY AND PREVIEW** Colombia's history includes the Chibcha, Spanish conquest, and independence. Today, Colombia's people are dealing with a long civil war. Next, you will learn about Colombia's neighbor, Venezuela.

### Section 2 Assessment

hmhsocialstudies.com
ONLINE QUIZ

### Reviewing Ideas, Terms, and Places

1. **a. Recall** Who were the Chibcha?
   **b. Draw Conclusions** Why did Spain want land in Colombia?
2. **a. Describe** What factors make Colombia ideal for growing coffee?
   **b. Interpret** In what part of the country do most Colombians live?
   **c. Predict** How might Colombia solve the problem of **guerrillas** trying to control the country?

### Critical Thinking

3. **Analyzing** Using your notes, write a sentence about the topic of each box in a diagram like this one.

| Music | → | |
| Sports | → | |
| Religion | → | |
| Language | → | |

### FOCUS ON WRITING

4. **Writing about Colombia** What information about the history, culture, and daily life of Colombia might your pen pal like to learn? Add these details to your notes.

# Venezuela and the Guianas

## What You Will Learn...

### Main Ideas

1. Spanish settlement shaped the history and culture of Venezuela.
2. Oil production plays a large role in Venezuela's economy and government today.
3. The Guianas have diverse cultures and plentiful resources.

### The Big Idea

European settlement, immigration, and natural resources have greatly influenced the culture and economy of Venezuela and the Guianas.

### Key Terms and Places

llaneros, *p. 196*
Lake Maracaibo, *p. 196*
Caracas, *p. 197*
strike, *p. 198*
referendum, *p. 198*

hmhsocialstudies.com
TAKING NOTES

Use the graphic organizer online to organize your notes on Venezuela and the Guianas.

## If YOU lived there...

You've come from your home in eastern Venezuela to visit the nearby country of Suriname. Your visit is full of surprises. As you walk along the streets of the country's capital, Paramaribo, people are not speaking Spanish, but Dutch, English, and some languages you don't even recognize. You see Hindu temples and Muslim mosques alongside Christian churches.

**Why is Suriname so different from Venezuela?**

**BUILDING BACKGROUND** Venezuela, like Colombia, was once a Spanish colony, but the Guianas were colonized by other nations—Great Britain, the Netherlands, and France. When these countries gained independence, British Guiana became Guyana and Dutch Guiana became Suriname.

## History and Culture of Venezuela

Venezuela was originally the home of many small tribes of South American Indians. Those groups were conquered by the Spanish in the early 1500s. Though Venezuela became independent from Spain in the early 1800s, those three centuries of Spanish rule shaped the country's history and culture.

### Spanish Settlement and Colonial Rule

The Spanish came to Venezuela hoping to find gold and pearls. They forced the native Indians to search for these treasures, but they finally realized there was little gold to be found. Then the Spanish turned to agriculture, once again forcing the Indians to do the work. They grew indigo (IN-di-goh), a plant used to make a deep blue dye. Because the work was very hard, many of the Indians died. Then the Spanish began bringing enslaved Africans to take the Indians' places. Eventually, some of the slaves escaped, settling in remote areas of the country.

## Venezuela's Independence

Each year, Venezuelans celebrate Simon Bolívar's efforts in achieving Venezuela's independence. Independence Day is filled with parades and parties.

## Simon Bolívar
(1783–1830)

Known as the "George Washington of South America," Simon Bolívar was a revolutionary general. In the early 1800s he led the liberation of several South American countries from Spanish rule.

Beginning in 1811 Bolívar helped free his native Venezuela. He was president of Gran Colombia (present-day Venezuela, Colombia, Panama, and Ecuador) and then Peru. Because Bolívar also helped free Bolivia, the country was named in his honor. People across South America admire Bolívar for his determination in achieving independence for the former Spanish colonies. Today in both Venezuela and Bolivia, Bolívar's birthday is a national holiday.

**Drawing Inferences** Why do you think Bolívar is often compared to George Washington?

## Independence and Self-Rule

Partly because the colony was so poor, some people in Venezuela revolted against Spain. Simon Bolívar helped lead the fight against Spanish rule. Bolívar is considered a hero in many South American countries because he led wars of independence throughout the region. Bolívar helped win Venezuelan independence from Spain by 1821. However, Venezuela did not officially become independent until 1830.

Throughout the 1800s Venezuelans suffered from dictatorships and civil wars. Venezuela's military leaders ran the country. After oil was discovered in the early 1900s, some leaders kept the country's oil money for themselves. As a result, the people of Venezuela did not benefit from their country's oil wealth.

## People and Culture

The people of Venezuela are descended from native Indians, Europeans, and Africans. The majority of Venezuelans are of mixed Indian and European descent. Indians make up only about 2 percent of the population. People of European descent tend to live in the large cities. People of African descent tend to live along the coast. Most Venezuelans are Spanish-speaking Roman Catholics, but the country's Indians speak 25 different languages and follow the religious practices of their ancestors.

Venezuelan culture includes dancing and sports. Venezuela's national dance, the *joropo*, is a lively foot-stomping couples' dance. Large crowds of Venezuelans attend rodeo events. Baseball and soccer are also popular throughout Venezuela.

**READING CHECK** **Summarizing** How did the Spanish contribute to Venezuela's history?

FOCUS ON
READING

In the paragraphs under Venezuela Today, what details support the main idea that oil production plays a large role in Venezuela's economy and government?

# Venezuela Today

Many Venezuelans make a living by farming and ranching. However, most wealthy Venezuelans have made money in the country's oil industry. In addition, Venezuela's government has also benefited from oil wealth.

## Agriculture and Ranching

Rural areas of Venezuela are dotted by farms and ranches. Northern Venezuela has some small family farms as well as large commercial farms. **Llaneros** (yah-NAY-rohs)—or Venezuelan cowboys—herd cattle on the many ranches of the Llanos region. However, some small communities of Indians practice traditional agriculture.

## Economy and Natural Resources

In the 1960s Venezuela began earning huge sums of money from oil production. This wealth allowed part of the population to buy luxuries. However, the vast majority of the population still lived in poverty. Many of Venezuela's poor people moved to the cities to try to find work. Some settled on the outskirts in communities of shacks. They had no running water, sewers, or electricity.

Venezuela's wealth attracted many immigrants from Europe and other South American countries. These immigrants, like most other Venezuelans, suffered in the 1980s when the price of oil dropped sharply. Without the money provided by high oil prices, the economy couldn't support the people. Oil prices recovered in the 1990s, and the Venezuelan economy continues to be based on oil production.

As you can see on the map on the next page, the Orinoco River basin and **Lake Maracaibo** (mah-rah-KY-boh) are rich in oil. Venezuela is the only South American member of the Organization of Petroleum

## FOCUS ON CULTURE

### The Feast of Corpus Christi

One day each summer, men dressed as devils dance in the streets of the Venezuelan town of San Francisco de Yare. On this day, people here honor the Roman Catholic feast day of Corpus Christi. Spanish settlers brought the tradition of dressing up as devils to Venezuela. This tradition includes the making of elaborate, colorful masks that the dancers wear. These masks usually resemble pigs or jaguars. Dancing through the town's streets to the beat of drums, the dancers shake musical instruments called maracas. They believe their dancing, music, and scary masks will keep evil away from their town.

**Summarizing** How do some Venezuelans celebrate the Feast of Corpus Christi?

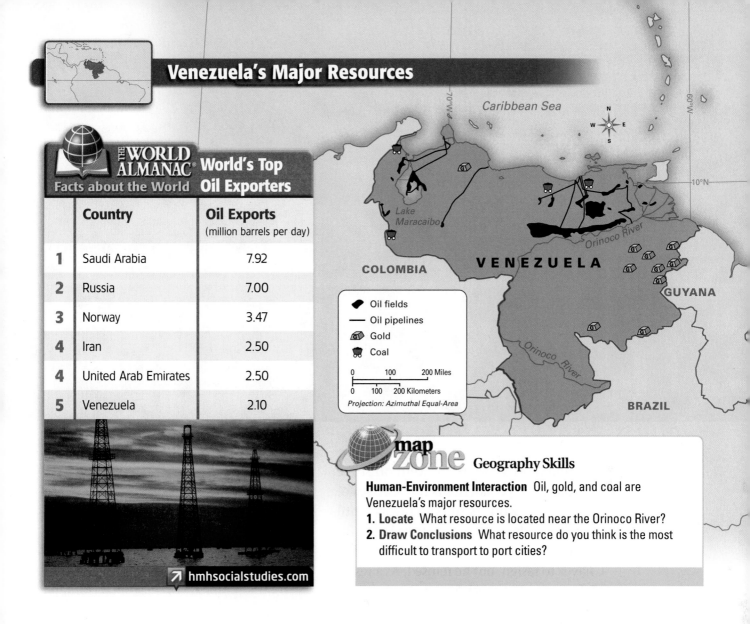

THE WORLD ALMANAC
Facts about the World
World's Top Oil Exporters

| | Country | Oil Exports (million barrels per day) |
|---|---|---|
| 1 | Saudi Arabia | 7.92 |
| 2 | Russia | 7.00 |
| 3 | Norway | 3.47 |
| 4 | Iran | 2.50 |
| 4 | United Arab Emirates | 2.50 |
| 5 | Venezuela | 2.10 |

hmhsocialstudies.com

Oil fields
Oil pipelines
Gold
Coal

0    100    200 Miles
0    100    200 Kilometers
Projection: Azimuthal Equal-Area

Caribbean Sea
Lake Maracaibo
COLOMBIA
VENEZUELA
Orinoco River
GUYANA
Orinoco River
BRAZIL

**map zone Geography Skills**

**Human-Environment Interaction** Oil, gold, and coal are Venezuela's major resources.
1. **Locate** What resource is located near the Orinoco River?
2. **Draw Conclusions** What resource do you think is the most difficult to transport to port cities?

Exporting Countries (OPEC). The member countries in this organization attempt to control world oil production and keep oil prices from falling too low.

The Guiana Highlands in the southeast are rich in other minerals, such as iron ore for making steel. Gold is also mined in remote areas of the highlands. Dams on tributaries of the Orinoco River produce hydroelectricity.

**Caracas** (kah-RAH-kahs) is Venezuela's capital and the economic and cultural center of the country. It is a large city with a modern subway system, busy expressways, and tall office buildings. Still, neither Caracas nor Venezuela has escaped poverty.

Caracas is encircled by slums, and many Venezuelans living in the rural areas of the country are also poor.

## Government

After years of suffering under military dictatorships, the people of Venezuela elected their first president in 1959. Since then, Venezuela's government has dealt with economic turmoil and political protests.

In 2002 Venezuela's president, Hugo Chavez, started to distribute the country's oil income equally among all Venezuelans. Before Chavez's presidency, only a small percentage of wealthy Venezuelans benefited from the country's oil income.

## Caracas, Venezuela

With a population of more than 4 million, Venezuela's capital city, Caracas, is the country's financial and cultural center.

**ANALYZING VISUALS** Why do you think Caracas is located in this mountain valley?

Millions of Venezuelans went on strike to protest the president's actions. A **strike** is a group of workers stopping work until their demands are met. The strike lasted for about two months. The protestors wanted Chavez to resign, but he refused. As a result of the strike, Venezuela's economy suffered and oil exports fell dramatically.

Many Venezuelans opposed to President Chavez called for a **referendum**, or recall vote. The referendum was defeated. In 2006 about 63 percent of Venezuelans re-elected Chavez president. In his second term, Chavez adopted new **policies** aimed at bringing an end to poverty, illiteracy, and hunger. Chavez has also supported changing his nation's constitution to end presidential term limits. Many Venezuelans fear that Chavez has grown too powerful and might rule indefinitely.

**ACADEMIC VOCABULARY**
**policy** rule, course of action

**READING CHECK** Identifying Cause and Effect What effect did the workers' strike have on Venezuela's economy?

## The Guianas

The countries of Guyana, Suriname, and French Guiana are together known as the Guianas (gee-AH-nuhz). Dense tropical rain forests cover much of this region, which lies east of Venezuela.

### Guyana

Guyana (gy-AH-nuh) comes from a South American Indian word that means "land of waters." About one-third of the country's population lives in Georgetown, the capital. Nearly all of Guyana's agricultural lands are located on the flat, fertile plains along the coast. Guyana's most important agricultural products are rice and sugar.

Guyana's population is diverse. About half of its people are descended from people who migrated to Guyana from India. These immigrants came to Guyana to work on the country's sugar plantations. Most Guyanese today farm small plots of land or run small businesses. About one-third of the population is descended from former African slaves. These people operate large businesses and hold most of the government positions.

## Suriname

The resources and economy of Suriname (soohr-uh-NAHM) are similar to those of Guyana. Like Guyana, Suriname has a diverse population. The country's population includes South Asians, Africans, Chinese, Indonesians, and Creoles—people of mixed heritage. The capital, Paramaribo (pah-rah-MAH-ree-boh), is home to nearly half of the country's people.

## French Guiana

French Guiana (gee-A-nuh) is a territory of France and sends representatives to the government in Paris. French Guiana's roughly 200,000 people live mostly in coastal areas. About two-thirds of the people are of African descent. Other groups include Europeans, Asians, and South American Indians. The country depends heavily on imports for its food and energy.

**READING CHECK** **Contrasting** How is French Guiana different from the rest of the Guianas?

Creole women carry gifts to a party in downtown Paramaribo. About 30 percent of Suriname's population is Creole.

**SUMMARY AND PREVIEW** In this section, you learned that Venezuela's history was largely shaped by Spanish settlement. Today Venezuela's economy is based on oil. You also learned that to the east, the Guianas are home to a diverse population. In the next chapter, you will learn about the history and people of Atlantic South America.

## Section 3 Assessment

hmhsocialstudies.com
ONLINE QUIZ

### Reviewing Ideas, Terms, and Places

1. **a. Recall** What did Spanish settlers hope to find in Venezuela?
   **b. Explain** Who led Venezuela's revolt against Spain?
2. **a. Describe** What does the landscape of **Caracas** include?
   **b. Explain** How is oil important to Venezuela's economy?
   **c. Elaborate** Why did some Venezuelans go on **strike**?
3. **a. Describe** What are Guyana's agricultural lands and products like?
   **b. Contrast** How is population of the Guianas different from that of Colombia and Venezuela?

### Critical Thinking

4. **Identifying Cause and Effect** Using your notes on Venezuela's natural resources and this diagram, list the effects of oil production on Venezuela's people, economy, and government.

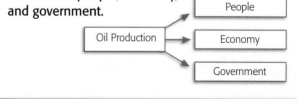

### FOCUS ON WRITING

5. **Writing about Venezuela and the Guianas** Collect details about Venezuela and the Guianas for your letter. What is interesting about these cultures?

# Social Studies Skills

# Using Latitude and Longitude

## Learn

The pattern of imaginary lines that circle the globe in east-west and north-south directions is called a grid. Geographers measure the distances between the lines of the grid in degrees.

Look at the diagram to the right. As you can see, lines that run east to west are lines of latitude. These lines measure distance north and south of the equator. Lines that run north to south are lines of longitude. These lines measure distance east and west of the prime meridian.

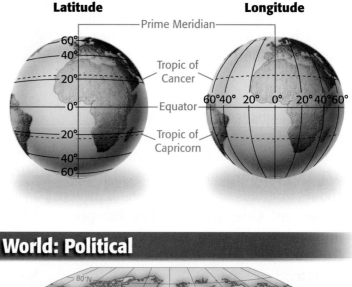

**Latitude**

**Longitude**

Prime Meridian

Tropic of Cancer

Equator

Tropic of Capricorn

## Practice

Look at the world map to the right. Use these guidelines to read latitude and longitude.

❶ Pick a city on the map.

❷ To find the latitude of the city you picked, first look at the equator. From there, look at the city's location. Then find the closest line of latitude to see how many degrees the city is north or south of the equator.

❸ To find the longitude of the city, first look at the prime meridian. Then find the closest line of longitude to see how many degrees the city is east or west of the prime meridian.

### World: Political

map zone

## Apply

Using an atlas, find a map of the United States and a map of the world. On the map of the United States, find the line of latitude that is located near your hometown. Then look at a world map and follow this line of latitude across the world. Which countries share the same latitude as your hometown?

# Chapter Review

## Visual Summary

*Use the visual summary below to help you review the main ideas of the chapter.*

QUICK FACTS

Caribbean South America's physical features include rivers, plains, mountains, and the world's highest waterfall.

A country rich in history and culture, Colombia is enduring a civil war today.

Venezuela is an oil-rich nation that has a population of mostly mixed Indian and European descent.

## Reviewing Vocabulary, Terms, and Places

*For each statement below, write T if it is true and F if it is false.*

1. The Andes is a river system.

2. The Orinoco River flows 1,300 miles (2,100 km) through Venezuela.

3. Caribbean South America's location near the equator means that the region is very cold.

4. The Chibcha were the first people to settle Colombia.

5. Colombian culture includes traditional African songs and dances.

6. Most Venezuelans are of mixed Indian and European descent.

7. Venezuela gained its independence from France.

8. Venezuela's economy depends on oil production.

## Comprehension and Critical Thinking

**SECTION 1** *(Pages 186–189)*

9. **a. Recall** What is the region's longest river?

   **b. Analyze** How does the temperature vary in the Andes?

   **c. Evaluate** Why do you think it would be hard to live in the rain forest of Colombia?

**SECTION 2** *(Pages 190–193)*

10. **a. Describe** How did the Chibcha treat their ruler?

    **b. Draw Conclusions** What created a problem for all Colombians after independence?

    **c. Elaborate** Why do most Colombians live in fertile valleys and river basins?

**SECTION 3** *(Pages 194–199)*

11. **a. Define** What is a strike?

b. **Draw Conclusions** Why did people from India immigrate to Guyana?

c. **Predict** Do you think Venezuela's government will continue to use oil wealth to help the country's people? Explain your answer.

## Using the Internet

12. **Activity: Writing a Journal Entry** Ride with the llaneros! Pack your bags and prepare for a trek through the South American countryside. Explore the vast grasslands, visit villages, and learn about the life and work of the cowboys, or llaneros, of the Venezuelan plains. Through your online textbook, research and take notes that will help you describe your adventure. Use the interactive template to write your journal entry. Describe what you have learned about the people and places you visited.

> **↗ hmhsocialstudies.com**

## Social Studies Skills

13. **Using Latitude and Longitude** Look at the physical map in Section 1. Find the lines of latitude and longitude. What line of latitude, shown on the map, runs through both Venezuela and Colombia? Which country in Caribbean South America is partly located on the equator?

## Map Activity

14. **Caribbean South America** On a separate sheet of paper, match the letters on the map with their correct labels.

Llanos                  Andes

Guiana Highlands        Orinoco River

Lake Maracaibo

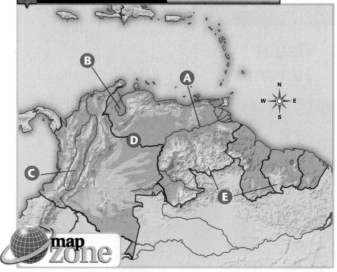

**↗ hmhsocialstudies.com  INTERACTIVE MAP**

## FOCUS ON READING AND WRITING

15. **Identifying Supporting Details** Look back over Section 2 on Colombia. Then make a list of details you find to support the section's main ideas. Make sure you include details about the Spanish conquest, independence, culture, resources, and civil war.

16. **Writing a Letter** By now you have information about the region and the country you have chosen to live in. Begin your letter to your pen pal by describing the most interesting physical and cultural features of the whole region. Then write a second paragraph telling your pen pal about the special physical and cultural features of the country you've chosen to live in. Try to keep your pen pal interested in reading by including fascinating details and descriptions.

# Standardized Test Prep

DIRECTIONS: *Read questions 1 through 7 and write the letter of the best response. Then read question 8 and write your own well-constructed response.*

**1** Temperatures in Caribbean South America remain warm year-round because of the region's location near the

A  equator.

B  Caribbean Sea.

C  Amazon Basin.

D  Tropic of Cancer.

**2** What valuable natural resource were the Chibcha known for using?

A  silver

B  gold

C  copper

D  iron

**3** What Colombian city was a major naval base and commercial port in the Spanish empire?

A  Bogotá

B  Cali

C  Caracas

D  Cartagena

**4** Venezuela's economy is based on

A  oil production.

B  flower exports.

C  small farms.

D  silver mining.

**5** Simon Bolívar helped several South American countries gain independence from

A  Britain.

B  Brazil.

C  Spain.

D  Mexico.

## Volcanoes of Colombia

**6** Based on the map above, active volcanoes are located in Colombia's

A  rivers.

B  mountains.

C  plains.

D  coastal areas.

**7** The physical geography of the Guianas includes

A  dense rain forests.

B  deserts.

C  the Orinoco River.

D  the Andes.

**8** **Extended Response** Look at the table of the world's oil exporters and the map of Venezuela's major resources in Section 3. Write a paragraph explaining why oil is Venezuela's most important resource. Identify at least two reasons.

# Atlantic South America

## What You Will Learn...

In this chapter you will learn about the plains and rain forest of Atlantic South America. You will also study the histories of the different countries and how different influences have shaped their cultures. In addition, you will learn about life, landscapes, and issues in Brazil, Argentina, Uruguay, and Paraguay today.

## FOCUS ON READING AND WRITING

**Using Context Clues** As you read, you may find some unknown words. You can usually figure out what a word means by using context clues. Look at the words and sentences around the unknown word—its context—to figure out the definition. **See the lesson, Using Context Clues, on page 524.**

**Creating a Web Site** You are a Web designer at a travel agency. Read this chapter and then use what you learn to create a Web site about Atlantic South America. The goal of your Web site will be to convince viewers to visit the region.

PACIFIC OCEAN

110°W
100°W
0° Equator
20°S

◉ National capital
● Other cities

0   300   600 Miles
0   300   600 Kilometers

Projection:
Lambert Azimuthal Equal-Area

### map zone

**Geography Skills**

**Place** Brazil and Argentina are South America's largest countries.
1. **Identify** What city lies on the Amazon River?
2. **Analyze** What would be some benefits of the location of Buenos Aires?

**Culture** During Carnival, Brazilians celebrate with music, dancing, and costumes.

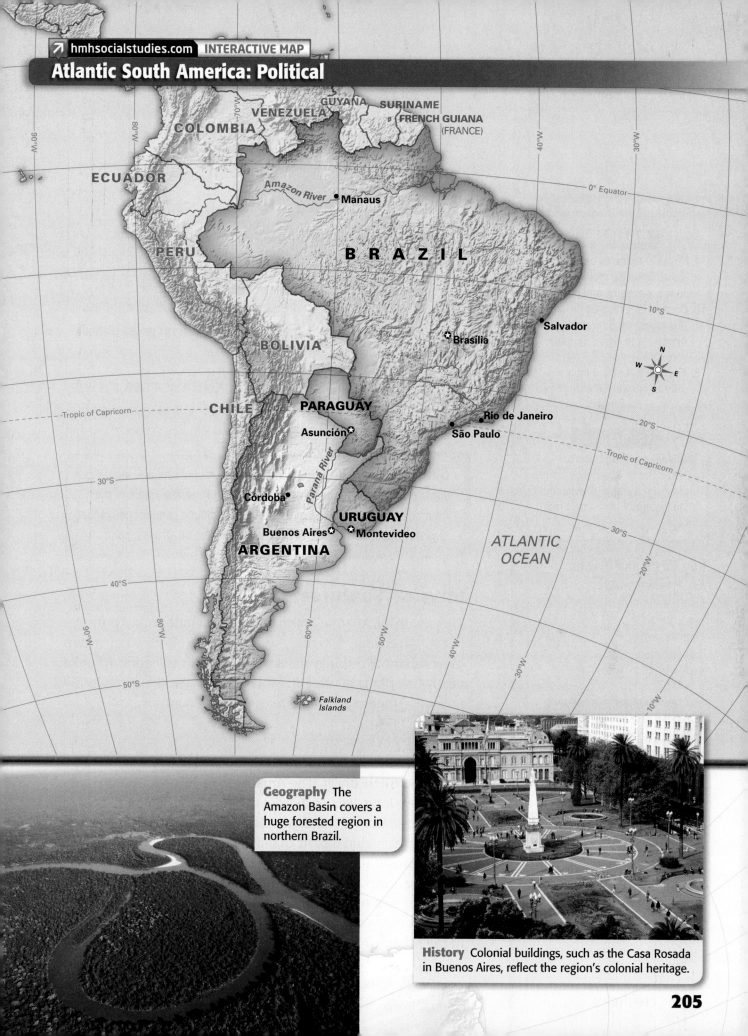

COLOMBIA

VENEZUELA

GUYANA

SURINAME

FRENCH GUIANA (FRANCE)

ECUADOR

PERU

Amazon River    • Manaus

B R A Z I L

BOLIVIA

✪ Brasília

• Salvador

CHILE

PARAGUAY

Asunción ✪

Paraná River

• Rio de Janeiro

São Paulo

0° Equator

10°S

20°S

Tropic of Capricorn

Tropic of Capricorn

30°S

Córdoba •

URUGUAY

Buenos Aires ✪  ✪ Montevideo

ARGENTINA

ATLANTIC OCEAN

40°S

50°S

Falkland Islands

N
W    E
S

80°W    70°W    60°W    50°W    40°W    30°W    20°W    10°W    90°W

**Geography** The Amazon Basin covers a huge forested region in northern Brazil.

**History** Colonial buildings, such as the Casa Rosada in Buenos Aires, reflect the region's colonial heritage.

# Physical Geography

## If YOU lived there...

You live on the coast of Brazil, near the mouth of the Amazon River. Now you are taking your first trip up the river deep into the rain forest. The river is amazingly wide and calm. Trees on the riverbanks seem to soar to the sky. Your boat slows as you pass a small village. You notice that all the houses rest on poles that lift them 8 to 10 feet out of the water.

**What would it be like to live in the rain forest?**

**BUILDING BACKGROUND** While rugged mountains and highlands dominate the lansdcape of Caribbean South America, much of the Atlantic region is made up of broad interior plains. Landscapes in this region range from tropical rain forest to temperate, grassy plains.

## Physical Features

The region of Atlantic South America includes four countries: Brazil, Argentina, Uruguay, and Paraguay. This large region covers about two-thirds of South America. Brazil alone occupies nearly half of the continent. Most of the physical features found in South America are found in these four countries.

### Major River Systems

The world's largest river system, the Amazon, flows eastward across northern Brazil. The **Amazon River** is about 4,000 miles (6,440 km) long. It extends from the Andes Mountains in Peru to the Atlantic Ocean. Hundreds of tributaries flow into it, draining an area that includes parts of most South American countries.

Because of its huge drainage area, the Amazon carries more water than any other river in the world. About 20 percent of the water that runs off Earth's surface flows down the Amazon. Where it meets the Atlantic, this freshwater lowers the salt level of the Atlantic for more than 100 miles (160 km) from shore.

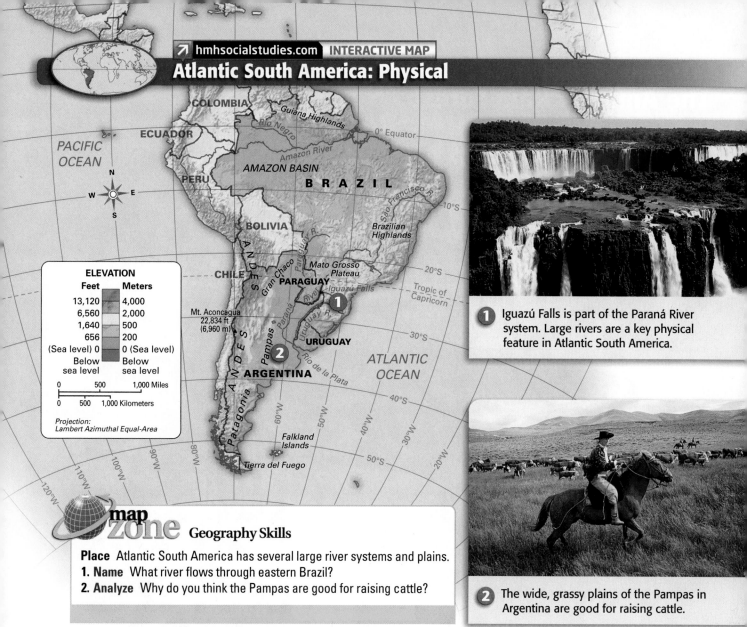

## Atlantic South America: Physical

hmhsocialstudies.com **INTERACTIVE MAP**

**ELEVATION**

| Feet | Meters |
|---|---|
| 13,120 | 4,000 |
| 6,560 | 2,000 |
| 1,640 | 500 |
| 656 | 200 |
| (Sea level) 0 | 0 (Sea level) |
| Below sea level | Below sea level |

0    500    1,000 Miles
0    500    1,000 Kilometers

Projection:
Lambert Azimuthal Equal-Area

**map zone Geography Skills**

**Place** Atlantic South America has several large river systems and plains.
**1. Name** What river flows through eastern Brazil?
**2. Analyze** Why do you think the Pampas are good for raising cattle?

1 Iguazú Falls is part of the Paraná River system. Large rivers are a key physical feature in Atlantic South America.

2 The wide, grassy plains of the Pampas in Argentina are good for raising cattle.

The Paraná (pah-rah-NAH) River drains much of the central part of South America. Water from the Paraná River eventually flows into the **Río de la Plata** (REE-oh day lah PLAH-tah) and the Atlantic Ocean beyond. The Río de la Plata is an estuary. An **estuary** is a partially enclosed body of water where freshwater mixes with salty seawater.

## Plains and Plateaus

As you can see on the map, this region's landforms mainly consist of plains and plateaus. The Amazon Basin in northern Brazil is a giant, flat floodplain. South of the Amazon Basin are the Brazilian Highlands, a rugged region of old, eroded mountains, and another area of high plains called the Mato Grosso Plateau.

Farther south, a low plains region known as the Gran Chaco (grahn CHAH-koh) stretches across parts of Paraguay and northern Argentina. In central Argentina are the wide, grassy plains of the **Pampas**. South of the Pampas is Patagonia—a region of dry plains and plateaus. All of these southern plains rise in the west to form the high Andes Mountains.

**FOCUS ON READING**
Where can you find the definition of *Pampas*?

**READING CHECK** **Summarizing** What are the region's major landforms and rivers?

The Amazon rain forest covers more than one-third of South America. Seen from the air, it looks like a big, green carpet. The top level of tree branches is called the canopy. Most action in the forest takes place in the canopy, but plenty of life also exists below.

hmhsocialstudies.com
ANIMATED GEOGRAPHY

Animals such as monkeys and sloths can spend their entire lives in the canopy.

People have cleared parts of the rain forest for farming, ranching, and logging.

Parts of the forest are flooded for half the year, and trees stand in water up to 40 feet (12 m) deep.

ANALYSIS
SKILL ANALYZING VISUALS

What kinds of animals could not survive living in the canopy?

# Climate and Vegetation

Atlantic South America has many climates. Generally, cool climates in southern and highland areas give way to tropical, moist climates in northern and coastal areas.

In southern Argentina Patagonia has a cool, desert climate. North of Patagonia, rich soils and a humid subtropical climate make parts of the Pampas good for farming. Farther north in Argentina, the Gran Chaco has a humid tropical climate. There, summer rains can turn some parts of the plains into marshlands.

North of Argentina, in Brazil, a large part of the central region has a tropical savanna climate with warm grasslands. The northeastern part of the country has a hot, dry climate, while the southeast is cooler and more humid.

In northern Brazil the Amazon Basin's humid tropical climate supports the world's largest tropical rain forest. Rain falls almost every day in this region. The Amazon rain forest contains the world's greatest variety of plant and animal life.

**READING CHECK** **Finding Main Ideas** What is the climate like in the rain forest?

# Natural Resources

The Amazon rain forest is one of the region's greatest natural resources. It provides food, wood, rubber, plants for medicines, and other products. In recent years **deforestation**, or the clearing of trees, has become an issue in the forest.

The region's land is also a resource for commercial farming, which is found near coastal areas of Atlantic South America. In some areas, however, planting the same crop every year has caused **soil exhaustion**, which means the soil is infertile because it has lost nutrients needed by plants.

Atlantic South America also has good mineral and energy resources such as gold, silver, copper, iron, and oil. Dams on some of the region's large rivers also provide hydroelectric power.

**READING CHECK** **Summarizing** What resources does the rain forest provide?

**SUMMARY AND PREVIEW** Physical features of Atlantic South America include great river systems and plains. The Amazon rain forest makes up a huge part of the region. Next you will learn about Brazil, the country of the Amazon.

## Section 1 Assessment

hmhsocialstudies.com
ONLINE QUIZ

### Reviewing Ideas, Terms, and Places

1. **a. Define** What is an **estuary**?
   **b. Explain** How does the **Amazon River** affect the Atlantic Ocean at the river's mouth?
   **c. Elaborate** What benefits do you think the rivers might bring to Atlantic South America?
2. **a. Recall** What kind of climate does Patagonia have?
   **b. Make Inferences** Why are temperatures in the south generally cooler than temperatures in the north?
3. **a. Identify** What resources does the rain forest provide?
   **b. Analyze** What is one benefit and one drawback of practicing commercial agriculture in the rain forest?
   **c. Elaborate** **Soil exhaustion** might lead to what kinds of additional problems?

### Critical Thinking

4. **Categorizing** Look back over your notes. Then use a table like this one to organize the physical geography of Atlantic South America by country.

| | Geography |
|---|---|
| Brazil | |
| Argentina | |

### FOCUS ON WRITING

5. **Describing Physical Geography** Jot down notes about the physical features, climate and vegetation, landscapes, and resources of this area. Identify one or two images you could use for your Web site.

# Brazil

## If YOU lived there...

You live in Rio de Janeiro, Brazil's second-largest city. For months your friends have been preparing for Carnival, the year's biggest holiday. During Carnival, people perform in glittery costumes and there is dancing all day and all night in the streets. The city is packed with tourists. It can be fun, but it is hectic! Your family is thinking of leaving Rio during Carnival so they can get some peace and quiet, but you may stay in Rio with a friend if you like.

**Would you stay for Carnival? Why or why not?**

**BUILDING BACKGROUND** Carnival is a tradition that is not unique to Brazil, but it has come to symbolize certain parts of Brazilian culture. Brazilian culture differs from cultures in the rest of South America in many ways. Brazil's unique history in the region is responsible for most of the cultural differences.

## History

Brazil is the largest country in South America. Its population of more than 188 million is larger than the population of all of the other South American countries combined. Most Brazilians are descended from three groups of people who contributed in different ways throughout Brazil's history.

### Colonial Brazil

The first people in Brazil were American Indians. They arrived in the region many thousands of years ago and developed a way of life based on hunting, fishing, and small-scale farming.

In 1500 Portuguese explorers became the first Europeans to find Brazil. Soon Portuguese settlers began to move there. Good climates and soils, particularly in the northeast, made Brazil a large sugar-growing colony. Colonists brought a third group of people—Africans—to work as slaves on the plantations. Sugar plantations made Portugal rich, but they also eventually replaced forests along the Atlantic coast.

## What You Will Learn...

### Main Ideas

1. Brazil's history has been affected by Brazilian Indians, Portuguese settlers, and enslaved Africans.
2. Brazil's society reflects a mix of people and cultures.
3. Brazil today is experiencing population growth in its cities and new development in rain forest areas.

### The Big Idea

The influence of Brazil's history can be seen all over the country in its people and culture.

### Key Terms and Places

São Paulo, *p. 212*
megacity, *p. 212*
Rio de Janeiro, *p. 212*
favelas, *p. 213*
Brasília, *p. 213*
Manaus, *p. 213*

**hmhsocialstudies.com**
TAKING NOTES

Use the graphic organizer online to take notes on Brazil.

Other parts of Brazil also contributed to the colonial economy. Inland, many Portuguese settlers created cattle ranches. In the late 1600s and early 1700s, people discovered gold and precious gems in the southeast. A mining boom drew people to Brazil from around the world. Finally, in the late 1800s southeastern Brazil became a major coffee-producing region.

### Brazil Since Independence

Brazil gained independence from Portugal without a fight in 1822. However, independence did not change Brazil's economy much. For example, Brazil was the last country in the Americas to end slavery.

Since the end of Portuguese rule, Brazil has been governed at times by dictators and at other times by elected officials. Today the country has an elected president and legislature. Brazilians can participate in politics through voting.

**READING CHECK** **Summarizing** What was Brazil's colonial economy like?

## People and Culture

The people who came to Brazil over the years brought their own traditions. These traditions blended to create a unique Brazilian culture.

### People

More than half of Brazilians consider themselves of European descent. These people include descendants of original Portuguese settlers along with descendants of more recent immigrants from Spain, Germany, Italy, and Poland. Nearly 40 percent of Brazil's people are of mixed African and European descent. Brazil also has the largest Japanese population outside of Japan.

Because of its colonial heritage, Brazil's official language is Portuguese. In fact, since Brazil's population is so huge, there are more Portuguese-speakers in South America than there are Spanish-speakers, even though Spanish is spoken in almost every other country on the continent. Other Brazilians speak Spanish, English, French, Japanese, or native languages.

**FOCUS ON READING**
What context clues in this paragraph help you understand the meaning of *descent*?

FOCUS ON CULTURE

### Soccer in Brazil

To Brazilians, soccer is more than a game. It is part of being Brazilian. Professional stars are national heroes. The national team often plays in Rio de Janeiro, home of the world's largest soccer stadium. Some fans beat drums all through the games. But it is not just professional soccer that is popular. People all over Brazil play soccer—in cleared fields, on the beach, or in the street. Here, boys in Rio practice their skills.

**Analyzing** Why do you think soccer is so popular in Brazil?

## Regions of Brazil

Brazil's regions differ from each other in their people, climates, economies, and landscapes.

**ANALYZING VISUALS** Which region appears to be the wealthiest?

**1** The southeast has the country's largest cities, such as Rio de Janeiro.

↗ hmhsocialstudies.com
**ANIMATED GEOGRAPHY**
Present-Day Brazil

### Religion

Brazil has the largest population of Roman Catholics of any country in the world. About 75 percent of Brazilians are Catholic. In recent years Protestantism has grown in popularity, particularly among the urban poor. Some Brazilians practice macumba (mah-KOOM-bah), a religion that combines beliefs and practices of African and Indian religions with Christianity.

### Festivals and Food

**ACADEMIC VOCABULARY**

aspects parts

Other **aspects** of Brazilian life also reflect the country's mix of cultures. For example, Brazilians celebrate Carnival before the Christian season of Lent. The celebration mixes traditions from Africa, Brazil, and Europe. During Carnival, Brazilians dance the samba, which was adapted from an African dance.

Immigrant influences can also be found in Brazilian foods. In parts of the country, an African seafood dish called vatapá (vah-tah-PAH) is popular. Many Brazilians also enjoy eating feijoada (fay-ZHWAH-dah), a stew of black beans and meat.

**READING CHECK** Analyzing How has cultural borrowing affected Brazilian culture?

## Brazil Today

Brazil's large size creates opportunities and challenges for the country. For example, Brazil has the largest economy in South America and has modern and wealthy areas. However, many Brazilians are poor.

While some of the same issues and characteristics can be found throughout Brazil, other characteristics are unique to a particular region of the country. We can divide Brazil into four regions based on their people, economies, and landscapes.

### The Southeast

Most people in Brazil live in the southeast. **São Paulo** is located there. Almost 19 million people live in and around São Paulo. It is the largest urban area in South America and the fourth largest in the world. São Paulo is considered a **megacity**, or a giant urban area that includes surrounding cities and suburbs.

**Rio de Janeiro**, Brazil's second-largest city, lies northeast of São Paulo. Almost 12 million people live there. The city was the capital of Brazil from 1822 until 1960. Today Rio de Janeiro remains a major port city. Its spectacular setting and exciting culture are popular with tourists.

2 About one third of Brazilians live in the dry northeast, the nation's poorest region.

3 Rivers provide resources and transportation for people living in the Amazon region.

In addition to having the largest cities, the southeast is also Brazil's richest region. It is rich in natural resources and has most of the country's industries and productive farmland. It is one of the major coffee-growing regions of the world.

Although the southeast has a strong economy, it also has poverty. Cities in the region have huge slums called **favelas** (fah-VE-lahz). Many people who live in favelas have come to cities of the southeast from other regions of Brazil in search of jobs.

## The Northeast

Immigrants to Brazil's large cities often come from the northeast, which is Brazil's poorest region. Many people there cannot read, and health care is poor. The region often suffers from droughts, which make farming and raising livestock difficult. The northeast has also had difficulty attracting industry. However, the region's beautiful beaches do attract tourists.

Other tourist attractions in northeastern Brazil are the region's many old colonial cities. These cities were built during the days of the sugar industry. They have brightly painted buildings, cobblestone streets, and elaborate Catholic churches.

## The Interior

The interior region of Brazil is a frontier land. Its abundant land and mild climate could someday make it an important area for agriculture. For now, few people live in this region, except for those who reside in the country's capital, **Brasília**.

In the mid-1950s government officials hoped that building a new capital city in the Brazilian interior would help develop the region. Brasília has modern buildings and busy highways. More than 2 million people live in Brasília, although it was originally designed for only 500,000.

## The Amazon

The Amazon region covers the northern part of Brazil. **Manaus**, which lies 1,000 miles (1,600 km) from the mouth of the Amazon, is a major port and industrial city. More than 1 million people live there. They rely on the river for transportation and communication.

Isolated Indian villages are scattered throughout the region's dense rain forest. Some of Brazil's Indians had little contact with outsiders until recently. Now, logging, mining, and new roads are bringing more people and development to this region.

# Deforestation in the Amazon

Deforestation is changing the landscape of the Amazon rain forest. This satellite image shows new roads and cleared areas where people have taken resources from the forest.

Many people depend on the industries that result in deforestation. For example, people need wood for building and making paper. Also, farmers, loggers, and miners need to make a living. However, deforestation in the Amazon also threatens the survival of many plant and animal species. It also threatens hundreds of unique ecosystems.

**Making Inferences** What do you think might be some effects of building roads in the rain forest?

This new development provides needed income for some people. But it destroys large areas of the rain forest. It also creates tensions among the Brazilian Indians, new settlers, miners, and the government.

**READING CHECK** **Contrasting** How does the northeast of Brazil differ from the southeast?

**SUMMARY AND PREVIEW** In this section you read about Brazil—a huge country of many contrasts. Brazil reflects the mixing of people and cultures from its history. In the next section you will learn about Brazil's neighbors—Argentina, Uruguay, and Paraguay.

## Section 2 Assessment

hmhsocialstudies.com
ONLINE QUIZ

### Reviewing Ideas, Terms, and Places

1. **a. Recall** What European country colonized Brazil?
   **b. Make Inferences** Why did the colonists bring Africans to work on plantations as slaves?
   **c. Elaborate** Why do you think the main basis of Brazil's colonial economy changed over the years?
2. **a. Identify** What religion is most common in Brazil?
   **b. Explain** Why is so much of Brazil's culture influenced by African traditions?
3. **a. Define** What is a **megacity**, and what is an example of a megacity in Brazil?
   **b. Make Inferences** Why might development in the Amazon cause tensions between Brazilian Indians and new settlers?
   **c. Elaborate** How might life change for a person who moves from the northeast to the southeast?

### Critical Thinking

4. **Finding Main Ideas** Review your notes on Brazil. Then, write a main idea statement about each region. Use a graphic organizer like this one.

|  | Main Idea |
|---|---|
| The Southeast |  |
| The Northeast |  |
| The Interior |  |
| The Amazon |  |

### FOCUS ON WRITING

5. **Writing about Brazil** What information about the history, people, and culture of Brazil will draw readers to the country? What regions do you think they would like to visit? List details and ideas for possible images for your Web site.

# Connecting Ideas

## Learn

You have already used several types of graphic organizers in this book. Graphic organizers are drawings that help you organize information and connect ideas.

One type of graphic organizer is a word web. A word web like the one at right helps you organize specific facts and details around a main topic. Notice that information gets more detailed as it gets farther away from the main topic.

## Practice

Use the word web here to answer the following questions. You may also want to look back at the information on Brazilian culture in your textbook.

❶ How can a graphic organizer help you connect ideas?

❷ What is the main topic of this word web?

❸ What three main ideas does this graphic organizer connect?

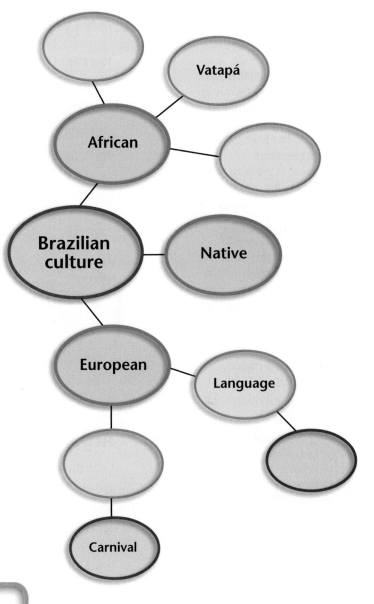

## Apply

Copy the graphic organizer shown here in your notebook. Use the information on Brazilian culture in your textbook to fill in the blank circles with additional details about the main topic.

# Argentina, Uruguay, and Paraguay

## What You Will Learn...

### Main Ideas

1. European immigrants have dominated the history and culture of Argentina.
2. Argentina's capital, Buenos Aires, plays a large role in the country's government and economy today.
3. Uruguay has been influenced by its neighbors.
4. Paraguay is the most rural country in the region.

### The Big Idea

Argentina, Uruguay, and Paraguay have been influenced by European immigration, a tradition of ranching, and large urban populations.

### Key Terms and Places

gauchos, *p. 217*
Buenos Aires, *p. 218*
Mercosur, *p. 218*
informal economy, *p. 219*
landlocked, *p. 220*

hmhsocialstudies.com
**TAKING NOTES**

Use the graphic organizer online to organize your notes on Argentina, Uruguay, and Paraguay.

## If YOU lived there...

You live in Montevideo, the capital of Uruguay. On weekends you like to visit the old part of the city and admire its beautiful buildings. You also enjoy walking along the banks of the Río de la Plata and watching fishers bring in their catch. Sometimes you visit the parks and beaches along the banks of the river.

**How do you think the river has influenced Montevideo?**

**BUILDING BACKGROUND** The southern countries of Atlantic South America—Argentina, Uruguay, and Paraguay—have all been influenced by their locations and European culture. Neither Spanish influence nor Indian culture is as strong in the southern part of South America as in other parts of the continent.

## Argentina's History and Culture

Like most of South America, Argentina was originally home to groups of Indians. Groups living in the Pampas hunted wild game, while farther north Indians built irrigation systems for farming. However, unlike most of South America, Argentina has very few native peoples remaining. Instead, Argentina's culture has been mostly influenced by Europeans.

### Early History

The first Europeans to come to Argentina were the Spanish. In the 1500s Spanish conquerors spread from the northern part of the continent into southern South America in search of silver and gold. They named the region Argentina. *Argentina* means "land of silver" or "silvery one."

## Gauchos on the Pampas

Gauchos were a popular subject in Argentine art. In this painting from 1820, gauchos gather to watch a horse race.

**ANALYZING VISUALS** Why would horses be important to a gaucho?

The Spanish soon built settlements in Argentina. The Spanish monarch granted land to the colonists, who in turn built the settlements. These landowners were also given the right to force the Indians living there to work.

During the colonial era, the Pampas became an important agricultural region. Argentine cowboys, called **gauchos** (GOW-chohz), herded cattle and horses on the open grasslands. Although agriculture is still important on the Pampas, very few people in Argentina live as gauchos today.

In the early 1800s Argentina fought for independence from Spain. A period of violence and instability followed. Many Indians were killed or driven away by fighting during this time.

### Modern Argentina

As the Indians were being killed off, more European influences dominated the region. New immigrants arrived from Italy, Germany, and Spain. Also, the British helped build railroads across the country. Railroads made it easier for Argentina to transport agricultural products for export to Europe. Beef exports, in particular, made the country rich.

Argentina remained one of South America's richest countries throughout the 1900s. However, the country also struggled under dictators and military governments during those years.

Some political leaders, like Eva Perón, were popular. But many leaders abused human rights. During the "Dirty War" in the 1970s, they tortured and killed many accused of disagreeing with the government. Both the country's people and its economy suffered. Finally, in the 1980s, Argentina's last military government gave up power to an elected government.

### BIOGRAPHY

### Eva Perón
(1919–1952)

Known affectionately as Evita, Eva Perón helped improve the living conditions of people in Argentina, particularly the poor. As the wife of Argentina's president, Juan Perón, Evita established thousands of hospitals and schools throughout Argentina. She also helped women gain the right to vote. After years of battling cancer, Evita died at age 33. All of Argentina mourned her death for weeks.

**Analyzing** Why was Eva Perón able to help many people?

### People and Culture

Argentina's historical ties to Europe still affect its culture. Most of Argentina's roughly 40 million people are descended from Spanish, Italian, or other European settlers. Argentine Indians and mestizos make up only about 3 percent of the population. Most Argentines are Roman Catholic.

Beef is still a part of Argentina's culture. A popular dish is parrilla (pah-REE-yah), which includes grilled sausage and steak. Supper is generally eaten late.

**READING CHECK** **Generalizing** What kind of governments did Argentina have in the 1900s?

## Argentina Today

Today many more of Argentina's people live in **Buenos Aires** (BWAY-nohs EYE-rayz) than in any other city. Buenos Aires is the country's capital. It is also the second-largest urban area in South America. Much of Argentina's industry is located in and around Buenos Aires. Its location on the coast and near the Pampas has contributed to its economic development.

The Pampas are the country's most developed agricultural region. About 11 percent of Argentina's labor force works in agriculture. Large ranches and farms there produce beef, wheat, and corn for export to other countries.

Argentina's economy has always been affected by government policies. In the 1990s government leaders made economic reforms to help businesses grow. Argentina joined **Mercosur**—an organization that promotes trade and economic cooperation among the southern and eastern countries of South America. By the late 1900s and early 2000s, however, heavy debt and government spending brought Argentina into an economic crisis.

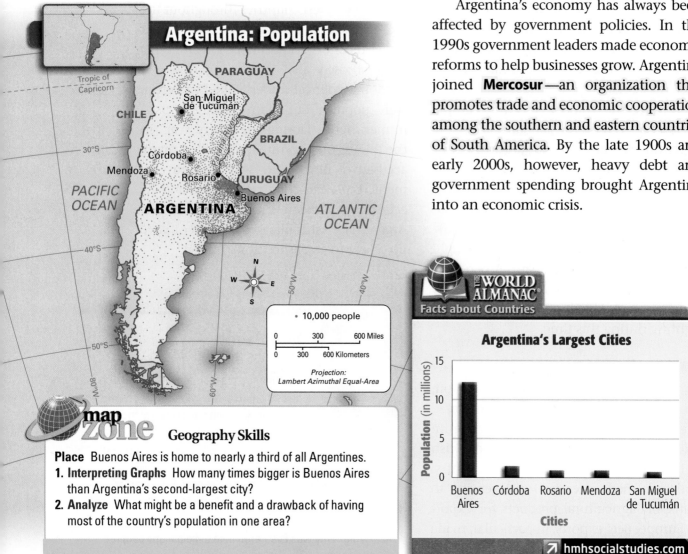

**Argentina: Population**

- 10,000 people

0 300 600 Miles
0 300 600 Kilometers

*Projection: Lambert Azimuthal Equal-Area*

**map zone** **Geography Skills**

**Place** Buenos Aires is home to nearly a third of all Argentines.
1. **Interpreting Graphs** How many times bigger is Buenos Aires than Argentina's second-largest city?
2. **Analyze** What might be a benefit and a drawback of having most of the country's population in one area?

**THE WORLD ALMANAC** **Facts about Countries**

**Argentina's Largest Cities**

Population (in millions) — Cities: Buenos Aires, Córdoba, Rosario, Mendoza, San Miguel de Tucumán

hmhsocialstudies.com

The economic crisis caused a political crisis. As a result, during 2001, Argentina's government changed hands four times as its leaders tried to solve the problems. By 2003 the economy had stabilized somewhat, but thousands of people's lives had changed forever. The crisis caused many people who once had professional careers to lose their jobs and join the informal economy. The **informal economy** is a part of the economy based on odd jobs that people perform without government regulation through taxes. Today many Argentines are still searching for ways to improve their economy.

**READING CHECK** **Comparing and Contrasting** What are some similarities and differences between Buenos Aires and the Pampas?

## Uruguay

Tucked between Argentina and Brazil lies Uruguay. Its capital, Montevideo (mawn-tay-vee-DAY-oh), is located on the north shore of the Río de la Plata, not far from Buenos Aires. Uruguay has always been influenced by its larger neighbors.

Portugal claimed Uruguay during the colonial era, but the Spanish took over in the 1770s. By that time, few Uruguayan Indians remained. A few years later, in 1825, Uruguay declared independence from Spain. Since then, military governments have ruled Uruguay off and on. In general, however, the country has a strong tradition of respect for political freedom. Today Uruguay is a democracy.

### People

As in Argentina, people of European descent make up the majority of Uruguay's population. Only about 12 percent of the population is mestizo, Indian, or of African descent. Roman Catholicism is the main religion in the country. Spanish is the official language, but many people also speak Portuguese because of Uruguay's location near Brazil.

More than 90 percent of Uruguay's people live in urban areas. More than a third of Uruguayans live in and near Montevideo. The country has a high literacy rate. In addition, many people there have good jobs and can afford a wide range of consumer goods and travel to Europe. However, many young people leave Uruguay to explore better economic opportunities elsewhere.

## Economy

**FOCUS ON READING**

Where can you find the definition of *landlocked*?

Just as Uruguay's culture is tied to its neighbors, its economy is tied to the economies of Brazil and Argentina. In fact, more than half of Uruguay's foreign trade is with these two Mercosur partners. Beef is an important export. As in Argentina, ranchers graze livestock on inland plains.

Agriculture, along with some limited manufacturing, is the basis of Uruguay's economy. Uruguay has few mineral resources. One important source of energy is hydroelectric power. Developing poor rural areas in the interior, where resources are in short supply, is a big challenge.

**READING CHECK** **Compare** In what ways is Uruguay similar to Argentina?

# Paraguay

Paraguay shares borders with Bolivia, Brazil, and Argentina. It is a landlocked country. **Landlocked** means completely surrounded by land with no direct access to the ocean. The Paraguay River divides the country into two regions. East of the river is the country's most productive farmland. Ranchers also graze livestock in some parts of western Paraguay.

Paraguay was claimed by Spanish settlers in the mid-1530s. It remained a Spanish colony until 1811, when it won independence. From independence until 1989, Paraguay was ruled off and on by dictators. Today the country has elected leaders and a democratic government.

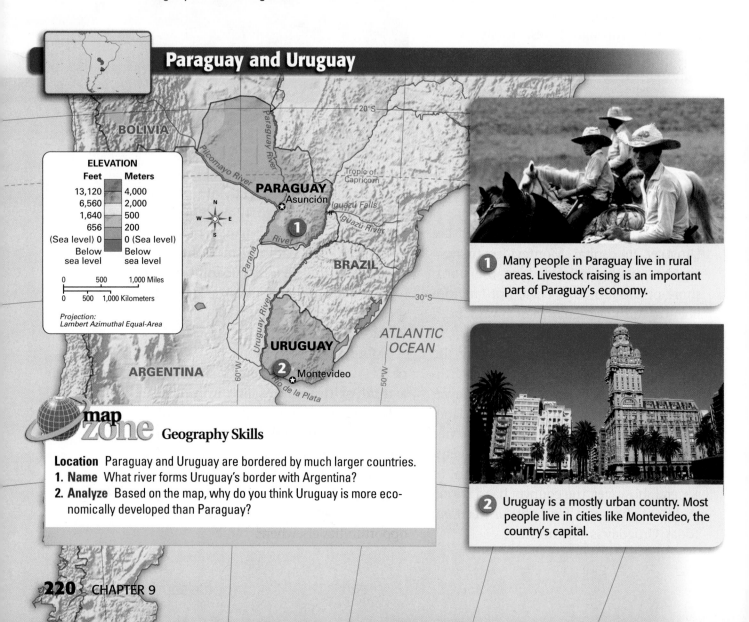

## Paraguay and Uruguay

**ELEVATION**

| Feet | Meters |
|------|--------|
| 13,120 | 4,000 |
| 6,560 | 2,000 |
| 1,640 | 500 |
| 656 | 200 |
| (Sea level) 0 | 0 (Sea level) |
| Below sea level | Below sea level |

0    500    1,000 Miles
0    500  1,000 Kilometers

*Projection: Lambert Azimuthal Equal-Area*

BOLIVIA

PARAGUAY
Asunción

PARAGUAY

BRAZIL

URUGUAY

ARGENTINA

Montevideo

ATLANTIC OCEAN

Pilcomayo River
Paraguay River
Iguazú Falls
Iguazú River
Paraná River
Uruguay River
Río de la Plata

20°S
Tropic of Capricorn
30°S
60°W
50°W

**① Many people in Paraguay live in rural areas. Livestock raising is an important part of Paraguay's economy.**

**② Uruguay is a mostly urban country. Most people live in cities like Montevideo, the country's capital.**

**map zone** **Geography Skills**

**Location** Paraguay and Uruguay are bordered by much larger countries.
1. **Name** What river forms Uruguay's border with Argentina?
2. **Analyze** Based on the map, why do you think Uruguay is more economically developed than Paraguay?

## People

A great majority—about 95 percent—of Paraguayans are mestizos. Indians and people of mostly European descent make up the rest of the population. Paraguay has two official languages. Almost all people in Paraguay speak both Spanish and Guarani (gwah-ruh-NEE), an Indian language. As in Uruguay, most people are Roman Catholic.

Paraguay's capital and largest city is Asunción (ah-soon-SYOHN). The city is located along the Paraguay River near the border with Argentina.

## Economy

Much of Paraguay's wealth is controlled by a few rich families and companies. These families and companies have tremendous influence over the country's government.

Agriculture is an important part of the economy. In fact, nearly half of the country's workers are farmers. Many of these farmers grow just enough food to feed themselves and their families. They grow crops such as corn, cotton, soybeans, and sugarcane. Paraguay also has many small businesses but not much industry.

Paraguay's future may be promising as the country learns how to use its resources more effectively. For example, the country has built large hydroelectric dams on the Paraná River. These dams provide more power than Paraguay needs, so Paraguay is able to sell the surplus electricity to Brazil and Argentina.

**READING CHECK** **Contrast** How are the people of Paraguay different from the people of Argentina and Uruguay?

**SUMMARY AND PREVIEW** The people of Paraguay, Argentina, and Uruguay share some aspects of their European heritage. Their economies are also closely tied. In the next chapter you will learn about these countries' neighbors to the west.

---

## Section 3 Assessment

### Reviewing Ideas, Terms, and Places

1. **a. Define** What is a **gaucho**?
   **b. Explain** Why is Argentina's population mostly of European descent?
2. **a. Identify** What is Argentina's biggest city?
   **b. Make Inferences** What benefits do you think being part of **Mercosur** brings to Argentina?
   **c. Elaborate** What are some benefits the **informal economy** provides, and what are some of its drawbacks?
3. **a. Recall** Where is Uruguay's capital located?
   **b. Summarize** How has Uruguay's location influenced its culture?
4. **a. Define** What does it mean to say a country is **landlocked**?
   **b. Explain** What is Paraguay's economy like?
   **c. Predict** What are some possible ways Paraguay may be able to improve its economy in the future?

### Critical Thinking

5. **Comparing and Contrasting** Look over your notes on Uruguay and Paraguay. Then draw a diagram like the one here and use it to show similarities and differences between the two countries.

Uruguay      Paraguay

### FOCUS ON WRITING

6. **Thinking about Argentina, Uruguay, and Paraguay** Add details about these countries to your notes for your Web site. What information on history, culture, and specific locations will you include? For each country, think of one image that would best illustrate it.

# from
# The Gaucho Martín Fierro

## by José Hernández

**About the Reading** *José Hernández spent part of his childhood on Argentina's Pampas. The gauchos lived freely on the plains there, herding cattle. In 1872 he published an epic poem about his days as an Argentine cowboy. The passage below is an excerpt.*

**AS YOU READ** Notice the emotion with which Hernández writes.

Gauchos spent a lot of time alone on the plains, but sometimes they got together for games and amusement.

### GUIDED READING

#### WORD HELP

**lassoing** catching with a rope
**steers** cattle
**keen** happy, eager

❶ Notice Hernández's description of the Pampas.

❷ Hernández describes the work of gauchos.

*What were some activities of gauchos?*

Even the poorest gaucho
had a string of matching horses;
he could always afford some amusement,
and people were ready for anything . . .
Looking out across the land
you'd see nothing but cattle and sky. ❶

When the branding-time came round
that was work to warm you up!
What a crowd! lassoing the running steers
and keen to hold and throw them . . . ❷
What a time that was! in those days surely
there were champions to be seen . . .

And the games that would get going
when we were all of us together!
We were always ready for them,
as at times like those
a lot of neighbors would turn up
to help out the regular hands.

## Connecting Literature to Geography

1. **Identifying Points of View** Hernández had happy memories of his days as a gaucho. What words and phrases demonstrate how Hernández felt?

2. **Analyzing** Although few people still work as gauchos, they are popular subjects in Argentine literature. What aspects of gaucho life do you think modern readers find appealing?

**Geography's Impact**
video series
Review the video to answer the closing question:
*What are some arguments for and against deforestation?*

## Visual Summary

*Use the visual summary below to help you review the main ideas of the chapter.*

QUICK FACTS

The lush Amazon rain forest covers a huge part of the region.

Brazil has many large cities as well as large rural areas.

Argentina, Uruguay, and Paraguay have large plains that are good for ranching.

## Reviewing Vocabulary, Terms, and Places

*For each group of terms below, write a sentence that shows how all the terms in the group are related.*

1. estuary
   Río de la Plata
   Buenos Aires
2. megacity
   favelas
   aspects
3. gauchos
   Pampas
4. soil exhaustion
   deforestation
   Amazon River
5. Rio de Janeiro
   São Paulo
   Manaus

## Comprehension and Critical Thinking

**SECTION 1** *(Pages 206–209)*

**6. a. Recall** What kind of climate does the Amazon Basin have?

**b. Contrast** How are northern Brazil and southern Argentina different?

**c. Elaborate** How might the region's major physical features have influenced development and daily life in Atlantic South America?

**SECTION 2** *(Pages 210–215)*

**7. a. Describe** What parts of Brazilian culture reflect African influences?

**b. Analyze** What factors lead people from the northeast of Brazil to move to the southeast?

**c. Evaluate** Is deforestation of the Amazon rain forest necessary? Explain your answer. What arguments might someone with a different opinion use?

**8. a. Describe** How is Argentina's culture different from other South American countries?

**b. Contrast** What is one difference between Uruguay and Paraguay?

**c. Predict** As Argentina's economy improves, what might happen to its informal economy?

## Social Studies Skills

**9. Connecting Ideas** Draw a graphic organizer to help you organize information about the economy in Atlantic South America. One has been started for you below. You will need to add more ovals to contain the information.

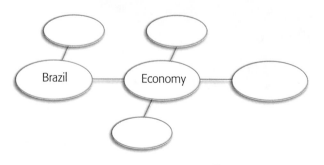

## Using the Internet 21ST CENTURY

**10. Activity: Creating a Poster** The Amazon River is the world's second-longest river. Through your online textbook, explore the many aspects of the river, including its wildlife, the rain forest it cuts through, the people who live alongside it, and the environmental issues surrounding it. Use the information you find and the interactive template provided to create a poster about the amazing Amazon River.

 hmhsocialstudies.com

## Map Activity 21ST CENTURY

**11. Atlantic South America** On a separate sheet of paper, match the letters on the map with their correct labels.

| | | |
|---|---|---|
| São Paulo | Pampas | Patagonia |
| Paraná River | Río de la Plata | Amazon River |

hmhsocialstudies.com **INTERACTIVE MAP**

**FOCUS ON READING AND WRITING**

**12. Using Context Clues** Look through the chapter and pick out two difficult words that you had to figure out by using context clues. Then, note the context clues you used to help you figure out the definitions of the difficult words.

**13. Creating a Web Site** You can create a real Web site or a paper version of a Web site. First, look back through your notes and choose key ideas about each country to include. In designing your site, first include a home page that briefly describes the region. Indicate links for pages about each of the countries in the region. Each of your country pages should include one short paragraph and one image. Remember to keep the pages simple—too much text might overwhelm your readers and send them off to another site!

# Standardized Test Prep

*DIRECTIONS: Read questions 1 through 7 and write the letter of the best response. Then read question 8 and write your own well-constructed response.*

**1** **In which country do most people speak Portuguese?**

   A Brazil

   B Argentina

   C Uruguay

   D Paraguay

**2** **What major river flows through northwestern Brazil?**

   A Río de la Plata

   B Uruguay River

   C Paraná River

   D Amazon River

**3** **Which of the following statements about Argentina is true?**

   A Most people are mestizos.

   B Most people in Argentina live on the Pampas.

   C Argentina is a member of Mercosur.

   D Argentina has had a stable government and economy since 2000.

**4** **Which of the following was an effect of the "Dirty War" in Argentina?**

   A The country's economy suffered.

   B Eva Perón became a popular political leader.

   C Many Indians were killed on the Pampas.

   D People elected military leaders to rule their country.

**5** **What is the most important part of the economy of Paraguay?**

   A mining

   B agriculture

   C manufacturing

   D logging

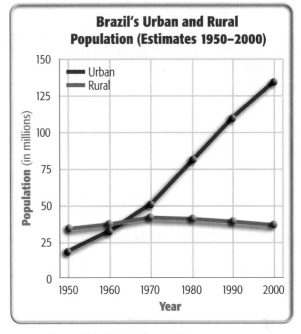

**Brazil's Urban and Rural Population (Estimates 1950–2000)**

Source: Instituto Brasileiro de Geografia e Estatística

**6** **Based on the graph above, which of the following statements is false?**

   A Brazil's urban population is increasing while the rural population is decreasing.

   B By 1960 more people in Brazil lived in urban areas than in rural areas.

   C In 1950 more people in Brazil lived in rural areas than in urban areas.

   D Brazil's total population is growing.

**7** **Based on the graph above, about how many people lived in urban areas of Brazil in 1990?**

   A 20 million

   B 135 million

   C 110 million

   D 40 million

**8** **Extended Response** Study the graph above and the information in your book about Brazil today. Then write a brief essay explaining how urban and rural landscapes in Brazil are changing. You will also want to discuss the causes and effects of this change.

# Pacific South America

CHAPTER 10

**Essential Question** How has political unrest shaped the nations of Pacific South America?

## What You Will Learn...

In this chapter you will learn about the Andes mountains that dominate the physical geography of Pacific South America. You will also study the history and culture of the region. In addition, you will learn about some of the struggles and progress happening today in Ecuador, Peru, Bolivia, and Chile.

### FOCUS ON READING AND SPEAKING

**Making Inferences** An inference is a kind of guess. Sometimes an author does not give you complete information, and you have to make an inference. As you read, try to fill in gaps in information. Make guesses about things the writer does not tell you directly. **See the lesson, Making Inferences, on page 525.**

**Interviewing** Interviews with experts are a great way to learn new information. As you read about Pacific South America, you will identify questions for an interview. Then, with a partner, you will create a script for an interview about the region. One of you will play the role of the interviewer, and one will play the regional expert.

**map zone**

**Geography Skills**

**Location** The countries of Pacific South America lie on the western side of South America.
1. **Identify** Which country is landlocked?
2. **Analyze** How do you think Chile's shape affects life in that country?

**Physical Geography** The Andes are the second-highest mountain range in the world. These peaks are in a national park in Chile.

# Pacific South America: Political

HISTORY

**Cliff Mummies of the Andes: Unwrapped**

↗ hmhsocialstudies.com  VIDEO

COLOMBIA

Quito ✪

ECUADOR

Guayaquil •

Amazon River

Equator — 0°

PERU

B R A Z I L

10°S

Lima ✪          • Cuzco

BOLIVIA

✪ La Paz

• Santa Cruz

✪ Sucre

CHILE          PARAGUAY

20°S

Tropic of Capricorn

URUGUAY

Valparaíso •
Santiago ✪

ARGENTINA

ATLANTIC
OCEAN

30°S

✪ National capital

• Other cities

0        300        600 Miles

0    300    600 Kilometers

*Projection:
Lambert Azimuthal Equal-Area*

**History** Early cultures made beautiful gold and silver art.

**Culture** Many people who live in the Andes still wear traditional dress and speak native languages. These women are from Peru.

**227**

# Physical Geography

## If YOU lived there...

You and your family fish for herring in the cold waters off the coast of Peru. Last year, however, an event called El Niño changed both the weather and the water. El Niño made the nearby ocean warmer. Without cold water, all the herring disappeared. You caught almost no fish at all. El Niño also caused terrible weather on the mainland.

**How might another El Niño affect you?**

## What You Will Learn...

### Main Ideas

1. The Andes are the main physical feature of Pacific South America.
2. The region's climate and vegetation change with elevation.
3. Key natural resources in the region include lumber, oil, and minerals.

### The Big Idea

The Andes dominate Pacific South America's physical geography and influence the region's climate and resources.

### Key Terms and Places

altiplano, *p. 229*
strait, *p. 229*
Atacama Desert, *p. 231*
El Niño, *p. 231*

**hmhsocialstudies.com**
**TAKING NOTES**

Use the graphic organizer online to take notes on the physical geography of Pacific South America.

**BUILDING BACKGROUND** Although most of the countries of Pacific South America lie along the coast, their landscapes are dominated by the rugged mountain range called the Andes. These mountains influence climates in the region. Ocean winds and currents also affect coastal areas here.

## Physical Features

The countries of Pacific South America stretch along the Pacific coast from the equator, for which the country of Ecuador is named, south almost to the Arctic Circle. One narrow country, Chile (CHEE-lay), is so long that it covers about half the Pacific coast by itself. Not all of the countries in Pacific South America have coastlines, however. Bolivia is landlocked. But all of the countries in this region do share one major physical feature—the high Andes mountains.

### Mountains

The Andes run through Ecuador, Peru, Bolivia, and Chile. Some ridges and volcanic peaks in the Andes rise more than 20,000 feet (6,800 m) above sea level. Because two tectonic plates meet at the region's edge, earthquakes and volcanoes are a constant threat. Sometimes these earthquakes disturb Andean glaciers, sending ice and mud rushing down mountain slopes.

Landscapes in the Andes differ from south to north. In southern Chile, rugged mountain peaks are covered by ice caps. In the north, the Andes are more rounded than rugged, and there the range splits into two ridges. In southern Peru and Bolivia these ridges are quite far apart. A broad, high plateau called the **altiplano** lies between the ridges of the Andes.

## Water and Islands

Andean glaciers are the source for many tributaries of the Amazon River. Other than the Amazon tributaries, the region has few major rivers. Rivers on the altiplano have no outlet to the sea. Water collects in two large lakes. One of these, Lake Titicaca, is the highest lake in the world that large ships can cross.

At the southern tip of the continent, the Strait of Magellan links the Atlantic and Pacific oceans. A **strait** is a narrow body of water connecting two larger bodies of water. The large island south of the strait is Tierra del Fuego, or "land of fire."

Chile and Ecuador both control large islands in the Pacific Ocean. Ecuador's volcanic Galápagos Islands have wildlife not found anywhere else in the world.

**READING CHECK** Contrasting How do the Andes differ from north to south?

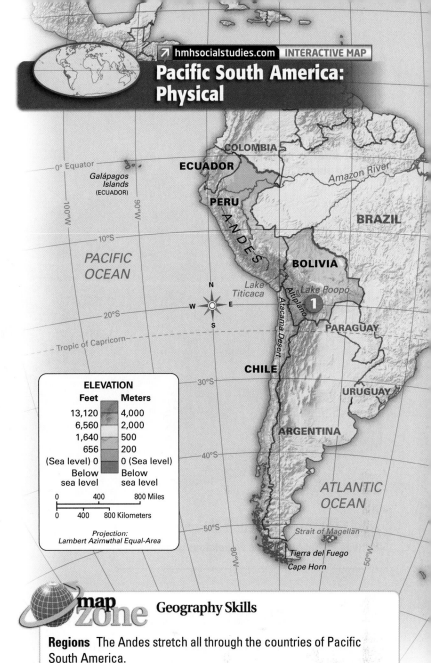

**Pacific South America: Physical**

### ELEVATION

| Feet | Meters |
|---|---|
| 13,120 | 4,000 |
| 6,560 | 2,000 |
| 1,640 | 500 |
| 656 | 200 |
| (Sea level) 0 | 0 (Sea level) |
| Below sea level | Below sea level |

0    400    800 Miles
0    400    800 Kilometers

Projection:
Lambert Azimuthal Equal-Area

**map Zone** Geography Skills

**Regions** The Andes stretch all through the countries of Pacific South America.
1. **Identify** To what country do the Galápagos Islands belong?
2. **Interpret** How do you think the Andes affect life in the region?

1 Llamas graze on the high, dry altiplano. The climate on the altiplano is too dry for trees to grow.

229

# Climate Zones in the Andes

Five climate zones exist in the Andes. The different elevations support different types of plant and animal life.

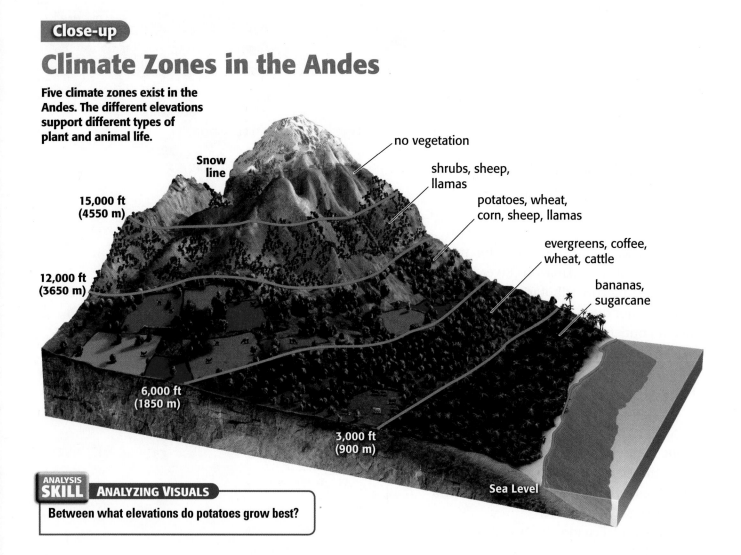

no vegetation

shrubs, sheep, llamas

potatoes, wheat, corn, sheep, llamas

evergreens, coffee, wheat, cattle

bananas, sugarcane

Snow line

15,000 ft (4550 m)

12,000 ft (3650 m)

6,000 ft (1850 m)

3,000 ft (900 m)

Sea Level

**ANALYSIS SKILL  ANALYZING VISUALS**

Between what elevations do potatoes grow best?

## Climate and Vegetation

FOCUS ON READING
What can you infer about the location of mountains in Ecuador?

Climate, vegetation, and landscapes all vary widely in Pacific South America. We usually think of latitude as the major factor that affects climate. However, in Pacific South America, elevation has the biggest effect on climate and vegetation.

### Elevation

Mountain environments change with elevation. For this reason, we can identify five different climate zones in the Andes. You can see these different climate zones on the diagram above.

The lowest zone includes the hot and humid lower elevations near sea level. Crops such as sugarcane and bananas grow well there. This first zone is often found along the coast, but it is also found inland in eastern Ecuador and Peru and northern Bolivia. These regions are part of the Amazon basin. They have a humid tropical climate with thick, tropical rain forests.

As elevation increases, the air becomes cooler. The second elevation zone has moist climates with mountain forests. This zone is good for growing coffee. In addition, many of Pacific South America's large cities are located in this zone.

Higher up the mountains is a third, cooler zone of forests and grasslands. Farmers grow potatoes and wheat there. Many people in Pacific South America live and farm in this climate zone.

At a certain elevation, the climate becomes too cool for trees to grow. This fourth climate zone above the tree line contains alpine meadows with grasslands and hardy shrubs. The altiplano region between the two ridges of the Andes lies mostly in this climate zone.

The fifth climate zone, in the highest elevations, is very cold. No vegetation grows in this zone because the ground is almost always covered with snow and ice.

### Deserts

Pacific South America also has some climates that are not typical of any of the five climate zones. Instead of hot and humid climates, some coastal regions have desert climates.

Northern Chile contains the **Atacama Desert**. This desert is about 600 miles (965 km) long. Rain falls there less than five times a century, but fog and low clouds are common. They form when a cold current in the Pacific Ocean chills the warmer air above the ocean's surface. Cloud cover keeps the air near the ground from being warmed by the sun. As a result, coastal Chile is one of the cloudiest—and driest—places on Earth.

In Peru, some rivers cut through the dry coastal region. They bring snowmelt down from the Andes. Because they rely on melting snow, some of these rivers only appear at certain times of the year. The rivers have made some small settlements possible in these dry areas.

### El Niño

About every two to seven years, this dry region experiences **El Niño**, an ocean and weather pattern that affects the Pacific coast. During an El Niño year, cool Pacific water near the coast warms. This change may cause extreme ocean and weather events that can have global effects.

As El Niño warms ocean waters, fish leave what is usually a rich fishing area. This change affects fishers. Also, El Niño **causes** heavy rains, and areas along the coast sometimes experience flooding. Some scientists think that air pollutants have made El Niño last longer and have more damaging effects.

ACADEMIC VOCABULARY

**cause** to make something happen

**READING CHECK** **Finding Main Ideas** How does elevation affect climate and vegetation?

## Natural Resources

The landscapes of Pacific South America provide many valuable natural resources. For example, forests in southern Chile and in eastern Peru and Ecuador provide lumber. Also, as you have read, the coastal waters of the Pacific Ocean are rich in fish.

### Satellite View

### Atacama Desert

The Atacama Desert lies between the Pacific coast and the Andes in northern Chile. In this image you can see two snowcapped volcanoes. The salt in the top right part of the image is formed from minerals carried there by rivers that only appear during certain months of the year. These seasonal rivers also support some limited vegetation.

**Drawing Conclusions** Why do you think there is snow on the volcanoes even though the desert gets hardly any precipitation?

## Bolivia: Resources

Gold  Tin
Lead  Zinc
Silver

0    100    200 Miles
0    100    200 Kilometers

Projection: Lambert
Azimuthal Equal-Area

BRAZIL

BOLIVIA

Lake
Titicaca

Lake
Poopó

—20°S

CHILE    ARGENTINA    PARAGUAY

### map zone Geography Skills

**Place** Bolivia has many valuable mineral resources.
1. **Locate** Where are most of Bolivia's gold resources found?
2. **Interpret** What do you notice about the location of the mineral resources and the rivers?

In addition, the region has valuable oil and minerals. Ecuador in particular has large oil and gas reserves, and oil is the country's main export. Bolivia has some deposits of tin, gold, silver, lead, and zinc. Chile has copper deposits. In fact, Chile exports more copper than any other country in the world. Chile is also the site of the world's largest open pit mine.

Although the countries of Pacific South America have many valuable resources, one resource they do not have much of is good farmland. Many people farm, but the region's mostly cool, arid lands make it difficult to produce large crops for export.

**READING CHECK Categorizing** What types of resources do the countries of Pacific South America have?

**SUMMARY AND PREVIEW** The Andes are the main physical feature of Pacific South America. Next, you will learn how the Andes have affected the region's history and how they continue to affect life there today.

## Section 1 Assessment

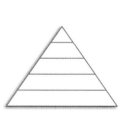
### Reviewing Ideas, Terms, and Places

1. **a. Identify** What is the main physical feature of Pacific South America?
   **b. Analyze** How is Bolivia's location unique in the region?
2. **a. Define** What is **El Niño**, and what are some of its effects?
   **b. Draw Conclusions** Why are parts of Ecuador, in the tropics, cooler than parts of southern Chile?
3. **a. Identify** What country in this region has large oil reserves?
   **b. Make Inferences** Why do you think much of the region is not good for farming?
   **c. Elaborate** What effects do you think copper mining in Chile might have on the environment?

### Critical Thinking

4. **Categorizing** Review your notes on climate. Then use a diagram like this one to describe the climate and vegetation in each of the five climate zones.

### Focus on Speaking

5. **Describing Physical Geography** Note information about the physical features, climate and vegetation, and resources of Pacific South America. Write two questions and answers you can use in your interview.

# Interpreting an Elevation Profile

## Learn

An elevation profile is a diagram that shows a side view of an area. This kind of diagram shows the physical features that lie along a line from point A to point B. Keep in mind that an elevation profile typically exaggerates vertical distances because vertical and horizontal distances are measured differently on elevation profiles. If they were not, even tall mountains would appear as tiny bumps.

Vertical measurements are given on the sides of the diagram.

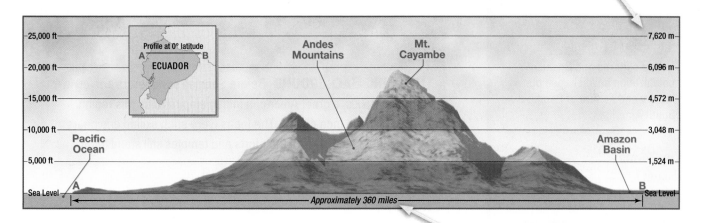

| 25,000 ft | | Andes Mountains | Mt. Cayambe | | 7,620 m |
| 20,000 ft | Profile at 0° latitude / A — B / ECUADOR | | | | 6,096 m |
| 15,000 ft | | | | | 4,572 m |
| 10,000 ft | Pacific Ocean | | | Amazon Basin | 3,048 m |
| 5,000 ft | | | | | 1,524 m |
| Sea Level | A | Approximately 360 miles | | B | Sea Level |

The horizontal measurement is given along the bottom of the diagram.

## Practice

Use the elevation profile above to answer the following questions.

1. What place does this elevation profile measure?

2. What is the highest point, and what is its elevation?

3. How can you tell that the vertical distance is exaggerated?

## Apply

Look at the physical map of Pacific South America in Section 1 of this chapter. Choose a latitude line and create your own elevation profile for the land at that latitude. Be sure to pay attention to the scale and the legend so that you use correct measurements.

# History and Culture

## If YOU lived there...

You live in Cuzco, the capital of the Inca Empire. You are required to contribute labor to the empire, and you have been chosen to work on a construction project. Hauling the huge stones will be difficult, but the work will be rewarding. You can either choose to help build a magnificent temple to the sun god or you can help build a road from Cuzco to the far end of the empire.

**Which project will you choose? Why?**

**BUILDING BACKGROUND** Before Spanish conquerors arrived in the early 1500s, a great American Indian empire ruled this region. Cuzco was the Inca capital. The Incas were such skilled engineers and builders that many of their forts and temples still stand today.

## History

Thousands of years ago, people in Pacific South America tried to farm on mountainsides as steep as bleachers. Other people tried to farm where there was almost no rain. These early cultures learned how to adapt to and modify their environments.

### Early Cultures

Peru's first advanced civilization reached its height in about 900 BC in the Andes. These people built stone terraces into the steep mountainside so they could raise crops. In coastal areas, people created irrigation systems to store water and control flooding.

Agriculture supported large populations, towns, and culture. In the Bolivian highlands one early culture, the Tiahuanaco (tee-uh-wuh-NAH-koh), made huge stone carvings near a lakeshore. In another civilization on the coast, people scratched outlines of animals and other shapes into the surface of the Peruvian desert. These designs, known as the Nazca lines, are so large they can only be recognized from the sky.

---

## What You Will Learn...

### Main Ideas

1. The countries of Pacific South America share a history influenced by the Inca civilization and Spanish colonization.
2. The culture of Pacific South America includes American Indian and Spanish influences.

### The Big Idea

Native cultures and Spanish colonization have shaped the history and culture of Pacific South America.

### Key Terms

viceroy, *p. 235*
Creoles, *p. 236*

hmhsocialstudies.com
**TAKING NOTES**

Use the graphic organizer online to take notes on the history and culture of Pacific South America.

## An Inca City

The Inca city of Machu Picchu lay undiscovered high in the Andes until 1911.

**ANALYZING VISUALS** Why do you think Machu Picchu was undiscovered for almost 400 years?

### The Inca Empire

Eventually, one group of people came to rule most of the region. By the early 1500s, these people, the Incas, controlled an area that stretched from northern Ecuador to central Chile. The Inca Empire was home to as many as 12 million people.

The huge Inca Empire was highly organized. Irrigation projects turned deserts into rich farmland. Thousands of miles of stone-paved roads connected the empire. Rope suspension bridges helped the Incas cross the steep Andean valleys.

As advanced as their civilization was, the Incas had no wheeled vehicles or horses. Instead, relay teams of runners carried messages from one end of the empire to the other. Working together, a team of runners could carry a message up to 150 miles (240 km) in one day. The runners did not carry any letters, however, because the Incas did not have a written language.

### Spanish Rule

In spite of its great organization, however, the Inca Empire did not last long. A new Inca ruler, on his way to be crowned king, met the Spanish explorer Francisco Pizarro. Pizarro captured the Inca king, who ordered his people to bring enough gold and silver to fill a whole room. These riches were supposed to be a ransom for the king's freedom. Instead, Pizarro ordered the Inca king killed. Fighting broke out, and by 1535 the Spaniards had conquered the Inca Empire.

The new Spanish rulers often dealt harshly with the South American Indians of the fallen Inca Empire. Many Indians had to work in gold or silver mines or on the Spaniards' plantations. A Spanish **viceroy**, or governor, was appointed by the king of Spain to make sure the Indians followed the Spanish laws and customs that had replaced native traditions.

**VIDEO**
Machu Picchu

hmhsocialstudies.com

**FOCUS ON READING**
How do you think the South American Indians felt about the viceroy?

## Independence

By the early 1800s, people in Pacific South America began to want independence. They began to revolt against Spanish rule. **Creoles**, American-born descendants of Europeans, were the main leaders of the revolts. The success of the revolts led to independence for Chile, Ecuador, Peru, and Bolivia by 1825.

**READING CHECK** **Evaluating** How did Inca civilization influence the history of the region?

## Culture

Spanish and native cultures have both left their marks on Pacific South America. Most people in the region speak Spanish, and Spanish is the official language in all of the countries of the region.

However, people in many parts of the region also maintain much of their native culture. Millions of South American Indians speak native languages in addition to or instead of Spanish. In Bolivia, two native languages are official languages in addition to Spanish.

The people and customs of Pacific South America also reflect the region's Spanish and Indian heritage. For example, Bolivia's population has the highest percentage of South American Indians of any country on the continent. Many Bolivian Indians follow customs and lifestyles that have existed for many centuries. They often dress in traditional styles—full skirts and derby hats for the women and colorful, striped ponchos for the men.

Another part of the region's culture that reflects Spanish and Indian influences is religion. Most people in Pacific

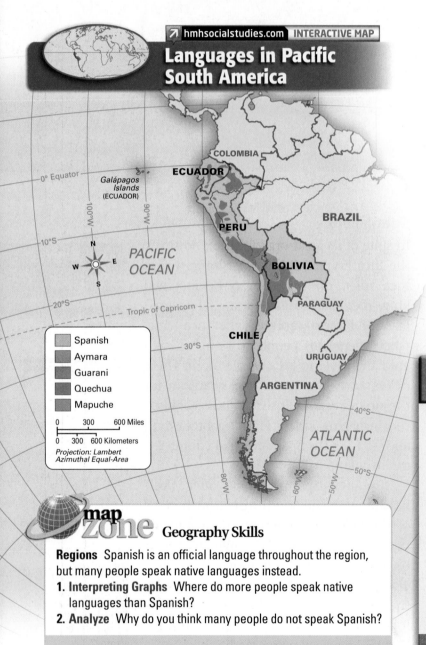

↗ hmhsocialstudies.com **INTERACTIVE MAP**

### Languages in Pacific South America

Spanish
Aymara
Guarani
Quechua
Mapuche

0    300    600 Miles
0    300    600 Kilometers
Projection: Lambert Azimuthal Equal-Area

**map zone** **Geography Skills**

**Regions** Spanish is an official language throughout the region, but many people speak native languages instead.
1. **Interpreting Graphs** Where do more people speak native languages than Spanish?
2. **Analyze** Why do you think many people do not speak Spanish?

**THE WORLD ALMANAC** Facts about Countries

**Languages in Pacific South America**

- Speak mostly Spanish
- Speak mostly a native language

↗ hmhsocialstudies.com

## Andean Culture

Every May, high in the Andes, Bolivians gather in Macha, Bolivia for Tinku, a festival honoring *Pachamama*, or mother earth.

**ANALYZING VISUALS** What do you think the climate is like in Macha?

Music played on wooden flutes like these is popular in the Andes.

South America practice the religion of the Spanish—Roman Catholicism. Some people in the Andes, however, also still practice ancient religious customs. Every June, for example, people participate in a festival that was celebrated by the Incas to worship the sun. During festivals people wear traditional costumes, sometimes with wooden masks. They also play traditional instruments, such as wooden flutes.

**READING CHECK** Generalizing What traditional customs do people in the region still practice today?

**SUMMARY AND PREVIEW** Pacific South America was home to one of the greatest ancient civilizations in the Americas—the Inca. The Spanish conquered the Incas. Today the region's culture still reflects Inca and Spanish influences. Next, you will learn more about the governments and economies of Ecuador, Bolivia, Peru, and Chile today.

## Section 2 Assessment

hmhsocialstudies.com
ONLINE QUIZ

### Reviewing Ideas, Terms, and Places

1. a. **Recall** What ancient empire built paved roads through the Andes?
   b. **Explain** What role did **Creoles** play in the history of Pacific South America?
   c. **Predict** How might the Inca Empire have been different if the Incas had had wheels and horses?
2. a. **Recall** What country has the highest percentage of South American Indians in its population?
   b. **Make Generalizations** What aspects of culture in Pacific South America reflect Spanish influence, and what aspects reflect Indian heritage?

### Critical Thinking

3. **Sequencing** Look over your notes on the region's history. Then draw a graphic organizer like the one here and use it to put major historical events in chronological order.

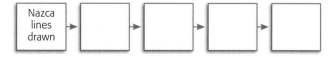

Nazca lines drawn →

### FOCUS ON SPEAKING

4. **Taking Notes on History and Culture** What information about the history and culture is important? Add two more questions, plus answers, to your notes.

# Pacific South America Today

## What You Will Learn...

### Main Ideas

1. Ecuador struggles with poverty and political instability.
2. Bolivia's government is trying to gain stability and improve the economy.
3. Peru has made progress against poverty and violence.
4. Chile has a stable government and a strong economy.

### The Big Idea

The countries of Pacific South America are working to overcome challenges of poverty and political instability.

### Key Terms and Places

Quito, *p. 239*
La Paz, *p. 239*
Lima, *p. 240*
coup, *p. 241*
Santiago, *p. 242*

hmhsocialstudies.com
TAKING NOTES

Use the graphic organizer online to take notes on Pacific South America today.

## If YOU lived there...

You are at a political rally in Valparaíso, Chile. Your family owns a vineyard nearby, so government policies about the economy affect you personally. You listen carefully to the speakers at the rally. Some politicians are in favor of more free trade with countries in North America. Others speak about different issues, such as housing and education.

**What would you like to ask the politicians?**

**BUILDING BACKGROUND** All the countries of Pacific South America have faced similar issues in recent years. These include poverty, unstable governments, economic development, and how to encourage development and still protect the environment. Several of these countries are making progress, while others still have problems.

## Ecuador Today

In recent decades, the countries of Pacific South America have all experienced periods of political instability. Ecuador, in particular, has faced recent instability. Widespread poverty is a constant threat to a stable government in this country.

### Government

Ecuador has been a democracy since 1979. Still, the country has experienced great political instability and corruption. From 1996–2007, the country had nine different presidents. In 2004, Ecuadorian president Lucio Gutiérrez fired the majority of the nation's supreme court judges because they did not support him. Soon after, to quiet his political opponents, Gutiérrez declared a state of emergency. In response, the Ecuadorian Congress forced Gutiérrez from power in 2005. In 2006, Ecuadorians elected Rafael Correa president. In 2009, Correa was the first Ecuadorian president to be re-elected in more than 30 years.

## Economic Regions

Ecuador has three different economic regions. One region, the coastal lowlands, has agriculture and industry. The country's largest city, Guayaquil (gwy-ah-KEEL), is located there. It is Ecuador's major port and commercial center.

The Andean region of Ecuador is poorer. **Quito**, the national capital, is located there. Open-air markets and Spanish colonial buildings attract many tourists to Quito and other towns in the region.

A third region, the Amazon basin, has valuable oil deposits. The oil industry provides jobs that draw people to the region. Oil is also Ecuador's main export. But the oil industry has brought problems as well as benefits. The country's economy suffers if the world oil price drops. In addition, some citizens worry that drilling for oil could harm the rain forest.

**READING CHECK** **Generalizing** Why has Ecuador's government been unstable?

## Bolivia Today

Like Ecuador, Bolivia is a poor country. Poverty has been a cause of political unrest in recent years.

### Government

After years of military rule, Bolivia is a democracy. Bolivia's government is divided between two capital cities. The supreme court meets in Sucre (SOO-kray), but the congress meets in **La Paz**. Located at about 12,000 feet (3,660 m), La Paz is the highest capital city in the world. It is also Bolivia's main industrial center.

In the early 2000s, many Bolivians disagreed with their government's plans for fighting poverty. National protests forced several presidents to resign. Then in 2005, Bolivians elected an indigenous leader, Evo Morales, as president. Re-elected president in 2009, Morales continues to work to improve the lives of Bolivia's poor.

### Economy

Bolivia is the poorest country in South America. In the plains of eastern Bolivia there are few roads and little money for investment. However, foreign aid has provided funds for some development. In addition, the country has valuable resources, including metals and natural gas.

**READING CHECK** **Analyzing** Why might political revolts slow development?

## CONNECTING TO Economics

### The Informal Economy

Many people in the countries of Pacific South America are part of the informal economy. Street vendors, like the ones shown here in Quito, are common sights in the region's cities. People visit street vendors to buy items like snacks, small electronics, or clothing. The informal economy provides jobs for many people. However, it does not help the national economy because the participants do not pay taxes. Without income from taxes, the government cannot pay for services.

**Analyzing** How does the informal economy affect taxes?

## Settlements around Lima

Lima has three main types of settlements. The wealthier people tend to live in houses and apartments in town. Poor people live mostly in slums or in recently built "young towns."

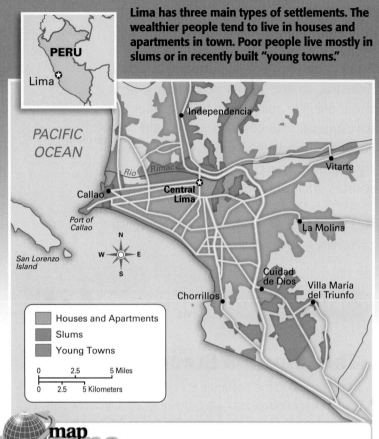

**Houses and Apartments** Most housing in Lima is made up of high-rise apartments and private houses, some of which are from the colonial era.

**map zone** **Geography Skills**

**Human-Environment Interaction** People have built three different basic types of housing in and around Lima.
1. **Use the Map** What is the most common type of housing?
2. **Draw Conclusions** Why are most young towns built far from central Lima?

## Peru Today

Peru is the largest and most populous country in Pacific South America. Today it is making some progress against political violence and poverty.

### Lima

Peru's capital, **Lima** (LEE-muh), is the largest city in the region. Nearly one-third of all Peruvians live in Lima or the nearby port city of Callao (kah-YAH-oh). Lima has industry, universities, and government jobs, which attract many people from the countryside to Lima.

Lima was the colonial capital of Peru, and the city still contains many beautiful old buildings from the colonial era. It has high-rise apartments and wide, tree-lined boulevards. However, as in many big urban areas, a lot of people there live in poverty.

In spite of the poverty, central Lima has few slum areas. This is because most poor people prefer to claim land on the outskirts of the city and build their own houses. Often they can get only poor building materials. They also have a hard time getting water and electricity from the city.

Settlements of new self-built houses are called "young towns" in Lima. Over time, as people improve and add to their houses, the new settlements develop into large, permanent suburbs. Many of the people in Lima's young towns are migrants from the highlands. Some came to Lima to escape violence in their home villages.

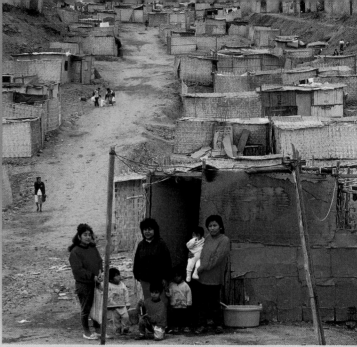

**Slums** Just outside downtown and near the port area, many people live in slum housing. These buildings are permanent, but run-down.

**Young Towns** Many poor people in recent years have taken over land on the outskirts of Lima and have built their own shelters.

## Government

In the 1980s and 1990s, a terrorist group called the Shining Path was active. This group carried out deadly attacks because it opposed government policies. Some 70,000 people died in violence between the Shining Path and government forces, and Peru's economy suffered. However, after the arrest of the group's leaders, Peru's government began making progress against political violence and poverty. The country has an elected president and congress.

## Resources

Peru's resources are key factors in its economic progress. Some mineral deposits are located near the coast, and hydroelectric projects on rivers provide energy. Peru's highlands are less developed than the coastal areas. However, many Peruvian Indians grow potatoes and corn there.

**READING CHECK** **Identifying Cause and Effect** How did the Shining Path affect Peru?

# Chile Today

Like Peru, Chile has ended a long violent period. Chile now has a stable government and a growing economy.

## Government

In 1970 Chileans elected a president who had some ideas influenced by communism. A few years later he was overthrown and died in a U.S.-backed military coup (KOO). A **coup** is a sudden overthrow of a government by a small group of people.

In the years after the coup, military rulers tried to crush their political enemies. Chile's military government was harsh and often violent. It imprisoned or killed thousands of people.

In the late 1980s Chile's military dictatorship weakened and Chileans created a new, democratic government. In 2006 Chileans elected their first female president, Michelle Bachelet, and in 2010 they elected business leader Sebastián Piñera president.

**FOCUS ON READING**

What can you infer about the reason for the end of the military government?

A man in Chile harvests grapes to be made into wine for export.

Mediterranean climate allows farmers to grow many crops. For example, grapes grow well there, and Chilean fruit and wine are exported around the world.

Farming, fishing, forestry, and mining form the basis of Chile's economy. Copper mining is especially important. It accounts for more than one-third of Chile's exports.

Chile's economic stability was rocked by a massive earthquake that struck on February 27, 2010. The quake killed about 500 Chileans and caused about $30 billion of damage to buildings, homes, and streets. Today, Chile's people and government continue to rebuild their nation.

**READING CHECK** Identifying Points of View Why might Chile want to join a free trade group?

**SUMMARY AND PREVIEW** In recent years Ecuador, Peru, Bolivia, and Chile have struggled with political violence and poverty. However, Peru and Chile are recovering. Next, you will study the culture and economy of the United States.

## Resources and Economy

Chile's economy is the strongest in the region. Poverty rates have decreased, and Chile's prospects for the future seem bright. Small businesses and factories are growing quickly. More Chileans are finding work, and wages are rising.

About one-third of all Chileans live in central Chile. This region includes the capital, **Santiago**, and a nearby seaport, Valparaíso (bahl-pah-rah-EE-soh). Its mild

## Section 3 Assessment

hmhsocialstudies.com
ONLINE QUIZ

### Reviewing Ideas, Terms, and Places

1. **a. Identify** What is Ecuador's largest city?
   **b. Make Generalizations** Why have Ecuadorians been unhappy with their government in recent years?
2. **a. Identify** What are Bolivia's two capital cities?
   **b. Analyze** Why might Bolivia's economy improve in the future?
3. **a. Recall** Why did many Peruvians move to Lima from the highlands in the 1980s?
   **b. Elaborate** What challenges do you think people who move to **Lima** from the highlands face?
4. **a. Define** What is a **coup**?
   **b. Make Inferences** What might happen to Chile's economy if the world price of copper drops?

### Critical Thinking

5. **Solving Problems** Review your notes. Then, in a diagram like the one here, write one sentence about each country, explaining how that country is dealing with poverty or government instability.

| Ecuador | |
|---------|--|
| Bolivia | |
| Peru | |
| Chile | |

### FOCUS ON SPEAKING

6. **Thinking about Pacific South America Today**
   Add questions about each country in Pacific South America to your notes. How might you answer these questions in your interview? Write down the answer to each question.

# Chapter Review

**Geography's Impact**
video series
Review the video to answer the closing question:
*Why do descendants of the Incas still live in the difficult high altitudes of the Andes?*

## Visual Summary

*Use the visual summary below to help you review the main ideas of the chapter.*

QUICK FACTS

The high Andes affect the climates and landscapes of Pacific South America.

Many South American Indians maintain traditional customs and ways of life in the Andes.

Today the countries of Pacific South America are working toward development and improved economies.

## Reviewing Vocabulary, Terms, and Places

*Write each word defined below, circling each letter that is marked by a star. Then write the word these letters spell.*

1. _ _ * _ _ _ _ _ _  _ _ _ _ _ _ _—a desert in northern Chile that is one of the cloudiest and driest places on Earth

2. * _ _ _ _ —the capital of Peru

3. _ _ _ * _ _—the capital of Ecuador

4. _ * _ _ _ _ _ _—a governor appointed by the king of Spain

5. _ _  * _ _ _—one of the capitals of Bolivia

6. _ _ _ _ _ * _ _—an American-born descendant of Europeans

7. _ _ _ _ * _ _ _—a narrow passageway that connects two large bodies of water

8. _ _  * _ _ _ _—an ocean and weather pattern that affects the Pacific coast

9. _ * _ _ _—a sudden overthrow of a government by a small group of people

## Comprehension and Critical Thinking

**SECTION 1** *(Pages 228–232)*

10. **a. Describe** What are climate and vegetation like on the altiplano?

**b. Compare and Contrast** What are two differences and one similarity between the Atacama Desert and the altiplano?

**c. Evaluate** What elevation zone would you choose to live in if you lived in Pacific South America? Why would you choose to live there?

**SECTION 2** *(Pages 234–237)*

11. **a. Describe** How did the Incas organize their huge empire?

**b. Analyze** How have Spanish and native cultures left their marks on culture in Pacific South America?

**c. Elaborate** Why do you think Pizarro killed the Inca king even though he had received riches as ransom?

## SECTION 3 (Pages 238–242)

**12. a. Identify** What country in Pacific South America has the healthiest economy?

**b. Analyze** What problems in Ecuador and Bolivia cause political unrest?

**c. Evaluate** What would be some benefits and drawbacks of moving from the highlands to one of Lima's "young towns"?

# Using the Internet

**13. Activity: Analyzing Climate** Chile has steep mountains, volcanoes, a desert, a rich river valley, and thick forests. These diverse areas contain many different climates. Click on the links given in your online textbook to explore the many climates of Chile. Then test your knowledge by taking an online quiz.

↗ hmhsocialstudies.com

# Social Studies Skills

**Interpreting an Elevation Profile** *Use the elevation profile on the Social Studies Skills page to answer the following questions.*

**14.** What is the purpose of an elevation profile?

**15.** Where can you find the vertical measurements on an elevation profile?

**16.** What horizontal distance does the elevation profile measure?

**17.** What is the elevation of the Amazon basin?

# Map Activity

**18. Pacific South America** On a separate sheet of paper, match the letters on the map with their correct labels.

| | |
|---|---|
| Strait of Magellan | Santiago, Chile |
| Quito, Ecuador | Atacama Desert |
| Andes | La Paz, Bolivia |

↗ hmhsocialstudies.com **INTERACTIVE MAP**

### FOCUS ON READING AND SPEAKING

**Making Inferences** *Use the information in this chapter to answer the following questions.*

**19.** What is an inference?

**20.** What can you infer about the size of the population in the Atacama Desert? What clues led you to make this inference?

**21. Presenting an Interview** Now that you have questions and answers, work with a partner to write an interview script. Read through your script several times so that you know it well enough to sound natural during the interview. Remember to use a lively tone as you speak so that your audience will pay attention.

*DIRECTIONS: Read questions 1 through 7 and write the letter of the best response. Then read question 8 and write your own well-constructed response.*

**1** **The main mountain range located in Pacific South America is called the**

A  altiplano.

B  Andes.

C  Strait of Magellan.

D  Pampas.

**2** **Which of the following conditions is a result of El Niño?**

A  increased greenhouse gases

B  more fish in a usually poor fishing area

C  drought on the Pacific coast

D  warmer waters near the Pacific coast

**3** **What early culture had a huge empire in Pacific South America in the early 1500s?**

A  Inca

B  Aztec

C  Tiahuanaco

D  Nazca

**4** **Which of the following statements about culture in Pacific South America is false?**

A  Most people speak Spanish.

B  Chile has a higher percentage of Indians than any other country in South America.

C  Religion in the region often combines Catholic and ancient native customs.

D  Wooden flutes and drums are traditional instruments.

**5** **Which country's main export is oil?**

A  Bolivia

B  Chile

C  Ecuador

D  Peru

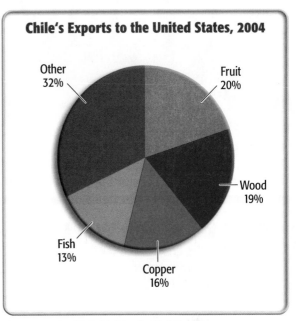

**Chile's Exports to the United States, 2004**

Other 32%
Fruit 20%
Wood 19%
Copper 16%
Fish 13%

Source: International Trade Administration, TradeStats Express

**6** **Based on the graph above, what one product is Chile's main export to the United States?**

A  fish

B  wood

C  fruit

D  copper

**7** **What has been a major cause of political unrest in the region?**

A  dissatisfaction with economic policies

B  arrest of the leaders of the Shining Path

C  development of "young towns" in Peru

D  high unemployment in Chile

**8** **Extended Response** Using the graph above and your knowledge of Pacific South America today, compare and contrast the economic situations in each of the four countries.

# CHAPTER 11

# The United States

## Essential Question
What are the unique characteristics of the different regions of the United States?

 ## What You Will Learn...

In this chapter you will learn about the physical features, climates, and resources of the United States. You will also discover how democratic ideas and immigration have shaped the United States. Finally, you will learn about our country's different regions, diverse population, and the challenges we face as a nation.

### FOCUS ON READING AND VIEWING

**Categorizing** A good way to make sense of what you read is to separate facts and details into groups, called categories. For example, you could sort facts about the United States into categories like natural resources, major cities, or rivers. As you read this chapter, look for ways to categorize details under each topic. **See the lesson, Categorizing, on page 526.**

**Creating a Collage** Artists create collages by gluing art and photographs onto a flat surface, such as a poster board. As you read this chapter, you will collect ideas for a collage about the United States. After you create your own collage, you will view and evaluate the collages of other students in your class.

**Culture** People of many different ethnic groups and cultures make up the population of the United States.

# The United States: Political

HISTORY  Paving America

↗ hmhsocialstudies.com  VIDEO

CANADA

River

ND
Fargo

MN

SD
Minneapolis

WI
Milwaukee

MI

L. Superior

L. Michigan

L. Huron

Detroit

Ontario

L. Erie

St. Lawrence R.

ME

VT
NH
Boston

NY

MA
CT
RI

40°N

WY

Cheyenne

NE
Lincoln

IA
Des Moines

Chicago

IN

IL
Indianapolis

OH

Cleveland

PA
Philadelphia
Baltimore

Washington,
D.C.

New York

NJ
DE
MD

Denver
CO

KS

Kansas
City

MO
St.
Louis

Missouri R.

Ohio  R.

Mississippi R.

Lexington

KY

WV

VA

Santa
Fe

OK
Oklahoma
City

AR
Little
Rock

Nashville
TN

Memphis

NC
Charlotte

SC

NM

TX  Dallas

MS

AL

Montgomery

Atlanta
GA

Charleston

Red R.

LA

Houston

New
Orleans

Rio Grande

FL

Jacksonville

Lake
Okeechobee

Gulf of
Mexico

N
W    E
S

90°W

Miami

80°W

30°N

ATLANTIC
OCEAN

MEXICO

National capital
Other cities

0        200        400 Miles
0    200    400 Kilometers

Projection: Albers Equal Area

map
zone

## Geography Skills

**Place** The United States is made up of 50 states.

1. **Locate** What two countries border the United States?
2. **Contrast** How is Maryland's size and location different from California's size and location?

**Geography** The Grand Canyon in Arizona is one example of the many spectacular landscapes in the United States.

**History** The Statue of Liberty in New York Harbor symbolizes our freedom and our history as a democratic nation.

# Physical Geography

## What You Will Learn...

### Main Ideas

1. Major physical features of the United States include mountains, rivers, and plains.
2. The climate of the United States is wetter in the East and South and drier in the West.
3. The United States is rich in natural resources such as farmland, oil, forests, and minerals.

### The Big Idea

The United States is a large country with diverse physical features, climates, and resources.

### Key Terms and Places

Appalachian Mountains, *p. 248*
Great Lakes, *p. 249*
Mississippi River, *p. 249*
tributary, *p. 249*
Rocky Mountains, *p. 250*
continental divide, *p. 250*

hmhsocialstudies.com
TAKING NOTES

Use the graphic organizer online to take notes on the physical geography of the United States.

## If YOU lived there...

You live in St. Louis, Missouri, which is located on the Mississippi River. For the next few days, you will travel down the river on an old-fashioned steamboat. The Mississippi begins in Minnesota and flows south through 10 states in the heart of the United States. On your trip, you bring a video camera to film life along this great river.

**What will you show in your video about the Mississippi?**

**BUILDING BACKGROUND** The United States stretches from sea to sea across North America. To the north is Canada and to the south lies Mexico. Because it is so large, the United States has a great variety of landscapes and climates.

## Physical Features

The United States is the third largest country in the world behind Russia and Canada. Our country is home to an incredible variety of physical features. All but two of the 50 states—Alaska and Hawaii—make up the main part of the country. Look at the physical map of the United States on the next page. It shows the main physical features of our country. Use the map as you read about America's physical geography in the East and South, the Interior Plains, and the West.

### The East and South

If you were traveling across the United States, you might start on the country's eastern coast. This low area, which is flat and close to sea level, is called the Atlantic Coastal Plain. As you go west, the land gradually rises higher to a region called the Piedmont. The **Appalachian Mountains**, which are the main mountain range in the East, rise above the Piedmont. These mountains are very old. For many millions of years, rain, snow, and wind

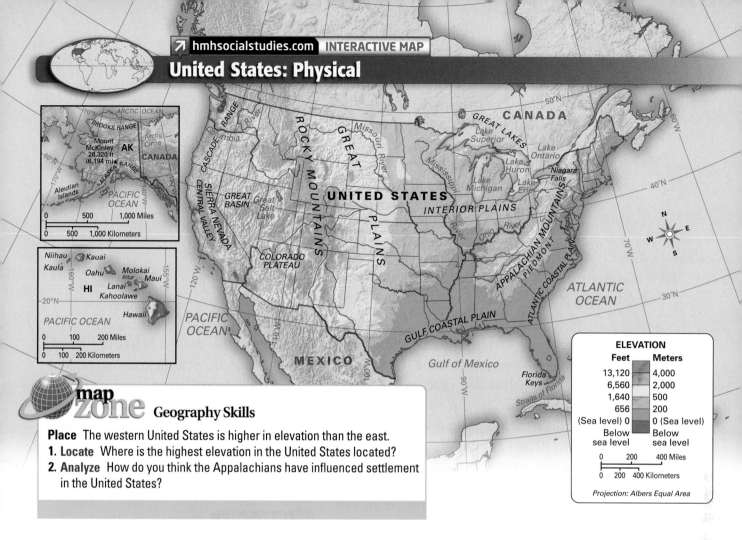

## United States: Physical

Mount McKinley 20,320 ft (6,194 m)

**ELEVATION**

| Feet | Meters |
|---|---|
| 13,120 | 4,000 |
| 6,560 | 2,000 |
| 1,640 | 500 |
| 656 | 200 |
| (Sea level) 0 | 0 (Sea level) |
| Below sea level | Below sea level |

0 200 400 Miles
0 200 400 Kilometers

*Projection: Albers Equal Area*

### map zone Geography Skills

**Place** The western United States is higher in elevation than the east.
1. **Locate** Where is the highest elevation in the United States located?
2. **Analyze** How do you think the Appalachians have influenced settlement in the United States?

---

have eroded and smoothed their peaks. As a result, the highest mountain in the Appalachians is about 6,700 feet (2,040 m).

### The Interior Plains

As you travel west from the Appalachians, you come across the vast Interior Plains that stretch to the Great Plains just east of the Rocky Mountains. The Interior Plains are filled with hills, lakes, and rivers. The first major water feature that you see here is called the **Great Lakes**. These lakes make up the largest group of freshwater lakes in the world. The Great Lakes are also an important waterway for trade between the United States and Canada.

West of the Great Lakes lies North America's largest and most important river, the **Mississippi River**. Tributaries in the interior plains flow to the Mississippi. A **tributary** is a smaller stream or river that flows into a larger stream or river.

**Appalachians** The smooth peaks of the Appalachian Mountains dominate the landscape of western North Carolina.

Along the way, these rivers deposit rich silt. The silt creates fertile farmlands that cover most of the Interior Plains. The Missouri and Ohio rivers are huge tributaries of the Mississippi. They help drain the entire Interior Plains.

Look at the map on the previous page. Notice the land begins to increase in elevation west of the Interior Plains. This higher region is called the Great Plains. Vast areas of grasslands cover these plains.

## The West

In the region called the West, several of the country's most rugged mountain ranges make up the **Rocky Mountains**. These enormous mountains, also called the Rockies, stretch as far as you can see. Many of the mountains' jagged peaks rise above 14,000 feet (4,270 m).

**FOCUS ON READING**
Into what two categories might you group the details on rivers?

In the Rocky Mountains is a line of high peaks called the Continental Divide. A **continental divide** is an area of high ground that divides the flow of rivers towards opposite ends of a continent.

Rivers east of the divide in the Rockies mostly flow eastward and empty into the Mississippi River. Most of the rivers west of the divide flow westward and empty into the Pacific Ocean.

Farther west, mountain ranges include the Cascade Range and the Sierra Nevada. Most of the mountains in the Cascades are dormant volcanoes. One mountain, Mount Saint Helens, is an active volcano. A tremendous eruption in 1980 blew off the mountain's peak and destroyed 150 square miles (390 sq km) of forest.

Mountains also stretch north along the Pacific coast. At 20,320 feet (6,194 m), Alaska's Mount McKinley is the highest mountain in North America.

Far out in the Pacific Ocean are the islands that make up the state of Hawaii. Volcanoes formed these islands millions of years ago. Today, hot lava and ash continue to erupt from the islands' volcanoes.

**READING CHECK** **Summarizing** What are the major physical features of the United States?

## Satellite View

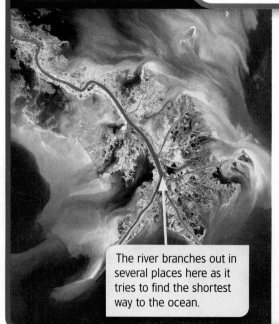

The river branches out in several places here as it tries to find the shortest way to the ocean.

## The Mississippi River Delta

From its source in Minnesota, the Mississippi River flows south across the central United States. It ends at the tip of Louisiana, which is shown here. This satellite image shows the area where the Mississippi River meets the Gulf of Mexico. This area is called a delta. A river's delta is formed from sediment that a river carries downstream to the ocean. Sediment is usually made up of rocks, soil, sand, and dead plants. Each year, the Mississippi dumps more than 400 million tons of sediment into the Gulf of Mexico.

The light blue and green areas in this image are shallow areas of sediment. The deeper water of the Gulf of Mexico is dark blue. Also, notice that much of the delta land looks fragile. This is new land that the river has built up by depositing sediment.

**Making Inferences** What natural hazards might people living in the Mississippi Delta experience?

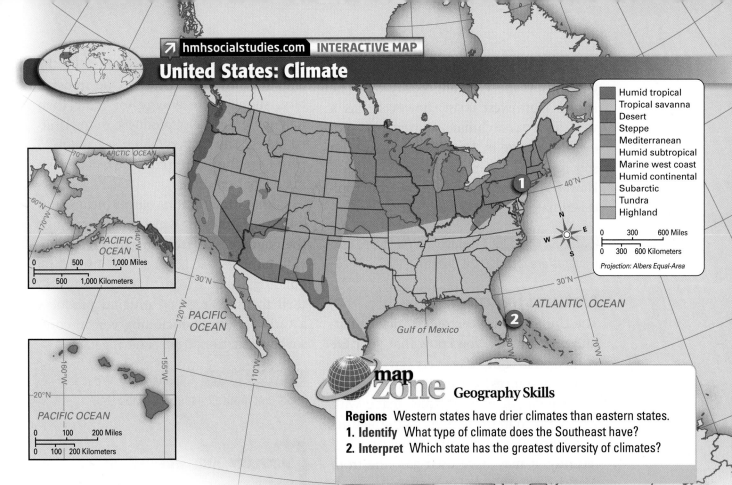

Humid tropical
Tropical savanna
Desert
Steppe
Mediterranean
Humid subtropical
Marine west coast
Humid continental
Subarctic
Tundra
Highland

Projection: Albers Equal-Area

**map zone Geography Skills**

**Regions** Western states have drier climates than eastern states.
1. **Identify** What type of climate does the Southeast have?
2. **Interpret** Which state has the greatest diversity of climates?

# Climate

Did you know that the United States has a greater variety of climates than any other country? Look at the map above to see the different climates of the United States.

## The East and South

The eastern United States has three climate regions. In the Northeast, people live in a humid continental climate with snowy winters and warm, humid summers. Southerners, on the other hand, experience milder winters and the warm, humid summers of a humid subtropical climate. Most of Florida is warm all year.

## The Interior Plains

Temperatures throughout the year can vary greatly in the Interior Plains. Summers are hot and dry in the Great Plains. However, most of the region has a humid continental climate with long, cold winters.

1 With a humid continental climate, New York City experiences cold winters with snowfall. In this climate people can ice skate during the winter.

2 With a humid subtropical climate, most of Florida has warm sunny days during most of the year. In this climate people can enjoy the region's beaches.

THE UNITED STATES **251**

### The West

Climates in the West are mostly dry. The Pacific Northwest coast, however, has a wet, mild coastal climate. The region's coldest climates are in Alaska, which has both subarctic and tundra climates. In contrast, Hawaii is the only state with a warm, tropical climate.

**READING CHECK** **Identifying** What types of climates are found in the United States?

## Natural Resources

The United States is extremely rich in natural resources. Do you know that your life is affected in some way every day by these natural resources? For example, if you ate bread today, it was probably made with wheat grown in the fertile soils of the Interior Plains. If you rode in a car or on a bus recently, it may have used gasoline from Alaska, California, or Louisiana.

The United States is a major oil producer but uses more oil than it produces. In fact, we import more than one half of the oil we need.

Valuable minerals are mined in the Appalachians and Rockies. One mineral, coal, supplies the energy for more than half of the electricity produced in the United States. The United States has about 25 percent of the world's coal reserves and is a major coal exporter.

Other important resources include forests and farmland, which cover much of the country. The trees in our forests provide lumber that is used in constructing buildings. Wood from these trees is also used to make paper. Farmland produces a variety of crops including wheat, corn, soybeans, cotton, fruits, and vegetables.

**READING CHECK** **Summarizing** What are important natural resources in the U.S.?

**SUMMARY AND PREVIEW** In this section you learned about the geography, climates, and natural resources of the United States. In the next section, you will learn about the history and culture of the United States.

---

## Section 1 Assessment

hmhsocialstudies.com
ONLINE QUIZ

### Reviewing Ideas, Terms, and Places

1. **a. Define** What is a **tributary**?
   **b. Contrast** How are the **Appalachian Mountains** different from the **Rocky Mountains**?
   **c. Elaborate** Why are the **Great Lakes** an important waterway?

2. **a. Describe** What is the climate like in the Northeast?
   **b. Draw Conclusions** What would winter be like in Alaska?

3. **a. Recall** What kinds of crops are grown in the United States?
   **b. Explain** Why is coal an important resource?
   **c. Predict** What natural resources might not be as important to your daily life in the future?

### Critical Thinking

4. **Categorizing** Copy the graphic organizer below. Use it to organize your notes on physical features, climate, and resources by region of the country.

| East and South | Interior Plains | West |
|---|---|---|

### FOCUS ON VIEWING

5. **Thinking about Physical Geography** Jot down key words that describe the physical features and climate of the United States. Think of at least three objects or images you might use to illustrate physical features and climate.

# Using a Political Map

## Learn

Many types of maps are useful in studying geography. Political maps are one of the most frequently used types of maps. These maps show human cultural features such as cities, states, and countries. Look at the map's legend to figure out how these features are represented on the map.

Most political maps show national boundaries and state boundaries. The countries on political maps are sometimes shaded different colors to help you tell where the borders of each country are located.

## Practice

Use the political map here to answer the following questions.

- What countries does this map show?
- How does the map show the difference between state boundaries and national boundaries?
- What is the capital of Canada?

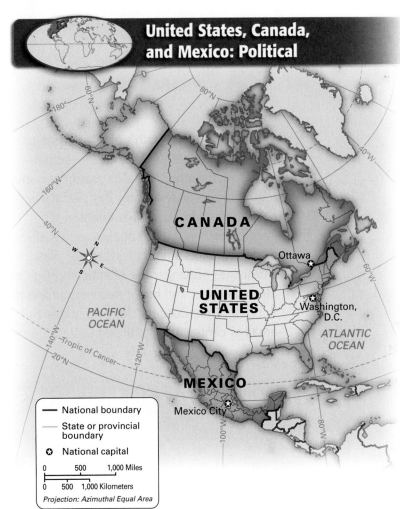

**United States, Canada, and Mexico: Political**

CANADA
Ottawa
UNITED STATES
Washington, D.C.
PACIFIC OCEAN
ATLANTIC OCEAN
MEXICO
Mexico City
Tropic of Cancer

— National boundary
— State or provincial boundary
⊛ National capital

0   500   1,000 Miles
0   500  1,000 Kilometers
*Projection: Azimuthal Equal Area*

## Apply

Using an atlas or the Internet, find a political map of your state. Use that map to answer the following questions.

1. What is the state capital and where is it located?
2. What other states or countries border your state?
3. What are two other cities in your state besides the capital and the city you live in?

# Case Study

# Natural Hazards
## in the United States

**Essential Elements**

The World in Spatial Terms
Places and Regions
**Physical Systems**
Human Systems
Environment and Society
The Uses of Geography

**Background** Earth's physical systems create patterns around us, and these patterns influence our lives. For example, every region of the United States has distinctive natural hazards. Volcanoes threaten the Pacific Northwest. Earthquakes rattle California. Wildfires strike forests in the West. Hurricanes endanger the Atlantic and Gulf of Mexico coasts, and major rivers are prone to flooding. Tornadoes regularly rip across flat areas of central and southeast United States.

In fact, the United States lies in danger of getting hit by an average of six hurricanes a year. Formed by the warm waters of the Atlantic Ocean and Caribbean Sea and the collision of strong winds, hurricanes are the most powerful storms on Earth. Most hurricanes look like large doughnuts with a hole, or eye, in the middle of the storm. Around the eye, high winds and rain bands rotate counterclockwise. Once the hurricane moves over land or cold water it weakens.

## Natural Hazards in the United States

Tornado Alley

| | | | |
|---|---|---|---|
| ◎ Earthquakes | ▲ Volcanoes | | |
| Wildfires | Tornadoes | | |
| ◎ Hurricanes | Tornado Risk | | |
| Flood areas | Moderate | | |
| | High | | |

map zone

After Hurricane Katrina hit New Orleans, people escaped the floodwaters by fleeing to rooftops and high-rise apartment buildings like this one.

Using satellite images like this one of Hurricane Katrina, scientists saw how large the storm was and warned people along the Gulf coast to evacuate.

## Hurricane Katrina

On August 29, 2005, one of the most destructive hurricanes ever hit the United States. Hurricane Katrina devastated coastal regions of Louisiana, the city of New Orleans, and the entire coast of Mississippi.

With winds as high as 145 mph (235 km), Katrina destroyed hundreds of thousands of homes and businesses. In addition, the force of Katrina's storm surge pushed water from the Gulf of Mexico onto land to a height of about two stories tall. As a result, low-lying areas along the Gulf coast experienced massive flooding.

The storm surge also caused several levees that protected New Orleans from the waters of Lake Pontchartrain to break. The loss of these levees caused the lake's waters to flood most of the city. About 150,000 people who did not evacuate before the storm were left stranded in shelters, high-rise buildings, and on rooftops. Using boats and helicopters, emergency workers rescued thousands of the city's people. Total damages from the storm along the Gulf coast was estimated to be nearly $130 billion. More than 1,300 people died and over a million were displaced.

## What It Means

Natural hazards can influence where we live, how we build our homes, and how we prepare for storms. In addition to hurricanes, other hazards affect the United States. For example, Tornado Alley is a region of the Great Plains that experiences a high number of tornadoes, or "twisters"—rapidly spinning columns of air that stay in contact with the ground. In Tornado Alley, special warning sirens go off when storms develop that might form a dangerous tornado.

### Geography for Life Activity

1. How are hurricanes formed?

2. Many people train and volunteer as storm chasers. They may follow storms for hundreds of miles to gather scientific data, take photographs, or file news reports. What might be the risks and rewards of such activity? Would it interest you?

3. **Comparing Windstorms** Do some research to find out how tornadoes and hurricanes differ. Summarize the differences in a chart that includes information about how these storms start, where and when they tend to occur in the United States, and their wind strength.

# History and Culture

## If YOU lived there...

It is 1803, and President Jefferson just arranged the purchase of a huge area of land west of the Mississippi River. It almost doubles the size of the United States. Living on the frontier in Ohio, you are a skillful hunter and trapper. One day, you see a poster calling for volunteers to explore the new Louisiana Territory. An expedition is heading west soon. You think it would be exciting but dangerous.

**Will you join the expedition to the West? Why or why not?**

**BUILDING BACKGROUND** From 13 colonies on the Atlantic coast, the territory of the United States expanded all the way to the Pacific Ocean in about 75 years. Since then, America's democracy has attracted immigrants from almost every country in the world. Looking for new opportunities, these immigrants have made the country very diverse.

## First Modern Democracy

Long before Italian explorer Christopher Columbus sailed to the Americas in 1492, native people lived on the land that is now the United States. These Native Americans developed many distinct cultures. Soon after Columbus and his crew explored the Americas, other Europeans began to set up colonies there.

### The American Colonies

Europeans began settling in North America and setting up colonies in the 1500s. A **colony** is a territory inhabited and controlled by people from a foreign land. By the mid-1700s the British Empire included more than a dozen colonies along the Atlantic coast. New cities in the colonies such as **Boston** and **New York** became major seaports.

Some people living in the British colonies lived on plantations. A **plantation** is a large farm that grows mainly one crop. Many of the colonial plantations produced tobacco, rice, or cotton. Thousands of enslaved Africans were brought to the colonies and forced to work on plantations.

By the 1770s many colonists in America were unhappy with British rule. They wanted independence from Britain. In July 1776, the colonial representatives adopted the Declaration of Independence. The document stated that "all men are created equal" and have the right to "life, liberty, and the pursuit of happiness." Although not everyone in the colonies was considered equal, the Declaration was a great step toward equality and justice.

To win their independence, the American colonists fought the British in the Revolutionary War. First, colonists from Massachusetts fought in the early battles of the war in and around Boston. As the war spread west and south, soldiers from all the American colonies joined the fight against Britain.

In 1781 the American forces under General George Washington defeated the British army at the Battle of Yorktown in Virginia. With this defeat, Britain recognized the independence of the United States. As a consequence, Britain granted all its land east of the Mississippi River to the new nation.

## Expansion and Industrial Growth

After independence, the United States gradually expanded west. Despite the challenges of crossing swift-moving rivers and traveling across rugged terrain and huge mountains, people moved west for land and plentiful resources.

### BIOGRAPHY

### George Washington
(1732–1799)

As the first president of the United States, George Washington is known as the Father of His Country. Washington was admired for his heroism and leadership as the commanding general during the Revolutionary War. Delegates to the Constitutional Convention chose him to preside over their meetings. Washington was then elected president in 1789 and served two terms.

**Drawing Inferences** Why do you think Washington was elected president?

## Fight for Independence

**This painting shows General George Washington leading American troops across the Delaware River to attack British forces.**

These first settlers that traveled west were called **pioneers**. Many followed the 2,000-mile Oregon Trail west from Missouri to the Oregon Territory. Groups of families traveled together in wagons pulled by oxen or mules. The trip was harsh. Food, supplies, and water were scarce.

ACADEMIC
VOCABULARY

**development** the process of growing or improving

While many pioneers headed west seeking land, others went in search of gold. The discovery of gold in California in the late 1840s had a major impact on the country. Tens of thousands of people moved to California.

By 1850 the population of the United States exceeded 23 million and the country stretched all the way to the Pacific Ocean. As the United States expanded, the nation's economy also grew. By the late 1800s, the country was a major producer of goods like steel, oil, and textiles, or cloth products. The steel industry grew around cities that were located near coal and iron ore deposits. Most of those new industrial cities were in the Northeast and Midwest. The country's economy also benefited from the **development** of waterways and railroads. This development helped industry and people move farther into the interior.

Attracted by a strong economy, millions of people immigrated, or came to, the United States for better jobs and land. Immigration from European countries was especially heavy in the late 1800s and early 1900s. As a result of this historical pattern of immigration, the United States is a culturally diverse nation today.

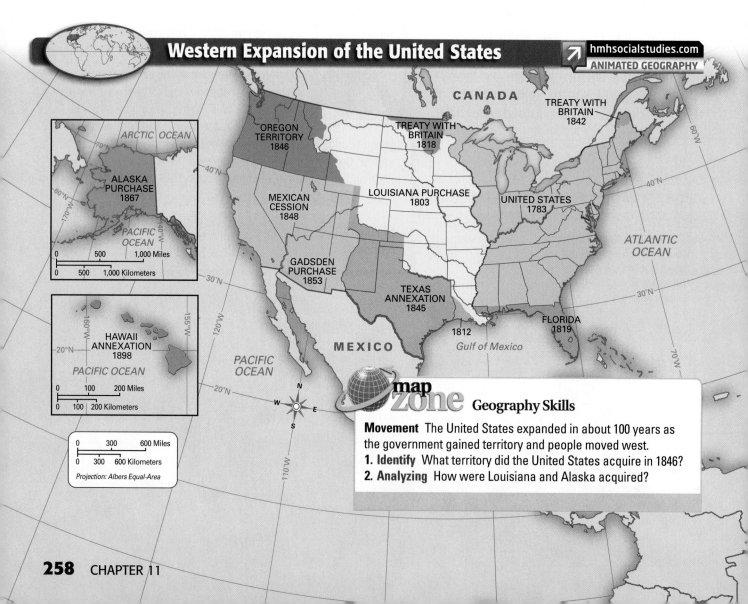

**Western Expansion of the United States**

hmhsocialstudies.com
ANIMATED GEOGRAPHY

CANADA

TREATY WITH BRITAIN 1842

ARCTIC OCEAN

OREGON TERRITORY 1846

TREATY WITH BRITAIN 1818

ALASKA PURCHASE 1867

PACIFIC OCEAN

MEXICAN CESSION 1848

LOUISIANA PURCHASE 1803

UNITED STATES 1783

UNITED STATES 1783

ATLANTIC OCEAN

GADSDEN PURCHASE 1853

TEXAS ANNEXATION 1845

FLORIDA 1819

0   500   1,000 Miles
0   500   1,000 Kilometers

1812

HAWAII ANNEXATION 1898

MEXICO

Gulf of Mexico

*PACIFIC OCEAN*

*PACIFIC OCEAN*

0   100   200 Miles
0   100   200 Kilometers

0   300   600 Miles
0   300   600 Kilometers

Projection: Albers Equal-Area

**map zone** Geography Skills

**Movement** The United States expanded in about 100 years as the government gained territory and people moved west.
**1. Identify** What territory did the United States acquire in 1846?
**2. Analyzing** How were Louisiana and Alaska acquired?

## Wars and Peace

The United States fought in several wars during the 1900s. Many Americans died in two major wars, World Wars I and II. After World War II, the United States and the Soviet Union became rivals in what was known as the Cold War. The Cold War lasted until the early 1990s, when the Soviet Union collapsed. U.S. troops also served in long wars in Korea in the 1950s and in Vietnam in the 1960s and 1970s. In 1991, the U.S. fought Iraq in the Persian Gulf War. More recently, the U.S. invaded Iraq in 2003 and is helping Iraqis rebuild their country today.

Today the United States is a member of many international organizations. The headquarters of one such organization, the United Nations (UN), is located in New York City. About 190 countries are UN members. The United States is one of the most powerful members.

## Government and Citizenship

The United States has a limited, democratic government based on the U.S. Constitution. This document spells out the powers and functions of the branches of the federal government. The federal government includes an elected president and Congress. In general, the federal government handles issues affecting the whole country, but many powers are left to the 50 state governments. Counties and cities also have their own local governments. Many of these local governments provide services to the community such as trash collection, road building, electricity, and public transportation.

## Rights and Responsibilities

American citizens have many rights and responsibilities, including the right to vote. Starting at age 18, U.S. citizens are allowed to vote. They are also encouraged

### HISTORIC DOCUMENT
# The Constitution

*On September 17, 1787, state delegates gathered in Philadelphia to create a constitution, a written statement of the powers and functions of the new government of the United States. The Preamble, or introduction, to the U.S. Constitution is shown below. It states the document's general purpose.*

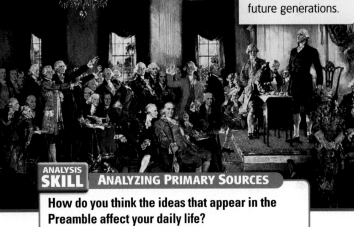

" **We the People** of the United States, in order to form a more perfect Union, establish justice, insure domestic tranquillity, provide for the common defense, promote the general welfare, and secure the blessings of liberty to ourselves and our posterity, do ordain and establish this Constitution for the United States of America. "

Americans wanted peace within the United States and a national military force.

They wanted to ensure freedoms for themselves and for future generations.

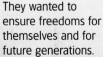

**ANALYSIS SKILL** ANALYZING PRIMARY SOURCES

How do you think the ideas that appear in the Preamble affect your daily life?

to play an active role in government. For example, Americans can call or write their public officials to ask them to help solve problems in their communities. Without people participating in their government, the democratic process suffers.

**READING CHECK** **Sequencing** What were some major events in the history of the United States?

# People and Culture

About 7 out of 10 Americans are descended from European immigrants. However, the United States is also home to people of many other cultures and ethnic groups. As a result, the United States is a diverse nation where many languages are spoken and different religions and customs are practiced. The blending of these different cultures has helped produce a unique American culture.

## Ethnic Groups in the United States

**FOCUS ON READING**
What details would be included under a category called *ethnic groups*?

Some ethnic groups in the United States include Native Americans, African Americans, Hispanic Americans, and Asian Americans. As you can see on the maps on the next page, higher percentages of these ethnic groups are concentrated in different areas of the United States.

For thousands of years, Native Americans were the only people living in the Americas. Today, most Native Americans live in the western United States. Many Native Americans are concentrated in Arizona and New Mexico.

Even though African Americans live in every region of the country, some areas of the United States have a higher percentage of African Americans. For example, a higher percentage of African Americans live in southern states. Many large cities also have a high percentage of African Americans. On the other hand, descendants of people who came from Asian countries, or Asian Americans, are mostly concentrated in California.

Many Hispanic Americans originally migrated to the United States from Mexico, Cuba, and other Latin American countries. As you can see on the map of Hispanic Americans, a higher percentage of Hispanic Americans live in the southwestern states. These states border Mexico.

## Language

What language or languages do you hear as you walk through the hall of your school? Since most people in the United States speak English, you probably hear English spoken every day. However, in many parts of the country, English is just one of many languages you might hear. Are you or is someone you know bilingual? People who speak two languages are **bilingual**.

Today more than 55 million U.S. residents speak a language in addition to English. These languages include Spanish, French, Chinese, Russian, Arabic, Navajo, and many others.

After English, Spanish is the most widely spoken language in the United States. About 34 million Americans speak Spanish at home. Many of these people live near the border between the United States and Mexico and in Florida.

## Religion

Americans also practice many religious faiths. Most people are Christians. However, some are Jewish or Muslim. A small percentage of Americans are Hindu or Buddhist. What religions are practiced in your community? Your community might have Christian churches, Jewish synagogues, and Islamic mosques, as well as other places of worship. Religious variety adds to our country's cultural diversity.

With so many different religions, many religious holidays are celebrated in the United States. These holidays include the Christian celebrations of Christmas and Easter and the Jewish holidays of Hanukkah, Yom Kippur, and Rosh Hashanah. Some African Americans also celebrate Kwanzaa, a holiday that is based on a traditional African festival. Muslims celebrate the end of the month of Ramadan with a large feast called 'Id al-Fitr.

# Distribution of Selected Ethnic Groups, 2000

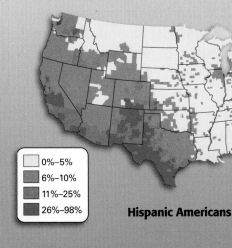

0%–5%
6%–10%
11%–25%
26%–98%

**Hispanic Americans**

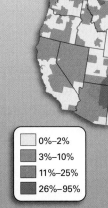

0%–2%
3%–10%
11%–25%
26%–95%

**Native Americans**

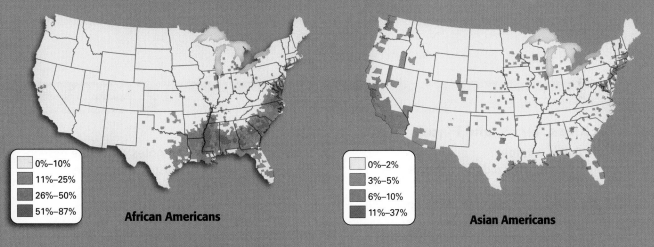

### Diverse America

**People of different ethnic groups enjoy a concert in Miami, Florida. Like most large American cities, Miami has a very diverse population. More than half of all Hispanic Americans of Cuban descent live in Miami.**

0%–10%
11%–25%
26%–50%
51%–87%

**African Americans**

0%–2%
3%–5%
6%–10%
11%–37%

**Asian Americans**

Source: U.S. Census Bureau, 2000

**map zone**
**Geography Skills**

**Regions** These maps show population information from the U.S. Census. Every 10 years, Americans answer census questions about their race or ethnic group.

1. **Locate** In what region of the United States does the highest percentage of African Americans live?
2. **Analyze** Why do you think many Hispanic Americans live in the southwestern United States?

## Foods and Music

Diversity shows itself through cultural practices. In addition to language and religion, cultural practices include the food we eat and the music we listen to.

America's food is as diverse as the American people. Think about some of the foods you have eaten this week. You may have eaten Mexican tacos, Italian pasta, or Japanese sushi. These dishes are now part of the American diet.

Different types of music from around the world have also influenced American culture. For example, salsa music from Latin America is popular in the United States today. Many American musicians now combine elements of salsa into their pop songs. However, music that originated in the United States is also popular in other countries. American musical styles include blues, jazz, rock, and hip hop.

## American Popular Culture

As the most powerful country in the world, the United States has tremendous influence around the world. American popular culture, such as movies, television programs, and sports, is popular elsewhere. For example, the *Star Wars* movies are seen by millions of people around the world. Other examples of American culture in other places include the popularity of baseball in Japan, Starbucks coffee shops in almost every major city in the world, and an MTV channel available throughout Asia. As you can see, Americans influence the rest of the world in many ways through their culture.

**READING CHECK** **Generalizing** How has cultural diversity enriched life in the United States?

**SUMMARY AND PREVIEW** The history of the United States has helped shape the democratic nation it is today. Drawn to the United States because of its democracy, immigrants from around the world have shaped American culture. In the next section, you will learn about the different regions of the United States and the issues the country is facing today.

---

## Section 2 Assessment

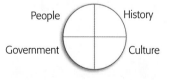
hmhsocialstudies.com
ONLINE QUIZ

### Reviewing Ideas, Terms, and Places

1. **a. Define** What is a **colony**?
   **b. Make Inferences** Why did the pioneers move west?
   **c. Elaborate** What is an example of the rights and responsibilities that American citizens have?
2. **a. Recall** What language other than English is widely spoken in the United States?
   **b. Summarize** What are some religions practiced in the United States?
   **c. Predict** How do you think American culture will be different in the future, and what influences do you think will bring about the changes?

### Critical Thinking

3. **Summarizing** Using your notes, write one descriptive sentence about the history, government, people, and culture of the United States.

People | History

Government | Culture

### FOCUS ON VIEWING

4. **Thinking about History and Culture** How would you describe the history and culture of the United States? Identify two images for your collage.

# from
# Bearstone

## by Will Hobbs

**In this book, a Native American boy named Cloyd learns more about his ancestors.**

**About the Reading** *In* Bearstone, *writer Will Hobbs tells about an orphaned Native American boy named Cloyd who lives on a Colorado farm. While roaming the nearby canyons, Cloyd finds a relic from his ancestors. The relic is a stone in the shape of a turquoise bear, which becomes his Bearstone, the title of this story.*

**AS YOU READ** Identify what the mountains mean to Cloyd.

. . . This was a shining new world. To the north and east, peaks still covered with snow shone in the cloudless blue sky. He'd never seen mountains so sharp and rugged, so fierce and splendid. Below him, an eagle soared high above the old man's field. It was a good sign.

Then he remembered his grandmother's parting words as he left for Colorado. She told him something he'd never heard before: their band of Weminuche Utes ❶ hadn't always lived at White Mesa. ❷ Colorado, especially the mountains above Durango, had been their home until gold was discovered there and the white men wanted them out of the way. Summers the people used to hunt and fish in the high mountains, she'd said; they knew every stream, places so out of the way that white men still hadn't seen them. 'So don't feel bad about going to Durango,' she told him.

Cloyd regarded the distant peaks with new strength, a fierce kind of pride he'd never felt before. These were the mountains where his people used to live.

## Connecting Literature to Geography

1. **Describing** What details in the first paragraph show us that Cloyd feels happy and at home in these mountains? Which details describe the physical features of these mountains?

2. **Making Inferences** Why did Cloyd's grandmother think he shouldn't feel bad about going to Durango? How does this fact affect his feelings about the mountains of Colorado?

# The United States Today

## What You Will Learn...

### Main Ideas

1. The United States has four regions—the Northeast, South, Midwest, and West.
2. The United States has a strong economy and a powerful military but is facing the challenge of world terrorism.

### The Big Idea

The United States has four main regions and faces opportunities and challenges.

## Key Terms and Places

megalopolis, *p. 265*
Washington, D.C., *p. 265*
Detroit, *p. 267*
Chicago, *p. 267*
Seattle, *p. 268*
terrorism, *p. 270*

hmhsocialstudies.com
TAKING NOTES

Use the graphic organizer online to take notes on the United States today.

## If YOU lived there...

You and your family run a small resort hotel in Fort Lauderdale, on the east coast of Florida. You love the sunny weather and the beaches there. Now your family is thinking about moving the business to another region where the tourist industry is important. They have looked at ski lodges in Colorado, lake cottages in Michigan, and hotels on the coast of Maine.

**How will you decide among these different regions?**

**BUILDING BACKGROUND** Geography, history, climate, and population give each region of the United States its own style. Some differences between the regions are more visible than others. For example, people in each region speak with different accents and have their favorite foods. Even with some differences, however, Americans are linked by a sense of unity in confronting important issues.

## Regions of the United States

Because the United States is such a large country, geographers often divide it into four main regions. These are the Northeast, South, Midwest, and the West. You can see the four regions on the map on the next page. Find the region where you live. You probably know more about your own region than you do the three others. The population, resources, and economies of the four regions are similar in some ways and unique in others.

### The Northeast

The Northeast shares a border with Canada. The economy in this region is heavily dependent on banks, investment firms, and insurance companies. Education also contributes to the economy. The area's respected universities include Harvard and Yale.

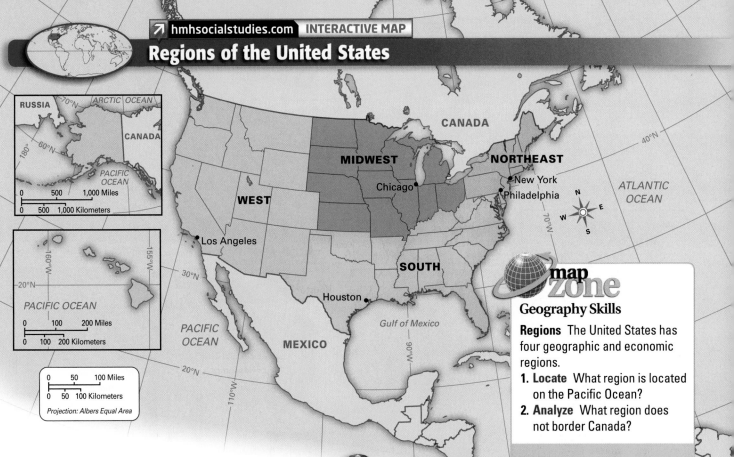

RUSSIA
ARCTIC OCEAN
CANADA
PACIFIC OCEAN
0  500  1,000 Miles
0  500  1,000 Kilometers

PACIFIC OCEAN
0  100  200 Miles
0  100  200 Kilometers

0  50  100 Miles
0  50  100 Kilometers
Projection: Albers Equal Area

CANADA

MIDWEST

NORTHEAST

Chicago

New York
Philadelphia

ATLANTIC OCEAN

WEST

Los Angeles

SOUTH

Houston

Gulf of Mexico

PACIFIC OCEAN

MEXICO

**map zone**

**Geography Skills**

**Regions** The United States has four geographic and economic regions.

1. **Locate** What region is located on the Pacific Ocean?
2. **Analyze** What region does not border Canada?

Some natural resources of the Northeast states include rich farmland and huge pockets of coal. Used in the steelmaking process, coal remains very important to the region's economy. The steel industry helped make Pittsburgh, in western Pennsylvania, the largest industrial city in the Appalachians.

Today fishing remains an important industry in the Northeast. Major seaports allow companies to ship their products to markets around the world. Cool, shallow waters off the Atlantic coast are good fishing areas. Cod and shellfish such as lobster are the most valuable seafood.

The Northeast is the most densely populated region of the United States. Much of the Northeast is a **megalopolis**, a string of large cities that have grown together. This area stretches along the Atlantic coast from Boston to **Washington, D.C.** The three other major cities in the megalopolis are New York, Philadelphia, and Baltimore.

THE WORLD ALMANAC
Facts about Countries

**Population of Major U.S. Cities**

| | City | Population |
|---|---|---|
| 1 | New York | 8,363,710 |
| 2 | Los Angeles | 3,833,995 |
| 3 | Chicago | 2,853,114 |
| 4 | Houston | 2,242,193 |
| 5 | Phoenix | 1,567,924 |

New York, New York

↗ hmhsocialstudies.com

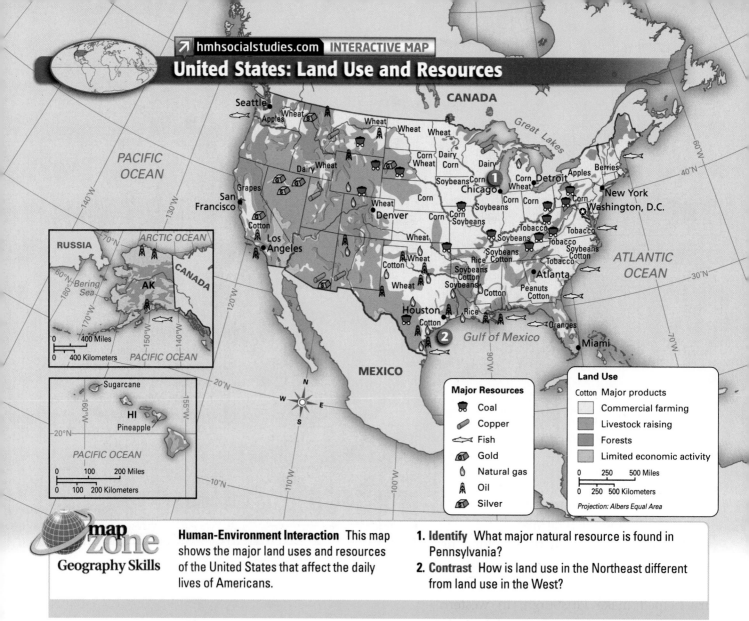

# United States: Land Use and Resources

hmhsocialstudies.com  INTERACTIVE MAP

CANADA

Great Lakes

PACIFIC OCEAN

Seattle
Apples
Wheat
Wheat
Wheat
Wheat
Wheat

Dairy
Wheat
Corn
Wheat
Dairy
Corn
Dairy

San Francisco
Grapes
Soybeans
Corn
Corn
Wheat
Corn
Detroit
Apples
Berries
New York

Corn
Corn
Corn
Washington, D.C.

Wheat
Denver
Corn
Soybeans

Los Angeles
Corn
Soybeans
Tobacco
Tobacco

Cotton
Wheat
Soybeans
Cotton
Tobacco
Soybeans
Cotton

ATLANTIC OCEAN

Cotton
Rice
Cotton
Tobacco

Soybeans
Cotton
Atlanta

Wheat
Soybeans
Peanuts
Cotton

Houston
Cotton
Rice
Cotton
Oranges

Gulf of Mexico
Miami

MEXICO

**RUSSIA**
ARCTIC OCEAN
CANADA
Bering Sea
AK
PACIFIC OCEAN
0   400 Miles
0   400 Kilometers

Sugarcane
HI
Pineapple
PACIFIC OCEAN
0   100   200 Miles
0   100   200 Kilometers

**Major Resources**

| | |
|---|---|
| Coal | |
| Copper | |
| Fish | |
| Gold | |
| Natural gas | |
| Oil | |
| Silver | |

**Land Use**

Cotton  Major products

Commercial farming
Livestock raising
Forests
Limited economic activity

0   250   500 Miles
0   250   500 Kilometers

Projection: Albers Equal Area

**map zone**
**Geography Skills**

**Human-Environment Interaction** This map shows the major land uses and resources of the United States that affect the daily lives of Americans.

1. **Identify** What major natural resource is found in Pennsylvania?
2. **Contrast** How is land use in the Northeast different from land use in the West?

---

At least 40 million people live in this urban area. All of these cities were founded during the colonial era. They grew because they were important seaports. Today these cities are industrial and financial centers.

## The South

The South is a region that includes long coastlines along the Atlantic Ocean and the Gulf of Mexico. Along the coastal plains rich soils provide farmers with abundant crops of cotton, tobacco, and citrus fruit.

In recent years, the South has become more urban and industrial and is one of the country's fastest-growing regions. The South's cities, such as Atlanta, have grown along with the economy. The Atlanta metropolitan area has grown from a population of only about 1 million in 1960 to more than 5 million today.

Other places in the South have also experienced growth in population and industry. The Research Triangle in North Carolina is an area of high-tech companies and several large universities. The Texas Gulf Coast and the lower Mississippi River area have huge oil refineries and petrochemical plants. Their products, which include gasoline, are mostly shipped from the ports of Houston and New Orleans.

1 Farms with fertile soils like this one in Wisconsin cover much of the rural Midwest.

2 Large white containers, shown here at the Port of Houston, store oil from the Gulf Coast.

Millions of Americans vacation in the South, which makes the travel industry profitable in the region. Warm weather and beautiful beaches draw many vacationers to resorts in the South. You may not think of weather and beaches when you think about industry, but you should. Resort areas are an industry because they provide jobs and help local economies grow.

Many cities in the South trade goods and services with Mexico and countries in Central and South America. This trade is possible because several of the southern states are located near these countries. For example, Miami is an important trading port and travel connection with Caribbean countries, Mexico, and South America. Atlanta, Houston, and Dallas are also major transportation centers.

## The Midwest

The Midwest is one of the most productive farming regions in the world. The Mississippi River and many of its tributaries carry materials that help create the region's rich soils, which are good for farming. Midwestern farmers grow mostly corn, wheat, and soybeans. Farmers in the region also raise livestock such as dairy cows.

The core of the Midwest's corn-growing region stretches from Ohio to Nebraska. Much of the corn is used to feed livestock, such as beef cattle and hogs.

To the north of the corn-growing region is an area of dairy farms. States with dairy farms are major producers of milk, cheese, and other dairy products. This area includes Wisconsin and most of Michigan and Minnesota. Much of the dairy farm region is pasture, but farmers also grow crops to feed dairy cows.

Many of the Midwest's farm and factory products are shipped to markets by water routes, such as those along the Ohio and Mississippi rivers. The other is through the Great Lakes and the Saint Lawrence Seaway to the Atlantic Ocean.

Most major cities in the Midwest are located on rivers or the Great Lakes. As a result, they are important transportation centers. Farm products, coal, and iron ore are easily shipped to these cities from nearby farms and mines. These natural resources support industries such as automobile manufacturing. For example, **Detroit**, Michigan, is the country's leading automobile producer.

One of the busiest shipping ports on the Great Lakes is **Chicago**, Illinois. The city also has one of the world's busiest airports. Chicago's industries attracted many immigrants in the late 1800s. People moved here to work in the city's steel mills. Today Chicago is the nation's third-largest city.

FOCUS ON READING

As you read about the Midwest, sort the details into three categories.

## The West

The West is the largest region in the United States. Many western states have large open spaces with few people. The West is not all open spaces, however. Many large cities are on the Pacific coast.

One state on the coast, California, is home to more than 10 percent of the U.S. population. California's mild climate and wealth of resources attract people to the state. Most Californians live in Los Angeles, San Diego, and the San Francisco Bay area. The center of the country's entertainment industry, Hollywood, is in Los Angeles. Farming and the technology industry are also important to California's economy.

The economy of other states in the West is dependent on ranching and growing wheat. Wheat is grown mostly in Montana, Idaho, and Washington.

Much of the farmland in the West must be irrigated, or watered. One method of irrigation uses long sprinkler systems mounted on huge wheels. The wheels rotate slowly. This sprinkler system waters the area within a circle. From the air, parts of the irrigated Great Plains resemble a series of green circles.

The West also has rich deposits of coal, oil, gold, silver, copper, and other minerals. However, mining these minerals can cause problems. For example, coal miners in parts of the Great Plains use a **process** called strip mining, which strips away soil and rock. This kind of mining leads to soil erosion and other problems. Today laws require miners to restore mined areas.

In Oregon and Washington, forestry and fishing are two of the most important economic activities. **Seattle** is Washington's largest city. The Seattle area is home to many important industries, including a major computer software company. More than half of the people in Oregon live in and around Portland.

Alaska's economy is largely based on oil, forests, and fish. As in Washington and Oregon, people debate over developing

**ACADEMIC VOCABULARY**

**process** a series of steps by which a task is accomplished

## Olympic National Park

One of the largest sections of coastal wilderness in the United States, shown here, stretches along the Pacific coast in Washington's Olympic National Park.

these resources. For example, some people want to limit oil drilling in wild areas of Alaska. Others want to expand drilling to produce more oil.

Hawaii's natural beauty, mild climate, and fertile soils are its most important resources. The islands' major crops are sugarcane and pineapples. Millions of tourists visit the islands each year.

**READING CHECK** **Comparing** How is the economy of the West different from the economy of the South?

# Changes in the Nation

Because of its economic and military strength, the United States is often called the world's only superpower. In recent years, however, the United States has faced many challenges and changes.

## Economy

An abundance of natural resources, technology, and plentiful jobs have helped make the U.S. economy strong. The United States also benefits by trading with other countries. The three largest trading partners of the United States are Canada, China, and Mexico. In 1992 the United States, Mexico, and Canada signed the North American Free Trade Agreement, or NAFTA. This agreement made trade easier and cheaper between the three neighboring nations.

Still, the U.S. economy has experienced significant ups and downs since the 1990s. In the 1990s the nation experienced the longest period of economic growth in its history. By the end of 2007, the United States faced a recession, or a sharp decrease in economic activity. In this recession, the housing market collapsed, major banks and businesses failed, and an estimated 8.4 million jobs were lost in the United States.

## The War on Terror

In the 1990s the United States began to experience acts of terrorism against its people. Terrorism is the threat or use of violence to intimidate or cause fear for political or social reasons. Some terrorists have been from foreign countries, whereas others have been U.S. citizens.

On September 11, 2001, the United States suffered the deadliest terrorist attack in the country's history. Wanting to disrupt the U.S. economy, 19 Islamic extremist terrorists hijacked four American jets. They crashed two into the World Trade Center and one into the Pentagon.

In response, U.S. President George W. Bush declared a "war on terrorism." He sent military forces to Afghanistan, to kill or capture members of a terrorist group called al-Qaeda, which had planned the September 11 attacks. The United States then turned its attention to Iraq. President Bush believed that Iraqi leader Saddam Hussein was another threat to Americans. In March 2003 Bush sent U.S. troops into Iraq to remove Hussein from power.

Today world leaders are working with the United States to combat terrorism. In the United States, the Department of Homeland Security was established to prevent terrorist attacks on American soil. Many other countries have also increased security within their borders, especially at international airports.

## Government

The 2008 presidential election pitted Republican senator John McCain and his running mate Governor Sarah Palin against Democratic senator Barack Obama and his running mate Joe Biden, a fellow senator. The two presidential candidates differed in many ways. For example, McCain was 25 years older than Obama and he held opposing views on the war in Iraq.

On election day, about 128 million people voted, the highest voter turnout for any election in U.S. history. Barack Obama won the election, winning 365 electoral votes to McCain's 173. Obama became the nation's first African American president.

**READING CHECK** **Summarizing** What issues shaped the 2008 presidential election?

The 2008 presidential campaign of Barack Obama captured the imagination of many Americans

McCain, a distinguished military veteran, thought that U.S. forces should stay in Iraq indefinitely. Obama supported plans to withdraw U.S. troops as soon as possible. The two also differed over how best to address the economy, taxes, and health care.

**SUMMARY AND PREVIEW** In this section, you learned about the geographic features, resources, and economic activities found in different regions of the United States. You also learned that the economy and terrorism are two important issues facing the country today. In the next chapter, you will learn about Canada, our neighbor to the north of the United States.

## Section 3 Assessment

hmhsocialstudies.com
ONLINE QUIZ

### Reviewing Ideas, Terms, and Places

1. **a. Define** What is a **megalopolis**? What major cities are part of the largest megalopolis in the United States?
   **b. Compare and Contrast** How is land use in the Midwest similar to and different from land use in the South?
   **c. Elaborate** How are the regions of the United States different from one another?
2. **a. Define** What is **terrorism**? What terrorist attack occurred in September 2001?
   **b. Explain** How did a recession affect the U.S. economy in 2007?
   **c. Elaborate** What steps are the United States and other countries taking in an attempt to combat world terrorism?

### Critical Thinking

3. **Finding Main Ideas** Use your notes to help you list at least one main idea about the population, resources, and economy of each region.

|  | Northeast | South | Midwest | West |
|---|---|---|---|---|
| Population |  |  |  |  |
| Resources |  |  |  |  |
| Economy |  |  |  |  |

### FOCUS ON VIEWING

4. **Thinking about the United States Today** You have read about the regions of the United States, as well as issues facing the country today. What key words, images, and objects might represent what you have learned?

**Geography's Impact**
video series
Review the video to answer the closing question:
*What do you think it would be like to live in a country that had no cultural diversity?*

## Visual Summary

*Use the visual summary below to help you review the main ideas of the chapter.*

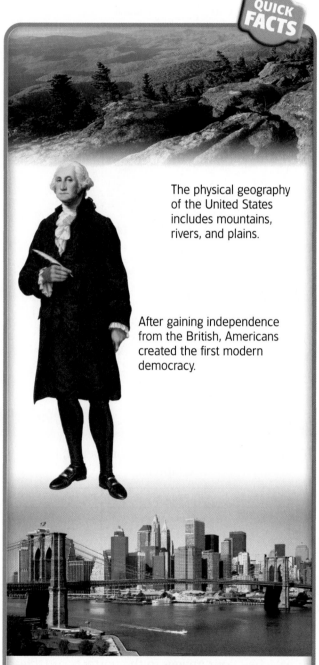

QUICK FACTS

The physical geography of the United States includes mountains, rivers, and plains.

After gaining independence from the British, Americans created the first modern democracy.

The United States has four geographic and economic regions—the Northeast, South, Midwest, and the West.

## Reviewing Vocabulary, Terms, and Places

*Match the terms or places with their definitions or descriptions.*

**a.** Boston
**b.** Great Lakes
**c.** tributary
**d.** Rocky Mountains
**e.** colony
**f.** Appalachian Mountains
**g.** pioneers
**h.** bilingual
**i.** megalopolis
**j.** Washington, D.C.
**k.** Chicago
**l.** terrorism

**1.** a string of cities that have grown together
**2.** major seaport in the British colonies
**3.** stream or river that flows into a larger stream or river
**4.** violent attacks that cause fear
**5.** first settlers
**6.** largest freshwater lake system in the world
**7.** major mountain range in the West
**8.** capital of the United States
**9.** third-largest city in the United States
**10.** major mountain range in the East
**11.** having the ability to speak two languages
**12.** territory controlled by people from a foreign land

## Comprehension and Critical Thinking

**SECTION 1** *(Pages 248–252)*

**13. a. Identify** What river drains the entire Interior Plains and is the longest river in North America?

## SECTION 1 (continued)

**b. Contrast** How are the Appalachians different from the Rocky Mountains?

**c. Elaborate** What natural resources affect your daily life?

**SECTION 2** (Pages 256–262)

**14. a. Define** Who were the pioneers?

**b. Draw Conclusions** Why do you think people immigrate to the United States?

**c. Elaborate** How has American culture influenced cultures around the world?

**SECTION 3** (Pages 264–270)

**15. a. Recall** What are the four regions of the United States?

**b. Compare** Is corn grown mostly in the Midwest or the South?

**c. Elaborate** How should the United States protect itself from terrorism?

## Using the Internet 21ST CENTURY

**16. Activity: Making a Brochure** The United States is a country with a diverse population. This diversity is seen in many of the holidays Americans celebrate. Through your online textbook, research holidays celebrated in the United States. Take notes on what you find. Then use your notes to create an illustrated brochure about three holidays. Be sure to tell about the history, background, and traditions of each holiday.

 hmhsocialstudies.com

## Social Studies Skills

**Reading a Political Map** Look at the political map of the United States at the beginning of this chapter. Then answer the following questions.

**17.** What four states border Mexico?

**18.** What river forms the boundary between Illinois and Missouri?

## Map Activity 21ST CENTURY

**19. The United States** On a sheet of paper, match the letters on the map with their correct labels.

Great Lakes      Rocky Mountains

Mississippi River      Pacific Ocean

Atlantic Ocean      Alaska

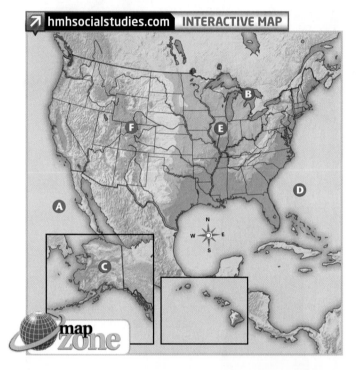

hmhsocialstudies.com    INTERACTIVE MAP

map zone

### FOCUS ON READING AND VIEWING

**20. Categorizing** For each category below, list details from the chapter.

| Geography | People | Regions |
|---|---|---|
|  |  |  |

**21. Creating a Collage** Gather the information and images you need to create a collage about the United States. Next, decide how to organize your collage. You might, for example, organize it by region or by time period. After you have attached your images to the poster board, create a label for each grouping. Finally, write a title for the entire collage. Be prepared to display your work and evaluate your classmates' collages for organization and clarity.

*DIRECTIONS: Read questions 1 through 7 and write the letter of the best response. Question 8 will require a brief essay.*

**1** What physical feature does the Mississippi River and its tributaries drain?

A Piedmont

B Rocky Mountains

C Interior Plains

D Great Lakes

**2** What country did the United States gain independence from?

A Britain

B France

C Canada

D Mexico

**3** Many pioneers moved west hoping to find

A silver.

B diamonds.

C coal.

D gold.

**4** People who are bilingual speak how many languages?

A one

B five

C two

D three

**5** NAFTA is a trade agreement among the United States, Mexico, and

A Brazil.

B Canada.

C Britain.

D Australia.

## Regions of the United States

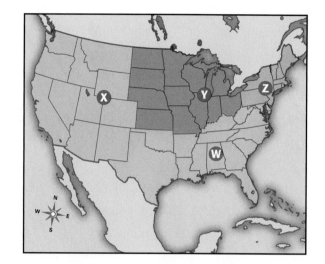

**6** Based on the map above, which region is the Midwest?

A X

B W

C Z

D Y

**7** Which region is known for its dense population?

A Z

B W

C Y

D X

**8** **Extended Response** Look at the map of U.S. regions and the chart of major U.S. cities in Section 3. Write a short essay describing the population, resources, and economies of each region of the United States.

# THE American REVOLUTION

**The American Revolution led to the formation of the United States of America in 1776.** Beginning in the 1760s, tensions grew between American colonists and their British rulers when Britain started passing a series of new laws and taxes for the colonies. With no representation in the British government, however, colonists had no say in these laws, which led to growing discontent. After fighting broke out in 1775, colonial leaders met to decide what to do. They approved the Declaration of Independence, announcing that the American colonies were free from British rule. In reality, however, freedom would not come until after years of fighting.

Explore some of the people and events of the American Revolution online. You can find a wealth of information, video clips, primary sources, activities, and more at ⏎ hmhsocialstudies.com.

*"I know not what course others may take; but as for me, give me liberty or give me death!"*

– Patrick Henry

**"Give Me Liberty or Give Me Death"**
Read an excerpt from Patrick Henry's famous speech, which urged the colonists to fight against the British.

**Seeds of Revolution**
Watch the video to learn about colonial discontent in the years before the Revolutionary War.

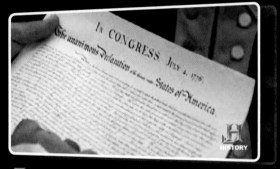

**Independence!**
Watch the video to learn about the origins of the Declaration of Independence.

**Victory!**
Watch the video to learn how the American colonists won the Revolutionary War.

# CHAPTER 12

# Canada

National capital
★ Provincial capitals
● Other cities

0        250        500 Miles
0      250      500 Kilometers

Projection:
Lambert Azimuthal Equal-Area

---

**Essential Question** How has geography and climate shaped the development of Canada's provinces?

## What You Will Learn...

In this chapter you will learn about the physical features, climates, and resources of Canada. You will study the history of Canada and the country's different cultures. Finally, you will learn about Canada's government, regions, and economy.

### FOCUS ON READING AND SPEAKING

**Understanding Lists** Identifying a list of the interesting facts that you read about may help you understand the topic you are studying. For example, you could identify facts about Canada's physical features, regions, government, or economy. As you read this chapter, look for lists of facts. **See the lesson, Understanding Lists, on page 527.**

**Creating a Radio Ad** You are a member of the Canadian tourism board and your job is to develop a radio ad to attract visitors to Canada. Read about Canada in this chapter. Then, write a script for a one-minute radio ad. Be ready to present your ad to the class.

**Culture** Ice hockey is Canada's national sport. Many Canadians grow up playing on frozen lakes.

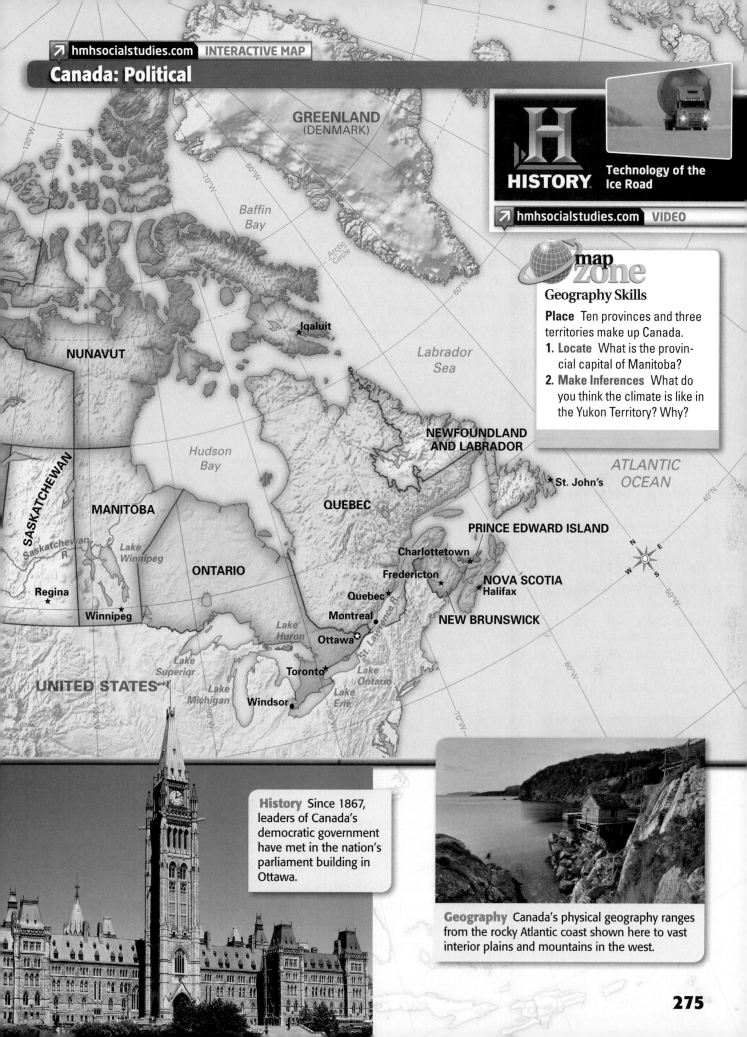

GREENLAND
(DENMARK)

Baffin
Bay

Arctic Circle

HISTORY™

**Technology of the Ice Road**

↗ hmhsocialstudies.com VIDEO

Iqaluit

Labrador
Sea

**map zone**

**Geography Skills**

**Place** Ten provinces and three territories make up Canada.

1. **Locate** What is the provincial capital of Manitoba?
2. **Make Inferences** What do you think the climate is like in the Yukon Territory? Why?

NUNAVUT

NEWFOUNDLAND
AND LABRADOR

Hudson
Bay

ATLANTIC
OCEAN

★ St. John's

SASKATCHEWAN

MANITOBA

QUEBEC

PRINCE EDWARD ISLAND

Saskatchewan R.

Lake
Winnipeg

Charlottetown ★

ONTARIO

Fredericton ★

NOVA SCOTIA
★ Halifax

Regina ★

Quebec ★

Winnipeg ★

Montreal ●

NEW BRUNSWICK

Lake
Huron

Ottawa ⍟

St. Lawrence R.

Lake
Superior

Toronto ★

Lake
Ontario

UNITED STATES →

Lake
Michigan

Windsor ●

Lake
Erie

N E W S

**History** Since 1867, leaders of Canada's democratic government have met in the nation's parliament building in Ottawa.

**Geography** Canada's physical geography ranges from the rocky Atlantic coast shown here to vast interior plains and mountains in the west.

# Physical Geography

## What You Will Learn...

### Main Ideas

1. A huge country, Canada has a wide variety of physical features, including rugged mountains, plains, and swamps.
2. Because of its northerly location, Canada is dominated by cold climates.
3. Canada is rich in natural resources like fish, minerals, fertile soil, and forests.

### The Big Idea

Canada is a huge country with a northerly location, cold climates, and rich resources.

### Key Terms and Places

Rocky Mountains, *p. 276*
St. Lawrence River, *p. 276*
Niagara Falls, *p. 276*
Canadian Shield, *p. 277*
Grand Banks, *p. 278*
pulp, *p. 279*
newsprint, *p. 279*

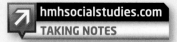
hmhsocialstudies.com
TAKING NOTES

Use the graphic organizer online to take notes on the physical geography of Canada.

## If YOU lived there...

You live in Winnipeg, Manitoba, in central Canada. Your hiking club is trying to decide where to go on a trip this summer. Since you live on the plains, some people want to visit the rugged Rocky Mountains in the west. Others want to travel north to Hudson Bay to see polar bears and other wildlife. Others would rather hike in the east near the Great Lakes and Niagara Falls.

**Which place will you choose for this year's trip?**

**BUILDING BACKGROUND** A long international boundary separates Canada and the United States. With the exception of the St. Lawrence River and the Great Lakes, there is no actual physical boundary between the two countries. Rivers, lakes, prairies, and mountain ranges cross the border.

## Physical Features

Did you know that Canada is the second-largest country in the world? Russia is the only country in the world that is larger than Canada. The United States is the third-largest country in the world and shares many physical features with Canada.

As you look at the map on the following page, see if you can find the physical features that the United States and Canada share. You may notice that mountains along the Pacific coast and the **Rocky Mountains** extend north into western Canada from the western United States. Broad plains stretch across the interiors of both countries. In the east, the two countries share a natural border formed by the **St. Lawrence River**. An important international waterway, the St. Lawrence links the Great Lakes to the Atlantic Ocean.

The United States and Canada also share a spectacular physical feature called **Niagara Falls**. The falls are located on the Niagara River between the province of Ontario and New York State.

Created by the waters of the Niagara River, the falls flow between two of the Great Lakes—Lake Erie and Lake Ontario. The falls here plunge an average of 162 feet (50 m) down a huge ledge. That is higher than many 15-story buildings!

Canada has a region of rocky uplands, lakes, and swamps called the **Canadian Shield**. See on the map how this feature curves around Hudson Bay. The Shield covers about half the country.

Farther north, Canada stretches all the way up to the Arctic Ocean. The land here is covered with ice year-round. Ellesmere Island is very rugged with snow-covered mountains and jagged coastlines. Very few people live this far north, but wildlife such as the polar bear and the Arctic wolf have adapted to the harsh environment.

**READING CHECK** **Summarizing** What are the major physical features of Canada?

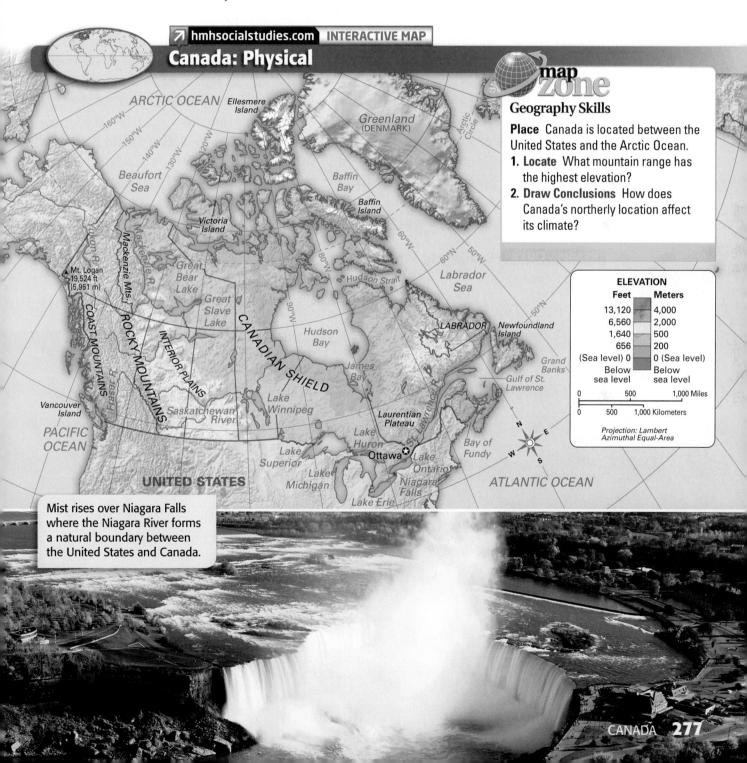

hmhsocialstudies.com INTERACTIVE MAP
**Canada: Physical**

map Zone
**Geography Skills**

**Place** Canada is located between the United States and the Arctic Ocean.
1. **Locate** What mountain range has the highest elevation?
2. **Draw Conclusions** How does Canada's northerly location affect its climate?

**ELEVATION**

| Feet | | Meters |
|---|---|---|
| 13,120 | | 4,000 |
| 6,560 | | 2,000 |
| 1,640 | | 500 |
| 656 | | 200 |
| (Sea level) 0 | | 0 (Sea level) |
| Below sea level | | Below sea level |

0    500    1,000 Miles
0   500   1,000 Kilometers

Projection: Lambert Azimuthal Equal-Area

Mist rises over Niagara Falls where the Niagara River forms a natural boundary between the United States and Canada.

## Climate

**FOCUS ON READING**

What climates would you include in a list of the climates of Canada?

Canada's location greatly influences the country's climate. Canada is located far from the equator at much higher latitudes than the United States. This more northerly location gives Canada cool to freezing temperatures year-round.

The farther north you go in Canada, the colder it gets. The coldest areas of Canada are located close to the Arctic Circle. Much of central and northern Canada has a subarctic climate. The far north has tundra and ice cap climates. About half of Canada lies in these extremely cold climates.

The central and eastern parts of southern Canada have a much different climate. It is humid and relatively mild. However, the mildest area of Canada is along the coast of British Columbia. This location on the Pacific coast brings rainy winters and mild temperatures. Inland areas of southern Canada are colder and drier.

**READING CHECK** **Categorizing** What are Canada's climates?

## Resources

Canada is incredibly rich in natural resources such as fish, minerals, and forests. Canada's Atlantic and Pacific coastal waters are among the world's richest fishing areas. Off the Atlantic coast lies a large fishing ground near Newfoundland and Labrador called the **Grand Banks**. Here, cold waters from the Labrador Sea meet the warm waters of the Gulf Stream. These conditions are ideal for the growth of tiny organisms, or plankton, that fish like to eat. As a result, large schools of fish gather at the Grand Banks. However, recent overfishing of this region has left many fishers in Canada unemployed.

Minerals are also valuable resources in Canada. The Canadian Shield contains many mineral deposits. Canada is a main source of the world's nickel, zinc, and uranium. Lead, copper, gold, and silver are also important resources. Saskatchewan has large deposits of potash, a mineral used to make fertilizer. Alberta produces most of Canada's oil and natural gas.

**Banff National Park**

Some of Canada's most spectacular scenery is found here in the Rockies at Banff National Park.

## Satellite View

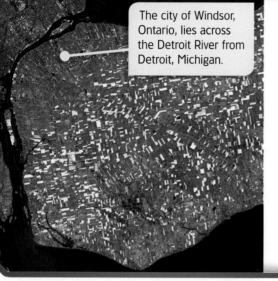

The city of Windsor, Ontario, lies across the Detroit River from Detroit, Michigan.

## Agriculture in Ontario

In this satellite image, crop fields in different stages of growth appear scattered throughout the province of Ontario. These rectangular fields of vegetation appear red at their height of growth and white after the crops are harvested. Rich soils and a mild climate in this region, which lies north of Lake Erie, make it one of Canada's most fertile regions. Crops grown here include wheat, soybeans, corn, and a variety of vegetables. Some of these crops are exported to the United States through the Canadian port of Windsor to Detroit, Michigan, just across the Detroit River. Both cities appear in this image as shades of blue and brown.

**Drawing Conclusions** What is the economy of southern Ontario based on?

---

Vast areas of forests stretch across most of Canada from Labrador to the Pacific coast. These trees provide lumber and pulp. **Pulp**—softened wood fibers—is used to make paper. The United States, the United Kingdom, and Japan get much of their newsprint from Canada. **Newsprint** is cheap paper used mainly for newspapers.

**READING CHECK** **Drawing Conclusions** How do Canada's major resources affect its economy?

**SUMMARY AND PREVIEW** In this section, you learned that Canada shares many physical features with the United States. However, Canada's geography is also different. Due to its northerly location, Canada has a cold climate. Fish, minerals, fertile soil, and forests are all important natural resources. In the next section, you will learn about the history and culture of Canada.

## Section 1 Assessment

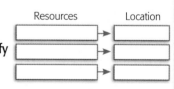

hmhsocialstudies.com
ONLINE QUIZ

### Reviewing Ideas, Terms, and Places

1. **a. Recall** What river links the Great Lakes to the Atlantic Ocean?
   **b. Explain** What physical features does **Niagara Falls** flow between?
   **c. Develop** If you were to live in Canada, where would you not want to live?
2. **a. Describe** How is Canada's climate related to its northerly location?
   **b. Draw Conclusions** Where would you expect to find Canada's coldest climate? Why?
3. **a. Define** What is the **Grand Banks**?
   **b. Interpret** How are Canada's forests a valuable resource?

### Critical Thinking

4. **Generalizing** Using your notes on Canada's resources, identify the location of each type of resource.

| Resources | | Location |
|---|---|---|
| | → | |
| | → | |
| | → | |

### FOCUS ON SPEAKING

5. **Writing about Physical Geography** What information about Canada's physical features, climate, and resources might visitors find appealing? Jot down what descriptions you want to include in your radio ad.

# History and Culture

## What You Will Learn...

### Main Ideas

1. Beginning in the 1600s, Europeans settled the region that would later become Canada.
2. Immigration and migration to cities have shaped Canadian culture.

### The Big Idea

Canada's history and culture reflect Native Canadian and European settlement, immigration, and migration to cities.

### Key Terms and Places

provinces, *p. 282*
Quebec, *p. 282*
British Columbia, *p. 282*
Toronto, *p. 284*

hmhsocialstudies.com
TAKING NOTES

Use the graphic organizer online to take notes on the history and culture of Canada.

## If **YOU** lived there...

You own a general store in Calgary, Alberta, in the early 1880s. Your town is a center for agriculture and ranching on the prairies around you. Still, it sometimes feels very isolated. You miss your family in Ontario. Now the news comes that the Canadian Pacific Railway will soon reach Calgary. It will connect the town with all of central and eastern Canada.

### How will the railroad change your life?

**BUILDING BACKGROUND** Canada is a close neighbor with the United States. The two countries are linked by a common language and a history of British colonial rule. But the two countries developed in different ways. Canada's diverse population developed its own culture and way of life.

## History

As the ice sheets of the ice ages melted, people moved into all areas of what is now Canada. As they did elsewhere in the Americas, these ancient settlers adapted to the physical environment.

### Canada's History

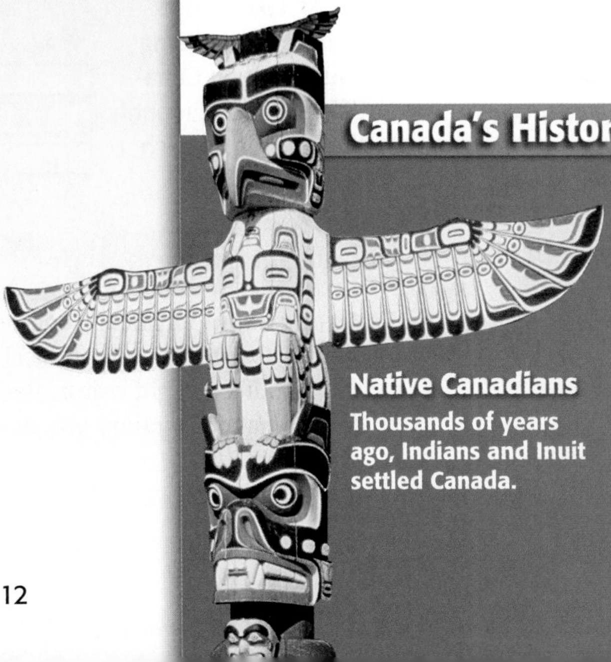

**Native Canadians**
Thousands of years ago, Indians and Inuit settled Canada.

**New France**
Known as the Father of New France, explorer Samuel de Champlain established Quebec in 1608.

## Native Canadians

Indians and the Inuit (IH-nu-wuht) people were the first Canadians. Over the years, some of these native peoples divided into groups that became known as the First Nations. One group living on Canada's vast interior plains, the Cree, were skilled bison hunters. In the far north the Inuit adapted to the region's extreme cold, where farming was impossible. By hunting seals, whales, walruses, and other animals, the Inuit could feed, clothe, and house themselves. Today about 400,000 Indians and Inuit live in Canada.

## European Settlement

Other people migrated to Canada from Europe. The first Europeans in Canada were the Vikings, or Norse. They settled on Newfoundland Island in about AD 1000, but later abandoned their settlements. In the late 1400s other Europeans arrived and explored Canada. Soon more explorers and fishermen from western Europe began crossing the Atlantic.

Trade quickly developed between the Europeans and Native Canadians. Europeans valued the furs that Native Canadians supplied. The Canadians wanted European metal goods like axes and guns. Through trading, they began to also exchange foods, clothing, and methods of travel.

## New France

France was the first European country to successfully settle parts of what would become Canada. The French **established** Quebec City in 1608. They called their new territories New France. At its height, New France included much of eastern Canada and the central United States.

New France was important for several reasons. It was part of the French Empire, which provided money and goods to French settlers. It also served as a base to spread French culture.

France had to compete with Britain, another European colonial power, for control of Canada. To defend their interests against the British, the French built trade and diplomatic relationships with Native Canadians. They exported furs, fish, and other products from New France to other parts of their empire. In addition, the French sent manufactured goods from France to New France. French missionaries also went to New France to convert people to Christianity.

All of these efforts protected French interests in New France for 150 years, until the British finally defeated the French. Although it did not last, New France shaped Canada's cultural makeup. The descendants of French settlers form one of Canada's major ethnic groups today.

**British Settlement**
The British built forts throughout Canada like this one in Halifax, Nova Scotia.

**Dominion of Canada**
After 1867, Canadians created their own government and a mounted police force patrolled the border with the United States.

## British Conquest

In the mid-1700s, the rivalry between France and England turned to war. The conflict was called the French and Indian War. This was the war that resulted in the British taking control of New France away from the French. A small number of French went back to France. However, the great majority stayed. For most of them, few changes occurred in their daily activities. They farmed the same land, prayed in the same churches, and continued to speak French. Few English-speaking settlers came to what is now called **Quebec**.

**Canadian Pacific Railroad**

Since 1885, the Canadian Pacific Railway has snaked through the Canadian Rockies on its way to the Pacific coast.

The British divided Quebec into two colonies. Lower Canada was mostly French-speaking, and Upper Canada was mostly English-speaking. The boundary between Upper and Lower Canada forms part of the border between the provinces of Quebec and Ontario today. **Provinces** are administrative divisions of a country. To the east, the colony of Nova Scotia (noh-vuh SKOH-shuh) was also divided. A new colony called New Brunswick was created where many of the British settlers lived.

## Creation of Canada

For several decades these new colonies developed separately from each other. The colonists viewed themselves as different from other parts of the British Empire. Therefore, the British Parliament created the Dominion of Canada in 1867. A dominion is a territory or area of influence. For Canadians, the creation of the Dominion was a step toward independence from Britain. The motto of the new Dominion was "from sea to sea."

How would Canadians create a nation from sea to sea? With railroads. When the Dominion was established, Ontario and Quebec were already well served by railroads. **British Columbia**, on the Pacific coast, was not. To connect British Columbia with the provinces in the east, the Canadians built a transcontinental railroad. Completed in 1885, the Canadian Pacific Railway was Canada's first transcontinental railroad.

After the Canadian Pacific Railway linked the original Canadian provinces to British Columbia, Canada acquired vast lands in the north. Much of this land was bought from the Hudson's Bay Company, a large British fur-trading business. Most of the people living in the north were Native Canadians and people of mixed European and native ancestry. With the building

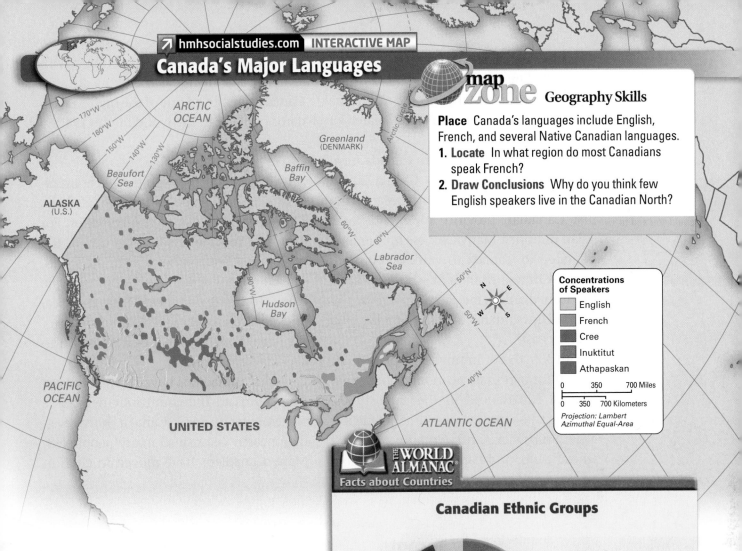

## Canada's Major Languages

hmhsocialstudies.com **INTERACTIVE MAP**

**map zone** Geography Skills

**Place** Canada's languages include English, French, and several Native Canadian languages.
1. **Locate** In what region do most Canadians speak French?
2. **Draw Conclusions** Why do you think few English speakers live in the Canadian North?

**Concentrations of Speakers**
- English
- French
- Cree
- Inuktitut
- Athapaskan

0    350    700 Miles
0    350    700 Kilometers
*Projection: Lambert Azimuthal Equal-Area*

ARCTIC OCEAN

Greenland (DENMARK)

Baffin Bay

Beaufort Sea

ALASKA (U.S.)

Labrador Sea

Hudson Bay

PACIFIC OCEAN

UNITED STATES

ATLANTIC OCEAN

**THE WORLD ALMANAC** Facts about Countries

**Canadian Ethnic Groups**

- British Isles origin — 28%
- French origin — 23%
- Other European — 15%
- Native Canadians — 2%
- Mixed background — 26%
- Other, mostly Asian, African, Arab — 6%

hmhsocialstudies.com

of the railroad and the signing of treaties with Native Canadians, early Canadian settlers created a way for more people to settle Canada's new territories.

**READING CHECK** **Summarizing** How was Canada linked from sea to sea?

## Culture

Canada's people reflect a history of British and French colonial rule. In addition, the country has experienced waves of immigration. The country is home to a great variety of people who belong to different ethnic groups and cultures. Although individual groups still keep their own cultural ways, many Canadians have tried to create a single national identity.

### Immigration

During the late 1800s and early 1900s, many immigrants came to Canada from Europe. Most were from Britain, Russia, and Germany. Some people also came from the United States. While most of these immigrants farmed, others worked in mines, forests, and factories.

CANADA **283**

Other immigrants were lured to Canada in 1897 by the discovery of gold in the Yukon Territory. Many people from the United States migrated north in search of Canada's gold.

**FOCUS ON READING**
What details of this paragraph could you add to a list of countries from which immigrants came?

Immigrants also came to Canada from Asian countries, especially China, Japan, and India. British Columbia became the first Canadian province to have a large Asian minority. Many Chinese immigrants migrated to Canada to work on the railroads. Chinese immigrants built most of the Canadian Pacific Railway, one of the railroad lines linking eastern Canada to the Pacific coast.

All of these immigrants played an important part in an economic boom that Canada experienced in the early 1900s. During these prosperous times, Quebec, New Brunswick, and Ontario produced wheat, pulp, and paper. British Columbia and Ontario supplied the country with minerals and hydroelectricity. As a result, Canadians enjoyed one of the highest standards of living in the world by the 1940s.

## Movement to Cities

After World War II, another wave of immigrants from Europe arrived in Canada. Many settled in Canada's large cities. For example, **Toronto** has become one of the most culturally diverse cities in the world. The Europeans were joined by other people from Africa, the Caribbean, Latin America, and particularly Asia. Asian businesspeople have brought a great deal of wealth to Canada's economy.

Many Canadians have recently moved from farms to the country's cities. Some settlements in rural Canada have even disappeared because so many people left. Many Canadians have moved to cities in

## Toronto

**With about 5 million people, Toronto is Canada's largest city.**

**ANALYZING VISUALS** How is Toronto's history reflected in this city square?

# Vancouver's Chinatown

If you walked around Vancouver, British Columbia, you would quickly realize when you entered the neighborhood of Chinatown. First you would notice that most signs are in Chinese and you would hear some people speaking Chinese. Then you would realize most restaurants serve Chinese food, and shops sell colorful silk clothing, herbs, and art imported from China. If you were in the city for the Chinese New Year, you would probably see a parade of people in traditional Chinese dress. Vancouver's Chinatown is a unique place where Chinese culture is kept alive in Canada today.

**Drawing Conclusions** How is Vancouver's Chinatown a unique neighborhood?

Ontario to find jobs. Others moved to Vancouver, British Columbia, for its good job opportunities, mild climate, and location near plentiful resources. Resources such as oil, gas, potash, and uranium have provided wealth to many cities in the Western Provinces. However, the political and economic center of power remains in the cities of Ottawa, Toronto, and Montreal.

**READING CHECK** **Analyzing** How has immigration changed Canada?

**SUMMARY AND PREVIEW** In this section, you learned that Canada was greatly influenced by British and French settlement, the building of the railroad to the Pacific coast, immigration, and movement to cities. In the next section you will learn about Canada's regions and economy today.

## Section 2 Assessment

hmhsocialstudies.com
ONLINE QUIZ

### Reviewing Ideas, Terms, and Places

1. **a. Recall** What is a **province**?
   **b. Summarize** How did Britain gain control of New France from the French?
   **c. Elaborate** How do you think the Canadian Pacific Railway changed Canada?
2. **a. Identify** What immigrant group helped build the railroads?
   **b. Draw Conclusions** Why did people migrate to Canada?
   **c. Elaborate** Why do you think many Canadians moved from farms to the cities?

### Critical Thinking

3. **Analyzing** Draw a diagram like the one below. Using your notes, write a sentence in each box about how each topic influenced the next topic.

Railroad → Immigration → Cities

### FOCUS ON SPEAKING

4. **Adding Details** Add information about the history and culture of Canada to your notes. Which details would most interest potential visitors?

# Canada Today

## If YOU lived there...

You and your family live in Toronto, Ontario. Your parents, who are architects, have been offered an important project in Montreal. If they accept it, you would live there for two years. Montreal is a major city in French-speaking Quebec. You would have to learn a new language. In Montreal, most street signs and advertisements are written in French.

**How do you feel about moving to a city with a different language and culture?**

**What You Will Learn...**

**Main Ideas**

1. Canada has a democratic government with a prime minister and a parliament.
2. Canada has four distinct geographic and cultural regions.
3. Canada's economy is largely based on trade with the United States.

**The Big Idea**

Canada's democratic government oversees the country's regions and economy.

**Key Terms and Places**

regionalism, *p. 287*
maritime, *p. 287*
Montreal, *p. 288*
Ottawa, *p. 289*
Vancouver, *p. 290*

hmhsocialstudies.com
TAKING NOTES

Use the graphic organizer online to take notes on present-day Canada.

**BUILDING BACKGROUND** Canada today has been shaped by both history and geography. Canada's first European settlers were French, but the British eventually controlled the territory. Differences in culture still remain, however. In addition, the four regions of Canada are separated by vast distances, economic activities, and culture.

## Canada's Government

"Peace, order, and good government" is a statement from Canada's constitution that Canadians greatly value. Canadians are proud of their democratic government, which is led by a prime minister. Similar to a president, a prime minister is the head of a country's government.

Canada's prime minister oversees the country's parliament, Canada's governing body. Parliament consists of the House of Commons and the Senate. Canadians elect members of the House of Commons. However, senators are appointed by the prime minister.

Canada's 10 provincial governments are each led by a premier. These provincial governments are much like our state governments. Canada's central government is similar to our federal government. The Canadian federal system lets people keep their feelings of loyalty to their own province.

**READING CHECK** **Comparing** How is Canada's government similar to that of the United States?

# Canada's Regions

Canada's physical geography separates the country into different regions. For example, people living on the Pacific coast in British Columbia are isolated from Canadians living in the eastern provinces on the Atlantic coast. Just as geographic distance separates much of Canada, differences in culture also define regions.

## Regionalism

The cultural differences between English-speaking and French-speaking Canadians have led to problems. English is the main language in most of Canada. In Quebec, however, French is the main language. When Canadians from different regions discuss important issues, they are often influenced by regionalism. **Regionalism** refers to the strong connection that people feel toward the region in which they live.

In some places, this connection is stronger than people's connection to their country as a whole. To better understand regionalism in Canada, we will now explore each region of the country. As you read, refer to the map below to locate each region.

## The Eastern Provinces

The region called the Eastern Provinces is a region that lies on the Atlantic coast of Canada. The provinces of New Brunswick, Nova Scotia, and Prince Edward Island are often called the Maritime Provinces. **Maritime** means on or near the sea. The province of Newfoundland and Labrador is usually not considered one of the Maritime Provinces. It includes the island of Newfoundland and a large region of the mainland called Labrador.

A short growing season limits farming in the Eastern Provinces. However, farmers in Prince Edward Island grow potatoes.

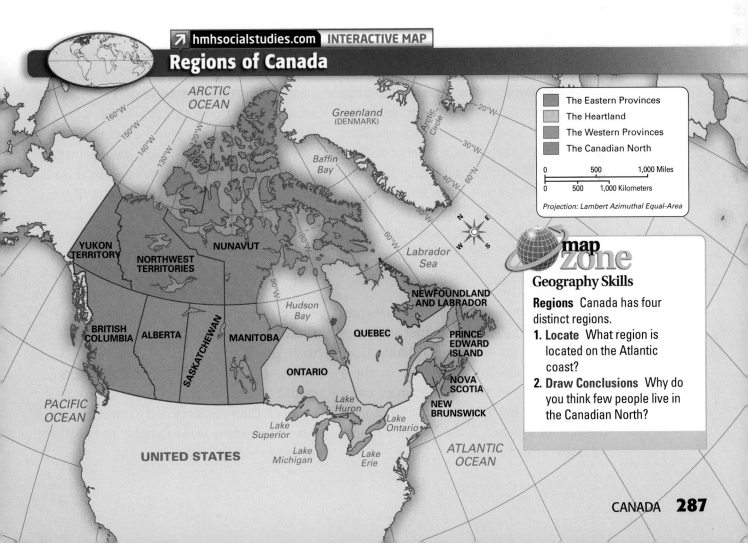

hmhsocialstudies.com **INTERACTIVE MAP**

## Regions of Canada

**Legend:**
- The Eastern Provinces
- The Heartland
- The Western Provinces
- The Canadian North

0    500    1,000 Miles
0    500    1,000 Kilometers

Projection: Lambert Azimuthal Equal-Area

### map zone

**Geography Skills**

**Regions** Canada has four distinct regions.

1. **Locate** What region is located on the Atlantic coast?
2. **Draw Conclusions** Why do you think few people live in the Canadian North?

# Quebec's Winter Carnival

At the annual Winter Carnival in the city of Quebec, millions of Canadians and visitors from around the world brave below-freezing temperatures to celebrate French Canadian culture.

The Inuit people traditionally used dogsleds as a means of transportation. Today dogsledding is a popular sport in Canada and a highlight of the carnival.

Most of the economy in Canada's Eastern Provinces is related to the forestry and fishing industries.

Many people in the Eastern Provinces are descendants of immigrants from the British Isles. In addition, French-speaking families have moved from Quebec to New Brunswick. Most of the region's people live in coastal cities. Many cities have industrial plants and serve as fishing and shipping ports. Along the Atlantic coast lies Halifax, Nova Scotia, the region's largest city.

## The Heartland

**FOCUS ON READING**

In the paragraphs under The Heartland sort the facts into different lists.

Inland from the Eastern Provinces are Quebec and Ontario, which together are sometimes referred to as the Heartland. More than half of all Canadians live in these two provinces. In fact, the chain of cities that extends from Windsor, Ontario, to the city of Quebec is the country's most urbanized region.

The provincial capital of Quebec is also called Quebec. The city's older section has narrow streets, stone walls, and French-style architecture. **Montreal** is Canada's second-largest city and one of the largest French-speaking cities in the world. About 3.5 million people live in the Montreal metropolitan area. It is the financial and industrial center of the province. Winters in Montreal are very cold. To deal with this harsh environment, Montreal's people use underground passages and overhead tunnels to move between buildings in the city's downtown.

In Canada many residents of Quebec, called Quebecois (kay-buh-KWAH), believe their province should be given a special status. Quebecois argue that this status would recognize the cultural differences between their province and the rest of Canada. Some even want Quebec to become an independent country.

Many of the city's buildings reflect French architecture.

ANALYSIS SKILL ANALYZING VISUALS

From the clues you see in this scene, what do you think is unique about French Canadian culture?

Ice sculptures created by Canadian and international artists line the carnival's grounds.

The carnival's mascot is a snowman who wears a traditional Canadian sash and hat.

On the other hand, many English-speaking Canadians think Quebec already has too many privileges. Most Canadians, however, still support a united Canada. Strong feelings of regionalism will continue to be an important issue.

With an even larger population than Quebec, the province of Ontario is Canada's leading manufacturing province. Hamilton, Ontario, is the center of Canada's steel industry. Canada exports much of its steel to the United States.

Ontario's capital, Toronto, is a major center for industry, finance, education, and culture. Toronto's residents come from many different parts of the world, including China, Europe, and India.

Canada's national capital, **Ottawa**, is also in Ontario. In Ottawa many people speak both English and French. The city is known for its grand government buildings, parks, and several universities.

## The Western Provinces

West of Ontario are the prairie provinces of Manitoba, Saskatchewan, and Alberta. On the Pacific coast is the province of British Columbia. Together, these four provinces make up Canada's Western Provinces.

More people live in Quebec than in all of the prairie provinces combined. The southern grasslands of these provinces are part of a rich wheat belt. Farms here produce far more wheat than Canadians need. The extra wheat is exported. Oil and natural gas production is a very important economic activity in Alberta. The beauty of the Canadian Rockies attracts many visitors to national parks in western Alberta and eastern British Columbia.

British Columbia is Canada's westernmost province and home to almost 4 million people. This mountainous province has rich natural resources, including forests, salmon, and valuable minerals.

Even in June, snow covers the small town of Pond Inlet, Nunavut. The Inuit here travel by snowmobile and enjoy ice fishing.

Nearly half of British Columbia's population lives in and around the coastal city of **Vancouver**. The city's location on the Pacific coast helps it to trade with countries in Asia.

### The Canadian North

Northern Canada is extremely cold due to its location close to the Arctic Circle. The region called the Canadian North includes the Yukon Territory, the Northwest Territories, and Nunavut (NOO-nuh-voot). These three territories cover more than a third of Canada but are home to only about 100,000 people.

Nunavut is a new territory created for the native Inuit people who live there. Nunavut means "Our Land" in the Inuit language. Even though Nunavut is part of Canada, the people there have their own **distinct** culture and government. About 30,000 people live in Nunavut.

The physical geography of the Canadian North includes forests and tundra. The frozen waters of the Arctic Ocean separate

**ACADEMIC VOCABULARY**

distinct separate

isolated towns and villages. During some parts of the winter, sunlight is limited to only a few hours.

**READING CHECK** **Drawing Conclusions** How does geography affect the location of economic activities in the Western Provinces?

## Canada's Economy

As you learned in Section 1, Canada has many valuable natural resources. Canada's economy is based on the industries associated with these resources. In addition, Canada's economy also benefits from trade.

### Industries

Canada is one of the world's leading mineral producers. Canadians mine valuable titanium, zinc, iron ore, gold, and coal. Canada's iron and steel industry uses iron ore to manufacture products like planes, automobiles and household appliances. However, most Canadians work in the services industry. For example, tourism is

Canada's fastest-growing services industry. Canada's economy also benefits from the millions of dollars visitors spend in the country each year.

## Trade

Canada's economy depends on trade. Many of Canada's natural resources that you have learned about are exported to countries around the world. Canada's leading trading partner is the United States.

As the world's largest trading relationship, Canada and the United States rely heavily on each other. About 60 percent of Canada's imported goods are from the United States. About 85 percent of Canada's exports, such as lumber, goes to the United States.

However, the United States placed tariffs, or added fees, on Canadian timber. American lumber companies accused Canada of selling their lumber at unfairly low prices. Canada argued that the tariffs were unfair according to the North American Free Trade Agreement (NAFTA).

The export of cattle to the United States is another area of dispute between the two countries. When a Canadian cow was discovered with mad cow disease in 2003, the United States banned the import of all cattle from Canada. Canadian ranchers now claim that all their cows are free of the disease. After a two-year ban, the United States imports Canadian cattle and beef again.

**READING CHECK** **Summarizing** What goods does Canada export?

**SUMMARY** In this section you learned that Canada has distinct regions that are separated by both geography and culture. The U.S. and Canada are trading partners that share a common colonial history, a border, and the English language.

**Trade with the United States**

| Major Exports | Major Imports |
|---|---|
| ■ Petroleum Products | ■ Automobiles and parts |
| ■ Automobiles and parts | ■ Chemicals |
| ■ Lumber | ■ Plastics |

## Section 3 Assessment

hmhsocialstudies.com
ONLINE QUIZ

### Reviewing Ideas, Terms, and Places

1. a. **Recall** What office heads Canada's government?
   b. **Summarize** How is Canada's parliament structured?
2. a. **Define** What is **regionalism**?
   b. **Contrast** How are Canada's Western Provinces different from the Canadian North?
   c. **Evaluate** Why do you think the Quebecois want to break away from Canada?
3. a. **Describe** How are Canada's natural resources important to the country's economy?
   b. **Draw Conclusions** Why do Canada and the United States rely on each other as trading partners?

### Critical Thinking

4. **Comparing and Contrasting** Use your notes to complete this chart. List the similarities and differences between the Eastern Provinces and Western Provinces.

| Similarities | Differences |
|---|---|
| 1. | 1. |
| 2. | |

**FOCUS ON SPEAKING**

5. **Presenting Canada Today** Add details about present-day Canada to your notes. Consider which images you will use to persuade your audience to visit Canada after they listen to your ad.

# Using Mental Maps and Sketch Maps

## Learn

We create maps in our heads of all kinds of places—our schools, communities, country, and the world. These images, or mental maps, are shaped by what we see and experience.

We use mental maps of places when we draw sketch maps. A sketch map uses very simple shapes to show the relationship between places and the relative size of places. Notice the sketch map of the world shown here. It may not look like any other map in your book, but it does give you an idea of what the world looks like.

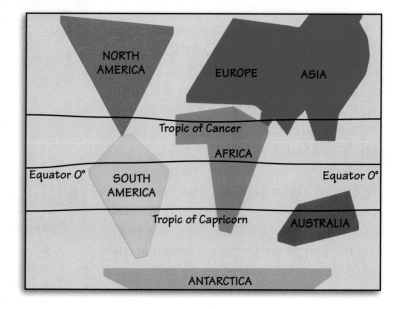

## Practice

Does your mental map of the world look like the sketch map here? It is alright if they do not look exactly alike. Now think about the places in your own neighborhood. Use your mental map to draw a sketch map of your neighborhood. Then use your sketch map to answer the following questions.

• What are the most important features of your map?

• What is the largest building in your neighborhood?

• What labels did you use on your map?

## Apply

Draw a sketch map of Canada. Make sure to include the cities and physical features you learned about in this chapter. Then exchange your map with another student. Ask your partner to make corrections to your map if he or she does not understand it.

**Geography's Impact**
**video series**
Review the video to answer the closing question:
*Why did the people of Nunavut want their own territory?*

## Visual Summary

*Use the visual summary below to help you review the main ideas of the chapter.*

QUICK FACTS

Native Canadian and European settlement has influenced Canadian culture.

Canada has cold climates and its physical features include rugged mountains.

Canada has distinctive cultural regions today.

## Reviewing Vocabulary, Terms, and Places

*Choose the letter of the answer that best completes each statement below.*

1. A physical feature of rocky uplands, lakes, and swamps in Canada is called the
   **a.** Niagara Falls.      **c.** Grand Banks.
   **b.** Great Lakes.       **d.** Canadian Shield.

2. Which part of Canada did the French settle?
   **a.** Ontario           **c.** Quebec
   **b.** New Brunswick     **d.** British Colombia

3. What province was the first to have a large Asian population?
   **a.** Manitoba          **c.** Quebec
   **b.** British Columbia  **d.** Saskatchewan

4. A strong connection that people feel toward their region is called
   **a.** maritime.         **c.** heartland.
   **b.** province.         **d.** regionalism.

## Comprehension and Critical Thinking

**SECTION 1** *(Pages 276–279)*

5. **a. Define** What is pulp?
   **b. Make Inferences** What is the coldest area in Canada?
   **c. Evaluate** What makes the Grand Banks an ideal fishing ground?

**SECTION 2** *(Pages 280–285)*

6. **a. Identify** Who were the first Canadians?
   **b. Draw Conclusions** Why did Canadians build a rail line across Canada?
   **c. Predict** Do you think Canada's cities will increase or decrease in population in the future? Explain your answers.

**SECTION 3** *(Pages 286–291)*

7. **a. Recall** What kind of government does Canada have?

## SECTION 3 (continued)

**b. Compare and Contrast** How are the Eastern Provinces different than the Western Provinces?

**c. Evaluate** Why do the Quebecois see themselves as different from other Canadians?

# Using the Internet

8. **Activity: Writing Newspaper Articles** You are a reporter for The Quebec Chronicle assigned to write articles for the next issue of the newspaper. Through your online textbook, explore the people of Quebec and find background information for your articles covering Quebec. Use the links provided to conduct your research and then write three short articles. Go to press using the interactive template and publish your Canadian newspaper.

# Social Studies Skills

9. **Using Mental Maps and Sketch Maps** Without looking at a map of Canada think about what the Eastern Provinces look like. Then create a sketch map of the Eastern Provinces. Make sure to include a compass rose and important physical features.

# Map Activity

10. **Canada** On a separate sheet of paper, match the letters on the map with their correct labels.

Rocky Mountains      Manitoba

Nunavut                    St. Lawrence River

Vancouver

## FOCUS ON READING AND SPEAKING

11. **Understanding Lists** Use your notes about Canada to create a list of important facts for each section. Organize your lists using this chart.

| Physical Geography | History and Culture | Canada Today |
|---|---|---|
|  |  |  |

12. **Creating a Tourism Ad** Now that you have collected notes on Canada's geography, history, and culture, choose the information you think will most appeal to visitors. Write a one-minute radio script, using descriptive and persuasive language to convince your audience to visit Canada. Describe Canada in a way that will capture your audience's imagination. Ask the class to listen carefully as you read your radio ad to them. Then ask the class to evaluate your ad on how persuasive it was or was not.

*DIRECTIONS: Read questions 1 through 7 and write the letter of the best response. Then read question 8 and write your own well-constructed response.*

**1** The United States and Canada share which physical feature?

A Canadian Shield

B Rocky Mountains

C Hudson Bay

D Saskatchewan River

**2** What resource in Canada provides pulp and newsprint?

A forests

B nickel

C potash

D fish

**3** Many Canadians moved from farms to cities to find

A gold.

B good schools.

C jobs.

D better weather.

**4** Canada's prime minister oversees the country's

A railroads.

B parliament.

C provincial governments.

D city governments.

**5** Canada's capital, Ottawa, is located in

A Northwest Territories.

B Nova Scotia.

C Ontario.

D British Columbia.

## Climate of British Columbia

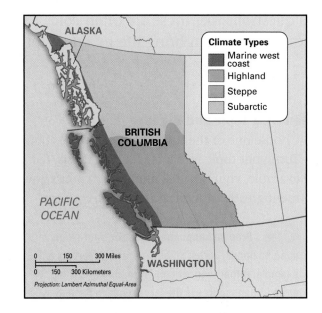

**6** Based on the map above, which climate type does the Pacific coast of British Columbia experience?

A subarctic

B marine west coast

C highland

D steppe

**7** About 60 percent of Canada's imported goods come from which country?

A Mexico

B Greenland

C Russia

D United States

**8** **Extended Response** Look at the political map of Canada at the beginning of this chapter. Using information from the map, explain why the United States and Canada are major trading partners.

# Describing a Place

**W**hat are the physical features of a country? What is the weather like? What drives the economy? The answers to questions like these are often cold, hard facts and statistics. But they can bring life to a description of a place.

## Assignment

Write a paper describing one of these places in the Americas:
- a city
- a country

## 1. Prewrite

### Identify a Topic and Big Idea

- Choose one of the topics above to write about.
- Turn your topic into a big idea, or thesis. For example, your big idea might be, "Cuba's government greatly influences life in the country."

> **TIP** **Precise Language** Describe your place with specific nouns, verbs, adjectives, and adverbs. For example, rather than writing "Buenos Aires is big," write "Buenos Aires is the largest city in Argentina."

### Gather and Organize Information

- Look for information about your place in the library or on the Internet. Organize your notes in groupings such as physical features, economy, or culture. Decide which facts about the place you are describing are most important or unique.

## 2. Write

### Use a Writer's Framework

> **A Writer's Framework**
>
> **Introduction**
> - Start with an interesting fact or question.
> - Identify your big idea and provide any necessary background information.
>
> **Body**
> - Write at least one paragraph for each category. Include facts that help explain each detail.
> - Write about each detail in order of importance.
>
> **Conclusion**
> - Summarize your description in your final paragraph.

## 3. Evaluate and Revise

### Review and Improve Your Paper

- Re-read your paper and use the questions below to identify ways to revise your paper.
- Make the changes needed to improve your paper.

### Evaluation Questions for a Description of a Place

1. Do you begin with an interesting fact or question?
2. Does your introduction identify your big idea? Do you provide background information to help your readers better understand your idea?
3. Do you have at least one paragraph for each category?
4. Do you use order of importance to organize the details of your description?
5. Are there more details you would like to know about your place? If so, what are they?

## 4. Proofread and Publish

### Give Your Description the Finishing Touch

- Make sure you used commas correctly when listing more than two details in a sentence.
- Check your spelling of the names of places.
- Share your description with classmates or with students in another social studies class.

## 5. Practice and Apply

Use the steps and strategies outlined in this workshop to write your description of a place. Share your description with classmates. With your classmates, group the descriptions by country and then identify the places you would like to visit.

# Europe and Russia

## The Alps

The Alps, one of Europe's major mountain ranges, stretch across the heart of central Europe.

## Islands and Peninsulas

Islands and peninsulas surround the edges of Europe, drawing people to the sea to work, travel, and trade.

## Northern European Plain

Rolling across northern Europe is a vast lowland called the Northern European Plain.

# UNIT 3

# Europe and Russia

**Explore the Satellite Image**
Land and sea are always close together in Europe. Islands and peninsulas are key features of this region. What can you learn about Europe's geography from this satellite image?

## The Satellite's Path

>44'56.08<

>>>>>>>>665.00'87<

+355    567.476.348    +766 +803 +966

456.094.

# Europe and Russia: Physical

ICELAND

Arctic Circle

Norwegian Sea

Kiolen Mountains

Kola Peninsula

Scandinavian Peninsula

FINLAND

Lake Onega

60°N

ATLANTIC OCEAN

BRITISH ISLES

Highlands

North Sea

Jutland Peninsula

NORWAY

SWEDEN

ESTONIA

Lake Ladoga

Volga River

EUROPEAN PLAIN

RUSSIA

URAL MOUNTAINS

Ob River

West Siberia Plain

Irtysh River

15°W

0°

45°E

45°E

DENMARK

Baltic Sea

LATVIA

LITHUANIA

RUSSIA

Kama River

Ural River

IRELAND

UNITED KINGDOM

NETHERLANDS

GERMANY

N O R T H E R N

POLAND

BELARUS

BELGIUM

Rhine R.

CZECH REPUBLIC

UKRAINE

LUXEMBOURG

Danube R.

AUSTRIA

SLOVAKIA

Carpathian Mts.

Donets Basin

Don R.

FRANCE

SWITZERLAND

A L P S

HUNGARY

SLOVENIA

MOLDOVA

Bay of Biscay

Mont Blanc ▲ 15,771 ft (4,807 m)

CROATIA

ROMANIA

Apennines

Mt. Elbrus 18,510 ft (5,642 m)

45°N

Pyrenees

ITALY

BOSNIA AND HERZEGOVINA

Dinaric Alps

SERBIA

▲ Caucasus Mts.

Caspian Sea

PORTUGAL

SPAIN

KOSOVO

BULGARIA

Black Sea

GEORGIA

MONTENEGRO

MACEDONIA

Iberian Peninsula

ALBANIA

Balkan Peninsula

ARMENIA

GREECE

AZERBAIJAN

M e d i t e r r a n e a n   S e a

15°E

30°E

SOUTHWEST ASIA

30°W

AFRICA

## THE WORLD ALMANAC® Facts about the World
### Geographical Extremes: Europe and Russia

| | |
|---|---|
| **Longest River** | Volga River, Russia: 2,290 miles (3,685 km) |
| **Highest Point** | Mount Elbrus, Russia: 18,510 feet (5,642 m) |
| **Lowest Point** | Caspian Sea, Russia/Azerbaijan: 92 feet (28 m) below sea level |
| **Highest Recorded Temperature** | Seville, Spain: 122°F (50°C) |
| **Lowest Recorded Temperature** | Ust'Shchugor, Russia: -67°F (-55°C) |
| **Wettest Place** | Crkvica, Bosnia and Herzegovina: 183 inches (464.8 cm) average precipitation per year |
| **Driest Place** | Astrakhan, Russia: 6.4 inches (16.3 cm) average precipitation per year |

↗ hmhsocialstudies.com

### ELEVATION

| Feet | Meters |
|---|---|
| 13,120 | 4,000 |
| 6,560 | 2,000 |
| 1,640 | 500 |
| 656 | 200 |
| (Sea level) 0 | 0 (Sea level) |
| Below sea level | Below sea level |

0       400       800 Miles

0   400   800 Kilometers

*Projection: Robinson*

# Europe and Russia

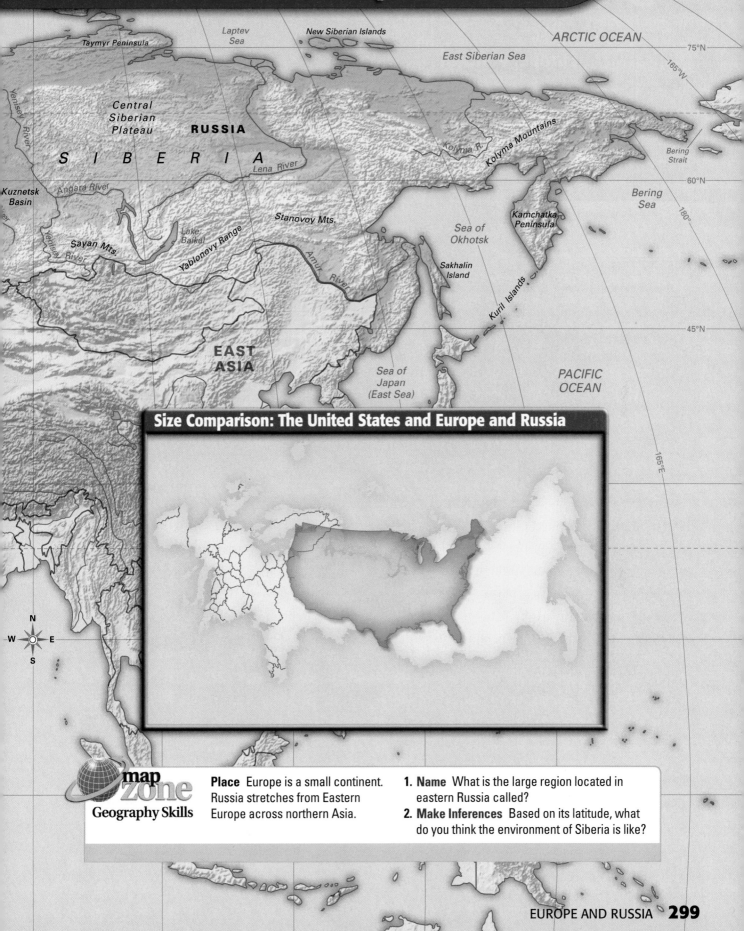

Taymyr Peninsula

Laptev Sea

New Siberian Islands

East Siberian Sea

ARCTIC OCEAN

75°N

165°W

Central Siberian Plateau

RUSSIA

S I B E R I A

Lena River

Kolyma R.

Kolyma Mountains

Bering Strait

Yenisey River

Kuznetsk Basin

Angara River

60°N

Bering Sea

180°

Sayan Mts.

Yenisey River

Lake Baikal

Yablonovy Range

Stanovoy Mts.

Amur River

Sea of Okhotsk

Kamchatka Peninsula

Sakhalin Island

Kuril Islands

165°E

45°N

EAST ASIA

Sea of Japan (East Sea)

PACIFIC OCEAN

## Size Comparison: The United States and Europe and Russia

N W E S

165°E

**map zone**

**Geography Skills**

**Place** Europe is a small continent. Russia stretches from Eastern Europe across northern Asia.

1. **Name** What is the large region located in eastern Russia called?

2. **Make Inferences** Based on its latitude, what do you think the environment of Siberia is like?

## Europe: Political

ARCTIC OCEAN

Denmark Strait

Reykjavik ✪ **ICELAND**

70°N

Arctic Circle

*Norwegian Sea*

Faeroe Islands (DENMARK)

✪ National capital
• Other city

| 0 | 200 | 400 Miles |
| 0 | 200 | 400 Kilometers |

*Projection: Azimuthal Equal-Area*

Shetland Islands (U.K.)

60°N

**NORWAY**

Oslo ✪

*North Sea*

**SWEDEN**

Stockholm •

**FINLAND**

Helsinki ✪

Tallinn •
**ESTONIA**

*Baltic Sea*

Riga ✪
**LATVIA**

**RUSSIA**

**IRELAND**

Dublin ✪

**UNITED KINGDOM**

50°N

London ✪

**NETHERLANDS**
• Amsterdam

**DENMARK**

Copenhagen ✪

Kaliningrad (RUSSIA)

**LITHUANIA**
Vilnius ✪

Minsk ✪

**BELARUS**

**ATLANTIC OCEAN**

Brussels ✪
**BELGIUM**

Berlin ✪

**GERMANY**

**POLAND**

Warsaw ✪

**LUXEMBOURG**
Luxembourg ✪

Prague ✪

Kiev ✪

*Dnieper River*

• Paris

Rhine R.

**CZECH REPUBLIC**

**SLOVAKIA**

**UKRAINE**

Danube R.

**LIECHTENSTEIN**

Bratislava ✪

**FRANCE**

Bern ✪

Vienna ✪

**AUSTRIA**

Budapest ✪

**MOLDOVA**

Chişinău ✪

**SWITZERLAND**

Ljubljana ✪ **SLOVENIA**

**HUNGARY**

**ROMANIA**

40°N

**PORTUGAL**

Lisbon ✪

**ANDORRA**

Madrid •

**SPAIN**

**MONACO**

**SAN MARINO**

**ITALY**

Zagreb ✪
**CROATIA**

**BOSNIA AND HERZEGOVINA**
Sarajevo ✪

Belgrade ✪

**SERBIA**

**KOSOVO**
Pristina ✪

Bucharest ✪

**BULGARIA**

Sofia ✪

*Black Sea*

Corsica (FRANCE)

*Adriatic Sea*

**VATICAN CITY**

Rome •

**MONTENEGRO**
Podgorica ✪

Skopje ✪
**MACEDONIA**

Balearic Islands (SPAIN)

Sardinia (ITALY)

Tirane ✪
**ALBANIA**

Strait of Gilbraltar

Gibraltar (U.K.)

0°

Sicily (ITALY)

**GREECE**

*Aegean Sea*

**ASIA**

**AFRICA**

**MALTA** ✪ Valletta

20°E

*Mediterranean Sea*

Athens ✪

Crete (GREECE)

30°E

map **zone**

**Geography Skills**

**Place** Europe includes many small countries.

**1. Name** Which European countries are island countries?

**2. Make Generalizations** Based on this map, which countries do you think might have the largest populations? Why?

# Europe and Russia

## Russia and the Caucasus: Political

ATLANTIC OCEAN

Arctic Circle

60°N

North Sea

Baltic Sea

EUROPE

Kaliningrad

St. Petersburg

Moscow ✪

Nizhniy Novgorod

Volga River

Samara

Yekaterinburg

Black Sea

GEORGIA
Tbilisi

ARMENIA
Yerevan ✪

Baku ✪

AZERBAIJAN

Caspian Sea

KAZAKHSTAN

Barents Sea

ARCTIC OCEAN

60°W  40°W  20°W  0°  20°E  40°E  60°E  80°E  100°E  120°E  80°N  140°E

80°W  100°W  120°W  140°W  160°W  180°  160°E

Bering Strait

Bering Sea

60°N

Ob River

Yenisey River

R U S S I A

Lena River

Sea of Okhotsk

Novosibirsk

MONGOLIA

Vladivostok

40°N

JAPAN

CHINA

PACIFIC OCEAN

Tropic of Cancer

20°N

✪ National capital
• Other city

0     300     600 Miles
0   300   600 Kilometers

Projection: Two-Point Equidistant

### map zone
### Geography Skills

**Place** Russia is the largest country in the world.
**1. Use the Map** About how many miles is Russia from west to east?

**2. Analyze** Where does Russia have access to the ocean? How do you think that affects trade?

## Europe: Population

ARCTIC OCEAN

Denmark Strait

70°N

Norwegian
Sea

Arctic Circle

60°N

North
Sea

Baltic Sea

Kaliningrad
(RUSSIA)

RUSSIA

ATLANTIC
OCEAN

50°N

London

Berlin

Warsaw

Kiev

Paris

Vienna

40°N

Madrid

Bucharest

Black Sea

Barcelona

Adriatic Sea

Rome

ASIA

Strait of
Gilbraltar

Aegean
Sea

AFRICA

Mediterranean Sea

| Persons per square mile | Persons per square km |
|---|---|
| 520 | 200 |
| 260 | 100 |
| 130 | 50 |
| 25 | 10 |
| 3 | 1 |
| 0 | 0 |

● Major cities over 2 million

0    150    300 Miles
0    150    300 Kilometers

Projection: Azimuthal Equal-Area

**map zone**
**Geography Skills**

**Place** Although Europe is small, it is densely populated.
1. **Use the Map** How does the population density of Northern Europe compare to the rest of Europe?
2. **Compare** Compare this map to the physical map. What large plain in Europe has a high population density?

## Russia and the Caucasus: Climate

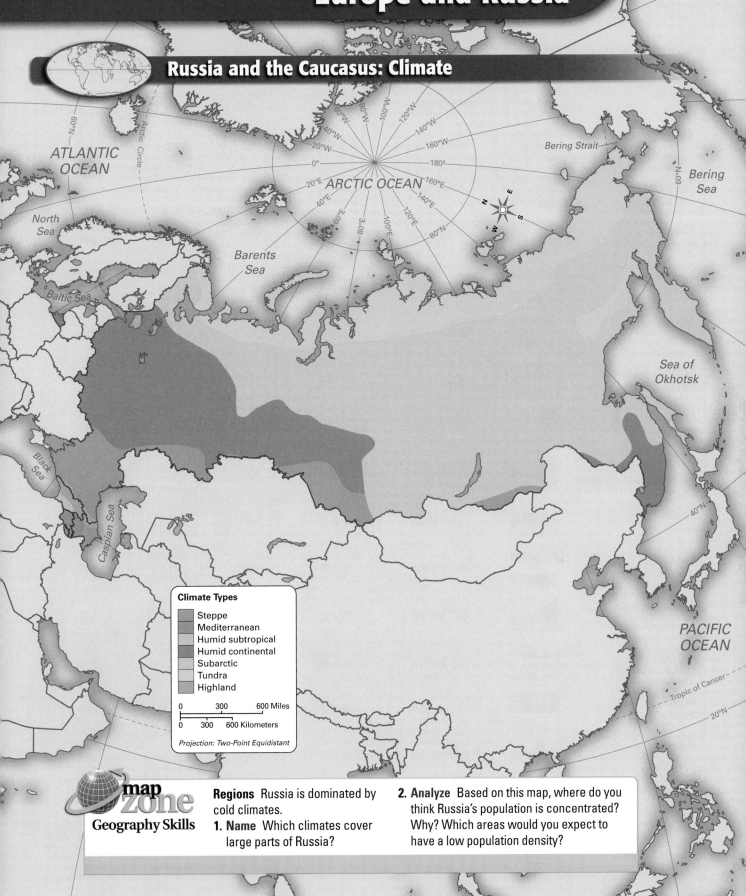

ATLANTIC OCEAN

North Sea

Baltic Sea

Arctic Circle

60°N

80°W

60°W

40°W

20°W

0°

20°E

40°E

60°E

80°E

100°E

120°E

140°E

160°E

180°

160°W

140°W

120°W

ARCTIC OCEAN

Barents Sea

Bering Strait

Bering Sea

60°N

N

E

S

W

80°N

Sea of Okhotsk

Black Sea

Caspian Sea

40°N

PACIFIC OCEAN

Tropic of Cancer

20°N

**Climate Types**

- Steppe
- Mediterranean
- Humid subtropical
- Humid continental
- Subarctic
- Tundra
- Highland

0     300     600 Miles

0     300     600 Kilometers

*Projection: Two-Point Equidistant*

**map zone**

**Geography Skills**

**Regions** Russia is dominated by cold climates.

**1. Name** Which climates cover large parts of Russia?

**2. Analyze** Based on this map, where do you think Russia's population is concentrated? Why? Which areas would you expect to have a low population density?

## Europe and Russia

| COUNTRY<br>Capital | FLAG | POPULATION | AREA<br>(sq mi) | PER CAPITA<br>GDP<br>(U.S. $) | LIFE<br>EXPECTANCY<br>AT BIRTH | TVS PER<br>1,000 PEOPLE |
|---|---|---|---|---|---|---|
| **Albania**<br>Tirana | | 3.6 million | 11,100 | $6,000 | 77.9 | 146 |
| **Andorra**<br>Andorra la Vella | | 83,888 | 181 | $42,500 | 82.7 | 440 |
| **Armenia**<br>Yerevan | | 3 million | 11,506 | $6,300 | 72.7 | 241 |
| **Austria**<br>Vienna | | 8.2 million | 32,382 | $40,200 | 79.5 | 526 |
| **Azerbaijan**<br>Baku | | 8.2 million | 33,436 | $9,500 | 66.6 | 257 |
| **Belarus**<br>Minsk | | 9.6 million | 80,155 | $11,800 | 70.5 | 331 |
| **Belgium**<br>Brussels | | 10.4 million | 11,787 | $37,400 | 79.2 | 532 |
| **Bosnia and Herzegovina:** Sarajevo | | 4.6 million | 19,741 | $6,500 | 78.5 | 112 |
| **Bulgaria**<br>Sofia | | 7.2 million | 42,823 | $12,900 | 73 | 429 |
| **Croatia**<br>Zagreb | | 4.5 million | 21,831 | $18,300 | 75.3 | 286 |
| **Czech Republic**<br>Prague | | 10.2 million | 30,450 | $25,900 | 76.7 | 487 |
| **Denmark**<br>Copenhagen | | 5.5 million | 16,639 | $37,100 | 78.2 | 776 |
| **Estonia**<br>Tallinn | | 1.3 million | 17,462 | $21,000 | 72.8 | 567 |
| **Finland**<br>Helsinki | | 5.3 million | 130,559 | $36,900 | 78.9 | 643 |
| **France**<br>Paris | | 64 million | 211,209 | $33,200 | 81 | 620 |
| **United States**<br>Washington, D.C. | | 307.2 million | 3,718,711 | $46,900 | 78.2 | 844 |

| COUNTRY Capital | FLAG | POPULATION | AREA (sq mi) | PER CAPITA GDP (U.S. $) | LIFE EXPECTANCY AT BIRTH | TVS PER 1,000 PEOPLE |
|---|---|---|---|---|---|---|
| **Georgia** T'bilisi | | 4.6 million | 26,911 | $4,600 | 76.8 | 516 |
| **Germany** Berlin | | 82.3 million | 137,847 | $35,400 | 79.2 | 581 |
| **Greece** Athens | | 10.7 million | 50,942 | $32,000 | 79.6 | 480 |
| **Hungary** Budapest | | 9.9 million | 35,919 | $19,800 | 73.3 | 447 |
| **Iceland** Reykjavik | | 306,694 | 39,769 | $41,800 | 80.6 | 505 |
| **Ireland** Dublin | | 4.2 million | 27,135 | $45,300 | 78.2 | 406 |
| **Italy** Rome | | 58.1 million | 116,306 | $31,300 | 80.2 | 492 |
| **Kosovo** Pristina | | 1.8 million | 4,203 | $2,300 | 69.5 | Not available |
| **Latvia** Riga | | 2.2 million | 24,938 | $17,300 | 72 | 757 |
| **Liechtenstein** Vaduz | | 34,761 | 62 | $118,000 | 80 | 469 |
| **Lithuania** Vilnius | | 3.6 million | 25,174 | $17,800 | 74.8 | 422 |
| **Luxembourg** Luxembourg | | 491,775 | 998 | $81,000 | 79.3 | 599 |
| **Macedonia** Skopje | | 2 million | 9,781 | $9,100 | 74.6 | 273 |
| **Malta** Valletta | | 405,165 | 122 | $24,700 | 79.4 | 549 |
| **Moldova** Chişinau | | 4.3 million | 13,067 | $2,500 | 70.6 | 297 |
| **United States** Washington, D.C. | | 307.2 million | 3,718,711 | $46,900 | 78.2 | 844 |

| COUNTRY<br>Capital | FLAG | POPULATION | AREA<br>(sq mi) | PER CAPITA GDP<br>(U.S. $) | LIFE<br>EXPECTANCY<br>AT BIRTH | TVS PER 1,000<br>PEOPLE |
|---|---|---|---|---|---|---|
| **Monaco**<br>Monaco | | 32,965 | 1 | $30,000 | 80.1 | 758 |
| **Montenegro**<br>Cetinje, Podgorica | | 672,180 | 5,415 | $10,100 | 77.3 | Not<br>available |
| **Netherlands**<br>Amsterdam | | 16.7 million | 16,033 | $40,400 | 79.4 | 540 |
| **Norway**<br>Oslo | | 4.7 million | 125,182 | $59,300 | 79.9 | 653 |
| **Poland**<br>Warsaw | | 38.5 million | 120,728 | $17,300 | 75.6 | 387 |
| **Portugal**<br>Lisbon | | 10.7 million | 35,672 | $22,200 | 78.2 | 567 |
| **Romania**<br>Bucharest | | 22.2 million | 91,699 | $12,200 | 72.3 | 312 |
| **Russia**<br>Moscow | | 140 million | 6,592,772 | $16,100 | 66.2 | 421 |
| **San Marino**<br>San Marino | | 30,324 | 24 | $41,900 | 82 | 875 |
| **Serbia**<br>Belgrade | | 7.4 million | 39,518 | $10,800 | 75.4 | 277 |
| **Slovakia**<br>Bratislava | | 5.5 million | 18,859 | $21,900 | 75.3 | 418 |
| **Slovenia**<br>Ljubljana | | 2 million | 7,827 | $29,600 | 76.9 | 362 |
| **Spain**<br>Madrid | | 40.5 million | 194,897 | $34,700 | 80.1 | 555 |
| **Sweden**<br>Stockholm | | 9 million | 173,732 | $38,100 | 80.8 | 551 |
| **Switzerland**<br>Bern | | 7.6 million | 15,942 | $41,800 | 80.8 | 457 |
| **United States**<br>Washington, D.C. | | 307.2 million | 3,718,711 | $46,900 | 78.2 | 844 |

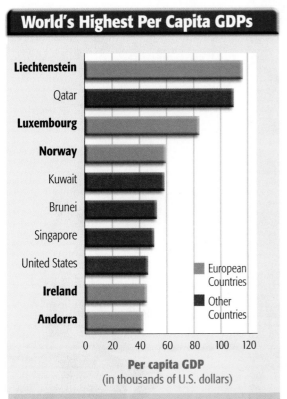

| COUNTRY / Capital | FLAG | POPULATION | AREA (sq mi) | PER CAPITA GDP (U.S. $) | LIFE EXPECTANCY AT BIRTH | TVS PER 1,000 PEOPLE |
|---|---|---|---|---|---|---|
| **Ukraine** Kiev | | 45.7 million | 233,090 | $7,400 | 68.2 | 433 |
| **United Kingdom** London | | 61.1 million | 94,526 | $36,500 | 79 | 661 |
| **Vatican City** Vatican City | | 826 | 0.17 | Not available | Not available | Not available |
| **United States** Washington, D.C. | | 307.2 million | 3,718,711 | $46,900 | 78.2 | 844 |

## World's Highest Per Capita GDPs

Liechtenstein
Qatar
Luxembourg
Norway
Kuwait
Brunei
Singapore
United States
Ireland
Andorra

0    20    40    60    80    100    120

**Per capita GDP**
(in thousands of U.S. dollars)

European Countries
Other Countries

Europe includes some of the wealthiest countries in the world. In fact, five of the ten countries with the highest per capita GDPs are in Europe.

## Densely Populated Countries: Europe

| Country | Population Density (per square mile) |
|---|---|
| Netherlands | 1,278 |
| Belgium | 891 |
| United Kingdom | 655 |
| Germany | 611 |
| Italy | 512 |
| Switzerland | 495 |
| Denmark | 336 |
| Poland | 327 |
| United States | 87 |

Many European countries are densely populated, especially when compared to the United States.

**ANALYSIS SKILL   ANALYZING INFORMATION**

1. What are the three most densely populated countries in Europe? How do their densities compare to that of the United States?
2. Which countries in Europe seem to have the lowest per capita GDPs? Look at the atlas political map. Where are these countries located in Europe?

# Early History of Europe

## 2000 BC–AD 1500

> **Essential Question** What are the major political and cultural legacies from Europe's early history?

## What You Will Learn...

In this chapter you will learn about three major periods in the early history of Europe. First you will learn about ancient Greece, a culture whose ideas still shape the world. Then you will learn about Rome, one of the most powerful civilizations in all of world history. Finally, you will read about the Middle Ages, a time of great changes in Europe.

### FOCUS ON READING AND WRITING

**Re-reading** Sometimes a single reading is not enough to fully understand a passage of text. If you feel like you do not fully understand a passage after you read it, it may help to re-read the passage more slowly. **See the lesson, Re-reading, on page 528.**

**Writing a Myth** A myth is a story that tries to explain why something happened. Throughout history, people have used myths to explain natural and historical events. After you read this chapter, you will write a myth that people might have used to explain a major event in European history.

---

### map zone

#### Geography Skills

**Place** Europe was home to some of the world's great civilizations.
1. **Locate** In what city was the Colosseum built?
2. **Analyze** Which of the buildings pictured on this map do you think is most impressive? Why?

W N E S

20°W

40°N

*ATLANTIC OCEAN*

**Greek trading ship**

10°W

30°N

**AFRICA**

**Greece** The ancient Greeks were known for their artwork. This vase shows Greek soldiers tending to horses.

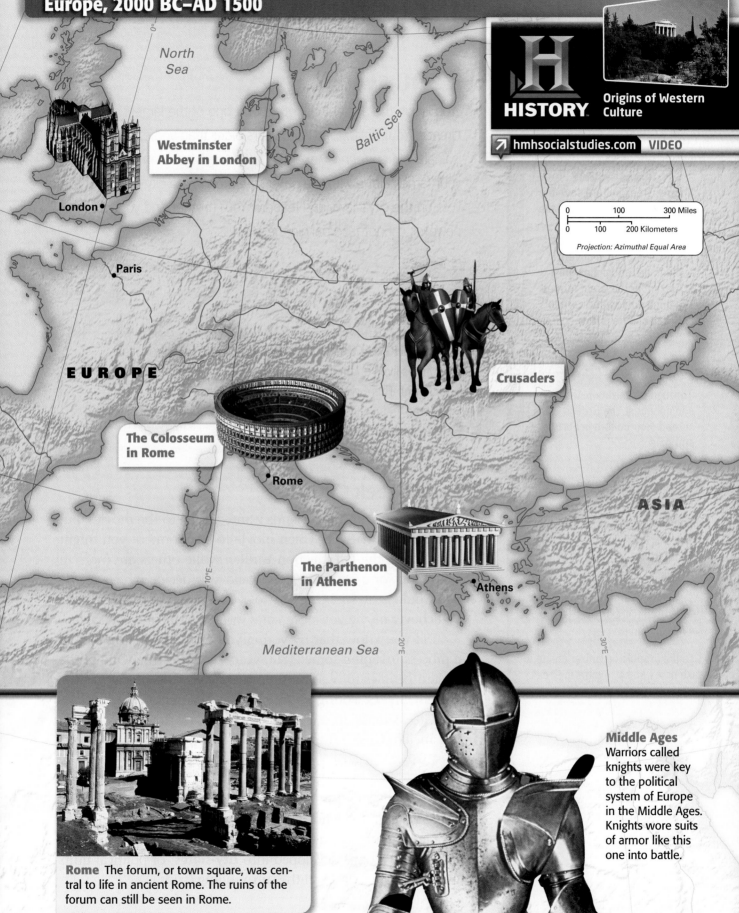

North
Sea

Baltic Sea

**Westminster Abbey in London**

London

Paris

E U R O P E

**The Colosseum in Rome**

Rome

**Crusaders**

A S I A

**The Parthenon in Athens**

Athens

Mediterranean Sea

10°E

20°E

30°E

**HISTORY** Origins of Western Culture

↗ hmhsocialstudies.com  VIDEO

0    100    300 Miles
0  100  200 Kilometers
*Projection: Azimuthal Equal Area*

**Rome** The forum, or town square, was central to life in ancient Rome. The ruins of the forum can still be seen in Rome.

**Middle Ages**
Warriors called knights were key to the political system of Europe in the Middle Ages. Knights wore suits of armor like this one into battle.

# Ancient Greece

## If YOU lived there...

You live in the ancient city of Athens, one of the largest cities in Greece. Your brother, just two years older than you, is excited. He is finally old enough to take part in the city's government. He and your father, along with the other free men in the city, will meet to vote on the city's laws and leaders. Your mother and your sisters, however, cannot take part in the process.

**Why is your brother excited about voting?**

**What You Will Learn...**

### Main Ideas

1. Early Greek culture saw the rise of the city-state and the creation of colonies.
2. The golden age of Greece saw advances in government, art, and philosophy.
3. Alexander the Great formed a huge empire and spread Greek culture into new areas.

### The Big Idea

Through colonization, trade, and conquest, the Greeks spread their culture in Europe and Asia.

### Key Terms and Places

city-states, *p. 310*
golden age, *p. 312*
Athens, *p. 313*
Sparta, *p. 315*
Hellenistic, *p. 316*

hmhsocialstudies.com
TAKING NOTES

Use the graphic organizer online to take notes on key events in Greek history.

**BUILDING BACKGROUND** In ancient times, people in most cultures lived under the rule of a king. In Greece, however, life was different. There was no ruler who held power over all of Greece. Instead, people lived in independent cities. Each of these cities had its own government, culture, and way of life.

## Early Greek Culture

Suppose you and some friends wanted to go to the movies, but you could not decide which movie to see. Some of you might want to see the latest action thriller, while others are more in the mood for a comedy. How could you decide which movie you would go to see? One way to decide would be to take a vote. Whichever movie got more votes would be the one you saw.

Did you know that by voting you would be taking part in a process invented some 2,500 years ago? It is true. One of the earliest peoples to use voting to make major decisions was the ancient Greeks. Voting was only one of the many contributions the Greeks made to our culture, though. In fact, many people call ancient Greece the birthplace of modern civilization.

### City-States

Early Greece could be a dangerous place. Waves of invaders swept through the land, and violence was common. Eventually, people began to band together in groups for protection. Over time, these groups developed into **city-states**, or political units made up of a city and all the surrounding lands.

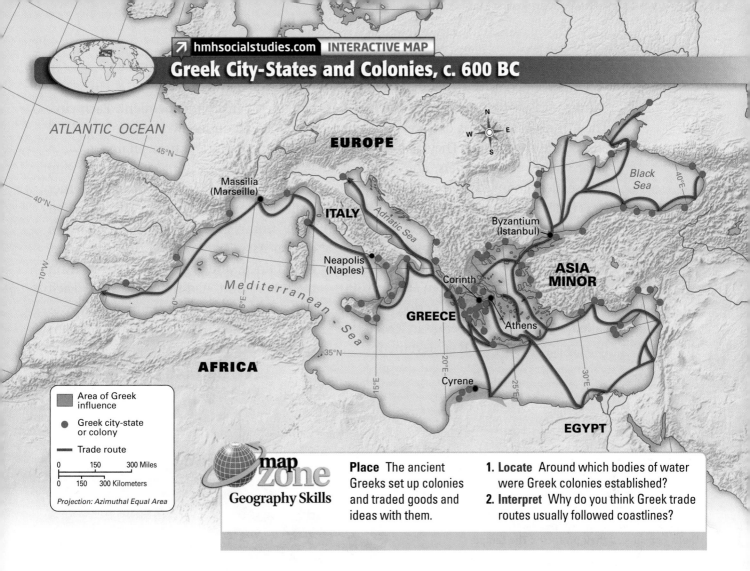

## Greek City-States and Colonies, c. 600 BC

ATLANTIC OCEAN

EUROPE

Massilia
(Marseille)

ITALY

Adriatic Sea

Byzantium
(Istanbul)

Black
Sea

Neapolis
(Naples)

Corinth

ASIA
MINOR

Mediterranean  Sea

GREECE

Athens

AFRICA

Cyrene

EGYPT

Area of Greek
influence

● Greek city-state
   or colony

— Trade route

0        150       300 Miles

0        150       300 Kilometers

Projection: Azimuthal Equal Area

**map zone Geography Skills**

**Place** The ancient Greeks set up colonies and traded goods and ideas with them.

1. **Locate** Around which bodies of water were Greek colonies established?
2. **Interpret** Why do you think Greek trade routes usually followed coastlines?

In the center of most city-states was a fortress on a hill. This hill was called the acropolis (uh-KRAH-puh-luhs), which is Greek for "top city." In addition to the fortress, many city-states built temples and other public buildings on the acropolis.

Around the acropolis was the rest of the city, including houses and markets. High walls usually surrounded the city for protection. In wartime, farmers who lived outside the walls could seek safety inside.

Living in city-states provided many advantages for the Greeks. The city was a place where people could meet and trade. In addition, the city-state gave people a new sense of identity. People thought of themselves as residents of a particular city-state, not as Greeks.

## Colonies

In time, some city-states established new outposts, or colonies, around the Black and Mediterranean seas. You can see these colonies on the map above. Some of them still exist today as modern cities, such as Naples, Italy, and Marseille, France.

Although they were independent, most colonies kept ties with the older cities of Greece. They traded goods and shared ideas. These ties helped strengthen the economies of both cities and colonies, and they kept Greek culture strong. Because they stayed in contact, Greek cities all over Europe shared a common culture.

**READING CHECK  Summarizing** Where did the ancient Greeks establish colonies?

## The Golden Age of Greece

When most people think of ancient Greek culture today, certain images come to mind. They think of the ruins of stately temples and of realistic statues. They also think of great writers, philosophers, and scientists whose ideas changed the world.

These images represent some of the many contributions the Greeks made to world history. Remarkably, most of these contributions were developed during a relatively short time, between 500 and 300 BC. For that reason, this period is often called a **golden age**, a period in a society's history marked by great achievements.

HISTORY

**VIDEO**
Mysteries and Discoveries

hmhsocialstudies.com

### The Growth of Greek Power

Early in Greece's history, city-states remained fiercely independent. Each city-state focused on its own concerns and did not interfere in the others' affairs.

Around 500 BC, however, an invading army caused the Greeks to band together against a common enemy. That invasion came from Persia, a powerful empire in central Asia. The Persian army was huge, well-trained, and experienced. Greece, on the other hand, had no single army. Each city-state had an army, but none was as large as Persia's. As a result, the Persians expected a quick victory.

**Close-up**

## The Parthenon

**The Parthenon is often seen as a symbol of ancient Athens. It was a beautiful temple to the goddess Athena, whom the people of Athens considered their protector. The temple is now in ruins, but this illustration shows how it may have looked when it was built around 440 BC.**

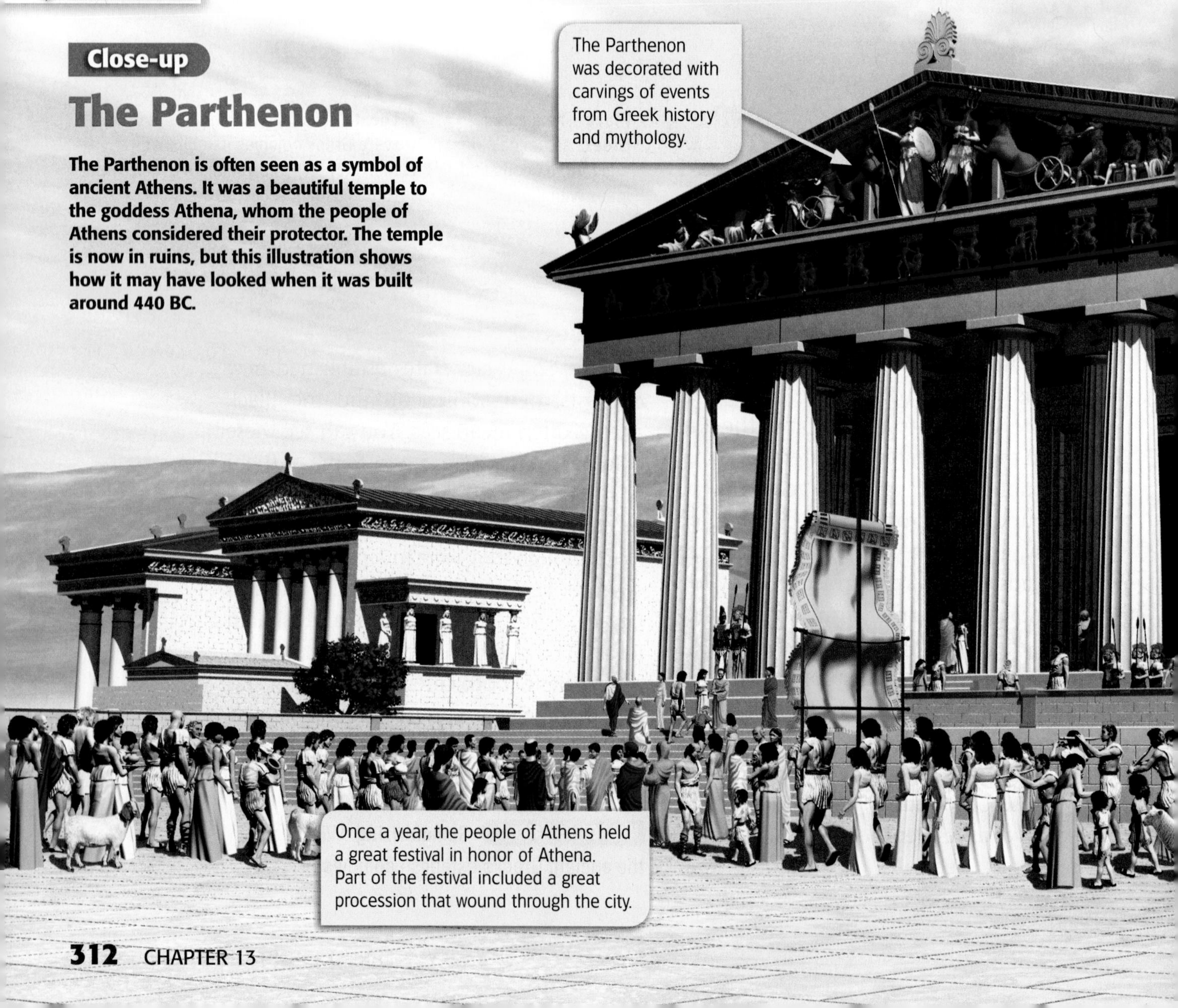

The Parthenon was decorated with carvings of events from Greek history and mythology.

Once a year, the people of Athens held a great festival in honor of Athena. Part of the festival included a great procession that wound through the city.

Nevertheless, the Greeks took up arms against the Persians. Led by **Athens**, a city-state in eastern Greece, the Greeks were able to defeat the Persians and keep Greece from being conquered. When the Persians invaded again 10 years later, the Athenians once again helped defeat them.

The victory over the Persians increased the confidence of people all over Greece. They realized that they were capable of great achievements. In the period after the Persian invasion, the people of Greece made amazing advances in art, writing, and thinking. Many of these advances were made by the people of Athens.

## Athenian Culture

In the century after the defeat of Persia, Athens was the cultural center of Greece. Some of history's most famous politicians, artists, and thinkers lived in Athens during this time.

One reason for the great advances the Athenians made during this time was their city's leadership. Leaders such as Pericles (PER-uh-kleez), who ruled Athens in the 400s BC, supported the arts and encouraged the creation of great works. For example, Pericles hired great architects and artists to construct and decorate the Parthenon, the temple shown below.

Inside the Parthenon was a magnificent statue of Athena by the sculptor Phidias. Many people consider him the greatest sculptor in all of Greece.

Like most Greek temples, the Parthenon had huge marble columns to support its roof.

**ANALYSIS SKILL** **ANALYZING VISUALS**

Why do you think people consider the Parthenon to be a symbol of ancient Athens?

# Athenian Democracy

Athens was governed as a democracy. Once a month, all adult men in the city gathered together in an assembly to make the city's laws.

Men spoke in the assembly to support or argue against ideas. Sometimes, people in the crowd argued with them.

Voting was done either by show of hands or by secret ballot. The ballots used were broken pieces of pottery.

## BIOGRAPHY

### Pericles
(c. 495–429 BC)

Pericles, the most famous leader in all of Athenian history, wanted the city's people to be proud of their city. In his speeches, he emphasized the greatness of Athenian democracy and encouraged everyone to take part. He also worked to make the city beautiful. He hired the city's best architects to build monuments, such as the Parthenon, and hired great artists to decorate them. He also supported the work of writers and poets in order to make Athens the cultural center of all Greece.

## Athenian Democracy

Leaders like Pericles had great power in Athens, but they did not rule alone. The city of Athens was a democracy, and its leaders were elected. In fact, Athens was the world's first democracy. No one else in history had created a government in which people ruled themselves.

In Athens most power was in the hands of the people. All the city's leaders could do was suggest ideas. Those ideas had to be approved by an assembly made up of the city's free men before they were enacted. As a result, it was vital that all the men of Athens took part in making government decisions.

The people of Athens were very proud of their democracy, and also of their city in general. This pride was reflected in their city's buildings and art.

Turn back to the previous page and look at the picture of the Parthenon again. Why do you think the temple was so large and so elaborately decorated? Like many Greek buildings, it was designed to be a symbol of the city. It was supposed to make people see Athens as a great and glorious city.

## Architecture and Art

The Parthenon may be the most famous building from ancient Greece, but it is only one of many magnificent structures built by the Greeks. All over Greece, builders created beautiful marble temples. These temples were symbols of the glory of the cities in which they were built.

Greek temples and other buildings were often decorated with statues and carvings. These works by Greek artists are still admired by people today.

Greek art is so admired because of the skill and careful preparation of ancient Greek artists. These artists wanted their works to look realistic. To achieve their goals, they watched people as they stood and moved. They wanted to learn exactly what the human body looked like while it was in motion. The artists then used what they learned from their observations to make their statues as lifelike as possible.

## Science, Philosophy, and Literature

Artists were not the only people in ancient Greece to study other people. Scientists, for example, studied people to learn how the body worked. Through these studies, the Greeks learned a great deal about medicine and biology. Other Greek scholars made great advances in math, astronomy, and other areas of science.

Greek philosophers, or thinkers, also studied people. They wanted to figure out how people could be happy. Three of the world's most influential philosophers—Socrates, Plato, and Aristotle—lived and taught in Athens during this time. Their ideas continue to shape how we live and think even today.

The ancient Greeks also made huge contributions to world literature. Some of the world's timeless classics were written in ancient Greece. They include stories of Greek heroes and their daring adventures, poems about love and friendship, and myths meant to teach lessons about life. Chances are that you have read a book, seen a film, or watched a play inspired by—or even written by—the ancient Greeks.

Actually, if you have ever seen a play at all then you have the Greeks to thank. The ancient Greeks were the first people to write and perform drama, or plays. Once a part of certain religious ceremonies, plays became one of the most popular forms of entertainment in Greece.

## The Decline of the City-States

As great as it was, the Greek golden age could not last forever. In the end, Greece was torn apart by a war between Athens and its rival city-state, **Sparta**.

Sparta was a military city with one of the strongest armies in Greece. Jealous of the influence Athens had over other city-states, the Spartans attacked Athens.

The war between these two powerful city-states devastated Greece. Other city-states joined the war, supporting one side or the other. For years the war went on. In the end, Sparta won, but Greece was in shambles. Thousands of people had been killed and whole cities had been destroyed. Weakened, Greece lay open for a foreign conqueror to swoop in and take over.

**READING CHECK** **Analyzing** Why is the period between 500 and 300 BC called a golden age in Greece?

### Greek Art

The ancient Greeks took great care to make their art lifelike. This statue shows Athena, a goddess from Greek mythology.

**ANALYZING VISUALS** What details make this statue lifelike?

# The Empire of Alexander

In fact, a conqueror did take over all of Greece in the 330s BC. For the first time in its history, all of Greece was unified under a single ruler. He was from an area called Macedonia just north of Greece, an area that many Greeks considered uncivilized. He was known as Alexander the Great.

## Alexander's Conquests

Alexander swept into Greece with a strong, well-trained army in 336 BC. In just a few years, he had conquered all of Greece.

Alexander, however, was not satisfied to rule only Greece. He wanted to create a huge empire. In 334 BC he set out to do just that. As you can see on the map, he was quite successful.

At its greatest extent, Alexander's empire stretched from Greece in the west all the way to India in the east. It included nearly all of central Asia—including what had been the Persian Empire—and Egypt. Alexander had dreams of extending his empire even farther east, but his troops refused to keep fighting. Tired and far from home, they demanded that Alexander turn back. He did, turning back toward home in 325 BC. On his way back home, however, Alexander became ill and died. He was 33.

## The Spread of Greek Culture

**FOCUS ON READING**

After you read this passage, reread it to make sure you understand all the details.

During his life, Alexander wanted Greek culture to spread throughout his empire. To help the culture spread, he built cities in the lands he conquered and urged Greek people to move there. He named many of the cities Alexandria after himself.

As Greek people moved to these cities, however, they mingled with the people and cultures in the area. As a result, Greek culture blended with other cultures. The result was a new type of culture that mixed elements from many people and places.

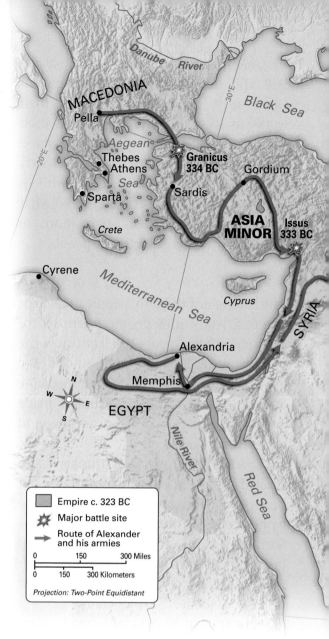

Empire c. 323 BC

Major battle site

Route of Alexander and his armies

0     150     300 Miles

0     150     300 Kilometers

Projection: Two-Point Equidistant

Because the Greek word for Greek is Hellenic, historians often refer to these blended cultures as **Hellenistic**, or Greek-like. Hellenistic culture helped shape life in Egypt, central Asia, and other parts of the world for many years.

**READING CHECK** Finding Main Ideas What lands were included in Alexander's empire?

**SUMMARY AND PREVIEW** Greece was the location of the first great civilization in Europe. In time, though, it was defeated by a new power, the Roman Empire.

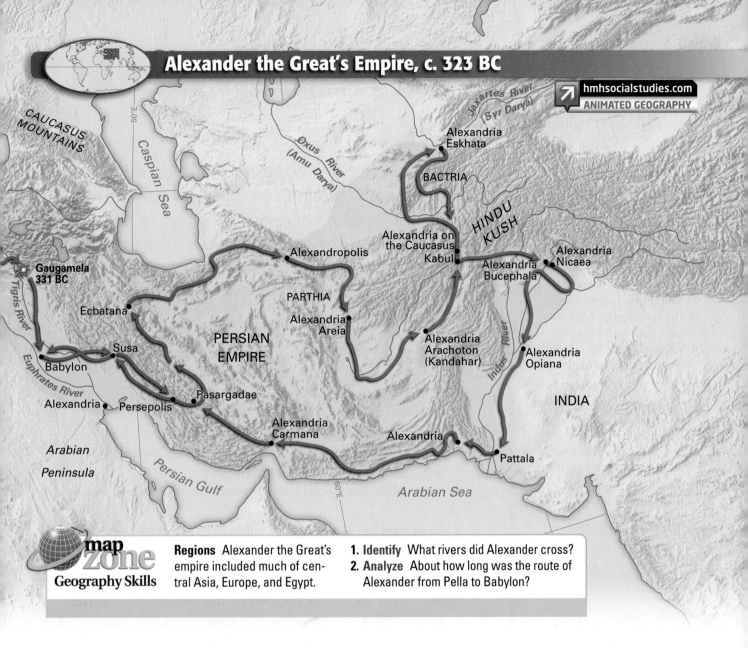

hmhsocialstudies.com
ANIMATED GEOGRAPHY

CAUCASUS MOUNTAINS

Caspian Sea

Jaxartes River (Syr Darya)

Oxus River (Amu Darya)

Alexandria Eskhata

BACTRIA

HINDU KUSH

Alexandropolis

Alexandria on the Caucasus
Kabul

Alexandria Nicaea

Alexandria Bucephala

Gaugamela 331 BC

Tigris River

PARTHIA

Ecbatana

PERSIAN EMPIRE

Alexandria Areia

Alexandria Arachoton (Kandahar)

Indus River

Alexandria Opiana

Euphrates River

Babylon

Susa

Alexandria

Persepolis
Pasargadae

Persian Gulf

INDIA

Alexandria Carmana

Alexandria

Pattala

Arabian Peninsula

Arabian Sea

60°E

map zone
Geography Skills

**Regions** Alexander the Great's empire included much of central Asia, Europe, and Egypt.

1. **Identify** What rivers did Alexander cross?
2. **Analyze** About how long was the route of Alexander from Pella to Babylon?

---

## Section 1 Assessment

hmhsocialstudies.com
ONLINE QUIZ

### Reviewing Ideas, Terms, and Places

1. **a. Describe** What did an ancient Greek **city-state** include?
   **b. Explain** Why did the Greeks form city-states?
2. **a. Identify** What were some major achievements in Greece between 500 and 300 BC?
   **b. Summarize** What was the government of ancient Athens like?
   **c. Evaluate** Would you have liked living in ancient Greece? Why or why not?
3. **a. Describe** How did Alexander the Great try to spread Greek culture in his empire?
   **b. Drawing Conclusions** How might Greek history have been different if Alexander had not existed?

### Critical Thinking

4. **Analyzing** Using your notes, draw a time line of major events in Greek history. For each event you list on your time line, write a sentence explaining why it was important.

### FOCUS ON WRITING

5. **Choosing Characters** Many ancient myths focused on the deeds of heroes or other great figures. What people from ancient Greece might feature in such a myth? Write some ideas in your notebook.

# The Roman World

## What You Will Learn...

### Main Ideas

1. The Roman Republic was governed by elected leaders.
2. The Roman Empire was a time of great achievements.
3. The spread of Chrisitianity began during the empire.
4. Various factors helped bring about the decline of Rome.

### The Big Idea

The Romans unified parts of Europe, Africa, and Asia in one of the ancient world's greatest civilizations.

### Key Terms and Places

Rome, *p. 318*
republic, *p. 319*
Senate, *p. 319*
citizens, *p. 319*
Carthage, *p. 320*
empire, *p. 320*
aqueducts, *p. 322*

hmhsocialstudies.com
**TAKING NOTES**

Use the graphic organizer online to take notes on Roman history and culture.

## If YOU lived there...

You live in Rome in about 50 BC. Times are difficult for ordinary Romans. Bread is scarce in the city, and you are finding it hard to find work. Now a popular general is mounting a campaign to cross the mountains into a territory called Gaul. He wants to try to conquer the barbarians who live there. It might be dangerous, but being a soldier guarantees work and a chance to make money.

**Will you join the army? Why or why not?**

**BUILDING BACKGROUND** Rome's well-trained army helped it conquer large parts of Europe, Africa, and Asia. Through these conquests, Rome built a long-lasting empire that left its mark on the languages, cultures, and government of Europe.

## The Roman Republic

"All roads lead to Rome." "Rome was not built in a day." "When in Rome, do as the Romans do." Have you heard these sayings before? All of them were inspired by the civilization of ancient Rome, a civilization that collapsed more than 1,500 years ago.

Why would people today use sayings that relate to so old a culture? They refer to Rome because it was one of the greatest and most influential civilizations in history. In fact, we can still see the influence of ancient Rome in our lives.

### Rome's Early History

Rome was not always so influential, however. At first it was just a small city in Italy. According to legend, the city of **Rome** was established in the year 753 BC by a group called the Latins.

For many years, the Romans were ruled by kings. Not all of these kings were Latin, though. For many years the Romans were ruled by a group called the Etruscans. The Romans learned a great deal from the Etruscans. For example, they learned about written language and how to build paved roads and sewers. Building on what they learned from the Etruscans, the Romans made Rome into a large and successful city.

## The Beginning of the Republic

Not all of Rome's kings were good leaders, or good people. Some were cruel, harsh, and unfair. The last king of Rome was so unpopular that he was overthrown. In 509 BC a group of Roman nobles forced the king to flee the city.

In place of the king the people of Rome created a new type of government. They formed a **republic**, a type of government in which people elect leaders to make laws for them. Once elected, these leaders made all government decisions.

To help make some decisions, Rome's leaders looked to the **Senate**, a council of rich and powerful Romans who helped run the city. By advising the city's leaders, the Senate gained much influence in Rome.

For Rome's republican government to succeed, **citizens**, or people who could take part in the government, needed to be active. Rome's leaders encouraged citizens to vote and to run for office. As a result, speeches and debates were common in the city. One popular place for these activities was in the forum, the city's public square.

**VIDEO**
The Glory of
Rome's Forum

↗ hmhsocialstudies.com

**Close-up**

# The Roman Forum

The forum was a large public square that stood in the center of the city. Roman citizens often met in the forum to discuss city affairs and politics.

Government buildings and temples stood on the hills around the forum.

Only citizens, or people who could vote, were allowed to wear this article of clothing, called a toga.

Many people met in the forum to discuss politics, current affairs, and other issues.

**ANALYSIS SKILL** **ANALYZING VISUALS**

What are some places in your local community that serve the same function as the forum did?

FOCUS ON
READING
After you read
this passage,
re-read it. Make a
list of details you
did not notice in
your first reading.

## Growth and Conquest

After the creation of the republic, the Romans began to expand their territory. They started this expansion in Italy. As the map at right shows, however, the republic kept growing. By 100 BC the Romans ruled much of the Mediterranean world.

The Romans were able to take so much land because of their strong, organized army. They used this army to conquer their rivals. For example, the Romans fought the people of **Carthage**, a city in North Africa, and took over their lands.

Rome's expansion did not stop in 100 BC. In the 40s BC a general named Julius Caesar conquered many new lands for Rome. Caesar's conquests made him very powerful and very popular in Rome. Afraid of Caesar's power, a group of Senators decided to put an end to it. They banded together and killed Caesar in 44 BC.

**READING CHECK** **Summarizing** How did the Romans expand their territory?

# The Roman Empire

The murder of Julius Caesar changed Roman society completely. The Romans were shocked and horrified by his death, and they wanted Caesar's murderers to be punished. One of the people they called on to punish the murderers was Caesar's adopted son, Octavian. Octavian's actions would reshape the Roman world. Under his leadership, Rome changed from a republic to an **empire**, a government that includes many different peoples and lands under a single rule.

## The First Emperor

Octavian moved quickly to punish his uncle's murderers. He led an army against them and, before long, defeated them all.

After defeating his enemies, Octavian became more powerful. One by one, he eliminated his rivals for power. Eventually, Octavian alone ruled the entire Roman world as Rome's first emperor.

## Roman Conquests

The Roman army was both powerful and flexible, which allowed it to take on and defeat many foes. Even the huge elephants ridden by the soldiers of Carthage were no match for the Romans' bravery and cleverness.

**ANALYZING VISUALS** What kind of equipment did the Roman army use?

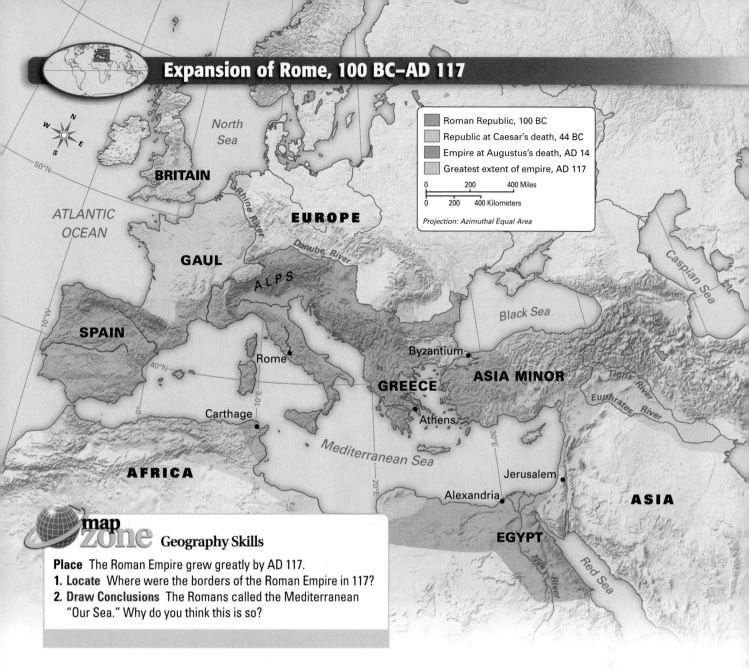

## Expansion of Rome, 100 BC–AD 117

Roman Republic, 100 BC
Republic at Caesar's death, 44 BC
Empire at Augustus's death, AD 14
Greatest extent of empire, AD 117

0      200      400 Miles
0    200    400 Kilometers

Projection: Azimuthal Equal Area

ATLANTIC OCEAN
North Sea
BRITAIN
EUROPE
GAUL
Rhine River
ALPS
Danube River
Black Sea
Caspian Sea
SPAIN
Rome
Byzantium
ASIA MINOR
GREECE
Tigris River
Euphrates River
Carthage
Athens
AFRICA
Mediterranean Sea
Jerusalem
ASIA
Alexandria
EGYPT
Nile River
Red Sea

### map zone Geography Skills

**Place** The Roman Empire grew greatly by AD 117.
**1. Locate** Where were the borders of the Roman Empire in 117?
**2. Draw Conclusions** The Romans called the Mediterranean "Our Sea." Why do you think this is so?

As emperor, Octavian was given a new name, Augustus, which means "honored one." The people of Rome respected and admired Augustus. This respect was mainly the result of his many accomplishments. As the map above shows, Augustus added a great deal of territory to the empire. He also made many improvements to lands already in the empire. For example, he built monuments and public buildings in the city of Rome. He also improved and expanded Rome's network of roads, which **facilitated** both travel and trade.

## The Pax Romana

The emperors who ruled after Augustus tried to follow his example. Some of them worked to add even more land to the empire. Others focused their attentions on improving Roman society.

Because of these emperors' efforts, Rome experienced a long period of peace and achievement. There were no major wars or rebellions within the empire, and trade increased. This period, which lasted for about 200 years, was called the Pax Romana, or the Roman Peace.

ACADEMIC VOCABULARY
**facilitate**
(fuh-SI-luh-tayt)
to make easier

## Built to Last

Think about the buildings in your neighborhood. Can you imagine any of them still standing 1,000 years from now? The ancient Romans could. Many structures that they built nearly 2,000 years ago are still standing today. How is that possible?

The Romans knew many techniques for building strong, long-lasting structures. Look at the Colosseum, pictured here. Notice how many arches were used in its design. Arches are one of the strongest shapes you can use in construction, a fact the Romans knew well. They also invented materials like cement to make their buildings stronger.

**Making Generalizations** How did technology help the Romans build strong and lasting structures?

hmhsocialstudies.com
ANIMATED
GEOGRAPHY
Roman
Aqueduct

## Roman Building and Engineering

Because the Pax Romana was a time of stability, the Romans were able to make great cultural achievements. Some of the advances made during this time continue to affect our lives even today.

One of the areas in which the Romans made visible advances was architecture. The Romans were great builders, and many of their structures have stood for centuries. In fact, you can still see Roman buildings in Europe today, almost 2,000 years after they were built. This is because the Romans were skilled engineers who knew how to make their buildings strong.

Buildings are not the only structures that the Romans built to last. Ancient roads, bridges, and **aqueducts**—channels used to carry water over long distances—are still seen all over Europe. Planned by skilled Roman engineers, many of these structures are still in use.

## Roman Language and Law

Not all Roman achievements are as easy to see as buildings, however. For example, the Romans greatly influenced how we speak, write, and think even today. Many of the languages spoken in Europe today, such as Spanish, French, and Italian, are based on Latin, the Romans' language. English, too, has adopted many words from Latin.

The Romans used the Latin language to create great works of literature. Among these works were some of the world's most famous plays, poems, and stories. Many of them are read and enjoyed by millions of people around the world today.

Even more important to the world than their literary achievements, however, were the Romans' political contributions. All around the world, people use legal systems based on ancient Roman law. In some countries, the entire government is based largely on the ancient Roman system.

One such country is the United States. The founders of our country admired the Roman government and used it as a model for our government. Like ancient Rome, the United States is a republic. We elect our leaders and trust them to make our laws. Also like the Romans, we require all people to obey a set of basic written laws. In ancient Rome, these laws were carved on stone tablets and kept on display. In the United States, they are written down in a document, the Constitution.

**READING CHECK** Finding Main Ideas What were some of the Romans' main achievements?

## The Spread of Christianity

In addition to art and law, the ancient Romans also had a tremendous influence on religion. One of the world's major religions, Christianity, first appeared and spread in the Roman world.

### The Beginnings of Christianity

Christianity is based on the life, actions, and teachings of Jesus of Nazareth. He and his early followers lived in the Roman territory of Judea in southwest Asia. They converted many people in Jerusalem and other cities in Judea to Christianity.

However, Christianity quickly spread far beyond the borders of Judea. Jesus's followers traveled widely, preaching and spreading his teachings. Through their efforts, communities of Christians began to appear in cities throughout the Roman world. Christian ideas spread quickly through these cities, as more and more people converted to Christianity.

### Persecution and Acceptance

The rapid spread of Christianity worried some Roman leaders. They feared that Christianity would soon grow larger than all other religions in the empire. If that ever happened, they feared, the Christians might rebel and take over Rome.

To prevent a rebellion, some emperors began to persecute, or punish, Christians. They arrested, fined, or even killed any Christians they found.

The persecution did not cause people to abandon Christianity, however. Instead, Christians began to meet in secret, hiding their religion from the government.

Eventually, the persecution was ended. In the 300s a powerful emperor named Constantine became a Christian himself. Once the emperor had converted, the Christian faith was openly accepted even more widely in the empire. Look at the map below to see how Christianity spread between 300 and 400.

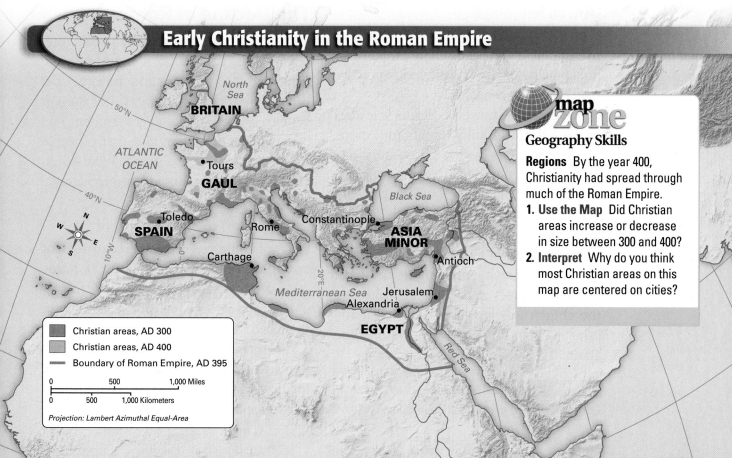

## Early Christianity in the Roman Empire

North Sea

BRITAIN

ATLANTIC OCEAN

Tours

GAUL

Toledo

SPAIN

Rome

Carthage

Constantinople

Black Sea

ASIA MINOR

Antioch

Jerusalem

Alexandria

Mediterranean Sea

EGYPT

Red Sea

50°N

40°N

10°W

20°E

- Christian areas, AD 300
- Christian areas, AD 400
- Boundary of Roman Empire, AD 395

0    500    1,000 Miles
0  500  1,000 Kilometers

Projection: Lambert Azimuthal Equal-Area

### map zone

**Geography Skills**

**Regions** By the year 400, Christianity had spread through much of the Roman Empire.

1. **Use the Map** Did Christian areas increase or decrease in size between 300 and 400?
2. **Interpret** Why do you think most Christian areas on this map are centered on cities?

## The Decline of Rome

Beginning around 200, the once-mighty Roman Empire began to weaken. Factors from inside and outside the empire caused many problems for Rome's leaders and led to the empire's collapse in the late 400s.

Barbarian invaders

### Reasons for the Decline of Rome

- Poor leaders cared less for the people of Rome than they did for their own happiness.
- Taxes and prices rose, increasing poverty.
- People became less loyal to Rome.
- Military leaders fought each other for power.
- The empire was too large for a single person to govern well.
- Barbarians invaded the empire from outside.

**ANALYSIS SKILL** **ANALYZING VISUALS**

Which factors in Rome's decline were internal? Which came from outside the empire?

### Official Religion

Even after Constantine became Christian, many people in the Roman Empire did not convert. Romans continued to practice many different religions.

Over time, however, Rome's leaders supported Christianity more and more. By the 380s, support for Christianity had grown so much that an emperor chose to ban all other religions. With that ban, Christianity was the only religion allowed in the Roman Empire.

By the end of the 300s, the Christian church had grown into one of the most influential forces in the Roman world. As the church was growing, however, many other parts of Roman society were falling apart. The Roman Empire was ending.

**READING CHECK** **Sequencing** How did the Christian church gain influence in Rome?

## The Decline of Rome

Rome's problems had actually started long before 300. For about a century, crime rates had been rising and poverty had been increasing. In addition, the Roman systems of education and government had begun breaking down, and many people no longer felt loyal to Rome. What could have happened to cause these problems?

### Problems in the Government

Many of Rome's problems were the result of poor government. After about 200, Rome was ruled by a series of bad emperors. Most of these emperors were more interested in their own happiness than in ruling well. Some simply ignored the needs of the Roman people. Others raised taxes to pay for new buildings or wars, driving many Romans into poverty.

Frustrated by these bad emperors, some military leaders tried to take over and rule Rome in their place. In most cases, though, these military leaders were no better than the emperors they replaced. Most of them were poor leaders. In addition, fighting between rival military leaders almost led to civil war on many occasions.

Rome did have a few good emperors who worked furiously to save the empire. One emperor feared that the empire had grown too large for one person to rule. To correct this problem, he divided the empire in half and named a co-ruler to help govern. Later, the emperor Constantine built a new capital, Constantinople, in what is now Turkey, nearer to the center of the Roman Empire. He thought that ruling from a central location would help keep the empire together. These measures helped restore order for a time, but they were not enough to save the Roman Empire.

## Invasions

Although internal problems weakened the empire, they alone probably would not have destroyed it. However, as the empire was getting weaker from within, invaders from outside also began to attack in the late 300s and 400s. Already suffering from their own problems, the Romans could not fight off these invasions.

Most Roman people considered the various groups who invaded their empire barbarians, uncivilized and backward. In truth, however, some of these so-called barbarian groups had their own complex societies and strong, capable leaders. As a result, they were able to defeat Roman armies and take lands away from the empire. In the end, the barbarians were even able to attack and destroy the city of Rome itself. In 476 the last emperor of Rome was overthrown and replaced by the leader of an invading group.

Most historians consider the capture of the Roman emperor in 476 the end of the Roman Empire in western Europe. Although people continued to think of themselves as Romans, there was no empire to tie them together. As a result, European society slowly broke apart.

**READING CHECK** **Generalizing** Why did the Roman Empire decline?

**SUMMARY AND PREVIEW** In this section you learned that the Romans brought a vast territory under one government. Next, you will learn what happened after that government collapsed, in a period called the Middle Ages.

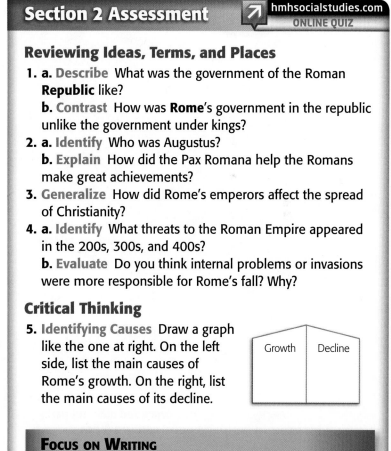

## Section 2 Assessment

### Reviewing Ideas, Terms, and Places

1. **a. Describe** What was the government of the Roman **Republic** like?
   **b. Contrast** How was **Rome**'s government in the republic unlike the government under kings?
2. **a. Identify** Who was Augustus?
   **b. Explain** How did the Pax Romana help the Romans make great achievements?
3. **Generalize** How did Rome's emperors affect the spread of Christianity?
4. **a. Identify** What threats to the Roman Empire appeared in the 200s, 300s, and 400s?
   **b. Evaluate** Do you think internal problems or invasions were more responsible for Rome's fall? Why?

### Critical Thinking

5. **Identifying Causes** Draw a graph like the one at right. On the left side, list the main causes of Rome's growth. On the right, list the main causes of its decline.

Growth | Decline

### FOCUS ON WRITING

6. **Finding a Setting** Where will your myth be set? Think back over this section and the previous one to find an appropriate location for your myth.

# Geography and History

# Roman Roads

The Romans are famous for their roads. They built a road network so large and well constructed that parts of it remain today, roughly 2,000 years later. Roads helped the Romans run their empire. Armies, travelers, messengers, and merchants all used the roads to get around. They stretched to every corner of the empire in a network so vast that people even today say that "all roads lead to Rome."

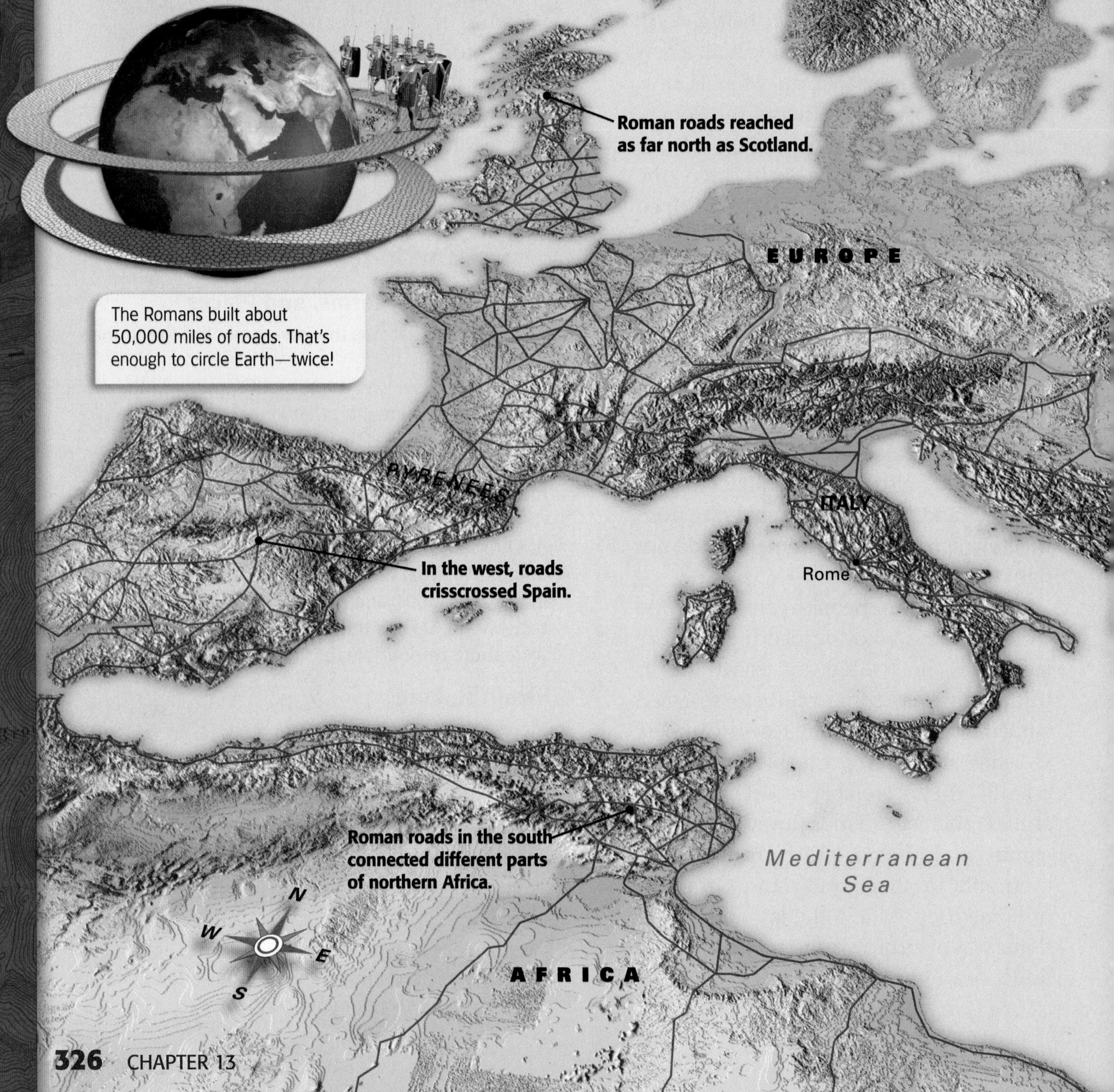

Roman roads reached as far north as Scotland.

The Romans built about 50,000 miles of roads. That's enough to circle Earth—twice!

EUROPE

PYRENEES

ITALY

Rome

In the west, roads crisscrossed Spain.

Roman roads in the south connected different parts of northern Africa.

Mediterranean Sea

AFRICA

N
W        E
S

Paving stones

Drainage ditch

Curbstones

Sand, clay, and gravel

Stone chips

Gravel concrete

Roman roads were built to last. They were constructed of layers of sand, concrete, rock, and stone. Drainage ditches let water drain off, preventing water damage.

The roads were built by and for the military. The main purpose of the roads was to allow Rome's armies to travel quickly throughout the empire.

**In the east, Roman roads stretched into Southwest Asia.**

The Romans built tall "milestones" along their roads to mark distances. Just like modern highway signs, the markers told travelers how far it was to the next town.

**ANALYSIS SKILL | ANALYZING VISUALS**

1. **Movement** Why did the Romans build their roads?
2. **Location** How does the map show that "all roads lead to Rome"?

# The Middle Ages

## What You Will Learn...

### Main Ideas

1. The Christian church influenced nearly every aspect of society in the Middle Ages.
2. Complicated political and economic systems governed life in the Middle Ages.
3. The period after 1000 was a time of great changes in medieval society.

### The Big Idea

Christianity and social systems influenced life in Europe in the Middle Ages.

### Key Terms and Places

Middle Ages, *p. 328*
pope, *p. 329*
Crusade, *p. 329*
Holy Land, *p. 329*
Gothic architecture, *p. 330*
feudal system, *p. 331*
manor, *p. 332*
nation-state, *p. 335*

hmhsocialstudies.com
**TAKING NOTES**

Use the graphic organizer online to take notes on medieval society.

## If YOU lived there...

You are the youngest child of a noble family in medieval France. One day your father tells you that you are being sent to the court of another noble family. There you will learn fine manners and proper behavior. You will also learn music and drawing. You know it is a great honor, but you will miss your own home.

**How do you feel about this change in your life?**

**BUILDING BACKGROUND** When people think of the Middle Ages today, they usually think of castles, princesses, and knights in shining armor. Although these were all part of the Middle Ages, they do not tell the whole story. The Middle Ages was a time of great change in Europe, as the influence of the ancient world faded away.

## The Christian Church and Society

When historians talk about the past, they often divide it into three long periods. The first period is the ancient world, the time of the world's earliest civilizations, such as Egypt, China, Greece, and Rome. The last period historians call the modern world, the world since about 1500. Since that time, new ideas and contacts between civilizations changed the world completely.

What happened between ancient and modern times? We call this period, which lasted from about 500 until about 1500, the **Middle Ages**. We also call it the medieval (mee-DEE-vuhl) period. The word *medieval* comes from two Latin words that mean "middle age." It was a time of great changes in Europe, many of them inspired by the Christian church.

### The Importance of the Church

When the Roman Empire fell apart in the late 400s, the people of Europe were left without a single dominant government to unite them. In the absence of strong leaders, Europe broke into many small kingdoms. Each of these kingdoms had its own laws, customs, and language. Europe was no longer the same place it had been under the Romans.

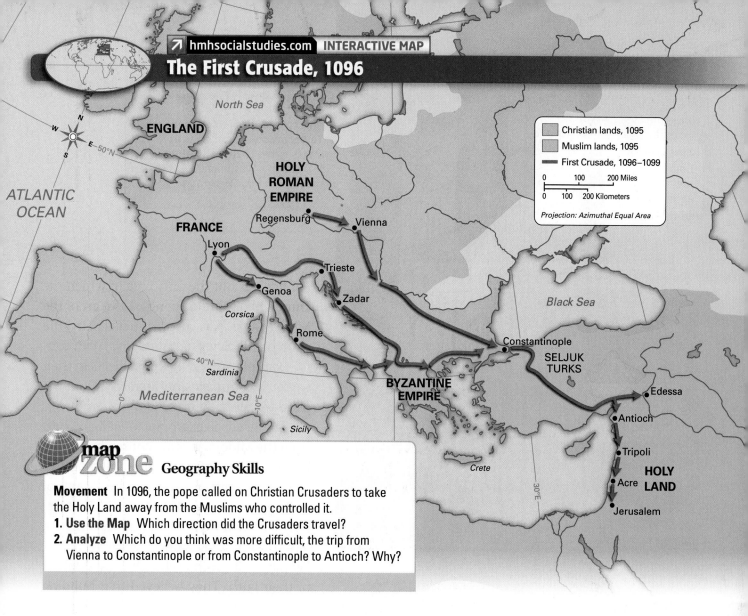

## The First Crusade, 1096

↗ hmhsocialstudies.com **INTERACTIVE MAP**

North Sea

ENGLAND

ATLANTIC OCEAN

HOLY ROMAN EMPIRE

FRANCE

Regensburg

Vienna

Lyon

Trieste

Genoa

Zadar

Corsica

Rome

Sardinia

Mediterranean Sea

Sicily

Black Sea

Constantinople

SELJUK TURKS

BYZANTINE EMPIRE

Crete

Edessa

Antioch

Tripoli

Acre

HOLY LAND

Jerusalem

Christian lands, 1095
Muslim lands, 1095
First Crusade, 1096–1099

0    100    200 Miles
0    100    200 Kilometers

Projection: Azimuthal Equal Area

### map zone Geography Skills

**Movement** In 1096, the pope called on Christian Crusaders to take the Holy Land away from the Muslims who controlled it.
1. **Use the Map** Which direction did the Crusaders travel?
2. **Analyze** Which do you think was more difficult, the trip from Vienna to Constantinople or from Constantinople to Antioch? Why?

One factor, however, continued to tie the people of Europe together—religion. Nearly everyone in Europe was Christian, and so most Europeans felt tied together by their beliefs. Over time, the number of Christians in Europe increased. People came to feel more and more like part of a single religious community.

Because Christianity was so important in Europe, the Christian church gained a great deal of influence. In time, the church began to influence the politics, art, and daily lives of people all over the continent. In fact, almost no part of life in Europe in the Middle Ages was unaffected by the church and its teachings.

## The Christian Church and Politics

As the Christian church gained influence in Europe, some church leaders became powerful. They gained political power in addition to their religious authority.

The most powerful religious leader was the **pope**, the head of the Christian church. The pope's decisions could have huge effects on people's lives. For example, one pope decided to start a religious war, or **Crusade**, against the church's enemies in Southwest Asia. He wanted Europeans to take over the **Holy Land**, the region in which Jesus had lived. For many years, the region had been in the hands of another religious group, the Muslims.

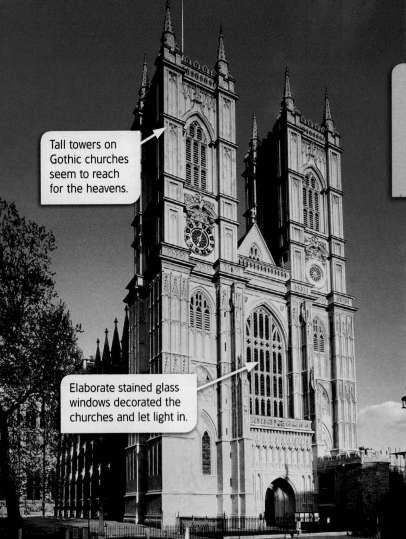

Tall towers on Gothic churches seem to reach for the heavens.

Elaborate stained glass windows decorated the churches and let light in.

## Gothic Architecture

Gothic churches were designed to tower over medieval cities as symbols of the church's greatness. This cathedral, Westminster Abbey, stands in London, England.

### The Church and Art

Politics was not the only area in which the church had great influence. Most art of the Middle Ages was also influenced by the church. Medieval painters and sculptors, for example, used religious subjects in their works. Most music and literature from the period is centered on religious themes.

The greatest examples of religious art from the Middle Ages are church buildings. Huge churches like the one shown on this page were built all over Europe. Many of them are examples of **Gothic architecture**, a style known for its high pointed ceilings, tall towers, and stained glass windows. People built Gothic churches as symbols of their faith. They believed that building these amazing structures would show their love for God. The insides of such churches are as elaborate and ornate as the outsides.

### The Church and Daily Life

Most people in Europe never saw a Gothic church, especially not the inside. Instead they worshipped at small local churches. In fact, people's lives often centered around their local church. Markets, festivals, and religious ceremonies all took place there. Local priests advised people on how to live and act. In addition, because most people could not read or write, they depended on the church to keep records for them.

**READING CHECK** **Summarizing** How did the Christian church shape life in the Middle Ages?

**HISTORY**

**VIDEO**
The Crusades' Aftermath

hmhsocialstudies.com

Thousands of people answered the pope's call for a Crusade. As the map on the previous page shows, they traveled thousands of miles to fight the church's enemies. This Crusade was the first of eight attempts by Christians over two centuries to win back the Holy Land.

In the end, the Crusades did not drive the Muslims from the Holy Land. They did, however, lead to sweeping changes in Europe. Crusaders brought new goods and ideas back to Europe with them. Europeans began to want more of these goods, so trade between Europe and Asia increased. At the same time, though, relations between Christians and Muslims grew worse. For years to come, followers of the religions distrusted and resented each other.

# Life in the Middle Ages

Christianity was a major influence on people's lives in the Middle Ages, but it was not the only one. Much of European society was controlled by two systems of relationships. They were the feudal (FYOO-duhl) system and the manor system.

## The Feudal System

Medieval Europe was divided into many small kingdoms. In most kingdoms, the king owned all the land. Sometimes, kings gave parts of their land to nobles—people born into wealthy, powerful families. In turn, these nobles gave land to knights, or trained warriors, who promised to help them defend both their lands and the king. This system of exchanging land for military service is called the **feudal system**, or feudalism (FYOO-duh-li-zuhm).

Everyone involved in the feudal system had certain duties to perform. The kings and nobles provided land and promised to protect the people who served them and to treat everyone fairly. In return, the knights who received land promised to serve the nobles dutifully, especially in times of war. The set of relationships between knights and nobles was the heart of Europe's feudal system.

The feudal system was very complex. Its rules varied from kingdom to kingdom and changed constantly. Feudal duties in France, for example, were not the same as those in Germany or England. Also, it was possible for one knight to owe service to more than one noble. If the two nobles he served went to war, the poor knight would be torn between them. In such situations, feudal relationships could be confusing or even dangerous.

**FOCUS ON READING**

After you read this passage, reread it. Make a list of details you did not notice in your first reading.

## Feudal Relationships

Europe's feudal system was based on relationships between knights and nobles. Each had certain duties that he or she had to perform.

**ANALYZING VISUALS** Who had to provide military service as one of his duties?

hmhsocialstudies.com
ANIMATED GEOGRAPHY

**Noble's duties**
- Provide knight with land
- Treat knights fairly and honestly

**Knight's duties**
- Provide military service
- Supply food and shelter for noble during visits

## The Manor System

The feudal system was only one set of guidelines that governed life in the Middle Ages. Another system, the manor system, controlled most economic activities in Europe during this period.

At the center of the manor system was the **manor**, a large estate owned by a noble or knight. Every manor was different, but most included a large house or castle, fields, pastures, and forests. A manor also had a village where workers lived. They traveled back and forth to the fields each day.

The owner of a manor did not farm his own land. Instead, he had workers to farm it for him. Most of the crops grown on the manor went to the owner. In exchange for their work, the workers got a place to live and a small piece of land on which they could grow their own food.

The workers on most manors included either free peasants or serfs. Peasants were free farmers. Serfs, on the other hand, were not free. Although they were not slaves, they were not allowed to leave the land on which they worked.

**Close-up**

# Life on a Manor

Manors were large estates that developed during the Middle Ages. Many manors were largely self-sufficient, producing most of the food and goods they needed. This picture shows what a manor in England might have looked like.

The owner of the manor lived in a large stone house called the manor house.

Peasants grew vegetables in small gardens located near their houses.

In late spring, peasants harvested crops like wheat.

## Towns and Trade

Not everyone in the Middle Ages lived on manors. Some people chose to live in towns and cities like Paris or London. Compared to our cities today, most of these medieval cities were small, dirty, and dark.

Many of the people who lived in cities were traders. They bought and sold goods from all over Europe and other parts of the world. Most of their goods were sold at trade fairs. Every year, merchants from many places in Europe would meet at these large fairs to sell their wares.

Before the year 1000, trade was not very common in Europe. After that year, however, trade increased. As it did, more people began to move to cities. Once small, these cities began to grow. As cities grew, trade increased even more, and the people who lived in them became wealthier. By the end of the Middle Ages, cities had become the centers of European culture and wealth.

**READING CHECK** **Finding Main Ideas** What were two systems that governed life in Europe during the Middle Ages? How did they differ?

The village church was built on a small piece of land that belonged to the lord.

Sheep grazed on grassy fields, and villagers used sheep's wool to make clothes.

The village blacksmith made iron tools for farming.

Peasants took wheat to the mill to be ground into flour, which they used to make bread.

**ANALYSIS SKILL** **ANALYZING VISUALS**

What goods can you see being produced on this manor? How do you think the lives of peasants on this manor differed from the life of the owner?

## Changes in Medieval Society

Life in the Middle Ages changed greatly after the year 1000. You have already seen how cities grew and trade increased. Even as these changes were taking place, bigger changes were sweeping through Europe.

**THE IMPACT TODAY**

The ideas of Magna Carta influenced later documents, including our Constitution.

### Political Changes in England

One of the countries most affected by change in the Middle Ages was England. In the year 1066 a noble from northern France, William the Conqueror, sailed to England and overthrew the old king. He declared himself the new king of England.

William built a strong government in England, something the English had not had before. Later kings of England built on William's example. For more than a century, these kings increased their power. By the late 1100s England's king was one of the most powerful men in Europe.

When William's descendant John took the throne, however, he angered many nobles by raising taxes. John believed that the king had the right to do whatever he wanted. England's nobles disagreed.

In 1215 a group of nobles forced King John to sign Magna Carta, one of the most important documents in English history. Magna Carta stated that the law, not the king, was the supreme power in England. The king had to obey the law. He could not raise taxes without the nobles' permission.

Many people consider Magna Carta to be one of the first steps toward democracy in modern Europe and one of history's most important documents. By stating that the king was not above the law, Magna Carta set limits on his power. In addition, it gave a council of nobles the power to advise the king. In time, that council developed into Parliament (PAHR-luh-muhnt), the elected body that governs England today.

---

**Primary Source**

### HISTORIC DOCUMENT
# Magna Carta

Magna Carta was one of the first documents to protect the rights of the people. Magna Carta was so influential that the British still consider it part of their constitution. Some of its ideas are also in the U.S. Constitution. Included in Magna Carta were 63 demands that English nobles made King John agree to follow. A few of these demands are listed here.

Demand number 31 defended people's right to property, not just wood.

Magna Carta guaranteed that free men had the right to a fair trial.

To all free men of our kingdom we have also granted, for us and our heirs for ever, all the liberties written out below, to have and to keep for them and their heirs, of us and our heirs.

(16) No man shall be forced to perform more service for a knight's 'fee,' or other free holding of land, than is due from it.

(31) Neither we nor any royal official will take wood for our castle, or for any other purpose, without the consent [permission] of the owner.

(38) In future no official shall place a man on trial upon his own unsupported statement, without producing credible [believable] witnesses to the truth of it.

—Magna Carta, from a translation by the British Library

**ANALYSIS SKILL  ANALYZING PRIMARY SOURCES**

In what ways do you think the ideas listed above influenced modern democracy?

## The Black Death

Not all of the changes that struck medieval Europe had such positive results. In 1347 a disease called the Black Death swept through Europe. Up to a third of Europe's people died from the disease. Even such a disaster, however, had some positive effects. With the decrease in population came a labor shortage. As a result, people could demand higher wages for their work.

## The Fight for Power

Even as the Black Death was sweeping across Europe, kings fought for power. In 1337 the Hundred Years' War broke out between England and France. As its name suggests, the war lasted more than 100 years. In the end, the French won.

Inspired by the victory, France's kings worked to increase their power. They took land away from nobles to rule themselves. France became a **nation-state**, a country united under a single strong government.

Around Europe, other rulers followed the French example. As nation-states arose around Europe, feudalism disappeared, and the Middle Ages came to an end.

**READING CHECK** Finding Main Ideas What changes occurred in Europe after 1000?

### BIOGRAPHY

## Joan of Arc
(c. 1412–1431)

One of the most famous war leaders in all of European history was a teenage girl. Joan of Arc, a leader of French troops during the Hundred Years' War, was only 16 when she first led troops into battle. She won many battles against the English but was captured in battle in 1430, tried, and executed. Nevertheless, her courage inspired the French, who went on to win the war. Today Joan is considered a national hero in France.

**Make Inferences** Why do you think Joan is considered a hero in France?

**SUMMARY AND PREVIEW** In this chapter you read about early Europe, a time that still influences how we live today. From the earliest civilizations of Greece and Rome to the Middle Ages, the people of Europe helped shape Western society. Next, you will learn about later periods that also affect our lives.

## Section 3 Assessment

hmhsocialstudies.com
ONLINE QUIZ

### Reviewing Ideas, Terms, and Places

1. a. **Recall** Why did the **pope** call for a **Crusade**?
   b. **Generalize** How did the Christian church affect art in the Middle Ages?
2. a. **Define** What was the **feudal system**?
   b. **Explain** How did the **manor** system work?
   c. **Elaborate** What made the feudal system so complex?
3. a. **Describe** How did the Black Death affect Europe?
   b. **Explain** How did England's government change after 1000?

### Critical Thinking

4. **Analyzing** Use your notes to complete a table like the one on the right. List ways the Church shaped medieval politics, life, and art.

```
        The Christian
           Church
          /        \
    Politics        Art
          \        /
         Daily
          Life
```

### FOCUS ON WRITING

5. **Selecting a Topic** Now you have read about events and people in the Middle Ages. Choose one that could be the subject of your myth.

## Geography and History

# The Black Death

"And they died by the hundreds," wrote one man who saw the horror, "both day and night." The Black Death had arrived. The Black Death was a series of deadly plagues that hit Europe between 1347 and 1351, killing millions. People didn't know what caused the plague. They also didn't know that geography played a key role in its spread—as people traveled to trade, they unwittingly carried the disease with them to new places.

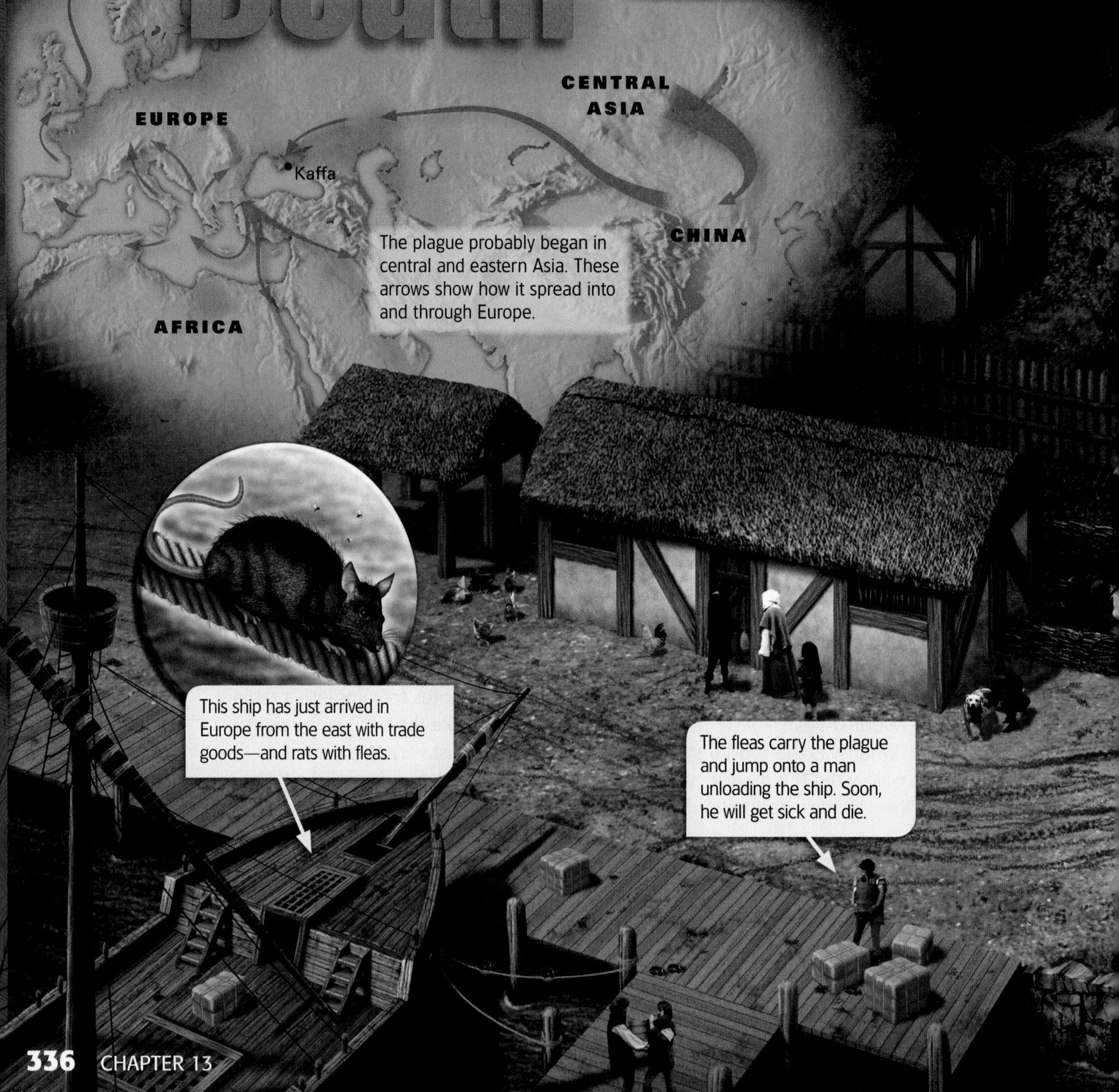
CENTRAL ASIA
EUROPE
Kaffa
CHINA
AFRICA
The plague probably began in central and eastern Asia. These arrows show how it spread into and through Europe.
This ship has just arrived in Europe from the east with trade goods—and rats with fleas.
The fleas carry the plague and jump onto a man unloading the ship. Soon, he will get sick and die.

The plague is so terrifying that many people think it's the end of the world. They leave town for the country, spreading the Black Death even further.

People dig mass graves to bury the dead. But often, so many victims are infected that there is no one left to bury them.

The garbage and dirty conditions in the town provide food and a home for the rats, allowing the disease to spread even more.

So many people die so quickly that special carts are sent through the streets to gather the bodies.

ANALYSIS
SKILL ANALYZING VISUALS

1. Movement  How did the Black Death reach Europe from Asia?
2. Place  What helped spread the plague within Europe?

# Interpreting a Historical Map

## Learn

History and geography are closely related. You cannot truly understand the history of a place without knowing where it is and what it is like. For that reason, historical maps are important in the study of history. A historical map is a map that shows what a place was like at a particular time in the past.

Like other maps, historical maps use colors and symbols to represent information. One color, for example, might represent the lands controlled by a certain kingdom or the areas in which a particular religion or type of government was common. Symbols might identify key cities, battle sites, or other major locations.

## Practice

Use the map on this page to answer the following questions.

❶ Read the map's title. What area does this map show? What time period?

❷ Check the map's legend. What does the color purple represent on this map?

❸ According to the map, what territory lay between France and the Holy Roman Empire at this time?

❹ What parts of Europe were Muslim in the year 1000?

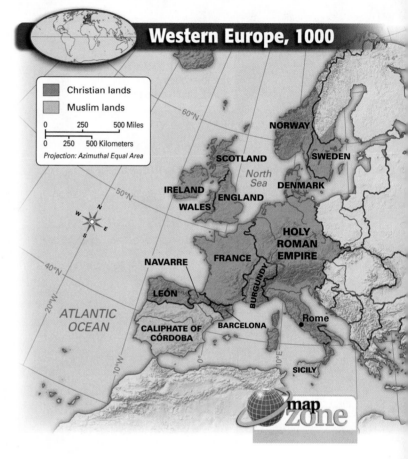

Western Europe, 1000

- Christian lands
- Muslim lands

0    250    500 Miles
0    250    500 Kilometers
Projection: Azimuthal Equal Area

NORWAY
SCOTLAND          SWEDEN
North Sea    DENMARK
IRELAND      ENGLAND
WALES
HOLY ROMAN EMPIRE
NAVARRE    FRANCE
BURGUNDY
LEÓN
ATLANTIC OCEAN
CALIPHATE OF CÓRDOBA    BARCELONA    Rome
SICILY

## Apply

Look back at the map called Early Christianity in the Roman Empire in Section 2 of this chapter. Study the map, and then write five questions that you might see about such a map on a test. Make sure that the questions you ask can be answered with just the information on the map.

# Chapter Review

**Geography's Impact**
video series
Review the video to answer the closing question:
*What are three ways in which Greek scholars have influenced education in America?*

## Visual Summary

*Use the visual summary below to help you review the main ideas of the chapter.*

QUICK FACTS

Ancient Greece was the birthplace of democracy, theater, and many other advances of Western society.

The Romans were master builders who created one of the largest empires in world history.

During the Middle Ages, new political and economic systems took hold in Europe, and religion dominated society.

## Reviewing Vocabulary, Terms, and Places

*For each group of terms below, write the letter of the term that does not relate to the others. Then write a sentence that explains how the other two terms are related.*

1. **a.** Athens
   **b.** Sparta
   **c.** Rome
2. **a.** feudal system
   **b.** aqueduct
   **c.** manor
3. **a.** Crusade
   **b.** republic
   **c.** empire
4. **a.** Senate
   **b.** citizen
   **c.** colony

## Comprehension and Critical Thinking

**SECTION 1** *(Pages 310–317)*

5. **a. Identify** What was the basic political unit in ancient Greece? What is one example?

   **b. Contrast** How was life in Greece different under Alexander than it had been during the golden age?

   **c. Evaluate** What do you think was the greatest achievement of the ancient Greeks? Why?

**SECTION 2** *(Pages 318–325)*

6. **a. Define** What was the Pax Romana? What happened during that time?

   **b. Summarize** How did Rome's government change after the republic fell apart?

   **c. Elaborate** What role did Rome's leaders play in the spread of Christianity?

**7. a. Describe** What were two changes that affected Europe in the late Middle Ages?

**b. Explain** What duties did knights have under the feudal system?

**c. Develop** Why do you think so much of the art created in the Middle Ages was religious?

# Using the Internet

**8. Activity: Exploring Ancient Greece** The golden age of Greece was an amazing time—the Greeks helped shape our government, art, philosophy, writing, and more! Through your online textbook, learn more about the ancient Greek world. Imagine you have traveled through time, back to ancient Greece. What are the people doing? What kinds of buildings do you see? What is the area like? Draw a picture or make a collage to record your observations.

↗ **hmhsocialstudies.com**

# Social Studies Skills

**Interpreting a Historical Map** *Use the map on the Expansion of Rome in Section 2 of this chapter to answer the following questions.*

**9.** What time period is shown on this map?

**10.** What does the orange color on this map represent?

**11.** Did the areas shown on the map in gold become part of Rome before or after the areas shown in light green?

**12.** Which was conquered by the Romans first—Spain or Gaul?

**13.** Between which two years did Egypt become a Roman territory?

# Map Activity

**14. Europe, 2000 BC–AD 1500** On a separate sheet of paper, match the letters on the map with their correct labels.

| Athens | Carthage | Rome |
| Gaul | Holy Land | Alexandria |

↗ **hmhsocialstudies.com** **INTERACTIVE MAP**

map zone

**FOCUS ON READING AND WRITING**

**15. Re-Reading** Read the passage titled The Manor System in Section 3. After you read, write down the main ideas of the passage. Then go back and re-read the passage carefully. Add to your list of main ideas anything more that you noticed in your second reading. How much more did you learn from the passage when you re-read it?

**16. Writing Your Myth** Now that you have learned about the events and people of ancient and medieval Europe, you can write a myth about one of them. Remember that your myth should try to explain the person or the event in a way that people of the time might have. For example, they might have thought that Caesar was the son of a goddess or that the Black Death was caused by a terrible unknown monster. Try to include descriptive details that will help bring your myth to life for the people who read it.

DIRECTIONS: *Read questions 1 through 7 and write the letter of the best response. Then read question 8 and write your own well-constructed response.*

**1** Democracy was first practiced in which city-state of ancient Greece?

A Athens

B Carthage

C Rome

D Sparta

**2** A large estate owned by a noble or knight in the Middle Ages was called a

A city-state.

B republic.

C empire.

D manor.

**3** The first Roman emperor to become a Christian was named

A Julius Caesar.

B Augustus.

C Constantine.

D Jesus of Nazareth.

**4** Which of the following was first created in the Middle Ages?

A aqueducts

B Gothic architecture

C drama

D democracy

**5** The blended culture that was created in Alexander the Great's empire is called

A Greek

B Hellenistic

C Roman

D Medieval

**Europe, AD 117**

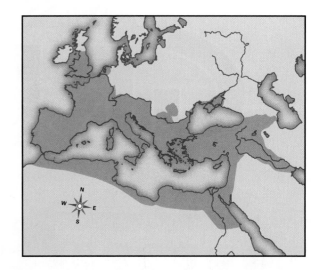

**6** Study the map above. The area shown in orange on this map was ruled by the

A Greeks

B Etruscans

C Romans

D French

**7** Which document limited the powers of the king of England?

A Black Death

B Crusade

C Feudal system

D Magna Carta

**8** **Extended Response** As the map above shows, much of Europe was unified under a single government in 117. By the Middle Ages, though, that government had fallen apart. Write a brief paragraph in which you explain two ways in which European society was different in the Middle Ages than it had been in earlier times.

# ANCIENT GREECE

**The Acropolis of Athens symbolizes the city and represents the architectural and artistic legacy of ancient Greece.** *Acropolis* means "highest city" in Greek, and there are many such sites in Greece. Historically, an acropolis provided shelter and defense against a city's enemies. The Acropolis of Athens—the best known of them all—contained temples, monuments, and artwork dedicated to the Greek gods. Archaeological evidence indicates that the Acropolis was an important place to inhabitants from much earlier eras. However, the structures that we see today on the site were largely conceived by the statesman Pericles during the Golden Age of Athens in the 5th century B.C.

Explore the Acropolis of ancient Greece and learn about the legacy of Greek civilization. You can find a wealth of information, video clips, primary sources, activities, and more at ↗ hmhsocialstudies.com.

### The Parthenon

Watch the video to see what the Parthenon, one of the most important temples on the Acropolis, might have looked like after it was completed.

### The Persian Wars

Watch the video to find out how Athens emerged as the principal Greek city-state at the conclusion of the Persian Wars.

### The Goddess Athena

Watch the video to learn how, according to Greek mythology, Athena became the protector of Athens.

### Legacy of Greece

Watch the video to analyze *The School of Athens*, a painting by the Italian Renaissance artist Raphael, which pays tribute to the legacy of ancient Greece in philosophy and science.

# CHAPTER 14

# History of Early Modern Europe

ATLANTIC
OCEAN

Explorer's ship

Madrid

AFRICA

**Essential Question** What important events shaped Europe from the Middle Ages to modern times?

## What You Will Learn...

In this chapter you will learn about European history from the end of the Middle Ages to 1900. During this period new ideas and innovations changed life and expanded knowledge across Europe.

### FOCUS ON READING AND WRITING

**Understanding Chronological Order** Chronological means "related to time." Many of the events in this chapter are described in sequence, or in the order in which they occurred. Words such as first, before, next, and later can signal chronological order. **See the lesson, Understanding Chronological Order, on page 529.**

**Creating a Travel Brochure** Your job is to encourage people to visit a time from Europe's exciting past. Read about Europe's history from the Renaissance through the Industrial Revolution. Then choose one time period and create a travel brochure to convince others to visit Europe during that period. What exciting changes might visitors see? What experiences might they have? Describe it all in your brochure.

**The Reformation** In 1517 Martin Luther, a German monk, posted problems he saw in the Catholic Church.

# Europe, 1500–1900

Steam train

*North Sea*

*Baltic Sea*

Printing press

Wittenberg

Paris

French Revolution

**EUROPE**

Milan

Venice

Florence

Rome

Duomo, a cathedral in Florence

*Mediterranean Sea*

10°E · 20°E · 30°E

0 — 100 — 300 Miles
0 — 100 — 200 Kilometers
*Projection: Azimuthal Equal Area*

**HISTORY** Da Vinci Tech

↗ hmhsocialstudies.com VIDEO

## map zone Geography Skills

**Place** The nations and kingdoms of Europe underwent many changes during this period.

1. **Identify** What city is connected with the French Revolution?
2. **Analyze** Based on the images on the map, what types of changes do you think occurred during this period of Europe's history?

**The Age of Exploration** Italian sailor Christopher Columbus led a voyage that reached the Americas in 1492.

**The Industrial Revolution** First used in factories, the steam engine later powered trains and ships. Inventions such as the steam engine changed life in Europe during the 1700s and 1800s.

# The Renaissance and Reformation

## What You Will Learn...

### Main Ideas

1. The Renaissance was a period of new learning, new ideas, and new advances in art, literature, and science.
2. The Reformation changed the religious map of Europe.

### The Big Idea

The periods of the Renaissance and the Reformation introduced new ideas and new ways of thinking into Europe.

### Key Terms and Places

Renaissance, *p. 344*
Florence, *p. 344*
Venice, *p. 344*
humanism, *p. 345*
Reformation, *p. 348*
Protestants, *p. 349*
Catholic Reformation, *p. 349*

hmhsocialstudies.com
**TAKING NOTES**

Use the graphic organizer online to take notes on the Renaissance and the Reformation.

## If YOU lived there...

You live in Florence, Italy, in the 1400s. Your father, a merchant, has just hired a tutor from Asia Minor to teach you and your sisters and brothers. Your new teacher starts by stating, "Nothing good has been written in a thousand years." He insists that you learn to read Latin and Greek so that you can study Roman and Greek books that were written long ago.

**What can you learn from these ancient books?**

**BUILDING BACKGROUND** The end of the Middle Ages brought important changes to European politics and society. These changes set the stage for an exciting new period of learning and creativity. During this period, new ideas influenced the arts, science, and attitudes toward religion.

## The Renaissance

Do you ever get the urge to do something creative? If so, how do you express your creativity? Do you like to draw or paint? Maybe you prefer to write stories or poems or create music.

At the end of the Middle Ages, people across Europe found the urge to be creative. Their creativity was sparked by new ideas and discoveries that were sweeping through Europe at the time. This period of creativity, of new ideas and inspirations, is called the **Renaissance** (REN-uh-sahns). It lasted from about 1350 through the 1500s. *Renaissance* is French for "rebirth." The people who named this period believed it represented a new beginning, or rebirth, in Europe's history and culture.

### New Ideas

The Renaissance started in Italy. During and after the Crusades, Italian cities such as **Florence** and **Venice** became rich through trade. Goods from faraway Asia moved through these cities.

These goods made the people who lived there curious about the larger world. At the same time, scholars from other parts of the world came to Italy. They brought books written by ancient Greeks and Romans.

Inspired by these books and by the ancient ruins around them, some people in Italy became interested in ancient cultures. These people began reading works in Greek and Latin and studying subjects that had been taught in Greek and Roman schools.

These subjects, known as the humanities, included history, poetry, and grammar. Increased study of the humanities led to a new way of thinking and learning known as humanism.

**Humanism** emphasized the abilities and accomplishments of human beings. The humanists believed that people were capable of great things. As a result, they admired artists, architects, leaders, writers, scientists, and other talented individuals.

**THE IMPACT TODAY**

American universities grant degrees in the humanities. You might one day get a degree in a humanities field.

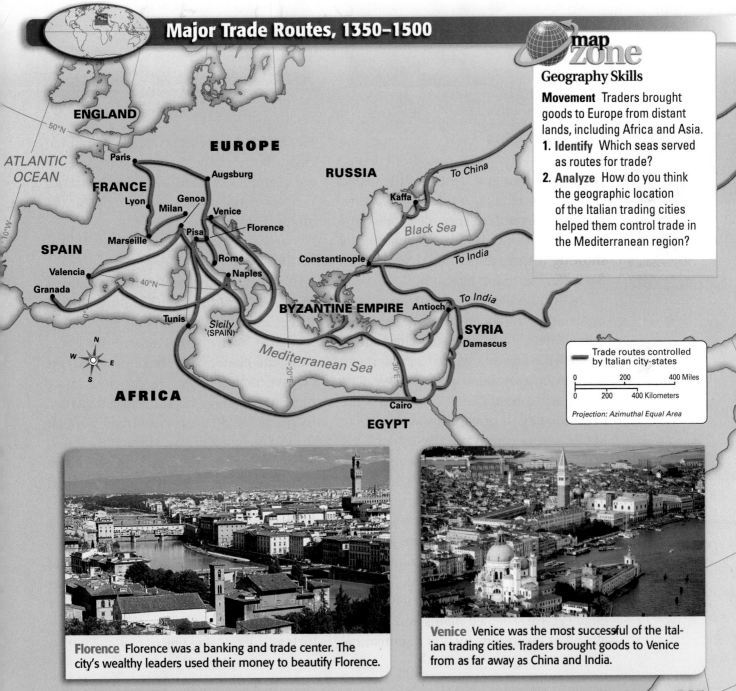

## Major Trade Routes, 1350–1500

**map zone**

### Geography Skills

**Movement** Traders brought goods to Europe from distant lands, including Africa and Asia.

1. **Identify** Which seas served as routes for trade?
2. **Analyze** How do you think the geographic location of the Italian trading cities helped them control trade in the Mediterranean region?

Trade routes controlled by Italian city-states

0    200    400 Miles
0    200    400 Kilometers

Projection: Azimuthal Equal Area

**Florence** Florence was a banking and trade center. The city's wealthy leaders used their money to beautify Florence.

**Venice** Venice was the most successful of the Italian trading cities. Traders brought goods to Venice from as far away as China and India.

# The Renaissance

**The Renaissance was a period of great creativity and advances in art, literature, and science.**

Renaissance sculptors were careful to show the tiniest details in their works. This statue by Michelangelo is of David, a king of ancient Israel.

Painters like Hans Holbein the Younger wanted to show what real life was like for people in Europe.

**VIDEO**
Humanism Triggers the Renaissance
hmhsocialstudies.com

## Renaissance Art

The Renaissance was a period of talented artistic achievements. Artists of the period created new techniques to improve their work. For example, they developed the technique of perspective, a method of showing a three-dimensional scene on a flat surface so that it looks real.

Many Renaissance artists were also humanists. Humanist artists valued the achievements of individuals. These artists wanted their paintings and sculptures to show people's unique personalities. One of the artists best able to show this sense of personality in his works was the Italian Michelangelo (mee-kay-LAHN-jay-loh). He was both a great painter and sculptor. His statues, like the one of King David above, seem almost to be alive.

Another famous Renaissance artist was Leonardo da Vinci. Leonardo achieved the Renaissance goal of excelling in many areas. He was not only a great painter and sculptor but also an architect, scientist, and engineer. He sketched plants and animals as well as inventions such as a submarine.

He collected knowledge about the human body. Both Leonardo and Michelangelo are examples of what we call Renaissance people—people who can do practically anything well.

## Renaissance Literature

Like artists, Renaissance writers expressed the attitudes of the time. The most famous Renaissance writer is probably the English dramatist William Shakespeare. He wrote excellent poetry, but Shakespeare is best known for his plays. They include more than 30 comedies, histories, and tragedies. In his plays, Shakespeare turned popular stories into great drama. His writing shows a deep understanding of human nature and skillfully expresses the thoughts and feelings of his characters. For these reasons, Shakespeare's plays are still highly popular in many parts of the world.

Renaissance writings were read and enjoyed by a larger audience than earlier writings had been. This change was largely due to advances in science and technology, such as the printing press.

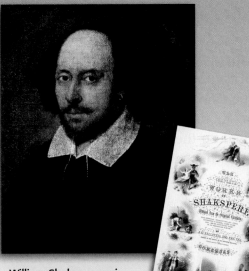

William Shakespeare is considered the greatest of all Renaissance writers. His plays are still read and performed today.

Leonardo da Vinci drew sketches of many devices that were not invented until centuries after his death. This model of a type of helicopter was based on the sketch by Leonardo shown below.

**ANALYSIS SKILL** **ANALYZING VISUALS**

Based on the sculpture of David and on the Holbein painting, how would you describe Renaissance art?

## Renaissance Science

Some of the ancient works rediscovered during the Renaissance dealt with science. For the first time in centuries, Europeans could read about early Greek and Roman scientific advances. Inspired by what they read, some people began to study math, astronomy, and other fields of science.

Using this new scientific knowledge, Europeans developed new inventions and techniques. For example, they learned how to build enormous domes that could rise higher than earlier buildings.

Another invention of the Renaissance was the movable type printing press. A German named Johann Gutenberg built the first movable type printing press in the mid-1400s. This type of printing press could print books quickly and cheaply. For the first time, people could easily share ideas with others in distant areas. The printing press helped the ideas of the Renaissance spread beyond Italy.

**READING CHECK** **Summarizing** How did life in Europe change during the Renaissance?

## CONNECTING TO Technology

# The Printing Press

Printing was not a new idea in Renaissance Europe. What was new was the method of printing. Johann Gutenberg designed a printing system called movable type. It used a set of tiny lead blocks, each carved with a letter of the alphabet. These blocks could then be used to spell out an entire page of text for printing. Once copies of the page were made, the printer could reuse the blocks to spell out another page. This was much faster and easier than earlier systems had been.

**Generalizing** How did movable type improve printing?

## The Reformation

By the early 1500s some Europeans had begun to complain about problems they saw in the Roman Catholic Church. For example, they thought the church had become corrupt. In time, their complaints led to a religious reform movement called the **Reformation** (re-fuhr-MAY-shuhn).

## The Protestant Reformation

Although people called for church reform in other places, the Reformation began in what is now Germany. This area was part of the Holy Roman Empire. Some people there thought church officials were too focused on their own power and had lost sight of their religious duties.

**hmhsocialstudies.com  INTERACTIVE MAP**

## Religion in Europe, 1600

Legend:
- Protestant
- Roman Catholic
- Roman Catholic with Protestant minorities
- Eastern Orthodox
- Muslim
- Boundary of the Holy Roman Empire

0    250    500 Miles
0   250   500 Kilometers

Projection: Lambert Azimuthal Equal-Area

**map zone Geography Skills**

**Regions** By the Reformation's end, parts of Europe were still Catholic, while others had become mostly Protestant.

1. **Locate** In which part of Europe were most people Protestant?
2. **Analyze** How were religious areas spread across the Holy Roman Empire?

One of the first people to express protests against the Catholic Church was a German monk named Martin Luther. In 1517 Luther nailed a list of complaints to a church door in the town of Wittenberg. Luther's protests angered church officials, who soon expelled him from the church. In response, Luther's followers formed a separate church. They became the first **Protestants**, Christians who broke from the Catholic Church over religious issues.

Other reformers who followed Luther began creating churches of their own as well. The Roman Catholic Church was no longer the only church in Western Europe. As you can see on the map, many areas of Europe had become Protestant by 1600.

## The Catholic Reformation

Protestants were not the only ones who called for reform in the Roman Catholic Church. Many Catholic officials wanted to reform the church as well. Even as the first Protestants were breaking away from the church, Catholic officials were launching a series of reforms that became known as the **Catholic Reformation**.

As part of the Catholic Reformation, church leaders began focusing more on spiritual concerns and less on political power. They also worked to make church teachings easier for people to understand. To tell people about the changes, church leaders sent priests and teachers all over Europe. Church leaders also worked to spread Catholic teachings into Asia, Africa, and other parts of the world.

## Religious Wars

The Reformation caused major changes to the religious map of Europe. Catholicism, once the main religion in most of Europe, was no longer so dominant. In many areas, especially in the north, Protestants now outnumbered Catholics.

In some parts of Europe, Catholics and Protestants lived together in peace. In some other places, however, this was not the case. Bloody religious wars broke out in France, Germany, the Netherlands, and Switzerland. Wars between religious groups left parts of Europe in ruins.

These religious wars led to political and social changes in Europe. For example, many people began relying less on what church leaders and other authority figures told them. Instead, people raised questions and began looking to science for answers.

FOCUS ON READING Dates in a text, such as the dates 1517 and 1600 in the text at left, help you keep events in order in your mind.

**READING CHECK** **Finding Main Ideas** How did Europe change after the Reformation?

**SUMMARY AND PREVIEW** In the 1300s through the 1500s, new ideas changed Europe. Next, you will learn about other ideas and events that brought changes.

## Section 1 Assessment

hmhsocialstudies.com
ONLINE QUIZ

### Reviewing Ideas, Terms, and Places

1. a. **Define** What was the **Renaissance**?
   b. **Summarize** What were some changes made in art during the Renaissance?
   c. **Elaborate** How did the printing press help spread Renaissance ideas?
2. a. **Describe** What led to the **Reformation**?
   b. **Explain** Why did church leaders launch the series of reforms known as the **Catholic Reformation**?

### Critical Thinking

3. **Finding Main Ideas** Draw a chart like the one shown. Use your notes to describe new ideas of the Renaissance and the Reformation. Add rows as needed.

| Idea | Description |
|------|-------------|
|      |             |
|      |             |
|      |             |

### FOCUS ON WRITING

4. **Describing the Renaissance and the Reformation** Note things about these two periods that might interest visitors. For example, visitors might want to see Renaissance art.

# Science and Exploration

## What You Will Learn...

### Main Ideas

1. During the Scientific Revolution, discoveries and inventions expanded knowledge and changed life in Europe.
2. In the 1400s and 1500s, Europeans led voyages of discovery and exploration.
3. As Europeans discovered new lands, they created colonies and new empires all over the world.

### The Big Idea

New inventions and knowledge led to European exploration and empires around the world.

### Key Terms

Scientific Revolution, *p. 351*
New World, *p. 355*
circumnavigate, *p. 355*

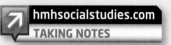
hmhsocialstudies.com
TAKING NOTES

Use the graphic organizer online to take notes on science and exploration.

## If **YOU** lived there...

You are an adviser to a European king in the 1500s. The rulers of several other countries have sent explorers to search for new trade routes. Your king does not want to fall behind. Now a young sea captain has come to the royal court with a daring plan. The king is interested, but funding such a voyage could be costly.

**What will you advise the king to do?**

**BUILDING BACKGROUND** The Renaissance made Europeans more curious about science and the world. This curiosity led to new inventions and technologies that helped people explore the world. As a result, a spirit of adventure swept across Europe.

## The Scientific Revolution

Can you imagine what your life would be like without science? Think of all the things that science has provided in our daily lives. Without it, we would have no electricity, no automobiles, no plastic. Our lives would be totally different.

### Scientific Advances and Exploration

Several inventions and technical advances enabled people to explore the world and to study the heavens.

**ANALYZING VISUALS** Why do you think these inventions and advances contributed to increased exploration of the world?

**Astrolabe** With an astrolabe, sailors could use the stars to calculate a ship's exact location.

Did you know that there was a time when people lived without the benefits of modern science? In fact, it was not until the 1500s and 1600s that most people in Europe began to appreciate what science and technology could do to improve life.

## A New View of Science

Before the 1500s, most educated people who studied the world relied on authorities such as ancient Greek writers and church officials. People thought these authorities could tell them all they needed to know. Europeans had little need for science.

Between about 1540 and 1700, though, European views about how to study the world changed. This widespread change in views was part of the **Scientific Revolution**, the series of events that led to the birth of modern science. People began placing more importance on what they observed and less on what they were told. They used their observations to come up with **logical** explanations for how the world worked. This new focus on observation marked the start of modern science.

Why is the birth of modern science called a revolution? The new approach to science was a radical idea. In the same way a political revolution changes a country, this new view of science changed society.

## Science and Religion

Not everyone was happy with the new role of science in society. Some people feared that scientific ideas would eventually lead to the breakdown of European society.

Many of the people who most feared the increasing influence of science were church officials. They tended to oppose science when it went against the teachings of the church. For example, the church taught that Earth was at the center of the universe. Some scientists, though, had observed through telescopes that Earth orbited the sun. This observation went against the church's teaching.

This growing tension between religion and science came to a head in 1632. That year, an Italian scientist named Galileo (gal-uh-LEE-oh) published a book in which he stated that Earth orbited the sun. He was arrested and put on trial. Afraid that the church would expel him, Galileo publicly stated that his writings were wrong. Privately, though, he held to his beliefs.

Despite conflicts such as these, science and religion were able to exist together in Europe. In fact, many scientists saw a connection between science and religion. These scientists believed that science could better explain church teachings. Science continued developing rapidly as a result.

**Compass** The compass, which always points north, helped sailors find their way at sea.

**Telescope** With the telescope, scientists could study the heavens like never before.

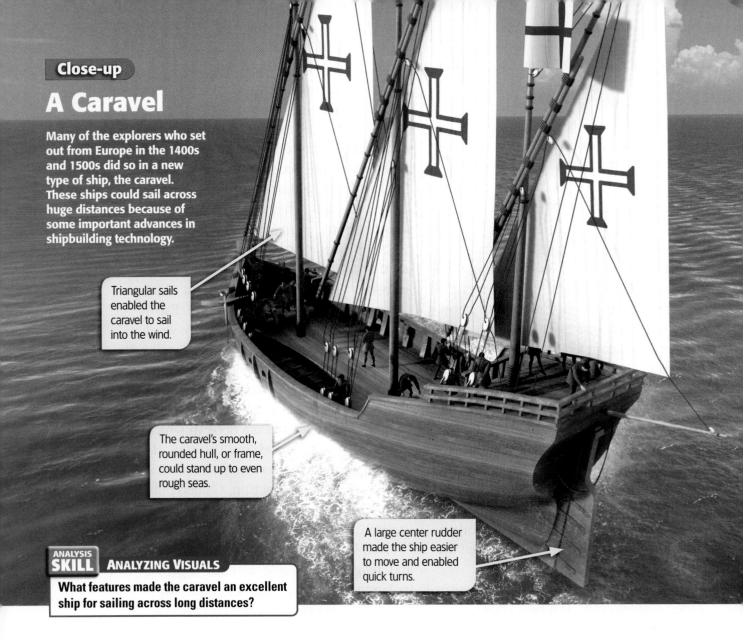

## Close-up

# A Caravel

Many of the explorers who set out from Europe in the 1400s and 1500s did so in a new type of ship, the caravel. These ships could sail across huge distances because of some important advances in shipbuilding technology.

Triangular sails enabled the caravel to sail into the wind.

The caravel's smooth, rounded hull, or frame, could stand up to even rough seas.

A large center rudder made the ship easier to move and enabled quick turns.

**ANALYSIS SKILL** **ANALYZING VISUALS**

What features made the caravel an excellent ship for sailing across long distances?

**VIDEO**
Sir Isaac Newton: The Gravity of Genius

hmhsocialstudies.com

## Discoveries and Inventions

The Scientific Revolution was a period of great advances in many fields of science. With increased interest in science came discoveries in astronomy, biology, physics, and other fields. For example, astronomers discovered how the stars and the planets move in the sky. Biologists learned how blood circulates throughout the human body. Physicists figured out how mirrors and pendulums worked.

Some of the greatest advances of the Scientific Revolution were made by one man, Sir Isaac Newton. He made exciting contributions to both math and physics.

Newton is probably best known today for his observations about gravity, the force that attracts objects to each other. Before his observations, scientists knew very little about how gravity works.

Many of the discoveries of the Scientific Revolution were possible because of new inventions. Devices such as the telescope, the microscope, and the thermometer were invented at this time. Some of these new inventions helped contribute to another exciting time—the Age of Exploration.

**READING CHECK** **Summarizing** What happened during the Scientific Revolution?

# The Voyages of Discovery

Some advances in science and technology enabled people to make longer, safer sea voyages. New compasses and astrolabes helped sailors figure out where they were even when far from land. Improvements in mapmaking helped people plan safer routes for their journeys. In addition, new ships, such as the caravel, made sea travel safer. The caravel could sail farther than earlier ships could.

Equipped with these new advances, many Europeans set out on great voyages of discovery. They sailed into unknown waters hoping to find new trade routes to faraway places. They would succeed in their quest, and their discoveries would change the world.

## The Drive to Discover

Why were Europeans so eager to explore? They had many reasons. Some explorers were curious about the unknown. They hoped to find out what lay beyond the horizon. Others sought adventure and the excitement of life at sea. Still others had religious reasons. These explorers wanted to spread the Christian faith.

Another reason to explore was the desire to get rich. Some explorers wanted to find new lands that had products they could sell in Europe. The explorers hoped to sell these goods for lots of money and to become rich.

In addition, some European leaders promoted exploration in hope it would benefit their countries. Prince Henry, a member of the Portuguese royal family, encouraged explorers to find a route to India's rich spice trade. Queen Isabella of Spain also promoted exploration. She paid for explorers to seek out new lands and claim them for Spain. She hoped these lands would bring Spain wealth.

## Voyages to the East

In the mid-1400s, explorers from Europe began searching for an all-water route to Asia. They wanted to reach Asia to get goods from China and India. During the Middle Ages, Europeans had discovered the exotic goods available in Asia. Many of them, such as silk and spices, were not found in Europe. These Asian goods were costly, because traders had to bring them long distances over land. Further, Italian traders controlled the sale of such goods in Europe—and these Italian traders had become very rich.

Other European countries wanted to break the hold the Italians had on trade with Asia. The Italians controlled all the trade routes in the eastern Mediterranean. If other countries could find an all-water route to Asia, they would not have to pay Italian traders to get exotic Asian goods.

## BIOGRAPHY

### Queen Isabella
(1451–1504)

Christopher Columbus's voyage to the Americas would not have been possible without the support of Queen Isabella of Spain. In 1492 Columbus approached the queen in search of money to pay for his voyage. He had already been turned down by the king of Portugal, who thought Columbus's plan was foolhardy. Isabella liked his plan, however. She gave Columbus money and ships to help make his voyage. With the support of the queen and others, he was able to complete his journey. It would change the history of Europe, the Americas, and the world forever.

**Analyzing** How did Isabella make Columbus's voyage possible?

353

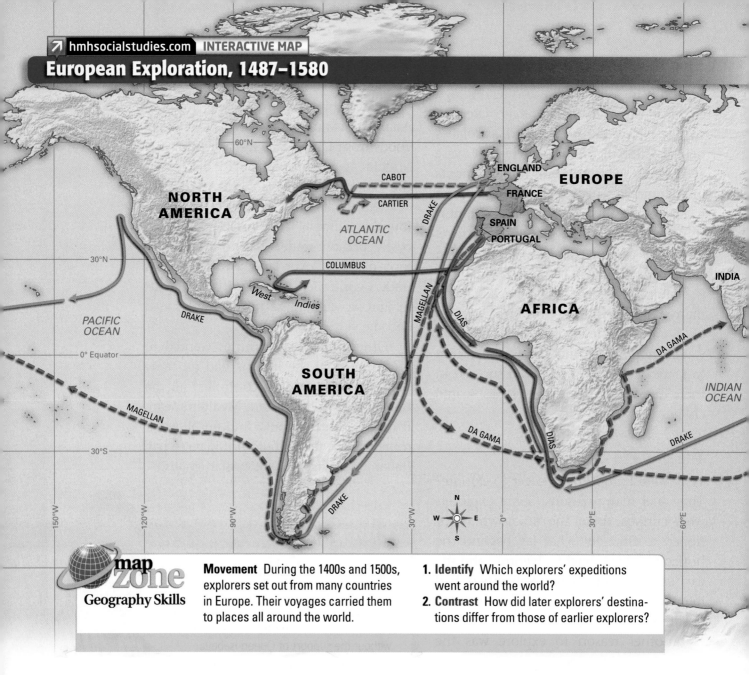

# European Exploration, 1487–1580

**map zone**
**Geography Skills**

**Movement** During the 1400s and 1500s, explorers set out from many countries in Europe. Their voyages carried them to places all around the world.

1. **Identify** Which explorers' expeditions went around the world?
2. **Contrast** How did later explorers' destinations differ from those of earlier explorers?

---

**FOCUS ON READING**

What signal words on this page give you clues about the chronological order of events?

The first explorers to search for a sea route to Asia were from Portugal. Under the direction of Prince Henry, they sailed south along Africa's west coast. As they went, they set up trading posts along the Atlantic coast of Africa. In time, explorers sailed farther south.

In 1497–1498 a Portuguese explorer named Vasco da Gama sailed around the southern tip of Africa and on to the west coast of India. You can see his route on the map above. Portugal had found a new sea route to Asia.

## Voyages to America

Meanwhile, other countries had also been sending explorers out to find new routes to Asia. The most important expedition came from Spain. In 1492 Queen Isabella of Spain helped pay for a voyage led by Christopher Columbus, an Italian sailor. Columbus hoped to reach Asia by sailing west across the Atlantic. The voyage was long and difficult, but he finally reached land after several months at sea. He landed on an island in what is now the Bahamas. Columbus had reached a new land.

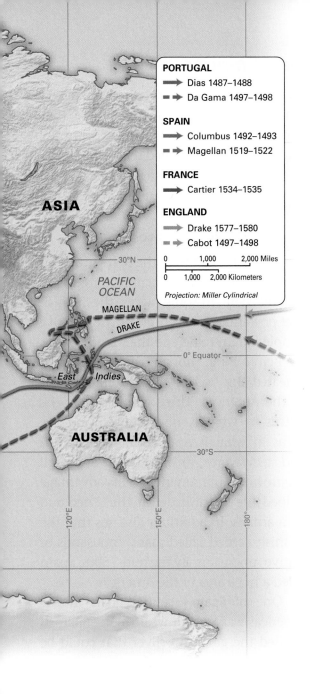

PORTUGAL
→ Dias 1487–1488
⇢ Da Gama 1497–1498

SPAIN
→ Columbus 1492–1493
⇢ Magellan 1519–1522

FRANCE
→ Cartier 1534–1535

ENGLAND
→ Drake 1577–1580
⇢ Cabot 1497–1498

0       1,000       2,000 Miles
0    1,000   2,000 Kilometers

Projection: Miller Cylindrical

ASIA

30°N

PACIFIC
OCEAN

MAGELLAN

DRAKE

0° Equator

East   Indies

AUSTRALIA

30°S

120°E    150°E    180°

Columbus thought he had found a route to Asia, which Europeans called the Indies. Europeans came to realize that he had reached a land unknown to them. They called this land, which in time came to be known as America, the **New World**.

Excited by the new discovery, explorers set out from Europe to learn more about the new land. Led by Spain, explorers from Portugal, France, England, and the Netherlands set sail for North and South America. Before long, little of the Americas would remain unexplored.

This wave of European exploration of the Americas had many different causes. Some explorers were still looking for the best water route to Asia. They hoped to find a passage through the Americas by which ships could sail to India or China.

Other explorers led voyages in search of riches. These explorers had heard that the native people of the Americas had lots of gold—more gold than most Europeans had ever seen. These explorers dreamed of the glory and riches they hoped to gain from conquering the lands and people of the Americas.

## Voyages around the World

For some Europeans, their new knowledge of the Americas made them more curious about the world. Since they had not known about the Americas, they wondered what else about the world they did not know. One way to learn more about the world, they decided, would be to **circumnavigate**, or travel all the way around, Earth.

The first person to try such a journey was Ferdinand Magellan (muh-JEHL-uhn), a Portuguese sailor. Magellan sailed west from Spain around the southern tip of South America. From there he continued into the Pacific Ocean, where no European had sailed before. Magellan made it as far as the Philippines, where he was killed in a conflict with natives. His crew pushed on, however, and finally reached Spain to complete their trip around the world.

The voyages of explorers like Magellan taught Europeans much about the world. In time, they even achieved the goal of Christopher Columbus—to reach Asia by sailing west from Europe. In addition, they paved the way for European settlement and colonization of the Americas.

**READING CHECK** Identifying Cause and Effect What were two causes of exploration?

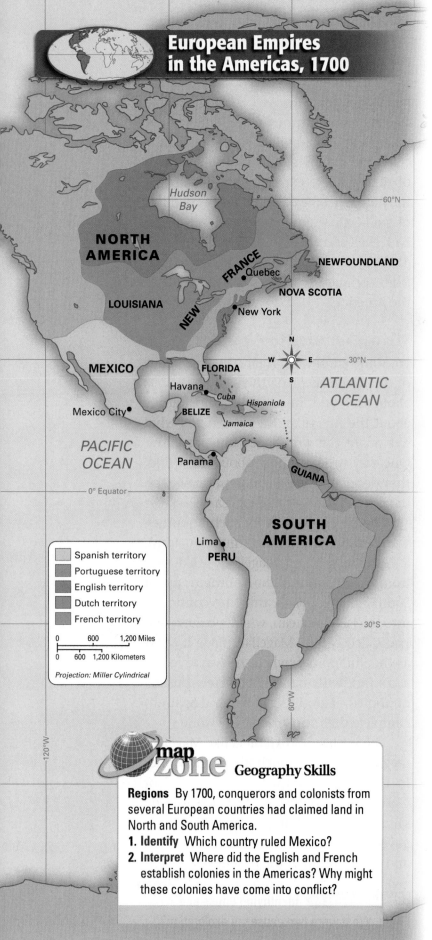

**European Empires in the Americas, 1700**

NORTH AMERICA

Hudson Bay

60°N

NEW FRANCE

Quebec

NEWFOUNDLAND

NOVA SCOTIA

LOUISIANA

New York

MEXICO

FLORIDA

30°N

Havana

Cuba

Hispaniola

ATLANTIC OCEAN

Mexico City

BELIZE

Jamaica

PACIFIC OCEAN

Panama

0° Equator

GUIANA

SOUTH AMERICA

Lima

PERU

30°S

60°W

120°W

Spanish territory
Portuguese territory
English territory
Dutch territory
French territory

0    600    1,200 Miles
0    600    1,200 Kilometers

Projection: Miller Cylindrical

**map zone Geography Skills**

**Regions** By 1700, conquerors and colonists from several European countries had claimed land in North and South America.

1. **Identify** Which country ruled Mexico?
2. **Interpret** Where did the English and French establish colonies in the Americas? Why might these colonies have come into conflict?

# New Empires

As European explorers discovered new lands in the Americas and elsewhere, they claimed these lands for their countries. These land claims formed the basis for new European empires that stretched across the sea into lands far from Europe.

## Conquests and Empires

The Spanish, who were the first Europeans to reach the Americas, claimed large areas of land there. In some places, the Spanish met powerful native empires. These native people fought to defend their lands.

Before long, though, the Spanish had defeated the two most powerful empires in the Americas. These empires were the Aztecs in what is now Mexico and the Incas in what is now Peru. The Spanish had steel swords, firearms, and horses—all unknown in the Americas. This advantage helped the Spanish defeat the Aztec and Inca armies. In addition, diseases that the Spanish carried killed many thousands of Native Americans. By the mid-1500s, Spain ruled a huge area in the Americas.

One of Spain's central goals in the Americas was to gain wealth. The Spanish wanted the gold and silver that could be found in Mexico and some other places. To get these riches, the Spanish enslaved Native Americans and forced them to work in mines. In addition, the Spanish brought African slaves to the Americas to work in the mines. Soon, ships full of gold and silver from these mines were crossing the Atlantic Ocean back to Spain.

Riches from the Americas made Spain the wealthiest country in Europe. Spain's rulers used this money to buy equipment for its armies and to produce ships for its navy. With this powerful military, Spain became Europe's mightiest country, the center of a huge empire.

## Other Colonies

Other European countries envied Spain's wealth and power. They wanted a share of the wealth that Spain was finding in the Americas. In hope of finding similar wealth, these countries began to establish colonies in the lands they explored. As the map shows, colonists from England, France, the Netherlands, and Portugal had settled in the Americas by 1700.

Like the Spanish, these colonists found Native Americans living in the places they settled. In some cases, new colonists lived peacefully with Native Americans. In other cases, conflict occurred, and colonists and Native Americans fought bloody wars.

Unlike the Spanish, other European colonists in the Americas did not find huge deposits of gold or silver. They did find other valuable resources, though. Among these resources were wood, furs, rich soil, and different foods. These resources helped the countries of England, France, Portugal, and the Netherlands grow wealthy.

**READING CHECK** ▶ **Analyzing** How did the Spanish create an empire in the Americas?

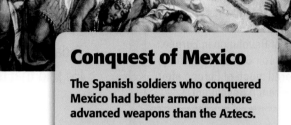

## Conquest of Mexico

The Spanish soldiers who conquered Mexico had better armor and more advanced weapons than the Aztecs.

**SUMMARY AND PREVIEW** The Scientific Revolution and the Age of Exploration expanded knowledge and led to changes around the world. Next, you will read about another time of great change. Called the Enlightenment, this period led to major political changes in Europe.

---

## Section 2 Assessment

hmhsocialstudies.com
ONLINE QUIZ

### Reviewing Ideas, Terms, and Places

1. **a. Describe** How did European attitudes toward science change in the 1500s and 1600s?
   **b. Evaluate** What do you think is the greatest advance of the **Scientific Revolution**? Why?

2. **a. Identify** Who was Christopher Columbus?
   **b. Explain** What drove Europeans to launch the voyages of discovery?
   **c. Elaborate** What challenges do you think made it difficult for explorers to **circumnavigate** the world for the first time?

3. **a. Describe** What enabled Spain to create a huge, powerful empire in the Americas?
   **b. Contrast** How did other countries' American colonies differ from Spain's?

### Critical Thinking

4. **Identifying Cause and Effect** Draw a diagram like the one shown. Using your notes for information, on the left list the causes of European exploration. On the right, list the effects of that exploration.

Causes → European Exploration → Effects

### FOCUS ON WRITING

5. **Describing the Scientific Revolution and the Age of Exploration** What were Europeans discovering and inventing? Where were Europeans traveling? How did these events change Europe? Take notes on events and changes that might interest visitors.

# Political Change in Europe

## What You Will Learn...

### Main Ideas

1. During the Enlightenment, new ideas about government took hold in Europe.
2. The 1600s and 1700s were an Age of Revolution in Europe.
3. Napoleon Bonaparte conquered much of Europe after the French Revolution.

### The Big Idea

Ideas of the Enlightenment inspired revolutions and new governments in Europe.

### Key Terms

Enlightenment, *p. 358*
English Bill of Rights, *p. 360*
Declaration of Independence, *p. 361*
Declaration of the Rights of Man and of the Citizen, *p. 362*
Reign of Terror, *p. 362*

hmhsocialstudies.com
**TAKING NOTES**

Use the graphic organizer online to take notes on Enlightenment ideas and the events they inspired.

## If **YOU** lived there...

You live in a village in northern France in the 1700s. Your father is a baker, and your mother is a seamstress. Like most people in your village, your family struggles to make ends meet. All your life you have been taught that the nobility has a right to rule over you. Today, though, a man made an angry speech in the village market. He said that the common people should demand more rights.

**How do you think your village will react?**

**BUILDING BACKGROUND** The Scientific Revolution and the Age of Exploration expanded Europeans' knowledge and changed life in many ways. The 1600s and 1700s brought still more changes. Some people began to use reason to improve government and society.

## The Enlightenment

Think about the last time you faced a problem that required careful thought. Perhaps you were working a complex math problem or trying to figure out how to win a game. Whatever the problem, when you thought carefully about how to solve it, you were using your power to reason, or to think logically.

### The Age of Reason

During the 1600s and 1700s a number of people began to put great importance on reason, or logical thought. They started using reason to challenge long-held beliefs about education, government, law, and religion. By using reason, these people hoped to solve problems such as poverty and war. They believed the use of reason could achieve three great goals—knowledge, freedom, and happiness—and thereby improve society. The use of reason in shaping people's ideas about society and politics defined a period called the **Enlightenment**. Because of its focus on reason, this period is also known as the Age of Reason.

# The Enlightenment

This 1764 painting shows a salon, a social gathering where people met to discuss Enlightenment ideas. The artist is Michel-Barthelemy Ollivier.

**INTERPRETING CHARTS** What were the key Enlightenment ideas about natural laws?

## Key Enlightenment Ideas

- The ability to reason is unique to humans.
- Reason can be used to solve problems and to improve people's lives.
- Reason can free people from ignorance.
- The natural world is governed by laws that can be discovered through reason.
- Natural laws also govern human behavior.
- Governments should reflect natural laws and encourage education and debate.

## New Ideas about Government

During the Enlightenment, some people used reason to examine government. They questioned how governments worked and what the purpose of government should be. In doing so, these people developed completely new ideas about government. These ideas would help lead to the creation of modern democracy.

At the time of the Enlightenment, monarchs, or kings and queens, ruled in most of Europe. Many of these monarchs believed they ruled through divine right. That is, they thought God gave them the right to rule however they chose.

Some people challenged rule by divine right. They thought rulers' powers should be limited to protect people's freedoms. These people said government's purpose was to protect and to serve the people.

John Locke, an English philosopher, had a major influence on Enlightenment thinking about the role of government.

Locke thought government should be a **contract** between a ruler and the people. A contract binds both sides, so it would limit the ruler's power. Locke also believed that all people had certain natural rights, such as life, liberty, and property. If a ruler did not protect these natural rights, people had the right to change rulers.

Other scholars built on Locke's ideas. One was Jean-Jacques Rousseau (roo-SOH). He said government should express the will, or desire, of the people. According to Rousseau, citizens give the government the power to make and enforce laws. But if these laws do not serve the people, the government should give up its power.

These Enlightenment ideas spread far and wide. In time, they would inspire some Europeans to rise up against their rulers.

**ACADEMIC VOCABULARY**
contract
a binding legal agreement

**READING CHECK** Contrasting How did Enlightenment ideas about government differ from the views of most monarchs?

# The Age of Revolution

The 1600s and 1700s were a time of great change in Europe. Some changes were peaceful, such as those in science. Other changes were more violent. In England, North America, and France, new ideas about government led to war and the Age of Revolution.

## Civil War and Reform in England

In England, Enlightenment ideas led to conflict between the monarchs, or rulers, and Parliament, the lawmaking body. For many years England's rulers had shared power with Parliament. The relationship was an uneasy one, however. As rulers and Parliament fought for power, the situation grew worse.

In 1642 the power struggle erupted in civil war. Supporters of Parliament forced King Charles I from power. He was later tried and beheaded. A new government then formed, but it was unstable.

**FOCUS ON READING**
Read the paragraph about Magna Carta. What date and signal words help you tell that this document was written long before the English Bill of Rights?

By 1660 many of the English were tired of instability. They wanted to restore the monarchy. They asked the former king's son to rule England as Charles II. However, Charles had to agree to let Parliament keep powers it had gained during the civil war.

In 1689 Parliament further limited the monarch's power. That year, it approved the **English Bill of Rights**. This document listed rights for Parliament and the English people. For example, it gave Parliament the power to pass laws and to raise taxes.

In addition, Parliament made the king promise to honor Magna Carta. Signed in 1215, this document limited the English ruler's power and protected some rights of the people. However, few monarchs had honored it during the previous 400 years. Parliament wanted to be sure future rulers honored Magna Carta.

By 1700 Parliament held most of the political power in England. Divine right to rule had ended for England's monarchy.

## Documents of Democracy

The key documents shown here greatly influenced the growth of modern democracy.

**ANALYZING VISUALS** Which two of the documents at right contain some of John Locke's ideas?

**Magna Carta** (1215)
- Limited the power of the monarchy
- Identified people's rights to property
- Established people's rights to trial by a jury

**The English Bill of Rights** (1689)
- Outlawed cruel and unusual punishment
- Guaranteed free speech for members of Parliament

## The American Revolution

In time, Enlightenment ideas spread to the British colonies in North America. There, the British ruler's power was not limited as it was in England. For this reason, many colonists had grown unhappy with British rule. These colonists began to protest the British laws that they thought were unfair.

In 1775 the protests turned to violence, starting the Revolutionary War. Colonial leaders, influenced by the ideas of Locke and Rousseau, claimed Great Britain had denied their rights. In July 1776 they signed the **Declaration of Independence**. Largely written by Thomas Jefferson, this document declared the American colonies' independence from Britain. A new nation, the United States of America, was born.

In 1783 the United States officially won its independence. The colonists had successfully put Enlightenment ideas into practice. Their success would inspire many other people, particularly in France.

## The French Revolution

The people of France closely watched the events of the American Revolution. Soon, they grew inspired to fight for their own rights in the French Revolution.

A major cause of the French Revolution was anger over the differences between social classes. In France, the king ruled over a society split into three classes called estates. The Catholic clergy made up the First Estate. They enjoyed many benefits. Nobles belonged to the Second Estate. These people held important positions in military, government, and the courts. The majority of the French people were members of the Third Estate. This group included peasants, craftworkers, and shopkeepers.

Many Third Estate members thought France's classes were unfair. These people were poor and often hungry. Yet, they paid the highest taxes. While they suffered, King Louis XVI held fancy parties, and Queen Marie-Antoinette wore costly clothes.

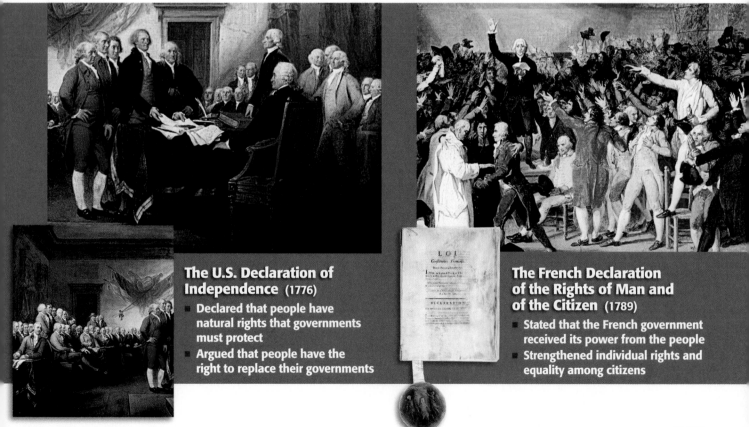

**The U.S. Declaration of Independence** (1776)
- Declared that people have natural rights that governments must protect
- Argued that people have the right to replace their governments

**The French Declaration of the Rights of Man and of the Citizen** (1789)
- Stated that the French government received its power from the people
- Strengthened individual rights and equality among citizens

Meanwhile, France's government was deeply in debt. To raise money, Louis XVI wanted to tax the wealthy. He called a meeting of the representatives of the three estates to discuss a tax increase.

The meeting did not go smoothly. Some members of the Third Estate were familiar with Enlightenment ideas. These members demanded a greater voice in the meeting's decisions. Eventually, the Third Estate members formed a separate group called the National Assembly. This group demanded that the French king accept a constitution limiting his powers.

Louis XVI refused, which angered the common people of Paris. On July 14, 1789, this anger led a mob to storm the Bastille, a prison in Paris. The mob released the prisoners and destroyed the building. The French Revolution had begun.

The French Revolution quickly spread to the countryside. In events called the Great Fear, peasants took revenge on landlords and other nobles for long years of poor treatment. In their rage, the peasants burned down houses and monasteries.

At the same time, other leaders of the revolution were taking peaceful steps. The National Assembly wrote and approved the **Declaration of the Rights of Man and of the Citizen**. This 1789 French constitution guaranteed French citizens some rights and made taxes fairer. Among the freedoms the constitution supported were the freedoms of speech, of the press, and of religion.

## The French Republic

In time, revolutionary leaders created a French republic. The new republic did not end France's many growing problems, however. Unrest soon returned.

In 1793 the revolutionaries executed Louis XVI. His execution was the first of many as the government began arresting anyone who questioned its rule. The result was the **Reign of Terror**, a bloody period of the French Revolution during which the government executed thousands of its opponents and others at the guillotine (GEE-uh-teen). This device beheaded victims with a large, heavy blade. The Reign of Terror finally ended when one of its own leaders was executed in 1794.

Although a violent period, the French Revolution did achieve some of its goals. French peasants and workers gained new political rights. The government opened new schools and improved wages. In addition, it ended slavery in France's colonies.

The French republic's leaders struggled, though. As problems grew worse, a strong leader rose up to take control.

**READING CHECK** Analyzing Why did many members of the Third Estate support revolution?

# The Storming of the Bastille

On July 14, 1789, a mob stormed and destroyed the Bastille, a prison in Paris. To many French people, this prison symbolized the king's harsh rule.

**ANALYZING VISUALS** What were some weapons used in the French Revolution?

## Napoleon Bonaparte

Jacques-Louis David painted this scene of Napoleon crowning his wife, Josephine, empress after crowning himself emperor. The coronation took place in 1804 in Notre Dame Cathedral in Paris, France.

**ANALYZING VISUALS** How does the event show Napoleon's power?

### Napoleonic Empire, 1812

North Sea

ATLANTIC OCEAN

Paris

Vienna

Madrid

Rome

Mediterranean Sea

# Napoleon Bonaparte

In 1799 France was ripe for a change in leadership. That year, Napoleon Bonaparte, a 30-year-old general, took control. Many French people welcomed him because he seemed to support the Revolution's goals. His popularity grew quickly, and in 1804 Napoleon crowned himself emperor.

## Military Conquests and Rule

Napoleon was a brilliant military leader. Under his command, the French army won a series of dazzling victories. By 1810 France's empire stretched across Europe.

In France, Napoleon restored order. He created an efficient government, made taxes fairer, and formed a system of public education. Perhaps his most important accomplishment was the creation of a new French legal system, the Napoleonic Code.

This legal code reflected the ideals of the French Revolution, such as equality before the law and equal civil rights.

With these many accomplishments, Napoleon sounds like a perfect leader. But he was not. He harshly punished anyone who opposed or questioned his rule.

## Napoleon's Defeat

In the end, bad weather contributed to Napoleon's downfall. In 1812 he led an invasion of Russia. The invasion was a disaster. Bitterly cold weather and smart Russian tactics forced Napoleon's army to retreat. Many French soldiers died.

Great Britain, Prussia, and Russia then joined forces and in 1814 defeated Napoleon's weakened army. He returned a year later with a new army, but was again defeated. The British then exiled him to an island, where he died in 1821.

## Europe after the Congress of Vienna, 1815

Boundary of the German Confederation

0    150    300 Miles
0    150    300 Kilometers
Projection: Azimuthal Equal Area

### map zone
**Geography Skills**

**Regions** After the defeat of Napoleon in 1814, the Congress of Vienna reorganized Europe.

1. **Name** What were Europe's largest empires in 1815?
2. **Analyze** How might France's location have contributed to Napoleon's rise and fall?

In 1814 European leaders met at the Congress of Vienna. There, they redrew the map of Europe. Their goal was to keep any country from ever becoming powerful enough to threaten Europe again.

**READING CHECK Drawing Inferences** Why did other countries want to defeat Napoleon?

**SUMMARY AND PREVIEW** You have read how new ideas about government arose out of the Enlightenment. These ideas led to revolutions and political change in Europe and elsewhere. Next, you will read about the growth of industry and how it changed European society.

---

## Section 3 Assessment

hmhsocialstudies.com
**ONLINE QUIZ**

### Reviewing Ideas, Terms, and Places

1. **a. Define** What does divine right mean?
   **b. Explain** What did **Enlightenment** thinkers believe the purpose of government should be?
2. **a. Describe** What was the significance of the **English Bill of Rights**?
   **b. Make Inferences** Why do you think many Americans consider Thomas Jefferson a hero?
   **c. Evaluate** How successful do you think the French Revolution was? Explain your answer.
3. **a. Identify** Who was Napoleon Bonaparte, and what were his main accomplishments?
   **b. Analyze** How were Napoleon's forces weakened and then defeated?

### Critical Thinking

4. **Sequencing** Review your notes. Then use a time line like the one here to list the main events of the Age of Revolution. List the events in the order in which they occurred.

### FOCUS ON WRITING

5. **Describing Political Change in Europe** Take notes on the political changes that occurred during this period. What exciting and dramatic events might interest visitors? For example, visitors might want to see the American Revolution firsthand.

# Making Economic Choices

## Learn

The economic choices that people make are a part of geography. For example, consider an economic choice you might make. You have a certain amount of spending money. You can either go to a movie with a friend or buy a CD. You cannot afford to do both, so you must make a choice.

Countries also must make economic choices. For example, a country might face a choice about whether to spend government money on improving defense, education, or health care.

Making economic choices involves sacrifices, or trade-offs. If you choose to spend your money on a movie, the trade-offs are the other things you want but cannot buy. By considering trade-offs, you can make better economic choices.

## Practice

You are on the school dance committee. The committee has enough money to upgrade one item for the dance. As the diagram below shows, the committee can spend the money on fancy decorations, a live band, or a ballroom. The committee votes and chooses the fancy decorations.

**1** Based on the diagram below, what are the trade-offs of the committee's choice?

**2** What would have been the trade-offs if the committee had voted to spend the money on a ballroom instead?

**3** How do you think creating a diagram like the one below might have helped the committee make its economic choice?

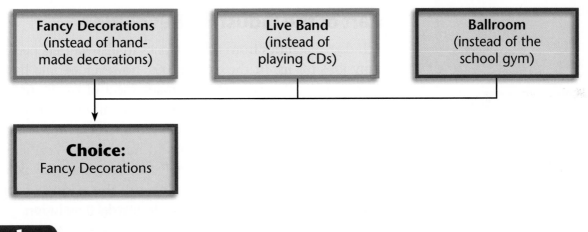

## Apply

1. Describe an example of an economic choice you might face that has three possible trade-offs.
2. For each possible economic choice, identify what the trade-offs are if you make that choice.
3. What final choice will you make? Why?
4. How did considering trade-offs help you make your choice?

# The Industrial Revolution

## If YOU lived there...

You live in Lancashire, England, in 1815. You and your family are weavers. You spin sheep's wool into thread. Then you weave the thread into fine woolen cloth to sell to local merchants. Now a mill is being built nearby. It will have large machines that weave cloth. The mill owner is looking for workers to run the machines. Some of your friends are going to work in the mill to earn more money.

**What do you think about working in the mill?**

**BUILDING BACKGROUND** In the mid-1700s great changes in industry revolutionized life in Europe. Like some earlier revolutions, the growth of industry was driven by new inventions and technology. This industrial growth would have far-reaching effects on society.

## Start of the Industrial Revolution

Each day, machines from alarm clocks to dishwashers perform many jobs for us. In the early 1700s, however, people had to do most work themselves. They made most of the items they needed by hand. For power, they used animals or water or their own muscles. Then around the mid-1700s, everything changed. People began inventing machines to make goods and supply power. These machines completely changed the way people across Europe worked and lived. We call this period of rapid growth in machine-made goods the **Industrial Revolution**.

### From Farmworker to Industrial Laborer

Changes in farming helped pave the way for industrial growth. Since the Middle Ages, farming in Europe had been changing. Wealthy farmers had started buying up land and creating larger farms. These large farms were more efficient. For this reason, many people who owned small farms lost their land. They then had to work for other farmers or move to cities.

At the same time, Europe's growing population was creating a need for more food. To meet this need, farmers began looking for ways to grow more and better crops. Farmers began to experiment with new methods. They also began improving farm technology. Englishman Jethro Tull, for example, invented a seed drill. This device made it possible to plant seeds in straight rows and at certain depths. As a result, more seeds grew into plants.

Better farming methods and technology had several effects. For one, farmers could grow more crops with less labor. With more crops available for food, the population grew even more. With less need for labor, however, many farmworkers lost their jobs. These workers then moved to cities. There, they created a large labor force for the coming industrial growth.

## Great Britain's Resources

Great Britain provided the setting for the Industrial Revolution's start. Britain and its colonies had the resources needed for industrial growth. These resources included labor, raw materials, and money to invest. For example, Britain had a large workforce, rich supplies of coal, and many rivers for waterpower.

In addition, Great Britain's colonial markets and its growing population were increasing the demand for manufactured goods. Increased demand led people to look for ways to make goods faster or more easily. In Britain all these things came together to start the Industrial Revolution.

**READING CHECK** **Identifying Cause and Effect** How did new technology and better farming methods affect agriculture in Europe?

## Inventions of the Industrial Revolution

Starting in the mid-1700s, inventions changed the way goods were made. James Hargreaves's spinning jenny, above, made thread quickly. The Bessemer furnace, at left, was an invention of the late Industrial Revolution. The furnace made steel from molten iron.

**ANALYZING VISUALS** What do you think operating a Bessemer furnace was like?

# Industrial Growth

New inventions continue to make communication faster and easier. Cell phones and e-mail are just two examples.

**FOCUS ON READING**

Which came first, Arkwright's invention or Bessemer's? How can you tell?

Industrial growth began with **textiles**, or cloth products. In the early 1700s people made cloth by hand. They used spinning wheels to make thread and looms to weave it into cloth. Given the time and effort this took, it is not surprising that people would want a way to make cloth quickly.

## The Textile Industry

A big step toward manufactured clothing came in 1769. That year, an Englishman, named Richard Arkwright invented a waterpowered spinning machine. Called a water frame, this machine could produce dozens of threads at one time. In contrast, a person using a traditional spinning wheel could produce only one thread at a time.

Other machines sped up production even more. With these new machines, workers could produce large amounts of cloth quickly. As a result, the price of cloth fell. Soon, the British were using machines to make many types of goods. People housed these machines in buildings called factories, and the factories needed power.

## Other Inventions

Most early machines ran on waterpower. Thus, factories had to be located by rivers. Although Britain had many rivers, they were not always in desirable locations.

Steam power provided a solution. In the 1760s James Watt, a Scot, built the first modern steam engine. Soon, steam powered most machines. Factories could now be built in better places, such as in cities.

Steam power increased the demand for coal and iron, which were needed to make machinery. Iron can be a brittle metal, though, and iron parts often broke. Then in 1855 Englishman Henry Bessemer developed a cheap way to convert iron into steel, which is stronger. This invention led to the growth of the steel industry.

In addition, new inventions improved transportation and communication. Steam engines powered riverboats and trains, speeding up transportation. The telegraph made communication faster. Instead of sending a note by boat or train, people could go to a telegraph office and instantly send a message over a long distance.

## The Factory System

Industrial growth led to major changes in the way people worked and lived. Before, most people had worked on farms or in their homes. Now, more people were going to work in factories. Many of these workers were young women and children, whom owners paid lower wages.

Factory work was long, tiring, and dangerous. Factory workers did the same tasks for 12 hours or more a day, six days a week. Breaks were few, and rules were strict. Although people made more than on farms, wages were still low.

To add to the toil, factory conditions were miserable and unsafe. Year-round, the air was thick with dust, which could harm workers' lungs. In addition, the large machines were dangerous and caused many injuries. Even so, factory jobs were desirable to people with few alternatives.

## Spread of Industry

In time, the Industrial Revolution spread from Great Britain to other parts of Europe. By the late 1800s, factories were making goods across much of Western Europe.

The growth of industry helped lead to a new economic system, **capitalism**. In this system, individuals own most businesses and resources. People invest money in businesses in the hope of making a profit.

**READING CHECK** **Evaluating** If you had lived at this time, would you have left a farm to work in a factory for more money? Why, or why not?

# A British Textile Factory

In early textile factories, workers ran machines in a large room. A supervisor kept a watchful eye. Conditions in factories were poor, and the work was long, tiring, and dangerous. Even so, young women and children as young as six worked in many early factories.

Factory owners keep windows shut to prevent air from blowing the threads. This creates a hot, stuffy room.

Dust and cotton fibers fill the air, causing breathing problems.

One task is to straighten threads as they come out of the machines. This task can cut workers' hands.

Machines are loud. Workers must shout to be heard over the deafening roar.

To avoid being injured or killed, girls must tie back their hair to keep it from getting caught in the machines.

**ANALYSIS SKILL** **ANALYZING VISUALS**

Why do you think the machines in early textile factories caused so many injuries?

Reform efforts addressed the workplace, society, and government. Here, British suffragettes campaign for the right to vote.

At the same time, industrial growth made life worse in other ways. Cities grew rapidly. They became dirty, noisy, and crowded. Many workers remained poor. They often had to live crammed together in shabby, unsafe apartments. In these conditions, diseases spread rapidly as well.

Such problems led to efforts to reform society and politics. People worked to have laws passed improving wages and factory conditions. Others worked to make cities cleaner and safer. Efforts to gain political power were led by **suffragettes**, women who campaigned to gain the right to vote. In 1928 British suffragettes won the right to vote for women in Great Britain. Changes like these helped usher in the modern age.

**READING CHECK** **Summarizing** How did the Industrial Revolution affect cities in Europe?

## Changes in Society

The Industrial Revolution improved life in Europe in many ways. Manufactured goods became cheaper and more available. Inventions made life easier. More people grew wealthier and joined the middle class. These people could afford to live well.

**SUMMARY AND PREVIEW** As you have read, industrial growth greatly changed how many Europeans lived and worked. In the next chapter you will learn about Europe's modern history.

---

**hmhsocialstudies.com**
ONLINE QUIZ

## Section 4 Assessment

### Reviewing Ideas, Terms, and Places

1. **a. Recall** In which country did the start of the **Industrial Revolution** take place?
   **b. Draw Conclusions** How did changes in farming help pave the way for industrial growth?
   **c. Develop** Write a few sentences defending the idea that Great Britain was ready for industrial growth in the early 1700s.
2. **a. Identify** What were two inventions that contributed to industrial growth during this period?
   **b. Make Inferences** How do you think work in a factory differed from that on a farm?
3. **a. Recall** What did the **suffragettes** achieve?
   **b. Summarize** What problems did industry create? How did people work to solve these problems?

### Critical Thinking

4. **Identifying Cause and Effect** Review your notes. Then use a diagram like the one shown to explain how each change in society led to the next.

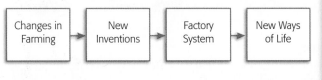

| Changes in Farming | New Inventions | Factory System | New Ways of Life |

### FOCUS ON WRITING

5. **Describing the Industrial Revolution** What might encourage people to visit Europe during the Industrial Revolution? Jot down some ideas in your notes. For example, people might want to see what it was like to work in an early factory.

**Geography's Impact**
video series
Review the video to answer the closing question:
*How did the Renaissance and Reformation change Europe?*

## Visual Summary

*Use the visual summary below to help you review the main ideas of the chapter.*

**QUICK FACTS**

The Renaissance and the Reformation introduced new ideas, art, and ways of thinking into Europe.

Advances of the Scientific Revolution, such as the astrolabe, led to European exploration and empires.

The new ideas of the Enlightenment led to European revolutions, such as the French Revolution.

Driven by new technologies, much of Europe developed industrial societies in the 1700s and 1800s.

## Reviewing Vocabulary, Terms, and Places

*Copy each sentence onto your own paper and fill in the blank with the word or place in the pair that best completes each sentence.*

**1.** Two important Italian trading cities were Venice and _____ (Florence/Wittenberg).

**2.** A way of thinking and learning that stresses the importance of human abilities is called _____ (humanism/perspective).

**3.** The _____ (Renaissance/Reformation) was a movement to reform the Catholic Church.

**4.** Magellan led a voyage that became the first to _____ (circumnavigate/navigate) Earth.

**5.** The first European country to build an American empire was _____ (Spain/Portugal).

**6.** The _____ (Renaissance/Enlightenment) is the period during which people used reason to examine society and politics.

**7.** John Locke thought government should be a _____ (contract/divine right) between the ruler and the people.

**8.** The Industrial Revolution began in _____ (steel/textiles).

**9.** Industrial growth led to a new economic system called _____ (capitalism/communism).

**10.** British women called _____ (suffragettes/reformers) campaigned for the right to vote.

## Comprehension and Critical Thinking

**SECTION 1** *(Pages 344–349)*

**11. a. Describe** What was the Reformation?

   **b. Summarize** How did the Renaissance affect art, literature, and science?

   **c. Evaluate** Do you think the Renaissance was truly a rebirth of Europe? Why, or why not?

## SECTION 2 (Pages 350–357)

**12. a. Identify** What did Christopher Columbus and Ferdinand Magellan achieve?

**b. Identify Cause and Effect** How did the Scientific Revolution help contribute to the Age of Exploration?

**c. Elaborate** How did European colonization of the Americas affect European society?

## SECTION 3 (Pages 358–364)

**13. a. Recall** What three goals did Enlightenment thinkers believe the use of reason could achieve?

**b. Compare** What ideas did John Locke and Jean-Jacques Rousseau share?

**c. Elaborate** How did the English Bill of Rights and the Declaration of the Rights of Man and of the Citizen change the power of monarchs?

## SECTION 4 (Pages 366–370)

**14. a. Recall** In which country did the Industrial Revolution start?

**b. Identify Cause and Effect** How did industrial growth lead to improvements in society?

**c. Evaluate** Which Industrial Revolution invention do you think was most significant? Why?

# Using the Internet 21ST CENTURY

**15. Activity: Creating a Biography** The period of the Renaissance saw many advances in art and literature. Through your online textbook, learn about some of the artists and writers of the Renaissance. Then choose one artist or writer to learn more about and write a brief biography of his or her life. Be sure to include information on the person's accomplishments and significance.

↗ hmhsocialstudies.com

# Social Studies Skills 21ST CENTURY

**Making Economic Choices** *You have enough money to buy one of the following items: shoes, a DVD, or a book.*

**16.** What are the trade-offs if you buy the DVD?

**17.** What are the trade-offs if you buy the book?

# Map Activity 21ST CENTURY

**18. Europe, 1500–1900** On a separate sheet of paper, match the letters on the map with their correct labels.

| | | |
|---|---|---|
| Florence | Madrid | Venice |
| London | Paris | Wittenberg |

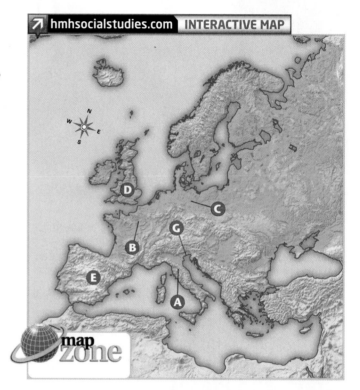

↗ hmhsocialstudies.com   INTERACTIVE MAP

### FOCUS ON READING AND WRITING

**19. Understanding Chronological Order** Create a time line that lists 10 significant events covered in this chapter. List the events in the order in which they occurred and provide a date and label for each event.

**20. Creating a Travel Brochure** By now you should know which time period you want to cover. Create a travel brochure to encourage people to visit Europe during that time period. Use images and descriptive language to convince your readers to travel to the period. In your brochure, highlight interesting historical events that visitors might witness, interesting people they might meet, or new ideas they might learn.

*DIRECTIONS: Read questions 1 through 7 and write the letter of the best response. Then read question 8 and write your own well-constructed response.*

**1** Which person played an important role in spreading the ideas of the Renaissance beyond Italy?

   A Johann Gutenberg

   B Leonardo da Vinci

   C Martin Luther

   D William Shakespeare

**2** What land did Christopher Columbus reach on his voyage in 1492?

   A America

   B China

   C India

   D Spain

**3** Which event marked the beginning of the French Revolution?

   A Congress of Vienna

   B Great Fear

   C Reign of Terror

   D Storming of the Bastille

**4** The Industrial Revolution began in which of the following countries?

   A France

   B Germany

   C Great Britain

   D Spain

**5** A period of rapid growth in machine-made goods during the 1700s and 1800s is the

   A American Revolution.

   B French Revolution.

   C Industrial Revolution.

   D Scientific Revolution.

**Religions in Europe, 1600**

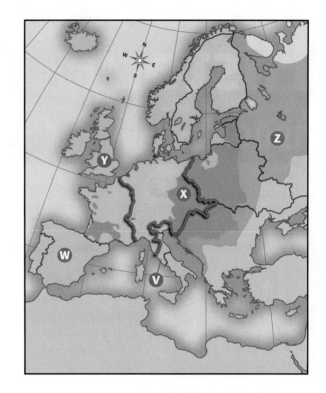

**6** On the map above, which letter marks a Protestant area?

   A V

   B W

   C Y

   D Z

**7** On the map, which letter indicates Rome?

   A V

   B W

   C X

   D Y

**8** **Extended Response**  Examine the Section 2 map European Exploration, 1487–1580. Select the two voyages that you think are most significant in European history. Describe each voyage, identify who led it, and explain its significance.

# Modern European History

## 1900–Today

**Essential Question** How have major conflicts shaped the history of modern Europe?

## What You Will Learn...

In this chapter you will learn about Europe since 1900. You will study the causes and effects of World Wars I and II. You will also learn about the Cold War and how it divided Europe. Finally, you will discover how Europe was reunited at the end of the Cold War.

### FOCUS ON READING AND WRITING

**Using Context Clues—Contrast** As you read, you may come across words you do not understand. When that happens, use context clues—words and sentences around the word—to guess at its meaning. Sometimes the clue to a word's meaning is a contrast clue. It tells you how the unknown word is different from a word you already know. **See the lesson, Using Context Clues—Contrast, on page 530.**

**Writing a Diary Entry** In this chapter you will read about European history since 1900. As you read, think about what it would have been like to live during this period. Later you will write a diary entry from the point of view of someone who lived during these times.

---

German U-boats

ATLANTIC OCEAN

Madrid

**map zone**

**Geography Skills**

**Place** Modern European history was marked by huge conflicts and later reunification.
1. **Identify** Into what country are the German soldiers marching?
2. **Make Inferences** What do the icons on the map indicate to you about modern European history?

AFRICA

**World War I** Soldiers from Europe's most powerful countries engaged in trench warfare during World War I.

# Europe, 1900–Today

North Sea

**European Union**

Baltic Sea

**HISTORY** Battle of Britain

hmhsocialstudies.com VIDEO

London

Berlin

**Bombing damage in Warsaw**

**Vladimir Lenin**

Paris

**EUROPE**

**German troops invade France**

Rome

Black Sea

100    300 Miles

0    100    200 Kilometers

*Projection: Azimuthal Equal Area*

10°E

ASIA

20°E    30°E

*Mediterranean Sea*

**World War II** The rise of strong dictators, like Germany's Adolf Hitler, led to the outbreak of the Second World War.

**Europe since 1945** The end of the Cold War and the fall of the Berlin Wall helped to reunite Europe by the end of the 1900s.

# World War I

## If YOU lived there...

It is 1914, and you live in London. For years you have heard about an important alliance between Great Britain, France, and Russia. Each country has promised to protect the others. Just days ago, you learned that war has broken out in Eastern Europe. Russia and France are preparing for war. People are saying that Britain will fight to protect its allies. If that happens, Europe's most powerful countries will be at war.

**How do you feel about the possibility of war?**

**BUILDING BACKGROUND** The 1800s were a time of rapid change in Europe. Industries grew quickly. Cities expanded. The countries of Europe raced to build empires and gain power. As each country tried to outdo the others, conflicts emerged. Europe was poised for war.

## The Outbreak of War

In the early 1900s Europe was on the brink of war. Rivalries were building among Europe's strongest nations. One small spark would be enough to start World War I.

### Causes of the War

During the 1800s nationalism changed Europe. **Nationalism is devotion and loyalty to one's country.** Some groups that were ruled by powerful empires wanted to build their own nation-states. For example, nationalism led some people in Bosnia and Herzegovina, a region in southeastern Europe, to demand their independence from the Austro-Hungarian Empire. Nationalism also created rivalries among many nations. By the early 1900s nationalism had grown so strong that countries were willing to go to war to prove their superiority over their rivals. A fierce competition emerged among the countries of Europe.

This competition for land, resources, and power drove many European countries to strengthen their armed forces. They built powerful armies and created stockpiles of new weapons. Each country wanted to show its strength and intimidate its rivals.

hmhsocialstudies.com
TAKING NOTES

Use the graphic organizer online to take notes on the causes and effects of World War I.

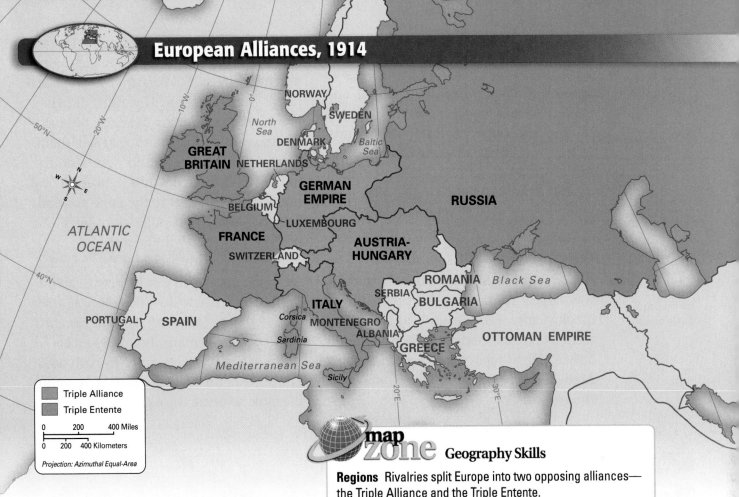

NORWAY
SWEDEN
North Sea
DENMARK
Baltic Sea
GREAT BRITAIN
NETHERLANDS
GERMAN EMPIRE
RUSSIA
BELGIUM
LUXEMBOURG
ATLANTIC OCEAN
FRANCE
SWITZERLAND
AUSTRIA-HUNGARY
ROMANIA
Black Sea
SERBIA
BULGARIA
PORTUGAL
SPAIN
ITALY
Corsica
MONTENEGRO
ALBANIA
GREECE
OTTOMAN EMPIRE
Sardinia
Mediterranean Sea
Sicily

Triple Alliance
Triple Entente

0    200    400 Miles
0  200  400 Kilometers

Projection: Azimuthal Equal-Area

**map zone** **Geography Skills**

**Regions** Rivalries split Europe into two opposing alliances—the Triple Alliance and the Triple Entente.
1. **Locate** Which alliance controlled central Europe?
2. **Draw Conclusions** Why do you think the location of the Triple Entente might have threatened the Triple Alliance?

Both Great Britain and Germany, for example, competed to build strong navies and powerful new battleships.

As tensions and suspicions grew, some European leaders hoped to protect their countries by creating alliances. An **alliance** is an agreement between countries. If one country is attacked, its allies—members of the alliance—help defend it. In 1882 Italy, Germany, and Austria-Hungary formed the Triple Alliance. In response, France, Great Britain, and Russia created their own alliance, the Triple Entente (ahn-TAHNT). As you can see in the map, these alliances divided Europe.

## The Spark for War

By the summer of 1914, war in Europe seemed certain. Tensions between Austria-Hungary and Serbia arose over the control of Bosnia and Herzegovina, a province of Austria-Hungary and Serbia's neighbor. On June 28, 1914, a Serbian assassin shot and killed Archduke Francis Ferdinand, the heir to the throne of Austria-Hungary. Seeking revenge, Austria-Hungary declared war on Serbia. After Serbia turned to Russia for help, the alliance system quickly split Europe into two warring sides. On one side was Austria-Hungary and Germany, known as the Central Powers. The Allied Powers—Serbia, Russia, Great Britain, and France—were on the other side.

**READING CHECK** **Finding Main Ideas** What were the causes of World War I?

## War and Victory

Germany struck the first blow in the war, sending a large army into Belgium and France. Allied troops, however, managed to stop the Germans just outside Paris. In the east, Russia attacked Germany and Austria-Hungary, forcing Germany to fight on two fronts. Hopes on both sides for a quick victory soon disappeared.

### A New Kind of War

**ACADEMIC VOCABULARY**

**strategy** a plan for fighting a battle or war

A new military **strategy**, trench warfare, was largely responsible for preventing a quick victory. Early in the war both sides turned to trench warfare. **Trench warfare** is a style of fighting in which each side fights from deep ditches, or trenches, dug into the ground.

Both the Allies and the Central Powers dug hundreds of miles of trenches along the front lines. Soldiers in the trenches faced great suffering. Not only did they live in constant danger of attack, but cold, hunger, and disease also plagued them. Sometimes soldiers would "go over the top" of their trenches and fight for a few hours, only to retreat to the same position. Trench warfare cost millions of lives, but neither side could win the war.

To gain an advantage in the trenches, each side developed deadly new weapons. Machine guns cut down soldiers as they tried to move forward. Poison gas, first used by the Germans, blinded soldiers in the trenches. It was later used by both sides. The British introduced another weapon, the tank, to break through enemy lines.

**Close-up**

# Trench Warfare

**Both the Allied Powers and the Central Powers relied on trenches for defense during World War I. As a result, the war dragged on for years with no clear victor. Each side developed new weapons and technology to try to gain an advantage in the trenches.**

Soldiers often threw or fired small bombs known as grenades.

Soldiers used gas masks to survive attacks of poison gas.

Trenches dug in zigzag patterns prevented the enemy from firing down the length of a trench.

At sea, Britain used its powerful navy to block supplies from reaching Germany. Germany responded by using submarines, called U-boats. German U-boats tried to break the British blockade and sink ships carrying supplies to Great Britain.

## The Allies Win

For three years the war was a stalemate—neither side could defeat the other. Slowly, however, the war turned in favor of the Allies. In early 1917 German U-boats began attacking American ships carrying supplies to Britain. When Germany ignored U.S. warnings to stop, the United States entered the war on the side of the Allies.

Help from American forces gave the Allies a fresh advantage. Soon afterward, however, the exhausted Russians pulled out of the war. Germany quickly attacked the Allies, hoping to put an end to the war. Allied troops, however, stopped Germany's attack. The Central Powers had suffered a great blow. In the fall of 1918 the Central Powers surrendered. The Allied Powers were victorious.

**READING CHECK** **Sequencing** What events led to the end of World War I?

# The War's End

After more than four years of fighting, the war came to an end on November 11, 1918. More than 8.5 million soldiers had been killed, and at least 20 million more were wounded. Millions of civilians had lost their lives as well. The war brought tremendous change to Europe.

## Making Peace

Shortly after the end of the war, leaders from the Allied nations met at Versailles (ver-SY), near Paris. There, they debated the terms of peace for the Central Powers.

The United States, led by President Woodrow Wilson, wanted a just peace after the war. He did not want harsh peace terms that might anger the losing countries and lead to future conflict.

**FOCUS ON READING**
What does the term *just peace* mean? How can you tell?

Other Allied leaders, however, wanted to punish Germany. They believed that Germany had started the war and should pay for it. They believed that weakening Germany would prevent future wars.

In the end, the Allies forced Germany to sign a treaty. The **Treaty of Versailles** was the final peace settlement of World War I. It forced Germany to accept the blame for starting the war. Germany also had to slash the size of its army and give up its overseas colonies. Additionally, Germany had to pay billions of dollars for damages caused during the war.

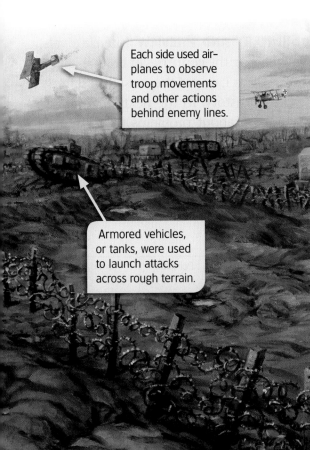

Each side used airplanes to observe troop movements and other actions behind enemy lines.

Armored vehicles, or tanks, were used to launch attacks across rough terrain.

**ANALYSIS SKILL** **ANALYZING VISUALS**

What advantages and disadvantages did trench warfare pose for soldiers?

Vladimir Lenin encouraged Russian workers to support his new Communist government.

over Russia's government and established a Communist government. **Communism** is a political system in which the government owns all property and controls all aspects of life in a country. An uprising toward the end of the war also forced the German emperor from power. A fragile republic replaced the German Empire.

World War I also altered the borders of many European countries. Austria and Hungary became separate countries. Poland and Czechoslovakia each gained their independence. Serbia, Bosnia and Herzegovina, and other Balkan states were combined to create Yugoslavia. Finland, Estonia, Latvia, and Lithuania, which had been part of Russia, became independent.

**READING CHECK** **Summarizing** How did World War I change Europe?

**SUMMARY AND PREVIEW** Intense rivalries among the countries of Europe led to World War I, one of the most devastating wars in history. In the next section you will learn about problems that plagued Europe and led to World War II.

## A New Europe

World War I had a tremendous effect on the countries of Europe. It changed the governments of some European countries and the borders of others. For example, in Russia the war had caused great hardship for the people. A revolution then forced the Russian czar, or emperor, to give up power. Shortly after, Vladimir Lenin took

## Section 1 Assessment

### Reviewing Ideas, Terms, and Places

1. a. **Identify** What event triggered World War I?
   b. **Analyze** How did **nationalism** cause rivalries between some European countries?
   c. **Evaluate** Do you think **alliances** helped or hurt most countries? Explain your answer.
2. a. **Describe** What was **trench warfare** like?
   b. **Draw Conclusions** What difficulties did soldiers face as a result of trench warfare?
   c. **Predict** How might the war have been different if the United States had not entered it?
3. a. **Recall** How did the **Treaty of Versailles** punish Germany for its role in the war?
   b. **Contrast** How did the Allied leaders' ideas for peace with Germany differ?
   c. **Elaborate** Why do you think the war caused changes in government in Russia and Germany?

### Critical Thinking

4. **Categorizing** Draw a chart like the one here. Use your notes to list the results of World War I in the appropriate category.

| Political | Economic |
|-----------|----------|
|           |          |

### FOCUS ON WRITING

5. **Writing about World War I** Think about the events of World War I. Imagine that you were present at one or more events during or after the war. What might you write about in your diary?

## from
# All Quiet on the Western Front

**by Erich Maria Remarque**

Soldiers prepare to rush over the top of a trench during a battle in World War I.

**About the Reading** *In* All Quiet on the Western Front, *author Erich Maria Remarque provides a fictional account of the lives of soldiers during World War I. The book is considered one of the most realistic accounts of the war. In this selection, the book's narrator, twenty-year-old German soldier Paul Bäumer, describes a battle between German and British forces.*

**AS YOU READ** Note the words the speaker uses to describe the battle.

Our trenches have now for some time been shot to pieces, and we have an elastic line, so that there is practically no longer any proper trench warfare. ❶ When attack and counter-attack have waged backwards and forwards there remains a broken line and a bitter struggle from crater to crater. The front-line has been penetrated, and everywhere small groups have established themselves, the fight is carried on from clusters of shell-holes.

We are buried in a crater, the English are coming down obliquely, they are turning our flank and working in behind us. ❷ We are surrounded. It is not easy to surrender, fog and smoke hang over us, no one would recognize that we wanted to give ourselves up, and perhaps we don't want to, a man doesn't even know himself at such moments. We hear the explosions of the hand-grenades coming towards us. Our machine-gun sweeps over the semicircle in front of us . . . Behind us the attack crashes ever nearer.

**GUIDED READING**

**WORD HELP**

**crater** a hole in the ground made by the explosion of a bomb or shell

**penetrated** passed into or through

**obliquely** indirectly or underhandedly

❶ An elastic line describes a battle line that is pushed back and forth by enemy forces.

❷ "Turning our flank" refers to a tactic in which one military force moves around the side of the opposing force in order to surround them.

## Connecting Literature to Geography

1. **Describing** What details in the first paragraph show that the technique of trench warfare is no longer working?

2. **Making Inferences** Why do you think the location of this trench is so important to the war and the people fighting in it?

# World War II

## If YOU lived there...

It is 1922, and you are part of a huge crowd in one of Rome's public squares. Everyone is listening to the fiery speech of a dynamic new leader. He promises to make Italy great again, as it was in the days of ancient Rome. You know that your parents and some of your teachers are excited about his ideas. Others are concerned that he may be too forceful.

**What do you think of this new leader's message?**

## What You Will Learn...

### Main Ideas

1. Economic and political problems troubled Europe in the years after World War I.
2. World War II broke out when Germany invaded Poland.
3. Nazi Germany targeted the Jews during the Holocaust.
4. Allied victories in Europe and Japan brought the end of World War II.

### The Big Idea

Problems in Europe led to World War II, the deadliest war in history.

### Key Terms

Great Depression, *p. 382*
dictator, *p. 383*
Axis Powers, *p. 385*
Allies, *p. 385*
Holocaust, *p. 385*

hmhsocialstudies.com
**TAKING NOTES**

Use the graphic organizer online to take notes on the important dates and events of World War II.

**BUILDING BACKGROUND** Many countries faced deep economic and political problems as a result of World War I. Dictators rose to power in a number of countries, but did not bring solutions. Instead, they attacked their neighbors and plunged the world back into war.

## Problems Trouble Europe

After World War I, Europeans began rebuilding their countries. Just as they had started to recover, however, many economic and political problems emerged. These problems threatened the peace and security of Europe.

### The Great Depression

World War I left much of Europe in shambles. Factories and farmland had been destroyed, and economies were in ruins. Countries that had lost the war, like Germany and Austria, owed billions in war damages. Many countries turned to the United States for help. During the 1920s the U.S. economy was booming. Loans from American banks and businesses helped many European nations recover and rebuild after World War I.

In 1929, however, the recovery fell apart. A stock market crash in the United States triggered a global economic crisis in the 1930s known as the **Great Depression**. As the U.S. economy faltered, American banks stopped lending to Europe. Without U.S. loans and investments, European economies declined. Unemployment skyrocketed as businesses and farms, as well as banks, went bankrupt.

## The Rise of Dictators

The Great Depression added to Europe's problems. Blaming weak governments for the hard times, some Europeans turned to dictators to strengthen their countries and improve their lives. A **dictator** is a ruler who has total control. Dictators rose to power in Russia, Italy, and Germany.

One of the first dictators in Europe was Russia's Vladimir Lenin. Lenin gained power as a result of a 1917 revolution. He formed the first Communist government and took control of businesses and private property. He also united Russia and other republics to create the Soviet Union. After Lenin's death in 1924, Joseph Stalin took power. As dictator, he made all economic decisions, restricted religious worship, and used secret police to spy on citizens.

Benito Mussolini of Italy was another powerful dictator during this period. In the 1920s Mussolini won control of the Italian government and made himself dictator. He promised to make Italy stronger and to revive the economy. He even spoke of restoring the glory of the former Roman Empire. As dictator, however, Mussolini suspended basic rights like freedom of speech and trial by jury.

By the 1930s many Germans had lost faith in their government. They turned to a new political party, the Nazi Party. The party's leader, Adolf Hitler, promised to strengthen Germany. He vowed to rebuild Germany's military and economy. After years of struggle, many Germans listened eagerly to his message. In 1933 Hitler rose to power and soon became dictator. He banned all parties except the Nazi Party. He also began discriminating against so-called inferior races, particularly Germany's Jews.

**READING CHECK** **Generalizing** Why did some people support the rise of dictators?

## European Dictators

Popular dictators rose to power in Europe in the 1920s and 1930s. Adolf Hitler in Germany and Benito Mussolini in Italy gained public support with promises to make life better and to strengthen their countries.

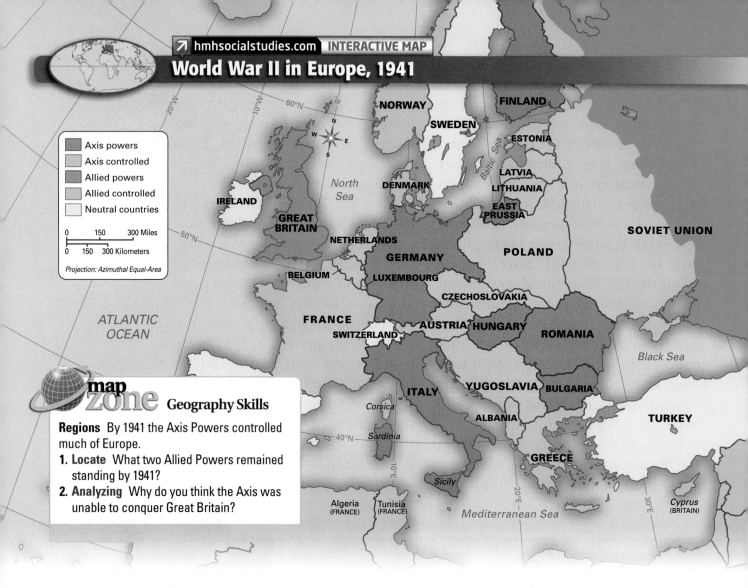

Axis powers
Axis controlled
Allied powers
Allied controlled
Neutral countries

| 0 | 150 | 300 Miles |
| 0 | 150 | 300 Kilometers |

Projection: Azimuthal Equal-Area

**map zone Geography Skills**

**Regions** By 1941 the Axis Powers controlled much of Europe.
1. **Locate** What two Allied Powers remained standing by 1941?
2. **Analyzing** Why do you think the Axis was unable to conquer Great Britain?

## War Breaks Out

As dictators, Hitler and Mussolini were determined to strengthen their countries at any cost. Their actions led to history's deadliest war—World War II.

### Threats to Peace

After World War I, European countries wanted peace. Many countries hoped to prevent another deadly war. By the late 1930s, however, attempts at peace had failed. Instead of peace, Italian and German aggression forced Europe into a second world war.

In 1935 Benito Mussolini ordered his Italian troops to invade Ethiopia, a country in East Africa. Other nations were shocked

by his actions, but none tried to turn back the invasion. Meanwhile, the Italian leader and Germany's Adolf Hitler joined together to form an alliance known as the Rome-Berlin Axis.

Hitler was next to act. In 1938 he broke the Treaty of Versailles when he annexed, or added, Austria to Germany's territory. Although Britain and France protested, they did not attempt to stop Germany.

Later that year, Hitler announced his plan to take Czechoslovakia as well. Many European leaders were worried, but they still hoped to avoid a war. They allowed Hitler to annex part of Czechoslovakia in return for his promise of peace. By the spring of 1939, however, Germany had conquered the rest of Czechoslovakia.

**FOCUS ON READING**
How do contrast clues help you understand the meaning of the word *aggression*?

Italy quickly moved to occupy Albania in the Balkans. Attempts to keep the peace had failed.

Eventually, Great Britain and France realized they could not ignore Hitler's actions. When Germany threatened to take Polish territory, the Allies vowed to protect Poland at all costs. On September 1, 1939, German forces launched an all-out attack on Poland. Two days later, Great Britain and France responded by declaring war on Germany. World War II had begun.

### Allies Lose Ground

Germany's invasion of Poland triggered the Second World War. Germany, Italy, and Japan formed an alliance called the **Axis Powers**. Against them stood the **Allies** —France, Great Britain, and other countries that opposed the Axis.

Germany struck first. After defeating Poland, Germany moved on to a series of quick victories in Western Europe. One by one, countries fell to German forces. In June 1940 Germany invaded and quickly defeated one of Europe's greatest powers, France. In less than a year, Hitler had gained control of almost all of Western Europe.

Next, Germany set its sights on Britain. The German air force repeatedly attacked British cities and military targets. Hitler hoped the British would surrender. Rather than give in, however, the British persevered.

Unable to defeat Great Britain, the Axis Powers turned their attention elsewhere. As German troops marched into Eastern Europe, Italian forces invaded North Africa. By the end of 1941 Germany had invaded the Soviet Union, and Japan had attacked the United States at Pearl Harbor, Hawaii. The Allies were losing ground in the war.

**READING CHECK** **Drawing Inferences** Why do you think the Axis Powers easily gained the advantage in the early years of the war?

## The Holocaust

One of the most horrifying aspects of the war was the Holocaust (HOH-luh-kawst). The **Holocaust** was the attempt by the Nazi government during World War II to eliminate Europe's Jews. Believing that the Germans were a superior race, the Nazis tried to destroy people who they believed were inferior, especially the Jews.

Even before the war began, the Nazi government began restricting the rights of Jews and others in Germany. For example, laws restricted Jews from holding government jobs or attending German schools. Nazis imprisoned countless Jews in camps.

### Primary Source

#### JOURNAL ENTRY
## The Diary of Anne Frank

*Anne Frank and her family fled to Amsterdam to escape Nazi persecution of Jews in Germany. In 1942, when Nazis began rounding up Jews in the Netherlands, the Franks were forced to hide. Anne kept a diary of her time in hiding.*

" Countless friends and acquaintances have gone to a terrible fate. Evening after evening the green and gray army lorries [trucks] trundle past. The Germans ring at every front door to inquire if there are any Jews living in the house. If there are, then the whole family has to go at once. If they don't find any, they go on to the next house. No one has a chance of evading them unless one goes into hiding. "

—from *The Diary of a Young Girl*

**ANALYSIS SKILL** **ANALYZING PRIMARY SOURCES**

What likely happened to the Jews that were rounded up by German officials?

# World War II

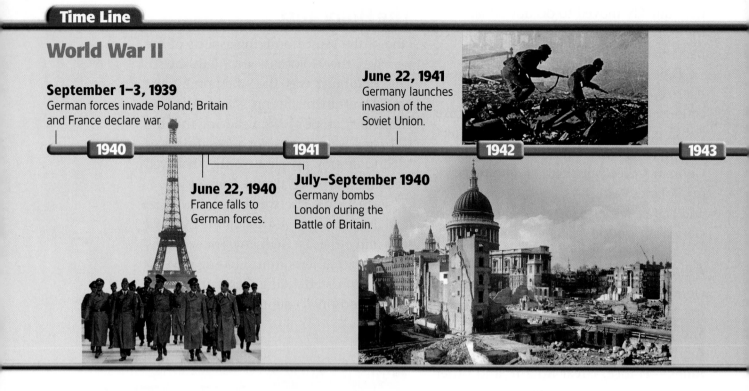

**September 1–3, 1939**
German forces invade Poland; Britain and France declare war.

**June 22, 1941**
Germany launches invasion of the Soviet Union.

**1940**

**1941**

**1942**

**1943**

**June 22, 1940**
France falls to German forces.

**July–September 1940**
Germany bombs London during the Battle of Britain.

Thousands of Jews fled Germany to escape persecution, but many had to remain behind because they were not allowed into other countries.

Germany's expansion into Eastern Europe brought millions more Jews under Hitler's control. In 1942 the Nazi government ordered the destruction of Europe's entire Jewish population. The Nazis used mass executions and concentration camps, like Auschwitz in Poland, to murder 6 million Jews.

The Nazis did face resistance. Some Jews fought back. For example, Jews in Warsaw, Poland, staged an uprising. Some non-Jewish Europeans tried to save Jews from the Nazis. German businessman Oskar Schindler, for example, saved Jews by employing them in his factories. By the time the Nazis were defeated, they had killed about two-thirds of Europe's Jews and several million non-Jews.

**READING CHECK** **Analyzing** Why did Hitler's Nazi government attempt to destroy the Jews?

# End of the War

The Allies did not fare well in the early years of the war. Victories in 1943 and 1944, though, helped them end World War II.

## Allies Are Victorious

In early 1943 U.S. and British forces gained control of North Africa and Italy, forcing Mussolini to surrender. That same year, the Allies defeated the Japanese in several key battles. In the east, Soviet troops forced Germany to retreat.

In June 1944 Allied forces landed on the beaches of Normandy, France. The invasion, or D-Day as it was called, dealt a serious blow to the Axis. It paved the way for Allied forces to advance on Germany.

By the spring of 1945 Allied troops had crossed into German territory. In May 1945 Germany surrendered. In August 1945 the United States used a powerful new weapon, the atomic bomb, to bring the war with Japan to an end. After almost six years of fighting, World War II was over.

**February 1945**
Allied leaders plan the final defeat of the Axis Powers.

**April 1945**
Allied troops begin liberation of Nazi concentration camps.

1944      1945      1946

**June 6, 1944**
Allied forces launch D–Day invasion in Normandy, France.

**May 7, 1945**
Germany surrenders to Allied Powers.

**HISTORY**

**VIDEO**
BBC Report on D-Day

↗ hmhsocialstudies.com

**ANALYSIS SKILL**   **READING TIME LINES**
About how long after the beginning of the war did Germany invade the Soviet Union?

## Results of the War

The war had a huge impact on the world. It resulted in millions of deaths, tensions between the Allies, and the creation of the United Nations.

World War II was the deadliest conflict in history. More than 50 million people lost their lives. Millions more were wounded.

The United States and the Soviet Union emerged from the war as the most powerful countries in the world. An intense rivalry developed between the two countries.

After the war, people hoped to prevent another deadly conflict. In 1945 some 50 nations formed the United Nations, an international peacekeeping organization.

**READING CHECK** **Summarizing** What were the main results of World War II?

**SUMMARY AND PREVIEW** World War II was the deadliest war in history. Next, you will learn about developments in Europe during the postwar period.

**Section 2 Assessment**

↗ hmhsocialstudies.com
ONLINE QUIZ

### Reviewing Ideas, Terms, and Places

1. **a. Define** What was the **Great Depression**?
   **b. Explain** How did economic problems in the United States lead to the Great Depression?
2. **a. Describe** What led to the outbreak of World War II?
   **b. Predict** What might have happened if Great Britain had fallen to Germany?
3. **a. Identify** What was the **Holocaust**?
   **b. Draw Inferences** Why did the Nazis target certain groups for elimination?
4. **a. Recall** What events led to Germany's surrender?
   **b. Analyze** How did World War II change Europe?

### Critical Thinking

5. **Sequencing** Draw a time line like this one. Using your notes on important events, place the main events and their dates on the time line.

   1917                            1945
   ←——┼———┼———┼———┼———┼———┼———→

### FOCUS ON WRITING

6. **Telling about World War II** Imagine that you are an adult during the Second World War. Where might you have lived? What might you have seen and done there? Write down some ideas in your notebook.

# Europe since 1945

## If YOU lived there...

It is November 1989, and you live on the East German side of Berlin. For years the Berlin Wall has divided your city in two. The government has carefully controlled who could cross the border. One night, you hear an exciting rumor—the gate through the Wall is open. People in East and West Berlin can now travel back and forth freely. Young Berliners are celebrating in the streets.

**What will this change mean for your country?**

## The Cold War

Although Europeans were relieved when World War II ended, new problems soon arose. Countries whose governments and economies had been weakened during the war had to work to strengthen them. Entire cities had to be rebuilt. Most importantly, postwar tensions between the Allies divided Europe.

### Superpowers Face Off

The United States and the Soviet Union emerged from World War II as the world's most powerful nations. Allies during the war, the two **superpowers**, or strong and influential countries, now distrusted each other. Growing hostility between the superpowers led to the **Cold War**, a period of tense rivalry between the United States and the Soviet Union.

Much of the hostility between the Soviet Union and the United States focused on political and economic differences. The United States is a democracy with an economy based on free enterprise. The Soviet Union was a Communist country, in which individual freedoms were limited. Its leaders exerted strict control over the political system and the economy. These basic differences separated the two countries.

### What You Will Learn...

#### Main Ideas

1. The Cold War divided Europe between democratic and Communist nations.
2. Many Eastern European countries changed boundaries and forms of government at the end of the Cold War.
3. European cooperation has brought economic and political change to Europe.

#### The Big Idea

After years of division during the Cold War, today Europe is working toward unity.

#### Key Terms

superpowers, *p. 388*
Cold War, *p. 388*
arms race, *p. 390*
common market, *p. 392*
European Union (EU), *p. 392*

hmhsocialstudies.com
**TAKING NOTES**

Use the graphic organizer online to take notes on events in Europe since 1945.

## A Divided Europe, 1955

NORWAY
FINLAND
SWEDEN
IRELAND
UNITED KINGDOM
DENMARK
NETHERLANDS
BELGIUM
EAST GERMANY
POLAND
SOVIET UNION
WEST GERMANY
CZECHOSLOVAKIA
FRANCE
SWITZERLAND
AUSTRIA
HUNGARY
ROMANIA
PORTUGAL
YUGOSLAVIA
SPAIN
ITALY
BULGARIA
ALBANIA
GREECE
TURKEY

North Sea
Baltic Sea
ATLANTIC OCEAN
Black Sea
Mediterranean Sea

NATO countries
Warsaw Pact countries
Other Communist countries
Neutral countries

0    200    400 Miles
0  200  400 Kilometers
Projection: Azimuthal Equal Area

**Geography Skills**

**Regions** The Cold War divided Europe into two distinct alliances—NATO and the Warsaw Pact.

1. **Identify** Which Communist country was not a member of the Warsaw Pact?
2. **Analyze** How was Germany affected by the alliances?

## Causes and Effects of the Cold War

| Causes | Effects |
|---|---|
| ■ Rivalry develops between the United States and the Soviet Union after World War II. | ■ Alliances divide Europe between Communist and non–Communist countries. |
| ■ Hostilities between democratic and Communist governments increase. | ■ Germany is divided into two separate countries. |
| ■ The superpowers dispute the division of Germany after World War II. | ■ The United States and the Soviet Union engage in a nuclear arms race. |

## A Divided Europe

The Cold War divided Europe into non-Communist and Communist countries. Most of Western Europe supported democracy and the United States. Much of Eastern Europe practiced Soviet-style communism. British prime minister Winston Churchill described the split that existed in Europe:

❝ ...an iron curtain has descended across the Continent. Behind that line lie all the capitals of the ancient states of Central and Eastern Europe. ...all are subject...not only to Soviet influence but to...control from Moscow. ❞
—from Winston Churchill's 1946 speech at Westminster College in Fulton, Missouri

Within this divided Europe was a divided Germany. After World War II, the Allies had separated Germany into four zones. By 1948 the Western Allies were ready to reunite their zones. However, the Soviet government feared the threat that a united Germany might pose. The next year, the Western zones were joined to form the Federal Republic of Germany, or West Germany. The Soviets helped to establish the German Democratic Republic, or East Germany. The city of Berlin, located within East Germany, was itself divided into East and West. In 1961 Communist leaders built the Berlin Wall to prevent any East Germans from fleeing to the West.

New alliances divided Europe even further. In 1949 the United States joined with several Western nations to create a powerful new alliance known as NATO, or the North Atlantic Treaty Organization.

**THE IMPACT TODAY**

NATO is still a powerful alliance today with 26 member nations in Europe and North America.

The members of NATO agreed to protect each other if attacked. In response, the Soviet Union formed its own alliance, the Warsaw Pact. Most Eastern European countries joined the Warsaw Pact. The two alliances used the threat of nuclear war to defend themselves. By the 1960s the United States, the Soviet Union, Britain, and France all had nuclear weapons.

The postwar division of Europe into East and West had a lasting effect on both sides. With U.S. assistance, many Western countries experienced economic growth. The economies of Communist Eastern Europe, however, failed to develop. Due to their lack of a market economy and strong industries, they suffered many shortages. They often lacked enough food, clothing, and automobiles to meet demand.

**READING CHECK** Summarizing How did the Cold War affect Europe?

## BIOGRAPHY

### Mikhail Gorbachev
( 1931–   )

Mikhail Gorbachev was a key figure in bringing the Cold War to an end. In 1985 Communist officials appointed Gorbachev the leader of the Soviet Union. He quickly enacted reforms to modernize his country. He expanded basic freedoms, such as freedom of speech and freedom of the press. His democratic reforms helped bring an end to communism in the Soviet Union. In 1990 Mikhail Gorbachev won the Nobel Peace Prize for his efforts to end the Cold War and promote peace.

**Evaluating** Do you think Gorbachev was a popular ruler? Why or why not?

# The End of the Cold War

In the late 1980s tensions between East and West finally came to an end. The collapse of communism and the end of the Cold War brought great changes to Europe.

### Triumph of Democracy

During the Cold War the United States and the Soviet Union competed against each other in an arms race. An **arms race** is a competition between countries to build superior weapons. Each country tried to create more-advanced weapons and to have more nuclear missiles than the other. This arms race was incredibly expensive. The high cost of the arms race eventually damaged the Soviet economy.

By the 1980s the Soviet economy was in serious trouble. Soviet leader Mikhail Gorbachev (GAWR-buh-chawf) hoped to solve the many problems his country faced. He reduced government control of the economy and introduced democratic elections. He improved relations with the United States. Along with U.S. president Ronald Reagan, Gorbachev took steps to slow the arms race.

In part because of these new policies, reform movements soon spread. Beginning in 1989, democratic movements swept through the East. For example, Poland and Czechoslovakia threw off Communist rule. Joyful Germans tore down the Berlin Wall that separated East and West. Several Soviet republics began to demand their independence. Finally, in December 1991 the Soviet Union broke apart.

### Changes in Eastern Europe

The end of the Cold War brought many changes to Eastern Europe. These changes resulted from Germany's reunification, the creation of new countries, and rising ethnic tensions in southeastern Europe.

## The Fall of Communism

Reforms in the Soviet Union in the 1980s encouraged support for democracy throughout Eastern Europe.

**ANALYZING VISUALS** What role did the people play in communism's collapse?

**Fall of the Berlin Wall** East and West Germans celebrate the fall of the Berlin Wall.

**Democracy in Czechoslovakia**
In 1989 pro-democracy demonstrations swept Czechoslovakia. Rallies like this one led to the collapse of Czechoslovakia's Communist government.

The reunification of East and West Germany was one of many changes in Eastern Europe that marked the end of the Cold War. After the fall of the Berlin Wall in 1989, thousands of East Germans began demanding change. In early 1990 the Communist government crumbled. A few months later, the governments of East and West Germany agreed to reunite. After 45 years of division, Germany was reunited.

Other important changes occurred in Eastern Europe after the Cold War. The breakup of the Soviet Union created more than a dozen independent nations. The Russian Federation is the largest and most powerful of these new countries. Ukraine, Lithuania, Belarus, and others also emerged from the former Soviet Union.

Ethnic conflicts have also transformed Eastern Europe since the end of the Cold War. For example, tensions between ethnic groups in Czechoslovakia and Yugoslavia led to the breakup of both countries.

In Czechoslovakia, ethnic tensions divided the country. Disputes between the country's two main ethnic groups emerged in the early 1990s. Both the Czechs and the Slovaks **advocated** separate governments. In January 1993 Czechoslovakia peacefully divided into two countries—the Czech Republic and Slovakia.

While ethnic problems in the former Czechoslovakia were peaceful, ethnic tension in Yugoslavia triggered violence. After the collapse of communism, several Yugoslav republics declared their independence. Different ethnic groups fought each other for control of territory. Yugoslavia's civil wars resulted in years of fighting and thousands of deaths. By 1994 Yugoslavia had split into five countries—Bosnia and Herzegovina, Croatia, Macedonia, Serbia and Montenegro, and Slovenia.

**ACADEMIC VOCABULARY**

**advocate**
to plead in favor of

**READING CHECK** **Drawing Conclusions** How did the end of the Cold War affect Europe?

| Country | Year Admitted | Monetary Unit | Representatives in the European Parliament |
|---|---|---|---|
| Austria | 1995 | Euro | 17 |
| Belgium | 1952 | Euro | 22 |
| Bulgaria | 2007 | Lev | 17 |
| Cyprus | 2004 | Pound | 6 |
| Czech Republic | 2004 | Koruna | 22 |
| Denmark | 1973 | Krone | 13 |
| Estonia | 2004 | Kroon | 6 |
| Finland | 1995 | Euro | 13 |
| France | 1952 | Euro | 72 |
| Germany | 1952 | Euro | 99 |
| Greece | 1979 | Euro | 22 |
| Hungary | 2004 | Forint | 22 |
| Ireland | 1973 | Euro | 12 |
| Italy | 1952 | Euro | 72 |
| Latvia | 2004 | Lats | 8 |
| Lithuania | 2004 | Litas | 12 |
| Luxembourg | 1952 | Euro | 6 |
| Malta | 2004 | Lira | 5 |
| The Netherlands | 1952 | Euro | 25 |
| Poland | 2004 | Zloty | 50 |
| Portugal | 1986 | Euro | 22 |
| Romania | 2007 | Leu | 33 |
| Slovakia | 2004 | Koruna | 13 |
| Slovenia | 2004 | Euro | 7 |
| Spain | 1986 | Euro | 50 |
| Sweden | 1995 | Krona | 18 |
| United Kingdom | 1973 | Pound | 72 |

**Drawing Conclusions** What are the most powerful countries in the European Parliament?

↗ hmhsocialstudies.com

# European Cooperation

Many changes shaped postwar Europe. One of the most important of those changes was the creation of an organization that now joins together most of the countries of Europe.

## A European Community

Two world wars tore Europe apart in the 1900s. After World War II many of Europe's leaders began to look for ways to prevent another deadly war. Some people believed that creating a feeling of community in Europe would make countries less likely to go to war. Leaders like Great Britain's Winston Churchill believed the countries of Europe should cooperate rather than compete. They believed strong economic and political ties were the key.

Six countries—Belgium, France, Italy, Luxembourg, the Netherlands, and West Germany—took the first steps toward European unity. In the early 1950s these six countries joined to create a united economic community. The organization's goal was to form a **common market**, a group of nations that cooperates to make trade among members easier. This European common market, created in 1957, made trade easier among member countries. Over time, other nations joined. Europeans had begun to create a new sense of unity.

## The European Union

Since its beginning in the 1950s, many new nations have become members of this European community, now known as the European Union. The **European Union (EU)** is an organization that promotes political and economic cooperation in Europe. Today the European Union has more than 25 members. Together, they deal with a wide range of issues, including trade, the environment, and migration.

The European Union has executive, legislative, and judicial branches. The EU is run by a commission made up of one representative from each member nation. Two legislative groups, the Council of the European Union and the European Parliament, debate and make laws. Finally, the Court of Justice resolves disputes and enforces EU laws.

Through the European Union, the countries of Europe work together toward common economic goals. The EU helps its member nations compete with economic powers like the United States and Japan. In 1999 the EU introduced a common currency, the euro, which many member countries now use. The euro has made trade much easier.

The European Union has helped unify Europe. In recent years many countries from Eastern Europe have joined the EU. Other countries hope to join in the future. Despite difficulties, EU leaders hope to continue their goal to bring the nations of Europe closer together.

**READING CHECK** **Finding Main Ideas** How has cooperation in Europe affected the region?

In 2005 French and Dutch voters rejected a proposed constitution for the European Union. Here, voters in France demand that their vote be upheld.

**SUMMARY AND PREVIEW** In this section you learned how the European Union helped unify much of Europe after years of division during the Cold War. In the next chapter, you will learn about Southern Europe's physical geography and culture.

## Section 3 Assessment

### Reviewing Ideas, Terms, and Places

1. a. **Recall** What was the **Cold War**?
   b. **Analyze** Why was Europe divided during the Cold War?
2. a. **Identify** What new countries were formed after the end of the Cold War?
   b. **Compare and Contrast** How were ethnic tensions in Czechoslovakia and Yugoslavia similar and different?
   c. **Evaluate** Do you think the end of the Cold War helped or hurt the nations of Eastern Europe?
3. a. **Define** What is a **common market**?
   b. **Make Inferences** Why did some Europeans believe stronger economic and political ties could prevent war in Europe?

### Critical Thinking

4. **Summarizing** Use your notes and the chart below to summarize the effect that each event had on the different regions of Europe. Write a sentence that summarizes the effect of each event.

|  | Cold War | End of Cold War | European Union |
|---|---|---|---|
| Western Europe |  |  |  |
| Eastern Europe |  |  |  |

### FOCUS ON WRITING

5. **Thinking about Europe since 1945** You are now in your mid-80s. How might events during and after the Cold War have affected your life?

# Interpreting Political Cartoons

## Learn

Political cartoons are drawings that express views on important political or social issues. The ability to interpret political cartoons will help you understand issues and people's attitudes about them.

Political cartoons use images and words to convey a message about a particular event, person, or issue in the news. Most political cartoons use symbols to represent those ideas. For example, political cartoonists often use Uncle Sam to represent the United States. They also use titles and captions to express their point of view.

## Practice

Examine the cartoon on this page. Then, answer the following questions to interpret the message of the cartoon.

1. Read any title, labels, or captions to identify the subject of the cartoon. What information does the caption for this cartoon give you? To what event does this cartoon refer?

2. Identify the people and symbols in the cartoon. What person is pictured in this cartoon? What does the crushed hammer and sickle represent?

3. What message is the cartoonist trying to convey?

Soviet leader Mikhail Gorbachev examines a broken hammer and sickle.

## Apply

Use your new skills to interpret a recent political cartoon. Locate a political cartoon that deals with an issue or event that has been in the news recently. Then answer the questions below.

1. What issue or event does the cartoon address?

2. What people or symbols are represented in the cartoon?

3. What point is the cartoon attempting to make?

**Geography's Impact**
video series
Review the video to answer the closing question:
*Why do you think the creation of the European Union was important to many Europeans?*

## Visual Summary

*Use the visual summary below to help you review the main ideas of the chapter.*

QUICK FACTS

World War I introduced many changes to Europe, including a new type of fighting called trench warfare.

The Allied and Axis powers faced off in World War II, the deadliest war in the world's history.

After years of division, the end of the Cold War finally reunited the nations of Europe.

## Reviewing Vocabulary, Terms, and Places

*Match the words or names with their definitions or descriptions.*

**1.** arms race      **4.** nationalism

**2.** Axis Powers      **5.** strategy

**3.** dictator      **6.** trench warfare

**a.** a powerful ruler that exerts complete control and often rules by force

**b.** a style of fighting in which each side fights from deep ditches dug into the ground

**c.** a plan for fighting a battle or war

**d.** the alliance of Germany, Italy, and Japan in World War II

**e.** devotion and loyalty to one's country

**f.** a competition between countries for superior weapons

## Comprehension and Critical Thinking

**SECTION 1** *(Pages 376–380)*

**7. a. Recall** What causes led to the outbreak of World War I?

   **b. Draw Conclusions** How did the U.S. entry into World War I affect the war's outcome?

   **c. Elaborate** Why do you think World War I led to revolutions in some countries?

**SECTION 2** *(Pages 382–387)*

**8. a. Identify** What two alliances fought in World War II? What countries belonged to each?

   **b. Compare** In what ways were Joseph Stalin, Benito Mussolini, and Adolf Hitler similar?

   **c. Elaborate** In your opinion, how were the Allies able to win World War II?

**SECTION 3** *(Pages 388–393)*

**9. a. Identify** Into what alliances was Europe divided during the Cold War?

**SECTION 3** *(continued)*

**b. Analyze** How did the Cold War come to an end?

**c. Predict** Do you think that the European Union will hurt or help Europe? Explain.

## Using the Internet

**10. Activity: Creating a Poster** The D-Day invasion of Normandy was crucial to the Allies' victory in World War II. Through your online textbook, find out more about D-Day. Then create a poster that celebrates the anniversary of the D-Day invasion. Be sure to include a short statement explaining why the invasion was important and images that grab your audience's attention.

⌐ hmhsocialstudies.com

## Social Studies Skills

**Interpreting Political Cartoons** *Examine the political cartoon below, then answer the questions that follow.*

**11.** What event does the cartoon depict?

**12.** What symbols does the cartoon use? To what do those symbols refer?

**13.** What point is the artist trying to make?

## Map Activity

**14. Europe, 1989** On a separate sheet of paper, match the letters on the map with their correct labels.

| | | |
|---|---|---|
| Berlin | Poland | West Germany |
| London | Moscow | Yugoslavia |
| Paris | | |

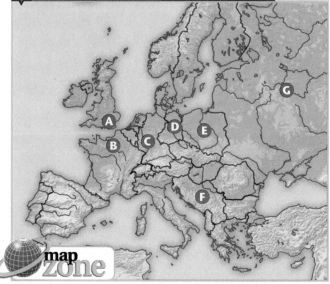

⌐ hmhsocialstudies.com  **INTERACTIVE MAP**

**FOCUS ON READING AND WRITING**

**Using Context Clues—Contrast** *Use context clues to determine the meaning of the underlined words in the sentences below.*

**15.** During World War II, people who aided Jews were often <u>detained</u> rather than set free.

**16.** Many celebrations at the end of the Cold War were <u>frenzied</u>, not calm and orderly.

**17.** European dictators who rose to power were <u>ruthless</u> as opposed to kind.

**Writing a Diary Entry** Use your notes and the directions below to write a diary entry.

**18.** Review your notes to organize the diary of your imaginary person. Divide your diary into three periods—World War I, World War II, and 1945–today. Describe the events your imaginary person experienced from his or her point of view. Remember to describe his or her thoughts and feelings about each event.

# Standardized Test Prep

*DIRECTIONS: Read questions 1 through 7 and write the letter of the best response. Question 8 will require a brief essay.*

**1** **Which world leader was *most* involved in the end of the Cold War?**

A   Francis Ferdinand

B   Joseph Stalin

C   Mikhail Gorbachev

D   Winston Churchill

**2** **The fall of the Berlin Wall is an important symbol of**

A   the Communist revolution in Russia.

B   the Allied victory in World War II.

C   the collapse of communism in Europe.

D   the formation of the European Union.

**3** **Which of the following was a result of World War II?**

A   The United Nations was formed.

B   Adolf Hitler was charged with war crimes.

C   A Communist revolution took place in Russia.

D   The U.S. economy collapsed.

**4** **Which of the following was a key cause of World War I?**

A   The United Nations failed to negotiate a peaceful settlement between East and West.

B   Germany and Italy launched invasions.

C   Competition between the countries of Europe created fierce rivalries.

D   Countries feared that communism would spread throughout Europe.

**5** **Who was the first leader of Communist Russia?**

A   Benito Mussolini

B   Joseph Stalin

C   Mikhail Gorbachev

D   Vladimir Lenin

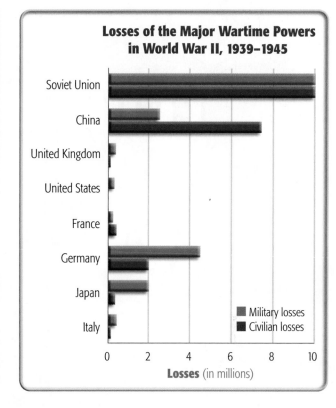

**Losses of the Major Wartime Powers in World War II, 1939–1945**

Losses (in millions)

Military losses
Civilian losses

**6** **Based on the information in the chart above, which Allied power lost the *fewest* civilians in World War II?**

A   France

B   United Kingdom

C   Italy

D   United States

**7** **Ethnic tensions at the end of the Cold War divided which of the following countries?**

A   France

B   Germany

C   United States

D   Yugoslavia

**8** **Extended Response** Tensions after World War II led to the Cold War between the United States and the Soviet Union. Use the map in Section 3 to explain how the Cold War affected Europe.

# *Dear home:* LETTERS FROM WWI

**When U.S. troops arrived in Europe in 1917 to fight in World War I, the war had been dragging on for nearly three years.** The American soldiers suddenly found themselves in the midst of chaos. Each day, they faced the threats of machine gun fire, poison gas, and aerial attacks. Still, the arrival of American reinforcements had sparked a new zeal among the Allies, who believed the new forces could finally turn the tide in their favor. The letters soldiers wrote to their families back home reveal the many emotions they felt on the battlefield: confusion about their surroundings, fear for their own safety, concern for friends and loved ones, and hope that the war would soon be over.

Explore World War I online through the eyes of the soldiers who fought in it. You can find a wealth of information, video clips, primary sources, activities, and more at ⬈ hmhsocialstudies.com .

"*I have been on every front in France. You cant imagine how torn up this country really is. Every where there are wire entanglements and trenches and dugouts. Even out of the war zone there are entanglements and dugouts to protect the civilians from air raids.*"

*-Corp. Albert Smith, U.S. soldier*

### Letter from France

Read the document to learn about one soldier's observations of wartime life.

### Over There

Watch the video to learn about the experiences of American soldiers on the way to Europe and upon their arrival.

### War on the Western Front

Watch the video to hear one soldier's vivid account of battle and its aftermath.

### Surrender!

Watch the video to experience soldiers' reactions to the news that the war was finally over.

# Southern Europe

## FOCUS ON READING AND WRITING

**Asking Questions** As you read a text, it can be helpful to ask yourself questions about what you are reading to be sure you understand it. One set of questions that you can use to test your understanding of a passage is the five Ws—who, what, when, where, and why. **See the lesson, Asking Questions, on page 531.**

**Writing a News Report** You are a newspaper reporter on special assignment in Southern Europe. Your editor has told you that many readers know about Southern Europe's past but not about the region today. After you read this chapter, you will write a news report about an imaginary event in a Southern European country today.

**Geography** Mountains cover large areas of Southern Europe. The Dolomites, shown here, are in northern Italy.

# Southern Europe: Political

GERMANY

FRANCE

SWITZERLAND

AUSTRIA

Milan

Venice

Po River

Genoa

ANDORRA

ITALY

SAN MARINO

Florence

Tiber River

Barcelona

VATICAN CITY

Rome

Adriatic Sea

Naples

Thessaloníki

Balearic Islands

Sardinia

Tyrrhenian Sea

GREECE

TURKEY

Ionian Sea

Aegean Sea

Palermo

ALGERIA

Sicily

Athens

MALTA

TUNISIA

Crete

Mediterranean Sea

10°E

20°E

**HISTORY**

Humanism Triggers the Renaissance

↗ hmhsocialstudies.com **VIDEO**

## map zone **Geography Skills**

**Place** Southern Europe occupies three large peninsulas and thousands of small islands in the Mediterranean Sea.
1. **Identify** What is the capital of Greece?
2. **Interpret** Why is Southern Europe also called Mediterranean Europe?

**History** Greece was the home of Europe's first great civilization. The ruins in Delphi are more than 2,300 years old.

**Culture** Bullfights are popular events in parts of Spain. Bullfighters, called matadors, are honored members of society.

399

# Physical Geography

## What You Will Learn...

### Main Ideas

1. Southern Europe's physical features include rugged mountains and narrow coastal plains.
2. The region's climate and resources support such industries as agriculture, fishing, and tourism.

### The Big Idea

The peninsulas of Southern Europe have rocky terrains and sunny, mild climates.

### Key Terms and Places

Mediterranean Sea, *p. 400*
Pyrenees, *p. 401*
Apennines, *p. 401*
Alps, *p. 401*
Mediterranean climate, *p. 402*

hmhsocialstudies.com
**TAKING NOTES**

Use the graphic organizer online to take notes on the physical geography of Southern Europe.

## If YOU lived there...

You are in a busy fish market in a small town on the coast of Italy, near the Mediterranean Sea. It is early morning. Colorful fishing boats have just pulled into shore with their catch of fresh fish and seafood. They unload their nets of slippery octopus and wriggling shrimp. Others bring silvery sea bass. You are looking forward to lunch—perhaps a tasty fish soup or pasta dish.

**How does the Mediterranean affect your life?**

**BUILDING BACKGROUND** The Mediterranean Sea has shaped the geography, climate, and culture of Southern Europe. All of these countries have long coastlines, with good harbors and beautiful beaches. Because much of the interior is rugged and mountainous, the sea has also been a highway for trade and travel.

## Physical Features

The continent of Europe has often been called a peninsula of peninsulas. Why do you think this is so? Look at the map of Europe in this book's Atlas to find out. Notice how Europe juts out from Asia like one big peninsula. Also, notice how smaller peninsulas extend into the many bodies of water that surround the continent.

Look at the map of Europe again. Do you see the three large peninsulas that extend south from Europe? From west to east, these are the Iberian Peninsula, the Italian Peninsula, and the Balkan Peninsula. Together with some large islands, they form the region of Southern Europe.

Southern Europe is also known as Mediterranean Europe. All of the countries of Southern Europe have long coastlines on the **Mediterranean Sea**. In addition to this common location on the Mediterranean, the countries of Southern Europe share many common physical features.

## Landforms

The three peninsulas of Southern Europe are largely covered with rugged mountains. In Greece, for example, about three-fourths of the land is mountainous. Because much of the land is so rugged, farming and travel in Southern Europe can be a challenge.

The mountains of Southern Europe form several large ranges. On the Iberian Peninsula, the **Pyrenees** (PIR-uh-neez) form a boundary between Spain and France to the north. Italy has two major ranges. The **Apennines** (A-puh-nynz) run along the whole peninsula, and the **Alps**—Europe's highest mountains—are in the north. The Pindus Mountains cover much of Greece.

Southern Europe's mountains extend into the sea as well, where they rise above the water to form islands. The Aegean Sea east of Greece is home to more than 2,000 such islands. Southern Europe also has many larger islands formed by undersea mountains. These include Crete, which is south of Greece; Sicily, at the southern tip of Italy; and many others.

Not all of Southern Europe is rocky and mountainous, though. Some flat plains lie in the region. Most of these plains are along the coast and in the valleys of major rivers. It is here that most farming in Southern Europe takes place. It is also here that most of the region's people live.

**FOCUS ON READING**

As you read, ask yourself this question: Where are the Pyrenees?

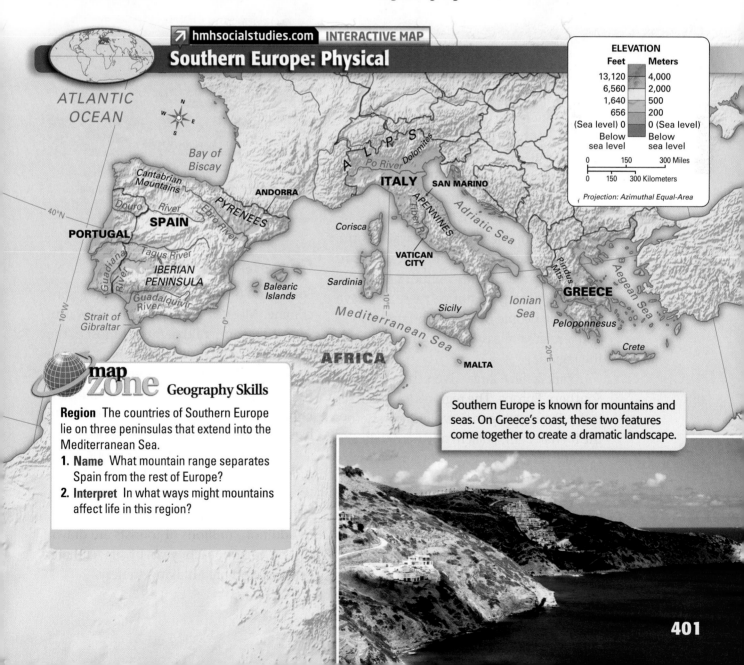

↗ hmhsocialstudies.com **INTERACTIVE MAP**

**Southern Europe: Physical**

**ELEVATION**

| Feet | | Meters |
|---|---|---|
| 13,120 | | 4,000 |
| 6,560 | | 2,000 |
| 1,640 | | 500 |
| 656 | | 200 |
| (Sea level) 0 | | 0 (Sea level) |
| Below sea level | | Below sea level |

0    150    300 Miles
0    150    300 Kilometers

*Projection: Azimuthal Equal-Area*

**Geography Skills**

**Region** The countries of Southern Europe lie on three peninsulas that extend into the Mediterranean Sea.

1. **Name** What mountain range separates Spain from the rest of Europe?
2. **Interpret** In what ways might mountains affect life in this region?

Southern Europe is known for mountains and seas. On Greece's coast, these two features come together to create a dramatic landscape.

**401**

# Mediterranean Climate

**Southern Europe is known for its Mediterranean climate, which features warm, dry summers and mild, wet winters. This climate affects nearly every aspect of life in the region.**

**1 Agriculture** The climate of Southern Europe is ideal for growing many crops. Here, Portuguese farmers harvest grapes.

**2 Tourism** The region's mild and sunny climate draws millions of tourists to places like this beach in Ibiza, Spain.

PORTUGAL 1  SPAIN  2

## Water Features

Since Southern Europe is mostly peninsulas and islands, water is central to the region's geography. No place in Southern Europe is very far from a major body of water. The largest of these bodies of water is the Mediterranean, but the Adriatic, Aegean, and Ionian seas are also important to the region. For many centuries, these seas have given the people of Southern Europe food and a relatively easy way to travel around the region.

Only a few large rivers run through Southern Europe. The region's longest river is the Tagus (TAY-guhs), which flows across the Iberian Peninsula. In northern Italy, the Po runs through one of Southern Europe's most fertile and densely populated areas. Other rivers run out of the mountains and into the many surrounding seas.

**READING CHECK Finding Main Ideas** What are the region's major features?

## Climate and Resources

Southern Europe is famous for its pleasant climate. Most of the region enjoys warm, sunny days and mild nights for most of the year. Little rain falls in the summer, falling instead during the mild winter. In fact, the type of climate found across Southern Europe is called a **Mediterranean climate** because it is common in this region.

The region's climate is also one of its most valuable resources. The mild climate is ideal for growing a variety of crops, from citrus fruits and grapes to olives and wheat. In addition, millions of tourists are drawn to the region each year by its climate, beaches, and breathtaking scenery.

ITALY

3

GREECE

4

**4 Architecture** Climate also affects architecture in Southern Europe. Buildings, like these in Greece, are airy and made of light materials to reflect sunlight and heat.

**ANALYSIS SKILL** **ANALYZING VISUALS**

What are four ways in which the Mediterranean climate affects life in Southern Europe?

**3 Vegetation** This field in Tuscany, a region of Italy, shows the variety of plants that thrive in Southern Europe's climate.

The sea is also an important resource in Southern Europe. Many of the region's largest cities are ports, which ship goods all over the world. In addition, the nearby seas are full of fish and shellfish, which provide the basis for profitable fishing industries.

**READING CHECK** Generalizing How is a mild climate important to Southern Europe?

**SUMMARY AND PREVIEW** In this section you learned about the physical features of Southern Europe. In the next section you will learn how those features affect life in one country—Greece.

**Section 1 Assessment** hmhsocialstudies.com
ONLINE QUIZ

**Reviewing Ideas, Terms, and Places**

1. **a. Recall** Which three peninsulas are in Southern Europe?
   **b. Explain** Why is the sea important to Southern Europe?
   **c. Elaborate** Why do you think most people in Southern Europe live on coastal plains or in river valleys?
2. **a. Describe** What is the **Mediterranean climate** like?
   **b. Generalize** How is climate an important resource for the region?

**Critical Thinking**

3. **Finding Main Ideas** Draw a diagram like the one shown here.

Landforms       Climate

In the left oval, use your notes to explain how landforms affect life in Southern Europe. In the right oval, explain how climate affects life in the region.

**FOCUS ON WRITING**

4. **Describing the Setting** Your news report will be about an imaginary event someplace in Southern Europe. That event might happen on a beach, in the mountains, or on a farm. Write some ideas in your notebook.

# Reading a Climate Map

## Learn

Geographers use many different types of maps to study a region. One type that can be very useful is a climate map. Because climate affects so many aspects of people's lives, it is important to know which climates are found in a region.

## Practice

Use the climate map of Europe below to answer the following questions.

1. What does orange mean on this map?
2. What city has a highland climate?
3. What is the dominant climate in the countries of Southern Europe?

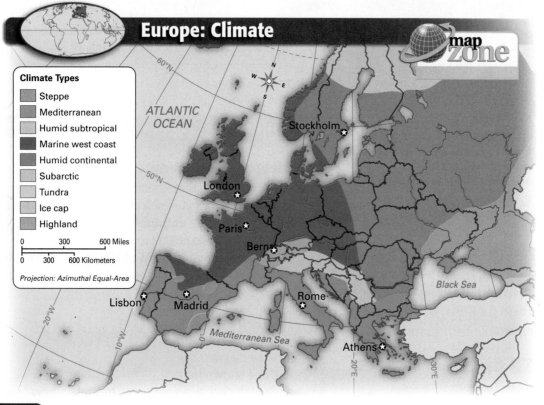

Europe: Climate
map zone
Climate Types
Steppe
Mediterranean
Humid subtropical
Marine west coast
Humid continental
Subarctic
Tundra
Ice cap
Highland
0 300 600 Miles
0 300 600 Kilometers
Projection: Azimuthal Equal-Area
ATLANTIC OCEAN
60°N
50°N
20°W
10°W
0°
20°E
30°E
N
S
E
W
Stockholm
London
Paris
Bern
Lisbon
Madrid
Rome
Athens
Black Sea
Mediterranean Sea

## Apply

Choose one of the cities shown on the map above. Imagine that you are planning a trip to that city and need to know what the climate is like so you can prepare. Use the map to identify the type of climate found in your chosen city. Then use the library or the Internet to find out more about that type of climate. Write a short description of the climate and how you could prepare for it.

# Greece

## If **YOU** lived there...

You live in a small town on one of the many Greek islands. White houses perch on steep streets leading down to the sea. Many tourists come here by boat after visiting the busy capital city of Athens. They tell you about the beautiful ancient buildings they saw there. But your island has ancient statues and temple sites too. Still, some of your friends talk about moving to the city.

**What might make people move to the city?**

**BUILDING BACKGROUND** In recent years, many people have moved out of Greece's small towns and villages into cities, especially Athens. Now the capital of Greece, Athens is an ancient city. It was home to one of Europe's greatest civilizations, one whose influence is still felt today all around the world.

## History

Greece is a country steeped in history. Home to one of the world's oldest civilizations, it has been called the birthplace of Western culture. Even today, remnants of ancient Greece can be found all over the country, and ideas from ancient thinkers continue to affect people's lives today.

### Ancient Greece

Theater. Philosophy. Democracy. These are just a few of the ideas that the modern world owes to ancient Greece. The Greeks were pioneers in many fields, and their contributions still affect how we live and think.

In art, the Greeks created lifelike paintings and statues that served as examples for later artists to imitate. In architecture, they built stately temples of marble that continue to inspire architects around the world.

**An ancient Greek jar**

### What You Will Learn...

**Main Ideas**

1. Early in its history, Greece was the home of a great civilization, but it was later ruled by foreign powers.
2. The Greek language, the Orthodox Church, and varied customs have helped shape Greece's culture.
3. In Greece today, many people are looking for new economic opportunities.

**The Big Idea**

The home of one of the Western world's oldest civilizations, Greece is trying to reclaim its place as a leading country in Europe.

**Key Terms and Places**
Orthodox Church, *p. 407*
Athens, *p. 408*

hmhsocialstudies.com
**TAKING NOTES**

Use the graphic organizer online to take notes on Greek history and culture.

## CONNECTING TO Math

# Proportion

The ancient Greeks were great admirers of mathematics. They thought math could be used in many areas of their lives. For example, they used it to design temples and other buildings.

Greek builders believed in a concept called the Golden Mean. This concept said that the height of a building should be a particular fraction of the building's width. If the building were too tall, they thought it would look flimsy. If it were too wide, it would look squat and ugly. As a result, these builders were very careful in planning their buildings. The Parthenon, the temple pictured below, was built using the Golden Mean. Many consider it to be the greatest of all Greek temples.

**Generalizing** How did mathematical ideas influence ancient Greek architecture?

They invented new forms of literature, including history and drama, and made advances in geometry and other branches of math that we still study. In philosophy, they created a system of reasoning that is the foundation for modern science. In government, they created democracy, which inspired the government embraced by most people around the world today.

No ancient civilization lasted forever, though. In the 300s BC Greece became a part of Alexander the Great's empire, which also included Egypt and much of Southwest Asia. Under Alexander, Greek culture spread throughout his empire.

**FOCUS ON READING**

As you read, ask yourself this question: Who conquered Greece in the 300s BC?

## The Romans and the Turks

Alexander's empire did not last very long. When it broke up, Greece became part of another empire, the Roman Empire. For about 300 years, the Greeks lived under Roman rule.

After about AD 400 the Roman Empire was divided into two parts. Greece became part of the Eastern, or Byzantine, Empire. The rulers of the Byzantine Empire admired Greek culture and encouraged people to adopt the Greek language and customs. They also encouraged people to adopt their religion, Christianity.

Greece was part of the Byzantine Empire for about 1,000 years. In the 1300s and 1400s, however, Greece was taken over by the Ottoman Turks from central Asia. The Turks were Muslim, but they allowed the people of Greece to remain Christian. Some elements of Greek culture, though, began to fade. For example, many people began speaking Turkish instead of Greek.

## Independent Greece

Many Greeks were not happy under Turkish rule. They wanted to be free of foreign influences. In the early 1800s, they rose up against the Turks. The rebellion seemed likely to fail, but the Greeks received help from other European countries and drove the Turks out. After the rebellion, Greece became a monarchy.

Greece's government has changed many times since independence. The country's first kings took steps toward restoring democracy, but for most of the 1900s the nation experienced instability. A military dictatorship ruled from 1967 to 1974. More recently, democracy has once again taken root in the country where it was born nearly 2,500 years ago.

**READING CHECK** **Sequencing** What groups have ruled Greece throughout history?

## Culture

Over the course of its history, many factors have combined to shape Greece's culture. These factors include the Greek language, Christianity, and customs adopted from the many groups who have ruled Greece.

### Language and Religion

The people of Greece today speak a form of the same language their ancestors spoke long ago. In fact, Greek is one of the oldest languages still spoken in Europe today. The language has changed greatly over time, but it was never lost.

Although the Greeks maintained their language, their ancient religions have long since disappeared. Today nearly everyone in Greece belongs to the **Orthodox Church**, a branch of Christianity that dates to the Byzantine Empire. Religion is important to the Greeks, and holidays such as Easter are popular times for celebration.

### Customs

Greek customs reflect the country's long history and its physical geography. Greek food, for example, is influenced both by products native to Greece and by groups who have ruled Greece over time.

Ingredients such as lamb, olives, and vegetables are easily available in Greece because they grow well there. As a result, the Greeks use lots of these ingredients in their cooking. Greek cuisine was later enhanced with ideas borrowed from other people. From the Turks, the Greeks learned to cook with yogurt and honey, and from the Italians they learned about pasta.

Greek meals are often eaten at family gatherings. For centuries, family has been central to Greek culture. Even as Greece is becoming more modernized, the family has remained the cornerstone of society.

**READING CHECK** **Summarizing** What are two dominant elements of Greek culture?

## Easter in Greece

Easter is one of the most sacred days of the year for Orthodox Christians. All over Greece, people celebrate Easter with festivals, feasts, and special rituals.

**ANALYZING VISUALS** What evidence in this photo suggests that Easter is a major celebration?

The priests carry containers of holy water. Later, they will sprinkle this holy water on crowds as part of a blessing.

Priests wear richly decorated robes as part of their Easter celebration.

Many Easter ceremonies are led by an archbishop, a high-ranking official in the Orthodox Church.

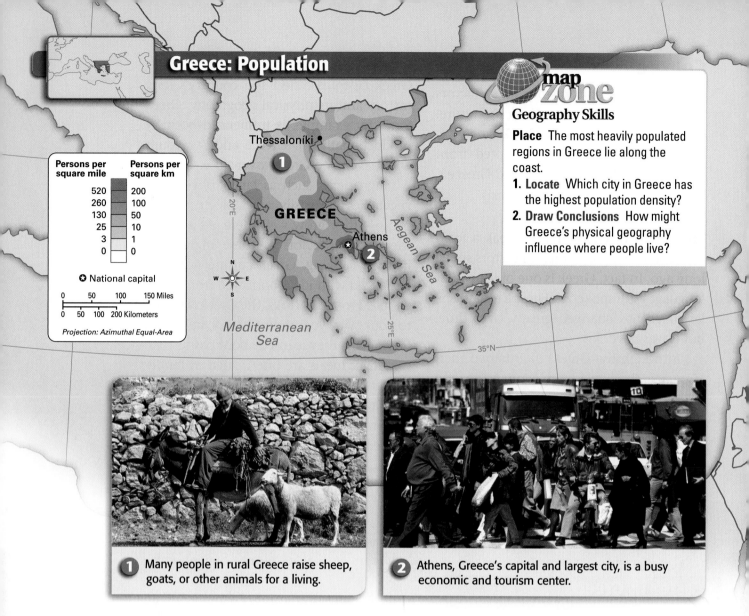

# Greece: Population

## map zone
### Geography Skills

**Place** The most heavily populated regions in Greece lie along the coast.

1. **Locate** Which city in Greece has the highest population density?
2. **Draw Conclusions** How might Greece's physical geography influence where people live?

| Persons per square mile | Persons per square km |
|---|---|
| 520 | 200 |
| 260 | 100 |
| 130 | 50 |
| 25 | 10 |
| 3 | 1 |
| 0 | 0 |

⊙ National capital

0    50    100    150 Miles

0    50    100    200 Kilometers

Projection: Azimuthal Equal-Area

Thessaloníki

GREECE

Athens

Aegean Sea

Mediterranean Sea

① Many people in rural Greece raise sheep, goats, or other animals for a living.

② Athens, Greece's capital and largest city, is a busy economic and tourism center.

## Greece Today

When many people think of Greece now, they think about the country's history. In fact, Greece's past often overshadows its present. Today, though, Greece is a largely urbanized society with a rapidly growing and diverse economy.

### Urban and Rural Greece

About three-fifths of all people in Greece today live in cities. Of these cities, **Athens**—the nation's capital—is by far the largest. In fact, almost one-third of the country's entire population lives in or around the city of Athens.

Athens is a huge city where old and new mix. Modern skyscrapers rise high above the ancient ruins of Greek temples. Most of the country's industry is centered there. However, this industry has resulted in air pollution, which damages the ancient ruins and causes health problems.

Outside of the city, Greek life is very different. People in rural areas still live largely as people have lived for centuries. Many live in isolated mountain villages, where they grow crops and raise sheep and goats. Village life often centers around the village square. People meet there to discuss local events and make decisions.

## Greece's Economy

Although Greece is experiencing rapid economic growth, it still lags behind some other European nations. This lag is largely caused by a lack of resources. Greece has few mineral resources, and only about one-fifth of its land can be farmed. The rest of the land is too rugged.

One industry in which Greece excels is shipping. Greece has one of the largest shipping fleets in the world. Greek ships can be found in ports all around the world, loaded with cargo from countries in Europe and other parts of the world.

Another profitable industry in Greece is tourism. Millions of people from around the world visit every year. Some are drawn to ancient ruins in Athens and other parts of the country. Others prefer the sunny, sandy beaches of Greece's many islands. The Greek government actively promotes this tourism, and more people visit the country every year. Largely due to this tourism, Greece's GDP—the value of all its goods and services—has risen steadily in recent years.

**READING CHECK** **Finding Main Ideas** What are the most important industries in Greece?

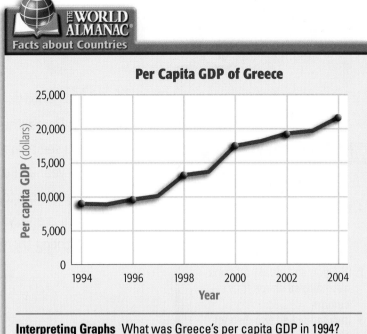

**THE WORLD ALMANAC** **Facts about Countries**

**Per Capita GDP of Greece**

**Interpreting Graphs** What was Greece's per capita GDP in 1994? What was it in 2004?

↗ hmhsocialstudies.com

**SUMMARY AND PREVIEW** In this section you learned about Greece, a country with a long and varied history that still shapes its culture and economy today. In the next section you will learn about Italy, another country in the region that has been shaped by history.

---

## Section 2 Assessment

↗ hmhsocialstudies.com
**ONLINE QUIZ**

### Reviewing Ideas, Terms, and Places

1. a. **Identify** What were two major achievements of the ancient Greeks?
   b. **Sequence** What steps did the Greeks take to gain their independence?
2. a. **Define** What is the **Orthodox Church**?
   b. **Generalize** What is one way in which Greece's history affects its culture today?
3. a. **Describe** What is life like in **Athens** today?
   b. **Explain** Why is manufacturing not a major industry in Greece?
   c. **Evaluate** Would you rather live in Athens or in rural Greece? Why?

### Critical Thinking

4. **Categorizing** Draw a table like the one here. Use the table to organize your notes into columns about Greece's history, its culture, and Greece today.

| Greece | | |
|---------|---------|-------|
| History | Culture | Today |
| | | |
| | | |

### FOCUS ON WRITING

5. **Introducing Greece** If you choose Greece for the site of your news report, what would be a good topic? The movement of people to the cities? An event at a historic site? Jot down your ideas.

# Italy

## What You Will Learn...

### Main Ideas

1. Italian history can be divided into three periods: ancient Rome, the Renaissance, and unified Italy.
2. Religion and local traditions have helped shape Italy's culture.
3. Italy today has two distinct economic regions—northern Italy and southern Italy.

### The Big Idea

Once the center of a huge empire, Italy is now one of the most prosperous countries in Europe.

### Key Terms and Places

pope, *p. 412*
Vatican City, *p. 412*
Sicily, *p. 413*
Naples, *p. 413*
Milan, *p. 413*
Rome, *p. 414*

**TAKING NOTES**

Use the graphic organizer online to take notes on Italian history, life, and culture.

## If **YOU** lived there...

You live in Rome, the historic heart of Italy. Wherever you walk in Rome, you see reminders of the city's long and rich history. It may be a 600-year-old church or a 2,000-year-old market. One of your favorite spots to visit is the Colosseum. When you sit inside this ancient arena, you can imagine fierce gladiators and wild animals fighting there long ago.

### How does history affect life in Italy?

**BUILDING BACKGROUND** Italian history continues to affect life in Italy today, but its influence extends far beyond that one country. All around the world, people owe their ideas about art, government, law, and language to Italy and its people. Many of these ideas are ancient, but even today Italians help shape the world's culture.

## History

Greece may have been the birthplace of the first civilization in Europe, but Italy was the home of the continent's greatest empire. For centuries, Italy was the heart of one of the largest and most powerful states the world has ever seen. Even after that state collapsed, Italy remained a major influence on Europe and other parts of the world.

### Ancient Rome

The great civilization that developed in Italy was Rome. Built in the 700s BC as a tiny village, Rome grew to control nearly all the land around the Mediterranean Sea. At the height of the Roman Empire, the Romans controlled an empire that stretched from Britain in the northwest to the Persian Gulf. It included most of Europe as well as parts of southwest Asia and northern Africa.

Roman influences in the world can still be seen today. The Romans' art, architecture, and literature are still admired. Their laws and political ideas have influenced the governments and legal systems of many countries. In addition, the Romans helped spread Christianity, one of the world's major religions.

## The Renaissance

The Roman Empire collapsed in the AD 400s, largely due to weak leadership and invasions from outside. With no central government to unite them, Italy's cities formed their own states. Each had its own laws, its own government, and its own army. Wars between them were common.

As time passed, the cities of Italy became major centers of trade. Merchants from these cities traveled to far-off places like China to bring goods back to Europe.

Many merchants became very rich from this trade. With the money they made, these merchants sponsored artists and architects. Their support of the arts helped lead to the Renaissance, a period of great creativity in Europe. It lasted from about 1350 through the 1500s. During the Renaissance artists and writers—many of them Italian—created some of the world's greatest works of art and literature.

## Unified Italy

Italy remained divided into small states until the mid-1800s. At that time, a rise in nationalism, or strong patriotic feelings for a country, led people across Italy to fight for unification. As a result of their efforts, Italy became a unified kingdom in 1861.

In the 1920s a new government came to power. Under Benito Mussolini, Italy became a dictatorship. That dictatorship was short-lived, however. Mussolini joined Hitler to fight other countries of Europe in World War II. In 1945 Italy was defeated.

After World War II, Italy became a democracy. Since that time, power has rested in an elected Parliament and prime minister. Also since the end of the war, Italy has developed one of the strongest economies in Europe.

**READING CHECK** **Summarizing** What are some key periods in the history of Italy?

## Italian History

The history of Italy stretches back nearly 3,000 years. This long span includes several key periods.

### Ancient Rome

- According to legend, the city of Rome was built in the 700s BC.
- The Romans created a huge empire. At its height, the empire included parts of Europe, Southwest Asia, and northern Africa.
- Roman art, architecture, literature, and law still influence people today.
- Christianity arose and spread in the Roman Empire.

**Roman statue**

### The Renaissance

- The Renaissance was a period of great advances in art, architecture, and literature.
- The Renaissance began in the 1300s in cities like Florence.
- From Italy, the Renaissance spread to other parts of Europe.
- Some of the world's greatest works of art were created at this time.

**Leonardo da Vinci's *Mona Lisa***

### Unified Italy

- Since the Middle Ages, Italy had been divided into small states.
- In the mid-1800s, increased feelings of nationalism led people across Italy to fight for unification.
- The fight for unification was led by Giuseppe Garibaldi.
- Italy was officially unified in 1861.

**Giuseppe Garibaldi**

# Culture

For centuries, people around the world have admired and borrowed from Italian culture. Italy's culture has been shaped by many factors. Among these factors are the Roman Catholic Church, local traditions, and regional geography.

## Religion

Most people in Italy belong to the Roman Catholic Church. Historically, the church has been the single strongest influence on Italian culture. This influence is strong in part because the **pope**, the spiritual head of the Roman Catholic Church, lives on the Italian Peninsula. He resides in **Vatican City**, an independent state located within the city of Rome.

ACADEMIC VOCABULARY

contemporary
modern

The lasting importance of the church can be seen in many ways in Italy. For example, the city of Rome alone is home to hundreds of Catholic churches from all periods of history. In addition, religious holidays and festivals are major events.

## Local Traditions

In addition to religion, local traditions have influenced Italian culture. Italian food, for example, varies widely from region to region. These variations are based on local preferences and products. All over Italy, people eat many of the same foods—olives, tomatoes, rice, pasta. However, the ways in which people prepare this food differ. In the south, for example, people often serve pasta with tomato sauces. In the north, creamy sauces are much more common.

Other traditions reflect Italy's past. For example, Italy has always been known as a center of the arts. The people of Italy have long been trendsetters, shaping styles that are later adopted by other people. As a result, the Italians are leaders in many **contemporary** art forms. For example, Italy has produced some of the world's greatest painters, sculptors, authors, composers, fashion designers, and filmmakers.

**READING CHECK** **Finding Main Ideas** What are two major influences on Italian culture?

## Major Cities of Italy

Milan, Rome, and Naples are the three largest cities in Italy. Because of their varied histories and locations, each city has a distinct landscape and culture.

**ANALYZING VISUALS** Which city would you most like to visit?

**Milan** Milan, the largest city in Italy, is a global fashion capital. The clothes created there influence fashion designers around the world.

# Italy Today

A shared language, the Roman Catholic Church, and strong family ties help bind Italians together. At the same time, though, major differences exist in the northern and southern parts of the country.

## Southern Italy

Southern Italy is the country's poorer half. Its economy has less industry than the north and depends heavily on agriculture. Farming is especially important in **Sicily**, an island at the peninsula's tip. Tourism is also vital to the south's economy. Among the region's attractions are its dazzling beaches and ancient Roman ruins.

In recent decades, Italy's government has tried to promote industry in the south. It has offered **incentives**, such as lower taxes, to private companies that will build factories there. Many of these government efforts center on the city of **Naples**, a busy port and the largest city in southern Italy. Thanks to government programs, Naples is now also an industrial center.

## Northern Italy

In contrast to southern Italy, the northern part of the country has a strong economy. Northern Italy includes the country's most fertile farmlands, its major trade centers, and its most popular tourist destinations.

The Po River valley in northern Italy has the country's most productive farmland. For decades, the Po valley has been called the breadbasket of Italy because most of the country's crops are grown there. Despite its fertile soils, farmers cannot grow enough to support Italy's population. Italy has to import much of its food.

The north is also home to Italy's major industrial centers. Busy factories in such cities as Turin and Genoa make appliances, automobiles, and other goods for export. **Milan** is also a major industrial center as well as a worldwide center for fashion design. The location of these cities near central Europe helps companies sell their goods to foreign customers. Railroads, highways, and tunnels make the shipment of goods through the Alps easy.

**ACADEMIC VOCABULARY**

**incentive** something that leads people to follow a certain course of action

**Rome** Rome, the capital of Italy, is in the central part of the country. A major center of banking and industry, Rome is also one of the world's most popular tourist sites.

**Naples** Naples is the most important city in southern Italy. Less glamorous than many northern cities, it is a port and manufacturing center.

## Venice

Venice, in northeastern Italy, is one of the country's most visited tourist attractions. Look at the image of Venice above, taken by an orbiting satellite. Does it look like other cities you have seen? What may not be obvious is that the paths that wind their way through the city are not roads, but canals. In fact, Venice has very few roads. This is because the city was built on islands—118 of them! People move about the city on boats that navigate along the canals. Every year, millions of tourists travel to Venice to see the sights as they are rowed along the scenic waterways.

**Contrasting** How is Venice unlike other cities you have studied?

Tens of millions of tourists visit the cities of northern Italy every year. They are drawn by the cities' rich histories and unique cultural features. Florence, for example, is a center of Italian art and culture. It was there that the Renaissance began in the 1300s. To the west of Florence is Pisa, famous for its Leaning Tower—the bell tower of the city's church. On the coast of the Adriatic Sea lies the city of Venice. Tourists are lured there by the romantic canals that serve as roads through the city.

Nestled in the center of the country is Italy's capital, **Rome**. With ties to both north and south, Rome does not fully belong to either region. From there, the country's leaders attempt to bring all the people of Italy together as one nation.

**READING CHECK** **Contrast** How are northern and southern Italy different?

**SUMMARY AND PREVIEW** In this section you read about Italy. The country's long history continues to affect life in Italy even today. Next, you will study two other countries whose pasts still affect life there—Spain and Portugal.

---

## Section 3 Assessment

hmhsocialstudies.com
ONLINE QUIZ

### Reviewing Ideas, Terms, and Places

1. **a. Describe** What was Renaissance Italy like?
   **b. Interpret** How did nationalism influence Italian history?
2. **a. Identify** What religion has had a major impact on Italian culture?
   **b. Explain** How have local traditions helped shape Italian culture?
3. **a. Recall** What is the main economic activity of southern Italy?
   **b. Contrast** How are the economies of **Milan**, **Rome**, and **Naples** different?
   **c. Rate** If you could visit any one city in Italy, which would it be? Why?

### Critical Thinking

4. **Comparing and Contrasting** Draw two circles like the ones here. Using your notes, list details about southern Italy in the left circle and about northern Italy in the right circle. Where the circles overlap, list common features of the two.

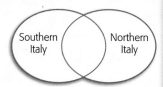

### FOCUS ON WRITING

5. **Investigating Italy** What Italian event could you report on? Perhaps it could be a fashion show or a religious service at the Vatican. Make a list of events that could make an interesting report.

# Spain and Portugal

## If YOU lived there...

You have just moved to southern Spain from a town in the far north. You cannot help noticing that many of the buildings here look different from those in your hometown. Many of the buildings here have rounded arches over the doorways and tall towers in front of them. In addition, some are decorated with ornate tiles.

**Why do you think the buildings look different?**

**BUILDING BACKGROUND** Throughout history, many different groups have ruled parts of Spain and Portugal. Each group brought elements of its own culture to the region. As a result, parts of the two countries have cultures unlike those found anywhere else.

## History

The countries of Spain and Portugal share the Iberian Peninsula, or **Iberia**, the westernmost peninsula in Europe. Although the two are different in many ways, they share a common history.

Across the centuries, several powerful empires controlled all or part of the Iberian Peninsula. By 700 BC, the Phoenicians, from the eastern Mediterranean, had colonized coastal areas of what is now Spain. After the Phoenicians came the Greeks. A few centuries later, all of Iberia became part of the Roman Empire.

After the Roman Empire fell apart, Iberia was invaded by the Moors, a group of Muslims from North Africa. For about 600 years, much of the Iberian Peninsula was under Muslim rule.

### What You Will Learn...

#### Main Ideas

1. Over the centuries, Spain and Portugal have been part of many large and powerful empires.
2. The cultures of Spain and Portugal reflect their long histories.
3. Having been both rich and poor in the past, Spain and Portugal today have growing economies.

#### The Big Idea

Spain and Portugal have rich cultures, stable governments, and growing economies.

#### Key Terms and Places

Iberia, *p. 415*
parliamentary monarchy, *p. 418*
Madrid, *p. 418*
Barcelona, *p. 418*
Lisbon, *p. 418*

hmhsocialstudies.com
TAKING NOTES

Use the graphic organizer online to take notes on Spain and Portugal.

Moorish structures, such as this tower outside of Lisbon, Portugal, can still be seen all over Iberia.

## Spain and Portugal: Languages

Many Basque speakers take part in rallies like this one in support of independence. The banner in this photo reads "Basque Nation Arise" in the Basque language.

### Languages
- Spanish
- Portuguese
- Catalan
- Galician
- Basque

Bay of Biscay

Bilbao

Barcelona

Madrid

**SPAIN**

PORTUGAL

Lisbon

Balearic Islands

Mediterranean Sea

ATLANTIC OCEAN

40°N

10°W

0   100   200 Miles
0   100   200 Kilometers
Projection: Azimuthal Equal-Area

#### map zone Geography Skills

**Place** Spanish and Portuguese are the most common languages of Spain and Portugal, but not the only ones.
1. **Identify** Which language is spoken in Barcelona?
2. **Draw Conclusions** Based on this map, which country do you think has a more unified culture? Why?

By the end of the 1400s, however, the Muslims were driven out of Iberia. The rulers of the Christian kingdoms of Spain and Portugal banded together to force non-Christians to leave Iberia. Those who refused to leave were made to convert or face severe punishments.

Spain and Portugal went on to build large empires that spanned the oceans. Both countries ruled huge territories in the Americas as well as smaller areas in Africa and Asia. These territories made the two kingdoms rich and powerful until most of their colonies broke away and became independent in the 1800s and 1900s.

**READING CHECK** **Summarizing** What empires have ruled Spain and Portugal?

## Culture

In some ways, the cultures of Spain and Portugal are like those of other southern European countries. For example, the Spanish, Portuguese, Greeks, and Italians all cook with many of the same ingredients. The Catholic Church is very influential in Italy as well as Spain and Portugal. In other ways, Iberian cultures are unique.

### Language

The most spoken languages in Iberia are, of course, Spanish and Portuguese. Various dialects of these languages are spoken in different parts of the peninsula. In addition, other languages are also spoken by many people in Iberia. The Catalan language of eastern Spain is similar to Spanish. Galician, which is spoken in northwest Spain, is more closely related to Portuguese.

In addition, the Basque (BASK) people of the Pyrenees have their own language, which is not related to either Spanish or Portuguese. The Basques also have their own customs and traditions, unlike those of the rest of Spain. As a result, many Basques have long wanted to form their own independent country.

### Religion

Most people in both Spain and Portugal are Roman Catholic. People in both countries celebrate Christian holidays like Christmas and Easter. In addition, many towns hold fiestas, or festivals, in honor of their patron saints. At these festivals, people may gather to dance or to watch a bullfight.

### Music and Art

Music and art have been central to Iberian culture for centuries. The Portuguese are famous for sad folk songs called fados. The Spanish are known for a style of song and dance called flamenco.

Many elements of Iberia's art and architecture reflect its Muslim past. Many buildings in the peninsula have elements of Muslim design, such as round arches and elaborate tilework.

**READING CHECK** **Comparing** What is one culture element that Spain and Portugal share?

## Spain and Portugal Today

Like other countries in Western Europe, Spain and Portugal have rather strong economies. They do have some problems, however, problems that were largely brought on by past events.

### Challenge of the Past

Spain and Portugal were once Europe's richest countries. Their wealth came from gold and silver found in their colonies.

When other countries in Europe began to build industrial economies, Spain and Portugal continued to rely on gold from their colonies. As those colonies became independent, that source of income was lost. As a result, Spain and Portugal were late in developing manufacturing.

Although Spain and Portugal are still poorer than other countries in Western Europe, they are growing rapidly. New industries such as tourism are making this new growth possible.

**FOCUS ON READING**
As you read, ask yourself this question: Why did Spain and Portugal fall behind other countries economically?

## FOCUS ON CULTURE

### Flamenco

Complex guitar rhythms, a heavy beat, and whirling dancers—these are all part of the traditional Spanish art form known as flamenco. The word *flamenco* refers both to a style of music and a style of dance. The most important instrument in the music is the guitar, which was itself a Spanish invention. Most of the time, the guitar is accompanied by other musical instruments and by singers.

When most people think of flamenco, however, they picture dancers. Flamenco dancers perform alone, in pairs, or in large groups. They wear brightly colored costumes as they perform complex steps. It is not unusual for dancers to clap their hands or snap their fingers to the beat or to play castanets as they dance. Castanets are small, hinged wooden instruments. The dancers clap the castanets together to make a clicking noise.

**Finding Main Ideas** What are the major elements of flamenco music and dancing?

Spanish culture blends old and new ideas. Here, modern vehicles drive by historic buildings in Barcelona.

In other ways, Spain has become a more modern country. Agriculture was once the major economic activity, but factories now create automobiles and other high-tech products. Cities such as **Madrid**—the capital—and **Barcelona** are centers of industry, tourism, and culture.

## Portugal Today

Unlike Spain, Portugal is not a monarchy. It is a republic with elected leaders. As in Spain, the economy is based largely on industries centered in large cities, especially **Lisbon**. In many rural areas, though, people depend on agriculture. Farmers there grow many crops but are most famous for grapes and cork. Farmers harvest cork from the bark of a particular type of oak tree. Once it is dried, the cork is used to make bottle stoppers and other products.

**READING CHECK** **Contrasting** How are Spain and Portugal's governments different?

**SUMMARY AND PREVIEW** You have just learned about the countries of Southern Europe. Next, you will move north to study West-Central Europe.

## Spain Today

The people of Spain have kept many aspects of their history alive. For example, Spain is still governed by a king, a descendant of the kings who ruled the country long ago. Unlike in the past, however, Spain today is a **parliamentary monarchy**, which means that the king rules with the help of an elected parliament.

hmhsocialstudies.com
ONLINE QUIZ

## Section 4 Assessment

### Reviewing Ideas, Terms, and Places

1. **a. Recall** What is **Iberia**? What two countries are located there?
   **b. Sequence** What people have ruled Iberia, and in what order did they rule it?
2. **a. Identify** What is the most common religion in Spain and Portugal?
   **b. Generalize** How is Spain's history reflected in its architecture?
   **c. Elaborate** Why do you think many Basques want to become independent from Spain?
3. **a. Identify** What are two crops grown in Portugal?
   **b. Analyze** What is Spain's government like?

### Critical Thinking

4. **Categorizing** Draw a diagram like the one here. Using your notes, record information about the cultures and economies of Spain and Portugal.

|  | Spain | Portugal |
|---|---|---|
| Culture |  |  |
| Economy |  |  |

### FOCUS ON WRITING

5. **Writing about Spain and Portugal** What details about Spain and Portugal will grab your readers' attention? Look back through your notes to choose the topic for your article.

**Geography's Impact**
**video series**
Review the video to answer the
closing question:
*Why did the 2004 Olympics
have so great an impact
on Athens?*

## Visual Summary

*Use the visual summary below to help you review
the main ideas of the chapter.*

QUICK FACTS

**Greece**
The birthplace of democracy, Greece is
working to improve its economy.

**Italy**
Italy is one of Europe's leading cultural
and economic countries.

**Spain and Portugal**
The rich cultures of Spain and Portugal
are shaped by their histories.

## Reviewing Vocabulary, Terms, and Places

*Fill in the blanks with the correct term or location from
this chapter.*

1. The climate found in most of Southern Europe
   is the _____.

2. The _____ is the head of the Roman
   Catholic Church.

3. The highest mountains in Europe are the
   _____.

4. _____ is the capital of Greece.

5. A _____ is a government in which a king
   rules with the help of an elected body.

6. Italy's capital, _____, was the birthplace of
   an ancient civilization.

7. _____ is an independent state located
   within the city of Rome.

8. Spain and Portugal are located on a peninsula
   known as _____.

## Comprehension and Critical Thinking

**SECTION 1** *(Pages 400–403)*

9. **a. Describe** What are two physical features that
   all the countries of Southern Europe have in
   common?

   **b. Draw Conclusions** Why has Southern
   Europe's climate been called its most valuable
   resource?

   **c. Predict** How would daily life in Southern
   Europe be different if it were not a coastal
   region?

**SECTION 2** *(Pages 405–409)*

10. **a. Identify** What is the largest city in Greece?
    How would you describe the city?

    **b. Generalize** How has Greece's economy
    changed in the last decade? What is largely
    responsible for this change?

    **c. Elaborate** How does Greek history still affect
    the country today?

## SECTION 3 (Pages 410–414)

**11. a. Recall** Which region of Italy has the stronger economy? Why?

**b. Sequence** What periods followed the Roman Empire in Italy? What happened during those periods?

**c. Elaborate** What are some ways in which the Italians have influenced world culture?

## SECTION 4 (Pages 415–418)

**12. a. Identify** Who are the Basques?

**b. Compare and Contrast** How are Spain and Portugal alike? How are they different?

**c. Elaborate** How do you think Iberia's history makes it different from other places in Europe?

# Social Studies Skills

**Reading a Climate Map** *Use the climate map from the Social Studies Skills lesson of this chapter to answer the following questions.*

**13.** What type of climate does London have?

**14.** What climate is found only in the far north?

**15.** Where in Europe would you find a humid subtropical climate?

# Using the Internet

**16. Activity: Exploring Italian Cuisine** Pizza. Pasta. Mozzarella. Olive oil. These are some of the most popular elements of Italian food, one of the world's favorites. Through your online textbook, learn more about the history and variety of Italian cooking. Then test your knowledge with the interactive activity.

↗ **hmhsocialstudies.com**

# Map Activity

**17. Southern Europe** On a separate sheet of paper, match the letters on the map with their correct labels.

| | |
|---|---|
| Mediterranean Sea | Lisbon, Portugal |
| Athens, Greece | Po River |
| Sicily | Rome, Italy |
| Spain | Aegean Sea |

↗ **hmhsocialstudies.com** **INTERACTIVE MAP**

## FOCUS ON READING AND WRITING

**Asking Questions** *Read the passage below. After you read it, answer the questions below to be sure you have understood what you read.*

Spain is a democracy, but it has not always been. From 1939 to 1975, a dictator named Francisco Franco ruled the country. He came to power as a result of a bloody civil war and was unpopular with the Spanish people.

**18.** Who is this paragraph about?

**19.** What did the people in this passage do?

**20.** When did the events described take place?

**21.** Where did the events described take place?

**22.** Why did the events happen?

**Writing Your News Report** *Use your notes and the instructions below to help you create your news report.*

**23.** Select a topic for your news report. Create a plan for your report by answering these questions: What is the scene or setting of the event? Who is there? Why is it important enough to include in the news? What happened? Start your news report with a dateline, for example: Rome, May 5, 2009. Begin your first paragraph with an interesting observation or detail. Explain the event in two or three short paragraphs. Close with an important piece of information or interesting detail.

*DIRECTIONS: Read questions 1 through 7 and write the letter of the best response. Then read question 8 and write your own well-constructed response.*

**1** **In which country of Southern Europe is the Orthodox Church dominant?**

A Portugal

B Spain

C Italy

D Greece

**2** **Two of the most common foods in Southern European cooking are**

A grapes and olives.

B corn and barley.

C beans and squash.

D beef and pork.

**3** **The form of government for which ancient Greece is best known is**

A monarchy.

B dictatorship.

C democracy.

D parliamentary monarchy.

**4** **The Moors were Muslims who conquered**

A Spain.

B Greece.

C Crete.

D Italy.

**5** **Which of these cities is in Portugal?**

A Rome

B Athens

C Lisbon

D Madrid

## Spain and Portugal: Climates

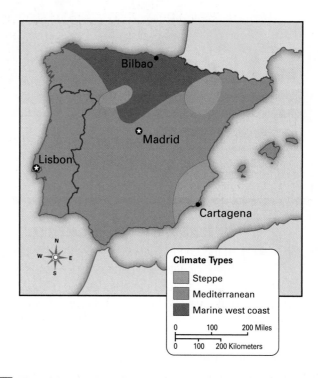

**6** **Based on the map above, which city in Spain lies in an area with a steppe climate?**

A Bilbao

B Cartagena

C Lisbon

D Madrid

**7** **Based on the map on this page, which is the most common climate in Spain?**

A Steppe

B Mediterranean

C Marine west coast

D Tropical

**8** **Extended response** Climate influences many aspects of people's lives in Southern Europe. Write a short paragraph that describes the region's climate. At the end of the paragraph, list two ways in which climate affects how people live.

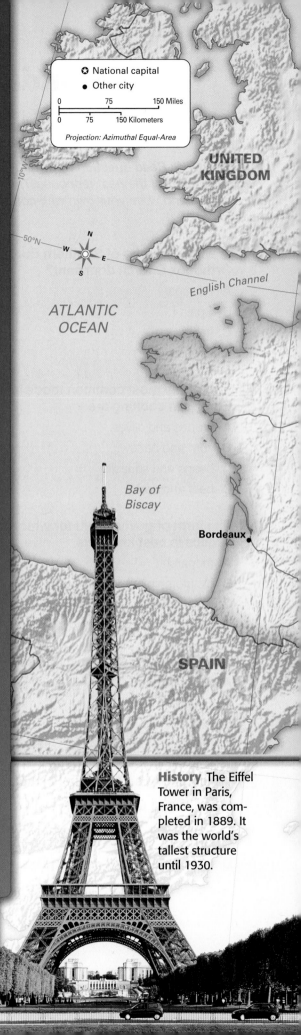

# CHAPTER 17

# West-Central Europe

**Essential Question** What geographic and cultural features characterize West-Central Europe?

## What You Will Learn...

In this chapter you will learn about the physical features, climate, and natural resources of West-Central Europe. You will also study the histories and cultures of the countries in this region. Finally, you will learn about life in these countries today.

### FOCUS ON READING AND SPEAKING

**Recognizing Word Origins** Many of the words we use today came into English from other languages, such as Latin, French, or German. As you read this chapter, think about the origin, or sources, of words. Knowing a word's origin can help you remember the word's meaning. **See the lesson, Recognizing Word Origins, on page 532.**

**Writing a Persuasive Speech** As you read about West-Central Europe, you will discover some issues. Issues are topics that people disagree about. Think about which of the issues seem important to you. Later, you will take a stand on one of these issues by writing and presenting a persuasive speech.

**History** The Eiffel Tower in Paris, France, was completed in 1889. It was the world's tallest structure until 1930.

North Sea

Kiel Canal

Hamburg

NETHERLANDS

Amsterdam

Rotterdam

RUHR

Elbe River

Weser River

Oder River

Neisse River

Berlin

GERMANY

Rhine River

Antwerp

Lille

Brussels

BELGIUM

Frankfurt

LUXEMBOURG

Luxembourg

CZECH REPUBLIC

Seine River

Paris

Danube River

Loire River

Munich

Vienna

LIECHTENSTEIN

Salzburg

AUSTRIA

HUNGARY

FRANCE

Zurich

Bern

Innsbruck

SWITZERLAND

Lake Geneva

Geneva

Lyon

Rhone River

Adriatic Sea

ITALY

MONACO

Marseille

Corsica (FRANCE)

Mediterranean Sea

10°E

20°E

**map zone** Geography Skills

**Regions** The countries of West-Central Europe are some of the most industrialized and richest countries in the world.
1. **Identify** Which countries make up this region?
2. **Make Inferences** Why do you think some of the countries in this region might want to join together to promote economic growth?

**Geography** The Netherlands is famous for its fields of brightly colored tulips.

**Culture** A German teen participates in a Bavarian cow festival.

# Physical Geography

## What You Will Learn...

### Main Ideas

1. The physical features of West-Central Europe include plains, uplands, mountains, rivers, and seas.
2. West-Central Europe's mild climate and resources support agriculture, energy production, and tourism.

### The Big Idea

West-Central Europe has a range of landscapes, a mild climate, and rich farmland.

### Key Terms and Places

Northern European Plain, *p. 424*
North Sea, *p. 426*
English Channel, *p. 426*
Danube River, *p. 426*
Rhine River, *p. 426*
navigable river, *p. 426*

hmhsocialstudies.com
TAKING NOTES

Use the graphic organizer online to take notes on the physical geography of West-Central Europe.

## If YOU lived there...

You are a photographer planning a book about the landscapes of West-Central Europe. You are trying to decide where to find the best pictures of rich farmland, forested plateaus, and rugged mountains. So far, you are planning to show the colorful tulip fields of the Netherlands, the hilly Black Forest region of Germany, and the snow-covered Alps in Switzerland.

### What other places might you want to show?

**BUILDING BACKGROUND** The countries of West-Central Europe are among the most prosperous and powerful countries in the world. The reasons include their mild climates, good farmland, many rivers, market economies, and stable governments. In addition, most of these countries cooperate as members of the European Union.

## Physical Features

From fields of tulips, to sunny beaches, to icy mountain peaks, West-Central Europe offers a wide range of landscapes. Even though the region is small, it includes three major types of landforms—plains, uplands, and mountains. These landforms extend in wide bands across the region.

### Plains, Uplands, and Mountains

Look at the map at right. Picture West-Central Europe as an open fan with Italy as the handle. The outer edge of this imaginary fan is a broad coastal plain called the **Northern European Plain**. This plain stretches from the Atlantic coast into Eastern Europe.

Most of this plain is flat or rolling and lies less than 500 feet (150 m) above sea level. In the Netherlands, parts of the plain dip below sea level. There, people must build walls to hold back the sea. In Brittany in northwestern France, the land rises to form a plateau above the surrounding plain.

The Northern European Plain provides the region's best farmland. Many people live on the plain, and the region's largest cities are located there.

The Central Uplands extend across the center of our imaginary fan. This area has many rounded hills, small plateaus, and valleys. In France, the uplands include the Massif Central (ma-SEEF sahn-TRAHL), a plateau region, and the Jura Mountains.

This range is on the French-Swiss border. In Germany, uplands cover much of the southern two-thirds of the country. Dense woodlands, such as the Black Forest, blanket many of the hills in this area.

The Central Uplands have many productive coalfields. As a result, the area is important for mining and industry. Some valleys provide fertile soil for farming, but most of the area is too rocky to farm.

**FOCUS ON READING**

Look up the origin of *massif* in a dictionary. How does its origin relate to the description of the Massif Central?

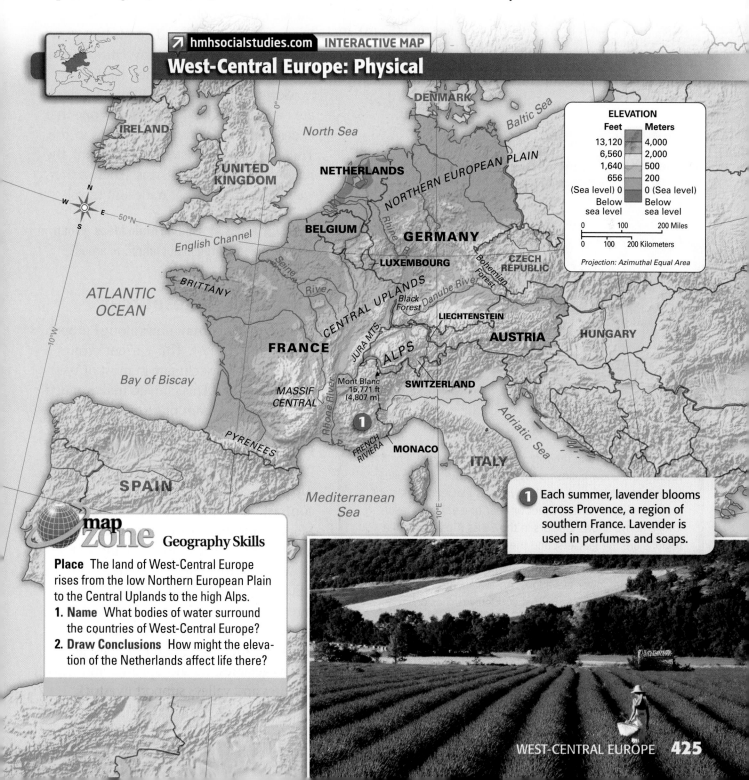

↗ hmhsocialstudies.com  INTERACTIVE MAP

## West-Central Europe: Physical

ELEVATION

| Feet | | Meters |
|---|---|---|
| 13,120 | | 4,000 |
| 6,560 | | 2,000 |
| 1,640 | | 500 |
| 656 | | 200 |
| (Sea level) 0 | | 0 (Sea level) |
| Below sea level | | Below sea level |

Projection: Azimuthal Equal Area

IRELAND

UNITED KINGDOM

North Sea

DENMARK

Baltic Sea

NETHERLANDS

NORTHERN EUROPEAN PLAIN

BELGIUM

GERMANY

English Channel

ATLANTIC OCEAN

BRITTANY

Seine River

LUXEMBOURG

Rhine

Bohemian Forest

CZECH REPUBLIC

CENTRAL UPLANDS

Black Forest

Danube River

LIECHTENSTEIN

JURA MTS.

ALPS

AUSTRIA

HUNGARY

FRANCE

Bay of Biscay

MASSIF CENTRAL

Rhône River

Mont Blanc 15,771 ft (4,807 m)

SWITZERLAND

1

Adriatic Sea

PYRENEES

FRENCH RIVIERA

MONACO

ITALY

SPAIN

Mediterranean Sea

1 Each summer, lavender blooms across Provence, a region of southern France. Lavender is used in perfumes and soaps.

**map zone** Geography Skills

**Place** The land of West-Central Europe rises from the low Northern European Plain to the Central Uplands to the high Alps.

1. **Name** What bodies of water surround the countries of West-Central Europe?
2. **Draw Conclusions** How might the elevation of the Netherlands affect life there?

Along the inner part of our imaginary fan, the land rises dramatically to form the alpine mountain system. This system includes the Alps and the Pyrenees, which you read about in the last chapter.

As you have read, the Alps are Europe's highest mountain range. They stretch from southern France to the Balkan Peninsula. Several of the jagged peaks in the Alps soar to more than 14,000 feet (4,270 m). The highest peak is Mont Blanc (mawn BLAHN), which rises to 15,771 feet (4,807 m) in France. Because of the height of the Alps, large snowfields coat some peaks.

## Satellite View

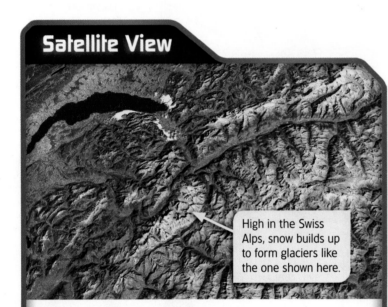

High in the Swiss Alps, snow builds up to form glaciers like the one shown here.

## The Swiss Alps

At high elevations in the Alps, snow does not melt. For this reason, the snow builds up over time. As the snow builds up, it turns to ice and eventually forms glaciers. A glacier is a large, slow-moving sheet or river of ice. The satellite image above shows glaciers in the Swiss Alps. The white regions are the glaciers, and the blue areas are alpine lakes.

The buildup of snow and ice in the Alps can cause avalanches at lower elevations. An avalanche is a large mass of snow or other material that suddenly rushes down a mountainside. Avalanches pose a serious danger to people.

**Analyzing** Why do glaciers sometimes form at higher elevations in the Alps?

## Water Features

Several bodies of water are important to West-Central Europe's physical geography. The **North Sea** and **English Channel** lie to the north. The Bay of Biscay and Atlantic Ocean lie to the west. The Mediterranean Sea borders France to the south.

Several rivers cross the region as well. Look at the map on the previous page to identify them. Two important rivers are the **Danube** (DAN-yoob) and the **Rhine** (RYN). For centuries people and goods have traveled these rivers, and many cities, farms, and industrial areas line their banks.

Several of West-Central Europe's rivers are navigable. A **navigable river** is one that is deep and wide enough for ships to use. These rivers and a system of canals link the region's interior to the seas. These waterways are important for trade and travel.

**READING CHECK** **Finding Main Ideas** What are the region's three major landform areas?

## Climate and Resources

A warm ocean current flows along Europe's northwestern coast. This current creates a marine west coast climate in most of West-Central Europe. This climate makes much of the area a pleasant place to live. Though winters can get cold, summers are mild. Rain and storms occur often, though.

At higher elevations, such as in the Alps, the climate is colder and wetter. In contrast, southern France has a warm Mediterranean climate. Summers are dry and hot, and winters are mild and wet.

West-Central Europe's mild climate is a valuable natural resource. Mild temperatures, plenty of rain, and rich soil have made the region's farmlands highly productive. Farm crops include grapes, grains, and vegetables. In the uplands and Alps, pastures and valleys support livestock.

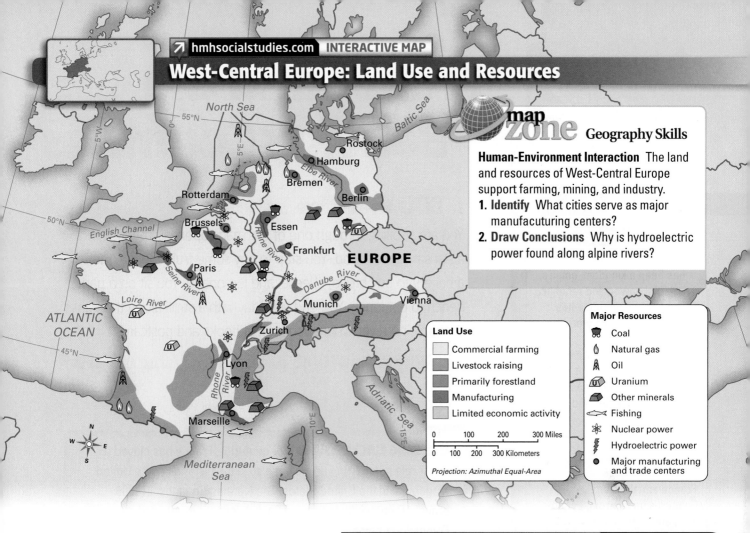

North Sea
55°N
Baltic Sea
Rostock
Hamburg
Bremen
Rotterdam
Berlin
Brussels
Essen
Rhine River
Frankfurt
**EUROPE**
English Channel
50°N
Paris
Seine River
Danube River
Loire River
Munich
Vienna
ATLANTIC OCEAN
45°N
Zurich
Lyon
Rhone River
Marseille
Adriatic Sea
15°E
Mediterranean Sea

W N E S

**map zone** Geography Skills

**Human-Environment Interaction** The land and resources of West-Central Europe support farming, mining, and industry.
1. **Identify** What cities serve as major manufacuturing centers?
2. **Draw Conclusions** Why is hydroelectric power found along alpine rivers?

**Land Use**
☐ Commercial farming
☐ Livestock raising
☐ Primarily forestland
☐ Manufacturing
☐ Limited economic activity

0   100   200   300 Miles
0  100  200  300 Kilometers
*Projection: Azimuthal Equal-Area*

**Major Resources**
⛏ Coal
◊ Natural gas
♨ Oil
⬓ Uranium
⬢ Other minerals
🐟 Fishing
✳ Nuclear power
⚡ Hydroelectric power
● Major manufacturing and trade centers

Energy and mineral resources are not evenly distributed across the region, as the map shows. France has coal and iron ore, Germany also has coal, and the Netherlands has natural gas. Fast-flowing alpine rivers provide hydroelectric power. Even so, many countries must import fuels.

Another valuable natural resource is found in the breathtaking beauty of the Alps. Each year, tourists flock to the Alps to enjoy the scenery and to hike and ski.

**READING CHECK** **Summarizing** What natural resources contribute to the region's economy?

**SUMMARY AND PREVIEW** West-Central Europe includes low plains, uplands, and mountains. The climate is mild, and natural resources support farming, industry, and tourism. Next, you will read about France and the Benelux Countries.

## Section 1 Assessment

↗ hmhsocialstudies.com
**ONLINE QUIZ**

### Reviewing Ideas, Terms, and Places

1. **a. Describe** What are the main physical features of the **Northern European Plain**?
   **b. Analyze** How does having many **navigable** rivers benefit West-Central Europe?
2. **a. Recall** What is the region's main climate?
   **b. Make Inferences** How might an uneven distribution of mineral resources affect the region?

### Critical Thinking

3. **Categorizing** Draw a fan like this one. Label each band with the landform area in West-Central Europe it represents. Using your notes, identify each area's physical features, climate, and resources.

### FOCUS ON SPEAKING

4. **Noting the Physical Geography** What issues related to land use and resources can you think of? Could mining coal or importing fuel be an issue? Jot down ideas.

# France and the Benelux Countries

## If YOU lived there...

You are strolling through one of the many open–air markets in a Paris neighborhood. You stop to buy some fruit, then go into a bakery to buy bread, cheese, and lemonade. You sit on a park bench to eat lunch. You end your day with a stroll along the banks of the Seine River, where you look at books and postcards.

**Why do you think people enjoy living in Paris?**

**BUILDING BACKGROUND** For centuries, France has played a major role not only in Europe but also in the histories of the United Kingdom and the United States. The Norman Conquest in 1066 brought French influences into English language, law, and culture. France later helped the American colonists win their independence.

## History of France

In southwest France, Lascaux (lah-SKOH) Cave holds a treasure from the past. Inside, prehistoric paintings of bulls run and jump along the stone walls. More than 15,000 years old, these paintings show how long people have lived in what is now France.

### Early History

In ancient times, France was part of a region called Gaul (GAWL). Centuries ago, Celtic peoples from eastern Europe settled in Gaul. In the 50s BC, the Romans conquered the region. They introduced Roman law. The Romans also established a Latin-based language that in time developed into French.

Roman rule in Gaul lasted until the AD 400s. The Franks, a Germanic people, then conquered much of Gaul. It is from the Franks that France gets its name. The Franks' greatest ruler was Charlemagne (SHAHR-luh-mayn), who built a powerful Christian empire. After he had conquered much of the old Roman Empire, the pope crowned him Emperor of the Romans in 800.

After Charlemagne's death, many invaders attacked the Franks. One such group, the Normans, settled in northwestern France. This area is called Normandy.

In 1066 the Normans conquered England. William the Conqueror, the duke of Normandy, became king of England. He now ruled England as well as part of France. In the 1300s England's king tried to claim the French throne to gain control of the rest of France. This event led to the Hundred Years' War (1337–1453). The French eventually drove out the English.

## Revolution and Empire

From the 1500s to the 1700s, France built a colonial empire. The French established colonies in the Americas, Africa, and Asia. At this time, most French people lived in poverty and had few rights. For these reasons, in 1789 the French people overthrew their king in the French Revolution.

A few years later a brilliant general named Napoleon took power. In time, he conquered much of Europe. Then in 1815 several European powers joined forces and defeated Napoleon. They exiled him and chose a new king to rule France.

## Modern History

During both World War I and World War II, German forces invaded France. After each war, France worked to rebuild its economy. In the 1950s it experienced rapid growth.

During the 1950s and 1960s, many of of the French colonies gained their independence. Some people from these former colonies then moved to France.

France is now a republic with a parliament and an elected president. France still controls several overseas territories, such as Martinique in the West Indies.

**READING CHECK** **Summarizing** Which foreign groups have affected France's history?

# France's History

During its long history, France has gone from strong kingdom to great empire, to colonial world power, to modern republic.

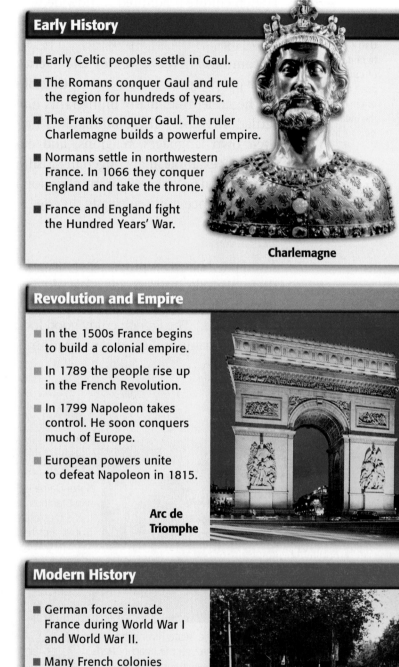

### Early History

- Early Celtic peoples settle in Gaul.
- The Romans conquer Gaul and rule the region for hundreds of years.
- The Franks conquer Gaul. The ruler Charlemagne builds a powerful empire.
- Normans settle in northwestern France. In 1066 they conquer England and take the throne.
- France and England fight the Hundred Years' War.

Charlemagne

### Revolution and Empire

- In the 1500s France begins to build a colonial empire.
- In 1789 the people rise up in the French Revolution.
- In 1799 Napoleon takes control. He soon conquers much of Europe.
- European powers unite to defeat Napoleon in 1815.

Arc de Triomphe

### Modern History

- German forces invade France during World War I and World War II.
- Many French colonies declare independence in the 1950s and 1960s.
- Today France is a republic with a president and a democratic government.

WWII German occupation

## The Culture of France

During their long history, the French have developed a strong cultural identity. Today French culture is admired worldwide.

**FOCUS ON READING**
Use a dictionary to find the origin of *cuisine*. How does the word's origin relate to the meaning of *cuisine* today?

### Language and Religion

A common heritage unites the French. Most people speak French and are Catholic. At the same time, many immigrants have settled in France. These immigrants have their own languages, religions, and customs. For example, many Algerian Muslims have moved to France. This immigration is making France more culturally diverse.

### Customs

The French have a phrase that describes their attitude toward life—*joie de vivre* (zhwah duh VEEV-ruh), meaning "enjoyment of life." The French enjoy good food, good company, and good conversation.

An enjoyment of food has helped make French cooking some of the best in the world. French chefs and cooking schools have worldwide reputations. The French have also contributed to the language of food. Terms such as *café*, *cuisine* (cooking), and *menu* all come from the French.

The French also enjoy their festivals. The major national festival is Bastille Day, held on July 14. On that date in 1789 a mob destroyed the Bastille, a Paris prison symbolizing the French king's harsh rule. The event began the French Revolution.

### Ideas and the Arts

The French have made major contributions to the arts and ideas. In the Middle Ages, the French built majestic cathedrals in the Gothic style. This style has high pointed ceilings, stained-glass windows, and tall towers that reach heavenward. Notre Dame Cathedral in Paris is an example.

**Close-up**

# Paris

Some 2,000 years old, Paris grew up along the banks of the Seine (SEN) River. Known as "the City of Light" for its gleaming beauty, Paris shines as one of Europe's most cultured cities. Wide tree-lined avenues, historic squares, and lovely gardens and parks grace the city center.

Notre Dame is France's most famous cathedral. It is a masterpiece of Gothic architecture.

The Seine River winds through the heart of Paris. Beautiful bridges cross the river, and in places booksellers line its banks.

In the 1700s France was a center of the Enlightenment, a period in which people used reason to improve society. French Enlightenment ideas about government inspired the American Revolution and the development of modern democracy.

In the 1800s France was the center of one of the most famous art movements of the modern age—impressionism. This style of painting uses rippling light to create an impression of a scene. During the same period, French authors wrote classics such as *The Three Musketeers* by Alexandre Dumas (doo-mah). Today France is known for art and its fashion and film industries.

**READING CHECK** **Summarizing** What are some main features of French culture?

## France Today

France is now West-Central Europe's largest country. It plays a leading role in Europe and in the European Union (EU).

Today about 75 percent of the French live in cities. **Paris**, the capital, is by far the largest city, with about 10 million people.

Fashionable with a quick pace, Paris is a center of business, finance, learning, and culture. It boasts world-class museums, art galleries, and restaurants as well as famous landmarks such as the Eiffel Tower and Notre Dame Cathedral.

Other major cities include Marseille (mar-SAY), a Mediterranean seaport, and Lyon (LYAWN), located on the Rhone River. A modern system of highways, canals, and high-speed trains links France's cities.

France has a strong economy. It is the EU's top agricultural producer, and its major crops include wheat and grapes. French workers are also highly productive. Rich soil and efficient workers have made France a major exporter of goods, such as its famous perfumes and wines.

The Paris Métro, or subway, is known for its decorative wrought-iron entrances, built in the early 1900s.

Paris is known for its many sidewalk cafés, where people meet to eat, socialize, and relax.

**ANALYSIS SKILL** **ANALYZING VISUALS**

**What examples do you see of the mixing of the new and the old in Paris?**

# Dutch Polders

More than 25 percent of the Netherlands lies below sea level. For centuries, the Dutch have reclaimed land from the sea. These reclaimed lands are called polders.

To create polders, the Dutch build dikes near the shoreline. They then use pumps to remove the water behind the dikes. A national system of dikes, dams, floodgates, and storm barriers now holds back the sea.

Unfortunately, creating polders has caused sinking lowlands and other environmental damage. The Dutch are working to address these problems. For example, they are considering restoring some of the polders to wetlands, lakes, and the seas.

**Finding Main Ideas** How have the Dutch modified their environment to live in a region that lies below sea level?

Tourism is also vital to the economy. Each year, millions of people visit Paris, the French Alps, and the sunny French Riviera, a resort area on the Mediterranean coast.

**READING CHECK** Drawing Conclusions Why do you think tourists might want to visit Paris?

## The Benelux Countries

Belgium, the Netherlands, and Luxembourg are called the Benelux Countries. *Benelux* combines the first letters of each country's name. They are also called the Low Countries because of their elevation.

### History

Many nations and empires dominated the Benelux region. In 1648 the Netherlands gained its independence. It ruled Belgium until 1830, and Luxembourg until 1867, when they gained independence.

In World War II, Germany occupied the Benelux Countries. After the war, they joined the North Atlantic Treaty Organization (NATO) for protection. NATO is an alliance of nations. In the 1950s the Benelux Countries joined the group of nations now known as the EU.

Today the Benelux Countries each have a parliament and ceremonial monarch. The tiny, densely populated countries lie between larger, stronger countries. This location has led to invasions but has also promoted trade. The Benelux Countries now have wealthy economies.

### The Netherlands

Bordering the North Sea, the Netherlands is low and flat. Some of the land lies below sea level. The Netherlands includes the historical region of Holland and is sometimes called Holland. The people here are the Dutch, and the language they speak is also called Dutch.

Excellent harbors on the North Sea have made the Netherlands a center of international trade. The city of Rotterdam is one of the world's busiest seaports. It is also part of a highly industrial and urban, or city-based, area. This area includes **Amsterdam**, the capital, and **The Hague** (HAYG), the seat of government. Agriculture is also important to the Dutch economy, and Dutch cheese and tulips are world famous.

## Belgium

Belgium is a highly urban country. More than 95 percent of the people of Belgium live in cities. The capital city, **Brussels**, serves as the headquarters for many international organizations, including the EU and NATO. The city of Brussels is as a result highly **cosmopolitan**, or characterized by many foreign influences.

Language divides Belgium. The coast and north are called Flanders. The people there speak Flemish. The southern interior is called Wallonia. The people there speak French and are called Walloons. These cultural differences have caused tensions.

Belgium is known for its cheeses, chocolate, cocoa, and lace. The city of Antwerp is a key port and diamond-cutting center.

## Luxembourg

Luxembourg is a forested, hilly country. Although smaller than Rhode Island, it has one of the world's highest standards of living. Most of the people in Luxembourg are Roman Catholic and speak either French or German.

Luxembourg earns much of its income from services such as banking. The region also produces steel and chemicals. Its small cities are cosmopolitan centers of international business and government.

**READING CHECK** **Comparing** What do the Benelux Countries have in common?

**SUMMARY AND PREVIEW** As you have learned, France and the Benelux Countries are modern and urban with strong economies. Next, you will read about Germany and the Alpine Countries.

---

## Section 2 Assessment

hmhsocialstudies.com
ONLINE QUIZ

### Reviewing Ideas, Terms, and Places

1. **a. Identify** Who was Charlemagne?
   **b. Explain** Why is Napoleon considered a significant figure in French history?
   **c. Develop** Why might the French be proud of their long history?
2. **a. Define** What is impressionism?
   **b. Summarize** What are some major contributions of French culture?
   **c. Elaborate** How has immigration influenced French culture?
3. **a. Describe** Why is **Paris** an important city?
   **b. Summarize** What is the French economy like?
4. **a. Describe** How does language divide Belgium?
   **b. Draw Conclusions** Why might **Brussels** be such a **cosmopolitan** city?

### Critical Thinking

5. **Categorizing** Draw a chart like the one here. Use your notes and enter information into each category. Within each category, organize the information by country.

History / Government / Culture / Economics

### FOCUS ON SPEAKING

6. **Describing France and the Benelux Countries** For each country, note one possible issue for your persuasive speech. For example, one issue might be language in Belgium. Should all Belgians have to speak the same language?

# The European Union

How can smaller countries compete with larger ones? One way is by working together. Since the 1950s, countries across Europe have been working to build a united community. Today this organization is called the European Union (EU). It promotes political and economic cooperation among member nations. The chart on the next page shows how the EU has changed life in Europe.

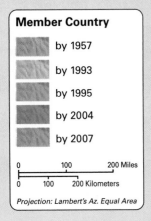

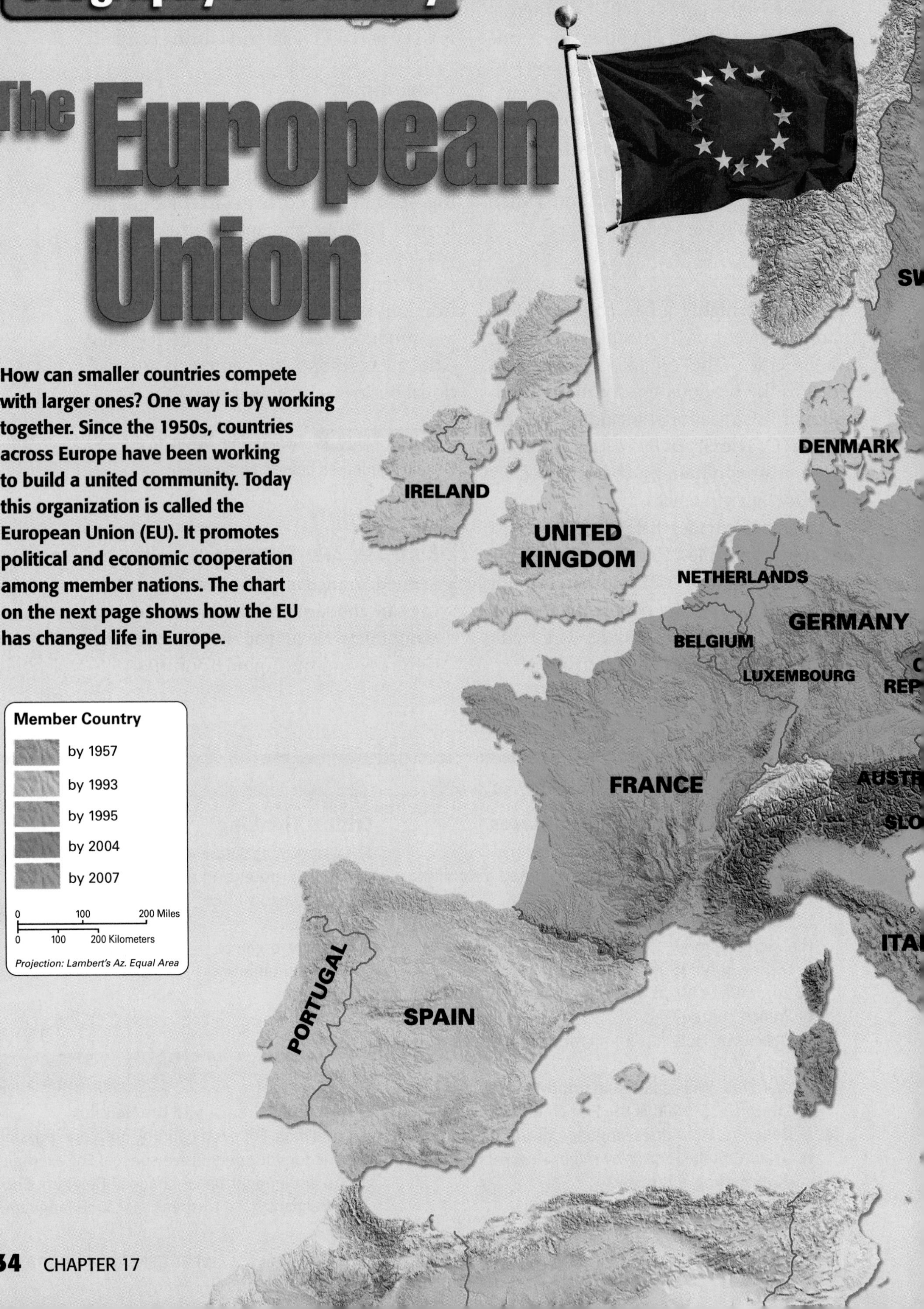

**Member Country**

| | |
|---|---|
| | by 1957 |
| | by 1993 |
| | by 1995 |
| | by 2004 |
| | by 2007 |

0   100   200 Miles
0   100   200 Kilometers

*Projection: Lambert's Az. Equal Area*

SW

DENMARK

IRELAND

UNITED KINGDOM

NETHERLANDS

BELGIUM

GERMANY

LUXEMBOURG

C REP

FRANCE

AUSTR

SLO

PORTUGAL

SPAIN

ITAL

FINLAND

ESTONIA

LATVIA

LITHUANIA

POLAND

SLOVAKIA

HUNGARY

ROMANIA

BULGARIA

TURKEY

GREECE

CYPRUS

## Benefits of Membership in the European Union

### Trade

| Before | After |
| --- | --- |
| ■ European countries had to pay customs duties, or taxes, on goods they traded with other European countries.<br><br>■ Many European countries' economies were small compared to those of larger nations such as the United States. | ■ EU countries are part of a common market. They can trade freely with each other without paying duties.<br><br>■ EU countries create a combined economy that is one of the largest in the world. |

### Currency

| Before | After |
| --- | --- |
| ■ Each European country had its own separate currency, or form of money.<br><br>■ European countries and their citizens had to exchange currencies to buy goods from other European countries. | ■ Most EU countries share one currency, the euro.<br><br>■ EU countries and their citizens can use the euro to buy goods and trade throughout the EU. |

### Work and Travel

| Before | After |
| --- | --- |
| ■ Europeans had to have passports or other special permits to travel from one European country to another.<br><br>■ Europeans had to obtain permission to live and work in other countries in Europe. | ■ Citizens of EU countries do not need passports or special permits to travel throughout most of the EU.<br><br>■ Citizens of EU countries can live and work anywhere in the EU without having to obtain permission. |

**The Euro** The front sides of euro coins all have the same image, but the backs feature a unique symbol for each country. Euro bills show symbols of unity.

**ANALYSIS SKILL** **ANALYZING VISUALS**

1. **Name** Which six countries were the first to unite?
2. **Make Inferences** How do you think democracy's spread in Eastern Europe has affected the EU?
3. **Interpreting Charts** Based on the chart above, what are two benefits of EU membership?

# Germany and the Alpine Countries

## If YOU lived there...

You are walking with your grandfather through Berlin, Germany. He begins telling you about a time when Germany was divided into two countries—one democratic and one Communist. A large wall even divided the city of Berlin. Germans could not pass freely through the wall. You think of your friends who live in eastern Berlin. They would have been on the other side of the wall back then.

**What do you think life in Berlin was like then?**

**BUILDING BACKGROUND** Since the Middle Ages, Germany and France have been the dominant countries in West-Central Europe. Both are large and prosperous with hardworking people and good farmland. The two countries have often been at war, but today they are partners in building a cooperative European Union.

## History of Germany

Some countries have had a strong influence on world events. Germany is one of these countries. From its location in the heart of Europe, Germany has shaped events across Europe and the world—for both good and bad.

### Growth of a Nation

In ancient times, tribes from northern Europe settled in the land that is now Germany. The Romans called this region Germania, after the name of one of the tribes. Over time, many small German states developed in the region. Princes ruled these states. With the support of the Roman Catholic Church, these states became part of the Holy Roman Empire.

For hundreds of years, Germany remained a loose association of small states. Then in 1871, Prussia, the strongest state, united Germany into one nation. As a unified nation, Germany developed into an industrial and military world power.

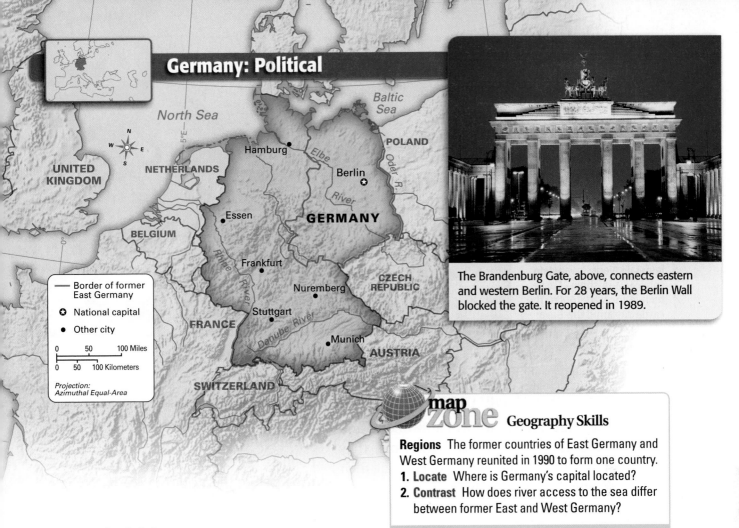

# Germany: Political

North Sea

Baltic Sea

UNITED KINGDOM

NETHERLANDS

POLAND

Hamburg

Elbe

Berlin ✪

River

Oder R.

Essen

**GERMANY**

BELGIUM

Frankfurt

Rhine River

Nuremberg

CZECH REPUBLIC

Stuttgart

Danube River

FRANCE

Munich

AUSTRIA

SWITZERLAND

— Border of former East Germany
✪ National capital
• Other city

0   50   100 Miles
0   50   100 Kilometers

Projection: Azimuthal Equal-Area

The Brandenburg Gate, above, connects eastern and western Berlin. For 28 years, the Berlin Wall blocked the gate. It reopened in 1989.

map zone  Geography Skills

**Regions** The former countries of East Germany and West Germany reunited in 1990 to form one country.
1. **Locate** Where is Germany's capital located?
2. **Contrast** How does river access to the sea differ between former East and West Germany?

## War and Division

In 1914–1918, Germany fought and lost World War I. Payments for war damages and a major depression severely hurt the German economy. Looking for a strong leader, Germans found Adolf Hitler and his Nazi Party. Hitler promised the Germans to restore their country to its former glory.

In 1939 Germany attacked Poland, starting World War II. Soon, Germany had conquered much of Europe. The Nazis also sought to kill all European Jews in what is called the Holocaust. Germany lost the war, though. By 1945 it lay in ruins, defeated.

After the war, British, French, and U.S. troops occupied West Germany. The Soviet Union's troops occupied East Germany. Over time, two countries emerged.

The city of **Berlin** was in Communist East Germany. Even so, West Germany kept control of the western part of the city.

In 1961 Communist leaders built the Berlin Wall. The Wall's **purpose** was to prevent East Germans from fleeing to West Berlin.

**ACADEMIC VOCABULARY**

**purpose** the reason something is done

## A Reunited Germany

After World War II, U.S. aid helped West Germany rebuild rapidly. It soon became an economic power. East Germany rebuilt as well, but its economy lagged. In addition, its people had limited freedoms.

In 1989 movements for democracy swept through Eastern Europe. Communist governments began collapsing. Joyful East Germans tore down the Berlin Wall. In 1990 East and West Germany reunited.

**READING CHECK** **Finding Main Ideas** What major challenges has Germany overcome?

## German Culture

Germany's long history has enriched its culture. Historic castles dot the landscape, and long-held traditions continue. Blending with this history is a modern culture that includes a love of sports.

**A Bavarian Castle** King Ludwig II of Bavaria had the fairy-tale Neuschwanstein (noy-SHVAHN-shtyn) Castle built in the mid-1800s. The castle sits amid the Bavarian Alps in southern Germany.

# Culture of Germany

Germans are known as hardworking and efficient people. At the same time, they enjoy their traditions and celebrating their cultural achievements.

## People

Most Germans share a common heritage. About 90 percent are ethnic German, and most speak German. In recent years, significant numbers of immigrants have come to Germany to live and work as well. These immigrants include Turks, Italians, and refugees from Eastern Europe. Their influence is making German culture more diverse.

## Religion

In 1517 Martin Luther, a German monk, helped start the Reformation. This religious reform movement led to the development of Protestant churches. Many Germanic states became Protestant; others remained Roman Catholic. Today in north and central Germany, most people are Protestant. In the south, most are Catholic. In eastern Germany, fewer Germans have religious ties, reflecting the area's Communist past.

## Customs

Festivals and holidays tell us much about German culture. Religious festivals are very popular. For example, many areas hold festivals before the Christian season of Lent. In addition, Christmas is a major family event. The tradition of the Christmas tree even began in Germany.

Each region has local festivals as well. The best known is Oktoberfest in Bavaria, the region of southeast Germany. This festival is held each fall in Munich (MYOO-nik) to celebrate the region's food and drink.

## The Arts and Sciences

Germany's contributions to the arts and sciences are widely admired. In music, Germany has produced famed classical composers, such as Johann Sebastian Bach and Ludwig van Beethoven. In literature, author Johann Wolfgang von Goethe (GOOH-tuh) ranks among Europe's most important writers. In science, Germans have made contributions in chemistry, engineering, medicine, and physics.

**READING CHECK** **Summarizing** What contributions have Germans made to world culture?

**Christmas Markets**
German Christmas markets and fairs like this one have been popular for centuries. Booths sell trees, crafts, and food. Rides and music provide entertainment.

## Germany Today

Despite a stormy history, Germany has endured. Today the country is a leading power in Europe and the world.

### Government and Economy

Germany is a federal republic. A parliament chooses a **chancellor**, or prime minister, to run the government. The parliament also helps elect a president, whose duties are largely ceremonial. On the world stage, Germany belongs to the EU and NATO.

Germany's market economy has helped the country become an economic giant. It is Europe's largest economy, producing nearly one-fifth of all goods and services in the EU. The nation exports a wide range of products. You may be familiar with German cars, such as BMWs or Volkswagens.

The German economy is based on industry, such as chemicals, engineering, and steel. The main industrial district is the Ruhr, located in western Germany. Fewer Germans farm than in the past, but agriculture remains important. Major crops include grain, potatoes, and grapes. Timber is harvested in the south.

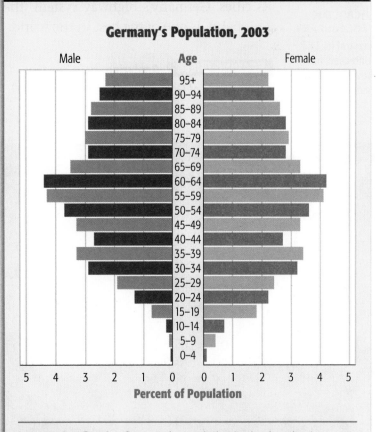

**Germany's Population, 2003**

**Interpreting Graphs** Germany's population is slowly aging because Germans are living longer and families are becoming smaller. Which age group in Germany is now the largest?

hmhsocialstudies.com

FOCUS ON
READING
Use a dictionary
to find the origin
of *lag.* How does
the word's origin
relate to its
meaning here?

Economic growth has slowed since East and West Germany reunited, however. The economy of former East Germany continues to lag. The region also suffers high unemployment. Germany's government is working to solve these problems.

### Cities

Most Germans live in cities. The largest city is Berlin, the capital. During World War II, Berlin suffered major destruction. Today Germans have restored their capital to its former splendor. A historic city, it has wide boulevards and many parks.

Other major German cities include Hamburg, a key port city on the North Sea, and Munich, a cultural and manufacturing center. Like France, Germany has an excellent transportation system that links its cities. Germany's highway system, the Autobahn, is one of the best in the world.

ACADEMIC
VOCABULARY
neutral (p. 145)
unbiased, not
favoring either
side in a conflict

**READING CHECK** **Analyzing** How has the reunification of Germany affected its economy?

## The Alpine Countries

The beauty of the Alps draws many tourists to Austria and Switzerland. These countries are called the Alpine Countries after the Alps, which cover much of them.

Austria and Switzerland have many similarities. Both are landlocked. Both are heavily influenced by German culture and were once part of the Holy Roman Empire. Yet, the countries have their differences.

### Austria

Austria was once the center of one of the most powerful empires in Europe. The royal Habsburg family came to control this empire. At its height, the Habsburg line ruled the Netherlands, Spain, and much of Germany, Italy, and Eastern Europe.

In 1918, however, the Habsburgs were on the losing side of World War I. After the war, Austria became a republic. Since then, Austria has grown into a modern, industrialized nation. Today it is a federal republic and EU member.

### The Alpine Countries

Austria and Switzerland draw millions of tourists each year. Above, tourists ride through Vienna, Austria, famous for its history and culture. At left, a mountain village shows the beauty of the Swiss Alps.

Most Austrians speak German and are Roman Catholic. The city of **Vienna** is Austria's capital and largest city. Located on the banks of the Danube, Vienna was once the center of Habsburg rule. Today historic palaces grace the city, which is a center of music and the fine arts.

Austria has a prosperous economy with little unemployment. Service industries, such as banking, are important and employ more than half of Austria's workforce. Tourism is important as well.

## Switzerland

Since the 1600s Switzerland has been an independent country. Today it is a federal republic with 26 districts called **cantons**. Citizens are active in local government. In addition, all male citizens serve for a period in the militia, a citizen army.

Switzerland's location in the Alps has helped it remain **neutral** for centuries. To stay neutral, Switzerland has not joined the EU or NATO. The Swiss are active in international organizations, however.

As the map shows, the Swiss speak several languages. The main languages are German and French. Switzerland's capital, **Bern**, is centrally located to be near both German- and French-speaking regions.

Switzerland has one of the world's highest standards of living. It is famous for its banks, watches and other precision devices, and chocolate and cheese.

**READING CHECK** **Contrasting** How are the countries of Austria and Switzerland different?

**SUMMARY AND PREVIEW** You have read that Germany is an economic power with a rich culture, while the Alpine Countries are prosperous with beautiful mountain scenery. In the next chapter you will learn about Northern Europe.

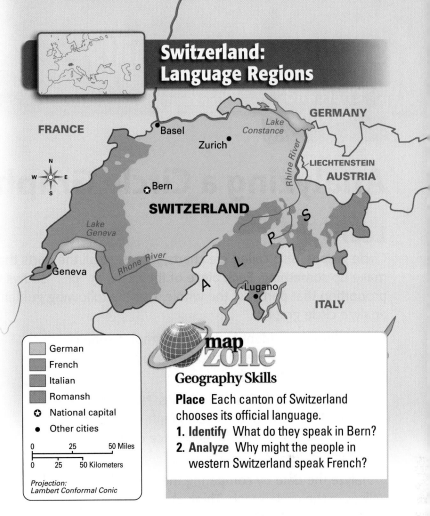

## Switzerland: Language Regions

**Legend:**
- German
- French
- Italian
- Romansh
- ✪ National capital
- • Other cities

0        25        50 Miles
0   25   50 Kilometers

Projection: Lambert Conformal Conic

### map zone

**Geography Skills**

**Place** Each canton of Switzerland chooses its official language.
1. **Identify** What do they speak in Bern?
2. **Analyze** Why might the people in western Switzerland speak French?

---

## Section 3 Assessment

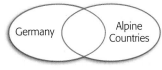

hmhsocialstudies.com
ONLINE QUIZ

### Reviewing Ideas, Terms, and Places

1. **a. Identify** Why is Adolf Hitler significant in history?
   **b. Sequence** What events led to German reunification?
2. **a. Recall** What are some popular festivals in Germany?
   **b. Contrast** How does religion differ across Germany?
3. **a. Describe** What is the role of Germany's **chancellor**?
   **b. Explain** Why has Germany's economy slowed?
4. **a. Define** What are **cantons**, and where are they found?
   **b. Analyze** How are the Alps a valuable resource?

### Critical Thinking

5. **Comparing and Contrasting** Draw a Venn diagram like this one. Use your notes to list the differences and similarities.

   Germany | Alpine Countries

### FOCUS ON SPEAKING

6. **Describing Germany and the Alpine Countries** For each country, note one issue for your speech. For example, you might argue that the Alps are the region's loveliest area.

# Analyzing a Circle Graph

## Learn

Circle graphs, also called pie charts, represent all the parts that make up something. Each piece of the circle, or "pie," shows what proportion that part is of the whole. Use the following guidelines to analyze circle graphs.

- Read the title to identify the circle graph's subject. The circle graph here shows the main languages spoken in Switzerland.

- Read the circle graph's other labels. Note what each part, or slice, of the circle graph represents. In the circle graph at right, each slice represents a different language.

- Analyze the data by comparing the size of the slices in the circle graph. Think about what the differences mean or imply.

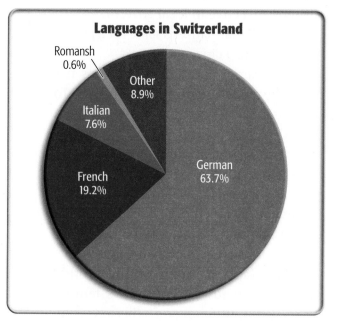

Languages in Switzerland

Source: Central Intelligence Agency, *The World Factbook 2002*

## Practice

❶ Based on the circle graph at right, what are the three main languages spoken in Switzerland?

❷ What language do less than 1 percent of the Swiss speak?

❸ What percentage of the Swiss speak other languages not listed individually?

## Apply

To answer the following questions, use the circle graph titled France's Current Export Partners in the Standardized Test Practice.

**1.** To which country does France send the highest percentage of its exports?

**2.** How many of France's main export partners belong to the European Union?

**3.** What percentage of French exports go to the United States?

# Chapter Review

**Geography's Impact**
video series
Review the video to answer the closing question:
*Do you think proximity to the sea has been more beneficial or harmful to the Netherlands?*

## Visual Summary

*Use the visual summary below to help you review the main ideas of the chapter.*

QUICK FACTS

France is a leading European nation and cultural center. The Benelux Countries are small, densely populated, and rich.

Germany is an industrial powerhouse with a rich culture. The landlocked Alpine Countries have stunning mountains.

## Reviewing Vocabulary, Terms, and Places

*Match each "I" statement below with the person, place, or thing that might have made the statement.*

| | |
|---|---|
| **a.** Berlin | **f.** Danube River |
| **b.** Brussels | **g.** dike |
| **c.** canton | **h.** navigable river |
| **d.** chancellor | **i.** North Sea |
| **e.** cosmopolitan city | **j.** Paris |

1. "I am the capital of France and a center of business, finance, learning, and culture."

2. "I am an important waterway in the region of West-Central Europe."

3. "I am a prime minister in Germany."

4. "I am an earthen wall used to hold back water."

5. "I am a type of river that is wide and deep enough for ships to use."

6. "I am a district in Switzerland."

7. "I am a city that has many foreign influences."

8. "I am an international city and the capital of Belgium."

9. "I am a large body of water located to the north of the Benelux Countries and Germany."

10. "I was divided into two parts after World War II and am now the capital of Germany."

## Comprehension and Critical Thinking

**SECTION 1** *(Pages 424–427)*

11. **a. Recall** From southeast to northwest, what are the major landforms in West-Central Europe?

    **b. Analyze** How have geographic features supported trade and travel across the region of West-Central Europe?

    **c. Elaborate** How does West-Central Europe's mild climate serve as a valuable resource and contribute to the economy?

## SECTION 2 *(Pages 428–433)*

**12. a. Identify** Where is the busiest seaport in the Netherlands located?

**b. Summarize** What are some products and cultural features for which France is famous?

**c. Develop** How have geographic features helped the Benelux Countries become centers of trade and international business?

## SECTION 3 *(Pages 436–441)*

**13. a. Recall** What are three major events in German history, and when did each one occur?

**b. Analyze** How is Switzerland's position in European affairs unique?

**c. Elaborate** How has the royal Habsburg family shaped Austria's history?

# Social Studies Skills

**Analyzing a Circle Graph** *Use the circle graph titled* Languages in Switzerland *in the Social Studies Skills to answer the following questions.*

**14.** Based on the circle graph, what percentage of the Swiss speak German?

**15.** What percentage of the Swiss speak French and Italian?

**16.** What fourth language do the Swiss speak?

# Using the Internet 21ST CENTURY

**17. Activity: Researching Schools** Imagine that your family is moving to Belgium or the Netherlands. In your new country you will be attending an international school. What kinds of classes will you have? What will your school day be like? What kinds of things might you see and do outside of school? Through your online textbook, research schools and daily life there. Then complete the online worksheet to record what you have learned. Finally, compare the schools you researched to the school you attend today.

↗ hmhsocialstudies.com

# Map Activity 21ST CENTURY

**18. West-Central Europe** On a separate sheet of paper, match the letters on the map with their correct labels.

| | |
|---|---|
| Alps | Paris, France |
| Berlin, Germany | Pyrenees |
| North Sea | Vienna, Austria |
| Northern European Plain | |

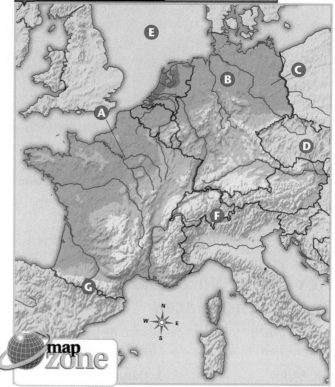

↗ hmhsocialstudies.com **INTERACTIVE MAP**

map zone

## FOCUS ON READING AND SPEAKING

**19. Recognizing Word Origins** Find the key term cosmopolitan in Section 2. Write the word's definition. Then use a good dictionary to research the word's origins. Explain how the word's origins relate to its definition.

**20. Writing a Persuasive Speech** Choose one of the issues you identified as you read the chapter. Write an opinion statement about the issue, such as "The Dutch polders should be restored to wetlands." Next, list three facts or examples that support your opinion. Use the chapter and other sources to find information. Then use the list to write your short persuasive speech. Practice delivering your speech using an assured tone of voice and a confident posture.

*DIRECTIONS: Read questions 1 through 7 and write the letter of the best response. Then read question 8 and write your own well-constructed response.*

**1** The alpine mountain system includes the Alps and the

**A** Black Forest.

**B** Jura Mountains.

**C** Massif Central.

**D** Pyrenees.

**2** What type of climate does *most* of West-Central Europe have?

**A** highland climate

**B** humid tropical climate

**C** marine west coast climate

**D** Mediterranean climate

**3** Which three countries make up the Benelux Countries?

**A** Belgium, the Netherlands, and Luxembourg

**B** France, Belgium, and Luxembourg

**C** France, Germany, and Austria

**D** Germany, Austria, and Switzerland

**4** Which French leader created a great empire only to be defeated in 1815?

**A** Adolf Hitler

**B** Charlemagne

**C** Napoleon

**D** William the Conqueror

**5** What capital city in West-Central Europe was divided after World War II?

**A** Berlin

**B** Brussels

**C** Paris

**D** Vienna

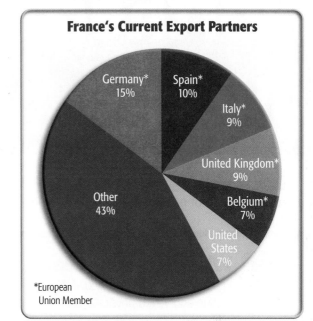

**France's Current Export Partners**

Germany* 15%
Spain* 10%
Italy* 9%
United Kingdom* 9%
Belgium* 7%
United States 7%
Other 43%

*European Union Member

Source: Central Intelligence Agency, *The World Factbook 2005*

**6** Based on the graph above, what percentage of French goods went to France's top two export partners?

**A** 10%

**B** 15%

**C** 25%

**D** 30%

**7** What is the main language spoken in both of the Alpine Countries?

**A** Dutch

**B** French

**C** German

**D** Italian

**8** **Extended Response** Examine the map of Germany in Section 3. Use the map to explain how the physical geography of former East and West Germany differed. Then analyze how you think each former country's physical geography affected its economy.

# CHAPTER 18

# Northern Europe

**Essential Question** How has location shaped the development of nations in Northern Europe?

## What You Will Learn...

In this chapter you will discover Northern Europe's unique and varied physical geography. You will also study the history and culture of Northern Europe's two main regions—the British Isles and Scandinavia. Finally, you will learn about the British Isles and Scandinavia today.

### FOCUS ON READING AND WRITING

**Using Context Clues—Synonyms** As you read, you may occasionally encounter a word or phrase that you do not know. When that happens, use the words and sentences around the unfamiliar word—context clues—to help you determine the word's meaning. As you read this chapter, look for words that are synonyms, or words that mean the same as the unfamiliar word. **See the lesson, Using Context Clues—Synonyms, on page 533.**

**Writing a Letter** Letters are a great way to stay in touch with friends and family. As you read this chapter, gather information about Northern Europe. Then imagine you are traveling through this region. Write a letter to your friends and family at home in which you describe what you have learned on your travels.

**Geography** Fertile plains like this one in Ireland provide Northern Europe with much of its farmland.

# Northern Europe: Political

70°N

ARCTIC OCEAN

Arctic Circle

Tromso

Norwegian Sea

NORWAY

SWEDEN

FINLAND

RUSSIA

Gulf of Bothnia

Bergen

Oslo

North Sea

Stockholm

Helsinki

Gulf of Finland

ESTONIA

Göteborg

LATVIA

DENMARK

Copenhagen

Baltic Sea

LITHUANIA

RUSSIA

BELARUS

NETHERLANDS

GERMANY

POLAND

**HISTORY** Winston Churchill

↗ hmhsocialstudies.com **VIDEO**

**map zone** Geography Skills

**Location** Much of Northern Europe is separated from the rest of the continent by the English Channel and the North and Baltic seas.

**1. Identify** What countries extend north of the Arctic Circle?

**2. Contrast** How does Northern Europe differ physically from the rest of Europe?

**History** The Palace of Westminster in London has been home to the British Parliament for over 600 years.

**Culture** Skiing and other forms of outdoor recreation are popular throughout much of Scandinavia.

**447**

# Physical Geography

## What You Will Learn...

### Main Ideas

1. The physical features of Northern Europe include low mountain ranges and jagged coastlines.
2. Northern Europe's natural resources include energy sources, soils, and seas.
3. The climates of Northern Europe range from a mild coastal climate to a freezing ice cap climate.

### The Big Idea

Northern Europe is a region of unique physical features, rich resources, and diverse climates.

### Key Terms and Places

British Isles, *p. 448*
Scandinavia, *p. 448*
fjord, *p. 449*
geothermal energy, *p. 450*
North Atlantic Drift, *p. 450*

hmhsocialstudies.com
TAKING NOTES

Use the graphic organizer online to take notes on the physical geography of Northern Europe.

## If YOU lived there...

Your family is planning to visit friends in Tromso, Norway. It is a city on the Norwegian Sea located 200 miles north of the Arctic Circle. You imagine a landscape covered in snow and ice. When you arrive, however, you discover green hills and ice-free harbors.

**What might explain the mild climate?**

**BUILDING BACKGROUND** Although located at high latitudes, Norway and the rest of Northern Europe have surprisingly mild temperatures. All the countries of Northern Europe are located on seas and oceans. As a result, they benefit from ocean currents that bring warm water north and keep the climate reasonably warm.

## Physical Features

From Ireland's gently rolling hills to Iceland's icy glaciers and fiery volcanoes, Northern Europe is a land of great variety. Because of this variety, the physical geography of Northern Europe changes greatly from one location to another.

Two regions—the British Isles and Scandinavia—make up Northern Europe. To the southwest lie the **British Isles**, a group of islands located across the English Channel from the rest of Europe. Northeast of the British Isles is **Scandinavia**, a region of islands and peninsulas in far northern Europe. The island of Iceland, to the west, is often considered part of Scandinavia.

**Hills and Mountains** Rough, rocky hills and low mountains cover much of Northern Europe. Rugged hills stretch across much of Iceland, northern Scotland, and Scandinavia. The jagged Kjolen (CHUH-luhn) Mountains on the Scandinavian Peninsula divide Norway from Sweden. The rocky soil and uneven terrain in these parts of Northern Europe make farming there difficult. As a result, fewer people live there than in the rest of Northern Europe.

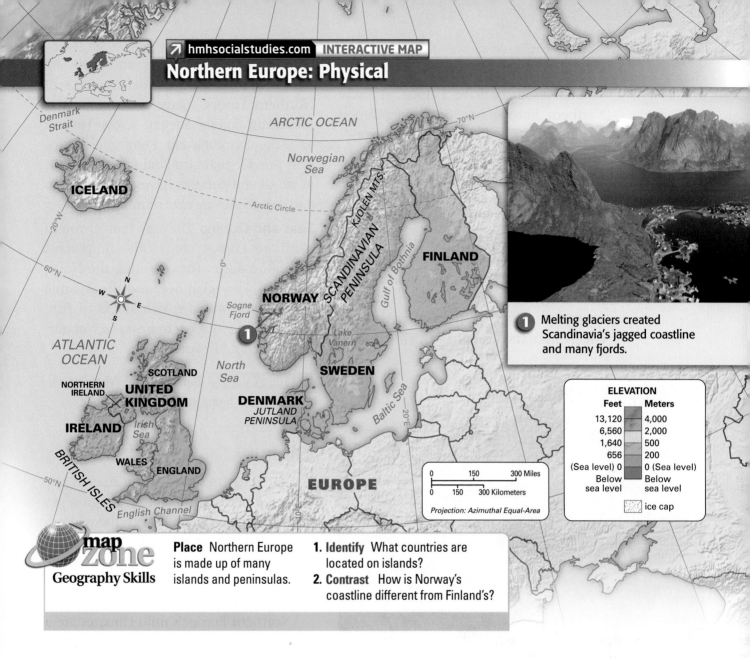

## Northern Europe: Physical

Denmark Strait

ARCTIC OCEAN

70°N

Norwegian Sea

ICELAND

Arctic Circle

20°W

60°N

KJØLEN MTS.

SCANDINAVIAN PENINSULA

FINLAND

Gulf of Bothnia

N
W    E
S

0°

Sogne Fjord

NORWAY

Lake Vanern

**1**

ATLANTIC OCEAN

North Sea

SWEDEN

Baltic Sea

20°E

SCOTLAND

NORTHERN IRELAND

UNITED KINGDOM

DENMARK
JUTLAND PENINSULA

IRELAND

Irish Sea

BRITISH ISLES

WALES

ENGLAND

50°N

EUROPE

English Channel

**1** Melting glaciers created Scandinavia's jagged coastline and many fjords.

| 0 | 150 | 300 Miles |
| 0 | 150 | 300 Kilometers |

Projection: Azimuthal Equal-Area

**ELEVATION**

| Feet | Meters |
|---|---|
| 13,120 | 4,000 |
| 6,560 | 2,000 |
| 1,640 | 500 |
| 656 | 200 |
| (Sea level) 0 | 0 (Sea level) |
| Below sea level | Below sea level |

ice cap

**map zone**

**Geography Skills**

**Place** Northern Europe is made up of many islands and peninsulas.

1. **Identify** What countries are located on islands?
2. **Contrast** How is Norway's coastline different from Finland's?

**Farmland and Plains** Fertile farmland and flat plains stretch across the southern parts of the British Isles and Scandinavia. Ireland's rolling, green hills provide rich farmland. Wide valleys in England and Denmark also have plenty of fertile soil.

**Effects of Glaciers** Slow-moving sheets of ice, or glaciers, have left their mark on Northern Europe's coastlines and lakes. As you can see on the map above, Norway's western coastline is very jagged. Millions of years ago, glaciers cut deep valleys into Norway's coastal mountains. As the glaciers melted, these valleys filled with water,

creating deep fjords. A **fjord** (fee-AWRD) is a narrow inlet of the sea set between high, rocky cliffs. Many fjords are very long and deep. Norway's Sogne (SAWNG-nuh) Fjord, for example, is over 100 miles (160 km) long and more than three-quarters of a mile (1.2 km) deep. Melting glaciers also carved thousands of lakes in Northern Europe. Sweden's Lake Vanern, along with many of the lakes in the British Isles, were carved by glaciers thousands of years ago.

**READING CHECK**  **Summarizing** What are some physical features of Northern Europe?

## Natural Resources

ACADEMIC VOCABULARY

primary
main, most
important

Natural resources have helped to make Northern Europe one of the wealthiest regions in the world. Northern Europe's **primary** resources are its energy resources, forests and soils, and surrounding seas.

**Energy** Northern Europe has a variety of energy resources. Norway and the United Kingdom benefit from oil and natural gas deposits under the North Sea. Hydroelectric energy is produced by the region's many lakes and rivers. In Iceland steam from hot springs produces **geothermal energy**, or energy from the heat of Earth's interior.

**Forests and Soils** Forests and soils are two other important natural resources in Northern Europe. Large areas of timber-producing forests stretch across Finland and the Scandinavian Peninsula. Fertile soils provide rich farmland for crops, such as wheat and potatoes. Livestock like sheep and dairy cattle are also common.

**Seas and Oceans** The seas that surround Northern Europe are another important natural resource. For centuries, the North Sea, the Norwegian Sea, and the Atlantic Ocean have provided rich stocks of fish. Today, fishing is a key industry in Norway, Denmark, and Iceland.

**READING CHECK** **Summarizing** What natural resources are found in Northern Europe?

## Climates

Locate Northern Europe on a map of the world. Notice that much of the region lies near the Arctic Circle. Due to the region's high latitude, you might imagine that it would be quite cold during much of the year. In reality, however, the climates in Northern Europe are remarkably mild.

Northern Europe's mild climates are a result of the **North Atlantic Drift**, an ocean current that brings warm, moist air across the Atlantic Ocean. Warm waters from this ocean current keep most of the region warmer than other locations around the globe at similar latitudes.

Much of Northern Europe has a marine west coast climate. Denmark, the British Isles, and western Norway benefit from mild summers and frequent rainfall. Snow and frosts may occur in winter but do not usually last long.

Central Norway, Sweden, and southern Finland have a humid continental climate. This area has four true seasons with cold, snowy winters and mild summers.

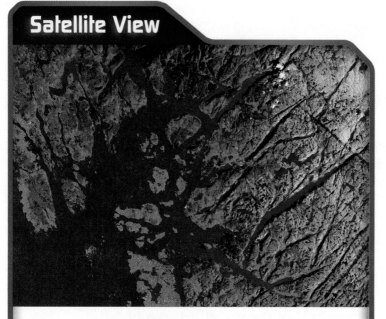

**Satellite View**

## Norway's Fjords

Millions of years ago much of Norway was covered with glaciers. As the glaciers flowed slowly downhill, they carved long, winding channels, or fjords, into Norway's coastline.

As you can see in this satellite image, fjords cut many miles into Norway's interior, bringing warm waters from the North and Norwegian seas. As warm waters penetrate inland, they keep temperatures relatively mild. In fact, people have used these unfrozen fjords to travel during the winter when ice and snow made travel over land difficult.

**Drawing Conclusions** How do fjords benefit life in Norway?

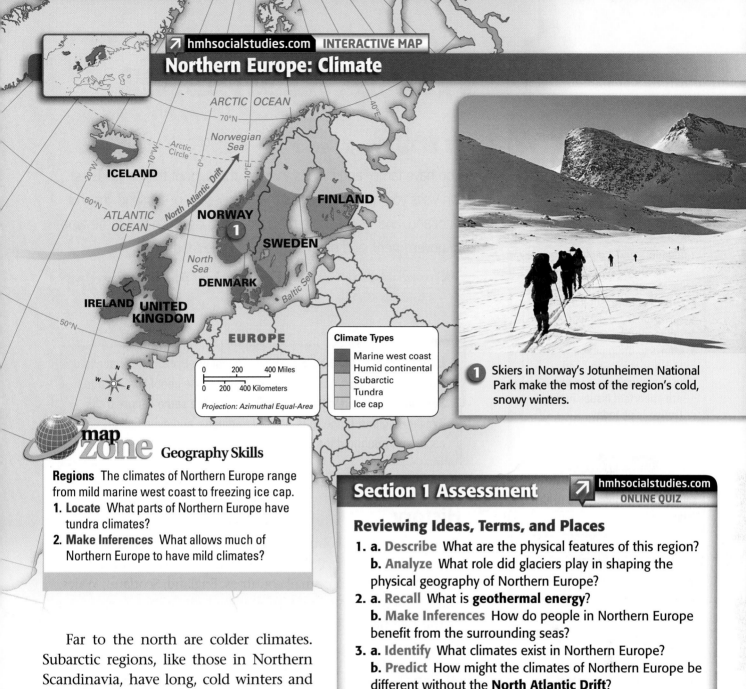

## Northern Europe: Climate

ARCTIC OCEAN
70°N
Norwegian Sea
Arctic Circle
ATLANTIC OCEAN
North Atlantic Drift
60°N
ICELAND
North Sea
NORWAY
①
FINLAND
SWEDEN
DENMARK
Baltic Sea
IRELAND
UNITED KINGDOM
50°N
EUROPE

N W E S

| 0 | 200 | 400 Miles |
| 0 | 200 | 400 Kilometers |

Projection: Azimuthal Equal-Area

**Climate Types**
- Marine west coast
- Humid continental
- Subarctic
- Tundra
- Ice cap

① Skiers in Norway's Jotunheimen National Park make the most of the region's cold, snowy winters.

### map zone Geography Skills

**Regions** The climates of Northern Europe range from mild marine west coast to freezing ice cap.
1. **Locate** What parts of Northern Europe have tundra climates?
2. **Make Inferences** What allows much of Northern Europe to have mild climates?

Far to the north are colder climates. Subarctic regions, like those in Northern Scandinavia, have long, cold winters and short summers. Iceland's tundra and ice cap climates produce extremely cold temperatures all year.

**READING CHECK** **Analyzing** How does the North Atlantic Drift keep climates mild?

**SUMMARY AND PREVIEW** Northern Europe has many different physical features, natural resources, and climates. Next, you will learn about the history and culture of the British Isles.

### Section 1 Assessment

#### Reviewing Ideas, Terms, and Places

1. a. **Describe** What are the physical features of this region?
   b. **Analyze** What role did glaciers play in shaping the physical geography of Northern Europe?
2. a. **Recall** What is **geothermal energy**?
   b. **Make Inferences** How do people in Northern Europe benefit from the surrounding seas?
3. a. **Identify** What climates exist in Northern Europe?
   b. **Predict** How might the climates of Northern Europe be different without the **North Atlantic Drift**?

#### Critical Thinking

4. **Comparing and Contrasting** Using your notes and a chart like the one below, compare and contrast the physical geography of the British Isles and Scandinavia.

|  | British Isles | Scandinavia |
|---|---|---|
| Physical Features |  |  |
| Resources |  |  |
| Climates |  |  |

#### FOCUS ON WRITING

5. **Describing the Physical Geography** Take notes on the physical features, resources, and climates of Northern Europe. In what season might you visit the region?

# The British Isles

## If YOU lived there...

You have family and friends that live throughout the British Isles. On visits you have discovered that the people of England, Ireland, Scotland, and Wales share the same language, use the same type of government, and eat many of the same foods.

**Why might culture in the British Isles be similar?**

**BUILDING BACKGROUND** The people of the British Isles have had close ties for thousands of years. As a result, the people of England, Scotland, Ireland, and Wales share many of the same culture traits. Similar religions, languages, literary traditions, and even holidays are common throughout the British Isles.

## History

Two independent countries—the Republic of Ireland and the United Kingdom—make up the British Isles. The United Kingdom is a union of four small countries: England, Scotland, Wales, and Northern Ireland. Throughout their history, the people of the British Isles have been closely linked together.

### Time Line

## History of the British Isles

**1558–1603**
England becomes a world power during the reign of Queen Elizabeth I.

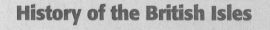

**3100 BC** | **1600**

**3100 BC** Ancient settlers in England build Stonehenge.

## Early History

The history of the British Isles dates back thousands of years. Early settlers built Stonehenge, an ancient monument, some 5,000 years ago. Around 450 BC, the Celts (KELTS) arrived in the British Isles and settled Scotland, Wales, and Ireland. Britain was even part of the ancient Roman Empire.

In the Middle Ages a series of invaders ruled the British Isles. The Angles, Saxons, and Vikings all established small kingdoms in Britain. Finally, in 1066, the Normans from northern France conquered England and established a strong kingdom there.

Over time, England grew in strength and power. It soon overshadowed its neighbors in the British Isles. By the 1500s strong rulers like Queen Elizabeth I had turned England into a world power.

## Rise of the British Empire

A strong economy and mighty navy helped England build a vast empire. Over time, England joined with Wales and Scotland to create the United Kingdom of Great Britain. Eventually, Ireland was annexed too. England also launched an overseas empire. By the 1800s Britain had colonies in the Americas, India, and Australia.

# BIOGRAPHY

## Sir Winston Churchill
( 1874–1965 )

One of Britain's greatest leaders, Sir Winston Churchill, guided the United Kingdom through the dark days of World War II. Churchill was appointed prime minister shortly after the beginning of World War II. He inspired the British to continue fighting despite Germany's defeat of much of Europe. During the Battle of Britain, Churchill gave fiery speeches. He encouraged British citizens to "never surrender." His creation of an alliance with the Soviet Union and the United States led to Germany's eventual defeat. Churchill's determination helped the Allies win the war.

**Evaluating** Do you think Churchill was important to British history? Why or why not?

The United Kingdom's economy soared in the 1700s and 1800s, thanks to the Industrial Revolution. Industries like iron, steel, and <u>textiles</u>, or cloth products, helped make the United Kingdom one of the world's richest countries.

Not everyone benefited, however. In the 1840s a severe food shortage devastated Ireland. Lack of support from the English government during the famine increased tensions between the two countries.

**HISTORY**

**VIDEO**
Winston Churchill

hmhsocialstudies.com

**FOCUS ON READING**
What are *textiles*? How can you tell?

**1730–1860**
The Industrial Revolution brings great wealth to England.

**1940**
London is bombed during the Battle of Britain in World War II.

1700        1800        1900        2000

**1858–1947**
The British Empire controls India, its most valuable colony.

**ANALYSIS SKILL** **READING TIME LINES**

About how many years ago was Stonehenge built?

By the late 1800s the British Empire spanned the globe. Africa, Asia, Australia, and the Americas were all home to British colonies. At its height, the British Empire was the largest empire in history.

### Decline of Empire

In the 1900s the British Empire began to fall apart. Both World War I and the Great Depression hurt the British economy. Rebellions in Ireland forced Britain to grant self-rule to all but the northern part of Ireland. In 1949 the Republic of Ireland gained full independence. Movements for independence also emerged in Britain's overseas colonies. After World War II, Great Britain gave up most of its colonies. The British Empire was no more.

**READING CHECK** **Sequencing** What major events mark the history of the British Isles?

## Culture

**People in different regions of the British Isles hold fast to regional traditions and customs. Here, Scots proudly display two symbols of Scottish culture—bagpipes and kilts.**

454

## Culture

For years the British ruled much of the world. As a result, the government, people, and popular culture of the British Isles have influenced people all around the globe.

### Government

The government of the United Kingdom is a **constitutional monarchy**, a type of democracy in which a king or queen serves as head of state but a legislature makes the laws. The English first limited the power of monarchs in the Middle Ages. A document known as **Magna Carta**, or Great Charter, limited the powers of kings. It also required everyone to obey the law. Today, a prime minister leads the British government. Most members of Britain's legislative body, known as Parliament, are elected.

The Republic of Ireland has a president as head of state. The president, who has limited powers, appoints a prime minister. Together with the Irish parliament, the prime minister runs the government.

### People

For hundreds of years, the countries of the British Isles have had close ties. As a result, the countries share many culture traits. One similarity is their common heritage. Many people in the British Isles can trace their heritage to the region's early settlers, such as the Celts, Angles, and Saxons. Sports like soccer and rugby are another shared trait among the people of Britain.

Although people in the British Isles share many culture traits, each region still maintains its own unique identity. This is particularly true in Ireland and Scotland. Unlike the rest of the British Isles, most Irish are Roman Catholic. Irish Gaelic, a Celtic language, is one of the country's official languages. The people of Scotland have also maintained their unique culture.

It is not unusual in Scotland to see people wearing kilts and playing bagpipes on special occasions.

Immigrants from all corners of the world have settled in Britain. Many immigrants from former British colonies, such as India and Jamaica, add to the rich culture of the British Isles.

## Popular Culture

British popular culture influences people all around the globe. For example, English is the language of business, education, and the Internet in many places. British music and literature are also popular. Millions of people around the globe listen to music by bands like Ireland's U2 and England's The Beatles and read works by British authors like William Shakespeare.

**READING CHECK** **Summarizing** What parts of British culture have spread around the world?

# British Isles Today

The British Isles face some challenges. Efforts to bring peace to Northern Ireland and to maintain a powerful economy are key issues in the British Isles today.

## Northern Ireland

One of the toughest problems facing the British Isles today is conflict in Northern Ireland. Disputes between the people of Northern Ireland have a long history.

In the 1500s Protestants from England and Scotland began settling in Northern Ireland. Over time, they outnumbered Irish Catholics in the area. When Ireland became a separate state, Northern Ireland's Protestant majority chose to remain part of the United Kingdom.

Since then, many Catholics in Northern Ireland believe they have not been treated fairly by Protestants. Some Catholics hope

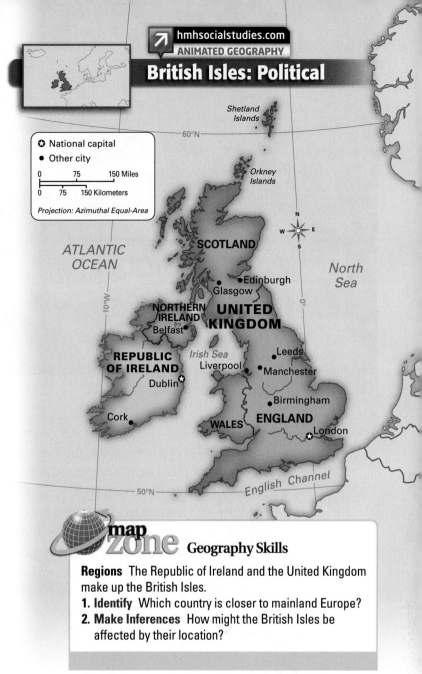

hmhsocialstudies.com
ANIMATED GEOGRAPHY
## British Isles: Political

⊕ National capital
● Other city

0    75    150 Miles
0    75    150 Kilometers

*Projection: Azimuthal Equal-Area*

Shetland Islands

ATLANTIC OCEAN

Orkney Islands

SCOTLAND

North Sea

Edinburgh
Glasgow

NORTHERN IRELAND
UNITED KINGDOM
Belfast

REPUBLIC OF IRELAND
Irish Sea
Liverpool
Leeds
Manchester

Dublin

Birmingham

Cork
WALES
ENGLAND
London

English Channel

**map zone** Geography Skills

**Regions** The Republic of Ireland and the United Kingdom make up the British Isles.
1. **Identify** Which country is closer to mainland Europe?
2. **Make Inferences** How might the British Isles be affected by their location?

to unite with the Republic of Ireland. For years the two sides have waged a bitter and violent struggle. In the late 1990s peace talks between the two warring sides began. An **agreement** eventually led to a cease-fire and the creation of a national assembly in Northern Ireland. However, the refusal of some groups to **disarm**, or give up all weapons, stalled the peace talks. Recently, however, hopes are once again high that peaceful relations between the groups will bring about a long-lasting peace.

**ACADEMIC VOCABULARY**
**agreement** a decision reached by two or more people or groups

The largest city in the British Isles, London serves as one of Europe's major financial centers.

## The Economy

The economies of the United Kingdom and the Republic of Ireland are among Europe's strongest. **London**, the capital of the United Kingdom, is a center for world trade and industry. North Sea energy reserves have made the United Kingdom a major producer of oil and natural gas. In Ireland, computer equipment and software have become major industries, especially near **Dublin**, Ireland's capital. The economies of the United Kingdom and the Republic of Ireland also rely on service industries like banking, tourism, and insurance.

**READING CHECK** **Summarizing** What has been the cause of conflict in Northern Ireland?

**SUMMARY AND PREVIEW** You have learned about the rich history and culture of the British Isles. Next, you will learn about the countries of Scandinavia.

---

## Section 2 Assessment

### Reviewing Ideas, Terms, and Places

1. **a. Identify** What peoples invaded the British Isles?
   **b. Make Inferences** How did the Industrial Revolution strengthen the British Empire?
2. **a. Describe** What elements of British culture are found around the world?
   **b. Explain** How did **Magna Carta** affect British government?
3. **a. Define** What does **disarm** mean?
   **b. Analyze** What are the central issues of the conflict in Northern Ireland?
   **c. Elaborate** Why do you think the economy of the British Isles is so strong?

### Critical Thinking

4. **Summarizing** Using your notes and a graphic organizer like the one here, summarize the history and culture of the British Isles in your own words.

### Focus on Writing

5. **Writing about the British Isles** What information about the British Isles do you think is most interesting? Take notes on what you could include in a letter to someone who has never visited the area.

# Social Studies Skills

# Writing to Learn

## Learn

Writing is an important tool for learning new information. When you write about what you read, you can better understand and remember information. For example, when you write a list of items you need from the grocery store, the act of writing can help you remember what to buy. Use the steps below to write to learn.

• Read the text carefully. Look for the main idea and important details.

• Think about the information you just read. Then summarize in your own words what you learned.

• Write a personal response to what you read. What do you think about the information? What questions might you have? How does this information affect you?

## Practice

Use the steps you just learned to practice writing to learn. Read the paragraph below carefully, then complete a chart like the one here.

Tromso, Norway, is one of Europe's northern-most cities. Because of Earth's tilt and Tromso's location north of the Arctic Circle, the city experiences unusual conditions in both summer and winter. During the summer, the sun stays above the horizon continuously from late May to late July. In winter, residents of Tromso do not see the sun from November to January.

| What I Learned | Personal Response |
| --- | --- |
| | |

## Apply

Read the information in Section 3 carefully. Then create a chart similar to the one above. In the first column, summarize the key ideas from the section in your own words. Use the second column to write your personal reaction to the information you learned.

# Scandinavia

## If YOU lived there...

You live in Copenhagen, the picturesque capital of Denmark. One of your favorite walks is along the waterfront, which is lined with colorful medieval buildings. Sailing boats of all sizes are anchored here. A famous statue in the harbor shows the Little Mermaid. But your favorite place of all is the huge amusement park called Tivoli Gardens, where you can enjoy fun and good food.

**What sights would you show to a visitor?**

**BUILDING BACKGROUND** After a long and warlike history, the modern countries of Scandinavia are models of peace and prosperity for the rest of Europe. Their cultures are similar in several ways, but each country has its own personality.

## History

Hundreds of years ago, Scandinavia was home to warlike Vikings. The **Vikings** were Scandinavian warriors who raided Europe and the Mediterranean in the early Middle Ages. Excellent sailors, the Vikings used quick and powerful longboats to attack villages along coasts or rivers. The Vikings conquered the British Isles, Finland, and parts of France, Germany, and Russia. They were some of the most feared warriors of their time.

The Vikings were also great explorers. They established the first settlements in Iceland in the 800s and in Greenland in the 900s. A short time later, Vikings led by Leif Eriksson became the first Europeans to reach North America. The ruins of a Viking colony have been found in present-day Newfoundland, off the southeast coast of Canada.

In the 1100s the Viking raids ended. Powerful Scandinavian chiefs instead concentrated on strengthening their kingdoms. During the Middle Ages three kingdoms—Norway, Sweden, and Denmark—competed for power in the region.

Denmark was the first to gain the upper hand. By the late 1300s Denmark ruled a union of all the Scandinavian kingdoms and territories. Eventually, Sweden challenged Denmark's power.

In time, Sweden left the Danish-led union, taking Finland with it. Many years later, Sweden won control of Norway as well.

By the 1900s Scandinavian countries wanted their independence. Norway won its independence from Sweden in the early 1900s. Soon after, Finland became independent after centuries of foreign <u>domination</u>, or control, by Sweden and later by Russia. Iceland, then a Danish territory, declared its independence in 1944. To this day, however, Greenland remains a part of Denmark as a self-ruling territory.

**READING CHECK** **Analyzing** What historical ties do the countries of Scandinavia have?

**FOCUS ON READING**

What other word has the same meaning as *domination*? How can you tell?

**Close-up**

# Viking Raids

The Vikings of Scandinavia launched raids on many European settlements in the early Middle Ages. Using powerful longships, Viking warriors attacked towns and villages near coasts and rivers. Vikings even sailed as far as North America in their longships.

NORTH AMERICA

Viking homeland

ASIA

EUROPE

NORTH ATLANTIC OCEAN

AFRICA

A large woolen sail helped increase the ship's speed.

Sometimes as many as 30 oars spanned each side of a longship.

Viking longships were designed the same at each end. As a result, warriors did not have to turn the ship around to make a quick escape.

**ANALYSIS SKILL** **ANALYZING VISUALS**

**What aspects of Viking longships might have frightened Europeans who saw them approaching?**

The longship's shallow design made river travel possible and allowed Viking raiders to sail their ships ashore.

NORTHERN EUROPE **459**

## Scandinavia Today

Today the countries of Scandinavia have much in common. Similar political views, languages, and religion unite the region. The countries of Scandinavia have large, wealthy cities, strong economies, and well-educated workers. Scandinavians enjoy some of the world's highest standards of living. Each country provides its citizens with excellent social programs and services, such as free health care. Sweden, Denmark, Greenland, Norway, Finland, and Iceland are among the world's most peaceful, stable, and prosperous nations.

### Sweden

Sweden is Scandinavia's largest and most populous country. Most Swedes live in the southern part of the country in large towns and cities. In fact, more than 84 percent of Swedes live in urban areas. **Stockholm**, Sweden's capital and largest city, is located on the east coast near the Baltic Sea. Often called a floating city, Stockholm is built on 14 islands and part of the mainland.

For almost 200 years, Sweden has been a neutral country. **Neutral** means that it has chosen not to take sides in an international conflict. Sweden does, however, play an active role in the United Nations as well as the European Union.

### Denmark

Denmark, once the most powerful country in Scandinavia, is also the smallest. It is Scandinavia's most densely populated country, with some 336 people per square mile (130 per square km).

## Scandinavia Today

Like most Scandinavians, the people of Oslo, Norway, enjoy one of the highest standards of living in the world. High per capita GDPs are one reason why.

**ANALYZING VISUALS** What elements in the photograph indicate a high standard of living?

### THE WORLD ALMANAC® Facts about Countries — Scandinavia's Per Capita GDP

| Country | Per Capita GDP (U.S. $) |
| --- | --- |
| Denmark | $37,100 |
| Finland | $36,900 |
| Iceland | $41,800 |
| Norway | $59,300 |
| Sweden | $38,100 |
| United States | $46,900 |

hmhsocialstudies.com

About 50 percent of Denmark's land is good for farming. Farm goods, especially meat and dairy products, are important Danish exports. Denmark also has modern industries, including iron, steel, textiles, and electronics industries.

## Greenland

The island of Greenland is geographically part of North America. However, it is a territory of Denmark. A thick ice sheet covers about 80 percent of the island. Because of this, much of Greenland is **uninhabitable**, or not able to support human settlement. Most people live on the island's southwest coast where the climate is warmest.

Recently, a movement for complete independence from Denmark has gained popularity. However, economic problems make independence unlikely, as Greenland relies heavily on imports and economic aid from Denmark.

## Norway

With one of the longest coastlines in the world, Norway takes advantage of its access to the sea. Fjords shelter Norway's many harbors. Its fishing and shipping fleets are among the largest in the world. **Oslo**, Norway's capital, is the country's leading seaport as well as its industrial center.

Norway has other valuable resources as well. Oil and natural gas provide Norway with the highest per capita GDP in Scandinavia. However, North Sea oil fields are expected to run dry over the next century. Despite strong economic ties to the rest of Europe, Norway's citizens have refused to join the European Union.

## Finland

Finland is Scandinavia's easternmost country. It lies between Sweden and Russia. The capital and largest city is **Helsinki**, which is located on the southern coast.

As with other countries in the region, trade is important to Finland. Paper and other forest products are major exports. Shipbuilding and electronics are also important industries in Finland.

## Iceland

Iceland is much greener than its name implies. Fertile farmland along the island's coast produces potatoes and vegetables and supports cattle and sheep.

Icelanders also make good use of their other natural resources. Fish from the rich waters of the Atlantic Ocean account for about 70 percent of Iceland's exports.

## Iceland

Iceland's geysers and hot springs produce great amounts of energy. Geothermal plants like this one near the Blue Lagoon hot spring provide heat for buildings and homes throughout the country.

In addition, steam from hot springs and geysers produces geothermal energy. **Geysers** are springs that shoot hot water and steam into the air. Geothermal energy heats many of Iceland's buildings. Each year thousands of tourists flock to see Iceland's many geysers, volcanoes, and glaciers.

**READING CHECK** Comparing and Contrasting In what ways are the countries of Scandinavia similar and different?

**SUMMARY AND PREVIEW** Scandinavia today is a region of relative peace and stability. A common history and culture link the people of the region. Today, Scandinavia is one of the wealthiest regions in Europe and in the world. In the next chapter, you will learn about the unique geography, history, and culture of another European region—Eastern Europe.

## Section 3 Assessment

hmhsocialstudies.com
ONLINE QUIZ

### Reviewing Ideas, Terms, and Places

1. **a. Identify** Who were the **Vikings**?
   **b. Analyze** What effect did the Vikings have on Scandinavian history?
   **c. Evaluate** Do you think the Vikings helped or hurt the future of Scandinavia? Explain your answer.
2. **a. Define** What does the term **neutral** mean?
   **b. Compare** What features do the countries of Scandinavia have in common today?
   **c. Elaborate** In which Scandinavian country would you prefer to live? Why?

### Critical Thinking

3. **Finding Main Ideas** Use your notes and this chart to identify two main ideas about Scandinavia's history and two about its culture today.

| History | Today |
|---------|-------|
|         |       |

### FOCUS ON WRITING

4. **Writing about Scandinavia** Where would you travel and what would you see in Scandinavia? Take notes on the details you might include in your letter.

**Geography's Impact**
video series
Review the video to answer the closing question:
*How have Icelanders made good use of their island's volcanoes?*

## Visual Summary

*Use the visual summary below to help you review the main ideas of the chapter.*

QUICK FACTS

Low mountains and plentiful resources are key features of Northern Europe's physical geography.

The British Isles are known around the world for their rich history, vibrant culture, and healthy economies.

The countries of Scandinavia are among the most peaceful and prosperous in the world.

## Reviewing Vocabulary, Terms, and Places

*Write each word defined below, and circle each letter marked by a star. Then write the word these letters spell.*

1. _ _ *_ _ _ _—to give up all weapons

2. _ _ _ _ _ _ _ _ _ *_—a decision reached by two or more people or groups

3. _ _ *_ _ _—a narrow inlet of the sea set between high, rocky cliffs

4. _ *_ _ _ _ _ _ _ _ _ _ _ _ _—a region in far Northern Europe that crosses the Arctic Circle

5. _ _ *_ _ _ _—warriors from Northern Europe who raided much of Europe and the Mediterranean during the early Middle Ages

6. _ _ _ _ *_ _ _ _ _ _ _ _—unable to support human settlement

7. _ _ *_ _ _ _ _ _ _ _ energy—energy produced by the heat of the planet's interior

8. _ _ _ *_ _ _—the capital of the Republic of Ireland

9. _ _ _ *_ _ _—main or most important

## Comprehension and Critical Thinking

**SECTION 1** *(Pages 448–451)*

10. **a. Identify** What are the major resources found in Northern Europe?

**b. Analyze** Explain how the North Atlantic Drift is responsible for the relatively mild climates in Northern Europe.

**c. Elaborate** In which region of Northern Europe would you prefer to live—the British Isles or Scandinavia? Why?

**SECTION 2** *(Pages 452–456)*

11. **a. Describe** What culture traits do the people of the British Isles share in common?

**b. Make Inferences** Why did the people of Ireland want to break away from the British Empire?

**c. Predict** How might the conflict in Northern Ireland affect the future of the United Kingdom?

**SECTION 3** *(Pages 458–462)*

**12. a. Recall** What countries make up Scandinavia?

**b. Compare and Contrast** In what ways are the countries of Scandinavia similar and different?

**c. Elaborate** Why do you think Scandinavian countries today are so prosperous and stable?

## Social Studies Skills

**13. Writing to Learn** Read the paragraph below carefully, then summarize it in your own words. Finally, write a personal response to what you learned in the paragraph.

> In the mid-1800s Ireland was devastated by a severe famine. For many Irish, the potato was a key part of their diet. When a disease infected potato crops around the country, millions were left without enough to eat. About 1.5 million Irish died as a result of the Irish Potato Famine.

## Map Activity

**14. Northern Europe** On a separate sheet of paper, match the letters on the map with their correct labels.

| | |
|---|---|
| Dublin | Oslo |
| English Channel | Reykjavik |
| Helsinki | Scandinavian Peninsula |
| London | Stockholm |

hmhsocialstudies.com  **INTERACTIVE MAP**

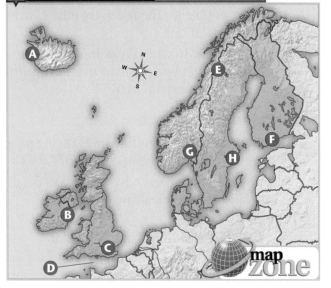

## Using the Internet 21ST CENTURY

**15. Activity: Creating a Poster** What does a medieval king have to do with modern democracy? Magna Carta was signed in 1215 by King John I of England. It established the principle that no one, including the king, is above the law. It also opened the door to a more democratic government in England. Centuries later, emerging democracies in the United States and France looked to Magna Carta for guidance. Through your online textbook, learn more about Magna Carta and its relationship with modern democracy. Then create a poster to display some of the ways this document has influenced modern governments.

hmhsocialstudies.com

**FOCUS ON READING AND WRITING**

**Using Context Clues—Synonyms** *Use context clues to determine the meaning of the underlined words in the sentences below.*

**16.** Wealthy in part because of its many natural resources, Scandinavia is one of the most <u>affluent</u> regions in Europe.

**17.** Thanks to the North Atlantic Drift, the British Isles are rarely affected by <u>inclement</u>, or harsh, weather.

**18.** <u>Dissent</u>, or disagreement, between Catholics and Protestants has caused years of conflict in Northern Ireland.

**Writing a Letter** *Use your notes from the chapter and the directions below to write a letter.*

**19.** Tell your friends and family members what you have seen on your travels in the British Isles and Scandinavia. You may want to organize the information by country. For example, you could start with a flight into London and end in Iceland. Include descriptions of fascinating physical features as well as any cities or cultural activities that are unusual or interesting.

*DIRECTIONS: Read questions 1 through 7 and write the letter of the best response. Then read question 8 and write your own well-constructed response.*

**1** **What group of people from Northern Europe raided Europe between 800 and 1100?**

A Anglo-Saxons

B Celts

C Sami

D Vikings

**2** **Which of the following accounts for the relatively mild climate throughout much of Northern Europe?**

A Arctic Ocean

B few mountains or hills

C North Atlantic Drift

D seasonal monsoons

**3** **Which Northern European city is a major European economic center?**

A Dublin

B Helsinki

C London

D Stockholm

**4** **What important energy source does Iceland use to heat buildings?**

A geothermal energy

B hydroelectric energy

C natural gas

D solar energy

**5** **Since the early 1900s, disputes and even violence have disrupted life in**

A Finland.

B Greenland.

C Northern Ireland.

D Scotland.

## Scandinavia: Population Density

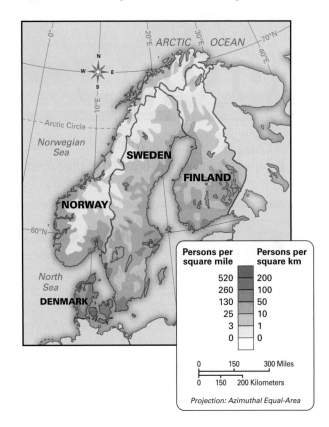

**6** **According to the map above, which part of Scandinavia is *least* densely populated?**

A Northern Scandinavia

B Southern Scandinavia

C Eastern Scandinavia

D Western Scandinavia

**7** **Which of the following characteristics do the countries of Scandinavia have in common?**

A high standards of living

B membership in the European Union

C status as neutral nations

D high unemployment rates

**8** **Extended Response Question** Use the climate map in Section 1 and the map above to write a paragraph explaining how climate might affect settlement patterns in Scandinavia.

# CHAPTER 19

# Eastern Europe

**Essential Question** What challenges has Eastern Europe faced since the breakup of the Soviet Union?

## What You Will Learn...

In this chapter you will learn about the countries of Eastern Europe. Once dominated by the Soviet Union, these countries have experienced major changes since the early 1990s. In some cases, those changes have been peaceful and have led to great economic success. In other places, the changes resulted in war, economic hardship, and political problems.

### FOCUS ON READING AND VIEWING

**Understanding Problems and Solutions** Writers sometimes organize information by stating a problem and then explaining the solution taken to solve it. To understand this type of writing, you need to identify both problems and solutions. **See the lesson, Understanding Problems and Solutions, on page 534.**

**Making a Presentation** After you read this chapter, you will present an oral report about one Eastern European country. You will also create a poster showing important features of the country. Finally, you will view and critique your classmates' reports and posters.

## map zone

### Geography Skills

**Place** Some of Eastern Europe's 20 countries are ancient, but others have been formed or changed more recently.

1. **Identify** What is the region's largest country?
2. **Make Inferences** Have you heard about any countries on this map in the news? What have you heard?

UNITED KINGDOM

North Sea

FRANCE

ATLANTIC OCEAN

SPAIN

⊛ National capital

| 0 | 100 | 200 Miles |
| 0 | 100 | 200 Kilometers |

*Projection: Azimuthal Equal-Area*

**Culture** Eastern Europe is home to dozens of cultures, each with its own unique customs.

## Eastern Europe: Political

Tallinn ✦
**ESTONIA**

*Baltic
Sea*

Riga ✦
**LATVIA**

**LITHUANIA**
Vilnius ✦

RUSSIA

Minsk ✦
**BELARUS**

**GERMANY**

**POLAND**
Warsaw ✦

Prague ✦
**CZECH
REPUBLIC**

**SLOVAKIA**
✦ Bratislava

**AUSTRIA**

✦ Budapest
**HUNGARY**

**SLOVENIA**
Ljubljana ✦
Zagreb ✦
**CROATIA**

**BOSNIA AND
HERZEGOVINA**
Sarajevo ✦
Belgrade ✦
**SERBIA**

**ITALY**

*Adriatic
Sea*

**MONTENEGRO**   **KOSOVO**
Podgorica ✦     ✦ Pristina
✦ Skopje
Tirana ✦   **MACEDONIA**

**ALBANIA**

**GREECE**

*Aegean
Sea*

RUSSIA

50°N

Kiev ✦

**UKRAINE**

**MOLDOVA**
Chişinau ✦

**ROMANIA**

Bucharest ✦
*Danube River*

**BULGARIA**
Sofia ✦

*Black Sea*

**TURKEY**

30°E

40°E

20°E

**H HISTORY** Chernobyl

↗ hmhsocialstudies.com **VIDEO**

**Geography** Like the Danube River shown here, many rivers flow through the mountains and plains of Eastern Europe.

**History** Buildings in cities like Prague, Czech Republic, are symbols of Eastern Europe's long history.

**467**

# Physical Geography

## What You Will Learn...

### Main Ideas

1. The physical features of Eastern Europe include wide open plains, rugged mountain ranges, and many rivers.
2. The climate and vegetation of Eastern Europe differ widely in the north and the south.

### The Big Idea

The physical geography of Eastern Europe varies greatly from place to place.

### Key Places

Carpathians, *p. 468*
Balkan Peninsula, *p. 469*
Danube, *p. 470*
Chernobyl, *p. 471*

hmhsocialstudies.com
TAKING NOTES

Use the graphic organizer online to take notes on the physical geography of Eastern Europe.

## If YOU lived there...

You are traveling on a boat down the Danube River, one of the longest in Europe. As you float downstream, you pass through dozens of towns and cities. Outside of the cities, the banks are lined with huge castles, soaring churches, and busy farms. From time to time, other boats pass you, some loaded with passengers and some with goods.

**Why do you think the Danube is so busy?**

**BUILDING BACKGROUND** The physical geography of Eastern Europe varies widely from north to south. Many of the landforms you learned about in earlier chapters, including the Northern European Plain and the Alps, extend into this region.

## Physical Features

Eastern Europe is a land of amazing contrasts. The northern parts of the region lie along the cold, often stormy shores of the Baltic Sea. In the south, however, are warm, sunny beaches along the Adriatic and Black seas. Jagged mountain peaks jut high into the sky in some places, while wildflowers dot the gently rolling hills of other parts of the region. These contrasts stem from the region's wide variety of landforms, water features, and climates.

### Landforms

As you can see on the map, the landforms of Eastern Europe are arranged in a series of broad bands. In the north is the Northern European Plain. As you have already learned, this large plain stretches across most of Northern Europe.

South of the Northern European Plain is a low mountain range called the **Carpathians** (kahr-PAY-thee-uhnz). These rugged mountains are an extension of the Alps of West-Central Europe. They stretch in a long arc from the Alps to the Black Sea area.

South and west of the Carpathians is another plain, the Great Hungarian Plain. As its name suggests, this fertile area is located mostly within Hungary.

South of the plain are more mountains, the Dinaric (duh-NAR-ik) Alps and Balkan Mountains. These two ranges together cover most of the **Balkan Peninsula**, one of the largest peninsulas in Europe. It extends south into the Mediterranean Sea.

## Water Features

Like the rest of the continent, Eastern Europe has many bodies of water that affect how people live. To the southwest is the Adriatic Sea, an important route for transportation and trade. To the east, the Black Sea serves the same **function**. In the far north is the Baltic Sea. It is another important trade route, though parts of the sea freeze over in the winter.

ACADEMIC VOCABULARY
function
use or purpose

↗ hmhsocialstudies.com **INTERACTIVE MAP**

### Eastern Europe: Physical

**ELEVATION**

| Feet | | Meters |
|---|---|---|
| 13,120 | | 4,000 |
| 6,560 | | 2,000 |
| 1,640 | | 500 |
| 656 | | 200 |
| (Sea level) 0 | | 0 (Sea level) |
| Below sea level | | Below sea level |

0    150    300 Miles
0    150    300 Kilometers

*Projection: Azimuthal Equal-Area*

1 The Carpathian Mountains run through the center of Eastern Europe.

2 Many rivers flow across the plains of Eastern Europe. The Vistula, shown here, is one of them.

**map zone**
**Geography Skills**

**Place** The physical features of Eastern Europe are arranged in alternating bands of rugged mountains and fertile plains.

1. **Locate** What large river flows through the southern part of the region?
2. **Interpret** Where do you think most of Eastern Europe's large cities are? Why?

In addition to these seas, Eastern Europe has several rivers that are vital paths for transportation and trade. The longest of these rivers, the **Danube** (DAN-yoob), begins in Germany and flows east across the Great Hungarian Plain. The river winds its way through nine countries before it finally empties into the Black Sea.

As you might expect, the Danube is central to the Eastern European economy. Some of the region's largest cities lie on the Danube's banks. Thousands of ships travel up and down the river every year, loaded with both goods and people. In addition, dams on the western parts of the river generate much of the region's electricity. Unfortunately, the high level of activity on the Danube has left it heavily polluted.

**READING CHECK** **Finding Main Ideas** What are the main bodies of water in Eastern Europe?

## Climate and Vegetation

Like its landforms, the climates and natural vegetation of Eastern Europe vary widely. In fact, the climates and landscapes found across Eastern Europe determine which plants will grow there.

### The Baltic Coast

The shores of the Baltic Sea are the coldest location in Eastern Europe. Winters there are long, cold, and harsh. This northern part of Eastern Europe receives less rain than other areas, but fog is common. In fact, some parts of the area have as few as 30 sunny days each year. The climate allows huge forests to grow there.

### The Interior Plains

The interior plains of Eastern Europe are much milder than the far north. Winters there can be very cold, but summers are generally pleasant and mild. The western parts of these plains receive much more rain than those areas farther east.

Because of this variation in climate, the plains of Eastern Europe have many types of vegetation. Huge forests cover much of the north. South of these forests are open grassy plains. In the spring, these plains erupt with colorful wildflowers.

---

**Primary Source**

### BOOK
# The Plains of Ukraine

*One of Russia's greatest novelists, Nikolai Gogol (gaw-guhl), was actually born in what is now Ukraine. Very fond of his homeland, he frequently wrote about its great beauty. In this passage from the short story "Taras Bulba," he describes a man's passage across the wide open fields of Ukraine.*

❝No plough had ever passed over the immeasurable waves of wild growth; horses alone, hidden in it as in a forest, trod it down. Nothing in nature could be finer. The whole surface resembled a golden-green ocean, upon which were sprinkled millions of different flowers. Through the tall, slender stems of the grass peeped light-blue, dark-blue, and lilac star-thistles; the yellow broom thrust up its pyramidal head; the parasol-shaped white flower of the false flax shimmered on high. A wheat-ear, brought God knows whence, was filling out to ripening. Amongst the roots of this luxuriant vegetation ran partridges with outstretched necks. The air was filled with the notes of a thousand different birds.❞

—from "Taras Bulba," by Nikolai Gogol

**ANALYSIS SKILL** **ANALYZING PRIMARY SOURCES**

**What features does Gogol describe on the plains of Ukraine?**

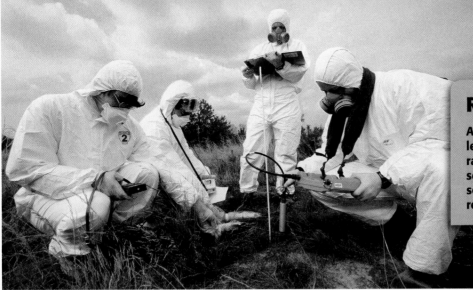

## Radiation Cleanup

A nuclear accident in 1986 leaked dangerous amounts of radiation into Eastern Europe's soil. Ukraine's government and scientists are still working to repair the damage.

Unfortunately, Eastern Europe's forests were greatly damaged by a terrible accident in 1986. A faulty reactor at the **Chernobyl** (chuhr-NOH-buhl) nuclear power plant in Ukraine exploded, releasing huge amounts of radiation into the air. This radiation poisoned millions of acres of forest and ruined soil across much of the region.

### The Balkan Coast

Along the Adriatic Sea, the Balkan coast has a Mediterranean climate, with warm summers and mild winters. As a result, its beaches are popular tourist destinations.

Because a Mediterranean climate does not bring much rain, the Balkan coast does not have many forests. Instead, the land there is covered by shrubs and hardy trees that do not need much water.

**READING CHECK** **Contrasting** How do the climates and vegetation of Eastern Europe vary?

**SUMMARY AND PREVIEW** The landforms of Eastern Europe vary widely, as do its cultures. Next you will study the cultures of the northernmost parts of the region.

**FOCUS ON READING**

What problems did the Chernobyl accident cause for Eastern Europe?

## Section 1 Assessment

hmhsocialstudies.com
**ONLINE QUIZ**

### Reviewing Ideas, Terms, and Places

1. **a. Identify** What are the major mountain ranges of Eastern Europe?
   **b. Make Inferences** How do you think the physical features of Eastern Europe influence where people live?
   **c. Elaborate** Why is the **Danube** so important to the people of Eastern Europe?
2. **a. Describe** What is the climate of the **Balkan Peninsula** like?
   **b. Explain** Why are there few trees in the far southern areas of Eastern Europe?
   **c. Predict** How do you think the lingering effects of the **Chernobyl** accident affect the plant life of Eastern Europe?

### Critical Thinking

3. **Categorizing** Draw a chart like the one shown here. In each column, identify the landforms, climates, and vegetation of each area in Eastern Europe.

|  | Landforms | Climates | Vegetation |
|---|---|---|---|
| Baltic coast |  |  |  |
| Interior plains |  |  |  |
| Balkan coast |  |  |  |

### FOCUS ON VIEWING

4. **Presenting Physical Geography** Until you decide what country you will report on, take notes about all of them. Make a list of the countries of Eastern Europe and the physical features found in each.

# Poland and the Baltic Republics

## What You Will Learn...

### Main Ideas

1. History ties Poland and the Baltic Republics together.
2. The cultures of Poland and the Baltic Republics differ in language and religion but share common customs.
3. Economic growth is a major issue in the region today.

### The Big Idea

The histories of Poland and the Baltic Republics, both as free states and as areas dominated by the Soviet Union, still shape life there.

### Key Terms and Places

infrastructure, *p. 475*
Warsaw, *p. 475*

hmhsocialstudies.com
**TAKING NOTES**

Use the graphic organizer online to take notes on Poland and the Baltic Republics.

## If **YOU** lived there...

You live in the beautiful and historic city of Krakow, Poland. Over the centuries, terrible wars have damaged many Polish cities, but Krakow is fIlled with cobblestone streets, romantic castles, and elaborate churches. The city is home to one of Europe's oldest shopping malls, the 500-year-old Cloth Hall. Glorious old Catholic churches also rise high above many parts of the city.

**What does the city suggest about Polish history?**

**BUILDING BACKGROUND** Located on the Northern European Plain, Poland and the Baltic Republics are caught between east and west. As a result, the region has often been a battlefield. On the other hand, this location at a cultural crossroads has helped each country develop its own distinctive culture, traditions, and customs.

## History

The area around the Baltic Sea was settled in ancient times by many different groups. In time, these groups developed into the people who live in the region today. One group became the Estonians, one became the Latvians and Lithuanians, and one became the Polish. Each of these groups had its own language and culture. Over the centuries, however, shared historical events have helped tie all these people together.

### Early History

By the Middle Ages, the people of the Baltics had formed many independent kingdoms. The kingdoms of Lithuania and Poland were large and strong. Together they ruled much of Eastern and Northern Europe. The smaller kingdoms of Latvia and Estonia, on the other hand, were not strong. In fact, they were often invaded by their more powerful neighbors. These invasions continued through the 1800s.

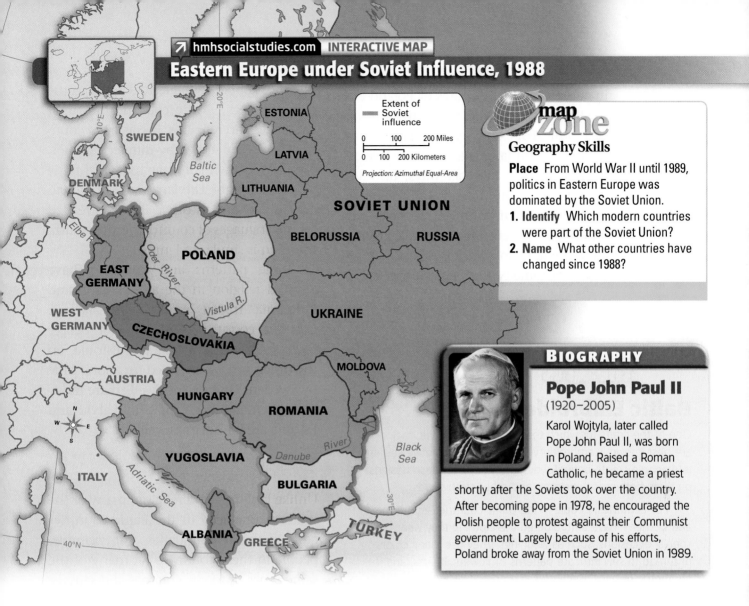

## Eastern Europe under Soviet Influence, 1988

Extent of
Soviet
influence

0    100    200 Miles

0    100    200 Kilometers

*Projection: Azimuthal Equal-Area*

SWEDEN

ESTONIA

LATVIA

LITHUANIA

Baltic
Sea

DENMARK

**SOVIET UNION**

BELORUSSIA          RUSSIA

POLAND

EAST
GERMANY

Oder
River

WEST
GERMANY

Elbe R.

Vistula R.

UKRAINE

CZECHOSLOVAKIA

AUSTRIA

MOLDOVA

HUNGARY

ROMANIA

Black
Sea

YUGOSLAVIA

Danube      River

ITALY

Adriatic
Sea

BULGARIA

ALBANIA          GREECE

TURKEY

### map zone

**Geography Skills**

**Place** From World War II until 1989, politics in Eastern Europe was dominated by the Soviet Union.

**1. Identify** Which modern countries were part of the Soviet Union?

**2. Name** What other countries have changed since 1988?

### BIOGRAPHY

## Pope John Paul II
(1920–2005)

Karol Wojtyla, later called Pope John Paul II, was born in Poland. Raised a Roman Catholic, he became a priest shortly after the Soviets took over the country. After becoming pope in 1978, he encouraged the Polish people to protest against their Communist government. Largely because of his efforts, Poland broke away from the Soviet Union in 1989.

## The World Wars

Both World War I and World War II were devastating for the Baltic people. Much of the fighting in World War I took place in Poland. As a result, millions of Poles—both soldiers and civilians—died. Thousands more were killed in the Baltic countries.

World War II began when the Germans invaded Poland from the west. As the Germans pushed through Poland from the west, the army of the Soviet Union invaded Poland from the east. Once again, Poland suffered tremendously. Millions of people were killed, and property all over Poland was destroyed. Estonia, Latvia, and Lithuania also suffered. All three countries were occupied by the Soviet army.

## Soviet Domination

As the map shows, the Soviet Union totally dominated Eastern Europe after World War II. Estonia, Latvia, and Lithuania became parts of the Soviet Union. Poland remained free, but the Soviets forced the Poles to accept a Communist government.

Many Eastern Europeans opposed Communist rule, and the Communist governments in the region eventually fell. Poland rejected Communism and elected new leaders in 1989. The Baltic Republics broke away from the Soviet Union in 1991 and became independent once more.

**READING CHECK** **Analyzing** How did the Soviet Union influence the region's history?

**FOCUS ON READING**

What problems were created in the Baltic region after World War II?

## Culture

In some ways, the cultures of Poland and the Baltic Republics are very different from each other. For example, people in the area speak different languages and practice different religions. In other ways, however, their cultures are actually quite similar. Because the four countries lie near each other, common customs have taken root in all of them. People cook similar foods and enjoy the same types of entertainment.

## Baltic Embroidery

One of the crafts for which the people of the Baltic region are best known is embroidery. This type of decorative sewing lets people create beautiful designs. They use these designs on their clothing, tablecloths, and other cloth goods.

For centuries, people in the Baltic countries—both men and women—have embroidered the clothing they wear on special occasions, such as weddings. They use many colors of thread to sew intricate patterns of flowers, hearts, and geometric designs. Because the embroidery is done by hand, it can take hours of work to create a single garment.

**Drawing Conclusions** Why do you think people embroider only clothing for special occasions?

## Cultural Differences

The most obvious differences between the cultures of the Baltic countries are their languages and religions. Because the countries were first settled by different groups, each has its own language today. Of these languages, only Latvian and Lithuanian are similar to each other. Polish is related to the languages of countries farther south. Estonian is similar to Finnish.

Trade patterns and invasions have affected religion in the area. Poland and Lithuania traded mostly with Roman Catholic countries, and so most people there are Catholic. Latvia and Estonia, on the other hand, were ruled for a long time by Sweden. Because the Swedish are mostly Lutheran, most people in Latvia and Estonia are Lutheran as well.

## Cultural Similarities

Unlike language and religion, many of the customs practiced in the Baltic countries cross national boundaries. For example, people in these countries eat many of the same types of foods. Potatoes and sausage are very popular, as is seafood.

Other shared customs tie the Baltic countries together as well. For example, people in all three countries practice many of the same crafts. Among these crafts are pottery, painting, and embroidery.

Also common to the countries of the Baltic Sea area is a love of music and dance. For centuries, people of the Baltics have been famous for their musical abilities. Frédéric Chopin (1810–1849), for example, was a famous Polish pianist and composer. Today, people throughout Poland and the Baltic Republics gather at music festivals to hear popular and traditional tunes.

**READING CHECK** **Comparing** How are the cultures of the Baltic countries similar?

## The Region Today

Estonia, Latvia, Lithuania, and Poland all still feel the effects of decades of Soviet rule. The economies of all four countries suffered because the Soviets did not build a decent infrastructure. An **infrastructure** is the set of resources, like roads, airports, and factories, that a country needs in order to support economic activities. The many factories built by the Soviets in Poland and the Baltics could not produce as many goods as those in Western Europe.

Today Poland and the Baltic Republics are working to rebuild and strengthen their economies. They are replacing the old and outdated factories built by the Soviets with new ones that take advantage of modern technology. As a result, cities like **Warsaw**, the capital of Poland, have become major industrial centers.

To further their economic growth, the countries of this region are also seeking new sources of income. One area in which they have found some success is tourism. Since the collapse of the Soviet Union in 1991, many Americans and Western Europeans have begun visiting. Polish cities like Warsaw and Krakow have long attracted tourists with their rich history and famous sites. Vilnius, Lithuania; Tallinn, Estonia; and Riga, Latvia, have also become tourist attractions. People are drawn to these cities by their fascinating cultures, cool summer climates, and historic sites.

**READING CHECK** Generalizing How has the region changed in recent years?

**SUMMARY AND PREVIEW** Poland and the Baltic Republics are still feeling the effects of decades of Soviet rule. In the next section, you will learn about more countries that feel the same effects.

## Tourism in the Baltics

Baltic cities such as Tallinn, Estonia, draw many tourists each year. These tourists are attracted to the cities' many churches and cultural sites.

## Section 2 Assessment

hmhsocialstudies.com
ONLINE QUIZ

### Reviewing Ideas, Terms, and Places

1. **a. Identify** What country ran the area after World War II?
   **b. Draw Conclusions** How do you think the two world wars affected the people of Poland?
2. **a. Describe** How do the languages spoken in Poland and the Baltic Republics reflect the region's history?
   **b. Elaborate** Why do you think that people across the region practice many of the same customs?
3. **a. Recall** What is one industry that has grown in the region since the fall of the Soviet Union?
   **b. Explain** How did Soviet rule hurt the area's economy?

### Critical Thinking

4. **Identifying Cause and Effect** Draw a chart like the one shown here. In each box on the right, explain how the event affected the cultures or economies of the region.

| Event | Effect |
|---|---|
| Soviet rule | |
| Breakup of the Soviet Union | |
| Growth of tourism | |

### FOCUS ON VIEWING

5. **Considering Poland and the Baltics** If you were to give your report about Poland or one of the Baltic Republics, what details would you include? Write down some ideas.

# Inland Eastern Europe

## What You Will Learn...

### Main Ideas

1. The histories and cultures of inland Eastern Europe vary from country to country.
2. Most of inland Eastern Europe today has stable governments, strong economies, and influential cities.

### The Big Idea

The countries of inland Eastern Europe have varied histories and cultures but face many of the same issues today.

### Key Terms and Places

Prague, *p. 477*
Kiev, *p. 477*
Commonwealth of Independent States, *p. 478*
Budapest, *p. 479*

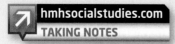
hmhsocialstudies.com
**TAKING NOTES**

Use the graphic organizer online to take notes on inland Eastern Europe.

## If **YOU** lived there...

You are a tourist visiting Budapest, the capital of Hungary. Early one morning, you stand on a bridge over the glittering water of the Danube River. You read in your guidebook that the two banks of the river were once separate cities. On the bank to your right, you see huge castles and churches standing on a tall hill. To your left is the Parliament building, obviously a much newer building.

### What might have brought the cities together?

**BUILDING BACKGROUND** The city of Budapest, like many of the cities of inland Eastern Europe, has a long, colorful history. Various parts of the city reflect wildly different eras in its past. Medieval churches, for example, stand near huge imperial fortresses and Soviet-built warehouses, all relics of the region's history.

## History and Culture

Located on the Northern European and Hungarian plains, inland Eastern Europe consists of six countries. They are the Czech (CHEK) Republic, Slovakia, Hungary, Ukraine, Belarus, and Moldova. Throughout history, many different peoples ruled these countries. Each ruling group influenced the culture and customs of the area.

### Czech Republic and Slovakia

The area that now includes the Czech Republic and Slovakia was once home to many small kingdoms. People called the Slavs founded these kingdoms. The Slavs were people from Asia who moved into Europe by AD 1000. Eventually, strong neighbors such as Austria conquered the Slavic kingdoms.

After World War I, the victorious Allies took land away from Austria to form a new nation, Czechoslovakia. About fifty years later, in 1993, it split into the Czech Republic and Slovakia.

Because of their location, these two countries have long had ties with Western Europe. As a result, Western influences are common. For example, many people in the two countries are Roman Catholic. The architecture of cities like **Prague** (PRAHG), the capital of the Czech Republic, also reflects Western influences.

## Hungary

In the 900s, a group of fierce invaders called the Magyars swept into what is now Hungary. Although they were conquered by the Austrians, the Magyars continued to shape Hungarian culture. The Hungarian language is based on the language spoken by the Magyars. In fact, people in Hungary today still refer to themselves as Magyars.

## Ukraine, Belarus, and Moldova

The Slavs also settled Ukraine, Belarus, and Moldova. Later other groups, including the Vikings of Scandinavia, invaded and conquered the Slavs.

A group called the Rus (RUHS) built a settlement in what is now **Kiev**, Ukraine, in the 800s. The rulers of Kiev eventually created a huge empire.

In the late 1700s, that empire became part of Russia. When the Soviet Union was formed in 1922, Ukraine and Belarus were made Soviet republics. Moldova became a republic two years later. They did not become independent until the breakup of the Soviet Union in 1991.

The long history of Russian influence in the region is reflected in the countries' cultures. For example, most people in these countries are Orthodox Christians, like the people of Russia. In addition, Ukrainian and Belarusian languages are written in the Cyrillic, or Russian, alphabet.

**READING CHECK** **Analyzing** Which groups have influenced the history of the region?

## The Kievan Empire

Kiev, now the capital of Ukraine, was once the capital of a large and powerful empire. At its height, the Kievan Empire stretched across much of Eastern Europe and Central Asia.

Kiev

According to an old legend, the city of Kiev was built by three brothers and their sister. This monument built in the 1980s honors the city's legendary founders.

The people of Kiev built Saint Sophia Cathedral in the 1000s. By that time, nearly everyone who lived in the Kievan Empire was Orthodox Christian.

## Close-up
# Budapest

Budapest, Hungary, is one of the largest cities of Eastern Europe. The city's two parts, Buda and Pest, are separated by the Danube River.

Once the poorer half of the city, Pest has grown quickly. Hungary's Parliament meets here.

Only a few bridges link the two halves of Budapest.

# Inland Eastern Europe Today

**FOCUS ON READING**

How might the CIS help solve problems in this region?

All of the countries of inland Eastern Europe were either part of the Soviet Union or run by Soviet-influenced governments. Since the end of Soviet domination, the people of inland Eastern Europe have largely overcome the problems created by the Soviets. Still, a few issues remain for the region's governments and economies.

## Government

During the Soviet era, the countries of inland Eastern Europe had Communist governments. Under the Communists, people had few freedoms. In addition, the Soviets were poor economic planners, and their policies caused many hardships.

Since the collapse of the Soviet Union, the governments of inland Eastern Europe have changed. Hungary, Slovakia, the Czech Republic, Ukraine, and Moldova are now republics in which the people elect their leaders. Belarus also claims to be a republic, but it is really a dictatorship.

The countries of inland Eastern Europe belong to several international alliances. One such alliance, the **Commonwealth of Independent States**, or CIS, meets to discuss issues such as trade and immigration that affect former Soviet republics. The CIS is based in Minsk, the capital of Belarus. Ukraine and Moldova are also members, as are many countries in Asia.

The Czech Republic, Slovakia, Hungary, Romania, and Bulgaria are not part of the CIS. They have sought closer ties to the West than to the former Soviet Union. As a result, all five belong to the EU.

## Economy

Economic development has been a major challenge for these countries since the collapse of the Soviet Union. The Czech Republic, Slovakia, Hungary, and Ukraine have been most successful. All four are thriving industrial centers. Ukraine, with rich, productive farmlands, grows grains, potatoes, and sugar beets.

Buda, the older half of the city, contains historic castles and churches.

The Danube is a key route for moving both goods and people in Eastern Europe.

ANALYSIS SKILL **ANALYZING VISUALS**

**How do you think the Danube affects daily life in Budapest?**

## Cities

Life in inland Eastern Europe is centered around cities, especially national capitals. In each country, the capital is both a key economic center and a cultural one.

Three cities in the region are especially important—Prague, Kiev, and **Budapest**, the capital of Hungary. They are the most prosperous cities in the region and home to influential leaders and universities. In addition, the cities are popular tourist destinations. People from all over the world visit Eastern Europe to see these cities' architectural and cultural sites.

**READING CHECK** **Generalizing** What are the countries of inland Eastern Europe like today?

**SUMMARY AND PREVIEW** Inland Eastern Europe has been successful in facing the challenges left by Soviet influence. Next, you will learn about a region that has faced more challenges, the Balkans.

## Section 3 Assessment

hmhsocialstudies.com
ONLINE QUIZ

### Reviewing Ideas, Terms, and Places

1. **a. Recall** In what country is **Prague** located?
   **b. Sequence** List the groups that ruled **Kiev** and the surrounding area in chronological order.
   **c. Elaborate** How has Hungary's history helped set it apart from other countries in inland Eastern Europe?
2. **a. Identify** What is the **Commonwealth of Independent States**? Which countries in this region are members?
   **b. Draw Conclusions** How have the economies of the region changed since the collapse of the Soviet Union?
   **c. Develop** Why do you think life is largely centered around cities in inland Eastern Europe?

### Critical Thinking

3. **Generalizing** Draw a diagram like the one shown here. In the left oval, describe the government and economy of inland Eastern Europe under the Soviet Union. In the right oval, describe them since the Soviet Union's collapse.

Russia Today

### FOCUS ON VIEWING

4. **Picturing Inland Eastern Europe** Which country sounds most interesting to you? Write down some details about it. Make a list of pictures you could use on your poster.

# The Balkan Countries

## What You Will Learn...

### Main Ideas

1. The history of the Balkan countries is one of conquest and conflict.
2. The cultures of the Balkan countries are shaped by the many ethnic groups who live there.
3. Civil War and weak economies are major challenges to the region today.

### The Big Idea

Life in the Balkans reflects the region's troubled past and its varied ethnic makeup.

### Key Terms

ethnic cleansing, *p. 482*

hmhsocialstudies.com
TAKING NOTES

Use the graphic organizer online to take notes on the Balkan countries.

## If YOU lived there...

As part of your summer vacation, you are hiking across the Balkan Peninsula. As you hike through villages in the rugged mountains, you are amazed at the different churches you see. There are small Roman Catholic churches, huge Orthodox churches with onion-shaped domes, and Muslim mosques with tall minarets.

**Why are there so many types of churches here?**

**BUILDING BACKGROUND** The Balkan countries are possibly the most diverse area in Europe. In addition to practicing many religions, the people there speak many languages and have different customs. At times, the area's diversity has led to serious problems.

## History

Like the rest of Eastern Europe, the Balkan Peninsula has been conquered and ruled by many different groups. The presence of these many groups continues to shape life in the area today.

### Early History

By the 600s BC the ancient Greeks had founded colonies on the northern Black Sea coast. The area they settled is now part of Bulgaria and Romania. Later, the Romans conquered most of the area from the Adriatic Sea to the Danube River.

When the Roman Empire divided into west and east in the late AD 300s, the Balkan Peninsula became part of the Eastern, or Byzantine, Empire. Under Byzantine rule, many people of the Balkans became Orthodox Christians. More than 1,000 years later, Muslim Ottoman Turks conquered the Byzantine Empire. Under the Ottomans, many people became Muslims.

The Ottomans ruled the Balkan Peninsula until the 1800s. At that time, the people of the region rose up and drove the Ottomans out. They then created their own kingdoms.

## World War I and After

Trouble between the Balkan kingdoms and their neighbors led to World War I. In the late 1800s the Austro-Hungarian Empire, which lay north of the Balkans, took over part of the peninsula. In protest, a man from Serbia shot the heir to the Austro-Hungarian throne, sparking the war.

After World War I, the Balkans changed dramatically. Europe's leaders divided the peninsula into new countries. Among these new countries was Yugoslavia, which combined many formerly independent countries under one government.

The nation of Yugoslavia lasted until the 1990s. The country eventually broke up, however, because of conflict between ethnic and religious groups.

**READING CHECK** **Summarizing** How did World War I affect the Balkan Peninsula?

# Culture

Culturally, the Balkans are the most diverse area of Europe. This diversity is reflected in the large number of religions practiced and languages spoken there.

## Religion

Most of the people of the Balkans, like most Europeans, are Christian. However, three types of Christianity are practiced in the area. Most Balkan Christians belong to the Orthodox Church. In the western part of the peninsula, there are many Roman Catholics. In addition, many countries also have large Protestant communities.

Christianity is not the only religion in the Balkans. Because of the Ottomans' long rule, Islam is also common. In fact, Albania is the only country in Europe in which most people are Muslims.

### Religion in the Balkans

Buildings from many religions can be found around the Balkans. This Orthodox church is in Bulgaria.

**THE WORLD ALMANAC**
Facts about the World

**Major Religions in the Balkans**

**Analyzing Graphs** What is the largest religion in the Balkans?

hmhsocialstudies.com

### Language

People in the Balkans speak languages from three major groups. Most languages in the region belong to the Slavic family and are related to Russian. In Romania, though, people speak a language that developed from Latin. It is more closely related to French, Italian, and Spanish than to Slavic languages. In addition, some people in Romania speak Germanic languages.

Some languages of the Balkans are not related to these groups. For example, Albanian is unlike any other language in the world. In addition, a group called the Roma have a language of their own.

**ACADEMIC VOCABULARY**

**implications**
consequences

**READING CHECK** Drawing Conclusions Why is Balkan culture so diverse?

## FOCUS ON CULTURE

# The Roma

The Roma are a nomadic people. For centuries, they have roamed from place to place in horse-drawn wagons, working as blacksmiths, animal trainers, and musicians. Although Roma live all over the world, the largest concentration of them is in southeastern Europe.

For centuries, many other Europeans did not trust the Roma. They were suspicious of the Roma's nomadic lifestyle and could not understand their language. As a result, many Roma have been subject to prejudice and discrimination.

**Summarizing** What is traditional Roma life like?

## The Balkans Today

The countries of the Balkan Peninsula, like most of Eastern Europe, were once run by Communist governments. Weak economic planning has left most of them poor and struggling to improve their economies. This area is still the poorest in Europe today.

Relations among religious and ethnic groups have had serious **implications** for the Balkans. When Yugoslavia broke apart, violence broke out among groups in some of the newly formed countries. Members of the largest religious or ethnic group in each country tried to get rid of all other groups who lived there. They threatened those who refused to leave with punishments or death. This kind of effort to remove all members of a group from a country or region is called **ethnic cleansing**.

The violence in the former Yugoslavia was so terrible that other countries stepped in to put an end to it. In 1995 countries around the world sent troops to Bosnia and Herzegovina to help bring an end to the fighting. The fighting between groups eventually ended and, in 2008, ten countries shared the Balkan Peninsula:

**Albania** The poorest country in Europe, Albania has struggled since the end of the Soviet period. High unemployment and crime rates have prevented the country's economy from improving.

**Macedonia** Once a part of Yugoslavia, Macedonia broke away in 1991. It was the first country to do so peacefully.

**Slovenia** Slovenia also broke from Yugoslavia in 1991. In 2004 it became the first Balkan country to join the EU.

**Croatia** When Croatia broke away from Yugoslavia, fighting broke out within the country. Ethnic Croats and Serbs fought over land for many years. In the end, many Serbs left Croatia, and peace was restored.

## Mostar

Fighting between ethnic groups left the city of Mostar in Bosnia and Herzegovina in ruins. After the war, the people of Mostar had to rebuild their city.

**ANALYZING VISUALS** What does this photo suggest about life in Mostar today?

**Bosnia and Herzegovina** Since the end of ethnic and religious violence, peace has returned to Bosnia and Herzegovina. The people there are working to rebuild.

**Serbia** Serbia is the largest nation to emerge from the former Yugoslavia. Like other Balkan countries, Serbia has seen fighting among ethnic groups.

**Kosovo** Formerly a province of Serbia, Kosovo declared independence in 2008. Its population is mostly ethnic Albanian.

**Montenegro** The mountainous country of Montenegro separated peacefully from Serbia in June 2006.

**Romania** Romania, the largest of the Balkan states, is working to recover from years of bad government. Poor leaders have left its government and economy in ruins.

**Bulgaria** Since the fall of the Soviet Union, Bulgaria has changed dramatically. People there are working to develop a capitalist economy based on industry and tourism.

**FOCUS ON READING**
What solutions are Bulgaria's leaders seeking to their economic problems?

**READING CHECK** **Generalizing** What issues does the Balkan region face today?

**SUMMARY AND PREVIEW** The Soviet Union had a huge effect on Eastern Europe. Next, you will read about the Soviet Union and Russia.

## Section 4 Assessment

### Reviewing Ideas, Terms, and Places

1. a. **Describe** What was Yugoslavia? When did it break apart?
   b. **Explain** What role did the Balkan countries play in starting World War I?
2. a. **Identify** What are the four most common religions in the Balkans?
   b. **Analyze** Why are so many different languages spoken in the Balkans?
3. a. **Define** What is **ethnic cleansing**?
   b. **Elaborate** Why do you think other countries sent troops to Bosnia and Herzegovina? How has the country changed since the war ended?

### Critical Thinking

4. **Summarizing** Draw a chart like this one. Use your notes to write a sentence about how each topic listed in the left column affected life in the Balkans after the breakup of Yugoslavia.

The Balkans Today

| | |
|---|---|
| Soviet influence | |
| Ethnic diversity | |
| Religion | |

### FOCUS ON VIEWING

5. **Choosing a Country** Now that you have studied all of Eastern Europe, choose your topic. What information and pictures will you include?

# The Breakup of Yugoslavia

**Essential Elements**

The World in Spatial Terms
Places and Regions
Physical Systems
**Human Systems**
Environment and Society
The Uses of Geography

**Background** A school playground has a limited amount of space. If many students want to use the playground at the same time, they have to work together and consider each other's feelings. Otherwise, conflict could break out.

Space on Earth is also limited. As a result, people are sometimes forced to live near people with whom they disagree. Like students on a playground, they must learn to work together to live in peace.

**Yugoslavia** The country of Yugoslavia was created after World War I. As a result, people from many ethnic groups—Serbs, Montenegrins, Bosnians, Croats, Slovenes, and Macedonians—lived together in one country. Each group had its own republic, or self-governed area, in the new country.

For decades, the republics of Yugoslavia worked together peacefully. People from various ethnic groups mixed within each republic. Then in 1991 Croatia, Macedonia, and Slovenia declared independence. The republic of Bosnia and Herzegovina did the same a year later. These republics were afraid Serbia wanted to take over Yugoslavia.

It appeared that they were right. Serbia's leader, Slobodan Milosevic (sloh-BOH-dahn mee-LOH-suh-vich), wanted to increase Serbia's power. He took land from other ethnic groups. He also called on Serbs who lived in other republics to vote to give Serbia more influence in the country.

**Refugees** Violence between ethnic groups led many people in Yugoslavia to leave their homes. The people in this photo are fleeing Bosnia to seek refuge in a safer area.

## The Former Yugoslavia, 2000

**Yugoslavia, 1991**

Zagreb
Belgrade
Sarajevo
**YUGOSLAVIA**
Adriatic Sea

SLOVENIA
Zagreb
CROATIA
Belgrade
BOSNIA AND HERZEGOVINA
Sarajevo
SERBIA AND MONTENEGRO
Adriatic Sea
MACEDONIA

**Ethnic Groups**
- Albanian
- Croat
- Macedonian
- Montenegrin
- Bosnian
- Serb
- Slovene
- Other or no majority

When the other republics broke away from Yugoslavia, Milosevic called on Serbs who lived there to rise up and demand that they rejoin the country. He also provided aid to Serbian military groups in these republics. In Bosnia and Herzegovina, Serbian rebels fought for three years against the Bosnian army in a destructive civil war.

Milosevic's actions caused other ethnic groups in Yugoslavia to resent the Serbs. As a result, additional violence broke out. In Croatia, for example, the army violently expelled all Serbs from their country. War raged in the area until 1995, when a peace accord was signed. As a result of that accord, Yugoslavia was dissolved. In its place were five countries that had once been Yugoslav republics.

**What It Means** The violent breakup of Yugoslavia has taught other countries some valuable lessons. First, it reinforced the idea that national borders are not permanent. Borders can and do change.

More importantly, however, the struggles in Yugoslavia have made some countries more aware of their people's needs. People want to feel that they have some say in their lives. When they feel as though another group is trying to take that say from them, as many in Yugoslavia felt the Serbs were doing, then trouble will often follow.

## Geography for Life Activity

1. What led to the breakup of Yugoslavia?

2. Look at the maps on this page. How did the pattern of ethnic groups in Yugoslavia change between 1991 and 2000? Why do you think this is so?

3. **Investigating Ethnic Relationships** Yugoslavia is not the only country in which multiple ethnic groups lived together. Research another country in which multiple groups live together, such as Switzerland or Indonesia. How do the groups who live there live together?

# Analyzing Benefits and Costs

## Learn

Decisions can be tough to make. A seemingly simple choice can have both positive effects, or benefits, and negative effects, or costs. Before you make a decision, it can be helpful to analyze all the possible benefits and costs that will result.

One way to analyze benefits and costs is to create a chart like the one below. On one side, list all the benefits that will result from your decision. On the other side, list the costs. Not all costs involve money. You must also consider opportunity costs, or the things that you might lose as a result of your decision. For example, going to a movie might mean that you have to miss a baseball game.

## Practice

The chart to the right could have been written by an official considering whether to develop a tourism industry in Croatia. Decide whether each of the numbered items listed here should be added to the benefits column or the costs column. Once you have determined that, use the chart to decide whether the benefits of tourism outweigh the costs. Write a short paragraph to support your decision.

**1** Would mean that tourist areas were not available for farming or industry

**2** Would improve Croatia's image to people in other parts of the world

| Tourism in Dalmatia, Croatia | |
|---|---|
| **Benefits** | **Costs** |
| ■ Would create much-needed income for towns in the region | ■ Would require building of hotels, airports, and roads |
| ■ Would not require much new investment, since tourists are drawn to region's beaches and climate | ■ Increase in tourism could lead to damaging of local environments |
| ■ | ■ |
| ■ | ■ |

## Apply

Imagine that city leaders in your area are trying to decide whether to build a new school. They cannot make a decision and have asked you to help analyze the benefits and costs of building the school. Create a chart like the one above to list those benefits and costs. Then write a brief paragraph stating whether the benefits of the plan outweigh its costs.

**Geography's Impact**
video series
Review the video to answer the closing question:
*How have the changing political borders in the Balkans affected people's lives?*

## Visual Summary

*Use the visual summary below to help you review the main ideas of the chapter.*

QUICK FACTS

**Poland and the Baltics**
The history of Poland and the Baltic Republics still shapes their culture, government, and economy.

**Inland Eastern Europe**
Once Communist, the countries of inland Eastern Europe have stable governments and strong economies.

**The Balkans**
Since the breakup of Yugoslavia, the Balkans have been faced with conflict and economic challenges.

## Reviewing Vocabulary, Terms, and Places

*Unscramble each group of letters below to spell a term that matches the given definition.*

1. **arwswa**—the capital of Poland

2. **neicht glncaenis**—the effort to remove all members of a group from a country or region

3. **ebndua**—the major river that flows through Eastern Europe, one of the longest on the continent

4. **ageurp**—the capital and largest city of the Czech Republic

5. **ncimlaitpiso**—consequences

6. **laknab**—the peninsula on which much of Eastern Europe is located

7. **ufrnrtriuacste**—the set of resources, like roads and factories, that a country needs to support economic activities

8. **nrhatcapias**—a mountain range in Eastern Europe

## Comprehension and Critical Thinking

**SECTION 1** *(Pages 468–471)*

9. **a. Identify** Name two major bodies of water that border Eastern Europe.

**b. Explain** How do the Danube and other rivers affect life for people in Eastern Europe?

**c. Evaluate** If you could live in any region of Eastern Europe, where would it be? Why?

**SECTION 2** *(Pages 472–475)*

10. **a. Identify** What are the three Baltic Republics? Why are they called that?

**b. Compare and Contrast** What are two cultural features that Poland and the Baltic Republics have in common? What are two features that are different in those countries?

**c. Elaborate** How did the collapse of the Soviet Union affect people in Poland and the Baltic Republics?

## SECTION 3 *(Pages 476–479)*

**11. a. Describe** What is the government of Belarus like? What type of government do the other countries of inland Eastern Europe have?

**b. Draw Conclusions** Why do you think that some countries in inland Eastern Europe have stronger economies than others?

**c. Elaborate** How has its location influenced the culture of the Czech Republic?

## SECTION 4 *(Pages 480–483)*

**12. a. Identify** What religions are common in the Balkan countries?

**b. Explain** Why did countries from around the world send troops to Kosovo?

**c. Predict** How do you think peace will affect life in the Balkans?

## Map Activity

**13. Eastern Europe** On a separate sheet of paper, match the letters on the map with their correct labels.

| | |
|---|---|
| Great Hungarian Plain | Kiev, Ukraine |
| Latvia | Warsaw, Poland |
| Albania | Danube River |

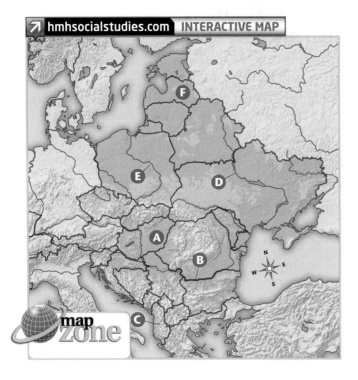

**hmhsocialstudies.com** INTERACTIVE MAP

## Using the Internet

**14. Activity: Writing a Report** For centuries the Balkans have been an arena of conflict. Through your online textbook, learn about the history and cultures of the Balkans and investigate recent conflicts there. Write a report on what you find.

**↗ hmhsocialstudies.com**

## Social Studies Skills

**15. Analyzing Costs and Benefits** Imagine that you are a government official in Ukraine. Your country cannot produce enough energy to meet its needs and has to buy energy from Russia. A company in Kiev has expressed interest in building nuclear power plants, but many people are leery of nuclear power since the Chernobyl incident. Make a list of the costs and benefits of nuclear power. Then write a statement that either supports or argues against the plan.

### FOCUS ON READING AND VIEWING

**16. Understanding Problems and Solutions** Re-read the first paragraph under the heading The Region Today in Section 2. Then write a short paragraph that explains the main problem facing Poland and the Baltics today. End your paragraph by suggesting a solution their governments might use to address the problem.

**17. Making a Presentation** Write a brief report about a country in Eastern Europe and prepare a poster that illustrates your main ideas. Find pictures of major features of your chosen country and arrange them on a poster board. Write a short caption that explains what each picture is. Present your report to the class. As you discuss each main idea, point out the pictures that illustrate it on your poster. Speak clearly and keep eye contact with your audience. Then, listen as your peers present their reports and posters. Note whether they speak clearly and maintain eye contact. Do their posters illustrate the main ideas in their reports?

*DIRECTIONS: Read questions 1 through 7 and write the letter of the best response. Then read question 8 and write your own well-constructed response.*

**1** **The country *most* influential in Eastern Europe after World War II was**

A the United States.

B the Soviet Union.

C France.

D Germany.

**2** **Which of the following countries violently broke apart in the 1990s?**

A Poland

B Romania

C Czechoslovakia

D Yugoslavia

**3** **The major river of Eastern Europe is the**

A Baltic River.

B Carpathian River.

C Danube River.

D Hungarian River.

**4** **Which of these countries is located on the Balkan Peninsula?**

A Croatia

B Poland

C Belarus

D Estonia

**5** **Which of these statements about religion in Eastern Europe is correct?**

A Nearly everyone in the region is Muslim.

B Nearly everyone in the region is Catholic.

C Nearly everyone in the region is Orthodox Christian.

D People in the region practice many different religions.

## Hungary

For those in search of the heart and soul of Europe, there's nowhere better. Hungarians, who call themselves Magyars, speak a language and revel in a culture unlike any other. Away from the cosmopolitan charms of Budapest, life in the provinces is more redolent of times past—simpler, slower, often friendlier. There are endless opportunities for those with special interests—from horse riding and cycling to bird-watching and "taking the waters" at the country's many thermal spas.

—from *Lonely Planet World Guide Online*

**6** **Read the passage above from a travel guide to Hungary. According to this passage, what do people from Hungary call themselves?**

A Hungarians

B Magyars

C Budapestians

D Europeans

**7** **Based on the above passage, which of the following statements is true?**

A Hungarian culture is similar to many others in Europe.

B There are few things to do in Hungary.

C People outside of Budapest live simpler and slower lives than people in the city.

D Hungary is the largest country in Europe.

**8** **Extended Response** Life in Eastern Europe is still influenced by the Soviet era, even though the Soviet Union collapsed many years ago. Consider what you have read in this chapter and write a paragraph in which you explain how Soviet influence is still felt in the region.

# CHAPTER 20

# Russia and the Caucasus

**Essential Question** What cultural and geographic features help define Russia and the Caucusus?

## What You Will Learn...

In this chapter you will learn about the physical features, climate, and natural resources of Russia and the Caucasus. You will also study the histories and cultures of these countries. Finally, you will learn about life in each of the countries today.

### FOCUS ON READING AND WRITING

**Making Generalizations** A generalization is a broad, general idea drawn from new information combined with what you already know. As you read this chapter, stop now and then to make a generalization. It will help you pull the pieces of information together and make sense of them. **See the lesson, Making Generalizations, on page 535.**

**Creating a Real Estate Ad** As you read this chapter, imagine you work for a real estate agency in Russia or the Caucasus. You are trying to sell a piece of property there. In order to sell the property, you must write an ad to be published in the newspaper and on the Internet. As you read, decide where your property would be located and what its characteristics would be.

**Geography** A volcano created Crater Bay in the Kuril Islands off the east coast of Russia. The islands have several active volcanoes.

# Russia and the Caucasus: Political

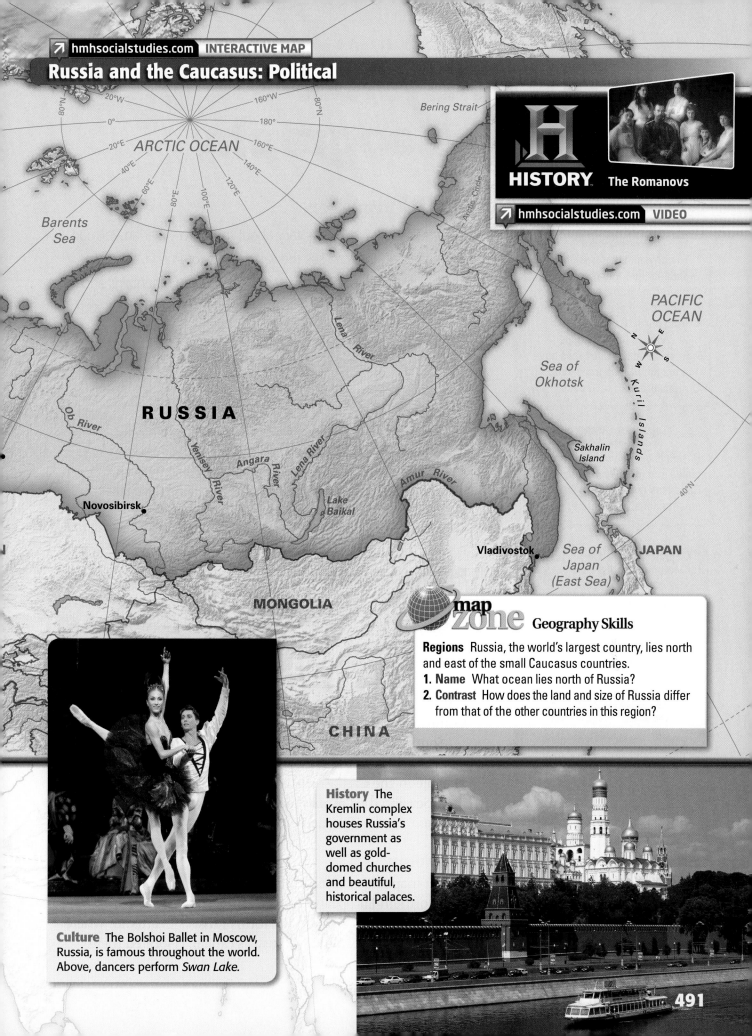

160°W

ARCTIC OCEAN

20°W

0°

20°E

40°E

60°E

80°E

100°E

120°E

140°E

160°E

180°

80°N

Bering Strait

Barents
Sea

Arctic Circle

PACIFIC
OCEAN

Lena
River

Sea of
Okhotsk

N
E
W
S

**R U S S I A**

Kuril Islands

Ob River

Yenisey River

Angara River

Lena River

Amur River

Sakhalin
Island

40°N

**Novosibirsk**

Lake
Baikal

**Vladivostok**

Sea of
Japan
(East Sea)

**JAPAN**

**MONGOLIA**

**map zone** Geography Skills

**Regions** Russia, the world's largest country, lies north and east of the small Caucasus countries.
1. **Name** What ocean lies north of Russia?
2. **Contrast** How does the land and size of Russia differ from that of the other countries in this region?

**CHINA**

**History** The Kremlin complex houses Russia's government as well as gold-domed churches and beautiful, historical palaces.

**Culture** The Bolshoi Ballet in Moscow, Russia, is famous throughout the world. Above, dancers perform *Swan Lake*.

# Physical Geography

## If YOU lived there...

You are making a documentary about the Trans–Siberian Railroad, a famous train that crosses the vast country of Russia. The train travels more than 5,700 miles across plains and mountains and through thick forests. As the train leaves the city of Moscow, you look out the window and see wheat fields and white birch trees.

**What scenes might you include in your film?**

> **BUILDING BACKGROUND** Look at a globe, and you will see that Russia extends nearly halfway around the world. Russia is the world's largest country. It is so vast that it spans 11 time zones. While huge, much of Russia consists of flat or rolling plains.

## Physical Features

Have you ever stood on two continents at once? In Russia's **Ural** (YOOHR-uhl) **Mountains**, you can. There, the continents of Europe and Asia meet. Europe lies to the west; Asia to the east. Together, Europe and Asia form the large landmass of Eurasia. On the map, you can see that a large chunk of Eurasia is the country of Russia. In fact, Russia is the world's largest country. Compared to the United States, Russia is almost twice as big.

South of Russia are three much smaller countries—Georgia, Armenia (ahr-MEE-nee-uh), and Azerbaijan (a-zuhr-by-JAHN). They lie in the Caucasus (KAW-kuh-suhs), the area between the Black Sea and the **Caspian Sea**. This area, which includes part of southern Russia, is named for the **Caucasus Mountains**.

### Landforms

As the map shows, Russia's landforms vary from west to east. The Northern European Plain stretches across western, or European, Russia. This fertile plain forms Russia's heartland, where most Russians live. **Moscow**, Russia's capital, is located there.

---

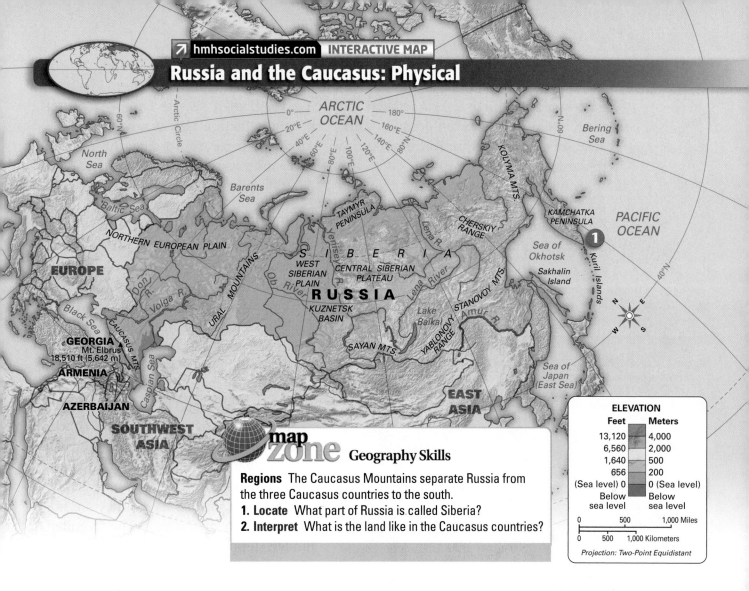

ARCTIC OCEAN

PACIFIC OCEAN

Bering Sea

North Sea

Barents Sea

Baltic Sea

NORTHERN EUROPEAN PLAIN

EUROPE

KOLYMA MTS.

KAMCHATKA PENINSULA

Kuril Islands

Sea of Okhotsk

TAYMYR PENINSULA

CHERSKIY RANGE

Sakhalin Island

SIBERIA

WEST SIBERIAN PLAIN

CENTRAL SIBERIAN PLATEAU

URAL MOUNTAINS

Ob River

Yenisey R.

Lena River

Lena R.

Don R.

Volga R.

RUSSIA

KUZNETSK BASIN

STANOVOY MTS.

Amur R.

Lake Baikal

YABLONOVY RANGE

Sea of Japan (East Sea)

Black Sea

GEORGIA
Mt. Elbrus
18,510 ft (5,642 m)

CAUCASUS MTS.

ARMENIA

Caspian Sea

SAYAN MTS.

AZERBAIJAN

SOUTHWEST ASIA

EAST ASIA

Arctic Circle

60°N

50°N

40°N

60°E

**map zone** Geography Skills

**Regions** The Caucasus Mountains separate Russia from the three Caucasus countries to the south.
1. **Locate** What part of Russia is called Siberia?
2. **Interpret** What is the land like in the Caucasus countries?

**ELEVATION**

| Feet | | Meters |
|---|---|---|
| 13,120 | | 4,000 |
| 6,560 | | 2,000 |
| 1,640 | | 500 |
| 656 | | 200 |
| (Sea level) 0 | | 0 (Sea level) |
| Below sea level | | Below sea level |

0   500   1,000 Miles
0   500   1,000 Kilometers

*Projection: Two-Point Equidistant*

To the east, the plain rises to form the Ural Mountains. These low mountains are worn down and rounded from erosion.

The vast area between the Urals and the Pacific Ocean is **Siberia**. This area includes several landforms, shown on the map. The West Siberian Plain is a flat, marshy area. It is one of the largest plains in the world.

East of this plain is an upland called the Central Siberian Plateau. Mountain ranges run through southern and eastern Siberia.

Eastern Siberia is called the Russian Far East. This area includes the Kamchatka (kuhm-CHAHT-kuh) Peninsula and several islands. The Russian Far East is part of the Ring of Fire, the area circling the Pacific.

**1** The Kamchatka Peninsula on Russia's east coast has many old and active volcanoes.

The Ring of Fire is known for its volcanoes and earthquakes, and the Russian Far East is no exception. It has several active volcanoes, and earthquakes can occur. In some areas, steam from within Earth breaks free to form geysers and hot springs.

South of Russia, the Caucasus countries consist largely of rugged uplands. The Caucasus Mountains cover much of Georgia and extend into Armenia and Azerbaijan.

## Russia's Climate and Plant Life

In the top photo, Russians bundled up in furs hurry through the snow and cold of Moscow, the capital. In the lower photo, evergreen forest called taiga blankets a Russian plain. In the distance, the low Ural Mountains mark the division between Europe and Asia.

These soaring mountains include Mount Elbrus (el-BROOS). At 18,510 feet (5,642 m), it is the highest peak in Europe. South of the mountains, a plateau covers much of Armenia. Gorges cut through this plateau, and earthquakes are common there. Lowlands lie along the Black and Caspian seas.

### Bodies of Water

Some of the longest rivers in the world flow through the region of Russia and the Caucasus. One of the most important is the **Volga** (VAHL-guh) **River** in western Russia. The longest river in Europe, the Volga winds southward to the Caspian Sea. The Volga has long formed the core of Russia's river network. Canals link the Volga to the nearby Don River and to the Baltic Sea.

Even longer rivers than the Volga flow through Siberia in the Asian part of Russia. The Ob (AWB), Yenisey (yi-ni-SAY), and Lena rivers flow northward to the Arctic Ocean. Like many of Russia's rivers, they are frozen for much of the year. The ice often hinders shipping and trade and closes some of Russia's ports for part of the year.

In addition to its rivers, Russia has some 200,000 lakes. Lake Baikal (by-KAHL), in south-central Siberia, is the world's deepest lake. Although not that large in surface area, Lake Baikal is deep enough to hold all the water in all five of the Great Lakes. Because of its beauty, Lake Baikal is called the Jewel of Siberia. Logging and factories have polluted the water, but Russians are now working to clean up the lake.

In the southwest part of the region, the Black and Caspian Seas border Russia and the Caucasus. The Black Sea connects to the Mediterranean Sea and is important for trade. The Caspian Sea holds saltwater and is the world's largest inland sea.

**READING CHECK** **Summarizing** What are the major landforms in Russia and the Caucasus?

# Climate and Plant Life

Russians sometimes joke that winter lasts for 12 months and then summer begins. Russia is a cold country. The reason is its northern location partly within the Arctic Circle. In general, Russia has short summers and long, snowy winters. The climate is milder west of the Urals and grows colder and harsher as one goes north and east.

Russia's northern coast is tundra. Winters are dark and bitterly cold, and the brief summers are cool. Much of the ground is permafrost, or permanently frozen soil. Only small plants such as mosses grow.

South of the tundra is a vast forest of evergreen trees called **taiga** (TY-guh). This huge forest covers about half of Russia. In Siberia, snow covers the taiga much of the year. South of the taiga is a flat grassland called the steppe (STEP). With rich, black soil and a warmer climate, the steppe is Russia's most important farming area.

Farther south, the Caucasus countries are warmer than Russia in general. Climate in the Caucasus ranges from warm and wet along the Black Sea to cooler in the uplands to hot and dry in much of Azerbaijan.

**READING CHECK** Finding Main Ideas How does Russia's location affect its climate?

# Natural Resources

Russia and the Caucasus have a wealth of resources. The Northern European Plain and the steppe provide fertile soil for farming. The taiga provides wood for building and paper products. Metals, such as copper and gold, and precious gems such as diamonds provide useful raw materials.

The region's main energy resources are coal, hydroelectricity, natural gas, and oil. Both Russia and Azerbaijan have large oil and gas fields. Oil also lies beneath the Caspian Sea.

The region's natural resources have been poorly managed, however. Until the early 1990s this region was part of the Soviet Union. The Soviet government put more importance on industry than on managing its resources. In Russia, many of the resources that were easy to access are gone. For example, most of the timber in western Russia has been cut down. Many remaining resources are in remote Siberia.

**READING CHECK** Analyzing Why are some of Russia's natural resources difficult to obtain?

**FOCUS ON READING**
What general idea can you draw from the text about natural resources? What facts or details support that idea?

**SUMMARY AND PREVIEW** Russia is big and cold, with vast plains and forests. The Caucasus countries are small, mountainous, and warmer. The region also has many natural resources. Next, you will read about Russia's history and culture.

## Section 1 Assessment

hmhsocialstudies.com
ONLINE QUIZ

### Reviewing Ideas, Terms, and Places

1. a. **Describe** Why are the **Ural Mountains** significant?
   b. **Draw Conclusions** Why might the Russian Far East be a dangerous place to live?
2. a. **Describe** What are winters like in much of Russia?
   b. **Analyze** How does climate affect Russia's plant life?
3. a. **Recall** What valuable resource is in the **Caspian Sea**?
   b. **Make Inferences** Why might resources located in remote, cold areas be difficult to use?

### Critical Thinking

4. **Generalizing** Draw a chart like the one here. Use your notes and enter one general idea for each topic in the chart.

| | |
|---|---|
| Physical Features | |
| Climate and Plants | |
| Natural Resources | |

### FOCUS ON WRITING

5. **Describing the Physical Geography** Now that you know the physical geography of the region, make a list of possible locations for the house or land you are selling.

# History and Culture of Russia

## What You Will Learn...

### Main Ideas

1. The Russian Empire grew under powerful leaders, but unrest and war led to its end.
2. The Soviet Union emerged as a Communist superpower with rigid government control.
3. Russia's history and diversity have influenced its culture.

### The Big Idea

Strict rule, unrest, and ethnic diversity have shaped Russia's history and culture.

### Key Terms and Places

Kiev, *p. 496*
Cyrillic, *p. 496*
czar, *p. 497*
Bolsheviks, *p. 497*
gulags, *p. 498*

**hmhsocialstudies.com**
**TAKING NOTES**

Use the graphic organizer online to take notes on the history and culture of Russia.

## If YOU lived there...

It is 1992, an exciting time in your home town of Moscow. At the end of 1991 the Soviet Union fell apart. Russia became independent. You watched on TV as people pulled down the red Soviet flag and knocked down statues of former leaders. Everyone is talking about new freedoms and a new kind of government.

**What new freedoms do you hope to have?**

**BUILDING BACKGROUND** The fall of the Soviet Union was not the first time Russia had experienced change. For centuries Russia was part of a great empire. Then in the early 1900s Communists overthrew the empire. The Soviet Union was born. Today it too is gone.

## The Russian Empire

Russia's roots lie in the grassy, windswept plains of the steppe. For thousands of years, people from Asia moved across the steppe. These groups of people included the Slavs. As you read in the last chapter, the Slavs settled in Eastern Europe, including what is now Ukraine and western Russia.

### Early History and Empire

The Slavs developed towns and began trading with people from other areas. In the AD 800s, Viking traders from Scandinavia invaded the Slavs. These Vikings were called Rus (ROOS), and the word *Russia* probably comes from their name. The Vikings shaped the first Russian state among the Slavs. This Russian state, called Kievan (KEE-e-fuhn) Rus, centered around the city of **Kiev**. This city is now the capital of Ukraine.

Over time, missionaries introduced the Orthodox Christian faith to Kiev. In addition, the missionaries introduced a form of the Greek alphabet called **Cyrillic** (suh-RI-lik). The Russians adopted this Cyrillic alphabet and still use it today.

# History of Russian Expansion

**Legend:**
- Russia, 1462–1533
- **Territory gained**
  - by 1689
  - by 1725
  - by 1801
  - by 1945
- Russian boundary, 1993

0  250  500 Miles
0  250  500 Kilometers

Projection: Two-Point Equidistant

Poland: Russian territory 1815–1918

Baltic republics: independent 1918–1940 and 1991

Finland: Russian territory 1809–1918

Russian territory 1871–1881

ARCTIC OCEAN

Bering Sea

Sea of Okhotsk

Sea of Japan (East Sea)

Black Sea

Caspian Sea

Baltic Sea

Arctic Circle

St. Petersburg

Moscow

## map zone Geography Skills

**Location** The colors in the map show the growth of the Russian Empire and of the Soviet Union over time.
1. **Name** What city is located in territory gained by 1725?
2. **Interpret** When was the period of greatest expansion?

In the 1200s, fierce Mongol invaders called Tatars (TAH-ters) swept out of Central Asia and conquered Kiev. The Mongols allowed Russian princes to rule over local states. In time, Muscovy became the strongest state. Its main city was Moscow.

After about 200 years Muscovy's prince, Ivan III, seized control from the Mongols. In the 1540s his grandson, Ivan IV, crowned himself **czar** (ZAHR), or emperor. *Czar* is Russian for "caesar." As czar, Ivan IV had total power. A cruel and savage ruler, he became known as Ivan the Terrible.

In time, Muscovy developed into the country of Russia. Strong czars such as Peter the Great (1682–1725) and Catherine the Great (1762–1796) built Russia into a huge empire and a world power. This empire included many conquered peoples.

In spite of its growth, Russia remained largely a country of poor farmers, while the czars and nobles had most of the wealth. In the early 1900s Russians began demanding improvements. The czar agreed to some changes, but unrest continued to grow.

## War and Revolution

In 1914 Russia entered World War I. The country suffered huge losses in the war. In addition, the Russian people experienced severe shortages of food. When the czar seemed to ignore the people's hardship, they rose up against him. He was forced to give up his throne in 1917.

Later that year the **Bolsheviks**, a radical Russian Communist group, seized power in the Russian Revolution. They then killed the czar and his family. In 1922 the Bolsheviks formed a new country, the Union of Soviet Socialist Republics (USSR), or the Soviet Union. It soon included 15 republics, the strongest of which was Russia. The first leader was Vladimir Lenin.

**READING CHECK** **Sequencing** What series of events led to the creation of the Soviet Union?

**VIDEO**
The Romanovs

🔗 hmhsocialstudies.com

## The Soviet Union

The Soviet Union, led by Lenin, became a Communist country. In this political system, the government owns all property and controls all aspects of life. In 1924 Lenin died. Joseph Stalin took power, ruling as a brutal and paranoid dictator.

### The Soviet Union under Stalin

**FOCUS ON READING**
Based on the Soviet Union's economy, what generalization might you make about command economies?

Under Stalin, the Soviet Union set up a command economy. In this system, the government owns all businesses and farms and makes all decisions. People were told what to make and how much to charge. Without competition, though, efficiency and the quality of goods fell over time.

The Soviet Union strictly controlled its people as well as its economy. Stalin had anyone who spoke out against the government jailed, exiled, or killed. Millions of people were sent to **gulags**, harsh Soviet labor camps often located in Siberia.

### Cold War and Collapse

During World War II, the Soviet Union fought with the Allies against Germany. Millions of Soviet citizens died in the war. Stalin's **reaction** to the war was to build a buffer around the Soviet Union to protect it from invasion. To do so, he set up Communist governments in Eastern Europe.

**ACADEMIC VOCABULARY**
**reaction**
a response to something

The United States opposed communism and saw its spread as a threat to democracy. This opposition led to the Cold War, a period of tense rivalry between the Soviet Union and the United States. The two rival countries became superpowers as they competed to have superior weapons.

In part because of the high costs of weapons, the Soviet economy was near collapse by the 1980s. Mikhail Gorbachev (GAWR-buh-chawf), the Soviet leader, began making changes. He reduced government control and introduced some democracy.

Despite his actions, the Soviet republics began pushing for independence. In 1991 the Soviet Union collapsed. It broke apart into 15 independent countries, including Russia. The Soviet Union was no more.

**READING CHECK** **Analyzing** How did the Cold War help lead to the Soviet Union's collapse?

## Culture

In the Soviet Union, the government had controlled culture just like everything else. Today, however, Russian culture is once again alive and vibrant.

### People and Religion

Russia is big and diverse, with more than 140 million people. About 80 percent are ethnic Russians, or Slavs, but Russia also has many other ethnic groups. The largest are the Tatars and Ukrainians. Russia's many ethnic groups are once again taking great pride in their cultures.

Like ethnic culture, religious worship has seen a revival. The Soviet government opposed religion and closed many houses of worship. Today many have reopened, including historic Russian cathedrals with their onion-shaped domes. The main faith is Russian Orthodox Christian. Other religions include Islam, Buddhism, and other forms of Christianity.

### Customs

Russian history has shaped its customs, such as holidays. Religious holidays, like Easter and Christmas, are popular. The main family holiday is New Year's Eve. To celebrate this holiday, families decorate a tree where, according to Russian folklore, Grandfather Frost and his helper the Snow Maiden leave gifts. A newer holiday is Russian Independence Day, which marks the end of the Soviet Union on June 12.

# St. Basil's Cathedral

Colorful St. Basil's Cathedral, in Moscow's Red Square, has become a symbol of Russia. Czar Ivan IV had the cathedral built between 1555 and 1561 in honor of Russian military victories. According to legend, Ivan had the architects blinded so they could never design anything else as magnificent.

Steeply sloped towers, called tent roofs, and onion-shaped domes easily shed snow.

St. Basil's Cathedral houses nine small, separate chapels.

Onion-shaped domes, based on Byzantine designs, decorate many early Russian churches.

In 1588 a chapel was added for the tomb of St. Basil the Blessed, a popular saint in Russia. In time, his name became linked to the cathedral.

**ANALYSIS SKILL** **ANALYZING VISUALS**

Besides onion domes, what other shapes and patterns are visible on the cathedral?

# Communist-era Poster

The Soviet Union used posters as propaganda. Propaganda is information designed to promote a specific cause or idea by influencing people's thoughts and beliefs. For example, Soviet posters often promoted the greatness and power of the Soviet state, its leaders, and their Communist policies.

The message of this 1924 poster reads, "Long live the Young Communist League! The young are taking over the older generation's torch!"

The color red in this poster symbolizes communism and the Russian Revolution.

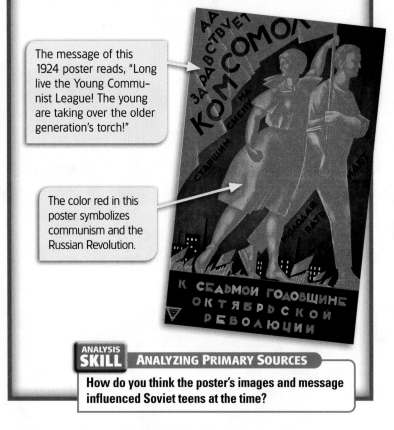

**ANALYSIS SKILL   ANALYZING PRIMARY SOURCES**

How do you think the poster's images and message influenced Soviet teens at the time?

## The Arts and Sciences

Russia has made great contributions in the arts and sciences. In the performing arts, Russia's ballet companies are world famous for their skill. In music, Peter Tchaikovsky (chy-KAWF-skee) is Russia's most famous composer. His many works include *The Nutcracker* ballet and the *1812 Overture*.

In the material arts, Russia's Fabergé eggs are priceless. Gifts for the czars, these eggs are made of precious metals and covered with gems such as emeralds and rubies. Each egg opens to reveal a tiny surprise.

In the sciences, Russia has contributed to space research. In 1957 the Soviet Union launched Sputnik, the first artificial satellite in space. Russian scientists now help work on the International Space Station.

**READING CHECK   Generalizing** How did the end of the Soviet Union affect Russian culture?

**SUMMARY AND PREVIEW** The history of Russia, from a great empire to a Communist superpower to a new nation, has shaped its rich culture. Next, you will read about life in Russia today.

---

## Section 2 Assessment

hmhsocialstudies.com
**ONLINE QUIZ**

### Reviewing Ideas, Terms, and Places

1. **a. Define** Who were the **czars**?
   **b. Analyze** What role did the city of **Kiev** play in Russian history?
   **c. Elaborate** What problems and events caused the Russian Empire to decline?
2. **a. Identify** Why are Vladimir Lenin and Joseph Stalin significant in Russian history?
   **b. Evaluate** Do you think life in the Soviet Union was an improvement over life in the Russian empire? Why, or why not?
3. **a. Recall** What is the main religion in Russia?
   **b. Summarize** How has Russian culture changed since the collapse of the Soviet Union in 1991?

### Critical Thinking

4. **Sequencing** Draw a chart like the one here. Use your notes to list the order of the major events leading up to the collapse of the Soviet Union.

○ → ○ → ○ → ○

**FOCUS ON WRITING**

5. **Considering Russia's History and Culture** Look at the locations you listed for Section 1. For the Russian locations, make notes about historical or cultural details you could include in your ad.

# Interpreting a Population Map

## Learn

Population maps give you a snapshot of the distribution of people in a region or country. Each color on a population map represents an average number of people living within a square mile or square kilometer. Sometimes symbols identify the cities with populations of a certain size. The map's legend identifies what the colors and symbols in the map mean.

## Practice

**1** Based on the map below, in which region of Russia do most of the country's people live?

**2** Which two cities in Russia have the largest population?

**3** How many Russian cities have more than 1 million people?

**Russia: Population**

| Persons per square mile | Persons per square km |
|---|---|
| 520 | 200 |
| 260 | 100 |
| 130 | 50 |
| 25 | 10 |
| 3 | 1 |
| 0 | 0 |

**Major cities**
- ● Over 2 million
- • 1 to 2 million
- · Under 1 million

0    500    1,000 Miles
0    500    1,000 Kilometers

*Projection: Two-Point Equidistant*

## Apply

Use an atlas to locate a current population map of the United States. Using the map, identify where the most and the least populated regions of the United States are. Then identify the number of U.S. cities or metropolitan areas with more than 2 million people.

# Russia Today

## If YOU lived there...

You live in St. Petersburg, a city of beautiful palaces and canals. You are looking forward to the end of school, when your family will go to their dacha, a cottage in the country. In midsummer, when the nights are long and the sun never really sets, you will go to concerts and other celebrations of the "White Nights" in your city.

**What do you like about living in St. Petersburg?**

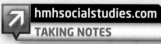
**BUILDING BACKGROUND** Russians have always had a special feeling for the countryside, from the wheat fields and birch forests in the west to the endless grasslands of the steppe. But Russia's great cities are exciting, too, with many shops, museums, and events.

## The Russian Federation

For decades, the Soviet Union reigned as a superpower, with Russia as its strongest republic. Then in 1991 the Soviet Union broke apart. Russia's leaders had to create a new government as they struggled to change from communism to democracy.

### Government

The Russian Federation is a federal republic, a system in which power is divided between national and local governments. The voters elect a president to serve as the country's chief executive, Russia's most powerful official. The president appoints a prime minister to serve as the head of the government. A legislature, called the Federal Assembly, makes the country's laws.

Increased democracy has led to more freedom for Russians. Voters can choose from several political parties. Information flows more freely. The government no longer seeks to control every aspect of life. In addition, the move toward democracy has improved relations between Russia and Western nations.

Changing to a democratic system has been difficult, though. Problems such as government corruption, or dishonesty, have slowed the development of a free society in Russia. Time will tell whether Russia will continue to grow as a democracy.

## Economy

With the move to democracy, Russia also began shifting to a market economy. This type of economy is based on free trade and competition. Today the Russian government has greatly reduced its control of the economy, and most businesses and farms are now privately owned. These changes have led to economic growth. At the same time, most of Russia's wealth is now in the hands of a small number of people.

Today Russia produces and exports oil, natural gas, timber, metals, and chemicals. Heavy industry, such as machinery, is still important. However, light industry, such as clothing and electronics, has grown. Furthermore, service industries now make up the largest part of Russia's economy.

In agriculture, Russia is now a major grower and exporter of grains. Other major crops are fruits, potatoes, and sugar beets.

## City and Rural Life

The changes sweeping Russia are visible in its cities. More restaurants and shopping centers are available. Stores offer a wider range of consumer goods, such as TVs. Some Russians have become wealthy and can afford luxuries. In fact, in 2005 Russia had more billionaires than any other European country. Nevertheless, the average Russian's standard of living remains low.

About 75 percent of all Russians live in cities. Most of these people live in small apartments in high-rise buildings. In rural areas, more people live in houses.

Although most Russians live in cities, they still have access to nature. Cities often have large parks and wooded areas in and around them. Many richer Russians own **dachas**, or Russian country houses, where they can garden and enjoy the fresh air.

**READING CHECK** **Summarizing** How has Russia changed since it became independent?

## CONNECTING TO Economics

### Kaliningrad

The small region of Kaliningrad—only slightly bigger than Connecticut—is more than 200 miles (320 km) from the rest of Russia. So why would Russia want this area? The reason has to do with the country's cold climate. Kaliningrad is Russia's only Baltic seaport that is free of ice all year. This important port provides Russia with year-round access to profitable European markets and trade. Railroads connect the port to Russia's major cities, as the map below shows.

**Drawing Conclusions** How do you think Russia's economy benefits from a Baltic seaport that is free of ice all year?

## Culture Regions

You have learned that Russia is vast and diverse. For this reason, we divide Russia into several culture regions, as the map on the next page shows. These regions differ in **features** such as population, natural resources, and economic activity.

The four western culture regions make up Russia's heartland. This area is home to the vast majority of Russia's people as well as to the country's capital and largest cities. In addition, the fertile plains of Russia's heartland are the country's most productive farming area.

**ACADEMIC VOCABULARY**

**features**
characteristics

## Russia: Culture Regions

**1** St. Petersburg's State Hermitage Museum, once the Winter Palace of the czars, now houses priceless works of art.

**2** Moscow is Russia's capital and largest city. It is a political, cultural, and transportation center.

**3** In Siberia, a Nenets woman leads a group of decorated reindeer as part of a village festival.

### The Moscow Region

Moscow is Russia's capital and largest city. The sprawling, modern city has wide boulevards and large public squares. Its many cultural attractions include the world-famous Bolshoi Ballet and Moscow Circus.

At Moscow's heart is the Kremlin, the center of Russia's government. In Russian, *kremlin* means "fortress." The Kremlin consists of several buildings surrounded by a wall and towers. The buildings include not only government offices but also palaces, museums, and gold-domed churches.

Next to the Kremlin is Red Square, an immense plaza. It is lined by many famous landmarks, such as St. Basil's Cathedral.

The Moscow region is Russia's most important economic area, and its factories produce a wide range of goods. The city is also a transportation center and links by road, rail, and plane to all parts of Russia.

### The St. Petersburg Region

**St. Petersburg** reflects Russians' desire for Western ways. Peter the Great founded the city and styled it after those of Western Europe. For some 200 years, St. Petersburg served as Russia's capital and home to the czars. It features wide avenues, grand palaces, and numerous canals. Theaters and museums enrich the city's cultural life.

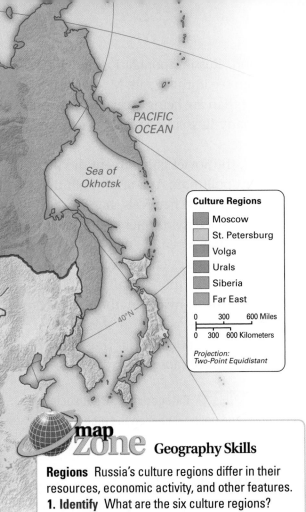

PACIFIC
OCEAN

Sea of
Okhotsk

40°N

**Culture Regions**

- Moscow
- St. Petersburg
- Volga
- Urals
- Siberia
- Far East

0    300    600 Miles

0    300    600 Kilometers

*Projection:*
*Two-Point Equidistant*

**map zone** **Geography Skills**

**Regions** Russia's culture regions differ in their resources, economic activity, and other features.
1. **Identify** What are the six culture regions?
2. **Interpret** What is the major defining feature in each of the four western culture regions?

St. Petersburg's location on the Gulf of Finland has made the city a major port and trade center. This northern location also produces "White Nights," a period during summer when it never gets totally dark.

## The Volga and Urals Regions

The Volga River and Ural Mountains are the third and fourth culture regions. The broad Volga is a major shipping route. Dams along its course form lakes and provide hydroelectric power. Factories in the area process oil and gas. In addition, a site on the Caspian Sea provides fish called sturgeon. The eggs of this fish are called black caviar, which is a costly delicacy, or rare and valued food.

The Ural Mountains are an important mining region and produce nearly every major mineral. **Smelters**, factories that process metal ores, process copper and iron. The Urals region is also known for gems and semiprecious stones.

## Siberia

East of the Urals lies the vast expanse of Siberia. In the Tatar language, *Siberia* means "Sleeping Land." Siberian winters are long and severe. As you have read, much of the land lies frozen or buried under snow for most or all of the year. The remote region has many valuable resources, but accessing them in the harsh climate is difficult.

Siberia's main industries are lumber, mining, and oil production. Large coal deposits are mined in southwest Siberia. Rivers produce hydroelectric power. The southern steppes, where the weather is warmer, are Siberia's main farmlands.

Because of Siberia's harsh climate, jobs there pay high wages. Even so, few people choose to live in Siberia. Most towns and cities are in the western and southern parts of the region. These cities tend to follow the **Trans-Siberian Railroad**. This rail line runs from Moscow to Vladivostok on the east coast, and is the longest single rail line in the world.

## The Russian Far East

Russia has a long coastline on the Pacific Ocean. There, in the Russian Far East, much land remains heavily forested. In the few cities, factories process forest and mineral resources. Farming occurs in the Amur River valley. The city of Vladivostok is a naval base and the area's main seaport. Islands off the coast provide oil, minerals, and commercial fishing.

**READING CHECK** **Finding Main Ideas** What areas make up Russia's culture regions?

**FOCUS ON READING**
Based on this description of Siberia, what generalization about human settlement can you make?

hmhsocialstudies.com

**ANIMATED GEOGRAPHY**
Trans-Siberian Railroad

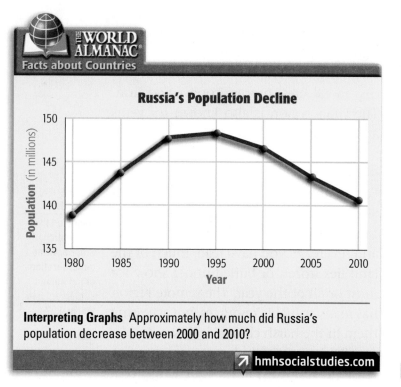

**Russia's Population Decline**

*Population (in millions)* — 150, 145, 140, 135

Year: 1980, 1985, 1990, 1995, 2000, 2005, 2010

**Interpreting Graphs** Approximately how much did Russia's population decrease between 2000 and 2010?

↗ hmhsocialstudies.com

Second, Russia's population is falling, as you can see in the graph. More Russians are dying than are being born. One reason is that many Russians cannot afford good health care.

Third, the Soviet government did little to prevent pollution. As a result pollution, such as industrial chemicals, has seriously harmed Russia's environment. The government must now repair the damage.

Last, Russia faces ethnic conflicts. One of the worst is in the Russian republic of **Chechnya** (CHECH-nyah) in the Caucasus Mountains. Some people in this Muslim area want independence. Fighting and terrorism there have caused many deaths.

**READING CHECK** **Categorizing** What social, economic, and political challenges face Russia?

## Russia's Challenges

Although Russia has made great progress since 1991, challenges remain. First, Russia's shift to a market economy has not been without problems. For example, prices and unemployment have risen, and the gap between rich and poor has widened.

**SUMMARY AND PREVIEW** As you have read, Russia is a federal republic working to build a market economy. The west is Russia's heartland, but Siberia has many valuable resources. In the next section, you will read about the Caucasus.

---

## Section 3 Assessment

↗ hmhsocialstudies.com
ONLINE QUIZ

### Reviewing Ideas, Terms, and Places

1. **a. Recall** What type of government does Russia now have?
   **b. Explain** How is Russia's economy changing?
2. **a. Recall** From west to east, what are Russia's major culture regions?
   **b. Draw Conclusions** Why do you think most Siberian towns and cities are located along the **Trans-Siberian Railroad**?
   **c. Rate** Which of Russia's culture regions would you most want to live in, and why?
3. **a. Identify** What are the main challenges that face Russia today?
   **b. Elaborate** What difficulties does **Chechnya** pose for Russia's leaders?

### Critical Thinking

4. **Categorizing** Draw a concept web like the one shown. Use your notes to list facts about each Russian culture region.

Russia's Culture Regions

### FOCUS ON WRITING

5. **Collecting Details about Russia Today** Based on conditions in Russia today, what location would you choose for your property? Review your notes from Section 2 and this section. Then choose one location in Russia for the property you are selling.

# from
# The Endless Steppe

## by Esther Hautzig

**About the Reading** *In* The Endless Steppe, *an autobiographical novel, Esther Hautzig writes about her own experiences as a teenage girl. In the novel, the girl Esther is from a wealthy Jewish family in Poland. In 1941 her family is deported to a labor camp in Siberia. In the excerpt below, Esther and her family are on the train to Siberia. She is dreading their destination.*

**AS YOU READ** Think about what Esther feels as she watches the passing landscape. What ideas does she already have about life in Siberia?

The flatness of this land was awesome. There wasn't a hill in sight; it was an enormous, unrippled sea of parched and lifeless grass.

"Tata, why is the earth so flat here?"

"These must be steppes, Esther."

"Steppes? But steppes are in Siberia."

"This is Siberia," he said quietly.

If I had been told that I had been transported to the moon, I could not have been more stunned.

"Siberia?" My voice trembled. "But Siberia is full of snow."

"It will be," my father said. ❶

Siberia! Siberia was the end of the world, a point of no return. Siberia was for criminals and political enemies, where the punishment was unbelievably cruel, and where people died like flies. ❷ Summer or no summer—and who had ever talked about hot Siberia?—Siberia was the tundra and mountainous drifts of snow. Siberia was *wolves*.

**GUIDED READING**

**WORD HELP**

**deported** forced to leave a country

**parched** very thirsty

**Tata** Polish word that means "daddy" or "papa"

**steppes** vast, grassy plains in southern Russia

**tundra** in subarctic climates, an almost treeless plain with permanently frozen subsoil

❶ At the time of the train journey, it is summer.

❷ The labor camps in Siberia, called gulags, were harsh places to live. Many people died at the camps.

## Connecting Literature to Geography

1. **Analyzing** Russian soldiers took Esther's family from their home in Poland to work in Siberia. How do you think this fact affects Esther's feelings as she views the landscape of Siberia from the train?

2. **Drawing Inferences** Why do you think Siberia was chosen as a place of exile? What made it a punishment to live there?

# The Caucasus

## If YOU lived there...

You live in Tbilisi, the capital of the country of Georgia. Several years ago, your sister and her college friends joined the Rose Revolution, a political protest that forced a corrupt president to resign. The protestors' symbol was a red rose. Since the protest, you have become more interested in politics.

**What kind of government do you want?**

**BUILDING BACKGROUND** Georgia is one of three republics in the area called the Caucasus. In 1991, when the Soviet Union ended, the Caucasus republics gained independence. Since then, the republics have struggled to become democracies with market economies.

## History

The Caucasus lies in the rugged Caucasus Mountains between the Black and Caspian seas. Located where Europe blends into Asia, the Caucasus reflects a range of cultural influences. At one time or another, Persians, Greeks, Romans, Arabs, Turks, and Mongols have all ruled or invaded the area. The Russians took control of much of the Caucasus in the early 1800s.

Russian control in the Caucasus did not include what is now western Armenia. The Ottoman Turks held this area. Over time, the Turks grew to distrust the Armenians, however; and in the late 1800s began abusing and killing them. During World War I (1914–1918), the Turks forced all Armenians to leave. Hundreds of thousands of Armenians died during this ethnic cleansing, or attempt to remove an ethnic group. The Turks lost World War I, though, and had to give up western Armenia.

After World War I, Armenia, Azerbaijan, and Georgia gained independence—but not for long. By the early 1920s they were part of the vast Soviet Union. Finally in 1991, when the Soviet Union fell, the Caucasus republics achieved true independence.

**READING CHECK** **Finding Main Ideas** Why do the countries in the Caucasus reflect a range of cultural influences?

The snow-capped peaks of the Caucasus Mountains rise above a mountain village and the remains of a fortress built in the 900s.

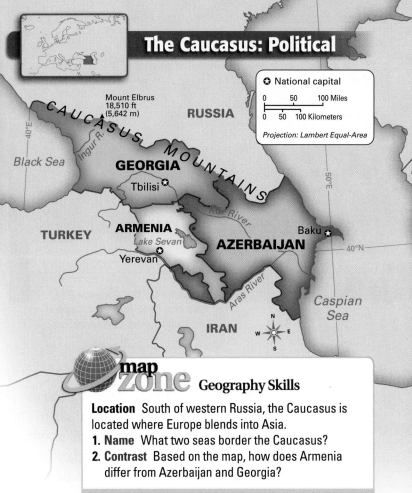

The Caucasus: Political

Mount Elbrus
18,510 ft
(5,642 m)

○ National capital

0    50    100 Miles
0    50    100 Kilometers

Projection: Lambert Equal-Area

RUSSIA

CAUCASUS MOUNTAINS

Black Sea

GEORGIA

Tbilisi ✪

Ingur R.

Kur River

TURKEY

ARMENIA
Lake Sevan

Yerevan

AZERBAIJAN

Baku ✪

Aras River

IRAN

Caspian Sea

40°N

mapzone Geography Skills

**Location** South of western Russia, the Caucasus is located where Europe blends into Asia.
1. **Name** What two seas border the Caucasus?
2. **Contrast** Based on the map, how does Armenia differ from Azerbaijan and Georgia?

## The Caucasus Today

The Caucasus may have a long history, but the Caucasus countries do not. Like other former Soviet republics, these young countries have had to create new governments and economies. Meanwhile, ethnic unrest and conflicts have slowed progress.

The Caucasus republics have similar governments. An elected president governs each nation, and an appointed prime minister runs each government. An elected parliament, or legislature, makes the laws.

### Georgia

The country of Georgia lies in the Caucasus Mountains east of the Black Sea. **Tbilisi** is the capital. About 70 percent of the people are ethnic Georgians, and most belong to the Georgian Orthodox Church. The official language is Georgian, a unique language with its own alphabet. However, many other languages are also spoken.

Since 1991 Georgia has struggled with unrest and civil war. In 2003 Georgians forced out their president in the peaceful Rose Revolution. Meanwhile, ethnic groups in northern Georgia were fighting for independence. Because these groups now hold parts of northern Georgia, division and unrest continues.

Although unrest has hurt Georgia's economy, international aid is helping it improve. Georgia's economy is based on services and farming. Major crops include citrus fruits, grapes, and tea. In addition, Georgia produces steel and mines copper and manganese. Georgia is also famous for its wines. The Black Sea is a resort area, and tourism contributes to the economy, too.

### Armenia

South of Georgia is the small, landlocked country of Armenia. The tiny country is slightly larger than the state of Maryland. **Yerevan** (yer-uh-VAHN) is the capital. Almost all the people are ethnic Armenian. Armenia prides itself as being the first country to adopt Christianity, and most people belong to the Armenian Orthodox Church.

### Baku

**Located on the Caspian Sea, the city of Baku is the capital and chief port of Azerbaijan.**

**FOCUS ON READING**

What general statements can you make about the Caucasus as a whole?

In the early 1990s, Armenia fought a bitter war with its neighbor Azerbaijan. The war involved an area of Azerbaijan where most people are ethnic Armenian. Armenia wanted this area to become part of its country. Although a cease-fire stopped the fighting in 1994, Armenian armed forces still control the area. The issue remained unsettled as of the early 2000s.

This conflict has greatly hurt Armenia's economy. However, international aid is helping Armenia's economy recover and expand. For example, diamond processing is now a growing industry in Armenia.

### Azerbaijan

East of Armenia is Azerbaijan. In contrast to the other Caucasus republics, Azerbaijan is largely Muslim. The Azeri (uh-ZE-ree) make up 90 percent of the population.

Azerbaijan's economy is based on oil, found along and under the Caspian Sea. **Baku**, the capital, is the center of a large oil-refining industry. This industry has led to strong economic growth. Corruption is high, though; and many people are poor. In addition, Azerbaijan has many refugees as a result of its conflict with Armenia.

**READING CHECK** **Summarizing** What challenges do the Caucasus republics face?

**SUMMARY** The Caucasus republics face challenges but are working to develop democracy and build their economies.

## Section 4 Assessment

hmhsocialstudies.com
ONLINE QUIZ

### Reviewing Ideas, Terms, and Places

1. **a. Identify** Which country controlled much of the Caucasus for most of the 1800s?
   **b. Identify Cause and Effect** How did Turkish rule affect Armenians in the Ottoman Empire?
   **c. Elaborate** How has location affected the history and culture of the Caucasus area?
2. **a. Recall** How does **Baku** contribute to the economy of Azerbaijan?
   **b. Compare and Contrast** How is religion in Georgia and Armenia similar? How does religion in these countries differ from that in Azerbaijan?
   **c. Elaborate** How has the war that occurred between Armenia and Azerbaijan affected each country?

### Critical Thinking

3. **Comparing and Contrasting** Draw a Venn diagram like the one here. Use your notes to identify the ways in which Georgia, Armenia, and Azerbaijan are similar and different.

### FOCUS ON WRITING

4. **Collecting Details about the Caucasus** You have narrowed Russian locations to one possibility. What features do the Caucasus countries have that might be attractive to potential buyers? Identify one Caucasus location you might use in your ad.

# Chapter Review

**Geography's Impact**
video series
Review the video to answer the closing question:
*Why was the Soviet Union so determined to become a major industrial power?*

## Visual Summary

*Use the visual summary below to help you review the main ideas of the chapter.*

QUICK FACTS

Russia is an immense, cold country with plains, mountains, and forest. The Caucasus is a small, mountainous area.

With a long history and a rich culture, Russia ranges from large modern cities to the vast plains and forests of Siberia.

The three small Caucasus republics lie between the Black and Caspian seas, and face ethnic unrest and conflict.

## Reviewing Vocabulary, Terms, and Places

*For each statement below, write T if it is true and F if it is false. If the statement is false, replace the boldfaced term with one that makes the sentence a true statement.*

1. The **Caucasus Mountains** separate European Russia from Asian Russia.

2. Russia's capital and largest city is **St. Petersburg**.

3. The Caucasus is bordered by the Black Sea to the west and **Lake Baikal** to the east.

4. Under the rule of the **Bolsheviks**, the Russian Empire expanded in size and power.

5. Much of the country of Georgia is located in the high, rugged **Ural Mountains**.

6. Many wealthier Russians have country houses, which are called **gulags**.

7. Russia's main government buildings are located in the **Kremlin** in Moscow.

8. Russia's culture regions differ in **features** such as cities, natural resources, and economic activity.

9. **Moscow** is a major port and was once home to Russia's czars.

10. The capital city of Armenia is **Yerevan**.

## Comprehension and Critical Thinking

**SECTION 1** *(Pages 492–495)*

11. **a. Recall** What is Russia's most important river, and to what major bodies of water does it link?

    **b. Identify Cause and Effect** How does Russia's location affect its climate?

    **c. Elaborate** Why might developing the many natural resources in Siberia be difficult?

**SECTION 2** *(Pages 496–500)*

12. **a. Identify** Who was Joseph Stalin?

    **b. Summarize** How has Russia contributed to world culture?

    **c. Elaborate** How was the end of the Soviet Union similar to the end of the Russian Empire?

## SECTION 3 (Pages 502–506)

**13. a. Identify** What four culture regions make up the Russian heartland?

**b. Compare and Contrast** How are Moscow and St. Petersburg similar and different?

**c. Elaborate** How might Siberia help make Russia an economic success?

## SECTION 4 (Pages 508–510)

**14. a. Recall** What is the capital of each of the Caucasus republics?

**b. Compare** What do the three Caucasus countries have in common?

**c. Elaborate** What issues and challenges do the Caucasus countries need to address to improve their economies?

## Using the Internet 21ST CENTURY

**15. Activity: Making a Map** The Trans-Siberian Railroad is the longest single rail line in the world. Climb aboard in Moscow and travel all the way across Russia. Through your online textbook, research the people, places, and history along the railroad's route. Then create an illustrated map of your journey. On the map, show the train's route, indicate the places where you stopped, and include images and descriptions about what you saw.

## Social Studies Skills

**Interpreting a Population Map** *Use a good atlas to find a population map of Europe. The map does not need to include Russia. Use the map to answer the following questions. Do not include the country of Russia when answering the questions.*

**16.** Not including the cities of Russia, how many cities or metropolitan areas in Europe have more than 2 million people?

**17.** Not including Russia, which regions of Europe are the most populated? Which regions of Europe are the least populated?

## Map Activity 21ST CENTURY

**18. Russia and the Caucasus** On a separate sheet of paper, match the letters on the map with their correct labels.

| | |
|---|---|
| Caucasus Mountains | Ural Mountains |
| Caspian Sea | Vladivostok, Russia |
| Kamchatka Peninsula | Volga River |
| Moscow, Russia | West Siberian Plain |
| St. Petersburg, Russia | |

### FOCUS ON READING AND WRITING

**19. Making Generalizations** Examine the information in Section 3 about the four culture regions that make up Russia's heartland. Based on the specific information about these regions, make two generalizations about western Russia.

**20. Creating a Real Estate Ad** Review your notes about locations in Russia and the Caucasus. Choose one location for the real estate you are selling. What are its best features? How would you describe the land and climate? What are the benefits of living there? If it is a building, what does it look like? What is nearby? Answer these questions in your real estate ad. Remember to include details that will make the property attractive to possible buyers.

*DIRECTIONS: Read questions 1 through 7 and write the letter of the best response. Then read question 8 and write your own well-constructed response.*

**1** **Which word below *best* describes Russia's overall climate?**

A Cold

B Dry

C Hot

D Wet

**2** **What is the name of the vast forest that covers much of Russia?**

A Siberia

B Steppe

C Taiga

D Tundra

**3** **What was the name of the second Soviet leader, who ruled as a brutal dictator?**

A Ivan III

B Ivan the Terrible

C Vladimir Lenin

D Joseph Stalin

**4** **The majority of Russians are descended from the**

A Bolsheviks.

B Slavs.

C Tatars.

D Ukrainians.

**5** **What are the Caucasus countries?**

A Armenia, Moscow, and St. Petersburg

B Azerbaijan, Georgia, and Russia

C Azerbaijan, Armenia, and Georgia

D Georgia, Moscow, and Russia

**The Caucasus: Climate**

**6** **Based on the map above, which of the following climates is found along part of the coast of the Black Sea?**

A Humid subtropical

B Mediterranean

C Steppe

D Tropical Savanna

**7** **What year did the Soviet Union collapse and break apart into 15 independent republics?**

A 1990

B 1991

C 2000

D 2001

**8** **Extended Response** Examine the Section 3 map of Russia's culture regions. Based on the map, describe how the physical geography in three of the culture regions contributes to the economic activity in those regions.

# A Biographical Narrative

**P**eople have shaped the world. Who are the important people in history? What were the critical events in their lives? How did geography or location affect those events? These are questions we ask as we try to understand our world.

## Assignment

Write a biographical narrative about a significant event in the life of a historical figure such as Queen Isabella, Martin Luther, Napoleon, or Mikhail Gorbachev.

## 1. Prewrite

### Choose a Topic

- Choose a person who affected European or Russian history in some way.
- Choose a specific event or incident in the person's life. For example, you might choose Napoleon at the Battle of Waterloo.

> **TIP** To choose the event, think about the person's importance or signficance. Choose an event that will help you make that point.

### Gather and Organize Information

- Look for information about your topic in the library or on the Internet. Book-length biographies about the person are a good source.
- Identify the parts of the event. Organize them in chonological, or time, order. Note details about people, actions, and the location of the event.

## 2. Write

### Use a Writer's Framework

> **A Writer's Framework**
>
> **Introduction**
> - Introduce the person and the event.
> - Identify the importance of the event.
>
> **Body**
> - Write at least one paragraph for each major part of the event. Include specific details.
> - Use chronological, or time, order to organize the parts of the event.
>
> **Conclusion**
> - Summarize the importance of the person and event in the final paragraph.

## 3. Evaluate and Revise

### Review and Improve Your Paper

- Read your first draft at least twice, and then use the questions below to evaluate your paper.
- Make the changes needed to improve your paper.

### Evaluation Questions for a Biographical Narrative

1. Do you introduce the person and event and identify the importance of each?
2. Do you have one paragraph for each major part of the event?
3. Do you include specific details about people, actions, and location?
4. Do you use chronological order, the order in time, to organize the parts of the event?
5. Do you end the paper with a summary of the importance of the person and event?

## 4. Proofread and Publish

### Give Your Explanation the Finishing Touch

- Make sure your transitional phrases—such as then, next, later, or finally—help clarify the order of the actions that took place.
- Make sure you capitalized all proper names.
- You can share your biographical narrative by reading it aloud in class or adding it to a class collection of biographies.

## 5. Practice and Apply

Use the steps and strategies outlined in this workshop to write your biographical narrative. Share your work with others, comparing and contrasting the importance of the people and events.

# References

Available @

↗ **hmhsocialstudies.com**

- Facts About the World
- Regions of the World Handbook
- Standardized Test-Taking Strategies
- Economics Handbook

515

# Using Prior Knowledge

## FOCUS ON READING

When you put together a puzzle, you search for pieces that are missing to complete the picture. As you read, you do the same thing when you use prior knowledge. You take what you already know about a subject and then add the information you are reading to create a full picture. The example below shows how using prior knowledge about computer mapping helped one reader fill in the pieces about how geographers use computer mapping.

In the past, maps were always drawn by hand. Many were not very accurate. Today, though, most maps are made using computers and satellite images. Through advances in mapmaking, we can make accurate maps on almost any scale, from the whole world to a single neighborhood, and keep them up to date.

*From Section 3, The Branches of Geography*

| Computer Mapping | |
|---|---|
| What I know before reading | What else I learned |
| • My dad uses the computer to get a map for trips.<br>• I can find maps on the Internet of states and countries. | • Maps have not always been very accurate.<br>• Computers help make new kinds of maps that are more than just cities and roads.<br>• These computer maps are an important part of geography. |

## YOU TRY IT!

Draw a chart like the one above. Think about what you know about satellite images and list this prior knowledge in the left column of your chart. Then read the passage below. Once you have read it, add what you learned about satellite images to the right column.

Much of the information gathered by these satellites is in the form of images. Geographers can study these images to see what an area looks like from above Earth. Satellites also collect information that we cannot see from the planet's surface. The information gathered by satellites helps geographers make accurate maps.

*From Section 1, Studying Geography*

# Using Word Parts

## FOCUS ON READING

Many English words are made up of several word parts: roots, prefixes, and suffixes. A root is the base of the word and carries the main meaning. A prefix is a letter or syllable added to the beginning of a root. A suffix is a letter or syllable added to the end to create new words. When you come across a new word, you can sometimes figure out the meaning by looking at its parts. Below are some common word parts and their meanings.

| Common Roots | | |
|---|---|---|
| **Word Root** | **Meaning** | **Sample Words** |
| -graph- | write, writing | autograph, biography |
| -vid-, -vis- | see | videotape, visible |

| Common Prefixes | | |
|---|---|---|
| **Prefix** | **Meaning** | **Sample Words** |
| geo- | earth | geology |
| inter- | between, among | interpersonal, intercom |
| in- | not | ineffective |
| re- | again | restate, rebuild |

| Common Suffixes | | |
|---|---|---|
| **Suffix** | **Meaning** | **Sample Words** |
| -ible | capable of | visible, responsible |
| -less | without | penniless, hopeless |
| -ment | result, action | commitment |
| -al | relating to | directional |
| -tion | the act or condition of | rotation, selection |

## YOU TRY IT!

Read the following words. First separate any prefixes or suffixes and identify the word's root. Use the chart above to define the root, the prefix, or the suffix. Then write a definition for each word.

| | | |
|---|---|---|
| **geography** | **visualize** | **movement** |
| **seasonal** | **reshaping** | **interact** |
| **regardless** | **separation** | **invisible** |

# Understanding Cause and Effect

## FOCUS ON READING

Learning to identify causes and effects can help you understand geography. A **cause** is something that makes another thing happen. An **effect** is the result of something else that happened. A cause may have several effects, and an effect may have several causes.  In addition, as you can see in the example below, causes and effects may occur in a chain.  Then, each effect in turn becomes the cause for another event.

**First cause** →

The Gulf Stream is a warm current that flows north along the U.S. East Coast. It then flows east across the Atlantic to become the North Atlantic Drift. As the warm current flows along northwestern Europe, it heats the air. Westerlies blow the warmed air across Europe. This process makes Europe warmer than it otherwise would be.

*From Section 1, Weather and Climate*

**Last effect** →

---

**Cause**
Gulf Stream

↓

**Effect**
Warm water flows along the coast of northwest Europe.

↓

**Effect**
Warm water raises temperature of the air above.

↓

**Effect**
Winds blow warm air across Europe.

↓

**Effect**
Warm winds make Europe warmer.

---

## YOU TRY IT!

Read the following sentences, and then use a graphic organizer like the one below right to analyze the cause and effects. Create as many boxes as you need to list the causes and effects.

Mountains also create wet and dry areas. . . A mountain forces wind blowing against it to rise.  As it rises, the air cools and precipitation falls as rain or snow.  Thus, the side of the mountain facing the wind is often green and lush.  However, little moisture remains for the other side.  This effect creates a rain shadow.

*From Section 1, Weather and Climate*

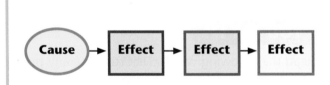

---

# Understanding Main Ideas

## FOCUS ON READING

Main ideas are like the hub of a wheel. The hub holds the wheel together, and everything circles around it. In a paragraph, the main idea holds the paragraph together and all the facts and details revolve around it. The main idea is usually stated clearly in a topic sentence, which may come at the beginning or end of a paragraph. Topic sentences always summarize the most important idea of a paragraph.

To find the main idea, ask yourself what one point is holding the paragraph together. See how the main idea in the following example holds all the details from the paragraph together.

A single country may also include more than one culture region within its borders. Mexico is one of many countries that is made up of different culture regions. People in northern Mexico and southern Mexico, for example, have different culture traits. The culture of northern Mexico tends to be more modern, while traditional culture remains strong in southern Mexico.

*From Section 1, Culture*

## YOU TRY IT!

Read the following paragraph, and then use a graphic organizer like the one above to identify the main idea. Create as many circles as you need to list the supporting facts and details.

At the same time, the United States is influenced by global culture. Martial arts movies from Asia attract large audiences in the United States. Radio stations in the United States play music by African, Latin American, and European musicians. We even adopt many foreign words, like *sushi* and *plaza*, into English.

*From Section 4, Global Connections*

# Setting a Purpose

## FOCUS ON READING

When you go on a trip, you have a purpose or a destination in mind before you start. Maps can help you get to your destination. When you read, you should also have a purpose in mind before you start. This purpose keeps you focused and moving toward your goal of understanding. Textbooks often provide "maps" to help you set a purpose for your reading. A textbook's "map" includes a chapter's headings, pictures, and study tips. To determine a purpose for your reading, look over the headings, pictures, and study tips. Then ask yourself a question that can guide you. See how looking over the chapter's first page can help you set a purpose.

### What You Will Learn...

*From Early History of the Americas*

In this chapter you will learn about the location, growth, and decline of the Maya, Aztec, and Inca civilizations in the Americas.

**Notice Headings, Pictures or Tips**
Here's a tip on what I should learn about in this chapter.

**Ask Questions**
What do I want to learn about these three civilizations?

**Set a Purpose**
I've never heard of these civilizations. I wonder what they were like and why they declined. I'll read to find out.

## YOU TRY IT!

You can also use the method described above to set a purpose for reading the main text in your book. Look at the heading for the following caption. Then write down one or two questions about what you will read. Finally, develop a purpose for reading about Tenochtitlán. State this purpose in one to two sentences.

### Tenochtitlán

The Aztecs turned a swampy, uninhabited island into one of the largest and grandest cities in the world. The first Europeans to visit Tenochtitlán were amazed. At the time, the Aztec capital was about five times bigger than London.

*From Section 2, The Aztecs*

# Predicting

## FOCUS ON READING

Predicting is guessing what will happen next based on what you already know. In reading about geography, you can use what you know about the place you live to help you make predictions about other countries. Predicting helps you stay involved with your reading as you see whether your prediction was right. Your mind follows these four steps when you make predictions as you read:

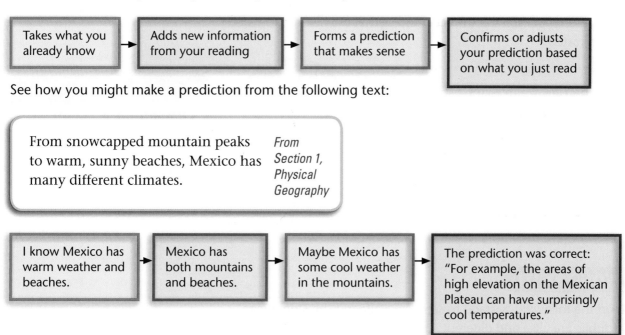

| Takes what you already know | → | Adds new information from your reading | → | Forms a prediction that makes sense | → | Confirms or adjusts your prediction based on what you just read |

See how you might make a prediction from the following text:

> From snowcapped mountain peaks to warm, sunny beaches, Mexico has many different climates.
>
> *From Section 1, Physical Geography*

| I know Mexico has warm weather and beaches. | → | Mexico has both mountains and beaches. | → | Maybe Mexico has some cool weather in the mountains. | → | The prediction was correct: "For example, the areas of high elevation on the Mexican Plateau can have surprisingly cool temperatures." |

## YOU TRY IT!

Read the following sentences. Then use a graphic organizer like the one below to help you predict what you will learn in your reading. Check the text in Section 3 to see if your prediction was correct.

> Mexico has a democratic government. However, Mexico is not like the United States where different political parties have always competed for power.
>
> *From Section 3, Mexico Today*

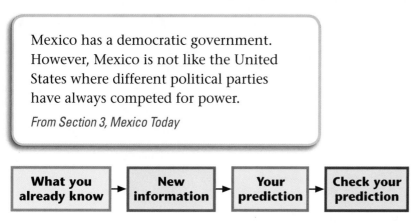

| What you already know | → | New information | → | Your prediction | → | Check your prediction |

READING SOCIAL STUDIES

# Understanding Comparison-Contrast

## FOCUS ON READING

Comparing shows how things are alike. Contrasting shows how things are different. You can understand comparison-contrast by learning to recognize clue words and points of comparison. Clue words let you know whether to look for similarities or differences. Points of comparison are the main topics that are being compared or contrasted.

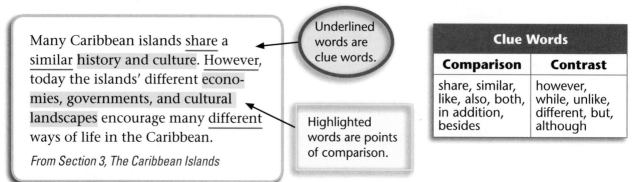

Many Caribbean islands <u>share</u> a <u>similar</u> history and culture. However, today the islands' <u>different</u> economies, governments, and cultural landscapes encourage many <u>different</u> ways of life in the Caribbean.

*From Section 3, The Caribbean Islands*

Underlined words are clue words.

Highlighted words are points of comparison.

| Clue Words | |
|---|---|
| **Comparison** | **Contrast** |
| share, similar, like, also, both, in addition, besides | however, while, unlike, different, but, although |

## YOU TRY IT!

Read the following passage to see how Haiti and the Dominican Republic are alike and different. Use a diagram like the one here to compare and contrast the two countries.

Haiti occupies the western part of the island of Hispaniola. Haiti's capital, Port-au-Prince, is the center of the nation's limited industry. Most Haitians farm small plots. Coffee and sugarcane are among Haiti's main exports.

The Dominican Republic occupies the eastern part of Hispaniola. The Dominican Republic is not a rich country. However, its economy, health care, education, and housing are more developed than Haiti's. Agriculture is the basis of the economy

*From Section 3, The Caribbean Islands*

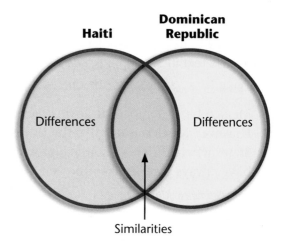

Haiti     **Dominican Republic**

Differences     Differences

Similarities

# Identifying Supporting Details

## FOCUS ON READING

Why believe what you read? One reason is because of details that support or prove the main idea. These details might be facts, statistics, examples, or definitions. In the example below, notice what kind of proof or supporting details help you believe the main idea.

> Colombia's economy relies on several valuable resources. Rich soil, steep slopes, and tall shade trees produce world-famous Colombian coffee. Other major export crops include bananas, sugarcane, and cotton. Many farms in Colombia produce flowers that are exported around the world. In fact, 80 percent of the country's flowers are shipped to the United States.
>
> *From Section 2, Colombia*

| Main Idea |
| --- |
| Colombia's economy relies on several valuable resources. |

| Supporting Details | | | |
| --- | --- | --- | --- |
| **Example** | **Fact** | **Fact** | **Statistic** |
| Colombian coffee | Other export crops | Export flowers | 80 percent shipped to U.S. |

## YOU TRY IT!

Read the following sentences. Then identify the supporting details in a graphic organizer like the one above.

> Caribbean South America is home to some remarkable wildlife. For example, hundreds of bird species, meat-eating fish called piranhas, and crocodiles live in or around the Orinoco River. Colombia has one of the world's highest concentrations of plant and animal species. The country's wildlife includes jaguars, ocelots, and several species of monkeys.
>
> *From Section 1, Physical Geography*

# Using Context Clues

## FOCUS ON READING

One practical way to tackle unfamiliar words you encounter is to look at the context. Reading the words and sentences surrounding the word will often help you because they give definitions, examples, or synonyms. For example, maybe you're not sure what the word *context* means. Just from reading the previous sentences, however, you probably understood that it means the "the part of a text surrounding a word or passage that makes its meaning clear." You have relied on the context to help you define the word. In reading geography, you may forget what some of the geographical terms mean. You can use context clues to figure them out. See how this process works in the example below with the word *tributary*.

The Amazon River is about 4,000 miles long. It extends from the Andes Mountains in Peru to the Atlantic Ocean. Hundreds of tributaries flow into it, draining an area that includes parts of most South American countries.

*From Section 1, Physical Geography*

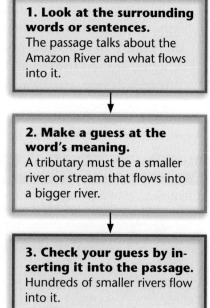

**1. Look at the surrounding words or sentences.**
The passage talks about the Amazon River and what flows into it.

**2. Make a guess at the word's meaning.**
A tributary must be a smaller river or stream that flows into a bigger river.

**3. Check your guess by inserting it into the passage.**
Hundreds of smaller rivers flow into it.

## YOU TRY IT!

Read the following sentences, and then use the three steps described above to help you define *hydroelectric*.

Atlantic South America also has good mineral and energy resources such as gold, silver, copper, iron, and oil. Dams on some of the region's large rivers also provide hydroelectric power.

*From Section 1, Physical Geography*

# Making Inferences

## FOCUS ON READING

Sometimes reading effectively means understanding both what the writer tells you directly and what the writer doesn't tell you. When you fill in the gaps, you are making inferences, or educated guesses. Why worry about what the writer doesn't tell you? Making inferences can help you make connections with the text. It can also give you a fuller picture of the information. To make an inference, think about the text and what you know or can guess from the information. The example below shows you the process.

> At the southern tip of the continent, the Strait of Magellan links the Atlantic and Pacific oceans. A strait is a narrow body of water connecting two larger bodies of water. The large island south of the strait is Tierra del Fuego, or "land of fire."
>
> *From Section 1, Physical Geography*

**1. Determine what the passage says:**
The Strait of Magellan connects the Atlantic and Pacific oceans. There is an island south of it.

↓

**2. Determine what you know about the topic or what you can connect to your experience.**
This sounds like a shortcut to me. It would keep boats from having to sail all the way around the island.

↓

**3. Make an inference.**
Many ships probably use the Strait of Magellan because it is a shortcut.

## YOU TRY IT!

Read the following sentences. Then use the three steps described above to make an inference about the Galápagos Islands.

> Chile and Ecuador both control large islands in the Pacific Ocean. Ecuador's volcanic Galápagos Islands have wildlife not found anywhere else in the world.
>
> *From Section 1, Physical Geography*

# Categorizing

### FOCUS ON READING

When you sort things into groups of similar items, you are categorizing. When you read, categorizing helps you to identify the main groups of information. Then you can find and see the individual facts in each group. Notice how the information in the paragraph below has been sorted into three main groups, with details listed under each group.

> If you were traveling across the United States, you might start on the country's eastern coast. This low area, which is flat and close to sea level, is called the Atlantic Coastal Plain. As you go west, the land gradually rises higher to a region called the Piedmont. The Appalachian Mountains, which are the main mountain range in the East, rise above the Piedmont.

*From Section 1, Physical Geography*

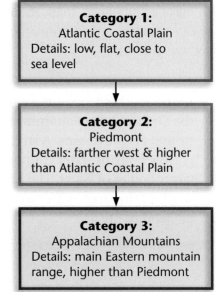

**Category 1:**
Atlantic Coastal Plain
Details: low, flat, close to sea level

**Category 2:**
Piedmont
Details: farther west & higher than Atlantic Coastal Plain

**Category 3:**
Appalachian Mountains
Details: main Eastern mountain range, higher than Piedmont

### YOU TRY IT!

Read the following paragraph, and then use a graphic organizer like the one above to categorize the group and details in the paragraph. Create as many boxes as you need to list the main groups.

> The eastern United States has three climate regions. In the Northeast, people live in a humid continental climate with snowy winters and warm, humid summers. Southerners, on the other hand, experience milder winters and the warm, humid summers of a humid subtropical climate. Most of Florida is warm all year.

*From Section 1, Physical Geography*

# Understanding Lists

## FOCUS ON READING

A to-do list can keep you focused on what you need to get done. Keeping lists while you read can keep you focused on understanding the main points of a text. In the example below, a list helps the reader identify and focus on the types of cold climates found in central and northern Canada.

The farther north you go in Canada, the colder it gets. The coldest areas of Canada are located close to the Arctic Circle. Much of central and northern Canada has a sub-arctic climate. The far north has tundra and ice cap climates. About half of Canada lies in these extremely cold climates.

*From Section 1, Physical Geography*

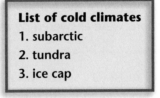

**List of cold climates**
1. subarctic
2. tundra
3. ice cap

## YOU TRY IT!

Read the sentences and then list the territories that make up the Canadian North region.

Northern Canada is extremely cold due to its location close to the Arctic Circle. The region called the Canadian North includes the Yukon Territory, the Northwest Territories, and Nunavut. These three territories cover more than a third of Canada but are home to only about 100,000 people.

*From Section 3, Canada Today*

# Re-reading

## FOCUS ON READING

Have you ever hit the rewind button on the VCR or DVD player because you missed an important scene or didn't quite catch what a character said? As you rewound, you probably asked yourself such questions as, "What did he say?" or "How did she do that?" Taking a second look helped you understand what was going on.

The same idea is true for reading. When you re-read a passage, you can catch details you didn't catch the first time. As you re-read, go slowly and check your understanding by asking yourself questions. In the example below, notice the questions the reader asked. Then see how the questions were answered by re-reading the passage.

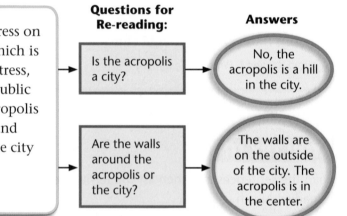

In the center of most city-states was a fortress on a hill. This hill was called the acropolis, which is Greek for "top city." In addition to the fortress, many city-states built temples and other public buildings on the acropolis. Around the acropolis was the rest of the city, including houses and markets. High walls usually surrounded the city for protection.

*From Section 1, Ancient Greece*

**Questions for Re-reading:**

Is the acropolis a city?

Are the walls around the acropolis or the city?

**Answers**

No, the acropolis is a hill in the city.

The walls are on the outside of the city. The acropolis is in the center.

## YOU TRY IT!

Read the following passage, and then develop two questions you can answer as you re-read the passage. Write down the questions and the answers.

When historians talk about the past, they often divide it into three long periods. The first period is the ancient world, the time of the world's earliest civilizations, such as Egypt, China, Greece, and Rome. The last period historians call the modern world, the world since about 1500. Since that time, new ideas and contacts between civilizations changed the world completely. What happened between ancient and modern times? We call this period, which lasted from about 500 until about 1500, the Middle Ages.

*From Section 3, The Middle Ages*

# Understanding Chronological Order

## FOCUS ON READING

History is full of fascinating events. Some of them happen quickly, while others take decades to unfold. Many events overlap. Sometimes it may be challenging to keep the sequence of events straight. One helpful strategy is to identify chronological order or the order in which events happened. Writers use dates or clue words such as *first, next, before, meanwhile,* and *then* to describe the order of events. Notice the words in the following passage that help show the sequence of events.

In **1812** Napoleon led an invasion of Russia. The invasion was a disaster. Bitterly cold weather and smart Russian tactics forced Napoleon's army to retreat. Many French soldiers died. Great Britain, Prussia, and Russia **then** joined forces and in **1814** defeated Napoleon's weakened army. He returned **a year later** with a new army, but was again defeated. The British **then** exiled him to an island, where he died in **1821**.

*From Section 3, Political Change in Europe*

**Time Markers/Dates**
1812
1814
1821

**Clue Words**
then
a year later

| First Event: Napoleon invades Russia. | → | Second Event: Countries join forces and defeat Napoleon. | → | Third Event: Napoleon returns with a new army. | → | Fourth Event: Napoleon exiled to an island and dies. |

## YOU TRY IT!

Read the passage below. Identify the three main events the passage describes and their chronological order. List the clue words or time markers that signal the order of the events.

In 1642 England's power struggle erupted in civil war. Supporters of Parliament forced King Charles I from power. . . A new government then formed, but it was unstable. By 1660 many of the English were tired of instability. They wanted to restore the monarchy. They asked the former king's son to rule England as Charles II.

*From Section 3, Political Change in Europe*

# Using Context Clues—Contrast

## FOCUS ON READING

Maybe you played this game as a young child: "Which of these things is not like the others?" This same game can help you understand new words as you read. Sometimes the words or sentences around a new word will show contrast, or how the word is not like something else. These contrast clues can help you figure out the new word's meaning. Look at how the following passage indicates that *persevered* means something different from *give in*.

> The German air force repeatedly attacked British cities and military targets. Hitler hoped the British would surrender. Rather than give in, however, the British *persevered*.
>
> *From Section 2, World War II*

**Contrast Clues:**

**1. Look for words or sentences that signal contrast.**
Words that signal contrast include *however, rather than, instead of,* and *not*. In this paragraph, the words *rather than* signal the contrast clues for the unfamiliar word *persevered*.

**2. Check the definition by substituting a word or phrase that fits.**
Persevere likely means to keep on trying. *Rather than give in, however, the British kept on trying.*

## YOU TRY IT!

Read the following paragraph, and then use the steps listed above to develop a definition for the word *compete*.

> Some people believed that creating a feeling of community in Europe would make countries less likely to go to war. Leaders like Great Britain's Winston Churchill believed the countries of Europe should cooperate rather than *compete*.
>
> *From Section 3, Europe since 1945*

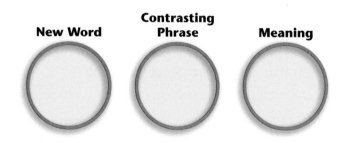

New Word          Contrasting Phrase          Meaning

# Asking Questions

## FOCUS ON READING

Reading is one place where asking questions will never get you in trouble. The five W questions – who, what, when, where, and why – can help you be sure you understand the material you read. After you read a section, ask yourself the 5 Ws: **Who** was this section about? **What** did they do? **When** and **where** did they live? **Why** did they do what they did? See the example below to learn how this reading strategy can help you identify the main points of a passage.

> Many Greeks were not happy under Turkish rule. They wanted to be free of foreign influences. In the early 1800s, they rose up against the Turks. The rebellion seemed likely to fail, but the Greeks received help from other European countries and drove the Turks out. After the rebellion, Greece became a monarchy.
>
> *From Section 2, Greece*

## The 5 Ws

| **Who?** Greeks | **What?** Led rebellion to become independent from Turks | **Where?** Greece | **When?** Early 1800s | **Why?** Wanted to be free of foreign influences |

## YOU TRY IT!

Read the following passage and answer the 5 Ws to check your understanding of it.

> Italy remained divided into small states until the mid-1800s. At that time, a rise in nationalism, or strong patriotic feelings for a country, led people across Italy to fight for unification. As a result of their efforts, Italy became a unified kingdom in 1861.
>
> *From Section 3, Italy*

# Recognizing Word Origins

## FOCUS ON READING

English is a language that loves to borrow words from other languages and cultures. From the French, we took *faceon* and changed it to *fashion*. From the German, we took *strollen* and changed it to *stroll*. From the Dutch, we took *koekje* and changed it to *cookie*. Below is a list of examples of other words that come from other languages.

| English Words from French | English Words from German | English Words from Latin |
|---|---|---|
| conquer | muffin | culture |
| brilliant | dollar | defeat |
| restaurant | rocket | general |
| republic | kindergarten | forces |
| fashion | hamburger | join |
| parliament | noodle | president |
| several | pretzel | elect |
| power | snorkel | control |
| exiled | hex | territory |

## YOU TRY IT!

Read the following sentences. Refer to the above word lists and make a list of the words in the passage below that originally came from other languages. After each word, list the original language.

> A few years later a brilliant general named Napoleon took power. In time, he conquered much of Europe. Then in 1815 several European powers joined forces and defeated Napoleon. They exiled him and chose a new king to rule France.
>
> France is now a republic with a parliament and an elected president. France still controls several overseas territories, such as Martinique in the West Indies.
>
> *From Section 2, France and the Benelux Countries*

# Using Context Clues—Synonyms

## FOCUS ON READING

You have probably discovered that geography is a subject with many new words and terms. What if you don't remember or don't know what a word means? You may be able to use context clues to determine its meaning. Context clues are words near the unfamiliar word that indicate its meaning.

One helpful context clue is the synonym—words or phrases that mean the same as the new word. Look for synonyms in the words and sentences surrounding an unfamiliar term. Synonyms can help you understand the meaning of the new word. They may come in the same sentence or in the sentence following the words they define. Notice how the following passage uses synonyms to define the word *urban*.

> Most Swedes live in the southern part of the country in large towns and cities. In fact, more than 80 percent of Swedes live in *urban* areas. Stockholm, Sweden's capital and largest city, is located on the east coast near the Baltic Sea.
>
> *From Section 3, Scandinavia*

**1. Look for words or phrases that mean the same thing.**
The first sentence uses the phrase large towns and cities to describe where most Swedes live.

**2. Substitute the synonym for the new word to confirm its meaning.**
More than 80 percent of Swedes live in large towns and cities.

## YOU TRY IT!

As you read the following sentences, look for synonyms that mean the same as the italicized words. Then use a graphic organizer like the one below to define each italicized word.

> Slow-moving sheets of ice, or *glaciers*, have left their mark on Northern Europe's coastlines and lakes.
>
> As the glaciers flowed slowly downhill, they carved long, winding channels, or *fjords*, into Norway's coastline.
>
> *From Section 1, Physical Geography*

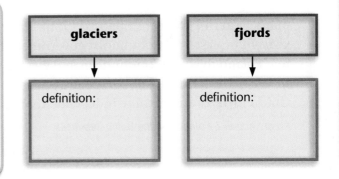

# Understanding Problems and Solutions

## FOCUS ON READING

Throughout history, people have faced problems and found solutions to them. As a result, writers who describe historical events often structure their writing by identifying a problem and then describing its solution. The ability to identify this pattern of writing will help you understand what you read. Notice how the following passage presents one problem with a two-pronged solution.

Estonia, Latvia, Lithuania, and Poland all still suffer from decades of Soviet rule. Under the Soviets, the economies of all four countries suffered.

Today, Poland and the Baltic Republics are working to rebuild and strengthen their economies. They are replacing the old and outdated factories built by the Soviets with new ones that take advantage of modern technology.

To further their economic growth, the countries of this region are also seeking new sources of income. One area in which they have found success is tourism.

*From Section 2, Poland and the Baltic Republics*

**Problem:**
Poor economies from Soviet rule

**Solution #1:**
Building new factories

**Solution #2:**
New source of income through tourism

## YOU TRY IT!

Read the following passage, and then use the process shown above to identify the problems and solutions the writer presents. Create as many boxes as you need.

Many Eastern Europeans opposed Communist rule. After years of protest, the Communist government in the region fell. Poland rejected Communism and elected new leaders in 1989. The Baltic Republics broke away from the Soviet Union in 1991 and became independent once more.

*From Section 2, Poland and the Baltic Republics*

# Making Generalizations

## FOCUS ON READING

As you read about different people and cultures, you probably realize that people share some similarities. Seeing those similarities may lead you to make a generalization. A generalization is a broad, general idea drawn from new information combined with what you already know, such as your own experience. Notice how this process works with the following passage.

> Russians sometimes joke that winter lasts for 12 months and then summer begins. Russia is a cold country. The reason is its northern location partly within the Arctic Circle. In general, Russia has short summers and long, snowy winters. The climate is milder west of the Urals and grows colder and harsher as one goes north and east.
>
> *From Section 1, Physical Geography*

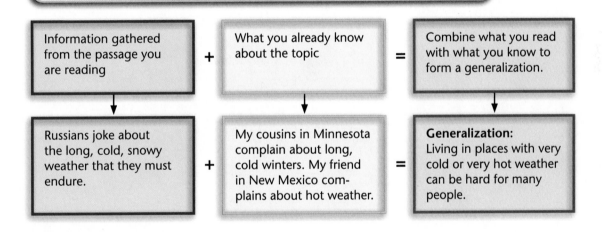

| Information gathered from the passage you are reading | + | What you already know about the topic | = | Combine what you read with what you know to form a generalization. |
|---|---|---|---|---|
| Russians joke about the long, cold, snowy weather that they must endure. | + | My cousins in Minnesota complain about long, cold winters. My friend in New Mexico complains about hot weather. | = | **Generalization:** Living in places with very cold or very hot weather can be hard for many people. |

## YOU TRY IT!

Read the following passage. Using the process described above, form a general idea about holidays. Write your generalization in one sentence.

> Russian history has shaped its customs, such as holidays. Religious holidays, like Easter and Christmas, are popular. The main family holiday is New Year's Eve. To celebrate this holiday, families decorate a tree where, according to Russian folklore, Grandfather Frost and his helper the Snow Maiden leave gifts. A newer holiday is Russian Independence Day, which marks the end of the Soviet Union on June 12.
>
> *From Section 2, History and Culture of Russia*

# United States: Physical

ATLAS

45°N

40°N

35°N

30°N

125°W

120°W

Strait of Juan de Fuca

Puget Sound

Mount Rainier
14,410 ft
(4,392 m)

Cape Mendocino

COAST RANGES

CASCADE RANGE

Columbia River

Klamath River

Goose Lake

Shasta Lake

Pyramid Lake

SIERRA NEVADA

Central Valley

Sacramento River

San Joaquin River

Lake Tahoe

Mount Whitney
14,494 ft
(4,419 m)

Death Valley

Mojave Desert

Coast Ranges

San Francisco Bay

Monterey Bay

PACIFIC OCEAN

Channel Islands

Salton Sea

Imperial Valley

Colorado River

Lake Mead

Grand Canyon

Franklin D. Roosevelt Lake

Pend Oreille Lake

Clark Fork

Flathead Lake

Bitterroot Range

Salmon River Range

Salmon River Mts.

Sawtooth Mts.

CONTINENTAL

Columbia Plateau

Snake River

LEWIS Range

ROCKY

Grand Tetons

Gannett Peak
13,804 ft
(4,207 m)

Wasatch Range

GREAT BASIN

Great Salt Lake

Utah Lake

Uinta Mts.

Green River

COLORADO

PLATEAU

Lake Powell

San Juan River

Painted Desert

Gila River

Sonoran Desert

Milk River

Missouri River

Fort Peck Lake

Yellowstone River

Yellowstone Lake

Bighorn Mts.

Bighorn River

Wind River Range

Wind River

Powder River

MOUNTAINS

Colorado River

Mount Elbert
14,433 ft
(4,400 m)

DIVIDE

Front Range

South Platte River

Pikes Peak
14,110 ft
(4,301 m)

San Luis Valley

Sangre De Cristo Mts.

DIVIDE

CONTINENTAL

Rio Grande

GREAT

Lake Sakakawea

Lake Oahe

Black Hills

Cheyenne River

White River

Niobrara River

North Platte River

Platte River

Republican River

Smoky Hill River

INTERIOR

PLAINS

Canadian River

Pecos River

Amistad Reservoir

Rio Grande

Nueces River

Colorado River

MEXICO

To understand the relative locations of Alaska and Hawaii, as well as the vast distances separating them from the rest of the United States, see the world map.

22°N

Kauai

Niihau

Oahu

HAWAII

Molokai

PACIFIC OCEAN

Lanai

Maui

Kahoolawe

Mauna Kea
13,796 ft
(4,206 m)

Hawaii

19°N

0    75    150 Miles
0    75    150 Kilometers
Projection: Mercator

ARCTIC OCEAN

RUSSIA

Bering Strait

Arctic Circle

BROOKS RANGE

Yukon River

St. Lawrence Island

St. Matthew Island

Nunivak Island

Kuskokwim River

ALASKA

Tanana River

RANGE

Mount McKinley
20,320 ft
(6,194 m)

CANADA

Bering Sea

Attu Island

ALEUTIAN ISLANDS

PACIFIC OCEAN

Kodiak Island

Gulf of Alaska

Alexander Archipelago

Gulf of California

0    250    500 Miles
0    250    500 Kilometers
Projection: Albers Equal Area

CANADA

Red River

Mesabi Range

Isle Royale

Lake Superior

Minnesota River

Mississippi River

Wisconsin River

Lake Michigan

Lake Huron

St. Lawrence River

St. Lawrence Seaway

Maine

Longfellow Mts.

Penobscot R.

Lake Champlain

Green Mts.

White Mts.

Connecticut River

Massachusetts

Cape Cod

Adirondack Mts.

Lake Ontario

New York

Catskill Mts.

PLATEAU

Allegheny R.

Susquehanna River

Pennsylvania

MOUNTAINS

Lake Erie

Long Island Sound

Long Island

40°N

Des Moines River

Missouri River

Illinois River

Wabash River

Indiana

Ohio

Scioto River

Ohio

Monongahela R.

Potomac River

ALLEGHENY

Kanawha River

Delaware River

Delaware Bay

Delaware

Maryland

Kansas R.

PLAINS

River

James River

Chesapeake Bay

ATLANTIC OCEAN

70°W

Lake of the Ozarks

OZARK PLATEAU

White River

Lake Barkley

Cumberland River

APPALACHIAN MOUNTAINS

Roanoke River

Pamlico Sound

Cape Hatteras

35°N

Keystone Lake

Arkansas River

Kentucky Lake

Cumberland River

Cumberland Plateau

Great Smoky Mts.

BLUE RIDGE MOUNTAINS

PIEDMONT

Eufaula Lake

Ouachita Mts.

Tennessee River

Lake Texoma

Trinity River

Saline River

Red River

Tombigbee River

Coosa River

Oconee River

Savannah River

Altamaha River

ELEVATION

| Feet | | Meters |
|---|---|---|
| 13,120 | | 4,000 |
| 6,560 | | 2,000 |
| 1,640 | | 500 |
| 656 | | 200 |
| (Sea level) 0 | | 0 (Sea level) |
| Below sea level | | Below sea level |

Mississippi River

Pearl River

Alabama R.

Chattahoochee River

PLAIN

Sea Islands

0          100          200 Miles
0     100     200 Kilometers

Projection: Albers Equal Area

Toledo Bend Reservoir

GULF

COASTAL

Chandeleur Islands

Mississippi Delta

Okefenokee Swamp

N
W        E
S

FLORIDA PENINSULA

Cape Canaveral

Gulf of Mexico

Lake Okeechobee

BAHAMAS

25°N

The Everglades

Cape Sable

Florida Keys

Straits of Florida

75°W

80°W

85°W

90°W

95°W

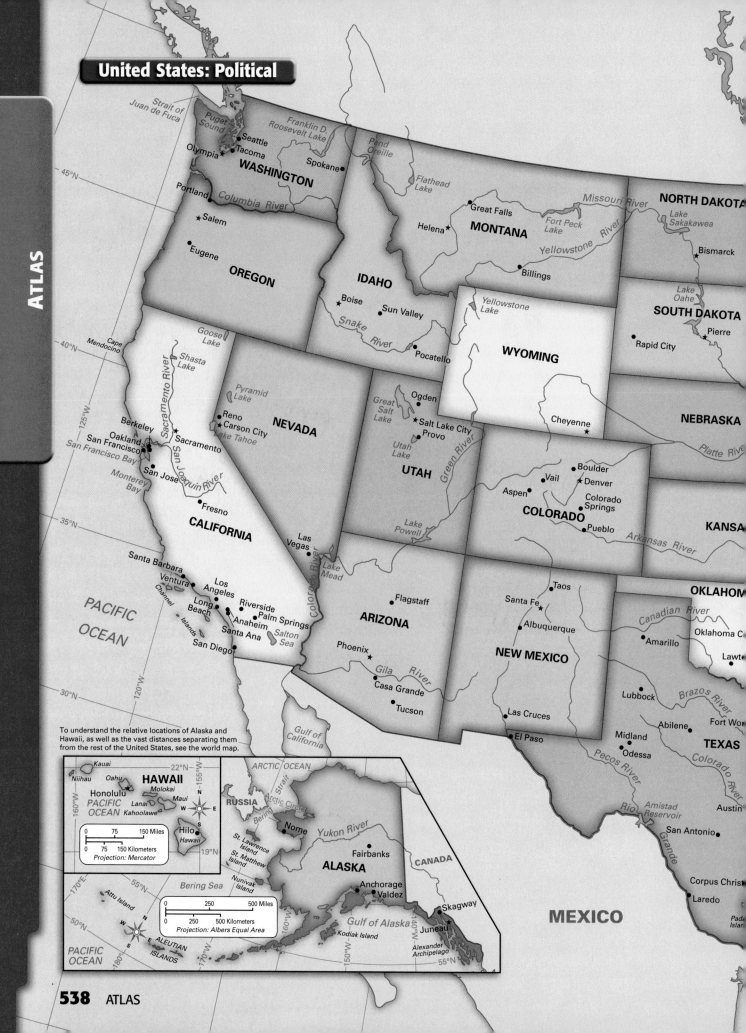

ATLAS

Strait of Juan de Fuca

Puget Sound
Seattle
Olympia ★ Tacoma
Franklin D. Roosevelt Lake
Spokane
**WASHINGTON**
Pend Oreille
Flathead Lake

45°N

Portland
Columbia River
★ Salem
**OREGON**
Eugene

Great Falls
Helena ★ **MONTANA**
Fort Peck Lake
Missouri River
Yellowstone River
Billings

**NORTH DAKOTA**
Lake Sakakawea
Bismarck

Boise ★
Sun Valley
**IDAHO**
Snake River
Pocatello

Yellowstone Lake
**WYOMING**
Cheyenne ★

**SOUTH DAKOTA**
Lake Oahe
Pierre ★
Rapid City

40°N
Cape Mendocino

Goose Lake
Shasta Lake
Sacramento River

Pyramid Lake
Reno ●
Carson City ●
Lake Tahoe
**NEVADA**

Great Salt Lake
Ogden ●
Salt Lake City ★
Provo
Utah Lake

Green River
**UTAH**

Aspen ●
Vail ●
Boulder ●
★ Denver
Colorado Springs ●
**COLORADO**
Pueblo ●

**NEBRASKA**
Platte River

125°W

Berkeley
Oakland ●
San Francisco ●
San Francisco Bay
San Jose ●
★ Sacramento
San Joaquin River
Monterey Bay

Fresno ●

35°N
**CALIFORNIA**

Las Vegas ●
Lake Mead
Colorado River

Lake Powell

Flagstaff ●
**ARIZONA**

Taos ●
Santa Fe ★
Albuquerque ●
**NEW MEXICO**

Canadian River
**OKLAHOMA**
Oklahoma C
Lawt

**KANSA**
Arkansas River

Santa Barbara ●
Ventura ●
Los Angeles ●
Long Beach ●
Anaheim ●
Santa Ana ●
San Diego ●
Riverside ●
Palm Springs ●
Salton Sea
Channel Islands

**PACIFIC OCEAN**

120°W

Phoenix ★
Casa Grande ●
Gila River
Tucson ●

Las Cruces ●
El Paso ●

Amarillo ●
Lubbock ●
Abilene ●
Midland ●
Odessa ●
Fort Wo
**TEXAS**
Brazos River
Colorado River
Pecos River

30°N

Gulf of California

Amistad Reservoir
Rio Grande
San Antonio ●
Austin

To understand the relative locations of Alaska and Hawaii, as well as the vast distances separating them from the rest of the United States, see the world map.

Kauai
Niihau
Oahu
Honolulu ★
**HAWAII**
Molokai
Maui
22°N
Lanai
Kahoolawe
**PACIFIC OCEAN**
160°W
Hilo ●
Hawaii
19°N

**ARCTIC OCEAN**
Strait
Arctic Circle
RUSSIA
Bering Strait
155°W

0   75   150 Miles
0   75   150 Kilometers
Projection: Mercator

Bering Sea
170°E
Attu Island
55°N

0   250   500 Miles
0   250   500 Kilometers
Projection: Albers Equal Area

St. Lawrence Island
St. Matthew Island
Nunivak Island

Nome ●
Yukon River
Fairbanks ●
**ALASKA**
Anchorage ●
Valdez ●
**CANADA**

Skagway ●
Juneau ★
Alexander Archipelago
55°N

Kodiak Island
Gulf of Alaska

50°N
180°
ALEUTIAN ISLANDS
170°W
160°W
150°W
140°W

**PACIFIC OCEAN**

Corpus Christ
Laredo ●

**MEXICO**

Pad
Islan

CANADA

MINNESOTA

Grand Forks

Red River

Fargo

Duluth

Lake Superior

Marquette

Sault Ste. Marie

MICHIGAN

Superior

WISCONSIN

Green Bay

Lake Huron

Lake Michigan

MAINE

Augusta

Lake Champlain

Burlington

Montpelier

Portland

VT

NH

Concord

Manchester

St. Lawrence River

Hudson River

Connecticut R.

Minneapolis

St. Paul

Madison

Milwaukee

Minnesota River

Grand Rapids

Lansing

Saginaw

Detroit

Ann Arbor

Lake Ontario

Rochester

Syracuse

Albany

Springfield

Boston

MA

Worcester

Providence

Cape Cod

Sioux Falls

Sioux City

IOWA

Cedar Rapids

Davenport

Des Moines

Mississippi River

Rockford

Chicago

South Bend

Gary

Fort Wayne

Toledo

Cleveland

Lake Erie

Buffalo

NEW YORK

Hartford

CT

RI

Bridgeport

New Haven

Long Island Sound

Jersey City

Yonkers

Long Island

Newark

New York City

40°N

Missouri River

naha

coln

Peoria

INDIANA

Springfield

ILLINOIS

Indianapolis

Illinois River

OHIO

Columbus

Dayton

Cincinnati

Youngstown

Akron

PENNSYLVANIA

Pittsburgh

Harrisburg

Allentown

Trenton

Camden

Philadelphia

NJ

Atlantic City

Susquehanna River

MISSOURI

peka

Kansas City

Kansas City

St. Louis

East St. Louis

Jefferson City

Lake of the Ozarks

Louisville

Evansville

Frankfort

Lexington

Ohio River

KENTUCKY

WEST VIRGINIA

Charleston

Baltimore

Washington, D.C.

MD

Annapolis

Dover

DE

VIRGINIA

Richmond

Newport News

Norfolk

Virginia Beach

Chesapeake Bay

Delaware Bay

ATLANTIC OCEAN

70°W

35°N

chita

Keystone Lake

Tulsa

Fayetteville

Lake Barkley

Kentucky Lake

Nashville

Mississippi River

TENNESSEE

Chattanooga

Knoxville

Asheville

Winston-Salem

Greensboro

Durham

Raleigh

Charlotte

NORTH CAROLINA

Cape Hatteras

faula Lake

ARKANSAS

Little Rock

Pine Bluff

Memphis

Huntsville

Greenville

SOUTH CAROLINA

Columbia

Charleston

Lake Texoma

Dallas

Shreveport

Red River

MISSISSIPPI

Vicksburg

Jackson

Meridian

ALABAMA

Birmingham

Montgomery

Columbus

GEORGIA

Macon

Atlanta

Savannah

Savannah River

Chattahoochee R.

Sea Islands

30°N

Waco

Toledo Bend Reservoir

LOUISIANA

Baton Rouge

Biloxi

Mobile

Pensacola

Tallahassee

Gainesville

Jacksonville

Beaumont

Houston

New Orleans

Chandeleur Islands

Galveston

Gulf of Mexico

N

W

E

S

FLORIDA

Orlando

Tampa

St. Petersburg

Lake Okeechobee

Cape Canaveral

80°W

BAHAMAS

25°N

Fort Myers

Fort Lauderdale

Miami

Cape Sable

Florida Keys

Straits of Florida

75°W

| Legend | |
|---|---|
| ✪ | National capital |
| ★ | State capitals |
| ● | Other cities |

0   100   200 Miles

0   100   200 Kilometers

Projection: Albers Equal Area

95°W   90°W   85°W

ATLAS

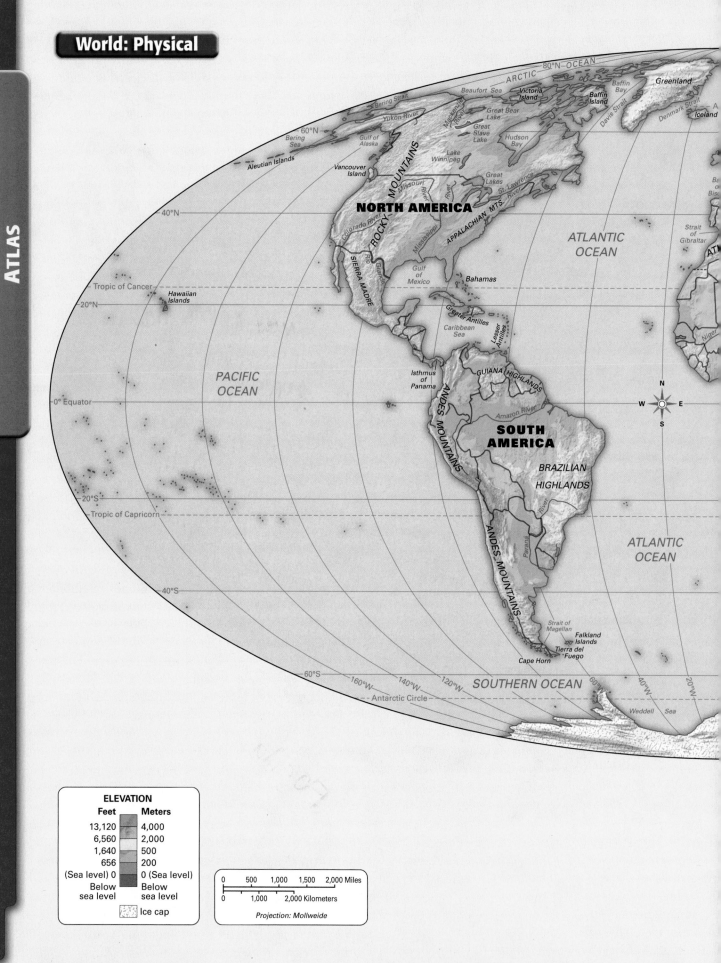

ARCTIC 80°N OCEAN
Greenland
Beaufort Sea
Victoria Island
Baffin Bay
Baffin Island
Davis Strait
Denmark Strait
Iceland
Bering Strait
Yukon River
Great Bear Lake
Mackenzie River
Great Slave Lake
Hudson Bay
60°N
Bering Sea
Gulf of Alaska
Aleutian Islands
Lake Winnipeg
Vancouver Island
Great Lakes
St. Lawrence River
NORTH AMERICA
40°N
ROCKY MOUNTAINS
Missouri River
Mississippi River
APPALACHIAN MTS.
ATLANTIC OCEAN
Strait of Gibraltar
Colorado River
SIERRA MADRE
Rio Grande
Gulf of Mexico
Bahamas
Tropic of Cancer
Hawaiian Islands
20°N
Greater Antilles
Caribbean Sea
Lesser Antilles
Niger
PACIFIC OCEAN
Isthmus of Panama
GUIANA HIGHLANDS
N
W  E
S
0° Equator
ANDES MOUNTAINS
Amazon River
SOUTH AMERICA
BRAZILIAN HIGHLANDS
20°S
Tropic of Capricorn
Paraná River
ATLANTIC OCEAN
40°S
ANDES MOUNTAINS
60°S
160°W
140°W
120°W
Strait of Magellan
Falkland Islands
Tierra del Fuego
Cape Horn
SOUTHERN OCEAN
60°W
40°W
20°W
Antarctic Circle
Weddell Sea

**ELEVATION**

| Feet | | Meters |
|---|---|---|
| 13,120 | | 4,000 |
| 6,560 | | 2,000 |
| 1,640 | | 500 |
| 656 | | 200 |
| (Sea level) 0 | | 0 (Sea level) |
| Below sea level | | Below sea level |

Ice cap

0    500    1,000    1,500    2,000 Miles
0         1,000         2,000 Kilometers

*Projection: Mollweide*

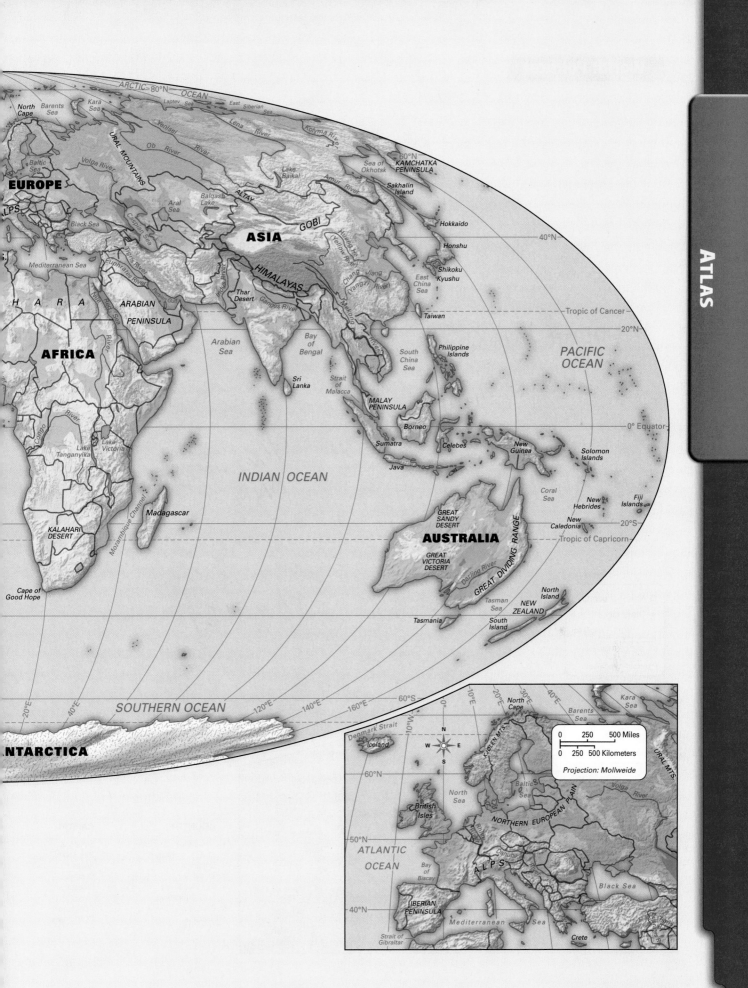

North Cape
Barents Sea
Kara Sea
ARCTIC—80°N OCEAN
Laptev Sea
East Siberian Sea
Baltic Sea
EUROPE
LPS
Volga River
URAL MOUNTAINS
Ob River
Yenisei River
Lena River
Kolyma River
60°N
Sea of Okhotsk
KAMCHATKA PENINSULA
Black Sea
Aral Sea
Caspian Sea
Balqash Lake
ALTAY
Lake Baikal
Amur River
Sakhalin Island
Mediterranean Sea
ASIA
GOBI
Hokkaido
40°N
S A H A R A
Tigris River
Euphrates River
Persian Gulf
HIMALAYAS
Indus River
Huang He (Yellow River)
Chang Jiang (Yangzi River)
Honshu
Shikoku
Kyushu
ARABIAN PENINSULA
Nile River
Red Sea
Thar Desert
Ganges River
Mekong River
East China Sea
Taiwan
Tropic of Cancer
AFRICA
Arabian Sea
Bay of Bengal
South China Sea
Philippine Islands
20°N
PACIFIC OCEAN
Congo River
Sri Lanka
Strait of Malacca
MALAY PENINSULA
Lake Tanganyika
Lake Victoria
Borneo
0° Equator
Sumatra
Celebes
New Guinea
Solomon Islands
Java
INDIAN OCEAN
Coral Sea
New Hebrides
Fiji Islands
Madagascar
Mozambique Channel
GREAT SANDY DESERT
GREAT DIVIDING RANGE
New Caledonia
20°S
KALAHARI DESERT
AUSTRALIA
Tropic of Capricorn
GREAT VICTORIA DESERT
Darling River
North Island
Cape of Good Hope
Tasman Sea
NEW ZEALAND
Tasmania
South Island
SOUTHERN OCEAN
60°S
20°E
40°E
120°E
140°E
160°E
NTARCTICA

Denmark Strait
Iceland
North Cape
Kara Sea
10°E
20°E
30°E
40°E
KJØLEN MTS.
Barents Sea
URAL MTS.
0 250 500 Miles
0 250 500 Kilometers
Projection: Mollweide
60°N
ATLANTIC OCEAN
British Isles
North Sea
Baltic Sea
Volga River
NORTHERN EUROPEAN PLAIN
50°N
Bay of Biscay
Danube
ALPS
Black Sea
40°N
IBERIAN PENINSULA
Mediterranean Sea
Crete
Strait of Gibraltar
N
W E
S

ATLAS

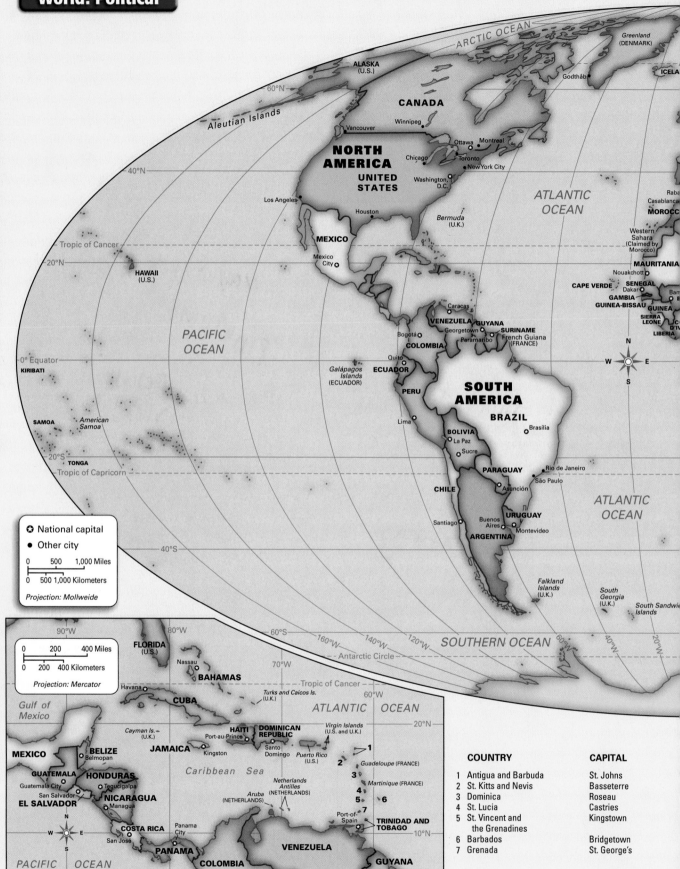

ARCTIC OCEAN

Greenland
(DENMARK)

ALASKA
(U.S.)

ICELA

Godthåb

60°N

Aleutian Islands

CANADA

Winnipeg

Vancouver

Ottawa    Montreal

NORTH
AMERICA

Chicago    Toronto

40°N

UNITED
STATES

Washington,
D.C.

New York City

ATLANTIC
OCEAN

Raba

Casablanca

MOROCC

Los Angeles

Houston

Bermuda
(U.K.)

Western
Sahara
(Claimed by
Morocco)

MEXICO

Tropic of Cancer

20°N

Mexico
City

MAURITANIA

Nouakchott

HAWAII
(U.S.)

CAPE VERDE

SENEGAL
Dakar

Ban

GAMBIA
GUINEA-BISSAU

GUINEA

Caracas

VENEZUELA    GUYANA

SIERRA
LEONE

C

D'IV

PACIFIC
OCEAN

Bogotá

Georgetown    SURINAME

LIBERIA

COLOMBIA

Paramaribo    French Guiana
(FRANCE)

Quito

N

0° Equator

KIRIBATI

Galápagos
Islands
(ECUADOR)

ECUADOR

W        E

PERU

Lima

SOUTH
AMERICA

S

SAMOA

American
Samoa

BRAZIL

Brasília

BOLIVIA

20°S

TONGA

La Paz

Sucre

Tropic of Capricorn

Rio de Janeiro

PARAGUAY

São Paulo

ATLANTIC
OCEAN

CHILE

Asunción

URUGUAY

Santiago

Buenos
Aires

Montevideo

40°S

ARGENTINA

Falkland
Islands
(U.K.)

South
Georgia
(U.K.)

South Sandwie
Islands

60°S

160°W    140°W    120°W

SOUTHERN OCEAN

60°

40°

20°

Antarctic Circle

⊗ National capital

● Other city

0    500    1,000 Miles

0    500 1,000 Kilometers

Projection: Mollweide

90°W        80°W

FLORIDA
(U.S.)

70°W

0    200    400 Miles

Nassau

Tropic of Cancer

60°W

0    200    400 Kilometers

BAHAMAS

Turks and Caicos Is.
(U.K.)

ATLANTIC    OCEAN

Projection: Mercator

Havana

20°N

Gulf of
Mexico

CUBA

Virgin Islands
(U.S. and U.K.)

Cayman Is.
(U.K.)

HAITI    DOMINICAN
REPUBLIC

1

MEXICO    BELIZE

Port-au-Prince

2

Guadeloupe (FRANCE)

Belmopan

JAMAICA

Santo
Domingo

3

GUATEMALA    HONDURAS

Kingston

Caribbean Sea

Puerto Rico
(U.S.)

Martinique (FRANCE)

4

Guatemala City    Tegucigalpa

Netherlands
Antilles
(NETHERLANDS)

5    6

San Salvador

NICARAGUA

Aruba
(NETHERLANDS)

7

EL SALVADOR

Managua

Port-of-
Spain

Panama

TRINIDAD AND
TOBAGO

COSTA RICA

City

10°N

San José

PANAMA

VENEZUELA

PACIFIC    OCEAN

COLOMBIA

GUYANA

| COUNTRY | CAPITAL |
|---|---|
| 1 Antigua and Barbuda | St. Johns |
| 2 St. Kitts and Nevis | Basseterre |
| 3 Dominica | Roseau |
| 4 St. Lucia | Castries |
| 5 St. Vincent and the Grenadines | Kingstown |
| 6 Barbados | Bridgetown |
| 7 Grenada | St. George's |

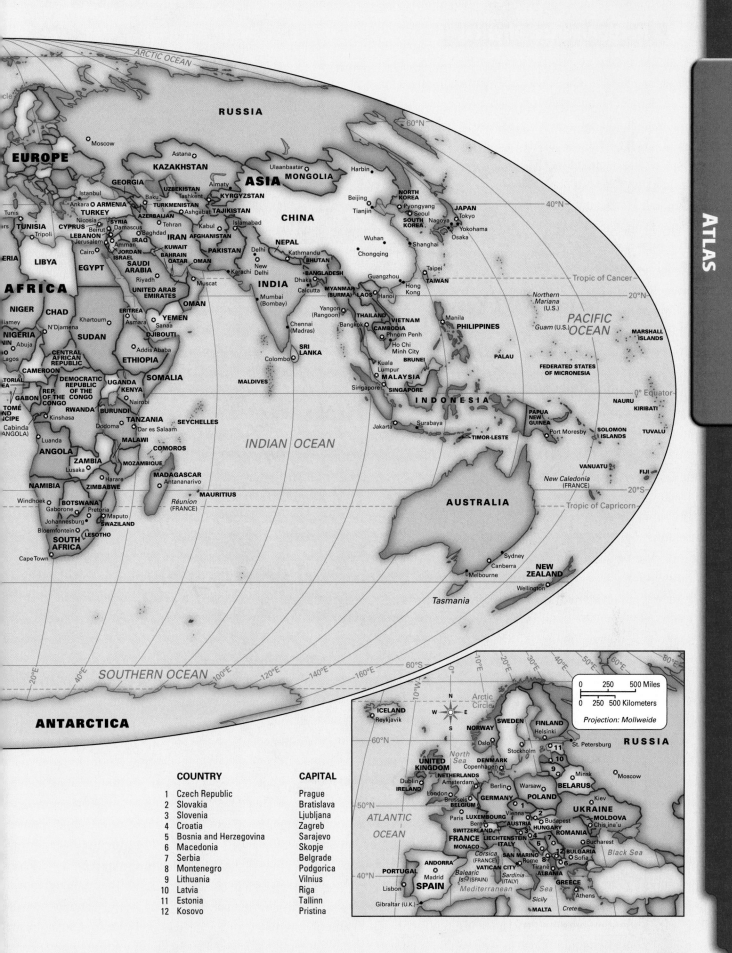

ARCTIC OCEAN

RUSSIA

EUROPE
Moscow

ASIA

KAZAKHSTAN
Astana
Ulaanbaatar
MONGOLIA
Harbin

GEORGIA
Istanbul
ARMENIA
Ankara
TURKEY
Nicosia
CYPRUS
LEBANON
Beirut
Damascus
SYRIA
Baku
AZERBAIJAN
TURKMENISTAN
Ashgabat
UZBEKISTAN
Tashkent
Almaty
KYRGYZSTAN
TAJIKISTAN
Beijing
Tianjin
NORTH
KOREA
Pyongyang
Seoul
SOUTH
KOREA
JAPAN
Tokyo
Nagoya
Yokohama
Osaka

Tunis
TUNISIA
Tripoli
ERIA
LIBYA
EGYPT
Cairo
Jerusalem
ISRAEL
JORDAN
Amman
IRAQ
Baghdad
KUWAIT
BAHRAIN
QATAR
SAUDI
ARABIA
Riyadh
Tehran
IRAN
Kabul
AFGHANISTAN
Islamabad
PAKISTAN
Delhi
New
Delhi
NEPAL
Kathmandu
BHUTAN
CHINA
Wuhan
Chongqing
Shanghai
Taipei
TAIWAN
Hong
Kong
Guangzhou

AFRICA
NIGER
CHAD
iamey
NIGERIA
BENIN
Abuja
Lagos
CAMEROON
TORIAL
EA
GABON
TOMÉ
AND
ICIPE
Kinshasa
DEMOCRATIC
REPUBLIC
OF THE
CONGO
REP. OF
THE
CONGO
Cabinda
(ANGOLA)
Luanda
ANGOLA
NAMIBIA
Windhoek
SUDAN
Khartoum
N'Djamena
CENTRAL
AFRICAN
REPUBLIC
ERITREA
Asmara
DJIBOUTI
Addis Ababa
ETHIOPIA
UGANDA
KENYA
Nairobi
RWANDA
BURUNDI
TANZANIA
Dodoma
Dar es Salaam
SOMALIA
SEYCHELLES
MALAWI
COMOROS
MOZAMBIQUE
ZAMBIA
Lusaka
MADAGASCAR
Antananarivo
ZIMBABWE
Harare
MAURITIUS
Réunion
(FRANCE)

UNITED ARAB
EMIRATES
Muscat
OMAN
YEMEN
Sanaa
Karachi
Muscat
Mumbai
(Bombay)
INDIA
Chennai
(Madras)
Calcutta
Dhaka
BANGLADESH
MYANMAR
(BURMA)
Yangon
(Rangoon)
LAOS
Hanoi
Bangkok
THAILAND
CAMBODIA
Phnom Penh
VIETNAM
Ho Chi
Minh City
SRI
LANKA
Colombo
MALDIVES
Kuala
Lumpur
MALAYSIA
Singapore
SINGAPORE
BRUNEI
Manila
PHILIPPINES
Guam (U.S.)
PALAU
Northern
Mariana
(U.S.)
PACIFIC
OCEAN
MARSHALL
ISLANDS
FEDERATED STATES
OF MICRONESIA
NAURU
KIRIBATI

Tropic of Cancer
20°N
0° Equator

INDONESIA
Jakarta
Surabaya
TIMOR-LESTE
PAPUA
NEW
GUINEA
Port Moresby
SOLOMON
ISLANDS
TUVALU
VANUATU
FIJI
New Caledonia
(FRANCE)

INDIAN OCEAN

20°S
Tropic of Capricorn

BOTSWANA
Gaborone
Pretoria
Johannesburg
Maputo
SWAZILAND
Bloemfontein
LESOTHO
SOUTH
AFRICA
Cape Town

AUSTRALIA
Sydney
Canberra
Melbourne
NEW
ZEALAND
Wellington
Tasmania

SOUTHERN OCEAN
20°E  40°E  100°E  120°E  140°E  160°E  60°S

ANTARCTICA

| COUNTRY | CAPITAL |
|---------|---------|
| 1 Czech Republic | Prague |
| 2 Slovakia | Bratislava |
| 3 Slovenia | Ljubljana |
| 4 Croatia | Zagreb |
| 5 Bosnia and Herzegovina | Sarajevo |
| 6 Macedonia | Skopje |
| 7 Serbia | Belgrade |
| 8 Montenegro | Podgorica |
| 9 Lithuania | Vilnius |
| 10 Latvia | Riga |
| 11 Estonia | Tallinn |
| 12 Kosovo | Pristina |

ATLAS

0  250  500 Miles
0  250  500 Kilometers
Projection: Mollweide

ICELAND
Reykjavik
Arctic
Circle
SWEDEN
FINLAND
Helsinki
NORWAY
Oslo
Stockholm
St. Petersburg
RUSSIA
60°N
UNITED
KINGDOM
Dublin
IRELAND
London
NETHERLANDS
Amsterdam
DENMARK
Copenhagen
Berlin
Warsaw
POLAND
Minsk
BELARUS
Moscow
Brussels
BELGIUM
GERMANY
Paris
LUXEMBOURG
Kiev
UKRAINE
50°N
FRANCE
Bern
SWITZERLAND
Vienna
AUSTRIA
LIECHTENSTEIN
Budapest
HUNGARY
ROMANIA
MOLDOVA
Chișinău
Bucharest
ATLANTIC
OCEAN
MONACO
Corsica
(FRANCE)
SAN MARINO
ITALY
Rome
VATICAN CITY
BULGARIA
Sofia
Black
Sea
ANDORRA
PORTUGAL
Lisbon
Madrid
SPAIN
Balearic
Is. (SPAIN)
Sardinia
(ITALY)
Tirané
ALBANIA
GREECE
Athens
40°N
Gibraltar (U.K.)
Mediterranean
Sea
Sicily
MALTA
Crete
North
Sea

ATLAS   543

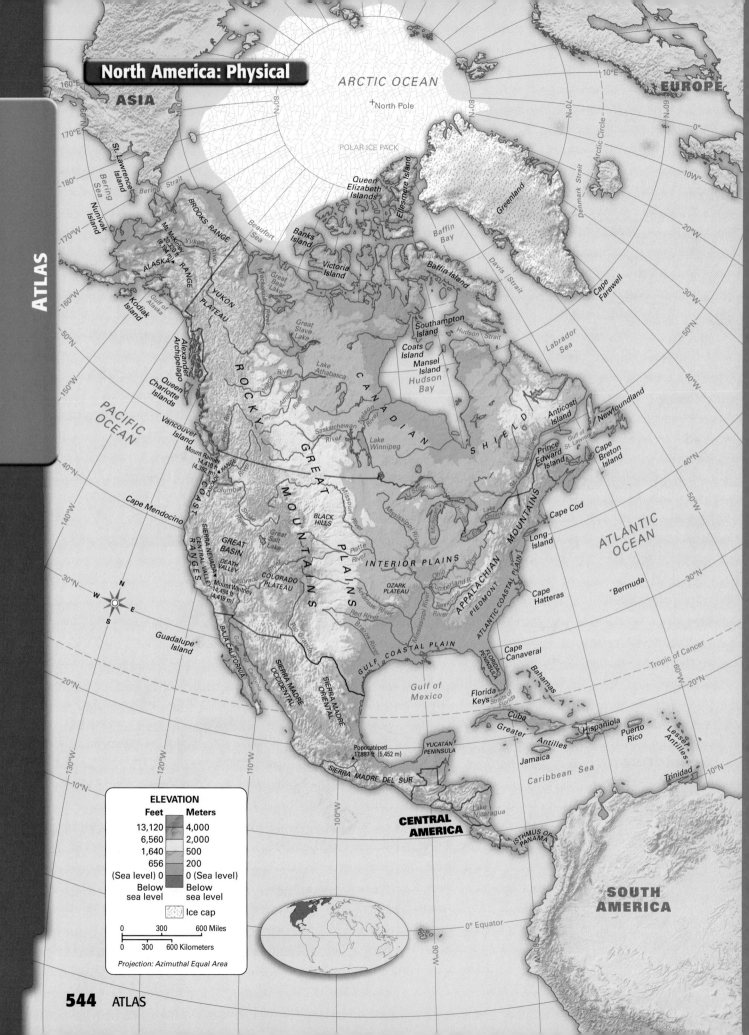

ARCTIC OCEAN

+ North Pole

EUROPE

ASIA

ATLAS

POLAR ICE PACK

St. Lawrence Island

Bering Strait

Bering Sea

Nunivak Island

BROOKS RANGE

Mt. McKinley 20,320 ft (6,194 m)

Yukon River

ALASKA RANGE

Kodiak Island

Gulf of Alaska

Alexander Archipelago

Queen Charlotte Islands

Vancouver Island

PACIFIC OCEAN

Cape Mendocino

COAST RANGES

CASCADE RANGE

Mount Rainier 14,410 ft (4,392 m)

Columbia River

Snake River

SIERRA NEVADA

CENTRAL VALLEY

GREAT BASIN

DEATH VALLEY

Mount Whitney 14,494 ft (4,419 m)

Great Salt Lake

COLORADO PLATEAU

Colorado River

Guadalupe Island

BAJA CALIFORNIA

Gulf of California

SIERRA MADRE OCCIDENTAL

SIERRA MADRE ORIENTAL

Rio Grande

Brazos River

Red River

Popocatépetl 17,887 ft (5,452 m)

SIERRA MADRE DEL SUR

YUCATÁN PENINSULA

YUKON PLATEAU

Mackenzie River

Great Bear Lake

Great Slave Lake

Lake Athabasca

Peace River

Athabasca River

Fraser River

ROCKY MOUNTAINS

Saskatchewan River

Nelson River

Lake Winnipeg

BLACK HILLS

Missouri River

Platte River

GREAT PLAINS

INTERIOR PLAINS

Arkansas River

Ohio River

OZARK PLATEAU

Tennessee River

Cumberland R.

Mississippi River

GULF COASTAL PLAIN

Gulf of Mexico

Queen Elizabeth Islands

Beaufort Sea

Banks Island

Victoria Island

Ellesmere Island

Greenland

Baffin Bay

Baffin Island

Davis Strait

Cape Farewell

Southampton Island

Coats Island

Mansel Island

Hudson Bay

Hudson Strait

CANADIAN SHIELD

Superior

L. Michigan

Huron

Lake Ontario

Erie

Labrador Sea

Anticosti Island

Newfoundland

Prince Edward Island

Gulf of St. Lawrence

Cape Breton Island

St. Lawrence R.

APPALACHIAN MOUNTAINS

PIEDMONT

ATLANTIC COASTAL PLAIN

Long Island

Cape Cod

Cape Hatteras

Cape Canaveral

FLORIDA PENINSULA

Florida Keys

Straits of Florida

Bahamas

Cuba

Jamaica

Greater Antilles

Hispaniola

Puerto Rico

Lesser Antilles

Trinidad

Caribbean Sea

Lake Nicaragua

CENTRAL AMERICA

ISTHMUS OF PANAMA

SOUTH AMERICA

ATLANTIC OCEAN

Bermuda

Arctic Circle

Tropic of Cancer

Equator

North Pole

## ELEVATION

| Feet | Meters |
|---|---|
| 13,120 | 4,000 |
| 6,560 | 2,000 |
| 1,640 | 500 |
| 656 | 200 |
| (Sea level) 0 | 0 (Sea level) |
| Below sea level | Below sea level |

Ice cap

0    300    600 Miles

0    300    600 Kilometers

Projection: Azimuthal Equal Area

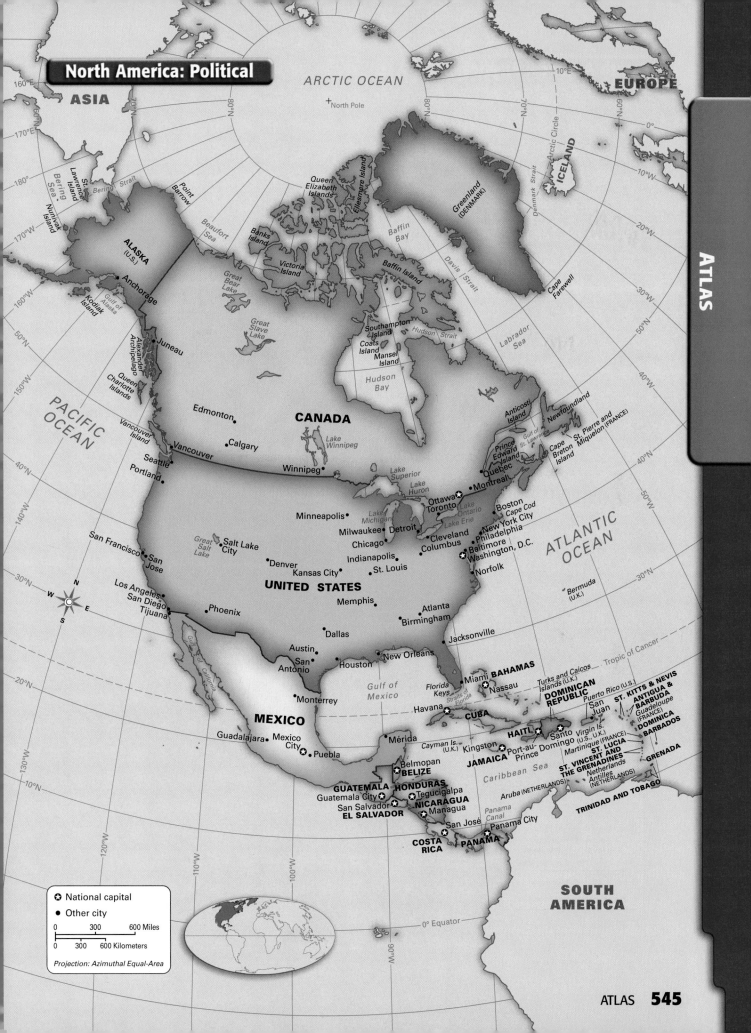

ASIA

ARCTIC OCEAN

+North Pole

EUROPE

ATLAS

Bering Strait

St. Lawrence Island

Nunivak Island

Point Barrow

Queen Elizabeth Islands

Ellesmere Island

Greenland (DENMARK)

ICELAND

Arctic Circle

Denmark Strait

ALASKA (U.S.)

Beaufort Sea

Banks Island

Victoria Island

Baffin Bay

Baffin Island

Anchorage

Gulf of Alaska

Kodiak Island

Great Bear Lake

Southampton Island

Davis Strait

Cape Farewell

Juneau

Alexander Archipelago

Great Slave Lake

Coats Island

Mansel Island

Labrador Sea

Queen Charlotte Islands

Hudson Strait

PACIFIC OCEAN

Vancouver Island

Edmonton

CANADA

Hudson Bay

Vancouver

Calgary

Lake Winnipeg

Anticosti Island

Newfoundland

St. Pierre and Miquelon (FRANCE)

Seattle

Winnipeg

Lake Superior

Prince Edward Island

Cape Breton Island

Gulf of St. Lawrence

Portland

Lake Huron

Quebec

Minneapolis

Lake Michigan

Ottawa

Toronto

Montreal

Boston

Cape Cod

Milwaukee

Detroit

Lake Ontario

Lake Erie

Cleveland

New York City

San Francisco

Great Salt Lake

Salt Lake City

Chicago

Columbus

Philadelphia

Baltimore

ATLANTIC OCEAN

San Jose

Denver

Indianapolis

Washington, D.C.

Kansas City

St. Louis

UNITED STATES

Norfolk

Los Angeles

San Diego

Tijuana

Phoenix

Memphis

Atlanta

Birmingham

Bermuda (U.K.)

Dallas

Jacksonville

Tropic of Cancer

Austin

San Antonio

Houston

New Orleans

Miami

BAHAMAS

Turks and Caicos Islands (U.K.)

Monterrey

Gulf of Mexico

Florida Keys

Nassau

DOMINICAN REPUBLIC

Puerto Rico (U.S.)

ST. KITTS & NEVIS

MEXICO

Havana

Straits of Florida

CUBA

San Juan

ANTIGUA & BARBUDA

Guadeloupe (FRANCE)

Guadalajara

Mexico City

Mérida

Cayman Is. (U.K.)

HAITI

Santo Domingo

Virgin Is. (U.S., U.K.)

DOMINICA

Puebla

Kingston

Port-au-Prince

Martinique (FRANCE)

BARBADOS

JAMAICA

ST. LUCIA

Belmopan

BELIZE

Caribbean Sea

ST. VINCENT AND THE GRENADINES

GRENADA

GUATEMALA

HONDURAS

Netherlands Antilles (NETHERLANDS)

Guatemala City

Tegucigalpa

Aruba (NETHERLANDS)

TRINIDAD AND TOBAGO

San Salvador

NICARAGUA

Managua

EL SALVADOR

Panama Canal

San José

Panama City

COSTA RICA

PANAMA

SOUTH AMERICA

⊛ National capital

● Other city

0    300    600 Miles

0    300    600 Kilometers

Projection: Azimuthal Equal-Area

Equator

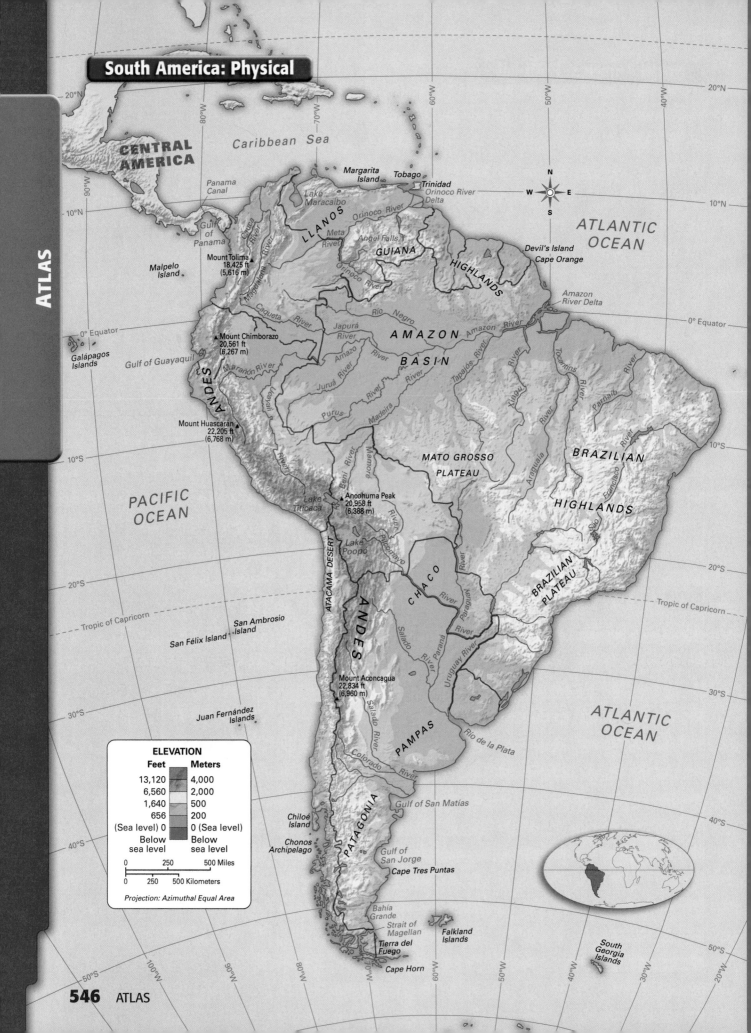

# South America: Physical

ATLAS

**CENTRAL AMERICA**

Caribbean Sea

Panama Canal

Gulf of Panama

Malpelo Island

Margarita Island

Tobago

Trinidad

Orinoco River Delta

Lake Maracaibo

LLANOS

Meta River

Orinoco River

Angel Falls

GUIANA

Cauca River

Magdalena River

Mount Tolima 18,425 ft (5,616 m)

HIGHLANDS

Devil's Island
Cape Orange

ATLANTIC OCEAN

Caquetá River

Orinoco River

Río Negro

AMAZON

Amazon River

Amazon River Delta

Japurá River

Amazon River

BASIN

Tapajós River

Tocantins River

Galápagos Islands

Gulf of Guayaquil

Mount Chimborazo 20,561 ft (6,267 m)

ANDES

Marañón River

Juruá River

Amazon River

Madeira River

Xingu River

Araguaia River

São Francisco River

BRAZILIAN

Ucayali River

Purus River

Mount Huascarán 22,205 ft (6,768 m)

Beni River

Mamoré River

MATO GROSSO PLATEAU

HIGHLANDS

PACIFIC OCEAN

Lake Titicaca

Ancohuma Peak 20,958 ft (6,388 m)

Lake Poopó

Pilcomayo River

CHACO

Paraguay River

Paraná River

BRAZILIAN PLATEAU

San Ambrosio Island

San Félix Island

Tropic of Capricorn

ATACAMA DESERT

ANDES

Salado River

Tropic of Capricorn

Juan Fernández Islands

Mount Aconcagua 22,834 ft (6,960 m)

Uruguay River

ATLANTIC OCEAN

Salado River

PAMPAS

Río de la Plata

Colorado River

**ELEVATION**

| Feet | | Meters |
|------|---|--------|
| 13,120 | | 4,000 |
| 6,560 | | 2,000 |
| 1,640 | | 500 |
| 656 | | 200 |
| (Sea level) 0 | | 0 (Sea level) |
| Below sea level | | Below sea level |

Gulf of San Matías

Chiloé Island

Chonos Archipelago

PATAGONIA

Gulf of San Jorge

Cape Tres Puntas

0    250    500 Miles

0    250    500 Kilometers

Projection: Azimuthal Equal Area

Bahía Grande

Strait of Magellan

Tierra del Fuego

Falkland Islands

South Georgia Islands

Cape Horn

# South America: Political

CENTRAL AMERICA

Caribbean Sea

Barranquilla
Cartagena
Caracas
VENEZUELA

Medellín
Bogotá
COLOMBIA
Cali

Georgetown
Paramaribo
GUYANA
Cayenne
SURINAME
French Guiana (FRANCE)

Lake Maracaibo

Malpelo Island (COLOMBIA)

Quito
ECUADOR
Guayaquil

Galápagos Islands (ECUADOR)

0° Equator

Belém

ATLANTIC OCEAN

PERU

Trujillo

BRAZIL

Recife

Callao
Lima
Arequipa

Lake Titicaca
La Paz
Lake Poopó
BOLIVIA
Sucre

Brasília

Salvador

PACIFIC OCEAN

Belo Horizonte

PARAGUAY
Asunción

Campinas
São Paulo
Rio de Janeiro
Curitiba

San Ambrosio Island (CHILE)
San Félix Island (CHILE)

CHILE

Juan Fernández Islands (CHILE)

Córdoba

Valparaíso
Santiago

Rosario

Buenos Aires

Pôrto Alegre

URUGUAY
Montevideo

ATLANTIC OCEAN

ARGENTINA

Strait of Magellan

Falkland Islands (U.K.)

Tierra del Fuego

South Georgia Island (U.K.)

Tropic of Capricorn

⊛ National capital
• Other city

0    250    500 Miles
0    250    500 Kilometers

Projection: Azimuthal Equal-Area

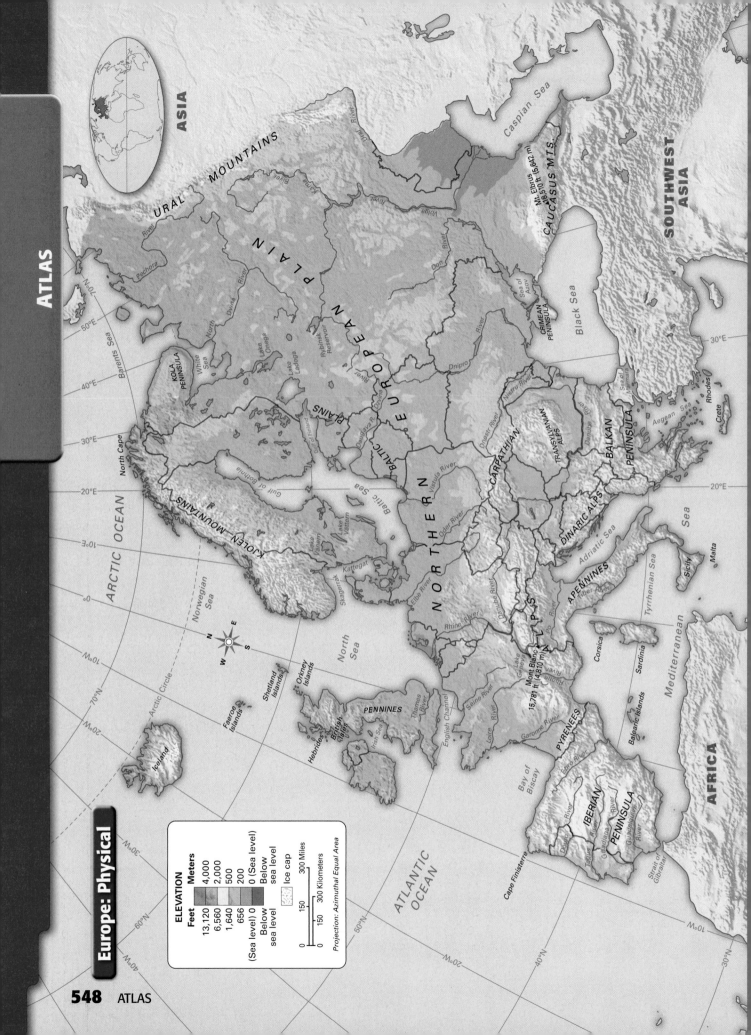

ASIA

SOUTHWEST ASIA

URAL MOUNTAINS

Pechora River

North Dvina River

Kama River

Volga River

Don River

Dnipro River

Caspian Sea

Mt. Elbrus (5,642 m)
18,510 ft

CAUCASUS MTS.

Sea of Azov

Black Sea

CRIMEAN PENINSULA

Barents Sea

KOLA PENINSULA

White Sea

Lake Onega

Lake Ladoga

Rybinsk Reservoir

NORTHERN EUROPEAN PLAIN

PLAINS

Gulf of Finland

Daugava R.

BALTIC

Vistula River

Oder River

CARPATHIAN

TRANSYLVANIAN ALPS

Nistru River

Dnestr River

Danube River

DINARIC ALPS

BALKAN PENINSULA

Sea of Marmara

Aegean Sea

Rhodes

Crete

North Cape

KJOLEN MOUNTAINS

Gulf of Bothnia

Lake Vänern

Lake Vättern

Baltic Sea

Kattegat

Skagerrak

ADRIATIC Sea

APENNINES

Tiber River

Tyrrhenian Sea

Sicily

Malta

Sea

ARCTIC OCEAN

Norwegian Sea

North Sea

Shetland Islands

Orkney Islands

Hebrides

British Isles

PENNINES

Irish Sea

Thames River

English Channel

Seine River

Loire River

Rhine River

A L P S

Lake Geneva

Mont Blanc
15,781 ft (4,810 m)

Rhône River

Po River

Danube River

Corsica

Sardinia

Mediterranean Sea

AFRICA

Arctic Circle

Faeroe Islands

Iceland

Bay of Biscay

Garonne River

PYRENEES

Ebro River

IBERIAN PENINSULA

Douro River

Tagus River

Guadiana River

Guadalquivir River

Cape Finisterre

Strait of Gibraltar

Balearic Islands

ATLANTIC OCEAN

70°N

60°N

50°N

40°N

70°E

50°E

40°E

30°E

20°E

10°E

0°

20°E

30°E

10°W

20°W

30°W

40°W

20°W

10°W

N
E
W
S

## Europe: Physical

ELEVATION

| Feet | Meters |
|---|---|
| 13,120 | 4,000 |
| 6,560 | 2,000 |
| 1,640 | 500 |
| 656 | 200 |
| (Sea level) 0 | 0 (Sea level) |
| Below sea level | Below sea level |

Ice cap

300 Miles
0        150        300
0    150    300 Kilometers

Projection: Azimuthal Equal Area

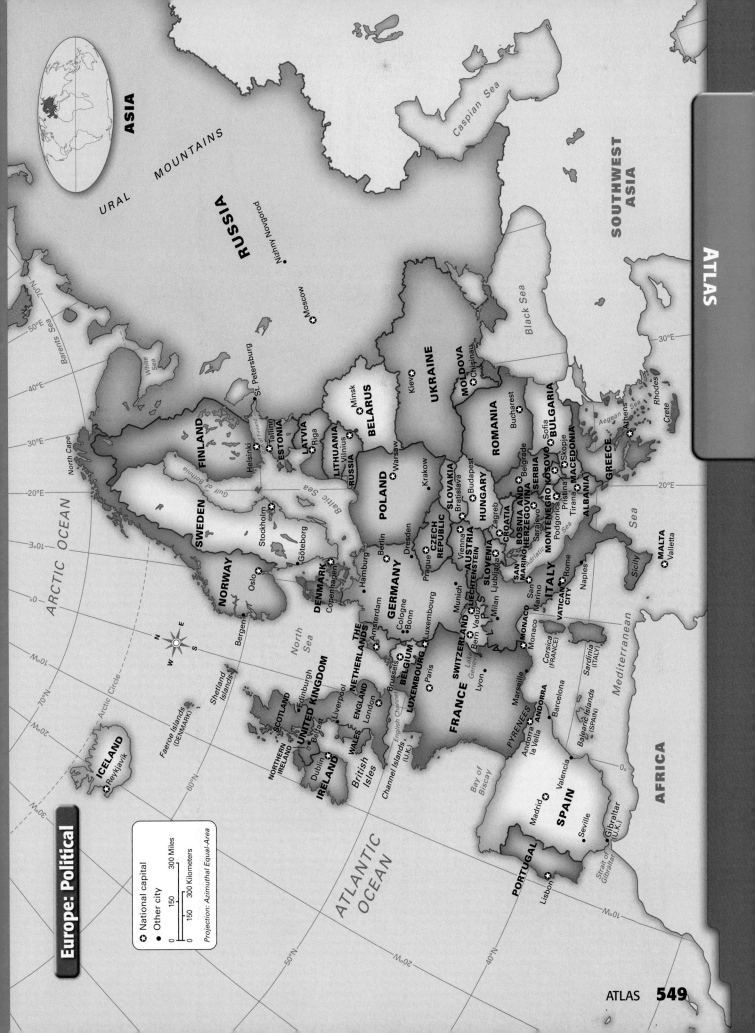

## Europe: Political

National capital ✪
Other city •

0      150      300 Miles
0      150      300 Kilometers

Projection: Azimuthal Equal-Area

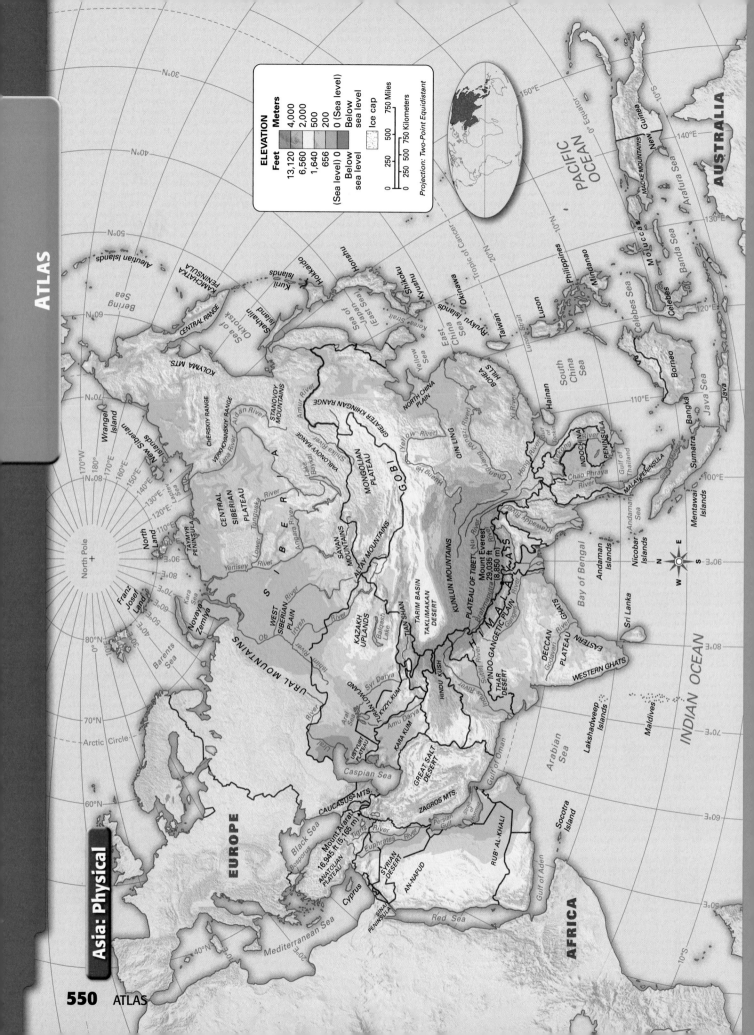

## Asia: Physical

**ELEVATION**

| Feet | Meters |
|------|--------|
| 13,120 | 4,000 |
| 6,560 | 2,000 |
| 1,640 | 500 |
| 656 | 200 |
| 0 (Sea level) | 0 (Sea level) |
| Below sea level | Below sea level |

Ice cap

Projection: Two-Point Equidistant

0 250 500 750 Miles
0 250 500 750 Kilometers

PACIFIC OCEAN

AUSTRALIA

New Guinea
MACKE MOUNTAINS
Arafura Sea
Banda Sea
Moluccas
Celebes
Celebes Sea
Mindanao
Philippines
Luzon
Luzon Strait
South China Sea
Borneo
Java Sea
Java
Bangka
Sumatra
Mentawai Islands
MALAY PENINSULA
Gulf of Thailand
INDOCHINA PENINSULA
Chao Phraya River
Hainan
Gulf of Tonkin
Hong (Red) River
Mekong River
Salween River
BOHEA HILLS
QIN LING
NORTH CHINA PLAIN
Yellow Sea
East China Sea
Taiwan
Tropic of Cancer
Okinawa
Ryukyu Islands
Korea Strait
Kyushu
Shikoku
Honshu
Japan Sea (East Sea)
Sea of Japan
Hokkaido
Kuril Islands
Sakhalin Island
KAMCHATKA PENINSULA
Sea of Okhotsk
Bering Sea
Aleutian Islands
CENTRAL RANGE

Huang He (Yellow River)
Chang Jiang (Yangzi River)
GREATER KHINGAN RANGE
GOBI
MONGOLIAN PLATEAU
Amur River
Shilka River
YABLONOV RANGE
Lake Baykal
Aldan River
STANOVOY MOUNTAINS
Lena River
VERKHOYANSKY RANGE
CHERSKIY RANGE
KOLYMA MTS.
Wrangel Island
New Siberian Islands
Laptev Sea

CENTRAL SIBERIAN PLATEAU
Lower Tunguska River
Angara River
Yenisey River
SAYAN MOUNTAINS
ALTAY MOUNTAINS
TIAN SHAN
TARIM BASIN
TAKLIMAKAN DESERT
KUNLUN MOUNTAINS
PLATEAU OF TIBET
Mount Everest 29,035 ft (8,850 m)
HIMALAYAS
Brahmaputra River
Nu River
Ganges River
Sutlej River
INDO-GANGETIC PLAIN
DECCAN PLATEAU
Godavari River
EASTERN GHATS
WESTERN GHATS
Bay of Bengal
Andaman Islands
Andaman Sea
Nicobar Islands
Sri Lanka

S I B E R I A

Taymyr Peninsula
North Land
North Pole
Franz Josef Land
Novaya Zemlya
Barents Sea
Kara Sea

WEST SIBERIAN PLAIN
Ob River
Irtysh River
Ishim River
URAL MOUNTAINS
KAZAKH UPLANDS
Balqash Lake
Syr Darya
TURAN LOWLAND
KYZYL KUM
Aral Sea
Amu Darya
KARA KUM
USTYURT PLATEAU
GREAT SALT DESERT
Caspian Sea
CAUCASUS MTS.
Mount Ararat 16,945 ft (5,165 m)
ANATOLIAN PLATEAU
Black Sea
Bosporus
Cyprus
Mediterranean Sea
Tigris River
Euphrates River
SYRIAN DESERT
ZAGROS MTS.
Persian Gulf
Gulf of Oman
Arabian Sea
Maldives
Lakshadweep Islands
THAR DESERT
Indus River
HINDU KUSH
SINAI PENINSULA
AN-NAFUD
RUB' AL-KHALI
Red Sea
Gulf of Aden
Socotra Island

EUROPE
AFRICA

Arctic Circle

INDIAN OCEAN

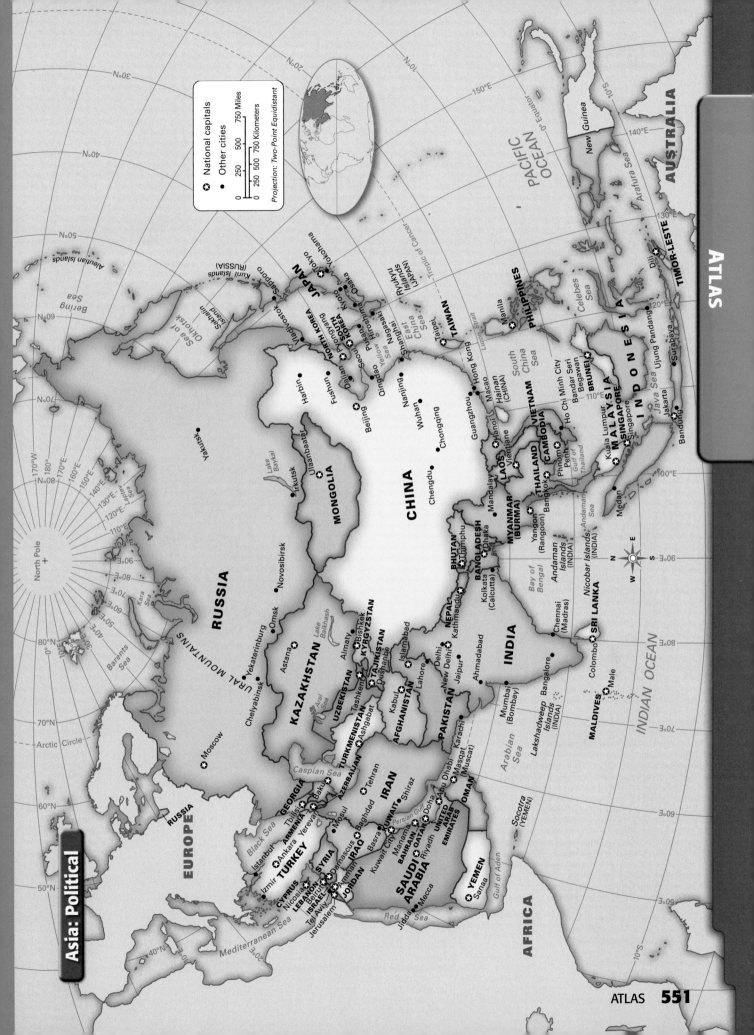

# Asia: Political

**Legend:**
- ✪ National capitals
- • Other cities

750 Miles
250 500 750 Kilometers

*Projection: Two-Point Equidistant*

**RUSSIA**

**EUROPE**

**AFRICA**

**AUSTRALIA**

**CHINA**

**INDIA**

**MONGOLIA**

**KAZAKHSTAN**

**JAPAN**

Tokyo
Yokohama
Sapporo
Osaka
Kyoto

**NORTH KOREA**
Pyongyang

**SOUTH KOREA**
Seoul
Pusan
Inchon

**TAIWAN**
Taipei

**PHILIPPINES**
Manila

**VIETNAM**
Hanoi
Ho Chi Minh City

**LAOS**
Vientiane

**THAILAND**
Bangkok

**CAMBODIA**
Phnom Penh

**MYANMAR (BURMA)**
Yangon (Rangoon)
Mandalay

**MALAYSIA**
Kuala Lumpur

**SINGAPORE**
Singapore

**BRUNEI**
Bandar Seri Begawan

**INDONESIA**
Jakarta
Bandung
Surabaya
Ujung Pandang
Medan

**TIMOR-LESTE**
Dili

**NEPAL**
Kathmandu

**BHUTAN**
Thimphu

**BANGLADESH**
Dhaka

**SRI LANKA**
Colombo

**MALDIVES**
Male

**PAKISTAN**
Islamabad
Karachi
Lahore

**AFGHANISTAN**
Kabul

**TAJIKISTAN**
Dushanbe

**KYRGYZSTAN**
Bishkek

**UZBEKISTAN**
Tashkent

**TURKMENISTAN**
Ashgabat

**IRAN**
Tehran
Shiraz

**IRAQ**
Baghdad
Basra
Mosul

**SYRIA**
Damascus

**JORDAN**
Amman

**ISRAEL**
Tel Aviv
Jerusalem

**LEBANON**
Beirut

**CYPRUS**
Nicosia

**TURKEY**
Ankara
Istanbul
Izmir

**GEORGIA**
Tbilisi

**ARMENIA**
Yerevan

**AZERBAIJAN**
Baku

**SAUDI ARABIA**
Riyadh
Jidda
Mecca

**YEMEN**
Sanaa

**OMAN**
Masqat (Muscat)

**UNITED ARAB EMIRATES**
Abu Dhabi

**QATAR**
Doha

**BAHRAIN**
Manama

**KUWAIT**
Kuwait City

Moscow
Novosibirsk
Omsk
Astana
Almaty
Yekaterinburg
Chelyabinsk
Yakutsk
Irkutsk
Ulaanbaatar
Vladivostok
Khabarovsk
Harbin
Fushun
Dalian
Qingdao
Beijing
Nanjing
Shanghai
Wuhan
Chengdu
Chongqing
Guangzhou
Hong Kong
Macao
Hainan (CHINA)

Delhi
New Delhi
Jaipur
Ahmadabad
Mumbai (Bombay)
Bangalore
Chennai (Madras)
Kolkata (Calcutta)

**Bodies of water:**
- Bering Sea
- Sea of Okhotsk
- Pacific Ocean
- East China Sea
- Yellow Sea
- South China Sea
- Celebes Sea
- Java Sea
- Arafura Sea
- Andaman Sea
- Bay of Bengal
- Indian Ocean
- Arabian Sea
- Gulf of Thailand
- Gulf of Aden
- Red Sea
- Persian Gulf
- Caspian Sea
- Black Sea
- Mediterranean Sea
- Barents Sea
- Kara Sea
- Aral Sea
- Lake Baykal
- Lake Balkhash
- Luzon Strait
- Tropic of Cancer

**Islands:**
- Aleutian Islands
- Kuril Islands (RUSSIA)
- Sakhalin Island
- Ryukyu Islands (JAPAN)
- Andaman Islands (INDIA)
- Nicobar Islands (INDIA)
- Lakshadweep Islands (INDIA)
- Socotra (YEMEN)
- New Guinea

**URAL MOUNTAINS**

North Pole
Arctic Circle

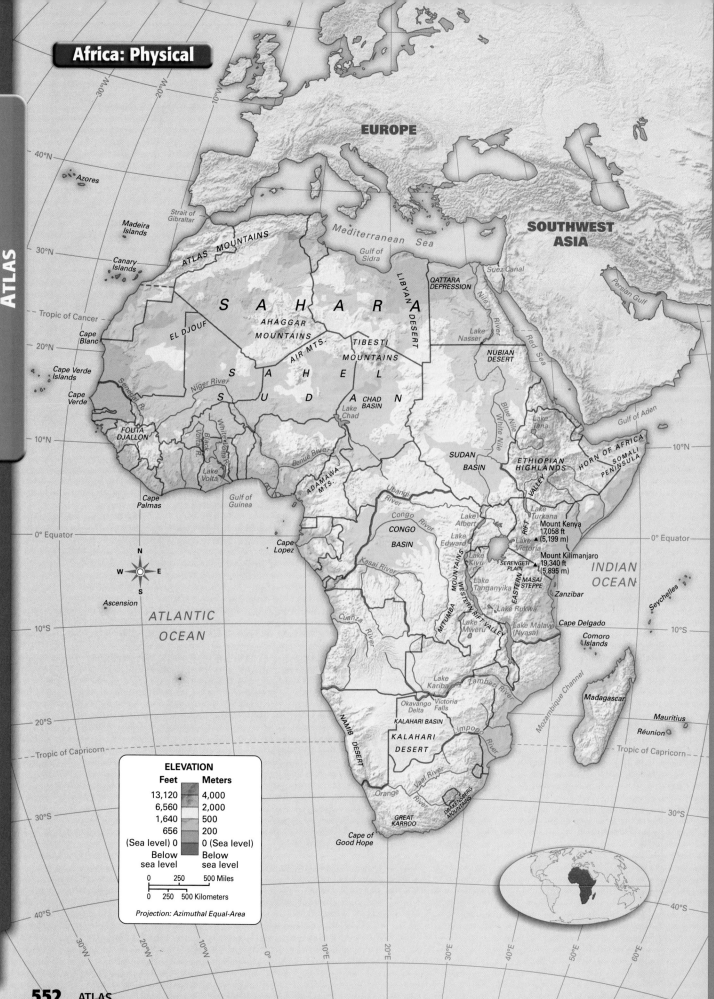

# Africa: Physical

EUROPE

SOUTHWEST ASIA

Azores

Madeira Islands

Strait of Gibraltar

Mediterranean Sea

Gulf of Sidra

QATTARA DEPRESSION

Suez Canal

Persian Gulf

ATLAS MOUNTAINS

Canary Islands

Tropic of Cancer

S A H A R A

LIBYAN DESERT

Cape Blanc

EL DJOUF

AHAGGAR MOUNTAINS

TIBESTI MOUNTAINS

Nile River

Lake Nasser

NUBIAN DESERT

Red Sea

Cape Verde Islands

AIR MTS.

S A H E L

Gulf of Aden

Cape Verde

Senegal R.

Niger River

S U D A N

CHAD BASIN

Lake Chad

Blue Nile

Lake Tana

ETHIOPIAN HIGHLANDS

HORN OF AFRICA

SOMALI PENINSULA

FOUTA DJALLON

White Volta R.

Black Volta R.

Benue River

SUDAN BASIN

White Nile

Lake Volta

ADAMAWA MTS.

Cape Palmas

Gulf of Guinea

Ubangi River

Congo River

Lake Albert

Lake Edward

Lake Victoria

Lake Turkana

RIFT VALLEY

Mount Kenya 17,058 ft (5,199 m)

Cape Lopez

CONGO BASIN

Kasai River

Lake Kivu

Lake Tanganyika

Lake Rukwa

SERENGETI PLAIN

MASAI STEPPE

EASTERN

Mount Kilimanjaro 19,340 ft (5,895 m)

Zanzibar

INDIAN OCEAN

Seychelles

0° Equator

0° Equator

N W E S

Ascension

ATLANTIC OCEAN

Cuanza River

MITUMBA MOUNTAINS

WESTERN RIFT VALLEY

Lake Mweru

Lake Malawi (Nyasa)

Cape Delgado

Comoro Islands

Mauritius

Lake Kariba

Zambezi River

Réunion

Okavango Delta

Victoria Falls

Madagascar

NAMIB DESERT

KALAHARI BASIN

Limpopo River

Mozambique Channel

KALAHARI DESERT

Tropic of Capricorn

Tropic of Capricorn

Orange River

Vaal River

DRAKENSBERG MOUNTAINS

GREAT KARROO

Cape of Good Hope

## ELEVATION

| Feet | | Meters |
|------|---|--------|
| 13,120 | | 4,000 |
| 6,560 | | 2,000 |
| 1,640 | | 500 |
| 656 | | 200 |
| (Sea level) 0 | | 0 (Sea level) |
| Below sea level | | Below sea level |

0    250    500 Miles

0    250    500 Kilometers

*Projection: Azimuthal Equal-Area*

# Africa: Political

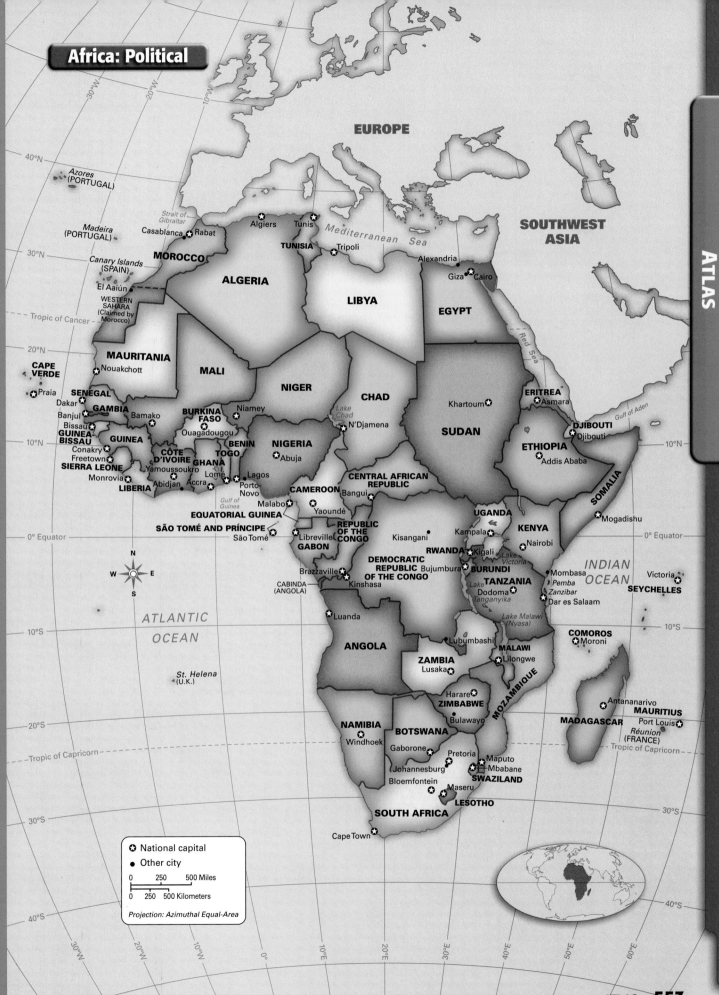

EUROPE

SOUTHWEST
ASIA

ATLAS

**Azores**
(PORTUGAL)

**Madeira**
(PORTUGAL)

Strait of
Gibraltar

*Mediterranean Sea*

Algiers • Tunis

Casablanca • Rabat

**MOROCCO**

**TUNISIA** • Tripoli

Alexandria

Giza • Cairo

**Canary Islands**
(SPAIN)

El Aaiún

**WESTERN
SAHARA**
(Claimed by
Morocco)

Tropic of Cancer

**ALGERIA**

**LIBYA**

**EGYPT**

*Red Sea*

**CAPE
VERDE**

• Praia

**MAURITANIA**

Nouakchott

**MALI**

**NIGER**

**CHAD**

Khartoum

**ERITREA**
• Asmara

*Gulf of Aden*

**SENEGAL**

Dakar

**GAMBIA**

Bamako

Banjul

Bissau

**GUINEA-
BISSAU**

**GUINEA**

Conakry

Freetown

**SIERRA LEONE**

Monrovia

**LIBERIA**

**BURKINA
FASO**

Niamey

Ouagadougou

**BENIN
TOGO**

**CÔTE
D'IVOIRE**

**GHANA**

Yamoussoukro

Lomé

Abidjan • Accra

**NIGERIA**

• Abuja

Lagos

Porto-
Novo

N'Djamena

*Lake
Chad*

**SUDAN**

**DJIBOUTI**
Djibouti

**ETHIOPIA**

Addis Ababa

**SOMALIA**

**CENTRAL AFRICAN
REPUBLIC**

**CAMEROON**

Malabo

Bangui

**UGANDA**

Kampala

Mogadishu

**EQUATORIAL GUINEA**

**SÃO TOMÉ AND PRÍNCIPE**

São Tomé

Yaoundé

**REPUBLIC
OF THE
CONGO**

**GABON**

Libreville

Kisangani

**RWANDA**

Kigali

*Lake
Victoria*

**KENYA**

• Nairobi

**INDIAN
OCEAN**

Victoria

**SEYCHELLES**

Brazzaville

**DEMOCRATIC
REPUBLIC
OF THE CONGO**

Bujumbura

**BURUNDI**

**TANZANIA**

Dodoma

Mombasa

Pemba

Zanzibar

Dar es Salaam

**CABINDA
(ANGOLA)**

Kinshasa

*Lake
Tanganyika*

**ATLANTIC
OCEAN**

Luanda

Lubumbashi

*Lake Malawi
(Nyasa)*

**COMOROS**
Moroni

**ANGOLA**

**ZAMBIA**

Lusaka

**MALAWI**
Lilongwe

**St. Helena**
(U.K.)

Harare

**ZIMBABWE**

Bulawayo

**MOZAMBIQUE**

Antananarivo

**MAURITIUS**

Port Louis

**MADAGASCAR**

**NAMIBIA**

Windhoek

**BOTSWANA**

Gaborone

Johannesburg

Pretoria

Maputo

Mbabane

**SWAZILAND**

Bloemfontein

Maseru

**LESOTHO**

*Réunion*
(FRANCE)

Tropic of Capricorn

**SOUTH AFRICA**

Cape Town

✪ National capital

• Other city

0    250    500 Miles

0  250  500 Kilometers

*Projection: Azimuthal Equal-Area*

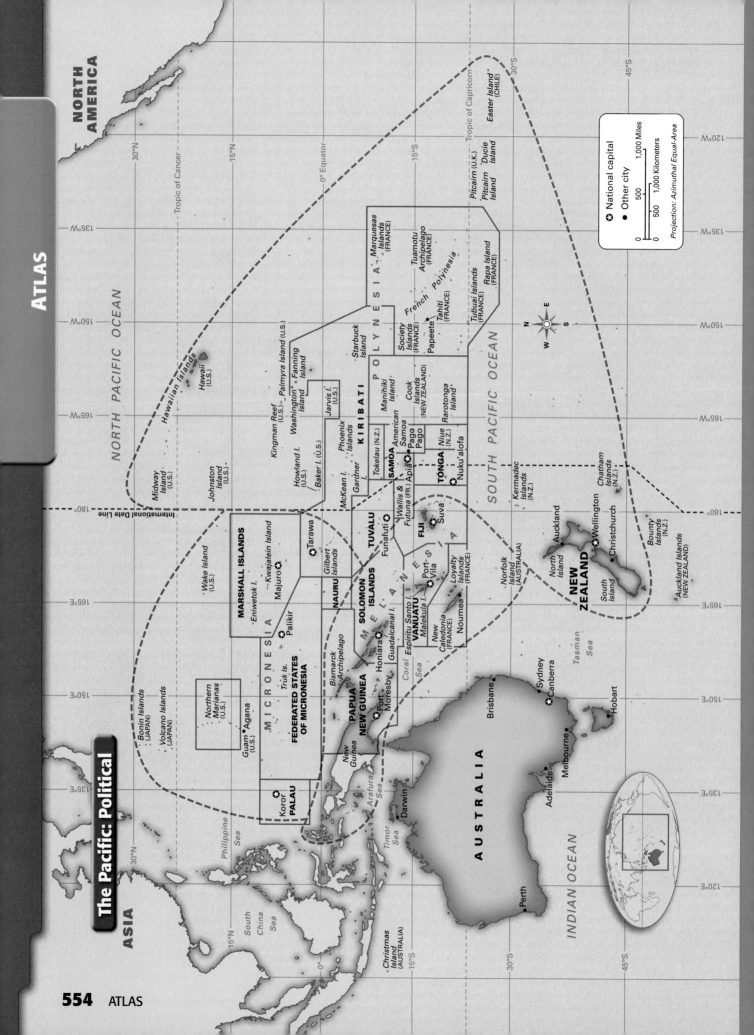

NORTH
AMERICA

ASIA

## The Pacific: Political

NORTH PACIFIC OCEAN

SOUTH PACIFIC OCEAN

INDIAN OCEAN

AUSTRALIA

NEW
ZEALAND

Tropic of Cancer

Tropic of Capricorn

0° Equator

International Date Line 180°

Projection: Azimuthal Equal-Area

National capital
Other city

1,000 Miles
1,000 Kilometers
500
500

M I C R O N E S I A

M E L A N E S I A

P O L Y N E S I A

KIRIBATI

MARSHALL ISLANDS

FEDERATED STATES
OF MICRONESIA

PALAU

NAURU

SOLOMON
ISLANDS

TUVALU

FIJI

VANUATU

SAMOA

TONGA

PAPUA
NEW GUINEA

Hawaiian Islands
Hawaii
(U.S.)

Midway
Island
(U.S.)

Johnston
Island
(U.S.)

Wake Island
(U.S.)

Eniwetok I.
Kwajalein Island
Majuro
Palikir

Bonin Islands
(JAPAN)

Volcano Islands
(JAPAN)

Northern
Marianas
(U.S.)

Guam Agana
(U.S.)

Truk Is.

Koror

New
Guinea

Port
Moresby

Darwin

Christmas
Island
(AUSTRALIA)

Philippine
Sea

South
China
Sea

Timor
Sea

Arafura
Sea

Coral
Sea

Bismarck
Archipelago

Guadalcanal I.
Honiara

Espiritu Santo I.
Malekula I.

Port-
Vila

New
Caledonia
(FRANCE)

Noumea

Loyalty
Islands
(FRANCE)

Norfolk
Island
(AUSTRALIA)

Tasman
Sea

Brisbane

Sydney
Canberra

Melbourne

Adelaide

Hobart

Perth

North
Island

South
Island

Auckland

Wellington
Christchurch

Chatham
Islands
(N.Z.)

Bounty
Islands
(N.Z.)

Auckland Islands
(NEW ZEALAND)

Kermadec
Islands
(N.Z.)

Kingman Reef
(U.S.)
Palmyra Island (U.S.)
Washington
Island
Fanning
Island

Jarvis I.
(U.S.)

Howland I.
(U.S.)
Baker I. (U.S.)

McKean I.
Gardner

Phoenix
Islands

Starbuck
Island

Tokelau (N.Z.)

Tarawa

Gilbert
Islands

Funafuti

Wallis &
Futuna (Fr.)

Suva

American
Samoa
Pago Pago

Apia

Nuku'alofa

Niue
(N.Z.)

Manihiki
Island

Cook
Islands
(NEW ZEALAND)

Rarotonga
Island

Marquesas
Islands
(FRANCE)

Tuamotu
Archipelago
(FRANCE)

French
Polynesia

Society
Islands
(FRANCE)

Papeete
Tahiti
(FRANCE)

Tubuai Islands
(FRANCE)

Rapa Island
(FRANCE)

Pitcairn (U.K.)
Pitcairn
Island
Ducie
Island

Easter Island
(CHILE)

N
W    E
S

30°N

15°N

30°N

15°N

0°

30°S

45°S

15°S

30°S

45°S

15°N

30°N

135°E

150°E

165°E

135°W

150°W

165°W

180°

165°W

150°W

135°W

120°W

120°E

135°E

150°E

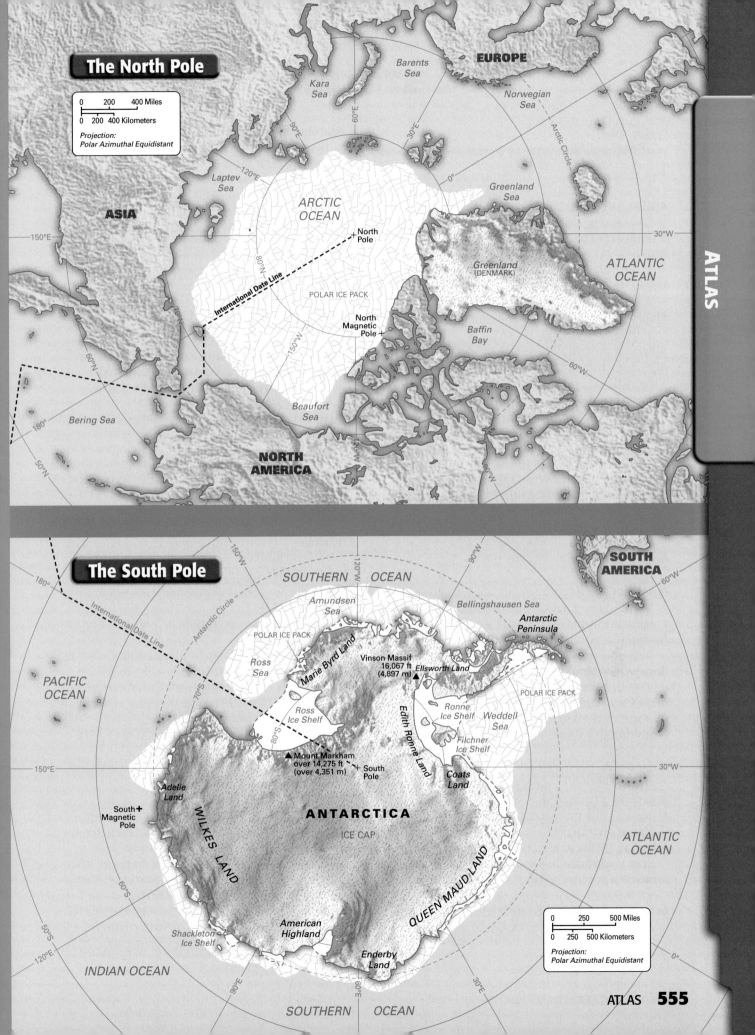

# The North Pole

Scale:
0 200 400 Miles
0 200 400 Kilometers

Projection:
Polar Azimuthal Equidistant

EUROPE

Kara Sea

Barents Sea

Norwegian Sea

Laptev Sea

ARCTIC OCEAN

Greenland Sea

Arctic Circle

ASIA

North Pole

Greenland (DENMARK)

ATLANTIC OCEAN

POLAR ICE PACK

30°W

North Magnetic Pole

Baffin Bay

International Date Line

60°W

Beaufort Sea

Bering Sea

NORTH AMERICA

90°W

# The South Pole

SOUTHERN OCEAN

SOUTH AMERICA

International Date Line

Amundsen Sea

Bellingshausen Sea

Antarctic Peninsula

Antarctic Circle

POLAR ICE PACK

Ross Sea

Marie Byrd Land

Vinson Massif 16,067 ft (4,897 m)

Ellsworth Land

POLAR ICE PACK

PACIFIC OCEAN

Ross Ice Shelf

Ronne Ice Shelf

Weddell Sea

Edith Ronne Land

Filchner Ice Shelf

Mount Markham over 14,275 ft (over 4,351 m)

South Pole

Coats Land

30°W

Adelie Land

South Magnetic Pole

WILKES LAND

ANTARCTICA

ICE CAP

QUEEN MAUD LAND

ATLANTIC OCEAN

Shackleton Ice Shelf

American Highland

Enderby Land

Scale:
0 250 500 Miles
0 250 500 Kilometers

Projection:
Polar Azimuthal Equidistant

INDIAN OCEAN

SOUTHERN OCEAN

# Gazetteer

**Afghanistan** a landlocked country in Central Asia (p. 559)

**Africa** the second-largest continent; surrounded by the Atlantic Ocean, Indian Ocean, and Mediterranean Sea (p. 552)

**Alabama** (AL) a state in the southern United States; admitted in 1819 (pp. 538–539)

**Alaska** (AK) a state in northwestern North America; admitted in 1959 (pp. 538–539)

**Albania** a country on the Balkan Peninsula in southeastern Europe (p. 467)

**Alberta** a province in western Canada (p. 274)

**Alps** a great mountain system in central Europe (p. 401)

**Amazon Basin** a huge basin in the heart of South America (p. 546)

**Amazon River** the major river in South America (p. 546)

**Amsterdam** (52°N, 5°E) the capital and largest city of the Netherlands (p. 433)

**Amur River** a river in Asia that forms part of the Russia-China border (p. 505)

**Andes** a mountain range along the west coast of South America (p. 546)

**Antarctica** the continent around the South Pole (p. 555)

**Antarctic Circle** the line of latitude located at 66.5° south of the equator; parallel beyond which no sunlight shines on the June solstice (p. 555)

**Apennines** (A-puh-nynz) the major mountain range on the Italian Peninsula (p. 401)

**Appalachian Mountains** a mountain system in eastern North America (p. 248)

**Arctic Circle** the line of latitude located at 66.5° north of the equator; parallel beyond which no sunlight shines on the December solstice (p. 555)

**Arctic Ocean** the ocean north of the Arctic Circle; the world's fourth-largest ocean (p. 540)

**Argentina** a country in South America (p. 205)

**Arizona** (AZ) a state in the southwestern United States; admitted in 1912 (pp. 538–539)

**Arkansas** (AR) a state in the south-central United States; admitted in 1836 (pp. 538–539)

**Armenia** a country in the Caucasus Mountains (p. 509)

**Asia** the world's largest continent; located between Europe and the Pacific Ocean (p. 550)

**Asia Minor** a large peninsula in Southwest Asia between the Black Sea and the Mediterranean Sea, forming most of Turkey (p. 311)

**Asunción** (ah-soon-SYOHN) (25°N, 58°W) the capital of Paraguay (p. 205)

**Atacama Desert** a desert located in northern Chile near the border with Peru (p. 231)

**Athens** (38°N, 24°E) an ancient city and the modern capital of Greece (p. 399)

**Atlanta** (33°N, 84°W) capital of Georgia (p. 266)

**Atlantic Ocean** the ocean between the continents of North and South America and the continents of Europe and Africa; the world's second-largest ocean (pp. 540–541)

**Australia** the only country occupying an entire continent (also called Australia); located between the Indian Ocean and the Pacific Ocean (p. 554)

**Austria** a country in West-Central Europe (p. 423)

**Azerbaijan** (a-zuhr-by-JAHN) a country in the Caucasus Mountains (p. 509)

**Bahamas** a country and group of islands located east of Florida in the Atlantic Ocean (p. 163)

**Baja California** a peninsula in Mexico (p. 142)

**Baku** (40°N, 48°E) the capital of Azerbaijan (p. 509)

**Balkan Peninsula** a peninsula in Southern Europe (p. 469)

**Baltic Sea** a shallow arm of the Atlantic Ocean in northern Europe (p. 449)

**Barbados** island country in the Caribbean (p. 161)

**Barcelona** (41°N, 2°E) a large port city in Spain on the Mediterranean Sea (p. 416)

**Basse-Terre** (16°N, 62°W) the capital of St. Kitts and Nevis (p. 161)

**Bavaria** a state and region in southern Germany (p. 438)

**Belarus** a country in Eastern Europe (p. 467)

**Belgium** a country in West-Central Europe (p. 423)

**Belgrade** (45°N, 21°E) the capital of Serbia (p. 467)

**Belize** a country in Central America (p. 160)

**Belmopan** (17°N, 90°W) capital of Belize (p. 160)

**Benelux** a term that refers to Belgium, the Netherlands, and Luxembourg (p. 432)

**Berlin** (53°N, 13°E) the capital of Germany (p. 423)

**Bern** (47°N, 7°E) the capital of Switzerland (p. 423)

**Bogotá** (4°N, 72°W) capital of Colombia (p. 184)

**Bolivia** a country in South America (p. 227)

**Bosnia and Herzegovina** a country on the Balkan Peninsula (p. 467)

**Boston** (42°N, 71°W) the capital of Massachusetts (p. 256)

**Brasília** (10°S, 55°W) the capital of Brazil (p. 213)

**Bratislava** (48°N, 17°E) the capital of Slovakia (p. 467)

**Brazil** a country in South America (p. 205)

**Brazilian Highlands** a region of rugged, old, eroded mountains in eastern Brazil (p. 207)

**British Columbia** a province in Canada (p. 274)

**British Isles** a group of islands off the northwestern coast of Europe including Britain and Ireland (p. 449)

**Brussels** (51°N, 4°E) the capital of Belgium (p. 423)

**Bucharest** (44°N, 26°E) the capital of Romania (p. 467)

**Budapest** (48°N, 19°E) the capital of Hungary (p. 467)

**Buenos Aires** (BWAY-nuhs y-reez) (36°S, 60°W) the capital of Argentina (p. 205)

**Bulgaria** a country in the Balkans (p. 467)

**Calgary** (51°N, 114°W) a large city in the province of Alberta in Canada (p. 274)

**California** (CA) a state in the western United States; admitted in 1850 (pp. 538–539)

**Canada** a country in North America (p. 274)

**Canadian Shield** a region of ancient rock that covers more than half of Canada (p. 277)

**Cancún** (21°N, 87°W) a popular resort on Mexico's Caribbean coast (p. 153)

**Caracas** (11°N, 67°W) the capital of Venezuela (p. 185)

**Caribbean Islands** a group of islands in the Caribbean Sea (p. 163)

**Caribbean Sea** an arm of the Atlantic Ocean between North and South America (p. 161)

**Carpathians** (kahr-PAY-thee-uhnz) a major mountain chain in central and eastern Europe (p. 468)

**Cartagena** (kahr-tah-HAY-nuh) (10°N, 74°W) a coastal city in northern Colombia (p. 184)

**Carthage** (KAHR-thij) (37°N, 10°E) an ancient Phoenician port city in North Africa in modern Tunisia (p. 321)

**Cascade Range** a mountain range in western North America (p. 250)

**Caspian Sea** a large inland sea located between Europe and Asia (p. 490)

**Caucasus Mountains** a mountain system in southeastern Europe between the Black Sea and Caspian Sea (p. 492)

**Cayenne** (4°N, 53°W) the capital of French Guiana (p. 185)

**Central America** a region in North America south of Mexico (p. 162)

**Central Uplands** an area of hills, plateaus, and valleys in central Europe (p. 425)

**Chechnya** (CHECH-nyuh) a republic in Russia that is fighting a violent struggle for independence (p. 506)

**Chernobyl** (51°N, 30°E) a city in Ukraine; the world's worst nuclear reactor accident occurred there in 1986 (p. 471)

**Chicago** (42°N, 88°W) a major U.S. city and port in northeastern Illinois on Lake Michigan (p. 265)

**Chile** (CHEE-lay) a country in western South America (p. 227)

**Chişinau** (47°N, 29°E) the capital of Moldova (p. 467)

**Coast Mountains** a mountain range in North America along the Pacific coast (p. 277)

**Colombia** a country in South America (p. 184)

**Colorado** (CO) a state in the southwestern United States; admitted in 1876 (pp. 538–539)

**Connecticut** (CT) a state in the northeastern United States; admitted in 1788 and one of the original 13 colonies (pp. 538–539)

**Copenhagen** (56°N, 13°E) the capital of Denmark (p. 447)

**Costa Rica** a country in Central America (p. 160)

**Croatia** a country in the Balkans (p. 467)

**Cuba** an island country in the Caribbean Sea south of Florida (p. 161)

**Cuzco** (KOO-skoh) (14°S, 72°W) a city in Peru and the former capital of the Inca Empire (p. 129)

**Czech Republic** a country in Eastern Europe (p. 467)

**Danube** (DAN-yoob) the second-longest river in Europe; it flows from Germany east to the Black Sea (p. 425)

**Delaware** (DE) a state in the eastern United States; admitted in 1787 and one of the original 13 colonies (pp. 538–539)

**Denmark** a country in Northern Europe (p. 447)

**Detroit** (42°N, 83°W) a large U.S. city in Michigan (p. 539)

**District of Columbia** (39°N, 77°W) a federal district between Maryland and Virginia; the capital of the United States (p. 247)

**Dominican Republic** a country in the Caribbean (p. 161)

**Dublin** (53°N, 6°W) the capital of Ireland (p. 446)

 **E**

**Eastern Hemisphere** the half of the globe between the prime meridian and 180° longitude that includes most of Africa and Europe as well as Asia, Australia, and the Indian Ocean (p. H3)

**Ecuador** a country in South America (p. 227)

**Edinburgh** (56°N, 3°W) the capital of Scotland (p. 455)

**Egypt** a country in North Africa on the Mediterranean Sea; home to one of the world's oldest civilizations (p. 553)

**El Salvador** a country in Central America (p. 160)

**England** a part of the United Kingdom occupying most of the island of Great Britain (p. 455)

**English Channel** a strait of the Atlantic Ocean between England and France (p. 426)

**equator** the imaginary line of latitude that circles the globe halfway between the North and South Poles (p. H2)

**Estonia** a Baltic country in Eastern Europe (p. 467)

**Europe** the continent between the Ural Mountains and the Atlantic Ocean (p. 548)

 **F**

**Finland** a country in Northern Europe (p. 447)

**Florence** (44°N, 11°E) a city in Italy that was a major center of the Renaissance (p. 345)

**Florida** (FL) a state in the southeastern United States; admitted in 1845 (p. 247)

**France** a country in West-Central Europe (p. 423)

**French Guiana** (gee-A-nuh) a region of France in northern South America (p. 185)

 **G**

**Galápagos Islands** a group of islands in the Pacific Ocean that are part of Ecuador (p. 229)

**Georgetown** (5°N, 59°W) capital of Guyana (p. 185)

**Georgia** (GA) a state in the southeastern United States; admitted in 1788 and one of the original 13 colonies (pp. 538–539)

**Georgia** a country in the Caucasus Mountains (p. 509)

**Germany** a country in West-Central Europe (p. 423)

**Grand Banks** (47°N, 52°W) a rich fishing ground near Newfoundland, Canada (p. 277)

**Grand Canyon** a large canyon in the southwestern United States (p. 536)

**Greater Antilles** an island group in the Caribbean that includes Cuba, Jamaica, Hispaniola, and Puerto Rico (p. 163)

**Great Lakes** a group of five large freshwater lakes in North America; they are Lake Superior, Lake Michigan, Lake Huron, Lake Erie, and Lake Ontario; the largest freshwater lake system in the world (p. 249)

**Great Plains** a large region of plains and grasslands in central North America (p. 249)

**Greece** a country in Southern Europe (p. 399)

**Greenland** a large island in North America controlled by Denmark that was settled by the Vikings (p. 275)

**Guadalajara** (21°N, 103°W) the second-largest city in Mexico (p. 141)

**Guadeloupe** a group of islands in the Caribbean that are part of France (p. 161)

**Guatemala** a country in Central America (p. 160)

**Guatemala City** (15°N, 91°W) the capital of Guatemala (p. 160)

**Guayaquil** (gwah-ah-KEEL) (2°S, 80°W) a city in Ecuador (p. 227)

**Guiana Highlands** (gee-YAH-nah) a large plateau region in northern South America (p. 187)

**Gulf of Mexico** a large gulf off the southeastern coast of North America (p. 141)

**Gulf Stream** a warm ocean current that flows north along the east coast of the United States (p. 52)

**Guyana** (gy-AH-nuh) a country in northern South America (p. 185)

**H**

**Haiti** a country in the Caribbean (p. 161)

**Havana** (23°N, 82°W) the capital of Cuba (p. 161)

**Hawaii** (HI) state in the Pacific Ocean comprised of the Hawaiian Islands; admitted in 1959 (pp. 546–547)

**Helsinki** (60°N, 25°E) the capital of Finland (p. 447)

**Hispaniola** (ees-pah-nee-O-lah) an island in the Caribbean (p. 163)
**Holland** a region in the Netherlands (p. 432)
**Honduras** a country in Central America (p. 160)
**Hudson Bay** a large bay in central Canada (p. 277)
**Hungary** a country in central Europe (p. 467)

**Iberian Peninsula** a large peninsula in Southern Europe; Spain and Portugal are located there (p. 415)
**Iceland** an island country in Northern Europe (p. 446)
**Idaho** (ID) a state in the northwestern United States; admitted in 1890 (pp. 538–539)
**Illinois** (IL) a state in the north-central United States; admitted in 1819 (pp. 538–539)
**India** a country in South Asia (p. 551)
**Indiana** (IN) a state in the north-central United States; admitted in 1816 (pp. 538–539)
**Indian Ocean** the world's third-largest ocean; located east of Africa, south of Asia, and west of Australia (p. 541)
**Interior Plains** a large plains region of North America (p. 249)
**Iowa** (IA) a state in the north-central United States; admitted in 1846 (pp. 538–539)
**Iraq** a country located between Iran and Saudi Arabia in Southwest Asia (p. 551)
**Ireland** a country west of Britain in the British Isles (p. 446)
**Italy** a country in Southern Europe (p. 399)

**Jamaica** an island country in the Caribbean (p. 161)
**Kaliningrad** (55°N, 21°E) a strategic city and port controlled by Russia (p. 503)
**Kamchatka Peninsula** a large, mountainous peninsula in eastern Russia on the Pacific Ocean (p. 493)
**Kansas** (KS) a state in the central United States; admitted in 1861 (pp. 538–539)
**Kentucky** (KY) a state in the east-central United States; admitted in 1792 (pp. 538–539)
**Kenya** a country in East Africa, south of Ethiopia (p. 553)

**Kiev** (50°N, 31°E) the capital of Ukraine (p. 467)
**Kjolen Mountains** a mountain range in Scandinavia along the Norway-Sweden border (p. 448)

**L**

**Lake Baikal** a huge freshwater lake in Russia; it is the deepest lake in the world (p. 493)
**Lake Maracaibo** (mah-rah-KY-boh) (10°N, 72°W) an oil-rich body of water in Venezuela (p. 197)
**Lake Texcoco** (tays-KOH-koh) an ancient lake in Mexico; it was the site of Tenochtitlán (p. 124)
**La Paz** (17°S, 65°W) the capital of Bolivia (p. 227)
**Latin America** a region in the Western Hemisphere; it includes countries where Spanish, Portuguese, or French culture shaped life (p. 142)
**Latvia** a Baltic country in Eastern Europe (p. 467)
**Lesser Antilles** a group of small islands in the Caribbean; they stretch from the Virgin Islands in the north to Trinidad in the south (p. 163)
**Lima** (10°S, 75°W) the capital of Peru (p. 227)
**Lisbon** (39°N, 9°W) the capital of Portugal (p. 398)
**Lithuania** a Baltic country in Eastern Europe (p. 467)
**Ljubljana** (46°N, 15°E) the capital of Slovenia (p. 467)
**Llanos** a plains region in South America (p. 187)
**London** (51°N, 1°W) the capital of England and the United Kingdom (p. 446)
**Louisiana** (LA) a state in the southeastern United States; admitted in 1812 (pp. 538–539)
**Luxembourg** a country in West-Central Europe (p. 423)
**Luxembourg City** (45°N 6°E) capital of Luxembourg (p. 423)

**M**

**Macedonia** a country on the Balkan Peninsula in southeastern Europe (p. 467)
**Machu Picchu** (MAH-choo PEEK-choo) (13°S, 73°W) a sacred city and fortress of the Incas (p. 131)
**Madrid** (40°N, 4°W) the capital of Spain (p. 398)
**Magdalena River** a river in Colombia (p. 184)
**Maine** (ME) a state in the northeastern United States; admitted in 1820 (pp. 538–539)
**Manaus** (3°S, 60°W) a major port and industrial city in Brazil's Amazon rain forest (p. 213)
**Manitoba** a province in central Canada (p. 275)

**Mariana Trench** the world's deepest ocean trench; located in the Pacific Ocean (p. 37)

**Marseille** (mar-SAY) (43°N, 5°E) a port city in France on the Mediterranean Sea (p. 423)

**Martinique** a group of islands in the Caribbean that are part of France (p. 175)

**Maryland** (MD) a state in the eastern United States; admitted in 1788 and one of the original 13 colonies (pp. 538–539)

**Massachusetts** (MA) a state in the northeastern United States; admitted in 1788 and one of the original 13 colonies (pp. 538–539)

**Massif Central** (ma-SEEF sahn-TRAHL) an upland region in south-central France (p. 425)

**Mato Grosso Plateau** a high plateau area in Brazil (p. 207)

**Mediterranean Sea** a sea surrounded by Europe, Asia, and Africa (p. 401)

**Mesoamerica** a region in North America; the first permanent farming settlements in the Americas developed in Mesoamerica (p. 118)

**Mexican Plateau** a high, mostly rugged region covering much of the interior of Mexico (p. 143)

**Mexico** a country in North America (p. 141)

**Mexico City** (23°N, 104°W) the capital of Mexico (p. 141)

**Michigan** (MI) a state in the north-central United States; admitted in 1837 (pp. 538–539)

**Mid-Atlantic Ridge** a mid-ocean ridge located in the Atlantic Ocean (p. 37)

**Minnesota** (MN) a state in the north-central United States; admitted in 1858 (pp. 538–539)

**Mississippi** (MS) a state in the southeastern United States; admitted in 1817 (pp. 538–539)

**Mississippi River** a major river in the central United States (p. 249)

**Missouri** (MO) a state in the central United States; admitted in 1821 (pp. 538–539)

**Moldova** a country in Eastern Europe (p. 467)

**Monaco** a small country in West-Central Europe (p. 423)

**Montana** (MT) a state in the northern United States; admitted in 1889 (pp. 538–539)

**Mont Blanc** (mawn BLAHN) (46°N, 7°E) a mountain peak in France; highest of the Alps (p. 426)

**Monterrey** (26°N, 100°W) a large city and industrial center in northern Mexico (p. 155)

**Montevideo** (mawn-tay-vee-DAY-oh) (35°S, 56°W) the capital of Uruguay (p. 205)

**Montreal** (46°N, 74°W) a major Canadian city in Quebec; founded by the French in 1642 (p. 288)

**Moscow** (56°N, 38°E) the capital of Russia (p. 490)

**Montenegro** (43°N, 19°E) a country in the Balkans (p. 171)

**Mount Elbrus** (el-BROOS) the highest peak of the Caucasus Mountains (p. 493)

**Mount Saint Helens** (46°N, 122°W) a volcano in Washington State that erupted in 1980 (p. 250)

**Nassau** (25°N, 77°W) the capital of the Bahamas (p. 161)

**Nebraska** (NE) a state in the central United States; admitted in 1867 (pp. 538–539)

**Netherlands** a country in West-Central Europe (p. 423)

**Nevada** (NV) a state in the western United States; admitted in 1864 (pp. 538–539)

**New Brunswick** a province in Canada (p. 275)

**Newfoundland and Labrador** an island province in eastern Canada (p. 275)

**New Hampshire** (NH) a state in the northeastern United States; admitted in 1788 and one of the original 13 colonies (pp. 538–539)

**New Jersey** (NJ) a state in the northeastern United States; admitted in 1787 and one of the original 13 colonies (pp. 538–539)

**New Mexico** (NM) a state in the southwestern United States; admitted in 1912 (pp. 538–539)

**New Orleans** (30°N, 90°W) a major U.S. port city located in southeastern Louisiana (p. 247)

**New York** (NY) a state in the northeastern United States; admitted in 1788 and one of the original 13 colonies (pp. 538–539)

**New York City** (41°N, 74°W) a city in the northeastern United States; the largest city in the United States (p. 539)

**Nicaragua** a country in Central America (p. 160)

**Normandy** a region in northwestern France (p. 386)

**North America** a continent including Canada, the United States, Mexico, Central America, and the Caribbean islands (p. 544)

**North Atlantic Current** a warm ocean current that flows across the Atlantic Ocean and along Western Europe (p. 52)

**North Carolina** (NC) a state in the southeastern United States; admitted in 1789 and one of the original 13 colonies (pp. 538–539)

**North Dakota** (ND) a state in the north-central United States; admitted in 1889 (pp. 538–539)

**Northern European Plain** a large plain across central and northern Europe (p. 425)

**Northern Hemisphere** the northern half of the globe, between the equator and the North Pole (p. H3)

**Northern Ireland** a part of the United Kingdom occupying the northeastern portion of the island of Ireland (p. 455)

**North Pole** (90°N) the northern point of Earth's axis (p. 555)

**North Sea** a shallow arm of the Atlantic Ocean in Northern Europe (p. 426)

**Northwest Territories** a territory in Canada (p. 274)

**Norway** a country in Northern Europe (p. 447)

**Nova Scotia** (noh-vuh SKOH-shuh) a province in eastern Canada (p. 275)

**Nunavut** (NOO-nah-VOOT) a territory in northern Canada created as a homeland for Canada's Inuit people (p. 275)

**Ob River** a long river in central Russia (p. 493)

**Ohio** (OH) a state in the north-central United States; admitted in 1803 (pp. 538–539)

**Oklahoma** (OK) a state in the south-central United States; admitted in 1907 (pp. 538–539)

**Ontario** a province in east-central Canada (p. 275)

**Oregon** (OR) a state in the northwestern United States; admitted in 1859 (pp. 538–539)

**Orinoco River** (OHR-ee-NOH-koh) a major river in Venezuela (p. 185)

**Oslo** (60°N, 11°E) the capital of Norway (p. 447)

**Ottawa** (45°N, 76°W) capital of Canada (p. 275)

**Pacific Ocean** the world's largest ocean; located between Asia and the Americas (pp. 540–541)

**Palenque** (pay-LENG-kay) (18°N, 92°W) an ancient Maya city in southern Mexico (p. 119)

**Pampas** a fertile plains region in southern South America located mainly in Argentina (p. 207)

**Panama** a country in Central America (p. 161)

**Panama Canal** (26°N, 80°W) a canal built by the United States in the early 1900s across the Isthmus of Panama (p. 172)

**Panama City** (8°N, 81°W) capital of Panama (p. 161)

**Paraguay** a country in South America (p. 205)

**Paraguay River** a river in South America (p. 207)

**Paramaribo** (6°N, 55°W) the capital of Suriname (p. 185)

**Paris** (46°N, 0°) the capital of France (p. 423)

**Patagonia** a region of dry plains and plateaus east of the Andes in southern Argentina (p. 207)

**Pennsylvania** (PA) a state in the eastern United States; admitted in 1787 and one of the original 13 colonies (pp. 538–539)

**Peru** a country in western South America (p. 227)

**Podgorica** (43°N, 19°E) capital of Montenegro (p. 171)

**Poland** a country in Eastern Europe (p. 467)

**Popocatépetl** (poh-poh-cah-TE-pet-uhl) (19°N, 99°W) a volcano near Mexico City (p. 143)

**Po River** a major river in northern Italy (p. 401)

**Port-au-Prince** (pohr-toh-PRINS) (19°N, 72°W) the capital of Haiti (p. 177)

**Port of Spain** (11°N, 61°W) the capital of Trinidad and Tobago (p. 161)

**Portugal** a country in Southern Europe on the Iberian Peninsula (p. 398)

**Prague** (50°N, 14°E) capital of the Czech Republic (p. 467)

**prime meridian** an imaginary line that runs through Greenwich, England, at 0° longitude (p. H2)

**Prince Edward Island** (46°N, 64°W) a small province in eastern Canada (p. 275)

**Puerto Rico** an island east of Cuba and southeast of Florida; it is a U.S. territory (p. 161)

**Pyrenees** (PIR-uh-neez) a high mountain range between Spain and France (p. 401)

**Q, R**

**Quebec** a province in eastern Canada (p. 275)

**Quito** (2°S, 78°W) the capital of Ecuador (p. 227)

**Reykjavik** (64°N, 22°W) the capital of Iceland (p. 446)

**Rhine** a major river in Europe; it begins in Switzerland and flows north to the North Sea (p. 425)

**Rhode Island** (RI) a state in the northeastern United States; admitted in 1790 and one of the original 13 colonies (pp. 538–539)

**Riga** (57°N, 24°E) the capital of Latvia (p. 467)

**Ring of Fire** a region that circles the Pacific Ocean; known for its earthquakes and volcanoes (p. 42)

**Río Bravo** the Mexican name for the river known as the Rio Grande in the United States; it forms the border between Mexico and Texas (p. 143)

**Río de Janeiro** (23°N, 43°W) the second-largest city in Brazil; it is a major port city and Brazil's former capital (p. 205)

**Río de la Plata** (REE-oh day lah PLAH-tah) a body of water in South America (p. 207)

**Rocky Mountains** a major mountain range in western North America (p. 249)

**Romania** a country in Eastern Europe (p. 467)

**Rome** (42°N, 13°E) the capital of Italy; it was the capital of the ancient Roman Empire (p. 399)

**Ruhr** a major industrial region in Germany (p. 439)

**Russia** a huge country that extends from Eastern Europe to the Pacific Ocean (p. 491)

## S

**St. Kitts and Nevis** country in the Caribbean (p. 179)

**St. Lawrence River** a river in North America that flows from the Great Lakes to the Atlantic Ocean (p. 276)

**San Andreas Fault** an area at the boundary of the Pacific tectonic plate where earthquakes are common; located in California (p. 38)

**San Francisco** (37°N, 122°W) a major U.S. port city in Northern California (p. 246)

**San Jose** (10°N, 84°W) capital of Costa Rica (p. 160)

**San Salvador** (14°N, 89°W) the capital of El Salvador (p. 160)

**Santiago** (33°S, 71°W) the capital of Chile (p. 227)

**Santo Domingo** (19°N, 71°W) the capital of the Dominican Republic (p. 161)

**São Paulo** (24°S, 47°W) the largest city in Brazil and South America (p. 205)

**Sarajevo** (44°N, 18°E) the capital of Bosnia and Herzegovina (p. 467)

**Saskatchewan** a province in Canada (p. 275)

**Scandinavia** a region of islands and peninsulas in far northern Europe; includes the countries of Norway, Sweden, Finland, and Denmark (p. 549)

**Scandinavian Peninsula** a large peninsula in Northern Europe that includes Norway and Sweden (p. 449)

**Scotland** a part of the United Kingdom located in the northern part of Great Britain (p. 455)

**Seattle** (48°N, 122°W) a major U.S. port and city in Washington State (p. 246)

**Serbia** a country in the Balkans (p. 467)

**Siberia** a huge region in eastern Russia (p. 493)

**Sierra Madre** (SYER-rah MAH-dray) the chief mountain range in Mexico (p. 143)

**Sierra Nevada** a large mountain range mainly in California (p. 249)

**Slovakia** a country in Eastern Europe (p. 467)

**Slovenia** a country in Eastern Europe (p. 467)

**Sofia** (43°N, 23°E) the capital of Bulgaria (p. 467)

**South America** a continent in the Western and Southern hemispheres (p. 546)

**South Carolina** (SC) a state in the southeastern United States; admitted in 1788 and one of the original 13 colonies (pp. 538–539)

**South Dakota** (SD) a state in the north-central United States; admitted in 1889 (pp. 538–539)

**Southern Hemisphere** the southern half of the globe, between the equator and the South Pole (p. H3)

**South Pole** (90°S) the southern point of Earth's axis (p. 563)

**Spain** a country in Southern Europe on the Iberian Peninsula; it colonized much of the Americas (p. 398)

**Sparta** (37°N, 22°E) an ancient city-state in Greece (p. 315)

**Stockholm** (59°N, 18°E) the capital of Sweden (p. 447)

**Strait of Magellan** a waterway through the southern tip of South America (p. 229)

**Sucre** (SOO-kray) (19°S, 65°W) the capital of Bolivia (p. 227)

**Suriname** (soohr-uh-NAHM) a country in northern South America (p. 185)

**Sweden** a country in Northern Europe (p. 447)

**Switzerland** a country in West-Central Europe (p. 423)

## T

**Tallinn** (59°N, 25°E) the capital of Estonia (p. 467)

**Tbilisi** (42°N, 45°E) the capital of Georgia (p. 509)

**Tegucigalpa** (15°N, 87°W) the capital of Honduras (p. 160)

**Tennessee** (TN) a state in the south-central United States; admitted in 1796 (pp. 538–539)

**Tenochtitlán** (tay-nawch-teet-LAHN) the capital of the Aztec Empire (p. 124)

**Texas** (TX) a state and former independent republic in the south-central United States; admitted in 1845 (pp. 538–539)

**Tierra del Fuego** a group of islands in southern South America (p. 229)

**Tigris River** a river in Southwest Asia (p. 558)

**Tirana** (41°N, 20°E) the capital of Albania (p. 467)

**Toronto** (44°N, 79°W) Canada's largest city (p. 275)

**Trinidad and Tobago** a country in the Caribbean just north of Venezuela (p. 161)

**Tropic of Cancer** the parallel 23.5° north of the equator; parallel on the globe at which the sun's most direct rays strike Earth during the June solstice (pp. 540–541)

**Tropic of Capricorn** the parallel at 23.5° south of the equator; parallel on the globe at which the sun's most direct rays strike Earth during the December solstice (pp. 540–541)

## U

**Ukraine** a country in Eastern Europe (p. 467)

**United Kingdom** a country in the British Isles that includes England, Wales, Scotland, and Northern Ireland (p. 446)

**United States of America** a country in North America located between Canada and Mexico (pp. 246–247)

**Ural Mountains** (YOOHR-uhl) a mountain range in Russia that separates Europe and Asia (p. 492)

**Uruguay** a country in South America (p. 205)

**Utah** (UT) a state in the western United States; admitted in 1896 (pp. 538–539)

## V

**Valley of Mexico** a large plateau region in central Mexico (p. 143)

**Vancouver** (49°N, 123°W) a city in western Canada just north of the U.S. border (p. 274)

**Vatican City** (42°N, 12°E) a small country in Rome that is the head of the Roman Catholic Church (p. 399)

**Venezuela** a country in South America (p. 185)

**Vermont** (VT) a state in the northeastern United States; admitted in 1791 (pp. 538–539)

**Vienna** (45°N, 12°E) the capital of Austria (p. 423)

**Vilnius** (55°N, 25°E) the capital of Lithuania (p. 467)

**Virginia** (VA) a state in the eastern United States; admitted in 1788 and one of the original 13 colonies (pp. 538–539)

**Virgin Islands** a group of small islands in the Caribbean (p. 161)

**Volga** (VAHL-guh) the longest river in Europe and Russia's most important commercial river (p. 493)

## W

**Wales** a part of the United Kingdom located west of England on the island of Great Britain (p. 455)

**Warsaw** (52°N, 21°E) the capital of Poland (p. 467)

**Washington** (WA) a state in the northwestern United States; admitted in 1889 (pp. 546–547)

**Washington, D.C.** (39°N, 77°W) the capital of the United States (p. 247)

**Western Hemisphere** the half of the globe between 180° and the prime meridian that includes North and South America and the Pacific and Atlantic oceans (p. H3)

**West Indies** a group of more than 1,200 islands in the Caribbean Sea (p. 174)

**West Virginia** (WV) a state in the east-central United States; admitted in 1863 (pp. 538–539)

**Wisconsin** (WI) a state in the north-central United States; admitted in 1848 (pp. 538–539)

**Wyoming** (WY) a state in the northwestern United States; admitted in 1890 (pp. 538–539)

## Y, Z

**Yerevan** (40°N, 45°E) the capital of Armenia (p. 509)

**Yucatán Peninsula** (yoo-kah-TAHN) a large peninsula that separates the Caribbean Sea from the Gulf of Mexico (p. 142)

**Yugoslavia** a former country in the Balkans that broke apart in the 1990s (p. 484)

**Yukon Territory** a territory in Canada (p. 274)

**Zagreb** (46°N, 16°E) the capital of Croatia (p. 467)

**Zurich** (47°N, 9°E) a city in Switzerland (p. 423)

GAZETTEER

# English and Spanish Glossary

| MARK | AS IN | RESPELLING | EXAMPLE |
|------|-------|-----------|---------|
| a | alphabet | a | *AL-fuh-bet |
| ā | Asia | ay | AY-zhuh |
| ä | cart, top | ah | KAHRT, TAHP |
| e | let, ten | e | LET, TEN |
| ē | even, leaf | ee | EE-vuhn, LEEF |
| i | it, tip, British | i | IT, TIP, BRIT-ish |
| ī | site, buy, Ohio | y | SYT, BY, oh-HY-oh |
| | iris | eye | EYE-ris |
| k | card | k | KAHRD |
| kw | quest | kw | KWEST |
| ō | over, rainbow | oh | OH-vuhr, RAYN-boh |
| ů | book, wood | ooh | BOOHK, WOOHD |
| ȯ | all, orchid | aw | AWL, AWR-kid |
| ȯi | foil, coin | oy | FOYL, KOYN |
| aů | out | ow | OWT |
| ə | cup, butter | uh | KUHP, BUHT-uhr |
| ü | rule, food | oo | ROOL, FOOD |
| yü | few | yoo | FYOO |
| zh | vision | zh | VIZH-uhn |

*A syllable printed in small capital letters receives heavier emphasis than the other syllable(s) in a word.

## Phonetic Respelling and Pronunciation Guide

Many of the key terms in this textbook have been respelled to help you pronounce them. The letter combinations used in the respelling throughout the narrative are explained in this phonetic respelling and pronunciation guide. The guide is adapted from *Merriam-Webster's Collegiate Dictionary, Eleventh Edition; Merriam-Webster's Geographical Dictionary;* and *Merriam-Webster's Biographical Dictionary.*

**absolute location** a specific description of where a place is located; absolute location is often expressed using latitude and longitude (p. 12)
  **ubicación absoluta** descripción específica del lugar donde se ubica un punto; con frecuencia se define en términos de latitud y longitud (pág. 12)

**alliance** an agreement to work together (p. 377)
  **alianza** acuerdo de colaboración (pág. 377)

**Allies** Great Britain, France, the Soviet Union, and the United States; they joined together in World War II against Germany, Italy, and Japan (p. 385)
  **Aliados** Gran Bretaña, Francia, la Unión Soviética y Estados Unidos; se unieron durante la Segunda Guerra Mundial contra Alemania, Italia y Japón (pág. 385)

**altiplano** a broad, high plateau that lies between the ridges of the Andes (p. 229)
  **altiplano** meseta amplia y elevada que se extiende entre las cadenas montañosas de los Andes (pág. 229)

**aqueduct** a human-made raised channel that carries water from distant places (p. 322)
  **acueducto** canal elevado hecho por el ser humano que trae agua desde lugares lejanos (pág. 322)

**archipelago** (ahr-kuh-PE-luh-goh) a large group of islands (p. 163)
  **archipiélago** grupo grande de islas (pág. 163)

**arms race** a competition between countries to build superior weapons (p. 390)
  **carrera armamentista** competencia entre países para construir armas mejores (pág. 390)

**Axis Powers** the name for the alliance formed by Germany, Italy, and Japan during World War II (p. 385)
  **Potencias del Eje** nombre de la alianza formada por Alemania, Italia y Japón durante la Segunda Guerra Mundial (pág. 385)

**bilingual** a term used to describe people who speak two languages (p. 260)
  **bilingüe** término utilizado para describir a las personas que hablan dos idiomas (pág. 260)

**birthrate** the annual number of births per 1,000 people (p. 88)
  **índice de natalidad** número de nacimientos por cada 1,000 personas en un año (pág. 88)

**Bolsheviks** a radical Russian Communist group that seized power in 1917 (p. 497)

bolcheviques grupo comunista ruso radical que obtuvo el poder en 1917 (pág. 497)

**canton** one of 26 districts in the republic of Switzerland (p. 441)

cantón uno de los 26 distritos de la república de Suiza (pág. 441)

**capitalism** an economic system in which individuals and private businesses run most industries (p. 368)

capitalismo sistema económico en el que los individuos y las empresas privadas controlan la mayoría de las industrias (pág. 368)

**cartography** the science of making maps (p. 19)

cartografía ciencia de crear mapas (pág. 19)

**cash crop** a crop that farmers grow mainly to sell for a profit (p. 153)

cultivo comercial cultivo que los agricultores producen principalmente para vender y obtener ganancias (pág. 153)

**Catholic Reformation** the effort of the late 1500s and 1600s to reform the Catholic Church from within; also called the Counter-Reformation (p. 349)

Reforma católica iniciativa para reformar la Iglesia católica desde dentro a finales del siglo XVI y en el XVII; también conocida como la Contrarreforma (pág. 349)

**causeway** a raised road across water or wet ground (p. 124)

carretera elevada camino construido sobre agua o terreno pantanoso (pág. 124)

**chancellor** a German prime minister (p. 439)

canciller primer ministro alemán (pág. 439)

**circumnavigate** to go all the way around (p. 355)

circunnavegar dar una vuelta completa (pág. 355)

**citizen** a person who has the right to take part in government (p. 319)

ciudadano persona que tiene el derecho de participar en el gobierno (pág. 319)

**city-state** a political unit consisting of a city and its surrounding countryside (p. 310)

cuidad estado unidad política formada por una ciudad y los campos que la rodean (pág. 310)

**civil war** a conflict between two or more groups within a country (p. 170)

guerra civil conflicto entre dos o más grupos dentro de un país (pág. 170)

**climate** a region's average weather conditions over a long period of time (p. 50)

clima condiciones del tiempo promedio de una región durante un período largo de tiempo (pág. 50)

**cloud forest** a moist, high-elevation tropical forest where low clouds are common (p. 164)

bosque nuboso bosque tropical de gran elevación y humedad donde los bancos de nubes son muy comunes (pág. 164)

**Cold War** a period of distrust between the United States and Soviet Union after World War II, when there was a tense rivalry between the two superpowers but no direct fighting (p. 388)

Guerra Fría período de desconfianza entre Estados Unidos y la Unión Soviética que siguió a la Segunda Guerra Mundial; existía una rivalidad tensa entre las dos superpotencias, pero no se llegó a la lucha directa (pág. 388)

**colony** a territory inhabited and controlled by people from a foreign land (p. 256)

colonia territorio habitado y controlado por personas de otro país (pág. 256)

**command economy** an economic system in which the central government makes all economic decisions (p. 94)

economía autoritaria sistema económico en el que el gobierno central toma todas las decisiones económicas (pág. 94)

**common market** a group of nations that cooperates to make trade among members easier (p. 392)

mercado común grupo de naciones que cooperan para facilitar el comercio entre los miembros (pág. 392)

**commonwealth** a self-governing territory associated with another country (p. 177)

mancomunidad o estado libre asociado territorio autogobernado asociado con otro país (pág. 177)

**Commonwealth of Independent States (CIS)** a union of former Soviet republics that meets about issues such as trade and immigration (p. 478)

Comunidad de Estados Independientes (CEI) unión de ex repúblicas soviéticas que se reúne para tratar temas como el comercio y la inmigración (pág. 478)

**Communism** an economic and political system in which the government owns all businesses and controls the economy (pp. 92, 380)

comunismo sistema económico y político en el que el gobierno es dueño de todos los negocios y controla la economía (págs. 92, 380)

**conquistadors** (kahn-KEES-tuh-dohrs) Spanish soldiers in the Americas who explored new lands, searched for gold and silver, and tried to spread Christianity (p. 128)

conquistadores soldados españoles en América que exploraron nuevas tierras, buscaron oro y plata e intentaron difundir el cristianismo (pág. 128)

**constitutional monarchy** a type of democracy in which a monarch serves as head of state, but a legislature makes the laws (p. 454)

**monarquía constitucional** tipo de democracia en la cual un monarca sirve como jefe de estado, pero una asamblea legislativa hace las leyes (pág. 454)

**continent** a large landmass that is part of Earth's crust; geographers identify seven continents (p. 36)

**continente** gran masa de tierra que forma parte de la corteza terrestre; los geógrafos identifican siete continentes (pág. 36)

**continental divide** an area of high ground that divides the flow of rivers towards opposite ends of a continent (p. 250)

**línea divisoria de aguas** zona de terreno elevado que divide el flujo de los ríos en dos direcciones, hacia los extremos opuestos de un continente (pág. 250)

**cooperative** an organization owned by its members and operated for their mutual benefit (p. 178)

**cooperativa** organización cuyos miembros son los propietarios y que es operada para beneficio de todos (pág. 178)

**cordillera** (kawr-duhl-YER-uh) a mountain system made up of roughly parallel ranges (p. 186)

**cordillera** sistema de cadenas montañosas aproximadamente paralelas entre sí (pág. 186)

**cosmopolitan** characterized by many foreign influences (p. 433)

**cosmopolita** caracterizado por muchas influencias extranjeras (pág. 433)

**coup** (KOO) a sudden overthrow of a government by a small group of people (p. 241)

**golpe de estado** derrocamiento repentino de un gobierno por parte de un grupo reducido de personas (pág. 241)

**Creole** an American-born descendant of Europeans (p. 236)

**criollo** persona de ascendencia europea y nacida en América (pág. 236)

**Crusades** a long series of wars between Christians and Muslims in Southwest Asia fought for control of the Holy Land; took place from 1096 to 1291 (p. 329)

**cruzadas** larga serie de guerras entre cristianos y musulmanes en el suroeste de Asia para conseguir el control de la Tierra Santa; tuvieron lugar entre 1096 y 1291 (pág. 329)

**cultural diffusion** the spread of culture traits from one region to another (p. 85)

**difusión cultural** difusión de rasgos culturales de una región a otra (pág. 85)

**cultural diversity** having a variety of cultures in the same area (p. 83)

**diversidad cultural** existencia de una variedad de culturas en la misma zona (pág. 83)

**culture** the set of beliefs, values, and practices that a group of people have in common (p. 80)

**cultura** conjunto de creencias, valores y costumbres compartidas por un grupo de personas (pág. 80)

**culture region** an area in which people have many shared culture traits (p. 82)

**región cultural** región en la que las personas comparten muchos rasgos culturales (pág. 82)

**culture trait** an activity or behavior in which people often take part (p. 81)

**rasgo cultural** actividad o conducta frecuente de las personas (pág. 81)

**Cyrllic** (suh-RIHL-ihk) a form of the Greek alphabet (p. 496)

**cirílico** forma del alfabeto griego (pág. 496)

**czar** (ZAHR) a Russian emperor (p. 497)

**zar** emperador ruso (pág. 497)

## D

**dachas** Russian country houses (p. 503)

**dachas** casas de campo rusas (pág. 503)

**Declaration of Independence** a document written in 1776 that declared the American colonies' independence from British rule (p. 361)

**Declaración de Independencia** documento escrito en 1776 que declaró la independencia de las colonias de América del Norte del dominio británico (pág. 361)

**Declaration of the Rights of Man and of the Citizen** a document written in France in 1789 that guaranteed specific freedoms for French citizens (p. 362)

**Declaración de los Derechos del Hombre y del Ciudadano** documento escrito en Francia en 1789 que garantizaba libertades específicas para los ciudadanos franceses (pág. 362)

**deforestation** the clearing of trees (pp. 69, 209)

**deforestación** tala de árboles (págs. 69, 209)

**democracy** a form of government in which the people elect leaders and rule by majority (p. 91)

**democracia** sistema de gobierno en el que el pueblo elige a sus líderes y gobierna por mayoría (pág. 91)

**desertification** the spread of desertlike conditions (p. 65)

**desertificación** ampliación de condiciones desérticas (pág. 65)

**developed countries** countries with strong economies and a high quality of life (p. 95)

**países desarrollados** países con economías sólidas y una alta calidad de vida (pág. 95)

**developing countries** countries with less productive economies and a lower quality of life (p. 95)

**países en vías de desarrollo** países con economías menos productivas y una menor calidad de vida (pág. 95)

**dialect** a regional variety of a language (p. 176)

**dialecto** variedad regional de un idioma (pág. 176)

**dictator** a ruler who has almost absolute power (p. 383)

**dictador** gobernante que tiene poder casi absoluto (pág. 383)

**disarm** to give up all weapons (p. 455)

**desarmarse** renunciar a todas las armas (pág. 455)

**E**

**earthquake** a sudden, violent movement of Earth's crust (p. 38)
　**terremoto** movimiento repentino y violento de la corteza terrestre (pág. 38)

**ecosystem** a group of plants and animals that depend on each other for survival, and the environment in which they live (p. 63)
　**ecosistema** grupo de plantas y animales que dependen unos de otros para sobrevivir, y el ambiente en el que estos viven (pág. 63)

**ecotourism** the practice of using an area's natural environment to attract tourists (p. 170)
　**ecoturismo** uso de regiones naturales para atraer turistas (pág. 170)

**El Niño** an ocean and weather pattern that affects the Pacific coast of the Americas; about every two to seven years, it warms normally cool ocean water and causes extreme ocean and weather events (p. 231)
　**El Niño** patrón oceánico y del tiempo que afecta a la costa del Pacífico de las Américas; aproximadamente cada dos a siete años, calienta las aguas normalmente frías del océano, y provoca sucesos oceánicos y climatológicos extremos (pág. 231)

**empire** a land with different territories and peoples under a single ruler (pp. 147, 320)
　**imperio** zona que reúne varios territorios y pueblos bajo un solo gobernante (págs. 147, 320)

**English Bill of Rights** a document approved in 1689 that listed rights for Parliament and the English people and drew on the principles of Magna Carta (p. 360)
　**Declaración de Derechos inglesa** documento aprobado en 1689 que enumeraba los derechos del Parlamento y del pueblo de Inglaterra, inspirada en los principios de la Carta Magna (pág. 360)

**Enlightenment** a period during the 1600s and 1700s when reason was used to guide people's thoughts about society, politics, and philosophy (p. 358)
　**Ilustración** período durante los siglos XVII y XVIII en el que la razón guiaba las ideas de las personas acerca de la sociedad, la política y la filosofía (pág. 358)

**environment** the land, water, climate, plants, and animals of an area; surroundings (pp. 12, 62)
　**ambiente** la tierra, el agua, el clima, las plantas y los animales de una zona; los alrededores (págs. 12, 62)

**erosion** the movement of sediment from one location to another (p. 39)
　**erosión** movimiento de sedimentos de un lugar a otro (pág. 39)

**estuary** a partially enclosed body of water where freshwater mixes with salty seawater (p. 207)
　**estuario** masa de agua parcialmente rodeada de tierra en la que el agua de mar se combina con agua dulce (pág. 207)

**ethnic cleansing** the effort to remove all members of an ethnic group from a country or region (p. 482)
　**limpieza étnica** esfuerzo por eliminar a todos los miembros de un grupo étnico de un país o región (pág. 482)

**ethnic group** a group of people who share a common culture and ancestry (p. 83)
　**grupo étnico** grupo de personas que comparten una cultura y una ascendencia (pág. 83)

**European Union (EU)** an organization that promotes political and economic cooperation in Europe (p. 392)
　**Unión Europea (UE)** organización que promueve la cooperación política y económica en Europa (pág. 392)

**extinct** no longer here; a species that has died out has become extinct (p. 64)
　**extinto** que ya no existe; una especie que ha desaparecido está extinta (pág. 64)

**F**

**favela** (fah-VE-lah) a huge slum in Brazil (p. 213)
　**favela** enorme barriada en Brasil (pág. 213)

**feudal system** the system of obligations that governed the relationships between lords and vassals in medieval Europe (p. 331)
　**sistema feudal** sistema de obligaciones que gobernaba las relaciones entre los señores feudales y los vasallos en la Europa medieval (pág. 331)

**fjord** (fyawrd) a narrow inlet of the sea set between high, rocky cliffs (p. 449)
　**fiordo** entrada estrecha del mar entre acantilados altos y rocosos (pág. 449)

**fossil fuels** nonrenewable resources that formed from the remains of ancient plants and animals; coal, petroleum, and natural gas are all fossil fuels (p. 69)
　**combustibles fósiles** recursos no renovables formados a partir de restos de plantas y animales antiguos; el carbón, el petróleo y el gas natural son combustibles fósiles (pág. 69)

**freshwater** water that is not salty; it makes up only about 3 percent of our total water supply (p. 31)
　**agua dulce** agua que no es salada; representa sólo alrededor del 3 por ciento de nuestro suministro total de agua (pág. 31)

**front** the place where two air masses of different temperatures or moisture content meet (p. 53)
　**frente** lugar en el que se encuentran dos masas de aire con diferente temperatura o humedad (pág. 53)

**ENGLISH AND SPANISH GLOSSARY**

## G

**gaucho** (GOW-choh) an Argentine cowboy (p. 217)
**gaucho** vaquero argentino (pág. 217)

**geography** the study of the world, its people, and the landscapes they create (p. 4)
**geografía** estudio del mundo, de sus habitantes y de los paisajes creados por el ser humano (pág. 4)

**geothermal energy** energy produced from the heat of Earth's interior (p. 450)
**energía geotérmica** energía producida a partir del calor del interior de la Tierra (pág. 450)

**geyser** a spring that shoots hot water and steam into the air (p. 462)
**géiser** manantial que lanza agua caliente y vapor al aire (pág. 462)

**glacier** a large area of slow moving ice (p. 31)
**glaciar** gran bloque de hielo que avanza con lentitud (pág. 31)

**globalization** the process in which countries are increasingly linked to each other through culture and trade (p. 97)
**globalización** proceso por el cual los países se encuentran cada vez más interconectados a través de la cultura y el comercio (pág. 97)

**globe** a spherical, or ball-shaped, model of the entire planet (p. 8)
**globo terráqueo** modelo esférico, o en forma de bola, de todo el planeta (pág. 8)

**golden age** a period in a society's history marked by great achievements (p. 312)
**edad dorada** período de la historia de una sociedad marcado por grandes logros (pág. 312)

**Gothic architecture** a style of architecture in Europe known for its high pointed ceilings, tall towers, and stained glass windows (p. 330)
**arquitectura gótica** estilo de arquitectura europea que se conoce por los techos altos en punta, las torres altas y los vitrales de colores (pág. 330)

**Great Depression** a global economic crisis that struck countries around the world in the 1930s (p. 382)
**Gran Depresión** crisis económica global que afectó a países de todo el mundo en la década de 1930 (pág. 382)

**gross domestic product (GDP)** the value of all goods and services produced within a country in a single year (p. 95)
**producto interior bruto (PIB)** valor de todos los bienes y servicios producidos en un país durante un año (pág. 95)

**groundwater** water found below Earth's surface (p. 32)
**agua subterránea** agua que se encuentra debajo de la superficie de la Tierra (pág. 32)

**guerrilla** a member of an irregular military force (p. 193)
**guerrillero** miembro de una fuerza militar irregular (pág. 193)

**gulag** a soviet labor camp (p. 498)
**gulag** campo soviético de trabajos forzados (pág. 498)

## H

**habitat** the place where a plant or animal lives (p. 64)
**hábitat** lugar en el que vive una planta o animal (pág. 64)

**hacienda** (hah-see-EN-duh) a huge expanse of farm or ranch land in the Americas (p. 148)
**hacienda** granja o rancho de gran tamaño en las Américas (pág. 148)

**Hellenistic** Greek-like; heavily influenced by Greek ideas (p. 316)
**helenístico** al estilo griego; muy influenciado por las ideas de la Grecia clásica (pág. 316)

**Holocaust** the Nazis' effort to wipe out the Jewish people in World War II, when 6 million Jews throughout Europe were killed (p. 385)
**Holocausto** intento de los nazis de eliminar al pueblo judío durante la Segunda Guerra Mundial, en el que se mató a 6 millones de judíos en toda Europa (pág. 385)

**human geography** the study of the world's people, communities, and landscapes (p. 18)
**geografía humana** estudio de los habitantes, las comunidades y los paisajes del mundo (pág. 18)

**humanism** the study of history, literature, public speaking, and art that led to a new way of thinking in Europe in the late 1300s (p. 345)
**humanismo** estudio de la historia, la literatura, la oratoria y el arte que produjo una nueva forma de pensar en Europa a finales del siglo XIV (pág. 345)

**humanitarian aid** assistance to people in distress (p. 100)
**ayuda humanitaria** ayuda a personas en peligro (pág. 100)

**humus** (HYOO-muhs) decayed plant or animal matter; it helps soil support abundant plant life (p. 65)
**humus** materia animal o vegetal descompuesta; contribuye a que crezca una gran cantidad de plantas en el suelo (pág. 65)

**hydroelectric power** the production of electricity from waterpower, such as from running water (p. 70)
**energía hidroeléctrica** producción de electricidad generada por la energía del agua, como la del agua corriente (pág. 70)

## I

**Industrial Revolution** the period of rapid growth in machine-made goods that changed the way people across Europe worked and lived; it began in Britain in the 1700s (p. 366)
**Revolución Industrial** período de rápido aumento de los bienes producidos con máquinas que cambió la forma de vivir y trabajar en toda Europa; comenzó en Gran Bretaña a comienzos del siglo XVIII (pág. 366)

**inflation** a rise in prices that occurs when currency loses its buying power (p. 152)
**inflación** aumento de los precios que ocurre cuando la moneda de un país pierde poder adquisitivo (pág. 152)

**informal economy** a part of the economy that is based on odd jobs that people perform without government regulation through taxes (p. 219)
**economía informal** parte de la economía basada en trabajos pequeños que se realizan sin el pago de impuestos regulados por el gobierno (pág. 219)

**infrastructure** the set of resources, like roads and factories, that a country needs to support economic activities (p. 475)
**infraestructura** conjunto de recursos, como carreteras o fábricas, que necesita un país para sostener su actividad económica (pág. 475)

**interdependence** a relationship between countries in which they rely on one another for resources, goods, or services (p. 99)
**interdependencia** una relación entre países en que dependen unos de otros para obtener recursos, bienes, o servicios (pág. 99)

**isthmus** a narrow strip of land that connects two larger land areas (p. 162)
**istmo** franja estrecha de tierra que une dos zonas más grandes (pág. 162)

**landform** a shape on the planet's surface, such as a mountain, valley, plain, island, or peninsula (p. 35)
**accidente geográfico** forma de la superficie terrestre, como una montaña, un valle, una llanura, una isla o una península (pág. 35)

**landlocked** completely surrounded by land with no direct access to the ocean (p. 220)
**sin salida al mar** completamente rodeado de tierra, sin acceso directo al océano (pág. 220)

**landscape** all the human and physical features that make a place unique (p. 4)
**paisaje** todas las características humanas y físicas que hacen que un lugar sea único (pág. 4)

**latitude** the distance north or south of Earth's equator (p. 27)
**latitud** distancia hacia el norte o el sur desde el ecuador (pág. 27)

**lava** magma that reaches Earth's surface (p. 37)
**lava** magma que llega a la superficie terrestre (pág. 37)

**llanero** (yah-NAY-roh) Venezuelan cowboy (p. 196)
**llanero** vaquero venezolano (pág. 196)

**Magna Carta** a document signed in 1215 by King John of England that required the king to honor certain rights (pág. 454)
**Carta Magna** documento firmado por el rey Juan de Inglaterra en 1215 que exigía que el rey respetara ciertos derechos (pág. 454)

**maize** corn (p. 118)
**maíz** cereal también conocido como elote o choclo (pág. 118)

**manor** a large estate owned by a knight or lord (p. 332)
**feudo** gran finca perteneciente a un caballero o señor feudal (pág. 332)

**map** a flat drawing that shows all or part of Earth's surface (p. 8)
**mapa** representación plana que muestra total o parcialmente la superficie de la Tierra (pág. 8)

**maquiladora** (mah-kee-lah-DORH-ah) a U.S. or other foreign-owned factory in Mexico (p. 155)
**maquiladora** fábrica estadounidense o de otro país establecida en México (pág. 155)

**maritime** on or near the sea (p. 287)
**marítimo** en o cerca del mar (pág. 287)

**market economy** an economic system based on free trade and competition (p. 94)
**economía de mercado** sistema económico basado en el libre comercio y la competencia (pág. 94)

**masonry** stonework (p. 131)
**mampostería** obra de piedra (pág. 131)

**Mediterranean climate** the type of climate found across Southern Europe; it features warm and sunny summer days, mild evenings, and cooler, rainy winters (p. 402)
**clima mediterráneo** tipo de clima de todo el sur europeo; se caracteriza por días de verano cálidos y soleados, noches templadas e inviernos lluviosos y más frescos (pág. 402)

**megacity** a giant urban area that includes surrounding cities and suburbs (p. 212)
**megaciudad** zona urbana enorme que incluye los suburbios y ciudades de alrededor (pág. 212)

**megalopolis** a string of large cities that have grown together (p. 265)
**megalópolis** serie de ciudades grandes que han crecido hasta unirse (pág. 265)

**Mercosur** an organization that promotes trade and economic cooperation among the southern and eastern countries of South America (p. 218)
**Mercosur** organización que promueve el comercio y la cooperación económica entre los países del sur y el este de América del Sur (pág. 218)

**mestizo** (me-STEE-zoh) a person of mixed European and Indian ancestry (p. 148)
**mestizo** persona de origen europeo e indígena (pág. 148)

**ENGLISH AND SPANISH GLOSSARY**

**meteorology** the study of weather and what causes it (p. 20)

**meteorología** estudio de las condiciones del tiempo y sus causas (pág. 20)

**Middle Ages** a period that lasted from about 500 to 1500 in Europe (p. 328)

**Edad Media** período que duró aproximadamente desde el año 500 hasta el 1500 en Europa (pág. 328)

**migration** the movement of people from one place to live in another (p. 89)

**migración** movimiento de personas de un lugar para ir a vivir a otro lugar (pág. 89)

**mission** a church outpost (p. 148)

**misión** asentamiento de la Iglesia (pág. 148)

**monsoon** a seasonal wind that brings either dry or moist air (p. 58)

**monzón** viento estacional que trae aire seco o húmedo (pág. 58)

**nationalism** a devotion and loyalty to one's country; develops among people with a common language, religion, or history (p. 376)

**nacionalismo** sentimiento de lealtad al país de uno; se desarrolla entre personas con un idioma, religión o historia en común (pág. 376)

**nation-state** a country united under a single strong government; made up of people with a common cultural background (p. 335)

**nación-estado** país unido bajo un solo gobierno fuerte; formado de personas con una cultura común (pág. 335)

**natural resource** any material in nature that people use and value (p. 68)

**recurso natural** todo material de la naturaleza que las personas utilizan y valoran (pág. 68)

**navigable river** a river that is deep and wide enough for ships to use (p. 426)

**río navegable** río que tiene la profundidad y el ancho necesarios para que pasen los barcos (pág. 426)

**neutral** not taking sides in an international conflict (p. 460)

**neutral** que no toma partido en un conflicto internacional (pág. 460)

**newsprint** cheap paper used mainly for newspapers (p. 279)

**papel de prensa** papel económico utilizado principalmente para imprimir periódicos (pág. 279)

**New World** a term used by Europeans to describe the Americas after the voyages of Christopher Columbus; the Americas were a "New World" to Europeans, who did not know they existed until Columbus's voyages (p. 355)

**Nuevo Mundo** término usado por los europeos para describir las Américas tras los viajes de Cristóbal Colón; las Américas eran un "Nuevo Mundo" para los europeos, que no sabían de su existencia hasta los viajes de Colón (pág. 355)

**nonrenewable resource** a resource that cannot be replaced naturally; coal and petroleum are examples of nonrenewable resources (p. 69)

**recurso no renovable** recurso que no puede reemplazarse naturalmente; el carbón y el petróleo son ejemplos de recursos no renovables (pág. 69)

**North Atlantic Drift** a warm ocean current that brings warm, moist air across the Atlantic Ocean to Northern Europe (p. 450)

**Corriente del Atlántico Norte** corriente oceánica cálida que trae aire cálido y húmedo a través del océano Atlántico al norte de Europa (pág. 450)

**observatory** a building from which people study the sky (p. 122)

**observatorio** edificio desde el cual las personas estudian el cielo (pág. 122)

**ocean currents** large streams of surface seawater; they move heat around Earth (p. 52)

**corrientes oceánicas** grandes corrientes de agua de mar que fluyen en la superficie del océano; transportan calor por toda la Tierra (pág. 52)

**Orthodox Church** a branch of Christianity that dates to the Byzantine Empire (p. 407)

**Iglesia ortodoxa** rama del cristianismo que data del Imperio bizantino (pág. 407)

**parliamentary monarchy** a type of government in which a king rules with the help of an elected parliament (p. 418)

**monarquía parlamentaria** tipo de gobierno en el que un rey gobierna con la ayuda de un parlamento electo (pág. 418)

**peninsula** a piece of land surrounded on three sides by water (p. 142)

**península** pedazo de tierra rodeado de agua por tres lados (pág. 142)

**permafrost** permanently frozen layers of soil (p. 61)
**permafrost** capas de tierra congeladas permanentemente (pág. 61)

**physical geography** the study of the world's physical features—its landforms, bodies of water, climates, soils, and plants (p. 16)
**geografía física** estudio de las características físicas de la Tierra: sus accidentes geográficos, sus masas de agua, sus climas, sus suelos y sus plantas (pág. 16)

**pioneer** an early settler; in the United States, people who settled the interior and western areas of the country were known as pioneers (p. 258)
**pionero** poblador; en Estados Unidos, las personas que se establecieron en el interior y el oeste del país se llamaron pioneros (pág. 258)

**plantation** a large farm that grows mainly one crop (p. 257)
**plantación** granja muy grande en la que se produce principalmente un solo tipo de cultivo (pág. 257)

**plate tectonics** a theory suggesting that Earth's surface is divided into a dozen or so slow-moving plates, or pieces of Earth's crust (p. 36)
**tectónica de placas** teoría que sugiere que la superficie terrestre está dividida en unas doce placas, o fragmentos de corteza terrestre, que se mueven lentamente (pág. 36)

**pope** the spiritual head of the Roman Catholic Church (pp. 329, 412)
**papa** jefe espiritual de la Iglesia Católica Romana (págs. 329, 412)

**popular culture** culture traits that are well known and widely accepted (p. 98)
**cultura popular** rasgos culturales conocidos y de gran aceptación (pág. 98)

**population** the total number of people in a given area (p. 86)
**población** número total de personas en una zona determinada (pág. 86)

**population density** a measure of the number of people living in an area (p. 86)
**densidad de población** medida del número de personas que viven en una zona (pág. 86)

**precipitation** water that falls to Earth's surface as rain, snow, sleet, or hail (p. 31)
**precipitación** agua que cae a la superficie de la Tierra en forma de lluvia, nieve, aguanieve o granizo (pág. 31)

**prevailing winds** winds that blow in the same direction over large areas of Earth (p. 51)
**vientos preponderantes** vientos que soplan en la misma dirección sobre grandes zonas de la Tierra (pág. 51)

**Protestant** a Christian who protested against the Catholic Church (p. 349)
**protestante** cristiano que protestaba en contra de la Iglesia católica (pág. 349)

**province** an administrative division of a country (p. 282)
**provincia** división administrativa de un país (pág. 282)

**pulp** softened wood fibers; used to make paper (p. 279)
**pulpa** fibras ablandadas de madera; usadas para hacer papel (pág. 279)

## Q

**Quechua** (ke-chuh-wuh) the official Inca language (p. 130)
**quechua** idioma oficial de los incas (pág. 130)

## R

**referendum** a recall vote (p. 198)
**referéndum** voto para quitar a alguien de su cargo (pág. 198)

**reforestation** planting trees to replace lost forestland (p. 69)
**reforestación** siembra de árboles para reemplazar los bosques que han desaparecido (pág. 69)

**Reformation** (re-fuhr-MAY-shuhn) a reform movement against the Roman Catholic Church that began in 1517; it resulted in the creation of Protestant churches (p. 348)
**Reforma** movimiento de reforma contra la Iglesia Católica Romana que comenzó en 1517; resultó en la creación de las iglesias protestantes (pág. 348)

**refugee** someone who flees to another country, usually for political or economic reasons (p. 177)
**refugiado** persona que escapa a otro país, generalmente por razones económicas o políticas (pág. 177)

**region** a part of the world that has one or more common features that distinguish it from surrounding areas (p. 6)
**región** parte del mundo que tiene una o más características comunes que la distinguen de las áreas que la rodean (pág. 6)

**regionalism** the strong connection that people feel toward the region in which they live (p. 287)
**regionalismo** gran conexión que las personas sienten con la región en la que viven (pág. 287)

**Reign of Terror** a bloody period of the French Revolution during which the government executed thousands of its opponents and others at the guillotine (p. 362)
**Reino del Terror** período sangriento de la Revolución Francesa durante el cual el gobierno ejecutó a miles de personas, oponentes y otros, en la guillotina (pág. 362)

**relative location** a general description of where a place is located; a place's relative location is often expressed in relation to something else (p. 12)
**ubicación relativa** descripción general de la posición de un lugar; la ubicación relativa de un lugar suele expresarse en relación con otra cosa (pág. 12)

**ENGLISH AND SPANISH GLOSSARY**

**Renaissance** (REN-uh-sahns) the period of "rebirth" and creativity that followed Europe's Middle Ages (p. 344)
**Renacimiento** período de "volver a nacer" y creatividad que siguió a la Edad Media en Europa (pág. 344)

**renewable resource** a resource that Earth replaces naturally, such as water, soil, trees, plants, and animals (p. 69)
**recurso renovable** recurso que la Tierra reemplaza por procesos naturales, como el agua, el suelo, los árboles, las plantas y los animales (pág. 69)

**republic** a political system in which people elect leaders to govern them (p. 319)
**república** sistema politico en el que el pueblo elige a los líderes que lo gobernarán (pág. 319)

**revolution** the 365 ¼ day trip Earth takes around the sun each year (p. 27)
**revolución** viaje de 365 ¼ días que la Tierra hace alrededor del Sol cada año (pág. 27)

**rotation** one complete spin of Earth on its axis; each rotation takes about 24 hours (p. 26)
**rotación** giro completo de la Tierra sobre su propio eje; cada rotación toma 24 horas (pág. 26)

## S

**savanna** an area of tall grasses and scattered trees and shrubs (p. 58)
**sabana** zona de pastos altos con arbustos y árboles dispersos (pág. 58)

**Scientific Revolution** a series of events that led to the birth of modern science; it lasted from about 1540 to 1700 (p. 351)
**Revolución Científica** serie de sucesos que produjeron el nacimiento de la ciencia moderna; duró desde alrededor de 1540 hasta 1700 (pág. 351)

**Senate** a council of rich and powerful Romans who helped run the city (p. 319)
**Senado** consejo de romanos ricos y poderosos que ayudaban a dirigir la ciudad (pág. 319)

**slash-and-burn agriculture** the practice of burning forest in order to clear land for planting (p. 153)
**agricultura de tala y quema** práctica de quemar los bosques para despejar el terreno y sembrar en él (pág. 153)

**smelters** factories that process metal ores (p. 505)
**fundiciones** fábricas que tratan menas de metal (pág. 505)

**smog** a mixture of smoke, chemicals, and fog (p. 154)
**smog** mezcla de humo, sustancias químicas y niebla (pág. 154)

**social science** a field that focuses on people and the relationships among them (p. 5)
**ciencias sociales** campo de estudio que se enfoca en las personas y en las relaciones entre ellas (pág. 5)

**soil exhaustion** the process of soil becoming infertile because it has lost nutrients needed by plants (p. 209)
**agotamiento del suelo** proceso por el cual el suelo se vuelve estéril porque ha perdido los nutrientes que necesitan las plantas (pág. 209)

**solar energy** energy from the sun (p. 26)
**energía solar** energía del Sol (pág. 26)

**steppe** a semidry grassland or prairie; steppes often border deserts (p. 59)
**estepa** pradera semiárida; las estepas suelen encontrarse en el límite de los desiertos (pág. 59)

**strait** a narrow passageway that connects two large bodies of water (p. 229)
**estrecho** paso angosto que une dos grandes masas de agua (pág. 229)

**strike** a work stoppage by a group of workers until their demands are met (p. 198)
**huelga** interrupción del trabajo por parte de un grupo de trabajadores hasta que se cumplan sus demandas (pág. 198)

**suffragettes** women who campaigned to gain the right to vote (p. 370)
**sufragistas** mujeres que hicieron campaña para obtener el derecho a votar (pág. 370)

**superpower** a strong and influential country (p. 388)
**superpotencia** país poderoso e influyente (pág. 388)

**surface water** water that is found in Earth's streams, rivers, and lakes (p. 31)
**agua superficial** agua que se encuentra en los arroyos, ríos y lagos de la Tierra (pág. 31)

## T

**taiga** (TY-guh) a forest of mainly evergreen trees covering much of Russia (p. 495)
**taiga** bosque de árboles de hoja perenne principalmente que cubre gran parte de Rusia (pág. 495)

**terrorism** violent attacks that cause fear (p. 270)
**terrorismo** ataques violentos que provocan miedo (pág. 270)

**textile** a cloth product (p. 368)
**textil** producto de tela (pág. 368)

**Trans-Siberian Railroad** a rail line in Russia that extends about 5,800 miles (9,330 km) from Moscow to Vladivostok; it is the longest single rail line in the world (p. 505)
**Ferrocarril Transiberiano** línea de ferrocarril rusa de 5,800 millas (9,330 km) de largo, desde Moscú hasta Vladivostok; es la vía de ferrocarril más larga del mundo (pág. 505)

**Treaty of Versailles** the final peace settlement of World War I (p. 379)
**Tratado de Versalles** acuerdo de paz final de la Primera Guerra Mundial (pág. 379)

**trench warfare** a style of fighting common in World War I in which each side fights from deep ditches, or trenches, dug into the ground (p. 378)
  guerra de trincheras forma de guerra comúnmente usada en la Primera Guerra Mundial, en la cual ambos bandos luchan desde profundas zanjas, o trincheras, cavadas en el suelo (pág. 378)

**tributary** a smaller stream or river that flows into a larger stream or river (p. 249)
  tributario río o corriente más pequeña que fluye hacia un río o una corriente más grande (pág. 249)

**tropics** regions close to the equator (p. 29)
  trópicos regiones cercanas al ecuador (pág. 29)

**uninhabitable** unable to support human settlement (p. 461)
  inhabitable que no puede sustentar asentamientos humanos (pág. 461)

**United Nations** an organization of countries that promotes peace and security around the world (p. 99)
  Naciones Unidas organización de países que promueve la paz y la seguridad en todo el mundo (pág. 99)

**viceroy** governor (p. 235)
  virrey gobernador (pág. 235)

**Vikings** Scandinavian warriors who raided Europe in the early Middle Ages (p. 458)
  vikingos guerreros escandinavos que atacaron Europa al principio de la Edad Media (pág. 458)

**water cycle** the movement of water from Earth's surface to the atmosphere and back (p. 33)
  ciclo del agua circulación del agua desde la superficie de la Tierra hacia la atmósfera y de regreso a la Tierra (pág. 33)

**water vapor** water occurring in the air as an invisible gas (p. 32)
  vapor de agua agua que se encuentra en el aire en estado gaseoso e invisible (pág. 32)

**weather** the short-term changes in the air for a given place and time (p. 50)
  tiempo cambios a corto plazo en la atmósfera en un momento y lugar determinados (pág. 50)

**weathering** the process by which rock is broken down into smaller pieces (p. 39)
  meteorización proceso de desintegración de las rocas en pedazos pequeños (pág. 39)

ENGLISH AND SPANISH GLOSSARY

# Index

INDEX

INDEX

INDEX

themes of, 10–12, 11f; global level, 7, 7p; human, 3, 17p, 18, 21; human-environment interaction theme, 10–12, 11f; landscape, 4; local level, 6, 6p; location theme, 10–12, 11f; movement theme, 10–12, 11f; physical, 3, 16–17, 17p, 21; place theme, 10–12, 11f; regional level, 6–7, 7p; region theme, 10–12, 11f; as science, 5; as social science, 5; studying, 4–9; urban, 19

**Geography and History:** The Black Death, 336–37f; Earth's Changing Environments, 66–67f; The European Union, 434–35f; Native Cultures of North America, 134–35f; The Panama Canal, 172–73f; Roman Roads, 326–27f

**Geography and Map Skills Handbook:** Geographic Dictionary, H10–H11; Geography Themes and Elements, H12–H13; Map Essentials, H6–H7; Mapmaking, H4–H5; Mapping the Earth, H2–H3; Working with Maps, H8–H9

**Geography Skills:** Analyzing Satellite Images, 15; Interpreting a Climate Graph, 180; Interpreting an Elevation Profile, 233; Interpreting a Historical Map, 338; Interpreting a Population Map, 501; Reading a Climate Map, 404; Using a Physical Map, 44; Using a Political Map, 253; Using Latitude and Longitude, 200; Using Mental Maps and Sketch Maps, 292

**Georgia,** 305c, 509; economy of, 509; history of, 508

**geothermal energy,** 71, 450; in Iceland, 462, 462p

**German Democratic Republic,** 389

**Germania,** 436

**Germany,** 305c, 436–40; arts, 438; Central Uplands, 425, 425m; cities in, 440; culture, 438, 438–39f; customs, 438; as developed country, 95; division of, after World War I, 389, 437; economy of, 439–40; in European Union, 392, 392c; fall of communism, 390, 437; government, 439; growth of nation, 436; history of, 436–37; Hitler, 383–86, 437; Holocaust, 385–86, 437; Holy Roman Empire, 436; industry and agriculture, 439; language, 438; Nazi Party, 383, 437; peace

agreement after World War I, 379; people of, 438; political map of, 437m; population, 438, 439c; Reformation, 348–49; religion, 438; reunification, 390–91, 437; rise of Hitler before World War I, 383; science, 438; today, 439–40; transportation, 440; in World War I, 377–79, 437; in World War II, 384–87, 437

**glaciers,** 31; Andean, 229; erosion by, 39; Northern Europe and, 449; in Swiss Alps, 426p

**globalization,** 79p, 97–100; defined, 97; global economy, 98–99f; global trade, 99; interdependence and, 99; popular culture and, 97–98; world community, 99–100

**global wind system,** 51–52, 51m

**globe,** H2; as geographer's tool, 8–9

**gold:** Mexico, 145, 148; Spanish colonization in Americas and, 356

**golden age,** 312; of ancient Greece, 312–15

**Gorbachev, Mikhail,** 390f, 498

**government:** Argentina, 217; Austria, 440–41; Benelux countries, 432; Bolivia, 239; Brazil, 211; British Isles, 454; Canada, 286; chancellor, 439; Chile, 241; city-state in ancient Greece, 310–11; communism, 92; communism in Russia after World War I, 380; constitutional monarchy, 454; Cuba, 178; democracy, 91–92; democracy in ancient Greece, 314; dictatorship, 92; Ecuador, 238; Enlightenment and, 359; Germany, 439; Greece, 406; Inca Empire, 130; Inland Eastern Europe, 478; Ireland, 454; Magna Carta in England, 334; Mexico, 152; monarchy, 92; nation-state, 335; Paraguay, 220; parliamentary monarchy, 418; Peru, 241; problems in Roman Empire government, 324–25; rise of dictators before World War I, 383; Roman government as model for United States, 322; Roman Republic, 319–20; Russia, 502; Spain, 418; Switzerland, 441; types of, 91–92; United Kingdom, 454; United States, 259; Uruguay, 219; Venezuela, 195, 197–98; world governments, 92m

**Gran Chaco,** 207, 207m; climate of, 209

**Gran Colombia,** 191

**Grand Banks,** 278

**Grand Canyon,** 247p; erosion and, 40

**graphs.** *See* charts and graphs

**grasslands,** 60

**Great Britain.** *See also* British Isles; England: Churchill and, 453f; colonies in United States, 256–57; colonization in Central America, 166–67; colonization of Canada, 282; French and Indian War, 282; Industrial Revolution, 367–68, 369f; Napoleon's defeat, 363–64; suffragettes, 370, 370p; in World War I, 377–79; in World War II, 384–87, 453

**Great Depression,** 382, 454

**Greater Antilles,** 163

**Greater Mexico City,** 154, 155p

**Great Hungarian Plain,** 469, 469m

**Great Lakes,** 31, 249, 249m, 277; temperature in Michigan, 53

**Great Plains,** 60, 250, 251, 268

**Great Salt Lake, Utah,** 31

**Greece,** 305c; agriculture, 408, 409; Byzantine Empire, 406; climate and resources of, 402–3; culture, 407; customs, 407; economy of, 409; in European Union, 392c; government of, 406; history of, 405–6; independent, 406; language, 407; Orthodox Church, 407, 407p; Ottoman Turks, 406; Per Capita GDP of Greece, 1994–2004, 409c; physical geography of, 400–402, 401m; religion, 407; resources, 409; Roman Empire, 406; shipping, 409; today, 408–9; tourism, 409; urban and rural, 408

**ancient Greece:** 310–17; acropolis, 311; Alexander the Great's Empire, c. 323 BC, 316–17m; architecture, 312–13f, 314–15, 405; art, 308p, 313–15, 315p, 405–06; Athenian culture, 313; Athenian democracy, 314; city-states, 310–11; culture of, 310–11; decline of city-states, 315; empire of Alexander, 316–17m; golden age of Greece, 312–15; Greek City-States and Colonies, c. 600 BC, 311m; growth of Greek power, 312–13; mathematics, 406f; Parthenon, 312–13f; science, philosophy and literature, 315; victory over Persians, 312–13; voting, 310, 314p

**Green Belt Movement,** 69

**Greenland,** 461; glaciers, 39; independence of, 459

**Grenada,** 113c

INDEX

INDEX

INDEX

INDEX

**INDEX**

### S

# T

# Credits and Acknowledgments

**For permission to reproduce copyrighted material, grateful acknowledgment is made to the following sources:**

*National Geographic Society:* From *Geography for Life: National Geography Standards 1994.* Copyright © 1994 by National Geographic Research & Exploration. All rights reserved.

*G. P. Putnam's Sons, a division of Penguin Group (USA) Inc.:* From *Time Enough for Love, the Lives of Lazarus Long* by Robert Heinlein. Copyright © 1973 by Robert Heinlein. All rights reserved.

*Random House Children's Books, a division of Random House, Inc.:* From *The River* by Gary Paulsen. Copyright © 1991 by Gary Paulsen.

*United Nations:* From the *Preamble to the Charter of the United Nations.* Copyright © 1945 by United Nations.

*Atheneum Books for Young Readers, an imprint of Simon & Schuster Children's Publishing Division:* From *Bearstone* by Will Hobbs. Copyright ©1989 by Will Hobbs. All rights reserved.

*Doubleday, a division of Random House, Inc.:* From *The Diary of a Young Girl, The Definitive Edition* by Anne Frank, edited by Otto H. Frank and Mirjam Pressler, translated by Susan Massotty. Copyright © 1995 by Doubleday, a division of Random House, Inc.

*HarperCollins Publishers: The Endless Steppe* by Esther Hautzig. Copyright © 1968 by Esther Hautzig.

*Lonely Planet:* From "Hungary" from the *Lonely Planet WorldGuide Online* Web site. Copyright © 2005 by Lonely Planet. Accessed at http://www.lonelyplanet.com/worldguide/destinations/europe/hungary/.

*Estate of Erich Maria Remarque:* From *All Quiet on the Western Front* by Erich Maria Remarque. Copyright 1929, 1930 by Little, Brown and Company; copyright renewed © 1957, 1958 by Erich Maria Remarque. All rights reserved. "Im Westen Nichts Neues" copyright 1928 by Ullstein A. G.; copyright renewed © 1956 by Erich Maria Remarque.

**Sources used by The World Almanac® for charts and graphs:**

Eruptions in the Ring of Fire: *The World Almanac and Book of Facts, 2005*; World Energy Production: Energy Information Administration of the U.S. Department of Energy; A Developed and a Developing Country: *The World Factbook, 2005*; U.S. Census Bureau; World Health Organization; Geographical Extremes: The Americas: *The World Almanac and Book of Facts, 2005*; *The World Factbook, 2005*; U.S.

Bureau of the Census; The Americas: *The World Factbook, 2005*; U.S. Bureau of the Census, International Database; United Nations Statistical Yearbook; World's Largest Cities: United Nations Population Division National Censuses; Urban Populations in the Americas: United Nations Population Division; Major Food Exports of the Americas: Food and Agriculture Organization of the United Nations; Languages of the Caribbean: Joshua Project; World's Top Oil Exporters: Energy Information Administration of the U.S. Department of Energy; Argentina's Largest Cities: National Institute of Statistics and Censuses, Argentina, 2001 Census; Languages in Pacific South America: Ethnologue: Languages of the World, 15th Edition; Population of Major U.S. Cities: U.S. Census Bureau; Canadian Ethnic Groups: The World Factbook, 2005; Geographical Extremes: Europe and Russia: *The World Almanac and Book of Facts, 2005*; *The World Factbook, 2005*; U.S. Bureau of the Census; Europe and Russia: *The World Factbook, 2005*; U.S. Bureau of the Census, International Database; United Nations Statistical Yearbook; World's Highest Per Capita GDPs: *The World Factbook, 2005*; Densely Populated Countries in Europe: *The World Factbook, 2005*; U.S. Bureau of the Census, International Database; The European Union: European Union, International Programs Center; U.S. Bureau of the Census, International Database; Per Capita GDP of Greece: *The World Factbook, 2005*; Scandinavia's Per Capita GDP: *The World Factbook, 2005*; U.S. Bureau of the Census, International Database; United Nations Statistical Yearbook; Major Religions in the Balkans: World Christian Database; Russia's Population Decline, 1980–2010: U.S. Census Bureau, International Programs Center; State Statistical Committee of Russia

## Illustrations and Photo Credits

**Cover: (bl),** Royalty-free/Corbis; (br), Mark Segal/Getty Images

**Front Matter:** ii, Victoria Smith/HMH Photo; iv (bl), Anthony Cassidy/Getty Images; v (br), Martin Harvey/Corbis; v (t), Age Fotostock/SuperStock; vi (t), Getty Images; viii (t), Macduff Everton/CORBIS; ix (tr), George Hunter/Pictures Colour Library Ltd.; x (br), Ron Watts/CORBIS; x (bl), Tom Grill/Photographer's Choice/Getty Images; xi, Dave Reede/First Light/Getty Images; xii (b), Christopher Groenhout/Lonely Planet Images; xiii (b), Bettmann/Corbis; xiii (tr), The Granger Collection, New York; xiv (b), Chad Ehlers/Alamy; xv (cr), Hans Strand/Corbis; xv (t), Hans Strand/Corbis; xvi (b), AP Photo/Amel Emric; xvii (br), Kurt Scholz/SuperStock; xvii (t), Michael Yamashita/Corbis; xix NASA/Photo Researchers, Inc.; xx, Renzo Gostoli/AP/Wide World Photos; xxiv

(bl), Carl & Ann Purcell/Corbis; xxiv (br), Glen Allison/Stone/Getty Images; H12 (t), Earth Satellite Corporation/Photo Researchers, Inc.; H12 (tc), Frans Lemmens/Getty Images; H12 (c), London Aerial Photo Library/Corbis; H12 (bc), Harvey Schwartz/Index Stock Imagery/Fotosearch; H12 (b), Tom Nebbia/Corbis.

**Unit 1:** 1 (bc), Robert Harding/Digital Vision/Getty Images; A, Taxi/Getty Images; B (bkgd), Planetary Visions; B (cr), Frans Lemmens/Image Bank/Getty Images; B (bl), Michael Melford/Getty Images.

**Chapter 1:** 2 (br), M. Colonel/Photo Researchers, Inc.; 2–3 (t), Age Fotostock/SuperStock; 3 (br), Anthony Cassidy/Getty Images; 3 (bl), Digital Vision/Getty Images; 5 (b), Frans Lemmens/Getty Images; 6 (b), Kim Sayer/Corbis; 7 (br), ESA/K.Horgan/Getty Images; 7 (bl), London Aerial Photo Library/Corbis; 8 (tl), Michael Newman/PhotoEdit; 11 (br), Morton Beebe/Corbis; 11 (bc), AFP/Getty Images; 11 (tr), Miles Ertman/Masterfile; 11 (tl), David R. Frazier/Photo Researchers, Inc.; 11 (bl), Corbis; 12–13 (br), Tom Nebbia/Corbis; 15 (l), M-SAT Ltd./Science Photo Library; 15 (r), Earth Satellite Corporation/Science Photo Library; 17 (tr), Penny Tweedie/Stone/Getty Images; 17 (tl), Torleif Svensson/Corbis; 19 (b), Donna Cox and Robert Patterson/NCSA; 20 (tl), Joe Raedle/Getty Images; 21 (tr), Donna Cox and Robert Patterson/NCSA; 21 (tc), Penny Tweedie/Stone/Getty Images; 21 (tl), Frans Lemmens/Getty Images.

**Chapter 2:** 24 (br), Pete Saloutos/Corbis; 24–25 (t), Earth Satellite Corporation/Science Photo Library; 25 (tr), 2010 A&E Television Networks, LLC. All rights reserved; 25 (bl), George H.H. Huey/Corbis; 25 (br), Royalty-Free/Corbis; 29 (tr), Paul A. Souders/Corbis; 30–31 (b), Doug Wilson/Corbis; 31 (br), Terje Rakke/The Image Bank/Getty Images; 34 (tr), Alan Sirulnikoff/Photo Researchers, Inc.; 34 (tl), Rick Doyle/Corbis; 37 (bl), Bettmann/Corbis; 38 (cr), Yann Arthus-Bertrand/Corbis; 38 (br), Roger Cracknell 01/classic/Alamy; 39 (br), Age Fotostock/SuperStock; 40 (bl), Owaki-Kulla/Corbis; 41 (t), Age Fotostock/SuperStock; 43 (tr), Gary Braasch/Corbis; 43 (tl), David Weintraub/Photo Researchers, Inc.; 45 (tr), Galen Rowell/Corbis; 45 (tc), Rick Doyle/Corbis; 45 (tl), W.H. Mueller/Zefa Images/Corbis; 45 (tr), Roger Cracknell 01/classic/Alamy.

**Chapter 3:** 48 (br), Kate Thompson/National Geographic/Getty Images; 48–49 (t), Warren Faidley/WeatherStock; 49 (tr), 2010 A&E Television Networks, LLC. All rights reserved; 49 (br), Bill Ross/Corbis; 49 (bl), L. Clarke/Corbis; 53 (br), Eric Meola/Getty Images; 53 (tr), William Thomas Cain/Getty Images; 56 (tl), Age FotoStock/SuperStock; 57 (cr),

Images; 314 (cl), Gjon Mili/Time & Life Pictures/Getty Images; 315 (br), Alinari/Art Resource, NY; 322 (cl), Comstock/Jupiter Images; 324 (tr), Richard T. Nowitz/National Geographic Image Collection; 327 (br), SEF/Art Resource, NY; 330 (tl), John Lamb/Getty Images; 334 (bl), Dept. of the Environment, London, UK/Bridgeman Art Library; 339 (tc), Jupiter Images; 339 (tl), Alinari/Art Resource, NY; 341 MC1-MC2, Goodshoot/Jupiter Images/Getty Images.

**Chapter 14:** 342 (br), AKG-Images; 343 (tr), 2010 A&E Television Networks, LLC. All rights reserved; 343 (br), Ali Meyer/Corbis; 343 (bl), The Granger Collection, New York; 345 (bl), age fotostock/SuperStock; 345 (br), Yann Arthus-Bertrand/Corbis; 346 (tr), Giraudon/Art Resource, NY; 346 (tl), Rabatti-Domingie/AKG-Images; 347 (br), Bettmann/Corbis; 347 (tr), The Granger Collection, New York; 347 (cl), The Granger Collection, New York; 347 (cl), Historical Picture Archive/Corbis; 347 (tl), National Portrait Gallery/SuperStock; 350 (br), HIP/Art Resource, NY; 351 (bl), Réunion des Musées Nationaux/Art Resource, NY; 351 (br), Royal Society, London, UK/Bridgeman Art Library; 357 (tr), Archivo Iconografico, S.A./Corbis; 359 (t), RÈunion des MusÈes Nationaux/Art Resource, NY; 360 (br), Custody of the House of Lords Record Office/Parliamentary Archives; 360 (cl), The Granger Collection, New York; 360 (bl), Dept. of the Environment, London, UK/Bridgeman Art Library; 360 (cl), Bettmann/Corbis; 361 (br), Document conserve au Centre Historique des Archives Nationales a Paris/Centre Historique des Archives Nationales (CHAN); 361 (cl), Réunion des Musées Nationaux/Art Resource, NY; 361 (bl), Joseph Sohm/Visions of America/Corbis; 361 (cl), Bettmann/Corbis; 362 (bl), Gianni Dagli Orti/Corbis; 363 (tr), Erich Lessing/Art Resource, NY; 367 (br), Hulton Archive/Getty Images; 367 (bl), The Granger Collection, New York; 370 (tl), Hulton Archive/Getty Images; 371 (cr), Gianni Dagli Orti/Corbis; 371 (cl), HIP/Art Resource, NY; 371 (tl), Rabatti-Domingie/AKG-Images.

**Chapter 15:** 374, (br), Hulton Archive/Getty Images; 375 (tr), 2010 A&E Television Networks, LLC. All rights reserved; 375 (br), Thomas Kienzle/AP/Wide World Photos; 375 (bl), Hugo Jaeger/Timepix/Time Life Pictures/Getty Images; 380 (tl), The Granger Collection, New York; 381 (tr), Hulton Archive/Getty Images; 383 (br), Hulton-Deutsch Collection/Corbis; 383 (b), The Granger Collection, New York; 385 (br), AKG-Images; 386 (tr), Hulton Archive/Getty Images; 386 (cl), Hulton-Deutsch Collection/Corbis; 386 (cl), Hulton Archive/Getty Images; 387 (tl), Bettmann/Corbis; 387 (tr), Margaret Bourke-White/Time Life Pictures/Getty Images; 387 (tc), Bettmann/Corbis; 390 (bl), Peter Turnley/Corbis; 391 (tr), David Turnley/Corbis; 391 (tl), Robert Maas/Corbis; 393 (tr), Alain Nogues/Corbis; 394 (c), Library of Congress; 395 (bl), Robert Maas/Corbis; 395 (cl), Hulton-Deutsch Collection/Corbis; 396 (bl), *The Tide Comes In*, 1944, by John Collins. M965.199.4595. McCord Museum of Canadian History, Montreal; 397 MC1-MC2, Bettman/Corbis.

**Chapter 16:** 398 (br), Richard Klune/Corbis; 399 (tr), 2010 A&E Television Networks, LLC. All rights reserved; 399 (bl), Carlos Cazalis/Corbis; 399 (br), Digital Vision/Robert Harding; 401 (br), Dmitry Kovyazin/Alamy; 402 (cl), Jeremy Lightfoot/Robert Harding; 402 (tl), Charles O'Rear/Corbis; 403 (tr), SIME s.a.s./eStock Photo; 403 (cl), IT Stock Free/eStock Photo; 405, Erich Lessing/Art Resource, NY; 406 (cl), Vega/Taxi/Getty Images; 407 (b), Roberto Meazza/IML Image Group; 408 (cl), Sylvain Grandadam/Robert Harding; 408 (cr), Mark Henley/Photolibrary; 411 (tc), Gianni Dagli Orti/Corbis; 411 (tr), Bildarchiv Preussischer Kulturbesitz/Art Resource, NY; 412 (br), Giuseppe Cacace/Getty Images; 413 (br), Martin Moos/Lonely Planet Images; 413 (bl), Steve Vidler/SuperStock; 414 (tl), WorldSat; 415 (b), Digital Vision/Getty Images; 416 (tr), AFP/Getty Images; 417 (br), Latin Focus/HRW; 418 (tl), Nigel Francis Photography; 419 (tr), Latin Focus/HRW; 419 (tc), Steve Vidler/SuperStock; 419 (tl), Roberto Meazza/IML Image Group.

**Chapter 17:** 422 (br), William Manning/Corbis; 423 (br), Elfi Kluck/Index Stock Imagery/PictureQuest/Jupiter Images; 423 (bl), Brian Lawrence/Image State; 425 (br), Chad Ehlers/Alamy; 426 (cl), WorldSat; 315 (br), Corbis; 429 (tr), SuperStock; 429 (cl), Vince Streano/Corbis; 432 (t), Goos van der Veen/Hollandse Hoogte/Pictures; 434 (br), PhotoDisc Collection/Getty Images; 435 (br), AFP/Getty Images; 437 Walter Bibikow/Taxi/Getty Images; 438 (tl), SuperStock RF/Superstock; 438–439 (tc), Sean Gallup/Getty Images; 439 (tr), Sean Gallup/Getty Images; 440 (br), Free Agents Limited/Corbis; 440 (bl), Ray Juno/Corbis; 443 (tl), Vince Streano/Corbis; 443 (tr), SuperStock RF/Superstock.

**Chapter 18:** 446 (br), Paul Harris/Stone/Getty Images; 447 (tr), 2010 A&E Television Networks, LLC. All rights reserved; 447 (br), Fredrik Naumann/Samfoto; 447 (bl), Steve Vidler/Image State; 449 (tr), Stefan Auth/Photolibrary; 450 (cl), WorldSat; 451 (tr), Espen Bratlie/Samfoto; 452 (cl), National Portrait Gallery/SuperStock; 452 (b), Steve Vidler/Image State; 453 (br), Hulton-Deutsch Collection/Corbis; 453 (bl), Hulton Archive/Getty Images; 453 (tr), Time Life Images/Getty Images; 454 (bl), SuperStock; 456 (t), Michael Duerinckx/Image State; 460 (b), Jon Arnold/DanitaDelimont.com; 461 (cl), Dave Houser/Image State; 462 (tl), Hans Strand/Corbis; 462 (tr), Hans Strand/Corbis; 463 (tr), Jon Arnold/DanitaDelimont.com; 463 (tc), Michael Duerinckx/Image State; 463 (tl), Stefan Auth/Photolibrary.

**Chapter 19:** 466 (br), Gregory Wrona/Alamy; 467 (tr), 2010 A&E Television Networks, LLC. All rights reserved; 467 (bl), Adam Woolfitt/Corbis; 467 (br), Paul Springett 09/Alamy; 469 (br), M. ou Me. Desjeux, Bernard/Corbis; 469 (cl), Liba Taylor/Corbis; 470 (bl), Fred Bruemmer/Photolibrary; 471 (tl), Reuters/Corbis; 473 (cl), Bettmann/Corbis; 474 (bl), Wally McNamee/Corbis; 475 (tr), Jon Arnold/DanitaDelimont.com; 477 (cl), John Farrar; 477 (br), Age Fotostock/SuperStock; 481 (b), Ethel Davies/Image State; 482 (bl), Barry Lewis/Corbis; 483 (t), AP Photo/Amel Emric; 484 (bl), David Turnley/Corbis; 487 (tr), David Turnley/Corbis; 487 (tl), Jon Arnold/DanitaDelimont.com.

**Chapter 20:** 490 (br), Michael Yamashita/Corbis; 491 (tr), 2010 A&E Television Networks, LLC. All rights reserved; 491 (bl), Robbie Jack/Corbis; 491 (br), Steve Vidler/Image State; 493 Mikhail V. Propp/Peter Arnold Images/Photolibrary; 494 (cl), Maxim Marmur/Getty Images; 494 (bl), Oxford Scientific/PictureQuest/Jupiter Images; 499, Kurt Scholz/SuperStock; 500 (tl), The Granger Collection, New York; 504 (cl), Maria Stenzel/National Geographic Image Collection; 504 (tl), Yogi, Inc./Corbis; 504 (cl), Harald Sund/The Image Bank/Getty Images; 507 (tr), Time Life Pictures/Getty Images; 509 (tl), Marc Garanger/Corbis; 510 (tl), Jeremy Horner/Corbis; 511 (tr), Marc Garanger/Corbis; 511 (tc), Kurt Scholz/SuperStock; 511 (tl), Maxim Marmur/Getty Images.

**Back Matter:** 541, Planetary Visions; 542–543 (t), Oriental Touch/Robert Harding; 543 (cl), Amanda Hall/Robert Harding.

## Staff Credits

The people who contributed to *Holt McDougal Social Studies: Western World* are listed below. They represent editorial, design, production, emedia, and permissions.

Melanie Baccus, Angela Beckmann, Julie Beckman-Key, Genick Blaise, Ed Blake, Jennifer Campbell, Henry Clark, Grant Davidson, Nina Degollado, Rose Degollado, Christine Devall, Michelle Dike, Lydia Doty, Chase Edmond, Mescal Evler, Susan Franques, Stephanie Friedman, Bob Fullilove, Matthew Gierhart, Bill Gillis, Ann Gorbett, Janet Harrington, Betsy Harris, Wendy Hodge, Tim Hovde, Cathy Jenevein, Carrie Jones, Kadonna Knape, Laura Lasley, Sarah Lee, Sean McCormick, Joe Melomo, Richard Metzger, Andrew Miles, Debra O'Shields, Jarred Prejean, Paul Provence, Shelly Ramos, Curtis Riker, Michael Rinella, Michelle Rimsa, Jennifer Rockwood, Carole Rollins, Beth Sample, Annette Saunders, Jenny Schaeffer, Kay Selke, Chris Smith, Jeremy Strykul, Jeannie Taylor, Terri Taylor, Joni Wackwitz, Mary Wages, Diana Holman Walker, Nadyne Wood, Robin Zaback